Communication Research Methods

Third Edition

Gerianne Merrigan
San Francisco State University

Carole L. Huston
University of San Diego

New York   Oxford
OXFORDS UNIVERSITY PRESS

Oxford University Press is a department of the University of Oxford.
It furthers the University's objective of excellence in research, scholarship,
and education by publishing worldwide.

Oxford   New York
Auckland   Cape Town   Dar es Salaam   Hong Kong   Karachi
Kuala Lumpur   Madrid   Melbourne   Mexico City   Nairobi
New Delhi   Shanghai   Taipei   Toronto

With offices in
Argentina   Austria   Brazil   Chile   Czech Republic   France   Greece
Guatemala   Hungary   Italy   Japan   Poland   Portugal   Singapore
South Korea   Switzerland   Thailand   Turkey   Ukraine   Vietnam

For titles covered by Section 112 of the US Higher Education
Opportunity Act,please visit www.oup.com/us/he for the
latest information about pricing and alternate formats.

Published in the United States of America by
Oxford University Press
198 Madison Avenue,
New York, NY 10016
http://www.oup.com

Library of Congress Cataloging-in-Publication Data
Merrigan, Gerianne.
   Communication Research Methods / Gerianne Merrigan,
San Francisco State University ; Carole L. Huston, University
of San Diego. -- Third edition.
      pages cm
   Includes bibliographical references and index.
   ISBN 978-0-19-933835-1 (acid-free paper) 1. Communication--
Research. I. Huston, Carole Logan. II. Title.
   P91.3.M46 2014
   302.2'0721--dc23
                                             2014013976

Printing number: 9 8 7 6 5 4 3 2 1

Printed in the United States of America
on acid-free paper

Geri dedicates this book in memory of her dad, James R. Merrigan, and to her mom and her siblings, without whose continuous love and support she would not have attempted to write, let alone complete, this book project.

Carole dedicates this book in memory of her mother, Arlene, and to her husband, Don, and her children, Sierra, Josh, and David. Their continued support and encouragement helped to make this project possible.

Brief Contents

v

Contents

Preface

This book started in conversations between two teacher-scholars. As both researchers and educators, we share a commitment to multiple ways of knowing. We believe that different research methodologies are useful for exploring different questions about communication. Since the early 1990s, we have taught undergraduate research methods courses at San Francisco State University (Merrigan) and the University of San Diego (Huston). Carole has taught multiple methods courses for undergraduate students, and Geri has taught undergraduate and graduate courses in quantitative and multiple methods. Together, we have amassed over 50 semesters' teaching experience with more than 1,500 research methodology students.

We developed this book to reflect changes that have happened over the past 65 years, as communication research grew from being predominately concerned with persuasion and media effects in the 1950s to the array of surveys, experiments, content analyses, ethnographies, rhetorical criticism, performance and textual deconstruction that our field now includes. We locate a variety of research methods within this historical context, and we highlight the role of different methodologies for making different types of research arguments (i.e., different kinds of claims, supported by different forms of data or evidence, and warranted in distinctly different ways). We hope to introduce undergraduate and introductory graduate students to a range of communication research methods. Those students should be upper-division majors in a communication-related program who have completed their university's graduation requirements in critical thinking, mathematical reasoning, and information competency. However, no other prerequisite background knowledge or skills are assumed (e.g., communication theory, statistics, or specific computer programs).

The Research-as-Argument Model

Because many departments require a research methods course for students majoring in communication (or speech, or media), this book treats communication research comprehensively. We've organized the book around three epistemological paradigms, each a response to the question, "How can we know about communication?" These include interpretation, criticism and discovery. If you are an experienced teacher of research methods, you will find the concepts you are used to teaching in this book. But you may find that those concepts are presented in a different order, or are organized somewhat differently than you have encountered in other texts. If you have used this book before, you will find the order of paradigms changed in this edition, a point we will return to in a moment.

Part I of this book gives readers an overview of "Some Essential Questions in Communication Research: Why and What to Study?" We have used Toulmin, Reike, and Janik's (1984) model of argument to talk about research as a way of making arguments. We think that model is applicable to quite different research methodologies. The research-as-argument model is embraced by scholars in a variety of disciplines. For example, here is what a Yale statistics professor of 42 years wrote about the approach:

> Rather than mindlessly trashing any and all statements with numbers in them, a more mature response is to learn enough about statistics to distinguish honest,

useful conclusions from skullduggery or foolishness. . . . My central theme is that good statistics involves principled argument that conveys an interesting and credible point. (Abelson, 1995, p. 1–2)

Similarly, in their textbook *The Craft of Research,* published by the University of Chicago Press, Booth, Colomb, and Williams (1995) wrote

People usually think of arguments as disputes. . . . But that is not the kind of argument that made them researchers in the first place (p. 86). When you make a claim, give good reasons, and add qualifications, you acknowledge your readers' desire to work with you in developing and testing new ideas. In this light, the best kind of argument is not verbal coercion but an act of co-operation and respect (p. 93).

In this book, we are using the Toulmin model to show that research methodology is a process of making claims about communication and supporting those claims with evidence and background reasoning. The reasoning is always based on the values of a particular way of knowing, whether that paradigm is criticism, discovery, or interpretation. Therefore, Part I of this book introduces students to "The What and Why of Communication Research." In Chapter 1, we consider links between communication theories and methods, and some audiences for communication research. We also introduce students to two types of primary source manuscripts including research reports and critical essays. In Chapter 2, we introduce our claim-data-warrant model and develop the three paradigms for communication research: interpretation, criticism, and discovery. In Chapter3, we turn to research ethics, its history in our field and some ethical choices students will face when they decide what to study, how to study it, and when they collect and report data or evidence. In Chapters 4–6, we outline the different kinds of claims made by communication researchers; introduce students to the most common sources, settings, and strategies for collecting and analyzing communication data or evidence, as well as to the notions of definitions and research designs; and we provide an extensive treatment of the ways that communication researchers warrant the value or worth of their studies.

Parts II and III of this book show students *how to conduct* communication research using the methodologies typically associated with each epistemological paradigm. Part II consists of four chapters, each concerned with how to conduct research using interpretive and critical paradigm methodologies. Part III consists of

seven chapters, each concerned with how to conduct discovery paradigm research, from designing causal and associative arguments, to using three specific research methods (content analysis, surveys, experiments), and then to statistical data analysis. We made this substantive change to the structure of the book for two reasons, both pedagogical.

First, Parks, Faw and Goldsmith's (2011) national survey of research methods instruction in the US showed that "over 85% of responding programs offered an empirical methods course" (p. 406). Nearly all of the 149 responding programs from undergraduate, master's and research institutions reported that they wanted students "to read published research and to evaluate the research that they encounter in everyday life," and they hoped to give "students research skills that will be useful in a career" (Parks et al., 2011, p. 411–412). But, only half of the responding programs listed "conduct original research," as a requirement in their research methods course. When students were required to do research activities, they typically developed "original research hypotheses," administered surveys, calculated descriptive statistics, and did content analysis (p. 414). Experiential activities for doing critical/cultural research were used less often in the empirical methods courses, except for "reading and critiquing primary source research articles" (p. 414; for more detail see Parks et al.'s Table 3, "Ranking of the Typical Hands-On Research Experiences Used in an Introductory Empirical Method Class"). In our experience, students are ready to create surveys, categorize messages, and statistically analyze those data nearer to the end of the academic term. That is why we have placed the chapters for "How to Discover Communication" in Part III of this edition.

Second, our experiences as teacher/scholars, and Parks et al.'s findings, suggest that communication programs need to better integrate instruction in all research methods, both because doing so would "better reflect actual research practice" and because it would help to "steer clear of polarized debates about methods" (Parks et al., 2011, p. 417). Broader and better integrated instruction in research methods also will help student and faculty researchers choose the most appropriate methods for the questions they hope to address with communication research. We have ordered the parts and chapters in this edition of *Communication Research Methods* to better fit these instructional trends.

Parks et al. (2011) cautioned, though, that "time constraints" and the sheer range of methods employed by communication scholars today make it unlikely that students can learn to *do* all research methods in one course. Instead, they advocated introducing students to research methods early in their programs and using course sequencing, or linked content across courses, to accomplish integration. This book will help students conduct their own survey and content analytic studies (perhaps the most practical methods for an introductory student to complete entirely in one term). It also will provide experiential exercises to give students a taste of other methods (e.g., participant-observation, interviewing, textual deconstruction, and narrative criticism). *Communication Research Methods* has been used successfully to integrate methods instruction across the curriculum (e.g., in two-term research course sequences such as quantitative-qualitative or empirical-critical/ cultural), as well as being used by students in their gateway and capstone courses.

Thus, the chapters in Part II of this edition of *CRM* begin with ethnography, an interpretive method for studying participants' communication meanings insitu, and the method that introductory students and teachers have found most approachable. Part II then proceeds with chapters devoted to conversation and discourse analysis, rhetorical and textual criticism.

Part III, Chapters 11–16, deal with the methods most often associated with the discovery paradigm, and begins with a brand new chapter, "Designing Discovery Research." We intend this chapter to help students understand and appreciate research arguments about cause-and-effect sequences, as well as to conceptualize and measure variables and design studies that control for competing explanations of change in a dependent variable. This chapter is followed by chapters about how to conduct content analyses, survey research, and experiments. We have placed the two chapters that address statistical data at the end of the book, simply because students will likely encounter data analysis for their own studies near the end of the term. We also have added step-by-step instructions and screen capture shots for using EXCEL and SPSS to conduct descriptive and simple inferential statistical tests in the Part III chapters, instead of putting those resources into the *Instructor's Manual*. This should help students and less-experienced research methods instructors navigate statistical data analysis for student projects. Each of the Part III chapters includes special attention to the ethical issues involved in making claims of explanation and prediction, collecting data or evidence to test those claims, and reporting the results of those studies. Most of those chapters (except Chapters 11, 15, and 16) are organized in parallel fashion, using the elements of research as argument (i.e., claims, data or evidence, and warrants). Chapters 11, 15, and 16 address broad issues of importance to survey, experimental, and content analytic researchers, and each of those chapters have their own internal structure.

New to This Edition

- Student learning outcomes have been added for every chapter;
- The how-to chapters have been divided into two parts (instead of one, as in CRM2e) with interpretive and critical paradigm methodologies in Part II and discovery paradigm methodologies in Part III;
- A new chapter, "Designing Discovery Research" has been added that directly precedes the how-to chapters for content analysis, surveys and experimental methods; it shows students how to design studies for cause-and-effect arguments and how to coneptualize and operationalize variables;
- Step-by-step instructions and screen capture shots for using SPSS and EXCEL have been added to the how-to chapters in Part III;
- Constructed data sets for running descriptive and simple inferential statistical tests have been added to the IRM;
- The paradigms chapter is more simplified, with less emphasis on the philosophies that undergird each paradigm;
- The claims are more clearly differentiated between paradigms as we have deleted descriptive claims entirely from this edition;
- The critical studies chapter is simplified by paring critical approaches down to deconstruction and narrative criticism (instead of the 10 critical approaches that were featured in CRM2e); two tables have been added to that chapter, giving students questions to ask when they evaluate texts and images;
- There is more emphasis on how proprietary and academic research is utilized in different industries and careers, and Chapter 1 contains a "Try It!" Activity that students can use to research their future careers online;
- There are several new "Try It!" Activities and Discussion Questions, and more examples designed to appeal to students and teachers in departments that emphasize media/mass communication.

Features of This Book

The style of presentation and writing in this book is similar to that of our previous editions, and the style modeled in other research methods texts. We've worked to provide more attention to proprietary research in this edition, and to show students how research skills will matter in their roles at work, as consumers, in healthcare and community contexts after they graduate. Each chapter begins with a short, reader-friendly introduction and we've added student-learning outcomes for each chapter. Many chapters conclude with a summary table, and each one has discussion questions, experiential exercises for students' hands-on learning, and a list of key terms. Each chapter provides readers with extensive examples from published communication research, examples that our many reviewers have said are accurate, current, and readable.

Teaching Ancillaries

Since the early 1990s, we have seen pedagogical choices for communication research methods courses change from almost exclusive reliance on lecture and examinations to more participatory teaching strategies and projects designed to demonstrate students' grasp of key concepts. Classroom instruction more often now includes computer laboratories or (when a class does not meet in a laboratory) students have access to data analysis programs like Excel, SPSS, VB-Pro, or NUD-IST. Furthermore, as the Internet websites and online databases have increased, our students are increasingly able to access and use these resources to supplement their learning about communication research methods (e.g., *Kahn Academy*). We provide several "Discussion Questions" and "Try It!" activities at the end of each chapter that will increase experiential learning for students.

This edition also includes a revised *Instructor's Manual* that we developed, and which our adopters indicate is quite helpful for teachers who have not taught the full breadth of communication research methods or who are novice teachers of research methods. The *Instructor's Manual* suggests ways of structuring the research methods courses(s) to allow integration of methods and to facilitate experiential learning. It includes in- and outside-class activities and a bank of sample test questions, as well as Internet research applications and activities. It also includes newly constructed data sets that instructors and students can use to conduct descriptive and inferential statistical tests with Excel and/or SPSS.

Acknowledgments

To all our students and teachers, we have learned from you, and we will continue to learn from you. We are grateful for the support of our families and friends over the 15 years we have worked together on this project. We appreciate and have benefited from the expertise of our reviewers, both the anonymous reviewers hired by Mark Haynes at Oxford University Press and our colleagues, who read chapters, suggested resources, and encouraged us in the writing of this book. Finally, we value the contributions made by Brian Spitzberg, both as a reviewer and critic and for writing the Foreword to this book. Any errors or omissions remain our own, however.

Our sincere thanks are extended to reviewers of this text, including:

Barbara Baker, University of Central Missouri
Gary Beck, Old Dominion University
Thomas Christie, University of Texas at Arlington
John Coward, University of Tulsa
Stephen Croucher, University of Jyväskylä
Corinne Dalelio, Coastal Carolina University
Douglas Ferguson, College of Charleston
Joseph Harasta, Kutztown University of Pennsylvania
Haley Horstman, University of Nebraska at Lincoln
Angela Jacobs, Eastern Illinois University
Kerk Kee, Chapman University
Mary LeAnne Lagasse, Texas Tech University
Irwin Mallin, Indiana University
Jennifer Marmo, Arizona State University
M. Chad McBride, Creighton University
Kevin Meyer, Illinois State University
Rick Olsen, University of North Carolina at Wilmington
Irene Paasch, University of Jamestown
David Park, Lake Forest College
Kendall Phillips, Syracuse University
Craig Stewart, University of Memphis
Anne Williams, Georgia State University

Foreword

Islands of Inquiry

Imagine an island archipelago in the vast, uncharted sea of science. Long ago intrepid explorers from a nation state far, far away settled the islands of this archipelago. Once the various islands were settled, the peoples found themselves separated by shark-infested waters, treacherous reefs, and inaccessible ports. Consequently, little commerce today occurs between natives of these separate islands. Over time, the peoples developed alternative customs, rituals, religions, values, dialects, and modes of exchange.

Because each island produces slightly different desirable natural resources, the various peoples of these islands face a fundamental choice: Do they compete to take the territories across the waters by force, or do they find sufficient commonality to negotiate normative and mutually compatible relations for continued commerce? Conflict is costly, but may be seen as a means to possess the entire archipelago, the entire territory with all the resources and power entailed by the success of such a conflict. In contrast, a negotiated cooperative arrangement may reduce the total resources available to each individual island, but enable greater benefits by avoiding the costs of waging war and arranging complementary exchanges of the best each culture has to offer. Conflict can make a group stronger by steeling the motives to pull together against the external enemies, yet it can also reveal the weaknesses and fractures of a given group, and potentially, the entire overthrow of one's own cherished culture.

The methodological "cultures" of social scientists are a lot like these separate island cultures. They each have their rules, customs, beliefs, and values. Each knows the others exist, but they engage in relatively little commerce and often view each other with suspicion and incredulity. Conflict, or at least indifference, has in the past often occurred more often than cooperation. There have also been periods of peace and collaboration, and there are signs that this may increasingly become the norm.

Social science began in the ancient, perhaps primal, desire to understand the world around us. Long ago, Eastern and Western traditions evolved across and into various eras, cultures, and locales of enlightenment. As it was increasingly realized that scientific methods for understanding the world could be cumulative and increasingly valid, the approaches to understanding the physical world were increasingly extended to investigating the social world.

These scholars eventually evolved into "tribes" of methodological and theoretical disciplines and associations. These tribes settled distinct islands of academe, often only dimly aware of the practices and beliefs of the tribes occupying the academic programs across continents, universities, colleges, departments, and even hallways and faculty room tables. The methods by which these tribes became acculturated and accustomed became claims to their natural resources of the "truth(s)" of the world, and the academic prestige implied by successful claims to this domain. Over time, these different methods have more often fomented indifference, alienation, and occasional struggles for respect, rather than negotiated cooperation. Scholars peer derisively at the alien practices of the heathen tribe across these methodological divides, and chant the righteousness of their own personal beliefs and customs.

The domain of truth is often viewed as a limited resource, and any successful claims by other tribes result in territory no longer available to conquer except through renewed conflict. These territorial skirmishes often strengthen the spirits of believers and sometimes eliminate more destructive or flawed cultural customs of certain tribes; but often the ongoing battles serve no higher purpose than to fuel the conflict itself. The tribes intuitively understand that identifying a foil, or a common enemy, helps reinforce the resolve of the group. The destructiveness of the conflicts is typically exacerbated by the tendency of the different cultures to employ distinct symbols, vocabularies, and dialects. Misunderstandings become common, even when negotiation efforts are pursued in the interest of cooperation.

Social scientists have developed different methodological idioms of scholarly inquiry. These methodological practices represent distinct cultures, sometimes cooperating, but more often competing, to claim the larger territory of social science. Even when representatives of these distinct cultures claim publicly the importance of "getting along," in private conversations with those of their own tribes, the rhetoric generally becomes incendiary and resentful of the others' intrusions into territories more "rightly" reserved for one's own endeavors.

Competition for the sake of competition may have reached the limits of its evolutionary value. Two millennia have helped hone a verdant array of methodological islands. Productive progress in the future may well require more than a mere truce. Instead, the academic archipelago of social sciences may need a common bill of rights, a common sense of collective purpose, and a common recognition of each other's contributions. Unfortunately, such a revolution is not in the immediate offing. Before such a revolution can occur, however, bridges must be forged between and among the

academic islands. This textbook lays the preliminary pontoons, in two important ways: First, by locating the nature of methods in the nature of argument, and second, by representing the broader scope of methods currently employed by the communication discipline.

By locating the central underlying architecture of all methods in the structure of arguments, this text helps decode the Rosetta Stone of methodological languages, the symbolic intersection through which negotiations for collective commerce in the pursuit of knowledge must progress. No matter what else a method attempts to accomplish, it must rely upon, and establish the validity of, its practices through argument. Every method guides the production, collection, and analysis of *data*, which consist of artifact(s), observation(s), case(s), example(s), or counts of something. But data alone prove nothing. Data only become meaningful in the crucible of argument, which connects the data through warrants to claims. *Warrants* are the reasons, rationale, or answer to the question "why" should I believe the claim being made by this research. The *claim* is the conclusion, or the particular proposition (e.g., hypothesis, value judgment, belief statement, etc.), which contextualizes the reasonableness of the data in connection with a claim. The claim, once established, may then become the warrant for subsequent arguments. Warrants are the bridges between data and claim, and claims so established serve as bridges to further arguments.

This textbook examines ways of knowing as arguments. When a scholar has reached a conclusion, it stands as a privileged claim—a claim that this scholar's method has provided specialized insight. Scholars apply a specialized method that they have apprenticed in their education to master, and this method serves as a way of privileging their voice compared to any given layperson's view of the world. This does not invalidate the layperson's views—it only suggests that methods provide a more reasoned or systematic approach to knowing than the average person will have had the opportunity or expertise to apply to making claims about some particular topic of investigation.

There are many ways of scholarly knowing, but four illustrative paradigms in the communication discipline consist of discovery, strict empiricist analysis, interpretation, and critical approaches. These will be defined and detailed more extensively throughout the text, but for now, they can be illustrated in general ways. The *discovery* method assumes a singular objective reality, and although no method can reveal this objective truth in the social world, the discovery method uses various methods of objectification, including experiments, control, and quantification in an attempt to inch ever closer to that reality. The *strict empiricist* method assumes that because communicators accomplish everyday life based only on the behaviors they display through their communication (as opposed to reading each other's minds), researchers can understand such behavior best by observing and precisely analyzing such naturally occurring activities. The *interpretive* method assumes that reality is socially constructed, that there are as many realities as there are people perceiving and influencing such perceptions through their communication. The *critical* method assumes that reality is always influenced by underlying systems of often hidden influence and power, and such structures must be evaluated through an evaluative perspective that reveals these hidden forces, thereby presenting opportunities for pursuing more noble or practical ends. If these paradigms are analyzed through the lens of the rationales they rely

upon, they might look something like the arguments shown in Figure 1.

Each paradigm or method can be further elaborated into its own particular rationale. The discovery paradigm presupposes that in any given process, there is a set of causes and effects, and that methods properly designed to manage or control for subjectivity of the researcher(s), and translating observations into quantifiable measurements, can reveal something about how causes associate with such effects. This approach to knowing implies an argument such those shown in Figure 2.

As another example, let's say that in meticulously observing everyday conversation, you recognize a highly complex process through which people achieve social life. That is, apologies, compliments, requests, and the "events" of everyday life are accomplished through a subtle choreography of move and countermove of behavior. In such a dance, thoughts, values, and beliefs are actually irrelevant to uncovering the structure of such accomplishments. An interactant cannot peer into your

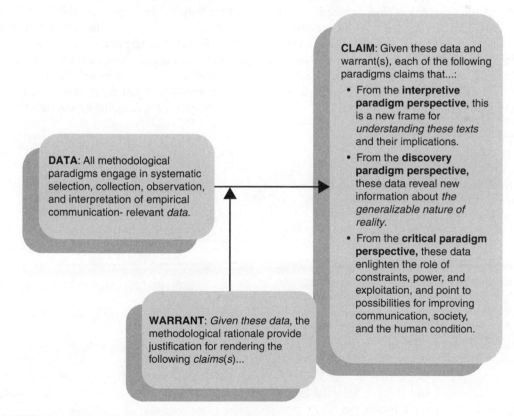

Figure 1 Diagramming the Underlying Arguments of Different Ways of Knowing

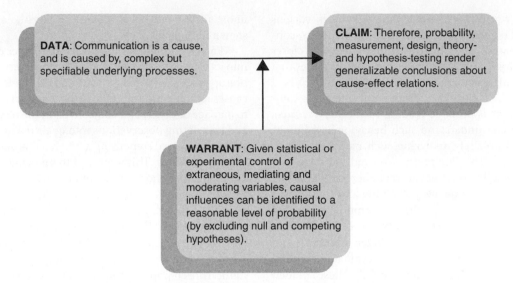

Figure 2 Diagramming the Underlying Argument for the Discovery Paradigm

mind during a conversation; he or she recognizes an apology through the structure of the behavior observed, and therefore, such behavior is also observable by a researcher. The data of everyday accomplishments exists in behavior. If this is accurate, then it seems reasonable that all inferences about what conversationalists are attempting to achieve through interaction are exclusively "available" to others through their behavior. Several arguments could be derived from this rationale, but consider for the moment shown in Figure 3:

In contrast, interactants often make judgments about what others are doing through their behavior. In so doing, sometimes making one attribution rather than another may be an important determinant of how a person behaves in response to others' behavior. For example, if you think you deserve an apology from someone, and this person provides what seems a cursory or inappropriate apology, you are likely to devalue this person's apology. If you think this person provided an insincere apology because he or she thought you didn't

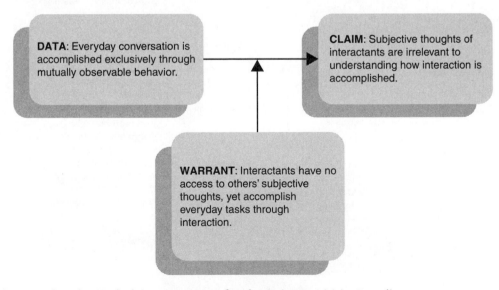

Figure 3 Diagramming the Underlying Argument for the Strict Empiricist Paradigm

deserve an apology, you might begin disliking this person. Further, you might respond by seeking further apology, or avoid interacting with this person in the future. In short, your attributions or subjective thoughts about this person's behavior directly influence your interaction with this person. Figure 4 illustrates this argument.

Finally, the world may reveal disparities and distortions that imply underlying forces at work, which sustain themselves through power, deception, manipulation, and bias. Such hidden forces require critics to expose them, and to provide an evaluative standard against which such exploitative practices might be revealed and the victims of such distortions thereby liberated to empower their own interests. The rationale underlying this paradigm might look like the one shown in Figure 5.

These various arguments lead to very different claims (i.e., methods) of understanding social interaction. For example, to the strict empiricist (typical of

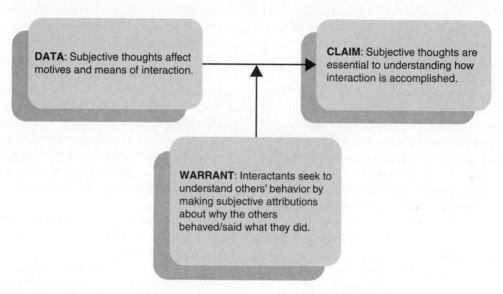

Figure 4 Diagramming the Underlying Argument for the Interpretive Paradigm

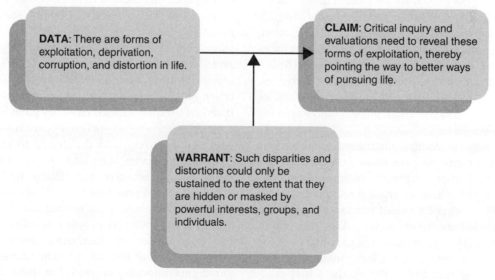

Figure 5 Diagramming the Underlying Argument for the Critical Paradigm

conversation analysts), only people's naturally occurring behaviors count as data, whereas in ethnographic or interpretive methods, both thoughts and behaviors count as data. Discovery researchers will experiment with people, whereas interpretive and strict empiricist researchers take people's behavior for what it is, or was, and do not seek to introduce new stimuli to the investigation context. It follows that what counts as a theory can differ substantially across these paradigms. In one, behavior explains behavior, whereas in another, perceptions and feelings explain behavior. Strict empiricist researchers don't see the relevance of the findings of survey (discovery) researchers, and survey researchers have difficulty seeing how to generalize the conclusions of strict empiricism without a cognitive theoretical context.

So it is with all methodological arguments—they are the ways we know, and the ways we choose to know often seem to preclude other ways of knowing. The collective practices and vocabularies of scholars represent what Thomas Kuhn (1970) referred to as *paradigms*, and he believed them to be incommensurable. That is, a paradigm answers all the questions it needs to, in much the same way a religion is meant to do, and consequently, there is no need to borrow from another paradigm, just as most people find no need to borrow religious beliefs from another religion.

So the islands upon which these researchers dwell are isolated by the arguments they make. But maybe, just maybe, if they recognize this fact, they can begin to understand *why* they reside on different islands in the first place, and how their respective tribes differ. Maybe they can begin to see how their arguments relate to each other, and begin a dialog through which cooperation, rather than conflict, can be begun (Craig, 1999). Perhaps they can learn to "talk each other's language" (Kuhn, 1970), and thereby better understand their differences. This textbook, by excavating the underlying basis of these differences, lays the initial bridges (and warrants) for this dialogue to begin.

This dialogue is facilitated to the extent the various tribes and their customs are known. Arguments are most competent when adapted to their audiences, including those with whom we argue (i.e., other practitioners), as well as other interested parties (e.g., granting agencies, foundations, the media, etc.). Another strength of this text is a fair representation of the domain of the discipline. Few survey textbooks, for example, do justice in characterizing and differentiating the actual practices of conversation and discourse analysts, or only give

shallow consideration of critical and rhetorical methods. In contrast, this textbook recognizes the legitimacy of these methods as equivalent because their endeavors are predicated on the same discourse of argument. As Walter Fisher (1978) claimed, all arguments are ultimately erected on the foundations of underlying values, and "no analytically grounded hierarchy of values will ever claim universal adherence" (p. 377). Nevertheless, having an understanding of the multiple cultures of values with which one may seek congress, the better the dialog can become in the service of that engagement.

Nowhere is this dialog more important than in the initial enculturation of students, beginning your own intrepid voyages into the often turbulent waters of the communication discipline. Just as it is easier developmentally to learn multiple languages early in the process of language learning, so it is easier to accept multiple methodologies before any single methodological argument has fortified its armaments and defenses against the other scholarly cultures with which it competes. Distinct cultural groups need not engage in similar practices to reap the benefits of mutual understanding and cooperation.

The potential distance and competition among islands of inquiry is an old concern. Scholars have previously suggested that the key differences are in the questions that each culture seeks to answer. The types of questions asked can be important frames for arguments—such as determining what kind of argument represents a sensible response. People have suggested, for example, that there need be no competition between religion and science (Gould, 1999) or science and humanities (Gould, 2003; Miller, 1975), because these *magisteria* ask different types of questions, and thereby avoid encroachment upon one another's territories. Others, however, have suggested that the differences between religion and science, for example, go far deeper than just the questions asked—they go to issues such as their orientation to skepticism, openness to new knowledge and discovery, and the degree to which faith is placed in preserving the past versus accumulating, revising, and correcting the past (Fuchs, 2001). In the case of the arguments posed for the methods encountered in this text, for the most part, the big questions addressed are the same—why do people communicate the ways they do, and how does such communication affect the human condition? Instead, the major differences in the paradigms of inquiry examined in this text have to do with *ways* of answering any such questions, and this "how" question is addressed by different methods, representing different kinds of arguments for pursuing understanding.

The journey is not an easy one. Forging relations with strange cultures and territories seldom is. There are many barriers that even the most motivated and capable among us face in building bridges across the waves and shoals of these methodological divides (Bryman, 2007). On the other hand, there are usually great benefits to developing an acquaintance and ongoing relationship with these cultures. Eventually, with enough trade, commerce, and experience in multiple cultures of research, scholars may become truly multilingual and multicultural, appreciating their indigenous culture and yet fully appreciating and engaging other cultures as well. There are many fruits of knowledge to taste and experiences to pursue that can only derive from encounters with those beyond the borders of our own comfortable domains.

Therefore, go forth, and may you find the value of the voyage worthwhile. And for the few of you who will ever get the privilege of applying such arguments in the service of knowledge, may you get some glimpse of the excitement that derives from knowing something no one else knows, of discovering something no one else has discovered, or of seeing further than anyone else has previously seen. The risks of being wrong are great, but the potential of charting new routes or discovering new islands, or even building new bridges, holds its own rewards for those willing to venture forth with a spirit of scholarly adventure. This text will help you greatly along your way, providing as it does the charts and compass needed for the voyage ahead.

Brian H. Spitzberg
School of Communication
San Diego State University
December 30, 2012

Part 1

The What and Why of
Communication Research

1 Introduction to Communication Research

Introduction

In this chapter, you will get an overview of communication research, including scholarly research conducted by academics and proprietary research conducted by professionals in communication-related industries like advertising, healthcare, media and marketing, public relations, and politics. We will start by distinguishing everyday ways of knowing about the world from the ways of knowing employed in research. Then we will introduce you to the idea of research as a way of making arguments. We will show you some of the ways that researchers think about the relationships among their theories and methods of studying communication, and how research findings are shared through professional associations and networks, as well as through publication in scholarly and trade journals and popular press outlets. The last part of the chapter will help you start to make sense of two types of academic manuscripts: research reports and critical essays.

Learning Outcomes

After completing this chapter, you should be able to:
- » Identify and find examples of communication research in academic and industry contexts.
- » Compare and contrast the advantages and disadvantages of tenacity, authority and a priori knowledge with science as a way of knowing.
- » Explain the three elements of the Toulmin model of argument: claim, data, and warrant.
- » Describe how communication theories and methods are related (for academic researchers) and how best practices serve as practical theories (for industry researchers).
- » Distinguish between research reports and critical essays, and identify the elements of each type of research manuscript.

Outline

How is social media being used by companies for branding, and how do customers view those efforts? Can a television program really reduce the teen pregnancy rate in the US? If you're trying to avoid getting the flu, will it matter whether you greet people with a handshake, a fist bump, a high five, or a hug? These communication questions, and many others, are being answered every day with research (e.g., Greer & Ferguson, 2011; Kearney & Levine, 2014; Ghareeb, Bourlai, Dutton, & McClellan, 2013).

Understanding communication research will help you to become a more competent and well-informed person. As a student, you are expected to read research studies in your major classes, and you may conduct your own research studies in some classes. For example, some communication studies majors at San Francisco State University collect and analyze messages that they find in different San Francisco neighborhoods (e.g., public health campaigns, advertisements, store front signage, or Yelp reviews of stores). They explain and interpret those messages using content analysis, and they survey neighborhood residents about their perceptions of the messages. You will learn more about those student research projects in Chapter 12, "Content Analysis," and Chapter 13, "Survey Research," respectively.

As a current or perhaps future employee in advertising, corporate communication, fundraising, human resource management, marketing, media, public relations,

politics, sales and training (some of the careers where communication, speech, and media program graduates work), you may be conducting research on behalf of your organization. If you work in management, you will need to interpret research evidence to help make policy decisions for your organization. As a consumer, a parent, and a community member, you need to understand research and be able make sense of studies that claim to explain, interpret, or criticize communication in all sorts of contexts (e.g., healthcare, politics, consumer behaviors).

Most communication programs today have identified student learning outcomes that are focused on skills you will need for your career and your role as a contributing member of society (Parks, Faw, & Goldsmith, 2011). Ask your professor where graduates of your program work, or look for alumni of your program on LinkedIn or Facebook. Use the "Try It!" activity at the end of this chapter to investigate the national and local outlook for your intended career; you will have begun to conduct your own communication research. It's challenging and fun!

Critical Thinking and Information Literacy

Understanding a range of humanistic and social scientific research methods will increase your critical thinking abilities and information literacy skills (Canary, 2003), which will help you in three ways: First, we all need to make sense of research findings as community members, consumers, jurors, parents, and voters. We have to understand the research findings we learn about in the news. Then we have to figure out whether those findings apply to us, and if so, how we might use the research findings to solve our particular problems. You may not have thought how often you already do research that requires information literacy and critical thinking (e.g., jumping on the web to MapQuest directions somewhere, Yelping about a favorite restaurant, or Googling just about anything).

Second, as a student, you need to be able to read research critically in your discipline. You probably are required to write term papers that have you read and apply academic research. You may even conduct your own communication research in this class or another class in your major. Academic communication research is the main focus of this book. Academic research is conducted by scholars and addresses a broad range of topic areas, including interpersonal and family communication, group and organizational communication, persuasion and social influence, and communication technology and media studies, as well as communication in particular contexts such as health, instruction, and the law or public policy. Chances are good that your department or major program emphasizes some of these areas of academic research but not all of them.

Third, most employees need to be able to conduct and critically evaluate research in the workplace. If you are working in a small family business or a large multinational corporation, government institution, or nonprofit organization, for example, you will need to survey coworkers and clients about their attitudes, analyze customer complaints, and recommend policy changes that will remedy those problems, track sales data or fundraising efforts, and so forth. If you work in a large organization, you may want to do a needs analysis to determine what sort of employee training to offer or figure out how to advertise and market your company's products. If you work for the government, you will use research to make decisions about public policies, grant funding, and political campaigns. All of these activities are heavily vested in research.

Just as communication research covers a range of topics it also uses a mixture of methodologies and theories, although this is true in slightly different ways for academic and industry research. Scholars who conduct academic research typically connect existing theories with different methods for investigating communication. Academic researchers make their procedures and findings available to everyone, so that any interested party can benefit from their studies. Check out http://www.communicationcurrents.com, a free, web-based magazine published by the National Communication Association, to see summaries of academic communication research. Or look at an academic online database such as *Communication & Mass Media Complete* to locate original academic research studies published in scholarly journals. You can follow your department's Facebook and Twitter pages to learn more about the academic research your department's faculty members are doing, too.

Proprietary research refers to research that is conducted in industry, where the procedures and findings are owned by the organization that paid to conduct the study. The methods and findings of proprietary studies may be kept secret in order to preserve the company's advantage over its competitors. Just as academic researchers are guided by scholarly theories, proprietary research is guided by **best practices**, the accumulated current wisdom of an industry about how to achieve results. Incidentally, best practices are established through research! **Benchmarking** is the process of measuring and validating strategic performance in a business or industry, and organizations use benchmarks as criteria against which to measure their own success. For example, the Arbitron and Nielsen ratings used to establish audience consumption of radio and television programs respectively are proprietary research endeavors that are used to benchmark the performance of media organizations, and the National Survey of Student Engagement (NSSE) is used to benchmark the performance of colleges and universities in the United States (McCormick, 2010). Check out *Communication World*, the magazine for communication management, to read about some additional examples of proprietary research.

In this book, you will learn about both academic and proprietary communication research methods, and you will learn how each method relates to communication theory. But before we embark on that journey, let's consider "What is a theory?"

Communication Theories

Theories are descriptions and explanations for how things work, what things mean, or how things ought to work differently. For instance, communication or speech majors often learn theories about how persuasion works, how meaning is coordinated among members of a social group, or how power relations tend to privilege dominant group members and oppress minority group members as well as how those situations might be changed. As a student, you may be required to take a course in rhetorical or communication theory, and you are also likely to encounter theories in your organizational, interpersonal, intercultural, group, health, or mass communication courses.

Some theories are really detailed and use formal logic. Those theories are made up of axioms and propositions. Axioms are statements about the relationships among two or more concepts, relationships that have been demonstrated in previous research. The term *axiom* comes from mathematics where it refers to a relationship that is uncontestable, accepted as law. In our field, axioms specify what we already know about a communication process. Propositions predict what relationships are likely between two or more concepts given what we already know (i.e., given the axioms of a theory). Berger and Calabrese's (1975) uncertainty reduction theory, which deals with interpersonal communication, and the popular uses and gratifications approach to media research (Palmgreen, 1984) are two examples of communication theories based on formal logic. Theories based on formal logic are often used to explain and predict how communication processes work: Uncertainty reduction theory has been used to show how interpersonal relationships develop and deteriorate, whereas uses and gratifications theory has been used to explain and predict consumers' mass media choices.

However, some theories are metaphoric, using one idea or a story rather than formal axioms and propositions to represent a communication process. For example, Baxter and Montgomery's (1998) dialectical theory uses the idea of paradox, or competing tensions between two opposing forces, to explore relationships between people, organizations, and even societies. In your family relationships, for instance, you probably want both connectedness and autonomy: You want to belong to your family group, but you sometimes want your separate, individual identity, too. How we manage tensions between two such competing desires is the subject of dialectical theory and research.

Another way of thinking about all the possible different communication theories is to ask what element of communication, or what parts of the process, are being theorized about? For example, there are theories about communicators themselves, but there are also theories about messages, conversations, relationships, groups, organizations, and the media and theories about whole cultures or societies (Littlejohn & Foss, 2005). Whether a theory uses formal logic or not, it is the way we organize what we know about anything.

When you first start to learn about communication theory, you may think that we already have all the theories we need to describe and explain everything about communication. Or you might think that the theories we used to believe in are now being replaced by newer, better theories. In fact, theories are more fluid and malleable than you might imagine. Communication theories, like communicators themselves, change constantly (Philipsen, 1997). So the topics that we try to understand and explain, and the ways that we conduct research, are still evolving.

Theory and Research Methods

In the field of communication, we sometimes think of theories as distinct from research methodologies; but sometimes theory and method are quite interconnected or even the same thing. Just as there are quite a large number of theories used to study human communication, so too can communication research methods take on many forms. Some researchers separate methodologies from the theories that their methods are designed to test, whereas other researchers in our field see theories and methods as thoroughly intertwined, so much so that theory and method are presented together in courses like rhetorical and media criticism, discourse analysis, or ethnography and communication. These different approaches highlight the fact that there is no one uniform approach to communication research methods.

Different methodologies come from profoundly different ways of thinking about what we know, what we believe communication is, and what we do as researchers when we study it. Each perspective represents a particular point of view. We hope to help you understand why treating research methods as if there is just one way of thinking about them is no longer an effective way of understanding communication.

When you are a researcher, you may simply come up with an idea for a study that answers a question you have about communication, like studying what makes someone really persuasive, without ever thinking about the merits of one particular methodology over another. But by choosing a methodology, you can't avoid tapping the underlying assumptions that go with it, assumptions about how we know what we know. In the next section, we consider some everyday ways of knowing, contrast them with a more rigorous way of knowing used in academic research, and introduce the idea of research as making an argument.

Everyday Ways of Knowing

As students of communication, we have to practice communication at the same time we are attempting to learn about it. So doing communication and knowing about it are inseparable. Ultimately, you will decide what you think communication means. But how you define communication influences what you think you know about it, just as what you know about communication will also influence the questions you want to investigate.

A philosopher by the name of Charles Sanders Peirce was interested in explaining the various ways we accept that we know things. Peirce believed that ordinary common sense could be distinguished from the methods of knowing we apply more rigorously in philosophy and in the sciences. He identified four general ways of knowing: tenacity, authority, a priori, and the method of science (Kerlinger, 1986).

Knowing by tenacity relies on customary knowledge. We know something is true because it is commonly held to be true. For example, you may believe some common assertions are true such as moon phases affect human moods and behavior, or planetary alignment at the moment of a person's birth can forecast the personality dispositions that appear later in that person's life. Today, beliefs in lunar influence and astrology are commonplace, and even though some people see them as superstitions, many people accept them as unquestionably true.

Sometimes your beliefs about reality can be influenced by what you hear and see around you. For example, if you watch very much television or are on the Internet every day, media portrayals of crime or world events may lead you to think that you are more likely to be a victim of crime or that Americans make up a larger proportion of the world population than they actually do. Studies by Gerbner and others (summarized in Gerbner, Gross, Morgan, & Signorelli, 1986) have actually tested the various ways media can cultivate or influence viewers to adopt certain perceptions of reality such

as those we just mentioned. The media, in effect, create the perception that certain beliefs are commonplace. Once a view of the world is accepted as the usual or ordinary pattern, it is accepted tenaciously. This means that even when we are shown quite strong evidence contradicting some of our basic assumptions, we are still unwilling to change our beliefs. Even though tenacity is difficult to shake as grounds for knowledge, it is the weakest method of knowing since it relies purely on belief without considering any other evidence. Because tenacious knowledge is grounded in belief, it cannot be questioned or challenged on any methodological grounds. It also cannot be verified.

The second general way of knowing that C. S. Peirce identified was **knowing by authority**, when we accept the truth or value of an idea because someone we regard as an expert says it is true. For example, we might listen to Dr. Oz and believe his advice on the latest diet or nutrition fad because we value his medical expertise. We might look on the Mayo Clinic's website for advice on dealing with a medical problem, or check an online dictionary to find the definition of a word. Since we cannot possibly develop expertise in every area of specialized knowledge, we rely heavily on the testimony of expert authorities: Building inspectors tell us when it is or is not safe to enter a building after it has been damaged in a hurricane or earthquake. Pharmaceutical researchers tell us which drugs to take to treat a physical condition. We pay our doctors to give us a diagnosis and lawyers to represent us knowledgeably in legal contexts. Every time we get into our cars and drive through an intersection, we depend on automobile and urban design experts to competently provide us with the means of getting from one point to another.

Knowing by authority is a trustworthy way of knowing things as long as the experts are correct. But what if they are wrong? There have been many cases of people who were prosecuted for claiming to be experts and misleading the people who trusted them; you don't have to look far to find a case like Bernie Madoff's investment embezzling scheme or Lance Armstrong's doping scandal. In both cases, thousands of people trusted their expertise and relied on their advice, until they were exposed as unethical and inaccurate authorities.

Sometimes, experts give advice in areas where they have only customary knowledge, but we attribute greater weight to what they say because of who they are. For example, entertainment celebrities sometimes use their public stature to advertise cars or medicine even though they have no specialized knowledge of these products. You may trust your teachers' knowledge not only about their areas of expertise, but also, because you admire them, you may find what they have to say about other topics influential as well. Even though we could not get along in life without relying on expert testimony and definitions, we sometimes have a difficult time determining when the experts are wrong and avoiding potentially harmful consequences as a result.

The last type of everyday knowledge is **knowing on a priori grounds**, which happens when we know something intuitively before we have experienced it. The a priori approach tests claims against standards of reasonableness. For example, we might establish criteria based on moral grounds for determining justifiable actions, such as "Is it honest?" Or our standards also could be based on aesthetic or artistic merits, such as "Is it beautiful?" But there are two main problems with this way of knowing. First, how do we determine what constitutes a *reasonable* standard of action? Can we figure that out using our minds alone, or do we need our body's sensory experiences to do so? If we need sensory observations, how can we ever separate *what* we sense from *our perception* of it? The second problem with a priori knowledge is that we will probably see as reasonable what we already know by tenacity: What we think is moral, or beautiful, for example, is probably influenced in great part by whatever our social predecessors have seen as having those merits.

The final way we know things, according to Peirce (1992), is through the **method of science**, which incorporates and builds upon tenacity, authority, and a priori knowledge. We've all been raised with some beliefs about science as a rigorous way of knowing (tenacity), and we've all benefited from scientific research (expertise). Like the a priori approach, the scientific method requires establishing standards by which any claim can be tested for its reasonableness. Here, Peirce said that in addition to logical consistency, researchers must also test their claims through observation and experience. He identified the following properties of reasoning in science: observations, experimentation, and generalization. These terms come out of a very specific paradigm of thought that represents just one approach to understanding science. In fact, all research methodologies are based on some form of observation and reflection, but not all methodologies are based on experimentation and generalization.

For Peirce (1992), tenacity, authority, and a priori reasoning, the everyday ways of knowing, were weak each in its own way compared to the scientific way of knowing because science relied on careful reasoning tested by experience. We agree with Peirce that researchers must reason carefully. But we expand his typology to include as research methodologies not only empirical methods but also more reflective methods of interpretation and evaluation. In fact, our everyday ways of knowing also play a role in research because researchers develop their own tenaciously held beliefs about the best ways to study communication, and some of their standards come from experts such as more experienced researchers. So we bring all our ways of knowing with us to the research process, where even the most careful reasoning leads us to express a point of view. We call this point of view making an argument, and in the next section, we introduce you to the idea of research methods as ways of making arguments about what you know.

Research Methods as Argument

We are not the only authors to approach studying research methods as different ways of constructing arguments (Abelson, 1995; Jackson, Jacobs, Burrell, & Allen, 1986). In fact, a statistics professor at Yale University, Robert Abelson (1995), maintained that research, "should make an interesting claim; it should tell a story that an informed audience will care about, and it should do so by intelligent interpretation of appropriate evidence" (p. 2).

We are about to introduce you to a classical Western form of argument (Toulmin, 1972; Toulmin, Rieke, & Janik, 1984) that will help you to distinguish research from everyday ways of knowing. Our research-as-argument model, represented by Figure 1.1 below, is a simplified version of Toulmin et al.'s (1984) extended form.

Whenever we make an argument, it is always based on some central assertion. This declarative statement is called the **claim**. For example, a very simple claim would be "This is my bicycle." As you will see in Chapter 4, "Making Claims," research assertions can take many different forms in our field. They can be specific statements about the relationship between two communication

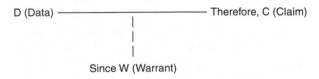

Figure 1.1 The Claim-Data-Warrant Model

phenomena, such as predicting that experience in different cultures will make one a more flexible communicator. They also can be phrased as questions, like asking whether women use different conflict strategies than men. Claims can represent the general purposes or goals of the research more broadly, such as claiming that the study of communication in one group will help us better understand what is happening in other groups. In Parts 2 and 3 of this book, you will learn a range of methodologies for investigating the different types of claims made in communication research.

Data, the second element of our research-as-argument model, refers to the evidence or grounds for a claim. Using our earlier example, you could say, "This is my bicycle. I have the receipt for the bike's purchase right here in my wallet." The receipt is direct evidence that supports your claim. In Chapter 5, "What Counts as Communication Data?" you will learn about many forms of evidence for communication research claims. For example, numerical ratings of communicator attitudes or counts of certain communication behaviors can be analyzed statistically. On the other hand, data may take the form of extensive field notes gathered by a researcher who hopes to explain how various groups of people talk with each other. Data may also refer to rhetorical texts that are analyzed for the speakers' motives or effects on audiences, although we usually call those texts evidence, rather than data, per se. You will learn much more about each of these approaches to data collection and analysis in the chapters of Parts 2 and 3.

The third element of an argument, the warrant, provides the crucial links between a researcher's claims and the data or evidence used to support them. **Warrants** are reasons for making a particular claim in view of specific evidence; they are standards for evaluating the evidence in light of a claim. The reasons themselves can take the form of rules, laws, principles, or formulas (Toulmin et al., 1984). Rules are "rules of thumb." They are the reasons that you, and any other person living in our society, would be likely to accept as a basis for some action. You can probably think of numerous rules that your department or university uses as a basis for their actions (e.g., students must pay fees to be officially enrolled in a class). **Laws** were briefly defined by Toulmin et al. as immutable, physical laws of nature (e.g., gravity), whereas **principles** referred specifically to legal rules and statutes (e.g., seat belts are required while driving a car). Finally, **formulas** referred to mathematical principles used in the physical and applied sciences (Toulmin

et al., 1984, p. 50). All of these rules, laws, principles, and formulas are warrants that allow us to apply standards of evaluation to some data and to use that data as evidence in support of a claim.

So in the bicycle example, you can make a claim of ownership based on the evidence you have provided, the receipt, because of the "receipt rule" that we have in our society. Your warrant depends on a large body of background information that clarifies how the rules are to be understood, applied, and relied on as the backing or support for an argument (Toulmin et al., 1984, p. 26). In other words, the warrants help us evaluate how good the argument that is being made. In the bicycle example, the rule of ownership based on printed receipts relies on a larger set of rules and beliefs we have generally about what constitutes legitimate ownership in our society. In Chapter 6, "Warrants for Research Arguments," we present the uniquely different ways of establishing warrants for particular types of communication research claims and data. Then, in each of the Parts 2 and 3 chapters, we show you how to apply those warrants for specific communication research methodologies.

The claim-data-warrant model is a useful way to distinguish general kinds of reasoning that we use to do research from the ordinary ways of knowing that we use every day. Although everyday thinking is similar to research reasoning in some ways, everyday thinking is not applied with the same systematic rigor that is characteristic of methodological inquiry. Moreover, everyday thinking frequently includes elements that are not used in research. To explore this idea more, let's talk about what makes a good argument.

Making Good Academic and Practical Arguments

You already know that arguments include the three elements of claim, data or evidence, and warrant. A good argument includes all three elements; however, not every argument that includes these elements is good. One way to evaluate an argument is to ask yourself these questions: "Who am I with respect to this argument? Who am I speaking *as*? Who am I speaking *for*? And who benefits?"

Let's say, for example, that you learn from a news report that coffee is good for your health. If you are a daily coffee drinker, you may be happy to find evidence that supports your habit, and you may have no problem with the fact that coffee producers are likely to benefit from the publication of such a finding. But if you are a tea drinker, you may feel less inclined to accept that argument, even with evidence.

In this book, we present communication research as a process of making good arguments. We help you learn to distinguish good claims, data or evidence, and warrants as they are used in different types of communication research methodologies. Because there are different methods, and different standards for evaluating the relationship between claims and evidence in those methods, a good way to begin learning about research arguments is to learn from example. Read the research articles you will find in scholarly, refereed journals. Those articles are written for particular audiences and in two main formats: research reports and critical essays. In the remainder of this chapter, we will profile some audiences for communication research, and introduce you to these two kinds of academic research manuscripts.

Audiences for Communication Research

The pursuit of knowledge is almost never wholly individual. Rather, research is intended to be shared with a community of interest. Whatever your research topic, you are probably trying to know about something that one or more communities of people also wants to know about. At a minimum, those communities might consist of other researchers, the research participants themselves, or the practitioners who apply and use the knowledge produced by research, including the decision-makers who determine organizational policies in government, education, healthcare, media, the law, and industry.

So, whenever you make an argument using research, considering your audience is one important part of the process. We need to write differently and target different publication outlets to reach different audiences since they don't all consume the same sources or even have the same criteria for effective writing (Canovar, 2012; Childress, 1998). Whether you are writing a research paper for a class assignment, for presentation at a professional association meeting, or for publication, it is important to consider your readers, just as you would consider your audience when you are preparing to give a speech. Professional association meetings and scholarly journals are the most common audiences and distribution outlets for academic research manuscripts written by communication scholars. Trade journals, popular press publications, websites, and textbooks are common distribution outlets for secondary reports of communication research that are consumed by nonacademics as well as by scholars. Let's consider each audience in turn.

Professional Associations

The first audience for written research reports and critical essays is typically the researcher's peer community of scholars in a given discipline or topic area. Original and unpublished research reports and critical essays are presented first at conferences. These conferences are often annual meetings sponsored by a **professional association**, a dues-paying group of academics in a particular field of study. Some of the professional associations frequented by scholars of communication, and their respective website addresses, are listed in Table 1.1.

In addition, we chose to also list some interdisciplinary professional associations that are frequented by communication scholars.

Professional association meetings help communication scholars stay abreast of the most recent developments in our field. In professional associations, we maintain ongoing dialogues about issues of interest as well as relationships with peers who share those interests. But professional associations also allow us, as researchers, to gain important feedback from our most important audience, our peers. The feedback we get from peers after we present our research at a professional association meeting helps us to revise our written manuscripts to determine what other audiences, if any, should be pursued for a given research report or critical essay. Feedback from peers, both formal and informal, also helps us to determine which research ideas or topics to pursue and how to pursue them in the future.

Scholarly Journals

Scholarly journals are published under the sponsorship of professional associations in a given discipline. Their purpose is to convey the very best theoretic and research scholarship in that field to a community of academic peers. Only a very small percentage of the research presented at professional meetings is ever published in a scholarly journal. Some of the papers presented at professional association meetings are works in progress, and some of the research presented at conferences never

Table 1.1 Professional Association Meetings Attended by Communication Scholars

Communication Disciplinary Associations

American Communication Association (ACA) (www.americancomm.org)

American Forensics Association (AFA) (www.americanforensics.org)

Association for Education in Journalism and Mass Communication (AEJMC) (http://www.aejmc.org/)

Broadcast Education Association (BEA) (http://www.beaweb.org/)

Communication Association of Japan

European Speech Communication Association (www.esca-speech.org)

International Association of Business Communicators (www.iabc.com)

International Communication Association (www.icahdq.org)

International Association for Intercultural Communication Studies (IAICS) (www.trinity.edu/org/ics)

International Listening Association (ILA) (www.listen.org)

International Network on Personal Relationships (INPR) (www.inpr.org)

International Society for the Study of Personal Relationships (ISSPR) (www.isspr.org)

Kenneth Burke Society (www.home.duq.edu/~thames/kennethburke)

National Communication Association (www.natcom.org)

Oral History Association (http://dickinson.edu/oha)

Organization for Research on Women and Communication (ORWAC) (http://www.orwac.org/)

Public Relations Society of America (www.prsa.org)

United States Regional Communication Associations

   Central States Communication Association (www.csca-net.org)

   Eastern States Communication Association (www.jmu.edu)

   Southern States Communication Association (http://ssca.net)

   Western States Communication Association (www.westcomm.org)

   Speech Communication Association of Puerto Rico

Interdisciplinary Associations Frequented by Communication Scholars

International Information Management Association (mass communication) (www.iima.org)

International Society for the Study of General Semantics (www.uiowa.edu)

Society for the Study of Symbolic Interaction (www.sun.soci.niu.edu/~sssi/)

Note: In addition to the preceding listings, many state-level communication associations exist in the United States (e.g., California Speech Communication Association).

will be submitted to scholarly journals. If a research report or critical essay is submitted for publication at a peer-reviewed scholarly journal, then two or more scholars who share the researcher's areas of theoretical, methodological, or topical expertise will closely evaluate the manuscript. Based on feedback from those reviewers, the journal editor will decide whether to publish the research study, usually with revisions suggested by the peer reviewers (Katzer, Cook, & Crouch, 1998). The journals sponsored by the NCA report over a 90% rejection rate. That means that fewer than 1 in 10 articles submitted for peer review are eventually accepted for publication.

Table 1.2 lists some of the scholarly journals that publish communication research. Notice that journals affiliated with professional associations in communication, as well as other relevant disciplines, are listed separately.

Trade Journals and Popular Press Publications

It is quite common to see summaries of communication research presented in trade journals and quoted in popular press publications. This makes sense because of the centrality of human communication to other aspects of

Table 1.2 Scholarly Journals That Publish Communication Research

Journals Affiliated with Communication Associations	
The American Communication Journal	Argumentation & Advocacy
Canadian Journal of Communication	Communication Education (CE)
Communication and the Law (CL)	Communication Monographs (CM)
Communication Quarterly (CQ)	Communication Reports (CR)
Communication Research	Communication Research Reports (CRR)
Communication Studies	Communication Teacher
Communication Theory (CT)	Communication Yearbook
Critical Studies in Mass Communication (CSMC)	Health Communication
Human Communication Research (HCR)	Journal of Applied Comm. Research (JACR)
Howard Journal of Communication (www.communicationarena.com)	Journal of CMC
	Journal of Film and Television
International Journal of Communication	Journal of Social & Personal Relationships (JSPR)
Journal of Communication & Religion	Journal of Popular Culture
Journal of Communication (JOC)	Mass Communication & Society
Journal of Health Communication	Philosophy & Rhetoric
Journal of Public Relations Research	Public Relations Journal (PRJ)
KB: A Journal of the Burke Society	Southern Communication Journal (SCJ)
National Forensic Journal	Text & Performance Quarterly (TPQ)
Political Communication (PC)	Written Communication (WC)
Quarterly Journal of Speech (QJS)	
The Review of Communication	
Western Journal of Communication (WJC)	

Journals Affiliated with Other Professional Associations	
Discourse and Society	Discourse Processes
Group and Organization Management	Journalism & Mass Comm. Quarterly
Journal of Business Communication	Journal of Broadcasting & Electronic Media
Journal of Contemporary Ethnography	Journal of Mixed Method Research
Journal of Social & Personal Relationships	Language and Society
Management Communication Quarterly	Qualitative Inquiry
Research on Language & Social Interaction	Sex Roles
Small Group Research	Society of Text & Discourse

our daily lives. **Trade journals** are print and digital publications aimed at practitioners in a particular business or industry. Just as scholarly journals are sponsored by the professional associations to which academics belong, trade journals are sponsored by the professional associations to which business and industry practitioners belong. And just as scholarly journals and professional associations function to maintain the community and interests of academic researchers and teachers, trade journals and associations work to preserve and carry out the interests of a business, educational, or other institutional community. Some examples of professional and trade journals that publish or refer to communication research include *Advertising Age, Communication World, Harvard Business Review, Public Relations Strategist,* and *Training & Development.*

Popular press publications are those secondary sources that are aimed at the general public, largely without regard to their readers' fields of academic study or particular occupations. Think of the magazines or other print and digital media that you consume, whether you purchase print format at a newsstand or visit the publication online. Chances are these are popular press publications. Both trade journals and popular press publications constitute secondary sources for communication research. Websites are among the fastest-growing types of secondary source for reporting research today.

The traditional academic view of research privileges the writing of academic manuscripts for the audience of a researcher's peers. In some cases, our peers are still the most desired audience to whom research findings are conveyed. But some of today's communication researchers privilege audiences other than or in addition to research peers. For example, participants in research projects have come to constitute a key audience for research findings and interpretations among interpretive scholars, who are concerned with understanding meaning in a particular context (Brodkey, 1987). Scholars whose claims address needed reforms of society sometimes target as their audience the policymakers in social situations of their concern. For example, the final reports filed to funding agencies who sponsor research are one avenue for researchers to influence research funding priorities, including the topics identified in future **requests for proposals**, the documents that funding agencies distribute to announce their funded research programs.

An **executive summary**, a brief one to two page overview of a study's purpose, methods, and key findings, can also serve to publicize communication research to audiences who do not regularly read scholarly journals. Executive summaries are provided to key decision-makers in a given institutional context, such as government lobbyists and legislators, educational accrediting agencies, or the boards that develop policy standards for particular industries (e.g., National Labor Relations Board). In some situations, the best access to policymakers may be through a trade journal. Or, if the researcher's goal is to raise awareness of a topic or research problem, then the most desirable source of publication may be the popular press periodical or book in which the greatest number and type of individuals will be exposed to the researcher's claims and conclusions.

At this early stage of your instruction in research methods, you may wonder how you will ever learn to write an academic research manuscript: "As most professional writers will affirm, the only way to learn to write is *to write*" (Spradley, 1980, p. 160). You cannot learn to write a research report or critical essay simply by reading published research studies, although that will be really helpful. Learning to write is analogous to learning to swim (Spradley, 1980).We don't learn to swim by watching other people swim, or even reading books about swimming, although instruction from a book or an experienced swimmer may be helpful. We learn to swim by watching it, trying it, and having someone more expert than our selves coach us as we do it! Learning to write research manuscripts is a lot like learning to swim. You may have trouble keeping your head above water when you are trying to write your first manuscript; but with practice, you will become much more competent and feel more at ease with the process. Writing research is a highly personal, yet skill-driven, activity, one that becomes easier with practice. It helps to pursue a project that engages you intellectually and emotionally so that your passion for the topic will keep you motivated when the going gets tough.

Two Academic Manuscripts: Research Reports and Critical Essays

Writing a research manuscript can be divided into a number of small tasks or steps, and the best manuscripts emerge over time, as the author repeatedly edits and reworks his or her ideas. In the next two sections, we compare and contrast two kinds of manuscripts, the research report and the critical essay. These are two fairly distinct types of writing that you are likely to encounter when reading academic journal articles. We use the term **research report** to refer to written summaries of research projects that include some form of data source collected from people's reports of their own, other people's beliefs or behaviors, observations of behavior, or some combination of those sources, perhaps with textual data analysis as well. We use the term **critical essay** to refer to manuscripts based primarily or only on textual data sources, whether the texts being analyzed are speeches, cultural artifacts, or the researcher's experiences as evidence and reasoning given in support of a claim. These two ways of writing academic manuscripts reflect different ways of thinking about research, something you will learn much more about in Chapter 2.

As a college student, you probably have to write term papers in which you use research findings to support your claims about a topic and to give speeches in which your teachers expect you to cite sources that support your claims. You may already know, then, about how academics in our field distinguish primary and secondary sources. **Primary sources** are original reports of research studies that have been published by the researcher, usually in a scholarly journal. Primary sources provide detailed descriptions of the researcher's claims and the data or evidence being used to support those claims, although in rhetoric and historical criticism, the artifact being analyzed is sometimes referred to as "the primary source." **Secondary sources** provide only general summaries of a researcher's claims, data, and findings. Examples of secondary sources for communication research include textbooks, encyclopedias, newspapers, television, Internet websites, and popular magazines. When you give a speech, you might cite both secondary and primary sources; but in your term papers, your teachers probably require you to cite original research articles (a.k.a., primary sources). In the last part of this chapter, you will learn a great deal more about research reports and critical essays, the two kinds of manuscripts found in scholarly communication journals. Our point here is that both primary and secondary sources can serve as evidence to support a claim.

If you are conducting your own research project in this class, ask your instructor for advice on writing a research report or critical essay. We will give you some tips on writing in each of the Part 2 and 3 chapters of this book (e.g., how to write up a survey or content analysis research project). When you write your own manuscripts, it will help you to read sample studies that employed the particular methodology you are using (e.g., experiment, discourse analysis, or rhetorical criticism). Those sample studies will give you models for how your manuscript should look and read. This is one of the best ways to get a sense of what constitutes an acceptable manuscript for a particular community of peers. Ask your instructor to suggest some exemplary articles for the methodology that you are using or select citations from the reference list in this textbook.

We will not provide you with instruction in library research strategies or sources in this book because every library and electronic database is somewhat unique. **Research strategies** are techniques for searching the communication literature at the library, on the Internet, or via electronic databases. Some of the **research sources** that you might find using those strategies include general sources, periodicals, and information compilations. If you need to learn more about research strategies and sources, ask your instructor for help, or check out R. B. Rubin, Rubin, and Haridakis's (2010) *Communication Research: Strategies and Sources*. You might also investigate your university's information literacy or library requirement. The ability to find, read, grasp, and evaluate research reports, critical essays, and secondary source publications about a variety of topics is a vital skill for most people in the world today.

Both research reports and critical essays typically begin with a title page and end with a **reference list**. For an unpublished paper, the **title page** includes the title of the paper, the writer's name and institutional affiliation, as well as contact information such as address, telephone number, and email address. Once published, the title of the paper, as well as the author name and affiliation, are listed on the first page. A reference list appears at the end of written research reports and critical essays, and it contains the full citations for all the works cited in your manuscript. Most of those citations will be the published works included in the literature review. Because one purpose of the reference list is to allow readers to locate and read all of the materials on which the author relied, a complete and accurate reference list is a must for both research reports and critical essays.

Communication scholars typically use one of two style manuals to guide their style choices about how to format source citations in the text and on the reference list. These published guidelines are the *Publication Manual of the American Psychological Association* (American Psychological Association, 2010), for social science research reports, and the *MLA Handbook for Writers of Research Papers* (Modern Language Association, 2009), for humanistic critical essays. Ask your research methods instructor which style guide you should be using if you are writing a research manuscript in this class, and check out the Online Writing Lab (OWL) at Purdue University for easily searchable advice about formatting your research report or critical essay.

Research Reports

The term *research report* refers to an investigator's written summary of a research project that included some data sources taken from self-reports, other-reports, or behavioral observations, possibly triangulated with textual or artifact analysis (see Chapter 5, "What Counts as Communication Data?" for more on data sources). Knowing something about the elements and characteristics of research reports will help you read and understand content analytic and survey and experimental research, as well as some conversation analytic research and some forms of rhetorical criticism. You will learn much more about each of those methods in Parts 2 and 3 of this book.

Research reports are written in "a formal and objective style" (Dangle & Haussman, 1963, p. 10), and they have clearly identifiable elements. In this section, we give you an overview of each element of the research report, which will help you to locate those elements as you start reading research reports. Later on in this section, we outline some characteristics of research reports, such as their precise, detailed, and objective tone. Those characteristics will help you most when you are writing your own research report.

Elements of Research Reports

There are five elements of a research report: (1) abstract; (2) review of previously published literature on the research topic; (3) methods section, with descriptions and warrants for the data collection sources, settings, and data collection and analytic strategies; (4) results section, which presents the key findings of the study; and (5) discussion section, with the researcher's interpretations of the findings, as well as the study's limitations, and suggested directions for future research.

The very first element of a research report, appearing right underneath the title and author name(s), is the **abstract**, a single paragraph of about 100 words that provides readers with an overview of the study. In much the same way that a speech introduction gives listeners an overview of the speaker's purpose, argument, and conclusions, the abstract greatly influences whether, and how, readers will consume the rest of the research report. It states in one sentence the problem investigated by a particular study. It then briefly describes the data collection sources, strategies, and data analytic procedures. Key findings and limitations of the study are outlined in the last sentence(s) of the abstract. Like a speech introduction, the abstract should be the last part of your research report to be written.

Immediately following the abstract is the literature review (Galvin, 1999). A review of literature provides your summary of previously published theories and research. That summary justifies, or establishes the context for your empirical study. Literature reviews begin with an introduction that should "introduce the problem area, establish its significance, and indicate the author's perspectives on the problem" (Pyrczak & Bruce, 1992, p. 33). A research project may be of personal, social, or theoretical significance, or it may be significant in all of these ways.

To establish personal significance, you might state why the study you are doing matters to you as an individual. To establish social significance, you'll want to identify a common problem that your research is designed to address and perhaps specify what harms will accrue or are already accruing, if the problem is not addressed. Finally, to establish theoretical significance, you will have to state precisely how you expect your study to contribute to communication theory by developing a new theory or by testing, extending, or refuting an existing theory. You already know that research reports are written for particular audiences (e.g., members of a professional association or readers of a scholarly journal). So you will need to adjust the amount of detail you include in your research report's introduction to suit the audience's knowledge of and interest in your research topic.

It is in the literature review that you will scrutinize previously published, academic research studies that are most closely related to your current research project. Research reports frequently have a heading that clearly identifies the literature review section. However, conducting and writing a literature review are two very different, albeit related, processes. To *conduct* a literature review, we locate and read all that we can on a given topic. Usually, the great bulk of this work occurs at the beginning of a research project, although for academic researchers who conduct and publish research over the course of their careers, locating and reading topic-relevant literature is an ongoing practice. If you are a beginning researcher, you will need to locate and read a number of existing studies on your topic before you can fully conceptualize your research project (i.e., what claims you want to make, the appropriate types of data to collect and analyze, methods of analysis, etc.). A well-founded literature search helps the researcher participate effectively in a conversation already taking place among the community of scholars or practitioners interested in that topic.

The literature review section of the research report typically includes the researcher's claim, which may be phrased in the form of a purpose statement, hypothesis, or research question. **Purpose statements** are declarative sentences that succinctly outline the researcher's goal for the study. If you, as the researcher, cannot state what the aim of your project is in one or two sentences, then you probably have not achieved enough clarity to be writing a research report. **Hypotheses** are also declarative statements, but hypotheses predict specific relationships among variables (e.g., visualization training reduces communication apprehension) or differences between two groups of people based on a single variable (e.g., male speakers interrupt more frequently than female speakers). **Research questions** are interrogative statements that ask, "What is the relationship . . ." or "Is there some relationship . . ." among communication variables or processes.

Following the literature review and purpose statement(s), the next section of the research report is labeled methodology, or sometimes, procedures. This section contains descriptions of the researcher's data sources, settings, data collection, and analytic strategies. You will learn much more about these topics in Chapter 5, "What Counts as Communication Data?" For now, it is enough for you to know that the methodology section contains detailed descriptions of the texts or participants whose observed behaviors or reported beliefs constituted the data for the study and the exact means by which those data were selected. The methodology section also will include, or will be followed by, descriptions of the *data analysis* procedures, the exact strategies by which the researcher made sense of the data he or she collected. Finally, the methodology section should include attention to the warrants for all these procedural choices.

Near the end of the research report, we present and discuss the key findings of a study, usually referring back to our purpose statement, hypotheses, or research questions. For statistical studies, the "*Results*" and "*Discussion*" sections are usually presented and labeled separately, and statistical symbols and tables are used in the results section to summarize numerical data so that well-informed readers can interpret the data themselves, given particular criteria that the author has provided. For qualitative field research, where the findings are not numerical, the researcher may summarize key findings and discuss their implications in a single section of the report, labeled "*Findings*." For rhetorical criticism, the researcher will usually present examples that show how she or he developed the conclusions regarding the events or artifacts that were examined. Within these sections, you will usually find the authors' cautionary notes about

the limitations of their research and their suggestions for future research and practice in the topic area.

Characteristics of Research Reports

In this section, we outline three principles by which research reports are evaluated (i.e., precise, detailed, and objective reporting). As you already know from the preceding section, "Elements of Research Reports," these manuscripts are characterized by their highly predictable outline sequence as well as their rational and formal tone. Authors of research reports typically make no reference to themselves, although such references are sometimes made in the third person (e.g., "The first author coded the transcripts").

To illustrate the three characteristics of research reports, let's consider Schrodt et al.'s (2007) examination of everyday talk in stepfamily systems. The abstract begins with a *precise* statement of the purpose of the study: "This study explored frequencies of everyday talk in stepfamilies and the extent to which such frequencies of talk differed according to family relationship type" (Schrodt et al., 2007, p. 216). The rest of the abstract succinctly presents the number and type of participants in the study and the key findings. Those findings are summarized in two sentences, one that lists the most frequent types of talk that occurred in all the stepfamilies, and one that notes that "relatively few differences emerged in stepchildren's reported frequencies of everyday talk with their stepparents and their nonresidential parents" (Schrodt et al., 2007, p. 216).

Following the abstract, Schrodt et al.'s (2007) literature review begins by situating communication research on personal relationships over the past decade within the constitutive view of communication, the idea that our "social world is constructed through everyday talk" (p. 216). After presenting their rationale for studying family communication as one particular aspect of social reality, Schrodt et al. move to articulate their specific theoretic perspective, a family systems approach. That section is marked by a bold heading, "Theoretic Perspective." In fact, each subsequent element of this research report is clearly marked with a bold heading, including "Method," "Results," and "Discussion." In the methods section, Schrodt et al. provide *detailed* descriptions of the study's participants and the instruments that were used to collect self-report data about everyday talk. The results section is explicitly organized around the study's two research questions. That section contains some complicated statistical symbols and tables that help well-informed readers interpret the data for themselves, given particular criteria that the authors have provided. (Ask your instructor for help understanding the results section of the article; you will learn much more about reading "results" sections in Chapters 16 and 17 of this book.) For now, you might just notice how *detailed* that section is and the *objective* voice in which the results section is written. For example, "relationship type had a significant effect on 19 of the 20 types of everyday talk" (Schrodt et al., 2007, p. 226). Reading this and other research reports will help you to see how precision, detail, and objectivity are enacted in academic manuscripts that are based on self-reports and other-reports and/or behavioral observation data.

In addition, some rhetorical criticism manuscripts, which are based solely on textual data (e.g., dramatistic criticism) also fit the characteristics of research reports. Of course, some rhetorical and critical studies manuscripts better fit the characteristics of the critical essay, which we outline later in this chapter. When you select a rhetorical artifact to represent some action or event, such as a speech or perhaps a website, you will want to describe that artifact in *precise detail* in your research report, since your readers may not have the same access to the artifact that you did. You also will need to articulate the structural components of that artifact that most interested you in your essay (see "Elements of the Critical Essay," following). If you are preparing a research report based on textual data only, you will be reporting, objectively and rationally, what you have discovered about the artifact or text in terms of those structural components.

Critical Essays

A critical essay is one scholar's summary of research for which the major evidence given in support of a claim is textual evidence. The text being analyzed may be a speech, a cultural artifact, or the text of the researcher's experiences and beliefs. Knowing something about the elements and characteristics of critical essays will help you read and understand the academic manuscripts that are written by critical and rhetorical scholars (i.e., methods you will learn about in Part 2 of this book). Understanding the characteristics of critical essays will help you to prepare your own manuscript if you are conducting rhetorical criticism or critical studies, and it may improve your analytic writing when you are not doing research, too.

Elements of Critical Essays

All of the elements of the research report also appear in critical essays. However, except for the abstract and literature review, the elements of a critical essay are presented very differently than the elements of a research report. In fact, writing a research report is usually seen as an activity to be completed after the research has been conducted, whereas the authors of critical essays are more likely to view writing as an emergent and iterative process. For example, many rhetorical critics, critical ethnographers, and discourse analytic scholars prefer to write as they go, so they can determine when they have enough evidence, what additional evidence or data is needed, and when new questions are arising from the evidence they have already begun to analyze. Because of this different organization of time and writing tasks, some scholars who write critical essays frame writing itself *as* a form of inquiry (e.g., Goodall, 2000).

In this section, we outline five elements of the critical essay: (1) abstract, (2) topic introduction, (3) description of the text and contexts, (4) unit of analysis, and (5) findings and conclusions. Unlike the plainly specified headings used in research reports, the elements of the critical essay "do not need to be presented in separate sections, or identified with headings, but in some way they should be included in the essay" (S. K. Foss, 1996, p. 16).

Critical essay writers tend to resist a standardizing form or structure, which is consistent with their philosophy that standardization always privileges some persons or values and oppresses others. Thus, you will see considerable variety in the ways that critical studies essays are organized. However, both research reports and critical essays tend to start with broad overviews of the topic area and proceed to the specific points their authors wish to present. The introduction to a rhetorical criticism essay generally functions to describe what rhetorical "artifact is being analyzed, the research question that is the impetus for analysis, and the contribution to rhetorical theory that will result from the analysis" (S. K. Foss, 1996, p. 16).

An **artifact** is any object made by human work: It could be a speech, a television commercial, or a blog posting. But artifacts are not limited to words. An artifact may be a piece of jewelry, a painting, or even a building, and an immense variety of artifacts can be read as texts. In some cases, the particular artifact a researcher has analyzed fits into a larger class of artifacts. For example, Martin Luther King's "I Have a Dream" speech fits into the general category of persuasive speeches by famous people. If you had analyzed that speech, you might begin your essay by referring to the ways that famous speakers have changed our views on important topics and our ideas about how to speak effectively. The introduction to the topic of study would orient your readers to the artifact you analyzed, starting at the broadest relevant level.

Once you have oriented readers to the context, you will be ready to describe the artifact that was analyzed in your particular study. Because readers of a critical essay do not necessarily have access to the artifact, text, or experience that the researcher analyzed, the next part of a critical essay is the author's full description of the textual evidence. For instance, if the artifact was a film, the author might describe its plot as well as its characters and any significant technical features (S. K. Foss, 1996). The researcher's description of the artifact, or text, and its context(s) should justify why it was "a particularly appropriate or useful one to analyze in order to answer the research question" (S. K. Foss, 1996, p. 17).

Critical scholars understand their essays to be rich representations of the actions, events, or texts they studied, which are inherently biased by their own experiences, values, and purposes. This does not mean that critical essays lack rigor or that their authors intentionally abuse their power of representing actions and events through language. In fact, rhetorical and critical scholarship is characterized by concerns about the *politics of representation:* Every choice about what is and is not said has ramifications that are linked to power and ideology, and the principle of rigorous self-reflection dictates that the writer examine the motives, word choices, and framing of an essay with immense care (Allen, 1996; Moreman & Persona Non Grata, 2011).

The next element of the critical essay should help readers to understand the unit of analysis that was used to analyze the text or artifact. You might think of the term unit of analysis in terms of the building blocks of evidence on which a study is based: Conversation analysts, for example, view units of analysis as "the building blocks of talk" (Sigman, Sullivan, & Wendell, 1988, p. 165). Survey researchers view the people that respond to a questionnaire as the building blocks of a sample. Similarly, the units of analysis in a critical essay are blocks of textual evidence on which the researcher assembles an argument in support of a claim.

The largest part of a critical essay consists of the findings. The goal in a critical essay is not to discover the one truth about an artifact or text but rather to substantiate

the *reasons* the author is making a particular claim. The concluding section of a critical essay should let the reader know what contribution the researcher feels his or her analysis makes to answering the research question or fulfilling the purpose.

Characteristics of Critical Essays

The critical essay's emphasis on textual data, rather than self-reports, other-reports, or behavioral observations, highlights one of the main ways that critical essays read differently than research reports. Whereas the research report author typically prefers to speak of how *data* supports, or fails to support, a claim, the critical essay writer is more likely to speak of how the text may be interpreted as *evidence* in support (or refutation) of a claim.

From a critical perspective, "even a simple literature review runs the risk of privileging existing patterns of thought" (Sprague, 1992, p. 181). In other words, the critical essay is an act of representation in itself and, as such, must be approached with the hermeneutics of suspicion. The critic begins the essay with an assumption of discursive domination, the idea that language itself, as used in a particular context, benefits some people in that context more than others. The critical scholar then proceeds to analyze the struggles among fluid, competing interests in terms of their various ways of representing actions and events (Mumby, 1997a). For example, you could analyze immigration discourse published in media sources that represent the conservative and liberal ends of the political spectrum to examine the ways that competing political interests drive word choice, problem definition, and the evidence used to support particular claims.

To illustrate the characteristics and organization of a critical essay, take a look at Watts and Orbe's (2002) analysis of the "*Whassup?!*" Budweiser commercials. Watts and Orbe (2002) began by speculating how the inventor of Budweiser's most successful 60-second commercial ever, "*Whassup?!*", must have felt:

> Charles Stone, III must have felt as though he had gone to sleep and awoken in Oz. It was three short years ago that he captured on film candid moments among three of his friends, and edited them into an engrossing and visually stunning short film called "True," and used it as a video resume. Stone was "floored" when Anheuser-Busch asked him to translate his film into a 60-second commercial spot for Budweiser beer.... It must have seemed even more surreal to be in Cannes ... and to hear his friends' greeting, now the world's most famous catchphrase, bouncing

off café walls and rippling along the beaches—"Whassup?!" It must have been bizarre to witness the usually stodgy Cannes judges joyfully exchanging the greeting in international accents" (p. 1).

Watts and Orbe (2002) presented their view of how Charles Stone III *must have felt* as a way to introduce the organizing concept on which their analysis was based, the concept of spectacular consumption.

Spectacular consumption treats "spectacle as a rhetorical construction" and "a mediated phenomenon that transforms persons' lived reality" (Watts & Orbe, 2002, p. 3). The "*Whassup?!*" Budweiser commercial, a simple "verbal high five" among friends, was at once "baffling" and the "Superbowl's most popular" ad (Watts & Orbe, 2002, p. 2). Watts and Orbe (2002) began their analysis with a suspicion that Budweiser's "ad campaign constitutes and administers cultural 'authenticity' as a market value" (pp. 2–3).

The next section of Watts and Orbe's (2002) essay is a **literature review**. First, the authors developed their definition of spectacular consumption based on previous theoretic works. Next, they examined and critiqued the "crossover appeal" (Watts & Orbe, 2002, p. 5) of the Budweiser commercial, deconstructing the dialectic tension underneath White America's appropriation of black communication styles. Using cites from previously published academic and nonacademic sources, Watts and Orbe (2002) argued that "white kids want to be as cool as black kids" (citing MTV's Chris Connelly, on p. 7), but "white folk do not want to *become* black" (citing bell hooks, 1992).

Next, Watts and Orbe (2002) conducted a textual analysis of the "*Whassup?!*" commercial itself, looking for any evidence of self-reflexivity. They wondered whether these three friends "recognize (that is, see) the ways that their 'play' is overvalued as an 'authentic' cultural performance" (p. 8). Finally they conducted focus groups with undergraduate communication students to see how the "*Whassup?!*" ads were consumed by different viewers. Watts and Orbe presented quotes from those students in the essay itself to illustrate interpretive themes that were based on repetition, recurrence, and forcefulness of a topic in the focus group interactions. The essay concluded with the authors' reiteration of their claim and summary of the evidence used to support their interpretations.

In writing a critical studies essay, you are creating another layer of text, another multiplicity of meanings that may be associated with that which you study. "In this sense, providing accounts of . . . phenomena is both a poetic and a political process" (Mumby, 1993, p. 20). It is poetic in that it gains credibility by adhering to the conventions or forms that are accepted by the researcher's **interpretive community** (i.e., an academic discipline or perhaps several disciplines). It is political because it usually separates researchers as "other," or different from, research participants and because there is no neutral representation of knowledge (Sprague, 1992).

One way to use writing as a form of inquiry is to explore, through writing, your identity as the author of an interpretive or critical essay. Why do you see things as you do? This notion is called *self-reflexivity*. Ellingson's (1998) autoethnographic account of an oncology clinic will illustrate the potential impact of self-reflexivity in ethnographic fieldwork. Herself a cancer survivor, Ellingson (1998) described her struggle to write about her research in a "new form" (p. 511):

> This piece integrates narrative and essay, embodying the dynamism of perspective within its structure. The narratives break into the essay in much the same way that they break into my train of thought as I write; my cancer experiences evoke narratives of patients and staff in the clinic, which evoke commentary from a researcher perspective, which evokes a personal illness narrative, and so forth (p. 511).

Ellingson (1998) noted that the use of experimental writing forms like hers "are becoming more common in academic journals, irreversibly contaminating the body of social science knowledge with the messiness of lived experience" (p. 511). However, despite her confident assertion, in the same year, Childress (1998) bemoaned the scarcity of "exemplary, compelling, whole ethnographies" in the published literature, "not because good ethnographic work doesn't exist, but because it doesn't easily get past editorial boards and journal reviewers and even library acquisition panels" (p. 249).

By being actively engaged with the phenomenon under study while writing the essay, you are helping to create the phenomenon you study. You are at least attempting to represent that phenomenon through language. Van Oosting (1996) argued that through writing, the writer comes to understand both performance and composition better, and differently, than is possible through performance alone. In your case, writing research can enhance your understanding of the phenomena you seek to study.

Summary

After reading this chapter, you should have a sense of the broad scope of communication research, both in academic and proprietary contexts. We have said that communication theories are descriptions and explanations for how things work or should work, what things mean, and whether they use formal logic, an idea, or even a story to represent a communication process. Because theories and research methods are in some cases quite distinct but other times interconnected, it is impossible to do research without representing a point of view. Thus, we have introduced the idea of research as making an argument, and we stressed that good arguments include claims, data or evidence, and warrants. We outlined three general ways of knowing (tenacity, authority, and a priori), and we contrasted them with the method of knowing used in academic research in which careful reasoning is tested by experience. We gave you an overview of three major outlets for communication research (professional association meetings, scholarly journals, and trade journals and other popular press publications), and we outlined the elements of two types of manuscripts that you might read in our scholarly journals: the research report and the critical essay.

Key Terms

Abstract	Knowing by authority	Requests for proposals
Academic research	Knowing by tenacity	Research questions
Artifact	Laws	Research report
Benchmarking	Literature review	Research sources
Best practices	Method of science	Research strategies
Claim	Popular press publications	Scholarly journals
Critical essay	Primary sources	Secondary sources
Data	Principles	Theories
Executive Summaries	Professional associations	Title page
Formulas	Proprietary research	Trade journals
Hypotheses	Purpose statements	Unit of analysis
Knowing on a priori grounds	Reference list	Warrant

Discussion Questions

1. What theories do you already know about from other classes you've taken in your major? Which of those theories use formal logic, and which are more conceptual or metaphorical?
2. Given your career aspirations, how might you use what you learn in *Communication Research Methods* now or after you graduate?
3. How might membership in a professional or trade association benefit you while you are still a student? What about after college?

"Try It!" Activity: Everyday Ways of Knowing

1. Listen to the following TED talk from the Filter Bubbles link below: http://www.ted.com/talks/eli_pariser_beware_online_filter_bubbles.
2. Identify the main claim or thesis of the speaker; be sure to include the issue (topic) and his position.
3. Identify the different forms of evidence this person cites (testimonials from eye witnesses or expert authority; case examples from personal and others' experiences; physical proof, analogies, and statistics; or other empirical evidence).

4. Conduct an information search of <u>nonacademic sources</u> on this topic and list three references that you find using APA style format. Ask your instructor which library databases available at your campus are best used to search for these sources.

5. A quick guide to APA format style can be found on Cornell University's website: http://www.library .cornell.edu/resrch/citmanage/apa. A more detailed description of APA formatting appears on the Purdue website: http://owl.english.purdue.edu/owl/resource/560/01/

   (a) The references you cite should help to clarify the position of the TED Talk speaker. Provide information that extends the topic.

   (b) Explain why you chose the references that you did and whether the authors generally support or contradict the speaker's position (i.e., what kind of evidence is provided in the article).

6. Next, conduct an information search of <u>academic sources</u> on this topic, and list three references that you find using APA style format.

   (a) At least one of the three references must come from the *Communication and Mass Media Complete* database (check out a list of frequently cited communication journals listed on p. 11 of the textbook to see if your references come from any of these).

   (b) The references should help to clarify the position of the TED Talk speaker in providing information that extends the speaker's topic.

   (c) Explain why you chose the references that you did and whether the authors generally support or contradict the speaker's position (i.e., what kind of evidence is provided in the article).

"Try It!" Activities: Research Reports & Critical Essays

1. Look at the print versions of two to three issues of a scholarly communication journal. Can you identify the elements of a research report and/or a critical essay? What else do you notice about each type of academic manuscript?

2. Now look at just the abstract for one academic research report: Can you identify the researcher's claim, method of investigation, and key result?

3. Look at just the abstract for a critical essay: Can you identify the topic, type of text analyzed, and key finding of the research, just from reading the abstract?

4. Read one research report and one critical essay. Then discuss your responses to the questions below in a small group, or write your responses in a short paper:

   (a) How easy or difficult was the report for you to read? What helped you read and grasp the report? What made it difficult?

   (b) How believable was the content of the report to you? Did your belief in the author's interpretations or conclusions change as you read the entire report?

   (c) How do you think reading this research report will impact you, if at all? Will you think, act, or communicate any differently as a result of having read this report?

(Adapted from Buchmann, 1992)

"Try It!" Activity: Investigating Communication-Related Careers

Part I: The National Picture for My Occupation

1. Go to http://www.bls.gov. Under the *Publications* link, choose the *Occupational Outlook Handbook*.

   (a) First, if you know your career goal after college, look at the *Occupation Groups* list at the left side of the handbook's homepage, and figure out which one of those groups best fits your career goal. Write down the name of that group, and your specific occupation, like this:

   Occupational Group = _____   Occupation = _____

(b) If you do not know what your career goals are, try looking at the links for these occupation groups: Community & Social Service; Education, Training & Library; Media & Communication; Office & Administrative Support; Protective Service; Sales. See if you can identify at least one occupation that fits your education, experiences, and interests. Write down the name of the occupation group and your new occupation goal like this:

Occupational Group = _____   Occupation = _____

2. Use http://www.bls.gov to learn more about your chosen occupation, beginning with the national level:
   (a) What is the job outlook for this occupation? Is the national demand for this occupation expected to grow, shrink, or remain about the same in the next 10 years?
   (b) What education and experience is required for this occupation at entry level?
   (c) What was the most recent median salary for this occupation in the United States? ($____/yr)
   (d) What is the work environment for this occupation? For example, which industries employ the most people with this occupation?
   (e) What about the work schedule for this occupation? Do most people in this occupation work full-time or part-time?
   (f) What advancement opportunities exist for people in this occupation?

3. Continuing to use http://www.bls.gov, next look at the Duties and Important Qualities listed for people in this occupation:
   (a) Which of these duties and/or qualities **best fit** your current strengths and abilities?
   (b) Which duties and/or qualities would you **need to develop** during your remaining college years in order to succeed at this occupation? Make notes of any steps you should take to develop those areas (e.g., selecting particular courses in your major, minor, or electives; part-time or internship experience, graduate school). For more help with this question, look at the *How to Become One* link for your chosen occupation.

Part II: Translating My Occupation to the Local Level

1. Go online to a mega-jobs database such as www.indeed.com/jobs or http://www.careerbuilder.com;
2. Type "communication degree" into the search engine for the database, or you might enter the specific name of your degree program (e.g., mass communication or theatre and speech). This will show you what jobs are available now related to your major.
3. To get more specific information, go back to the homepage for the database, and enter the name of your selected occupation into the search engine; now see what jobs are available. You can narrow your search by location (e.g., city, state) or even by company.
4. Finally, type the name of your city or town into a general search engine (e.g., Google); find the homepage for your city or town and look for a link to the Chamber(s) of Commerce. See if you can locate a Business Directory (i.e., a list of all the members). Those are the organizations seeking to advance commercial, industrial and civic interests in your area. Which of those organizations employs people in your chosen occupation?
5. Optional step: Use LinkedIn, YELP, Facebook, glassdoor.com, or another review site to see what others have to say about the organizations you are now exploring.

Write up a summary of your research using the elements of the research report described in this chapter (i.e., briefly describe your purpose, methods, findings, and interpretations). Alternately, prepare a speech for delivery to your research methods class, or to a student association at your school, that summarizes what you learned about your intended career.

2 Three Paradigms of Knowing

Introduction

This chapter begins by considering how we know what we know, an epistemological approach to understanding the research process, and why this approach is important. We will explore a common split between *quantitative* and *qualitative* characterizations of communication research and why this solution is incomplete. Alternatively, we describe three paradigms, three ways of knowing about communication: interpretation, criticism, and discovery. Each represents a different set of assumptions about the researchable world and as a result, they give us three sets of tools which equip us with distinctive approaches to studying communication. The chapter ends by considering how the paradigms have contributed to the unique methodologies within our field.

Learning Outcomes

After completing this chapter, you should be able to achieve the following outcomes through reflective analysis:

» Explain how epistemological paradigms are ways of knowing that can help distinguish among communication research methods.

» Describe the common split between quantitative and qualitative analysis and explain why this dichotomy is incomplete.

» Contrast the three main epistemological paradigms of research and articulate the underlying assumptions as points of contrast among the three paradigms.

» Associate communication methods with the three paradigms, explaining how paradigm assumptions can be used to analyze and differentiate among these.

Outline

The Dichotomy of Quantitative
and Qualitative Research

In the first chapter, we introduced you to the concepts of theory and method. Theories can be descriptions about what we observe or they can illustrate what things mean. The most effective and eloquent theories explain things or are interpretations; they can be assertions about what should be or should not be happening. They can be formal and contain rulelike propositions, or they can be in the form of a story. Theories are ideas we have about the way things really are. They organize what and how we think.

When you decide to do research, you will adopt a method that you can use to test your theories. In later chapters, you will see that sometimes the methods seem distinct from theories, and sometimes the theory and the method are thoroughly intertwined. The distinctiveness of the method is reflective of the assumptions the researcher makes about what can be known in exploring communication.

In Chapter 1, we introduced you to Toulmin's Claim-Data-Warrant model to help you understand how different methods compare, because every method can be explained by the elements of claim, data, and warrant. Said another way, every method is a form of argument. We will explore each element separately in the remaining chapters of this first section. But before we do, it is important to consider how the kind of argument you want to construct (or the process of research) is connected to the assumptions you make about what it means to do research.

Earlier, we distinguished the everyday common sense methods of knowing as distinct from those researchers apply more rigorously in the humanities, social sciences, and sciences. If you look at the studies reported in the wide variety of journals in our field, it is quickly apparent that there is no one standard way of doing research. These differences in methodologies come from profoundly different ways of thinking about what we know, how we understand communication, and what we do as researchers when we study it. Each of these different perspectives represents a particular set of assumptions. As a student of research, you may come up with an idea for studying communication through a particular method without realizing that the choice of method taps the set of assumptions that go with it.

These different perspectives or ways of knowing are called **paradigms**. Paradigms are like lenses that permit different worldviews (Kuhn, 1970). Just as you can use a prism or kaleidoscope to change what you see, paradigms of thinking help to organize your understanding of the world. Paradigms represent philosophic worldviews that impact the methods chosen for the research process: the questions you will ask, the data you will collect and analyze, and the way you will interpret the results. In the Foreword section of this book, Brian Spitzberg describes the paradigms as methodological "cultures" of social scientists, each with their own set of rules, customs, beliefs, and values. Little positive interchange among researchers from different paradigms characterized past relationships, but there is an increasing trend to shift from one perspective to the next, using paradigms collaboratively to enrich our understanding of complex research problems. We will explore these as paradigm bridges that show a blending of assumptions rather than a sharp demarcation.

Instead of examining the assumptions that underlie research, many social scientists have attempted to explain the differences very broadly by focusing on the ways in which data are collected and analyzed. These are identified by two approaches: quantitative research and qualitative research. In the next section, we will explore the dichotomy this split creates and why it presents an incomplete picture of communication research.

The Dichotomy of Quantitative and Qualitative Research

You are very likely to come across the terms quantitative and qualitative research either by hearing them from your instructors or students from other methods courses. Or you may read those terms in the research reports and critical essays you encounter in your classes. A simple way to understand the difference between these two is by the terms themselves. The term "quantitative" implies numerical measurement and is a data-focused term. In quantitative research, communication concepts are converted to numeric representations that can be analyzed using statistical procedures; even the articles reporting quantitative analyses have tended toward standard formats, making them more easily recognizable (Creswell, 2009; Babbie, 2013). You can review these features in our discussion of research reports from Chapter 1. Using "numbers" as the discriminating feature, you would be able to open many communication journals and quickly find a quantitative analysis with complex statistical tables and summaries. This broad approach provides you with a way to recognize some characteristics of quantitative research without understanding why researchers have adopted these methods. Without a deeper understanding, you would unfortunately be missing instances in which communication scholars share the same assumptions about knowledge and research but do not conduct statistical analyses. And even more perplexing, you would not understand how researchers who use methods typically thought of as "qualitative" might also employ some numerical measurement and analysis. Trumbo (2004) has argued that "the issue goes much deeper than 'to count or not to count.' The quantitative versus qualitative distinction is only the surface representation of a spectrum of fundamental orientations toward how the world may be known and how truth might be approached" (p. 418).

Your search for qualitative studies in communication research journals would yield even greater variation in methods. You could easily find instances of studies that do not contain statistical analyses, but aside from the absence of this one feature, many of these studies would have little in common. Some studies would reflect fieldwork in which communication researchers investigate communication practices as they occur in their natural environments; other studies would emphasize the analysis of communication media messages as "texts," using some sort of theoretical framework to explain the significance of these; still others would use their analyses to explain power inequities and urge social reform.

It is true that research scholars who use the terms "quantitative" and "qualitative" may distinguish between the two by describing the underlying philosophic perspectives and sets of assumptions associated with these terms (Denzin & Lincoln, 2003; Creswell, 2009; Babbie,

2013). Quantitative research is associated with positivism or postpositivism, philosophical perspectives characterized by the assumptions of an objective, fixed reality and the deductive application of control and measurement to determine the causes of outcomes under study (Creswell, 2009; Babbie, 2013). In contrast, the history of qualitative research reveals a reliance on assumptions of multiple, subjective realities and the emergence of understanding through observation and description. Qualitative research is accordingly characterized by multiple methods from multiple perspectives and traditions that include "ethnomethodology, phenomenology, hermeneutics, feminism, rhizomatics, deconstructionism, ethnography, interviews, psychoanalysis, cultural studies, survey research, and participant observation, among others" (Denzin & Lincoln, 2003, p. 10). However, this dichotomization does not explain traditional methods of rhetorical criticism that stem from discovery paradigm perspectives or statistical quantitative data analysis of a broken educational system as an argument for social reform.

As the philosophies and methods evolved, many scholars now point to a historical "crisis of representation" that differentiated "critical studies" perspectives from the traditional qualitative approaches to research. McLaren and Kincheloe (2007) argue that critical studies are "intensely concerned with the need to understand the various and complex ways that power operates to dominate and shape consciousness" as the primary basis for detailed analysis (p. 439). This historical emergence indicates a fundamental shift in qualitative research that requires a new set of paradigmatic assumptions. Because of these radical changes in philosophical perspectives, we believe that continuing to dichotomize communication research by quantitative and qualitative research creates more problems than it solves. In the next section, you will explore how paradigms are "ways of knowing" with sets of assumptions that help guide the process of research, and why **three** paradigms are necessary as the basic framework.

Methodological Ways of Knowing

Think of one thing that you know. One faculty member that we know uses the example of money. What do you know about money? Do you think what you know is the same as the person sitting next to you, or are your ideas unique to you? How did you come to have the ideas you do about money? Was it through your observations and experience? Will your conception of money and how it works make your life better? How will it affect the lives of people around you? Whatever it is you think you know, it's wise to remember that your knowledge represents one perspective of the way things are. Your struggle to know something is an attempt to make sense out of the world; your interpretations and conclusions can be very different from other people's views. And yet, even with our different perspectives, we can still find points of agreement in our ways of knowing.

Let's consider another example. Some people claim that violence on television and the Internet, in videogames, and in films make people more violent in real life. How do they know this is so? Do they know it from interpreting various audience reactions to violence portrayals in TV dramas or music videos? Do they view violence in the media as a symptom of a larger social problem, such as increasing alienation? Do groups like parents and teachers think that our social problems of alienation and violence can be solved by consumer action or legislative reform? Or are they basing this claim on their own experiences witnessing the connection between mediated violence and actual behavior?

With this one example, we can illustrate the three main paradigms of knowledge in communication research. We may see media violence as "symbolic texts" with multiple and equally valid interpretations of violence and its social significance. Focusing on these characteristics is the interpretive paradigm approach. Or we may see violence portrayals as signs of ideological privilege or oppression in our society, key features of the critical paradigm. Or we may emphasize the observable or general, common characteristics of media violence when watching particular types of television series or listening to music or playing video games. This emphasis is characteristic of the discovery paradigm. How we choose to study communication depends upon our paradigm assumptions.

What, then, do these paradigm assumptions entail? Understanding these for each of the three paradigms, interpretive, critical, and discovery, will help to clarify how paradigm perspectives affect your choice of research methods. Moreover, we spend the second section of the book illustrating how careful understanding and application of the methods will lead to more knowledge and better understanding of the questions you want answered, whether you work in an advertising firm, an organization that conducts surveys, or go on to graduate school with your academic interests. Before you begin reading about the three paradigms, try taking the quiz in Table 2.1.

This quiz will help orient you to the different ways of looking at reality that are described in each paradigm.

As you read about the paradigm assumptions in the sections that follow, think about your answers and how your own perspective may contribute to and influence the way that you think about research.

The three paradigms you learn about in this book emerged chronologically as discovery first, then interpretation, then criticism. Instead of a chronological order, we present interpretation and criticism first, followed by discovery, for basic pedagogical reasons: First and most importantly, we anticipate that you will be doing a research project in this class. Because of this assumption, the order of paradigms presented in this chapter and in the latter sections of this book allows you time for immersion in data collection and analysis and their warranting strategies, if you have chosen interpretive or critical projects, before you approach statistical data analysis if you are doing discovery paradigm projects.

Knowing by Interpretation

To know by interpretation implies several fundamental assumptions about the nature of reality and its study through the process of research; these are identified in Table 2.2. One guiding assumption is that there are multiple realities reflected in the interpretations that individuals construct about their experiences. You as the *knower* or researcher are inseparable from the people, events, and messages you observe because your perceptions and values affect what you see. Moreover, since each individual participant that you are observing or interviewing has a distinctive set of experiences, their views also represent multiple, equally legitimate interpretations of communication. Therefore, the purpose of research is to understand how individuals or groups of individuals (organizations, cultures) interpret or understand the meaning of communication in various social contexts; this is what Lindlof (1995) describes as the "insider's view."

Instead of treating knowledge as the pursuit of a single objective truth, your role as a researcher acknowledges how interpretation works in the process of research. Your subjective perspective is embraced wholeheartedly, and you might even be expected to become an active participant in the research context. The process of knowing is one of rich description in which you will use a broad range of data sources to show what and how communication

Table 2.1 Ways of Knowing Quiz

	Ways of Knowing: Choose the <u>one</u> alternative that best describes your point of view (even if you somewhat agree with several)	a, b, or c?
1a	I believe we all share one objective reality even though no one person can grasp its entirety.	
1b	I believe that our realities emerge out of our individual experiences and the groups most important to us: families, work, religion, culture, etc.	
1c	Social reality is shaped linguistically and through sociological, economic, and political memberships in society.	
2a	Who you are as a person will subjectively influence what you interpret as right and meaningful.	
2b	Your standpoint as an individual primarily reflects the broad cultural, political, and economic class memberships to which you belong.	
2c	The same set of truths is discoverable by anyone who wants to find out.	
3a	I think that the purpose of gaining new knowledge through research should be to try to uncover the power struggles in society and to work for social change.	
3b	I think that the purpose of gaining new knowledge is fulfilled when we accurately and objectively study reality.	
3c	I think that the purpose of gaining new knowledge happens when we understand how meaning is created, particularly from the views of the people we are studying.	
	Answers:	
	Interpretive: 1b, 2a, 3c	
	Critical: 1c, 2b, 3a	
	Discovery: 1a, 2c, 3b	

occurred, and what it meant to the participants in that particular context. The realities of the communication context emerge out of the process of research, a feature you will see later on in chapters that have adopted this paradigm approach.

These central assumptions arise out of a number of philosophical perspectives that include hermeneutics, phenomenology, symbolic interactionism, social construction, and naturalism (Bogdan & Biklen, 1982, pp. 10–14; Mertens, 1998, pp. 11–15; Smith, 1988, pp. 310–311). A discussion of these perspectives is beyond the scope of this book but we can summarize these in the "interpretive" paradigm perspective. Crotty (1998) identified three central assumptions of the constructivist perspective:

> 1) Meanings are constructed by human beings as they engage with the world that they are interpreting;
> 2) Humans engage with their world and make sense of it

based on their historical and social perspectives—we are all born into a world of meaning bestowed upon us by our culture; 3) The basic generation of meaning is always social, arising in and out of interaction with a human community. (Creswell, 2009, pp. 8–9)

Because the context provides the foundation for participants' understanding of interaction, your researcher role would require you to observe and interact with the participants across many instances. Your own experiences and background would also contribute to the research process and include a set of practices that will be explained in much greater detail in Parts 2 and 3 of this book.

To illustrate the interplay of multiple interpretations, Dollar & Zimmer (1998) presented ethnographic accounts of houseless young adult street speakers as to how they had come to be where they were, living on the

Table 2.2 Defining Assumptions of the Epistemological Paradigms

	Knowledge by Discovery	Knowledge by Interpretation	Knowledge by Criticism
Nature of reality	There is one knowable reality that can be discovered.	There are multiple realities that are socially constructed.	There are multiple realities that are socially constructed.
Role of knower	Reality can be known by any knower.	Reality is interpreted from the standpoint of a knower.	Reality is shaped by the knower's social, political, economic, ethnic, gender and ability values.
Role of context	The method of knowing is detached and decontextualized.	The method of knowing is subjective and contextual from the participants' perspective.	The method of knowing is subjective and broadly contextual.
Process characteristics	The process of knowing is precise, systematic, and repetitive.	The process of interpretation is creative and value-laden.	The process of interpretation is revelatory.
Purpose	The purpose of research is to accurately represent reality.	The purpose of research is to understand how meaning is created.	The purpose of research is to reveal hidden structures and instigate social change.
Goal accomplishment	Accurate representation is accomplished by classifying objects and identifying universal rules or laws.	Understanding meaning is accomplished by describing participants' perspective as contextually situated.	Instigating social change is accomplished by identifying historically and culturally situated hidden structures, especially as they relate to oppression.

street in Portland and Seattle. The authors coined the term *houseless youth* in order to avoid the term homeless, since many of these youth had homes, where they refused to go at night. The article analyzed the ways in which the community-at-large and street youth in particular are at odds in those cities because of conflicting definitions of youth identities. They showed that "youth and young adult street speakers rely on membership sets that conflict with those employed by parents, legislators, and other community members" (p. 596). For example, street youth see themselves as community members because they sleep consistently in the same area, and shop in the local stores; they see the police as defining community differently as those who own or rent a home, or have a business in the area. Each set of interpretations held equally legitimate interpretations of the community members' distinctive experiences, attitudes, and interests. As communication researchers, Dollar and

Zimmer provided an interpretive view of how these youth construct their contextually situated meanings of everyday life.

The interpretive paradigm orientation is also reflected in many forms of rhetorical criticism. The rhetorical critic often selects one or more interpretive frameworks as a basis for analyzing communication. In a recent study, Cox (2012) analyzed the use of metaphors as ways to create meaning in the minds of audience members. He argued that President Obama continuously used journey or movement metaphors in his speeches following the economic collapse of 2008 to help frame audience beliefs about recovery. As a rhetorical critic, Cox explored the meaning and significance of this set of metaphors as language choices over many of Obama's speeches in contributing to the understanding of these significant historical changes in the economy. The process of the rhetorical critic and several interpretive

Table 2.3 Communication Research Methods Affiliated with Paradigms

Discovery	Interpretative	Critical
Survey Research and Network Analysis	Discourse Analysis	Marxist Criticism
Experimental Research	Ethnography	Gender Criticism
Content Analysis	Narrative Criticism	Postmodern Criticism
Neoclassical Rhetorical Criticism	Metaphoric Criticism	Cultural Studies
Classical Genre Criticism	Dramatism in Rhetorical Criticism	Semiotic Criticism
Conversational Analysis		
	Critical bridges from discovery and interpretive paradigm methods	

frameworks will be explored in much greater detail in a later chapter.

The methods differ in ethnography and metaphoric rhetorical criticism but they share the assumption that meanings are constructed by the participants within the contextual frames that define the interactions or texts under study. Represented in the middle column of Table 2.3, typical research studies from the interpretive paradigm perspective include ethnographies, discourse analysis, metaphoric criticism, dramatism, and narrative criticism; this is not an exhaustive list of all interpretive methods in our field but it identifies those that you will learn in depth in later chapters.

As you review the table, *keep in mind that one type of methodology does not always ensure one paradigmatic view.* A number of researchers in our field conduct critical ethnographies. This methodology was at the center of the "crisis of representation" that challenged interpretivists with the critical paradigm perspective (e.g., Adelman & Frey, 1994; Conquergood, 1991; Harter, Berquist, Titsworth, Novak, & Brokaw, 2005).

In Part 2, you will explore these methods in great detail. You will begin to see, as you do, that while certain methods often originate from and are affiliated with certain paradigms they have been and can be adapted to other ends. So, for example, Littlefield and Quenette (2007) used a Burkean analysis of Hurricane Katrina's aftermath from interpretive rhetorical criticism to reveal how media could step out of the role of objective observer to social critic in examining the symbols of race, ethnicity, gender, and class. The Burkean framework originated

from an interpretive paradigm set of assumptions but the purposes and goals of the research represent clear bridges to the critical paradigm.

Knowing by Criticism

If you look at paradigm assumptions in Table 2.2, it is clear that critical researchers share several assumptions with interpretive scholars. Both agree that our individual perceptions and experiences influence what we see and that there are multiple and equally legitimate ways to view the world. Interpretive and critical researchers differ in an important respect. Those with an interpretive frame analyze systems and processes of meaning without evaluating the mechanisms of social value and power. By contrast, critical theorists explore multiple realities that are culturally and historically situated. Knowing by criticism, then, means that everything that we know is shaped by our values embedded within so much of what we are, such as our language, social practices, politics, economics, ethnicity, gender, sexual orientation, religion, and individual abilities. Critical research has two goals: the first is to make people aware of the ways in which these values shape reality. The second step is to instigate social change by revealing the values and behaviors that underlie social interaction. Both paradigms of research rely on rich description, but critical scholars reflect on the dynamics of power and privilege.

Knowledge by criticism is associated with the most recent changes in communication research. As a critique of knowledge by discovery and interpretation, the purpose of critical theory is to liberate individuals who have become alienated through oppression in modern society by increasing their social awareness of the ideological structures of power and domination (Rasmussen, 1996). The paradigm has its origins in the philosophies of critical theory, semiotics, structuralism, poststructuralism, postmodernism, postcolonialism, and deconstruction; some of these are discussed in much greater detail in a later chapter.

From a critical paradigm perspective, thought, discourse, and social interaction create what is known; just as in the interpretive paradigm, these constitute multiple realities (Lechte, 1994). Differing realities stem from the very nature of language or discourse in which meaning does not exist separate from its individual users. This way of thinking represented a radical shift from the rationalism of the Western world in which meaning was regarded as a fundamental, unchanging feature of words to its subjective location in individual users. Because of this philosophic shift, critical researchers contend that modern society uses communication as a symbolic system to create and reinforce its ideological structures of power and dominance.

As a critical researcher, you might engage in a systematic study of some social aspect of language, such as myths and narratives or cultural rules in social contexts that are used to convey status or power (Chandler, 1995). For example, you might study the ways in which parents outspend their budgets to send their children to prestigious schools or host an elaborate wedding reception. The "signs" of prestige and status clearly outweigh any utilitarian value that they may have and when social signs are expressed by social institutions such as the government or corporations, they cannot be anything but ideological (Lechte, 1994, pp. 233–37). From this perspective, you might study the ways in which media corporations control the ways in which information is controlled and conveyed. Additionally, some critical scholars have argued that material wealth of modern society is amassed and maintained through "first world" countries' cultural and racial oppression of "third world" countries. As a postcolonial scholar, you might show how stories of historical events (e.g., slavery or war) are contrasted between privileged and underbenefited perspectives.

Common to the philosophies above is the understanding that evaluation and criticism are not only impossible to avoid; they are desirable ends. Since the researcher cannot escape the subjective and interpretive view of reality, then this standpoint should be made explicit and clear.

Otherwise, the researcher misrepresents research as objective when it simply reinforces the existing privileged hierarchy of power. The feminist, Marxist, and cultural studies models of research explain how privileged groups exercise oppression of marginalized groups (such as women, targeted ethnicities, politically disfavored or economically disadvantaged groups, etc.).

From the critical paradigm perspective, the purpose of research often takes the form of identifying the implicit and dominant social structures of power so that real change in the sociocultural, political, and economic bases can be instigated. Some researchers may approach these social structures as material and verifiable; other researchers consider them experiential and subjective. Often, critical studies demonstrate the ways in which messages represent the dominant paradigms of communication in ways that minimally represent the experiences of marginalized groups. For example, Buzzanell and Liu (2005) argued that maternity leave was filled with gender "tensions and contradictions" in the negotiating of identities among the pregnant participants and others with whom they worked. They contended that the participants viewed the workplace as dominated by masculine interests, policies that stressed organizational efficiencies, and marginalization of feminine concerns and bodily requirements. Raising awareness of how these maternity leave practices may disadvantage women and discourage them from returning to work is the first step to changing those practices to ones that work for all employees.

Knowing by criticism, then, means that the researcher not only reveals his or her subjective view, but exposes social inequity and becomes an advocate for change. Critical scholars believe that if scholarship does not emphasize how dominance silences marginalized groups, then the research community is as guilty of perpetuating the existing hierarchy as the rest of society. Critical analysis must focus on the historical, political, and economic contexts that continually reinforce a social structure or system so that it can be studied, revealed, and changed. Various representations of critical methodologies appear in Table 2.3 and are discussed in much greater detail in a later chapter.

Knowing by Discovery

Historically, the paradigm of knowledge by discovery came from the earliest of the philosophic traditions and gave rise to the development of two newer paradigms of interpretation and criticism. But its chronological order does not mean you should value it or the philosophical perspectives associated with it any more than the others. Nor should you value the others intrinsically as better than the first simply because they are more contemporary. Each paradigm is a way of knowing that stands on its own merit. And every philosophical perspective within each paradigm brings a new facet to our understanding of how we might study communication.

Just as knowledge by interpretation and criticism emphasize subjective perceptions and experiences, the discovery paradigm researcher defines and measures what will be observed, and decides what conclusion can be derived from those observations. Knowledge obtained by discovery is starkly distinctive from the first two paradigms and is characterized by several fundamental assumptions found in Table 2.2. One assumption is centered in **objectivity**, the belief that things or objects exist in reality separate from our perceptions and interpretations of them. The world consists of physical objects and observable social interactions. Secondly, it is assumed that this reality is discoverable, that it is knowable through observation. A third assumption is that knowledge is testable through logical and empirical methods. Logical methods help us determine through rational means what is theoretically connected and free from contradiction, whereas empirical methods help us to identify what is probable based on our observations. The fourth assumption is that rigorous standards for testing our observations will result in an agreed upon system of evaluating our observations and our conclusions that we form (Bostrom, 2004; Corman, 2005; Pavitt, 2004).

The discovery paradigm has been the dominant paradigm in science and philosophy for many years, stemming from the philosophies of rationalism and empiricism. Rationalism stresses reliance on the mind for the underlying logic of an objective world while empiricism's central assumption emphasizes observing and explaining sensory information. Currently, many communication researchers from the discovery paradigm perspective adopt a "postpositivist" view. From a postpositivist perspective, the process of science became associated with the three emphases as tests of knowledge: (1) clarity or precision, (2) systematic inquiry, and (3) repetition for the purposes of verification (Mertens, 1998, pp. 6–10; Smith, 1988, pp. 307–309).

From a discovery paradigm perspective, the standards for reliability and validity that you will learn about in later chapters form the basis that you will use for evaluating your observations. As we have stated, these rigorous tests of knowledge can be accomplished by making precise, systematic, and repetitive observations of some event or thing. Following **precise** procedures means that you will employ them carefully and accurately. Being **systematic** means that you will follow clear, known procedures specified in sequence. Most discovery-based research begins with a deductive process in which claims are constructed from the evidence collected in many previous studies. Out of this past evidence, you will develop a prediction that will be tested through a series of observations that will provide you with new evidence. Finally, when you are **repetitive** in your research methods, it means that you make careful, systematic observations, over and over, to ensure that your findings are verifiable, that they are confirmable over many instances and observers. These three essential tests of knowledge form the basis for observations characteristic of research reports that we described in Chapter 1.

When you are conducting communication research, each of these properties is evident in the way you design your study. For example, Burleson, Holmstrom, & Gilstrap (2005) tested the effects of gender on the perceptions and motivations of providing support for distressed individuals. In their experiments, they carefully constructed conversation scenarios between college students that reflected different levels of support and changing genders of the support providers and receivers. In some conversation scenarios, the support provider or receiver was a female college student and in others, the student was a male. Additionally, some of the conversations reflected high levels of a quality called "person-centeredness"; other conversations reflected moderate or low levels. The researchers asked study participants reading the conversations a series of questions regarding how realistic the conversation seemed and how well they liked the support provider. They also had participants evaluate conversational goals, plans, and actions by changing the genders of the support provider and support receiver. Burleson and his colleagues were precise in the way that they constructed their tests, using the same questionnaire format and conversational contexts with all participants. They were systematic in varying the gender of each role to test the separate set of effects on perceived goals, plans, and actions in the conversations. Burleson et al. were also repetitive, conducting not just one but four separate experiments to make sure that it was the effects of gender and not some other explanation in determining more complex underlying motivations for providing and receiving support. You will learn much more about these characteristics of communication research methods in later chapters on survey, content analytic, experimental, and classical rhetorical criticism methods.

In the discovery process, observations become the basis for two processes: generalization and discrimination. **Generalization** is the process of grouping communication characteristics together based on their observed similarities or common properties. The process of **discrimination** entails contrasting communication characteristics by their differences. To illustrate how the process of generalization works in communication research, consider the study by Vevea, Pearson, Child, & Semlak (2009). They examined how students' unwillingness to communicate, self-esteem, and biological sex predicted their levels of communication apprehension in their public speaking classes. The researchers collected data from twenty-five sections of a basic public speaking course at one university and thirteen sections of another larger university; in all, data from 605 student participants were collected. The results showed that a student's unwillingness to communicate was the strongest predictor of communication apprehension, though students with lower self-esteem and female students were also more likely to be apprehensive. The researchers chose a large number of students from different sections of the public speaking course at separate universities so that they could generalize their findings from this study to other college students at other universities. Their results can be used by public speaking teachers to better understand students' problems with communication apprehension.

As a discovery paradigm researcher, you will use knowledge in discriminating ways to look for systematic differences in your observations. In a classic study of televised sports, Hallmark & Armstrong (1999) wanted to see if the media represent women and men's basketball championship games in different ways. Previous studies had shown that there were a variety of sex differences across broadcasts of men's and women's sports. Past observations revealed that men's sports generally occupied more airtime than women's sports, that women's team sports have been virtually ignored, and that announcers tended to make negative comments significantly more frequently during women's games than during men's. Although they cited progressive changes in media coverage of women's sports, Hallmark and

Armstrong wanted to explore whether some gender biases might be subtler, requiring a different level of discrimination. They focused on more specific features of media presentation: camera shot variation, the length of a shot, and the type and frequency of graphics in each broadcast of women's and men's basketball games during a championship division playoff. By refining their conceptualizations of media presentation, they were able to make finer discriminations about the types of sex differences that exist in sports media coverage.

In these three examples of research, the researchers emphasize discovery as their way of knowing. They began by reviewing past evidence from other studies to create a set of claims. They tested their claims deductively through observations using precise, systematic, and repetitive procedures. Through the processes of generalization and discrimination, the studies' results supported their conclusions, reflecting on what had been discovered. The discovery paradigm assumes that knowledge is discoverable through logical and empirical methods; that is, researchers who share the same standards of precision and systematic observation will observe the same patterns of results in repeated tests of the research claims. Knowledge is expanded, or discovered, through observable or rational means that minimize the subjective viewpoint of the researcher.

When taken together, the philosophical perspectives contributing to knowledge by discovery were combined to form several defining assumptions, which we review and summarize here: There is an objective reality that can be known by any observer, the method of knowing is through testing observations, the method depends on precise, systematic, and repetitive procedures, the purpose of research is to discover the probable through classifying objects based on their similarities and differences, and by identifying essential and universal structures and their interrelationships. Refer again to the defining assumptions for this paradigm that appear in Table 2.2. Many of the assumptions underlie certain types of studies in our field. For example, you can find experimental studies, survey studies, content and conversational analyses, and classical rhetorical analyses that all derive their central assumptions from the knowledge by discovery paradigm. Accordingly, you may find communication studied as quantifiable data in an experimental design, or as a speech in a neoclassical rhetorical theory. In either case, the grounding assumptions will be shared. Further exploration of specific methods is reserved for Parts 2 and 3 of this book.

Summary

In this chapter, you have learned about three epistemological paradigms: knowing by interpretation, knowing by criticism, and knowing by discovery. The paradigm that will inform your research choices depends a great deal on the kinds of research questions you want to ask about communication, as well as your assumptions about the nature of reality, the role of context, and the purpose of doing research. Understanding your own preferences usually follows after reading about studies you find interesting, a process that develops with time. Recognizing the paradigm implications of your choices will provide you with a framework for understanding the arguments you will make as a basis for your research project: constructing your claims (Chapter 4), deciding what will count as your communication data (Chapter 5), and understanding how you will warrant your claims (Chapter 6).

As points of contrast, we have emphasized distinctions among the three paradigms, but it is equally important to recognize the "fuzzy boundaries" between them. There are many studies that fit portions, but not all elements, of what we have described as the bases for each paradigm. Some may have more of an interpretive emphasis and be less politically motivated. Others may press overtly, or even exclusively for radical social change. Moreover, scholars in the communication field continue to debate the major tenets and assumptions common to all three perspectives. We are always in the state of flux as researchers, as theorists, as philosophers, as students and teachers!

The discussion in this section was intended to provide you with an encompassing view of the major paradigmatic changes happening in communication research, and more specifically, happening in our methodological approaches. In choosing to do research, you will select methods that have, at their core, basic assumptions about how you acquire knowledge. The assumptions for each paradigm were summarized in Table 2.2. The types of research methods most frequently associated with each paradigm are listed in Table 2.3. The methods researchers currently use were derived primarily out of the paradigm assumptions about what constitutes knowledge, claims, data, and warrant, as you will learn in the remaining chapters of the first part of this book. Often, researchers do not consciously think about the assumptions associated with each paradigm that characterizes their choice of methods, but the assumptions are there nonetheless. As a student relatively new to research, learning about all three paradigms will help to make you a better researcher and will enable you to appreciate research in all its forms and identify your own preferences.

Key Terms

Discrimination	Knowing by discovery	Paradigms
Generalization	Knowing by interpretation	Precise, systematic, and
Knowing by criticism	Objectivity	repetitive observations

Discussion Questions

1. In beginning this chapter, we asked you to identify one thing that you know and gave you an example of what you know about money. Write down your own example here. Try to identify which epistemological paradigm presented in this chapter best describes the way you came to your ideas about your example.
2. Some people may argue that research that comes from a paradigm other than their own is not *good* research. What are some of the points you can make to counter this argument?
3. Adopting a critical paradigm perspective, argue for/against a perspective of society represented in the media. See if you can find a research article that supports/refutes your point of view.

"Try It!" Activities: Paradigm Assumptions

In this activity, a paradigm perspective is explored and presented by one-third of the class. You will be divided into 2–4 teams per paradigm depending on the size of your class.

1. Discovery Paradigm: Each team should find a survey mentioned in any news or magazine article. Discuss what the article's author seemed to know as a result of the survey findings. What assumptions were made about the people who took the survey? About the survey itself? How are these related to discovery paradigm assumptions?

2. Interpretive Paradigm: With your instructor's help, each team representing this paradigm should read about a study of a cultural or organizational group. How did the author interpret the perspectives of the group's members? How do these reflect interpretive paradigm assumptions?

3. Critical Paradigm: With your instructor's help, each team should read about an issue in the news in which certain groups appear to be marginalized by one dominant social group. Identify dominant and marginalized groups explaining the basis for your identification. How does your explanation reflect critical paradigm assumptions?

Reporting Out: When your team has completed its task, you will present your findings to the rest of the class.

3 Ethics and Research

Introduction

In this chapter, you will get a brief history of communication research ethics that is grounded in classical rhetoric and you will learn about some instances of research misconduct during the last century. You will learn about ethical choices that you will face whenever you decide what to study, review prior research on your topic, implement your methodology, report your findings, and evaluate other people's research. Even if you never become a researcher yourself, understanding and appreciating research ethics will make you a more critical research consumer and it will help you to participate in civic processes more reflectively, too (Gale & Bunton, 2005; Jaksa & Pritchard, 1994; Kienzler, 2001, 2004).

Learning Outcomes

After completing this chapter, you should be able to:

» Recall two–three key historical instances of research misconduct and explain how those problems led to the development of Institutional Review Boards (IRBs) in the United States.

» Identify and explain the ethical choices that are involved at each of three stages of research: First, motives for choosing research topics or projects; second, ways of protecting research participants' rights to freely choose participation, be treated honestly, and maintain some level of privacy; and third, report and evaluate research ethically.

» Articulate and reasonably defend your position relative to particular ethical choices at each of the three stages of research (i.e., before, during, and after a research project).

» Given a published research study approved by an IRB, identify whether the study was likley treated as exempt or nonexempt: Was the study eligible for an expedited review, or was it likely to require full review by the IRB? Give reasons for your answer.

Outline

A Brief History of Communication Ethics

Ethical Choices in Communication Research
» Before Doing Research: Motives for Projects and Topics

» During Research Projects: Protecting the Rights of Research Participants
   Right to Freely Choose Research Participation

You probably took a critical thinking class early in your college studies, where you learned about some models of ethical reasoning. We have placed this chapter near the front of the book because we agree with George Cheney's (2004) observation that "Discussions of ethics and values should be integrated across topics and issues" (p. 38). Here, we will introduce you to some ethical choices that you will face before, during, and after doing research. But we will continue to address specific ethical issues in each chapter of Parts 2 and 3 of this book, when you learn how to conduct conversation and discourse analysis, ethnography, rhetorical criticism, content analysis, surveys, experiments, and so forth.

This chapter begins with how contemporary codes of ethical conduct for researchers came to exist. But we'll also help you think about how some recent changes in communications technology and in communication theory push the limits of those traditional codes of conduct. We will introduce you to ethical choices that you will make at three phases of the research process: Before doing research, you will need to examine your own motives for selecting particular topics and projects, and you will need to review previous theory and research. During a research study, you will have to protect the rights and responsibilities of your research participants. You also will need to think about how your research may benefit or harm society. Afterward, you'll make choices about how to ethically report and evaluate your research. Let's begin by reviewing the origins of our field in classical Greek and Roman rhetoric.

A Brief History of Communication Ethics

Classical scholars in ancient Greece and Rome were concerned about how values translate into social action,

concerns that are still addressed today in rhetorical studies. As Anderson (2000) pointed out, "For classical authors, the relationship between one's 'character' and communication effectiveness was clear and direct"; the Roman orator and critic, Quintilian, argued that the ideal rhetor was "a good man speaking well" (p. 132). Likewise, Aristotle linked living well with doing good, and more recently, Cheney (2004) pointed out that "Ethics is practical; what's more, it's necessary and not just nice" (p. 38). When you see all research methods as ways of making arguments, it becomes obvious why all researchers need to think about how they translate their values into social action.

For example, contemporary rhetorical critics have expanded the concept of moral character or ethos to include the right of access to communication in society and the participation of a multiplicity of voices (Nakayama, 1997). Consider the advantages and disadvantages of your own level of access to communication: If you own a personal computer or a smart phone, and you have free wireless networks on your campus, you have access to a wealth of resources that people with no computer and no Internet access lack. Access to communication becomes a moral issue in a representative democracy: We cannot participate if we cannot access the information or the interactions.

Furthermore, because all people don't participate in the same ways, the *common good* cannot be achieved just by giving everyone simple technological or physical access to information. Instead, ethical communication includes a range of socially and culturally constructed ways of speaking, writing, and performing communication. To that end, Asante (1999) developed an Afrocentric theory of communication; Perez (1997) discussed the construction of communication ethics in a Latin American context; and Hsieh, Hsieh, and Lehman (2003) articulated some of the ethical conflicts that arose when government-supported digitalization initiatives motivated Chinese and Western scholars to work together. Each of these scholar's works have challenged traditional assumptions about communication ethics by considering perspectives that were formerly marginalized. Scholarly inquiry about communication research ethics has continued to evolve from the Western tradition forward. Today, that inquiry has expanded considerably beyond the classical rhetorical frame. Some of that scholarship is theoretic and deals with what *ought* to be the case. But there are plenty of applied questions about communication ethics, too. For example, can loyalty go too far among public relations practitioners (Stoker, 2005)? When do a company's efforts to reduce its environmental impact count as *greening* versus *greenwashing*—that is, adopting environmentally friendly policies or practices chiefly or only to improve the company's credibility with consumers and investors (Munshi & Kurian, 2005)? What is ethical behavior for employers and job seekers in the application and interview processes (Ralston, 2000)? These are just three examples of ethical issues in specific contexts today. There are many other issues, including the ethical conduct of research involving human participants.

With the rise of social science in the nineteenth and early twentieth centuries, philosophers like C. S. Peirce and Karl Popper elaborated a unitary method of scientific research that was both amoral and neutral in its objectivity. According to Peirce (and other philosophers of social science like John Locke, John Stuart Mill, and Max Weber), ethical issues belonged to the realm of a priori knowledge, or intuition. These philosophers envisioned the ideal scientist as dispassionate and detached from human values and norms. For them, a true scientist approached research from a value-free perspective, and searched for objective truth in the empirical evidence. Science and morals were seen as two fundamentally separate dimensions of thought (Christians, 2003).

There were social critics. You may recall Mary Shelley's novel about Dr. Frankenstein, the scientist who pursued knowledge irrespective of the harm it caused to his subjects. Some members of the scientific community argued for guiding principles that would create the greatest good for the greatest number of people. These critics wanted researchers to exercise individual freedoms, so long as no harm was done to another person. This perspective, based on balancing the potential benefits and harms of scientific research, became known as **utilitarian ethics** (Christians, 2003).

But in the aftermath of World War I and II, there was an increasing awareness among researchers that a code of ethics was needed to guide the treatment of research participants and the conduct of researchers. For example, during World War II, Nazi physicians conducted medical experiments on thousands of concentration camp prisoners, "injecting people with gasoline and live viruses, immersing people in ice water, and forcing people to ingest poisons" (National Institute of Health [NIH], 2002, p. 5). Following the *Trials of War Criminals before the Nuremberg Military Tribunals*, twenty-three physicians and administrators involved in those experiments were convicted of crimes against humanity. Sixteen were found guilty; and seven were sentenced to death. The verdict included a section on "Permissible medical experiments," which later became known as the *Nuremberg Code*.

Other examples of inhumane and unethical research can be found in US history, including "a long term study of black males conducted at Tuskegee by the United States Public Health Service" (NIH, 2002, p. 6). From the early 1930s until 1972, more than 600 black men participated in that study of "the natural history of untreated syphilis" (NIH, 2002, p. 6). They were recruited without being told the true purpose of the research, and even when the researchers knew that penicillin was an effective treatment for syphilis, the men in the experiment were not told about the antibiotic or treated with it. When the study was first published, in 1972, public outrage helped to bring pressure on government agencies to insure that research institutions monitor their researchers' motives, treatment of research participants, and the consequences of the research (Veatch, 1996). "In acknowledgment of its responsibility, the Government continues to compensate surviving participants and the families of deceased participants" from the Tuskegee experiments (NIH, 2002, p. 7).

There were other examples of grossly unethical medical research: "In 1963, studies at New York's Jewish Chronic Disease Hospital were conducted to understand whether the body's inability to reject cancer cells was due to cancer or to debilitation" (NIH, 2002, p. 7). Live cancer cells were injected into patients hospitalized for various chronic, debilitating diseases. But the patients were not told that they would receive cancer cells. The Board of Regents for the State University of New York found the researchers guilty of fraud, deceit, and unprofessional conduct.

The Nuremburg Code and other instances of misconduct in research like the ones we just outlined significantly influenced the development of national standards for ethical research in the United States:

> [The] "National Commission for the Protection of Human Subjects in Biomedical and Behavioral Research . . . was established by the National Research Act of 1974 in response to public concern about unethical biomedical experiments." (Simmerling, Schwegler, Sieber, & Lindgren, 2007, p. 838)

The commissioners, most of whom were medical doctors and researchers, established three principles for ethical research, including beneficence, respect for the autonomy of persons, and justice. Those principles were outlined in the *Belmont Report*, named after the location where the Commission convened (Simmerling et al., 2007, p. 838). Later that year, the US federal government mandated that any organization receiving federal funds to support research (e.g., universities, hospitals, prisons) set up **Institutional Review Boards** (IRBs). An IRB is a working group that is responsible for establishing and implementing formal research codes of conduct (Madison, 2005).

Since 1974, a good number of scholarly professional associations like the National Communication Association have adopted their own codes of conduct. A **code of conduct** translates ethical values into social action (Christians, 2003, pp. 217–219). Yet most college and university IRBs still follow the values articulated by the National Commission for the Protection of Human Subjects in Biomedical and Behavioral Research and/or the National Institute of Health's online training for principal investigators. Research, as it is defined by NIH, is most consistent with the survey and experimental research methods that you will learn about in Part 3 of this book; the NIH view of *research* is sometimes at odds with other methods in this book, such as ethnography, discourse analysis, or critical studies. Nonetheless, the guidelines articulated by the NIH for biomedical research include beneficence, respect for autonomy of persons, and justice. Since those guidelines govern most universities' IRB practices across academic disciplines, we use them here as a frame for ethical conduct in communication research.

First, communication research should *benefit* people by maximizing the good for society and minimizing any potential harm to individuals. Second, research should *respect* people by preserving individual autonomy whenever possible. When you do research, think of participants as individuals who are capable of making their own decisions. If their ability to choose is compromised in any way (e.g., children, people with mental illness, prisoners), then you will need to take extra steps to respect their autonomy. Third, researchers should be concerned with *justice*. We should treat people fairly and consider who will bear the costs of research, as well as who will benefit from it. Each of these three values has been interpreted in ways that are distinctly US American (Madison, 2005) and in ways that privilege scientific research (if not biomedical research, per se). In other words, the ways that IRBs interpret beneficence, respect, and justice do not always fit social science research studies quite as well as they fit biomedical studies:

> It is a major leap from not harming subjects of biomedical research in the process of curing a disease or benefiting society with new health-giving technologies, to issues of whether one may inconvenience or upset subjects of social, educational or behavioral research in return for learning something about human behavior for the sake of knowledge, or for policy purposes. (Simmerling et al., 2007, p. 844)

This quote shows how seemingly straightforward issues like what to call the people who participate in your research (e.g., participants, human subjects, key informants) are more complicated than you may realize at first. That's one reason why IRBs are required to have members with varied backgrounds (i.e., gender, race/ethnicity, cultural heritage), including at least one nonscientific member, so that the interests of nonscientists will be represented. Furthermore, one IRB member must not be affiliated with the institution as a caution against institutional interests dominating research. These requirements work to ensure ethical communication in the IRB review process by requiring both access to IRB interactions and participation by multiple voices.

Research that involves human participants and is proposed on college campuses, then, must be reviewed by an IRB. The IRB will consider the potential risks and benefits of the project (i.e., utilitarian ethics). It will deem a study **exempt** if the project only includes educational settings and/or educational testing, if it uses existing data that is publicly available, or when it involves consumer taste-testing studies. In those cases, the risks to research participants are considered minimal because they are risks that people would take in the course of daily life activities or routine procedures, such as a medical exam. Exempt studies are given **expedited review**.

That means that the research protocol can be approved by the IRB chair or a subgroup of the full IRB.

A **research protocol** describes who you will invite to participate in your study and how you will recruit or select participants. The protocol also details your methods for collecting and analyzing data, any potential risks and benefits of your research, and how you will protect participants' rights to freely choose their participation, maintain some level of privacy, and be treated respectfully and honestly. Check your university's IRB website to see if there is a template or a sample research protocol posted there.

It is important for you to know two things about exempt research. First, the risks to participants go beyond their physical safety. There might be important risks that are economic, legal, psychological, or social. So when you think about your own research projects, or read published studies, consider what sort of risks the study may pose for participants. Second, the exempt category only applies to adults who can provide their own consent. In addition to children, and people with mental disabilities, people may be unable to consent to participate in research if they have "circumstances that severely restrict individual liberty (e.g., incarceration, military service)" (Simmerling et al., 2007, p. 848). Furthermore, in some cultural contexts, even an adult of sound mind can be constrained from autonomous consent (Madison, 2005). For example, consent of *the group* may be culturally mandated in some contexts, or a male member may give consent for females to participate in research in some tribal or marriage contexts. If you see those examples as either *good* or *bad*, notice that your values are being engaged. Your values may not match or may not be interpreted in the same ways as the values that guide IRB reviews. That's why we started this chapter with the ancient Greek and Roman rhetors' attempts to translate values into social action.

A research proposal is deemed **nonexempt**, and reviewed more closely by the full IRB, when the people involved in the study are not capable of independently giving their autonomous consent and/or when the potential risks to participants are greater than those that they would likely encounter in their daily life activities or routine procedures. Whether your study is deemed exempt or nonexempt, you must protect the rights of your research participants.

One way that protection typically happens is that NIH requires that women and minorities be included among the participants selected for biomedical research, so that the findings from those studies can be generalized to the entire population of the United States, and everyone will be able to benefit from the research. According to the justice ethic, if people are unlikely to benefit from the research, then they should not be subjected to the risks of participating in it. You may recognize this as the principle of **distributive justice**, which deems that the costs and benefits of a decision be distributed fairly. There are other justice principles (Simmerling et al., 2007). For example, **procedural justice** would decree that everyone gets to participate equally in the process, even though some people might benefit more from it than others. **Corrective justice** (or restorative justice) would mean that those who have benefited least in the past, or who have been harmed most by past practices, should be benefited most in present decisions. If you take a course in communication ethics or philosophy, you can learn much more about these ideas. Here, it's important to remember that IRBs typically operate on the principles of distributive justice and utilitarian ethics.

In the next section, we will outline some of the ways that you can attend to the values of beneficence, respect, and justice when you are conducting and reporting communication research. These choices start with you thinking about what to study and what not to study, and they matter as you review prior theory and research on your topic. We also make ethical choices as we go about conducting communication research and as we decide how to share our findings and evaluate other people's research. Table 3.2, at the end of this chapter, summarizes some of the ethical choices we make before, during, and after we conduct communication research studies.

Ethical Choices in Communication Research

Academic and other institutional researchers (e.g., in medicine, education, the judicial system, the media industry) have to complete ethics courses as a form of professional development before they can submit research protocols to an Institutional Review Board. Ask your research methods teacher what certification your institution requires from principal investigators prior to reviewing their research proposals. We have placed this chapter near the front of the book because we want you to start thinking about ethics right away by examining your own motives for doing research and for selecting particular research topics.

Before Doing Research: Motives for Projects and Topics

We must ask ourselves as researchers, "Why am I doing this research study?" In your case, it may be because your instructor, or your department, said you had to do so. Perhaps you want to answer some question you have about communication in a thoughtful, accurate, and generalizable way. Or you may want your research to help other people by telling your research participants' stories for them or with them, thus helping other people understand their meanings or perspectives. Perhaps you want to collaborate with your research participants in solving a social problem (Miles & Huberman, 1994; Best, 2013).

As you identify your own motives for doing research and their ethical consequences, you will need to consider several other criteria for developing sound, researchable questions. Chapter 4, "Making Claims," will help you start to think about the research process as a way of building good arguments. But before you can construct a strong argument, you will need to think about what kinds of communication questions peak your curiosity—and which of those questions can be explored or answered with communication research. At that point, you are ready to think about the ethics of pursuing particular communication research projects and topics.

Your primary interests are likely going to concern one or two subfields of communication (e.g., interpersonal, intercultural, or media communication, use of language and symbols). No matter what interests you about communication, your question should be broad enough to be socially significant. That is, research projects should matter to you and to other people! At the same time, your question must be narrow enough to be plausibly investigated in one research study. Ask your research methods instructor for help finding the right degree of specificity in stating your general research topic or question. You can also use the "Try It!" activity #4 at the end of this chapter to practice making your initial topic interests more and less specific. If your class is like most research methods classes for communication majors in the United States, your research project is likely to use some kind of survey or content analytic method (Parks, Faw, & Goldsmith, 2011).

Some research questions can be answered with data, and others can be explored, if not fully answered, by gathering certain kinds of evidence in support of a claim. Both of those kinds of questions are fine places to begin thinking about doing communication research. However, there are some questions that cannot be answered with data and so are not good questions with which to start a research project. Let's look at one simple example: The question, "What communication channels do college students most value?" is answerable with research. But the question, "What communication channels *should* college students value?" cannot be *answered*, per se, with research. The answers to what we *should* value (or do) can be explored through discussion. Research data might help to document different interpretations or opinions about such questions. But the question of what you should value cannot be tested or proven with research data.

Finally, you'll have to think about pragmatic issues like expertise, time, and money when you decide on a research question. There may be questions that fascinate you but that you lack the expertise to investigate. Likewise, you may have the curiosity and the expertise but lack the necessary time, money, or other resources needed to carry out a certain research project (e.g., software for data analysis or access to a field research setting).

In addition to pragmatic concerns, it's a good idea for you to consider the politics of selecting particular research questions or topics. If you work in a for-profit company that wants to develop research support for a new product that they are marketing, or if you are a campaign manager who aims to get someone elected, then you could end up designing a study to find the exact results that you or your supervisors hope to find. If you look on *YouTube* for "Milgram experiment" or "Stanford prison study" or even the recent military abuse of prisoners at Abu Graib, you will find videos about how obeying authority can lead to unethical conduct in research studies.

On the other hand, you might think that academic research is free of any such questionable motives. But what if you became a researcher in order to secure funding for your department? What if you are doing research because you have to *publish or perish* in order to get tenured and to be promoted? As students, professors, and practitioners, we have to consider our motives for doing research and our reasons for studying particular topics.

Virtually every arena of communication from interpersonal to the most public involves ethical issues.

There are ethical implications of selecting and avoiding particular research topics. For example, let's say you want to contribute to the good of society by studying interpersonal romantic relationships. Will you limit your study to married persons and long-term dating relationships? Will gay and lesbian couples be included in your research? How much of your findings will be shared with participants? How might that knowledge impact their relationships? If you use social media websites to collect your data, what potential risks and benefits might that pose? What if you end up documenting unethical or illegal behaviors in your study? In fact, does legal conduct equate to ethical conduct? How will you ensure that the benefits of your research study outweigh the potential costs to your research participants, or to you, the researcher?

These are just a few of the ethical questions we could mention related to one sample research topic in interpersonal communication. Think for a minute about communication in groups and teams. Imagine how a study of group decision making might honor, or threaten, the values of beneficence, respect, and autonomy. In public speaking and in mass-mediated contexts, there are countless ethical issues, such as how *respecting* ownership of intellectual property works for materials that we post on the Internet or how to preserve people's *autonomy* when using online surveys or even assessing "What's trending on Twitter?" We hope these examples start you thinking about the numerous ethical questions inherent in every research topic.

Before we consider how you can honor the values of beneficence, respect, and justice in your treatment of human research participants, let's look at one other kind of ethical dilemma you might face when beginning a research project. You will be faced with ethical choices when reviewing prior theory and research in your topic area. Have you searched diligently enough for prior work about your topic? Sometimes, you will need to read studies from other disciplines that are also involved in knowing about that topic. What if you read a study that supports your ideas, but has serious flaws or limitations? Will you point out those flaws in your literature review? Is it okay to cite studies you have only skimmed, or barely understand? How will you acknowledge the sources of your ideas (i.e., cite the theorists and authors of previous research whose key findings justify your purpose or research question)? You will need to follow established guidelines for crediting other people's ideas and contributions (e.g., the procedures published in either APA or MLA style guides). It is crucial that you avoid "fabrication, falsification, or plagiarism," the key elements of scientific **misconduct** as defined by the National Science Foundation.

Let's move on now, from thinking about your ethical behavior prior to conducting research (i.e., motives for doing research and choosing topics, as well as ethical choices in conducting literature reviews), to the specific actions that you might take in order to honor the values of beneficence, respect for individual autonomy, and justice as you conduct your research project.

During Research Projects: Protecting the Rights of Research Participants

Research participants have a right to be assured of treatment that is fair, just, and respectful. Public confidence in research findings depends greatly on our conducting research in an ethical manner. For both reasons, researchers must act with integrity and insure that participants' rights are protected (Jaksa & Pritchard, 1994; Scanlon, 1993). Notice that the word *right* to things such as informed choices about participating in research, privacy, justice, and respect derive from a theory of moral rights that goes beyond utilitarianism and argue that human beings are moral agents whose rights cannot justly be violated, regardless of the desirability of the outcome (Kant, 1785/1993; Noszick, 1974).

In fact, quite a few contemporary theorists have argued that our basic assumptions about ethics in social science research should be revisited (Bok, 1979; Gilligan, 1982; Johannesen, 2001; Perez, 1997). For example, Bok (1979) critiqued deception in social science research. Foucault (1979) argued that the research process cannot escape being value laden because the community of scholars exerts power over subjects that is neither equal nor neutral (see Spitzberg, 2000, on the related question of "what is *good* communication?"). Gilligan (1983) and others have critiqued justice as a dominant standard for ethical research, arguing that equal emphasis should be placed on an ethic of care for others. Denzin (1997) argued that social science research should include diverse perspectives and multiple voices, encourage critical thinking, and "promote social transformation" (Christians, 2003, pp. 228–229).

As you may have already gathered from these sample critiques, there are a number of potential ethical tensions among an individual researcher's goals, participants' goals, and societal goals. As the researcher, it is your responsibility to consider the ethical implications of your actions for yourself, for your participants, and for society. In this section, we introduce you to specific actions that are consistent with the IRB values of beneficence, respect, and justice, actions you can take to protect the rights of your research participants and the good of society. In particular, you will learn to protect your participants' rights to (1) freely choose whether to participate in research, (2) maintain their privacy, and (3) be treated honestly.

Right to Freely Choose Research Participation

As you already know, IRBs are charged with protecting the rights of people involved in research. The guiding principle of ethical research is to minimize harm and maximize benefit for participants and society. The first way you can avoid harming research participants is to protect their free choice about whether or not to participate in your study.

You can protect free choice by providing potential research participants with the opportunity to give their informed consent. **Informed consent** means that you communicate any potential risks and benefits of your research to potential study participants, in language that they can understand. You answer any questions that they may have, and you secure their written permission to collect their responses, video record their interactions, observe them, and so forth. Informed consent is a legal, ethical, and policy matter. It must be voluntary, not coerced. Table 3.1 contains a sample informed consent document.

The idea of getting people's informed consent to participate in research might seem simple at first. But it can be quite complicated. Let's consider the idea of informed consent documents being presented to participants in language they can understand. This might mean adapting your explanation of the potential risks and benefits of your study to your participants' age and education level. You will need to avoid technical jargon on the informed consent document. For instance, you can use readability statistics, like the Flesch-Kincaid Scale included many word-processing programs, to check the reading level of your informed consent documents and your survey questionnaires. Working with participants whose first language is not English presents another layer of complexity. As a case in point, Amason, Allen, & Holmes (1999) conducted interviews with employees in a multicultural organization about their experiences seeking social support at work. Some of the interviews were conducted with Hispanic employees who spoke in Spanish:

> When the interviews were conducted with Spanish speaking employees, a translator (not affiliated with the organization to protect employee confidentiality) was used. Translators were native Spanish speakers who either taught Spanish at the university level or provided translation services for the community through a local social service agency. (Amason et al., 1999, p. 316)

Communication researchers working with participants with different levels of education, expertise, or socioeconomic resources need to be concerned about status differentials. **Status differentials** are relevant whenever one party to an agreement has more power resources than the other(s). Those power differences can threaten participants' autonomous consent to participate in research (see the earlier reference to Milgram's obedience experiments). You and your research participants probably will vary in terms of money, time, expert knowledge, skills, and so on. Status differentials among participants, or between participants and the researcher, can open the way for potential power abuses (Scanlon, 1993). For example, inducements to participate in research studies can threaten autonomous consent if the participants really need whatever is being provided as an incentive, whether the incentive is cash or free services or extra-credit points. Likewise, experimental research that involves testing the effects of a treatment program by comparing people in the treatment group with participants who do not receive the same treatment raises ethical concerns about *justice*. It may be unjust to deny a potentially *beneficial* treatment to one group of people and provide it to another (e.g., training to reduce communication apprehension). Experimental groups can also threaten participants' *autonomous* consent to participate in research if they think they are getting treatment, when they're actually getting a placebo. At the same time, carefully controlled experiments allow researchers to isolate competing explanations about cause-and-effect relationships. We have all benefited from this type of research, not only in medicine (e.g., polio vaccine) but in communication research (e.g., advice regarding deception detection). So we have to balance potential costs with benefits.

Right to Privacy

As researchers, we also must think about how we will protect our research participants' privacy. In some cases,

Table 3.1 Sample Informed Consent Document

Informed Consent to Participate in a Research Study
College of _____
San Francisco State University
1600 Holloway Avenue
San Francisco, California 94132

Title of Research:
Name of Principal Investigator/Primary Researcher:
Phone Number of Principal Investigator/Primary Researcher:
Name and Phone Number of Committee Members:

A. PURPOSE AND BACKGROUND
Under the supervision of Dr. (insert faculty member's name), Professor of (insert Department name) at San Francisco State University (insert your whole name), a graduate student in research (insert Department name), is conducting research on (insert what the research is about.) The purpose of this interview is to help the researcher study (insert why you are doing this research.)

B. PROCEDURES
If I agree to participate in this research study, the following will occur: *(The following is sample information, <u>do not copy it</u>, instead, insert what is appropriate for your research.)*
  1. I will be asked to participate in an individual interview *(indicate the amount of time it will take to participate in the interview.)*
  2. I will be asked to discuss the following topics:
     a. stress in my life
     b. ways I deal with stress
     c. support systems
     d. personal resources for coping
  3. I will also be asked my age, gender, race, sexual orientation, socioeconomic status, and educational background.
  4. If I agree to participate in this research study, an audiotape of this interview will be made for research purposes.

C. RISKS (The following is sample information, <u>do not copy it</u>, instead insert what is appropriate for your research.) *If there are risks, you must state what they are:*
1. Risks:
I will be asked questions of a personal nature, and I might feel uncomfortable talking about some things. I am free to decline to answer any questions that I don't wish to answer, or I may stop my participation in the discussion at any time without penalty.
If there are no risks, state the following:
There are no known foreseeable risks or discomforts involved in participating in this study.
2. Confidentiality:
The records from this study will be kept as confidential as possible. No individual identities will be used in any reports or publications resulting from the study. All tapes, transcripts, and summaries will be given codes and stored separately from any names or other direct identification of participants. Research information will be kept in locked files at all times. Only research personnel will have access to the files and the audiotapes, and only those with an essential need to see names will have access to that particular file. After the study is completed and all data has been transcribed from the tapes, the tapes will be held for one year and then destroyed.
(Please note that <u>all informed consent forms</u> must have an explanation of the procedures by which the participants confidentiality will be protected.)
(Please note: Title of research and name of Principal Investigator/Primary Researcher must be on each page of an informed consent form no matter the length of the informed consent form. Also, the informed consent must contain sequential page numbers.)

(Continued)

Table 3.1 (*Continued*)

D. DIRECT BENEFITS (*The following is sample information, <u>do not copy it</u>, instead insert what is appropriate for your research.*)
There will be no direct benefit to me from participating in this research study. (*Note: if the preceding is true of your research, you may copy the aforementioned statement.*) The <u>anticipated</u> benefit of these procedures is a better understanding of what stress African American women who are HIV positive or have AIDS experience and how they cope with this stress.
Please note that direct benefits include free medical care, payment, and so forth. They do not include adding to a body of knowledge or any potential altruistic benefit.

E. ALTERNATIVES
I am free to choose not to participate in this research study.

F. COSTS
There will be no costs to me as a result of taking part in this research study.

G. COMPENSATION (if there is compensation)
I will be compensated $20.00 cash on completion of this interview.

H. QUESTIONS
I have spoken with (insert your whole name) about this study and have had my questions answered. If I have any further questions about the study, I can contact Dr. (insert faculty member's name), or (insert your whole name) by calling (insert Department phone number with area code) or write to them at the (insert Department name), San Francisco State University, 1600 Holloway Avenue, San Francisco, CA 94132.

I. CONSENT
I have been given a copy of this consent form to keep.

PARTICIPATION IN RESEARCH STUDY IS VOLUNTARY. I am free to decline to participate in this research study, or I may withdraw my participation at any point without penalty. My decision whether to participate in this research study will have no influence on my present or future status at San Francisco State University.

Signature _____ Date _____
Research Participant

Signature _____ Date _____
Interviewer

(Sample informed consent developed by Gilda M. Bloom, PhD, Chair, Committee for the Protection of Human Subjects, Spring 1998 and edited Spring 2001).

we protect participants' privacy by collecting data without any identifying information (e.g., names, ID numbers, addresses, photo or video images). In other cases, we promise participants **anonymity**, the assurance that neither the researcher nor anyone who sees the research data and final report will know their identities. This can be accomplished by coding data so that identifying information is eliminated early in the data collection and storage process.

In some cases, it may be enough to protect our participants' privacy by assuring them **confidentiality**, promising that the researcher is the only person who will know their identities and who will ensure that participants' responses can never be connected to their names, addresses, and so on. Assurances of confidentiality depend on how we store and report data (e.g., encrypted data storage; use of fictitious names; reporting data only in aggregate form, rather than using any individual's responses in our research reports). Of course, assuring anonymity is practically impossible when you collect photographs or video evidence of communicators in action. It is up to us as researchers, and to the IRB, to weigh the potential risks and benefits of how research participants are to be treated and to decide what degree of privacy to guarantee research participants.

Our rapid changes in communications technology bring with them new ethical considerations, as "web-based experiments, online focus groups, email questionnaires, and computerized assessments of face-to-face behaviors" relocate traditional research procedures into the electronic arena (Palomares & Flanagin, 2005, pp. 175–176). For example, there is still a lot of debate about the public or private nature of information obtained and given online. When information is posted in a blog or chat room, do the rules of public domain and fair use govern ethical use of that information? Or do IRB guidelines govern its use? If you post your survey on the web, with a hyperlink to an informed consent document, how will you ascertain that the persons who agree to participate in your study are autonomous, consenting adults (Palomares & Flanagin, 2005, p. 171)? If you collect and store data on a computer that is sometimes connected to the Internet, how will you protect against data leaks, hackers, or spyware (Voosen, 2013)? Questions like these are still very much in flux for communication researchers and for IRBs. Two common solutions today are to store research data in password-protected files that only the researcher(s) can access, and to destroy print or digital data files after the data analysis is completed. Storing data over multiple research projects, or for potential future projects, requires the explicit approval of an IRB. It may help you to think about these two questions together: How public is the data I am collecting? How risky is my use of that data to participants?

Because electronic technologies can be used to monitor information and its uses unobtrusively, the potential for privacy violations is significant. For example, a web camera can be used to collect information about someone who has consented to participate in research, but the camera may inadvertently collect images of other people in the immediate environment, people who have not consented to participate in research (Palomares & Flanagin, 2005). A mobile phone or personal data device can be used to audio- or videotape people who do not know that they are being recorded. Images of communicators may be posted to the Internet without their permission (e.g., *Facebook*, *Instagram*, *YouTube*). All of these are instances of potential privacy violations that must be avoided in research.

Furthermore, information is being collected about us every time we use the Internet. We do not have the same guarantees to privacy online that we have in other areas of our lives. For instance, G. Chung and Grimes (2005) explored the process of data mining, or collecting information for marketing purposes when children play games online. Those kinds of technological advances suggest how difficult it can be to apply any ethical standards to protect the privacy of research participants. Of course, it's also really hard for researchers and reporters to protect the confidentiality of informants when online communication is involved (Kennamer, 2005). These few examples start to show you how the *Belmont Report*, with its focus on biomedical research, failed to anticipate and account for some of the ethical issues inherent in studying human communication.

Many of the choices that you make as a researcher can simultaneously protect and threaten your participants' rights. For example, you may want to protect people's free choice to participate in your research. But you may not want to tell people your study's true purpose before they choose to participate, because you fear that knowledge would change their responses. That dilemma brings us to the issues of deception and omission in communication research.

Right to Be Treated with Honesty

In all communication research, the protection of human rights for those involved is paramount. "The value of the best research is not likely to outweigh injury" to a person harmed by the project (Stake, 1998, p. 103). Omitting information or deceiving research participants might harm them, whether directly or indirectly. An IRB will determine whether the benefits of gaining particular information or observations merits omitting information or deceiving participants. In some cases, information may be omitted or falsified, if the researcher provides a **debriefing**, telling participants the full truth after their responses have been collected and giving them a chance to withdraw their participation or data from the study.

We have to protect research participants' rights to freely consent to participate in research, to maintain some level of privacy, and to be treated honestly during a research study. Then we're ready to think about our ethical obligations as researchers after a study is completed. At that point, we have a duty to report our research in ethical ways, and to evaluate other people's research ethically.

Afterward: Reporting and Evaluating Research Ethically

We make choices about our motives for doing research and for selecting particular research topics. We also make choices about how we will conduct our studies. But ethics also means that we have to consider the impact of sharing our findings and evaluating other people's research. We must always assess the potential consequences that the conduct and publication of our research study has for ourselves and for others (Madison, 2005).

Research participants' rights to free choice, privacy, and honesty continue to be important as we present our research to audiences through performances or at professional association meetings and as we publish our research in scholarly or trade journals. As members of a research community, we also need to honor those rights when we evaluate other people's research.

Let's consider privacy, for example. Pollach (2005) analyzed websites' privacy policies to see whether the online policy statements communicated "clearly and unequivocally when, how and for what purpose data are collected, used or shared" (p. 221). In fact, Pollach found that the corporate policies she examined used persuasive appeals to increase the companies' perceived trustworthiness. Furthermore, she found that the language used in policy statements often disguised unethical data handling practices. Thus, her study showed how both the values (privacy) and the actions (policy for handling online users' contact information) demanded ethical choices.

The same link between values and actions holds true for us when we study people's ordinary talk. For example, it may be more accurate to download digital chat room data than it is to record people's conversations in real time, in a face-to-face context, and then transcribe those conversations. But if the people chatting online do not know that their talk is being used for research purposes, or if they do not know that their remarks might be published in your manuscript, then their rights to informed consent and privacy are being violated (Palomares & Flanagin, 2005).

Similarly, data mining, the practice of aggregating individuals' personal information from Internet commerce transactions for marketing purposes can threaten individual rights to privacy and freedom from harm (G. Chung & Grimes, 2005). The same problem exists when we aggregate information from social media websites for political or other persuasive projects. These privacy threats are equally important for communication researchers who aggregate electronic information about their students.

Plagiarism, the act of representing another person's words, ideas, or work as your own, is another big ethical issue when reporting and evaluating other people's research. Plagiarism violates professional codes of conduct. It also violates people's right to be treated honestly (e.g., your teachers expect you to be honest in your academic work. That usually means crediting the source of your ideas. It may also mean producing original work, not repurposing projects that you developed in previous classes). In addition to citing your sources of information accurately in a literature review, you must try to avoid misrepresenting information in your research report or critical essay. You will need to cite your sources fully and accurately. You'll also need to represent information as ethically as you can when presenting your research to an audience. For example, think about whether your representations of the participants and their communication are fair. When you are presenting your findings to colleagues, for example, would you do anything differently if your research participants were in the room during the presentation? If so, chances are that you may be violating one of the rights of your research participants. Conduct permitted by the IRB is legal conduct. So you may have to take steps beyond those dictated by your IRB to be both legal and ethical.

As a matter of fact, your responsibility to protect the rights of participants and the research community extends beyond avoiding plagiarism or misrepresenting research participants in presentations and manuscripts. As Madison (2005) advocated, you have to think about the effect of publicizing your research, too. For example, what are the likely policy implications of publishing your findings? If you report that a "stop smoking" program is ineffective, is the funding for the program likely to be cut? Who would benefit and who would be harmed if that happened? For some very sensitive research topics (e.g., communication around HIV/AIDS) or in studies with participants who are considered to be very vulnerable (e.g., prisoners, children), informed consent documents may be protected from legal subpoena—if the IRB grants a certificate of confidentiality prior to the start of the study. Absent that protection, your data could be subpoenaed and used in a court of law.

Finally, you need to consider how researchers who come after you might be affected by your presentations or publications. Avoid burning bridges during data collection and analysis, and when you present and publish your research. That way, you and other researchers will have the opportunity to participate with, and learn from, the people who contributed to your research studies (Madison, 2005).

Summary

After reading this chapter, you should have a clear sense of the history of communication ethics. You also should understand how historical instances of unethical behavior (aka research misconduct) led to the IRB review process and its values of beneficence, respect for autonomy of persons, and justice. You should be able to explain why your choice of a research topic, and your review of prior works on that topic, are ethical. Now you can describe some ways to protect research participants' privacy and autonomy, including informed consent procedures. You are prepared to start thinking about how you will treat research participants and to consider ethical issues that arise as you store, analyze, use, and report research findings. We hope this chapter helps you appreciate the complexities of communication ethics in practice. But most importantly, we hope you become an ethical scholar in your own research endeavors.

Table 3.2 Ethical Issues and Choices in Research

Phase of Research	Ethical Issues/Choices
Before doing research: Motives for projects and topics	• Why am I doing research? • What topics have I selected or rejected, and why? • Who will my research benefit or harm (Myself? Participants? Other people?) • Have I carefully searched the literature for relevant prior studies on this topic? • Have I properly credited the sources of my ideas (e.g., why this study matters, my research design, my methodological procedures)?
During research projects: Protecting the rights of participants	• Can my participants freely choose whether or not to participate in my study? • Do my participants understand what they are consenting to do? Do they understand the risks? • How might status differentials threaten my participants' right to freely choose their own participation? • How might any incentives to participate in my research project (e.g., money, extra-credit, access to free products or services, approval from an authority figure) threaten my participants' right to freely choose their own participation? • How will participants' rights to privacy be threatened or protected in my study? • How will I treat myself, my participants, and the research community with honesty and integrity during data collection and analysis? • Is any type of deception or omission merited in my study? • What differences exist, if any, between "legal" and "ethical" treatment of people in my study?
Afterward: Reporting and evaluating research ethically	• How will I treat myself, my participants, and the research community with honesty and integrity while writing my research report or critical essay? • How will I treat myself, my participants, and the research community with honesty and integrity while presenting or performing my findings to an audience? • If I document illegal or unethical behavior in my data collection, what will I do with that information (e/g/, nothing, report it to someone else, confront participants)? • [How] will I share research findings with the participants from my project? • Is each person who contributed substantially to my research report or critical essay credited (e.g., as an author or reviewer)?

Key Terms

Anonymity
Code of conduct
Confidentiality
Corrective justice principle
Debriefing
Distributive justice principle

Exempt versus nonexempt
    research
Expedited v. full IRB review
Informed consent
Institutional Review
    Board (IRB)

Misconduct
Plagiarism
Procedural justice principle
Research protocol
Status differentials
Utilitarian ethics

Discussion Questions

1. Pretend that your roommate, also a communication student, offers to edit your research manuscript if you perform a database search for articles she could use in her literature review. Do you agree to this exchange? If so, do you share that agreement with your teachers? Why or why not?
2. When, if ever, is it ethical to cite an article or book that you have not read or have only partially skimmed?
3. Why do researchers need to be concerned about status differentials (i.e., different amounts of expertise, skills, time, or financial resources) between researchers and participants?
4. Say you find a study whose results support your research claim, but that has at least one significant flaw (e.g., low reliability of measurement, lack of researcher credibility, incoherence). Do you include that study in your literature review? If so, what do you say about the study's flaws, if anything?
5. Students in your department receive extra credit for participating in research conducted on your campus. Under what conditions is this ethical or unethical?
6. Your school email address is owned by the university, just as your work email address is owned by your employer. Under what conditions is it ethical for researchers at the university to use your emails in a research study? Alternately, if you are in a class that uses a content-management system like Blackboard or Web-CT, when is it ethical for your teacher to use your comments or other contributions in a research study? What if the university's IRB approved the study before you enrolled in the class: Is your individual informed consent still required?

"Try It!" Activities

1. Regarding risks to research participants, choose one research study that you are assigned to read in your research methods or some other class, and make a list of the potential economic, legal, physical, psychological, or social risks that participants in that study might have faced.
2. Find out what ethics training researchers at your institution have to complete in order to serve as principal investigators (e.g., certification courses are offered by the National Institute of Health and the National Science Foundation). If permitted by your institution, complete the online training required of principal investigators.
3. Look at the website of a professional association for academics in your discipline (e.g., Broadcast Education Association. International Communication Association, National Communication Association, Public Relations Society of America). Can you tell whether any ethical code of conduct is explicitly endorsed by that association? If you check more than one site, how do their codes of conduct differ? How are they similar?
4. Use the major requirements in your department to identify one area of communication research that you care about (e.g., organizational communication):
   (a) Make a list of five possible research topics that fit within that area of study;

(b) Arrange your five possible topics in order from the most general or broad topic to the most narrow or specific topic;

(c) For the most general topic, identify two–three increasingly specific questions that could be studied within that subject area (e.g., in organizational communication, we can study supervisory communication, but more specifically, interactions between leaders and members);

(d) For your most specific topic, identify two–three increasingly general research projects (e.g., "What's wrong with my group?" might be expanded to "What makes student class project groups effective or ineffective?");

(e) Notice that when you narrow or broaden your topic area, the focus of investigation can shift (e.g., "What makes student project groups effective?" might shift to "How do students accomplish decision-making in class project groups?" That question could be expanded to "How do people in project teams make decisions effectively?" Alternately, your expansion of "What makes student project groups effective?" might shift "How do similarities or differences among group members impact group dynamics, specifically decision-making, social support, authority relations, etc.?"

(f) After completing this activity, you will have a list of about ten research topics that interest you: Assuming that your research methods class requires you to conduct a research project, which of your topics are pragmatically feasible (i.e., you will have enough expertise, time/money or other resources, and there are ethical ways to pursue your question or topic)?

5. Which of the communication research studies below is likely to be deemed exempt, and thus subject to review by only the IRB chair or a subgroup of IRB members? Which studies are likely to be deemed nonexempt and subject to full IRB review?

(a) Following people on Twitter and conducting content analysis of their topics;

(b) Observing children playing at a public park;

(c) Interviewing homeless people in the downtown area of a large city;

(d) Critiquing written political campaign speeches from the 1800s;

(e) Conducting a network analysis survey of employees in a corporate grocery chain;

(f) Surveying college students about their Facebook usage.

6. Working in small groups, identify at least one ethical dilemma in each situation given below: Discuss with your group members the potential harms and benefits of this dilemma, and develop a position statement that specifies the ethical standards you, as the researchers, would attend to. Identify the ethical behaviors you would select in this case as well as the potential harms that could ensue if you do not behave ethically:

(a) You are collecting observational and interview research data at a clothing manufacturing company. You are given hundreds of dollars worth of free clothing during your data collection. You really like the clothes and wear them proudly, but you don't know whether to tell people they were free or keep that a secret.

(b) You discover information during data collection that could hurt the research participants if you disclose it (e.g., either the participants are engaging in illegal behaviors, like underage drinking or the use of controlled substances, or they are behaving in ways that will be called to moral account by others, like committing certain sexual acts or making racial slurs).

(c) You want to conduct research in a group of which you are a member, but for your own personal reasons, you don't want to disclose your membership status (e.g., HIV positive, incest survivor, recovering alcoholic or drug addict).

(d) You have developed a treatment program for communication apprehension, based on visualization and systematic desensitization. You would like to see whether students in your department's basic course would benefit from your training program by providing your treatment program to some students and comparing their course performance against students who did not take your treatment program.

(e) You are interested in studying people's responses to communication rule violations in cross-cultural interactions. You want to collect actual instances of rule violations and responses from several different cultural contexts.

(f) As a way to insure plausible interpretations, you return to check your interpretations with your participants/informants, and they disagree. Should you publish your interpretations, with or without mentioning that you checked the interpretations with the participants?

4 Making Claims

Introduction

In this chapter, we address claims as the first component of the *research as argument* model that we identified in Chapter 1. We consider how different claims are framed as central assertions, thesis statements, or questions we ask as communication researchers. Moreover, we will explain that how we understand and use any one of these claim types depends upon our paradigmatic assumptions. We describe five different types of claims in communication research: interpretive, evaluative, reformist, explanatory, and predictive. You will learn how each is applied to different communication research methodologies across our three epistemological paradigms: interpretive, critical, and discovery communication research. You will also see that researchers may combine several different types of claims into one analysis (i.e., that a study may be based on two or more kinds of claims).

Learning Outcomes

After completing this chapter, you should be able to:

» Explain the process of making claims and its significance for each of the paradigms.

» Define the meaning of the term, claim, as a central component in the research-as-argument model.

» Identify, describe, and be able to recognize five different types of claims across multiple methodologies from the field of communication research.

» Compare and contrast the essential characteristics of each claim type and explain the association between claim types and paradigms.

» Using the concepts of independent and dependent variables, distinguish between causal and associative relationships.

» Analyze and evaluate at least two areas of boundary fuzziness in constructing and applying various types of claims.

Outline

The very first step toward doing research often involves thinking about some aspect of communication that peaks your curiosity or that is problematic in some way. You may not know why some friends regard "teasing" as a fundamental part of their relationship, whereas others try to avoid it. Or perhaps you would like to know how to create more favorable impressions during your various employment interviews. Or you might want to understand what makes some political campaigns more persuasive than others. Or maybe you are socially concerned that violence in visual media really is adversely affecting us generally in society. Or perhaps you wonder how your online presence will impact your future job searches. In each case, you are engaging in the first step in the process of making claims.

The Process of Making Claims

Our interests guide our decisions to engage in research. Suppose we take the teasing example; as a researcher, you might ask, "What are the effects of teasing?" wanting to explore its potential positive and negative impacts. Your research question will become the central claim of your research study. Much less apparent are the assumptions you have about how to conduct this research study, and yet those assumptions affect virtually every part of what happens next. You wouldn't say, for instance, "I want to do an experiment on the effects of three types of messages because I believe there is a discoverable objective

reality, that my purpose is to accurately represent reality, and that I will do so by precise, systematic, and repetitive methods." You would be thinking consciously of the ways in which you have seen and considered teasing as a form of communication. Nevertheless, the process of thinking about communication, what your questions are, and how you would study them are all informed by the three paradigms we described in Chapter 2 whether or not you are aware of these.

Suppose instead that you think of communication problems in a very different way beginning with the first step of research. Perhaps you decide that you want to study the unique communication patterns, such as teasing among college students, within a particular group or culture. You could focus on college roommates, or bilingual college students, or English language learners, for instance. You will not have claims at the start of your study; in fact, you may not even know how to adequately describe the community you are interested in studying before you begin. With this inductive approach, interpretive paradigm scholars are often interested in investigating such speech communities using ethnographic methods (i.e., observing, participating with, and interviewing members of the community). Examples of such speech communities are found in Petersen's (2009) study of rules for communicating positively in online social support groups for men living with HIV, Morgan's (2010) investigation of indirectness in the African American speech community, Dollar & Zimmers' (1998) study of identity and communicative boundaries in street youth, and Philipsen's (1975) influential study of male role enactment in an urban setting. We will focus on studies reflecting this methodology in more detail in Chapter 7 on ethnographic research. Alternatively, you might want to know how people from more than one group or community use discourse to accomplish particular goals in their interaction, such as switching styles of speaking, making requests, or giving and receiving compliments. These are all research questions or claims that you could explore with the methodologies that we cover in Chapter 8 on conversation and discourse analysis.

Perhaps you are more interested in great speeches given at important times in history, or you are generally intrigued by the concept of persuasion. This kind of exploration in communication research stems from rhetorical interpretive research that we will study in Chapter 9. In this form of research, you most often begin with an assertion or claim about a rhetorical text, such as a speech, and then apply a theoretical framework to reveal something about the text's social significance. For example, Moore (2006) used a Burkean conceptual framework to explain the rhetoric of Governor Ryan of Illinois, who reversed his position from a strong pro-death-penalty advocate to a staunch anti-death-penalty convert. As you will learn about in Chapter 9, the Burkean framework is one way rhetorical critics interpret texts.

Sometimes the central question you are interested in requires a different type of an answer than can be provided by either a discovery-paradigm perspective or an interpretive-paradigm perspective. If, as a researcher, you value the assumptions of the critical paradigm, you might begin by looking at communication very broadly in the political and social practices of both mainstream and marginalized groups. Your research questions might focus on how people in power use their interactions to maintain the status quo; your study might be the mechanism you use to reveal oppression and perhaps even instigate social change. In a comparison of rap music, Calhoun's (2005) research claims were about the ways in which Eminem's music constitutes a performance of "whiteness" around the intersections of race, gender, class, and sexuality that protected him from criticism, whereas Ice-T and 2 Live Crew were sanctioned for racist and sexist lyrics. Claims such as these evaluations are at the heart of many critical studies, which we explore in depth in Chapter 10.

Alternatively, if you begin the research process by constructing claims that can be measured and tested against observations, you are choosing a pattern evident in many kinds of discovery research. To return to the topic of teasing in interpersonal relationships as one of our earlier examples, Miller and Roloff (2007) tested effects of teasing vs. insulting romantic partners as forms of face loss. Their study began with the claims that individuals would suffer greater face loss (and experience hurt) when insulted instead of teased, in public vs. private contexts, and in front of known others. They tested their claims against the evidence that they collected to see if their claims could be supported. One of their claims appears in Table 4.4. We will have more to say about these types of studies in Chapter 11 when we discuss the concepts of measurement and research design and in the discovery methods' applications chapters on content analysis and survey and experimental research.

By understanding how these three epistemological paradigms guide us in making claims, it should be clear by now that we cannot tell you all communication research has the same, systematic set of practices, stages, or any other linear sequence of steps (Philipsen, 1977). Not all research begins with establishing a claim, testing that claim with data or evidence, and verifying that process with warrants. Some research begins with a claim, some with data, and some with describing the existing social warrants of specific social practices. The order depends again on the paradigmatic assumptions you have about the way knowledge is constructed.

Claims, too, arise in response to different assumptions about the world of research, which can result in different reasoning processes. You may have heard the terms inductive and deductive reasoning before if you have taken a class in logic or critical thinking. If you are a discovery paradigm researcher, you will tend to design research using **deductive reasoning**, an approach that begins with constructing testable claims, describing precise procedures for measurement, and reporting the results of testing your predictions. By contrast, if you have adopted the interpretive paradigm perspective, you will frequently use **inductive reasoning** in which you start with a set of observations and from these derive your claims or general interpretations about the communication you have observed. In the next sections of this chapter, we will consider the concept of claim in our *research as argument model* and how this concept is applied from each paradigm perspective.

Definition of Claim

One of the first assignments you might be asked to complete as a student of research is identifying the claims or

Table 4.1 Types of Claims Across the Paradigms

Discovery Paradigm	Interpretive Paradigm	Critical Paradigm
Explanatory claims	Interpretive claims	Evaluative claims
Predictive claims		Reformist claims

research questions in communication articles as well as eventually learning to construct your own claims. As we have just indicated in our previous discussion, claims depend on the way that the researcher conceives of the process of doing research, and so your ability to recognize them means that you will be learning from the start that they look and function very differently depending on the researcher's approach.

We can begin by saying that in every study, the **claim** is the central assertion of the researcher's argument. It often at least implicitly represents the study's purpose or goal as well. Claims, then, differ by the function that they perform. There are five different functions or types of claims: interpretive, evaluative, reformist, explanatory, and predictive claims (adapted from Smith, 1988, and Littlejohn, 1996). Not every type of claim can be found in every paradigm, nor is every type mutually exclusive. The interpretive paradigm emphasizes the claim as interpretation obviously, and to a lesser extent, a matter of inescapable evaluation, whereas the critical paradigm focuses explicitly on evaluation and social reform. Explanatory and predictive claims are concentrated in the discovery paradigm. The types of claims by paradigm are illustrated in Table 4.1, but keep in mind that with the fuzziness of paradigm boundaries, there will undoubtedly be exceptions. We will talk more about these in exploring each type.

Types of Claims

Claims have a function or a purpose in every research argument. Virtually every type of claim implies a description as a function through assertions about observations of people, messages, or events. Beyond description, every claim has a unique function. Some claims are interpretive; they describe and interpret the process of constructing meaning in the communication of a particular group or community. Studies generated by these claims help us understand what is accomplished in these communities. Some claims are assertions about inequities in the allocation or use of power resources and the ways in which society needs to change. And some claims explain and predict how communication will occur in cause and effect relationships.

Interpretive Claims

If you begin with an interpretive paradigm perspective, your claims will focus on exploring how communicators socially construct meanings and accomplish purposeful action within that system of shared meanings. You could construct interpretive claims by focusing on interpretations of rhetorical texts or by observing members of a community. Suppose you investigated how people greet each other in a particular cultural group. Unless you are a member of the group, you will have to observe the members many times over to begin to understand the greeting process from an insider's perspective. This approach is precisely what ethnographic researchers assume as a central purpose in their research; how meaningful actions, like greetings, are understood from the participants' perspectives. **Interpretive claims** often take the form of research questions which ask about what a practice means or how the relationship between communicators can be accomplished. Note that your concerns will extend beyond mere descriptions of events and people to their interpretations or meanings of those events and interactions.

Hermeneutic Circle

Interpretive claims are found in ethnographic studies, conversational and discourse analyses, and some forms of rhetorical criticism. They function to reveal the meaning of communication in a variety of social contexts, communities, groups, or texts. Interpretive researchers move back and forth between what they are observing and their descriptions and interpretations, changing these as they attempt to uncover emerging patterns of communication. This process is referred to as the **hermeneutic circle**. Suppose, for example, that you wanted to study how texting is used among a small group of teenage friends. You might begin with a simple research question as the claim: What is the function of texting among this group of friends? You study the group by observing the amount of time, frequency, times of day that they text each other; you examine who is texting whom; you conduct extensive interviews with the group about their practices of texting; you explore and interpret the content of the text messages. After multiple observations and interviews, you would begin to see various themes and patterns emerge about the communication: friends use texting for practical reasons, such as setting up meeting places and getting rides; they use texting to define who's in and who's out of the group; sometimes texts also serve as identity expressions to test what their friends might think of a certain idea. For each theme or pattern, you will test your interpretation inductively against many repeated observations and interviews until you are satisfied that your interpretive claims have been supported by the data.

Your goal as an interpretive researcher will be "to discover the meanings communicators have in mind when they talk with others in particular contexts" (Smith, 1988, p. 9). Interpretive paradigm researchers view the claim process inductively as creating socially agreed upon interpretations that arise out of the data. In many studies, interpretive claims depend upon three dimensions or levels of data collection: the observational domain, the interpretive schemes, and relations between observations (Smith, 1988, p. 9). At the first level, you can make a claim about *what* is occurring in communication—verbal/nonverbal, face-to-face/mediated, ritualized/unscripted, and so forth. For example, Monto, Machalek, and Anderson (2013) investigated male graffiti artists in Portland, Oregon. Through observations and interviews, the authors investigated how the actions of doing and talk about graffiti reinforced group membership and certain themes of masculinity. Graffiti artists are called *writers* and they frequently work together in groups called *crews*. The masculine theme of independence is reinforced through the valuing of individual identity and group membership is prized through joining a crew. Individual writers assume identities through the colorful names, such as OMEN and DEKOY in the group studied, and the actual performance of street art is called *bombing*. The verbal and nonverbal actions of the graffiti writers form the basis of understanding what is happening within this specific speech community, and are easily distinguishable from the broader mainstream communities that identify the same acts as *vandalism*. In this first level of analysis, the claim interprets action by identifying and labeling what is occurring.

Grounded Theory

At the second level of data collection, your task as an ethnographer is to construct the interpretive frameworks or schemes that communicators use to arrive at meaning.

Ethnographers use the **grounded-theory** approach developed by Glaser & Strauss (1967). This approach "entails an iterative, reflective process that moves back and forth between the data and categories so that the findings are theoretically grounded within the data" (Pepper & Larson, 2006, p. 56). In the previous example, Monto and his colleagues (2013) used the grounded-theory method by identifying the ways in which the graffiti speech community "reflects a particular version of masculinity and at the same time serves as a resource for constructing masculine identity and achieving status and respect among male peers" (p. 259). During the third level of data collection, interpretive claims are constructed out of emergent patterns or themes of interaction. Monto and his colleagues posed a central guiding research question, "why do people invest such effort and take such significant risks in order to participate in an activity that is risky, illegal, and likely to have only a temporary impact?" (p. 286) They showed that the practice of graffiti allows younger boys to be socialized into a community of older boys where they are able to gain respect and status by following a "code of honor among thieves" (p. 278), and that the expression of graffiti paradoxically is both transitory in nature and claims public space. Moreover, they demonstrated that the illegality of graffiti is an important element, woven into an outlaw version of masculinity that "values daring, risk, rebelliousness, ingenuity, commitment, and sacrifice, as well as a certain set of aesthetics" (p. 286). In this study, the claims were constructed inductively out of the process of observing and interviewing using the methodological framework of grounded theory.

Many other similar examples of interpretive claims in ethnographies can be found in communication research. For example, Tracy, Myers, & Scott (2006) were interested in exploring the role of humor in how members of an organization explore preferred and dispreferred identities within the organizational culture. Tracy et al.'s (2006) primary research question asked, "In what ways does humor assist employees in negotiating and affirming preferred identities?" (p. 284). The authors explored how humor provided safe ways in which members could test the acceptance of various self-presentations. In a similar study, Pepper & Larson (2006) explored cultural and organizational identities during a post-acquisition phase. They showed that transitions in ownership led to significant role redefinition and identity change that meant new identities were constructed, negotiated, and affirmed by old and new members. Both studies employed the Glaser and Strauss' constant comparison method for a grounded-theory approach described in our earlier example. You can see examples of interpretive research questions from these and other studies in Table 4.2. You will learn much more about ethnography of communication and speech communities in Chapter 7 on ethnographic research.

The role of technology in everyday interaction has also expanded enormously in the last decade. For example, the amount of time spent online and complexity of online networks frequently provide contexts for interpretive claims. For example, Soukup (2006) explored the designs of *fansites,* a new term for online Internet sites for *fan communities.* This researcher uncovered three themes during interviews with site designers: (a) a dialogue with the artist and the fan community, (b) controlling the representation of the celebrity, and (c) personal identification with the celebrity. In each facet, the site was explored for how fans interacted with the artist, how the depictions of the artist were implicitly regulated, and how the fans personally connected with the artist as part of the identity development process. In other recent studies of discourse analysis, Chua (2009) explored the regulation of speech in virtual communities (posting forums) and Skovholt and Svennevig (2006) investigated the potential impact of cc'ing third parties in email conversations; you will learn how to use discourse analysis to investigate online communication of these sorts in Chapter 8 of this book.

There are a variety of methods you can use in rhetorical criticism that also rely on interpretive claims. These will be explored more fully in Chapter 9, especially in distinguishing what we mean by the term rhetorical criticism (not to be confused with the critical paradigm perspective). Deciding which elements of a communication text to describe and how to represent a particular method are often considered to be interpretive decisions (Foss, 2004, p. 17). You will also be making an interpretive claim about a text if you explore its meaningfulness. In one study, Milford (2009) explored the rhetoric of Sarah Palin using the Burkean concept of *symbolic boasting* from his *dramatistic* framework. The concept of symbolic boasting "is an offshoot of identification that emphasizes a community's attempt to identify itself with a particular rhetor, functioning to reshape the community in the rhetor's image" (p. 44). In other words, speakers like Sarah Palin are persuasive because they provide specific appeal for a community who identifies with the values and images represented in the speaker's rhetoric. The audience forms a collective identity and the rhetor becomes its spokesperson, representing an idealized or desired identity. Milford claimed that "in the case of the Palinfacts community, their symbolic boasting of Palin served not to support her candidacy, but instead to solidify their own identity as frontier-oriented, tech savvy, culturally aware conservatives" (p. 44).

In another rhetorical essay from the interpretive paradigm, Stroud (2001) explored the story of the hero quest in the movie *The Matrix.* In a complex web of interconnections revealed throughout the film, Stroud claimed that the hero, Neo, maintained his individuality because he could use his technological expertise to stay free from the technologically trapped members of a futuristic society. Stroud (2001) used narrative theory as support for his claim that the film was "shown to be a powerful myth for alienated and disempowered individuals in technologically driven communities" (p. 416).

The essays of Milford (2009) and Stroud (2001) have offered unique interpretations and applications of rhetorical theories rather than arguing that one explanation was more justified or accurate than another. Likewise when you adopt the role of rhetorical interpreter, you are "not concerned with finding the one correct interpretation of the artifact because the critic recognizes the artifact does not constitute a reality that can be known and proved"; you can never "know what the artifact 'really' is" (Foss, 2004, p. 21). Instead, as an interpretive critic, you will argue for a new understanding of a theory as it is applied socially, culturally, and politically to a communication text. Examples of these interpretive rhetorical claims can be found in Table 4.2. When you move beyond interpretation to claims of evaluation and reform, your assumptions about the significance of communication change from the interpretive to the critical paradigm.

Evaluative and Reformist Claims

When you make **evaluative claims** as a researcher, you engage in the process of valuing the worth or importance of a social practice or communication behavior you have selected for study. You would frequently argue that a behavior, such as eating disorders, should be evaluated in terms of their extremely negative consequences for young women, or the conditions that permit such disorders to flourish in a society. Your evaluation could point to the irony of the proliferation of eating disorders

Table 4.2 Interpretive Paradigm Claims

Ethnographic and Discursive Interpretive Claims:
1. Why do people invest such effort and take such significant risks in order to participate in an activity that is risky, illegal, and likely to have only a temporary impact? (Monto, Machalek, & Anderson, 2013, p. 286).
2. In what ways does humor assist employees in negotiating and affirming preferred identities? (Tracy, Myers, & Scott, 2006, p. 284).
3. Via the identification processes associated with fansites, fans can significantly influence the meanings, uses, and even production-distribution of media texts and manipulate the complex iconography of celebrities to "visibly" participate in public discourse (Soukup, 2006, p. 319).

Rhetorical Interpretive Claims:
1. In the case of the Palinfacts community, their symbolic boasting of Palin served not to support her candidacy, but instead to solidify their own identity as frontier-oriented, tech savvy, culturally aware conservatives (Milford, 2009, p. 44).
2. This film [*The Matrix*] is shown to be a powerful myth for alienated and disempowered individuals in technologically driven communities, with potentially troubling consequences due to its theme of "solitary enlightenment" (Stroud, 2001, p. 416).

in a society rich enough to feed all of its members. You could also argue that any communication as a form of social protest should be valued positively as a necessary part of social growth. **Reformist claims** are not only evaluative; they identify negative consequences of the existing social system as a way of instigating change. Because evaluative and reformist claims require you to make explicit value judgments, they are associated only with the critical paradigm. Your purpose in critical research is to provide a framework for understanding power inequalities as the means of promoting social change. Your research should satisfy this basic common goal regardless of conducting analyses in critical ethnography, in feminist and cultural studies, or any other version of critical communication research you will explore more fully in Chapter 10.

In the last section, we discussed interpretive claims in ethnographic research. What distinguishes critical ethnography from conventional ethnography are the assumptions about the purposes of research. Your goal is not only to explain how members of a culture share their interpretations of reality, but to give voice to and represent members of marginalized cultures who are otherwise not represented in the mainstream (Thomas, 1993, p. 34). Thomas's (1993) study of prisoners revealed not only the way inmates used violence and the legal system to highlight their living conditions but illustrated clearly the broader social need for general prison reform.

As one brand of critical-paradigm research, feminist criticism is often based on the assumption that society must be reorganized "on the basis of equality for the sexes in all areas of social relations" (K. A. Foss, S. K. Foss, &

Griffin, 1999, p. 2). A prominent rhetorical critical theorist, bell hooks, has argued that resisting dominance is a central part of learning to think and speak freely, an essential quality of a truly democratic society (hooks, 1989, 1994, 2000). hooks refused to conform to capitalizing her name in the conventional ways as one of her many forms of personal protest. In a similar vein, Arnold & Doran's (2007) autoethnographic accounts of eating disorders in their families examined how themes of self-negation and self-control in women exacerbate these problems, particularly in their roles as mothers. By exploring socialization processes for women, the authors hope to identify the extent of negative effects of these disorders and provide practical assistance to mothers facing this set of issues. This investigation also permits the larger attention to gender socialization practices and how these might generally be improved.

As a critical researcher, you will emphasize both evaluation and reform openly acting as an advocate for your cause. You will make the general argument that no research can ever be value free and argue that scholars have an ethical obligation to improve social conditions through their efforts (K. K. Campbell, 1974; K. A. Foss & S. K. Foss, 1988; Madison, 2005; J. Thomas, 1993). In a recent study, Enck-Wanzer (2006) analyzed a social movement instigated by a group called the Young Lords Organization active during the late 1960s. Trash collectors did not make regular rounds in El Barrio of Manhattan for a variety of negative reasons. In protest, the Young Lords picked up trash and deposited it in several very busy intersections located elsewhere in the city. Enck-Wanzer (2006) claimed that their actions and rhetoric were inventive and decolonizing both in purpose and form (p. 174); by taking the problem outside of the neighborhood, they raised general awareness and instigated social action, a move that Enck-Wanzer argued was a necessary response to the constraints on their social choices as a group.

A more detailed analysis of one study will illustrate the frequently interweaving of evaluative and reformist claims. Forman (2013) investigated the functions of hip-hop as a means of authenticating African American urban youth identity with interventions from 'Hood workers. He argued that hip-hop was a "crucial mode of artistic and creative expression" while simultaneously serving as a "collective political agency" (p. 245). In response to a growing pool of disenfranchised African American youth, Forman identified an increasing number of 'Hood workers, men and women who may have some postsecondary education in the social sciences or liberal arts, but many whom are former street youth who have returned to their neighborhoods to "take new prosocial leadership roles in their communities" (p. 248). Many 'Hood workers have used hip-hop identified agencies to attract youth to a variety of programs that have a "shared mission to squash gang violence, promote teen peace in the city, develop safe and healthy communities, and meet other progressive social objectives through a combination of rational dialogue, focused action, and hip-hop creativity" (p. 249). Many are simply motivated to get teens together and off the streets in safe environments; toward this goal, they have devised "teen-led performance events, art displays, poetry and spoken-word jams, and dance-offs that involve teens from localized neighborhoods and that occasionally draw teens from across the city to central events" (p. 249).

In addition to creating safe places, many social agencies also have an active agenda for reform by getting the "boyz and girlz from the 'Hood thinking together about the possible roots of the social crises that most impact their lives and the lives of those around them and to help devise ways of responding effectively" (p. 249). 'Hood workers serve an important rhetorical function in assisting street youth to become critics of hip-hop discourse. Forman identified a genre of hip-hop, called "conscious rap" represented by artists such as Mos Def, Lupe Fiasco, Talib Kweli, Dead Prez, Paris, or early Public Enemy; these are contrasted with the lyrics of 50 Cent, Lil Wayne, or Nicki Minaj, which are interpreted as "problematic in terms of either their content or

Table 4.3 Critical Paradigm: Evaluative and Reformist Claims

1. Using cultural role expectations for women, we argue that the expectations of femininity and motherhood create a double bind that makes recovering from eating disorders extremely difficult. We consider the implications of this study . . . for practical attempts to assist mothers who are coping with these disorders (Arnold & Doran, p. 311).
2. The redistribution of trash by the Young Lords Organization was an inventive and decolonizing rhetorical move that heightened social awareness and instigated social change (Enck-Wanzer, 2006, p. 174).
3. Within what contexts are [HipHop's] meanings established and how are they negotiated among disparate or antagonistic forces? (Forman, 2013, p. 244).

their alignments with the Hip-Hop Industrial Complex" (p. 254). Forman's analysis is a comprehensive treatment exploring evaluative claims about hegemonic social practices that oppress street youth and reformist claims that 'Hood workers and conscious rap represent crucial instigators of positive social change.

When you come from the critical-paradigm perspective, you must decide not only whether your argument is logical but whether it also makes a positive contribution to society. As Brock, Scott, and Chesbro (1990) pointed out, the appeal for reform is often made on moral or ethical grounds, essential qualities of evaluative and reformist claims. You can see that, from the critical-paradigm perspective, your research will always be multifaceted. Your claims will be interpretive to some extent, evaluative and reformist, with these goals thoroughly intertwined. Examples of how these claims appear in their original articles can be found in Table 4.3.

We will explore how your focus as a critical researcher translates to these claim types in Chapter 10 on "Critical Studies." There, we will examine further how various forms of communication perpetuate dominant social constructions, marginalizing any voices in the minority, and how various social texts and performances can signify resisting dominance and reconstructing a new society. In the next section, you will explore the types of claims that are associated with the discovery paradigm: explanatory and predictive. There, the underlying assumptions require you to find and maintain a more detached and objective perspective when observing communication.

Explanatory and Predictive Claims

As we explained in the previous section, interpretive, evaluative, and reformist claims emerge by inductively arriving at these general assertions out of multiple observations of people, events, messages, or texts. Constructing claims from a discovery paradigm perspective is a different process. Researchers frequently begin with a theory about the way communication is occurring based on past research. Out of theories come communication concepts and ideas about the relationships between them. What do we mean by suspicion and how is it related to jealousy, for instance? How do we define media violence, and how does it affect perceptions of ethnic and age groups? **Explanatory claims** make clear the nature of a communication phenomenon by exploring its significance; they also explain the relationships between various communication phenomena, often by identifying reasons or causes for communication. When there is sufficient theory based on past research, the explanations can be advanced as **predictive claims**, and the process is deductive.

The process of making claims in the discovery paradigm is called deductive because claims are usually advanced first as general assertions and then these are tested against your observations. Earlier in this chapter, we introduced induction and deduction as two distinct processes, but in the discovery paradigm, these are often two steps in the same process. Researchers engage in an exploratory phase by using inductive means so that theory can be developed enough to support explanations and derive predictions. The full cycle is depicted in Figure 4.1, in which the process begins with observations that inductively produce generalizations; these

then provide the basis for theory development, from which predictions are produced.

In the interpretive and critical paradigms, the process can begin and end with induction. In the discovery paradigm, the process begins with induction and ends with the deductive phase; induction is only used as an exploratory preparation for formal theory testing as part of building causal arguments. This process is expected to extend over time across many studies conducted by different researchers working on the same topic area. Making causal arguments is the crux of the discovery paradigm view that knowledge is objective and that reality is discoverable. You would expect to find such claims in experimental and survey research, in content analysis, and even in the more classical approaches to rhetorical criticism, but you will not find them in interpretive and critical-paradigm research (see, e.g., Madison, 2005; Silverman, 1993; J. Thomas, 1993).

As a discovery paradigm researcher, you will focus on accurately representing an objective reality by discovering what rules explain whatever you observe happening in communication. Kerlinger (1986) elaborated on our figure by describing the research process in five parts: (1) development of theories, (2) testing of theories, (3) control of alternative explanations, (4) nature of relationships, and (5) testing theories with observable evidence. In this model, theories are the explanations that allow you to make certain causal predication; theories are "aimed at explanation, prediction, and control of human phenomena. Explanatory theories are composed of logically interrelated propositions" with an emphasis on testing these through a "logic of verification" (Jorgensen, 1989, p. 17), an essential part of causal reasoning as the preferred form of argument.

Research Questions and Hypotheses

Explanatory and predictive claims usually take the form of research questions (Smith, 1988; Mertens, 1998). **Research questions** ask how a concept chosen for study can be classified or defined, or they ask what relationship exists between various types of communication variables. Because they are generated from existing theory and research, **hypotheses** are considered more precise because they advance specific predictions about relationships between communication variables. Of all the various types of claims, these are often the most easily found offset by type and format in most articles with the abbreviations of RQs and Hs when the methods include content analyses, survey, and experimental research. Occasionally, however,

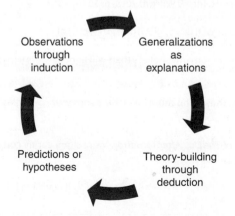

Figure 4.1 Cycle of Inductive/Deductive Inquiry

interpretive and critical methods may also identify their claims as research questions; that is why it is important for you to identify the paradigm assumptions and methods to determine exactly what type of claims and arguments underlie the studies you are examining.

To illustrate how the two claim forms are intertwined, Mongeau, Serewicz, & Therrien (2004) first used *research questions* to explore what types of goals college students have for first dates. They used open-ended questions in their surveys to obtain descriptions of these interaction goals. From participant responses, they developed a categorizing scheme or **taxonomy** for communication behaviors, events, and messages. Mongeau et al. (2004) found that romantic couples provided over 500 goals for their first dates! By using a statistical analysis to group the various reasons for going on a first date, five general categories of goals emerged: reduce uncertainty, relational escalation, companionship, sexual activity, and having fun. The results helped to explain the nature of this type of communication and to indicate which theories in interpersonal communication could help to explain how interaction goals develop.

In a second study reported in the same article, Mongeau et al. (2004) used *research questions* to explain how the goal categories are influenced by various contextual factors, such as the degree of intimacy and the availability of alcohol. In this study, they extended their knowledge about interaction goals to consider how these are related to other concepts and practices. Results from

the first and second studies permitted them to construct an experiment for the third study to test specific *hypotheses*, such as the effects of sex, alcohol availability, and relationship type on relational goals for first dates. Research questions were used in the first two studies because little previous theory and research explain interaction goals on first dates; *hypotheses* in the third study were specific predications made possible by the first two studies.

Similar examples proliferate in communication research. In a recent article, Hefner & Wilson (2013) described their first study as an exploration of ideals in popular romantic comedies. They derived four ideal themes from existing research on romantic love, and tested these themes by conducting a content analysis on the top (highest grossing) 52 romantic films of the past decade. In the first study, they constructed four guiding research questions which appear in Table 4.4. The authors not only wanted to confirm the existence of the romantic ideal themes but find out how prevalent they were, whether there were challenges to the ideal, what consequences followed and whether there were sex differences. By conducting a survey in study 2, the same authors used two media theories, cultivation and uses-and-gratification, to advance two predictions: "H_1: Heavy viewers of romantic comedies will report stronger endorsement of romantic beliefs than will light viewers (p. 163), and H_2: The association between viewing and beliefs will be strongest among those who report watching romantic comedies in order to learn" (p. 164).

Table 4.4 Discovery Paradigm: Explanatory/Predictive Claims

RQ$_1$: What goals will college students report for first dates? (Mongeau, Serewicz, & Therrien, 2004)
RQ$_1$: How prevalent are romantic ideals in popular romantic comedy films? (Hefner & Wilson, 2013, p. 154)
RQ$_3$: What are the consequences of romantic ideal and challenges expressions? (Hefner & Wilson, 2013, p. 154)
H$_1$: Heavy viewers of romantic comedies will report stronger endorsement of romantic beliefs than will light viewers (Hefner & Wilson, 2013, p. 163).
H$_2$: The association between viewing and beliefs will be strongest among those who report watching romantic comedies in order to learn (Hefner & Wilson, 2013, p. 164).
H$_2$: Web-traffic on global warming related websites and media coverage of *The Day After Tomorrow* were significantly correlated during the release period of *The Day After Tomorrow* (Hart & Leiserowitz, 2009, p. 359).
H$_3$: Changes in media coverage of *The Day After Tomorrow* preceded similar changes in web-traffic on global warming related websites (Hart & Leiserowitz, 2009, p. 359).

Note: RQ = research question; H = hypothesis.

Causal Relationships:
Independent and Dependent Variables

In the development of a model for television-viewing, Hmielowski, Holbert, & Lee (2011) were interested in explaining what makes people consume political satire. They used past research to identify successful predictors based on audience characteristics when viewing political satire. The present study expanded this list to include a new predictor, affinity for political humor. The authors conducted a telephone survey on a random sample generated professionally to test the effects of the predictors on viewing Jon Stewart's *The Daily Show* and *The Colbert Report*. When you are building a causal claim, such as the one in this study, the predictors that will change or influence other communication responses are called **independent variables**; in this study, these were classified into five groups: demographics (age, sex, etc.); political orientations; media exposure; need for humor; and affinity for political humor as the new variable (pp. 103–104). The researchers assumed that demographic factors such as sex and psychological factors such as "need for humor" would predict viewership of these two television shows. The **dependent variable** is the communication phenomenon presumed to be affected by the predictors; in this case, political TV satire exposure was measured by time spent viewing *The Daily Show* and *The Colbert Report*. When the claim you construct predicts that a change in the dependent variable is preceded and influenced by a change in the independent variable, you are describing the basis for a **causal claim**.

There is a decided preference for making causal arguments in discovery research, a process discussed in much more detail in Chapter 11. Briefly here, we will define the three conditions or criteria necessary for determining causality: time order, association, and control over competing claims. **Time order** means that the presumed cause must directly and logically precede the effects. In the example above, your age and gender as two possible causes are presumed to affect whether you watch *The Daily Show* and *The Colbert Report*. As the second condition for causality, **association** refers to the fact that both cause and effect must be related to each other. It must make logical sense to connect things like your demographic characteristics to the television shows you watch. Many studies have confirmed this association by showing that these two are correlated or they covary. The final condition for causality is the ability to **rule out competing claims** or hypotheses. This

latter condition requires careful design features that we will explore fully in Chapter 11 that strengthen the researcher's argument that the identified independent variables are indeed the causes of changes in the dependent variables, and not some other uncontrolled variable. In our example, perhaps people who gravitate toward irony and satire generally will also be more likely to view political satire.

Associative Relationships

Although discovery research emphasizes causality as the preferred form of argument, explanatory and predictive claims may meet only the second condition of causality, association. **Associative claims** predict relationships between two or more concepts or variables by asserting that they are related to each other or that changes in one variable are accompanied by changes in the other; this is called the **principle of covariation**. For the purposes of exploring the link between television viewing and Internet usage, Hart & Leiserowitz (2009) hypothesized that there would be associations between watching the TV film *The Day After Tomorrow* and web traffic on global warming websites (see Table 4.4 for the second and third hypotheses). They recognized that they were unable to control for many factors that weakened the case for making a causal argument, but they hoped to show with this exploration that the two phenomena were correlated in time and that media coverage of *The Day After Tomorrow* preceded similar changes in web traffic.

Time order is the first criterion for causality that we mentioned. In this study, the researchers did find a positive correlation between media coverage and global warming website traffic, but they were unable to confirm the time order dimension. If changes in variables either increase or decrease together, the relationship is described as a positive correlation. If one variable decreases as the other increases, or vice versa, the relationship is identified as a negative correlation. For example, Guerrero & Jones (2005) found important negative relationships between anxiety and avoidance, two dimensions related to attachment styles in interpersonal relationships, and communication skills. Participants with higher levels of anxiety scored lower on composure measures, and participants with higher levels of avoidance scored lower on measures of expressiveness and other-orientation (Guerrero & Jones, 2005, pp. 315–316).

Sometimes, the relationship is expected to be even more complex than a simple increase or decrease.

Relationships between variables can start to increase together and then level off, or even begin to decrease. This type of change is called a curvilinear relationship. For example, Duggan & Le Poire (2006) found a curvilinear relationship between depression and partners' verbal strategies. Some helping and encouraging strategies were reported before the diagnosis of depression was given, which then increased to the greatest amount of helping and encouraging strategies happening just following diagnosis, and finally helping and encouraging strategies dropped off again during a period of frustration after initial attempts to help. You will learn more about linear and curvilinear relationships in Chapter 16 when you discover how to test them statistically. It is important to stress again that associative claims usually lack one or more components of causal arguments that we shall detail in the discussion of research design and causal arguments from Chapter 11; we will also explore the application of associative and causal claims in the discovery methods chapters in the last section of the book.

Boundary Fuzziness

There are two areas of boundary fuzziness between paradigm claims that we should note before leaving this chapter. The first concerns a form of research, called action research, which challenges the traditional types of claims associated with the discovery paradigm. We have identified explanatory and predictive claims as the primary functions of claims in this paradigm. However, one general line of research is undertaken solely for the purpose of its more practical and applied outcomes rather than to develop theory or increase "pure knowledge." Called **action research** (S. J. Taylor & Bogdan, 1998, pp. 260–261), its objective is to evaluate some communication problem and what may be done to find a practical solution. In this sense, its claims can be seen as both evaluative and reformist, although the reform is often targeted to specific contexts rather than broad social change. If, for example, you were a researcher interested in testing the effectiveness of early intervention programs with students who are apprehensive about public speaking, you would be engaged in this type of research. Action research is specifically designed to find solutions in the short term, but it can also impact theory development. Program evaluations and assessment projects are other types of action research, and because of their goals, they often blur the boundary between explanatory research and evaluative-reformist research.

Bogdan & Biklen (1982) defined action research as "the systematic collection of information that is designed to bring about social change" (p. 215). When you do action research, you will collect and analyze data as evidence of negative effects from some current social problem. Researchers use both qualitative and quantitative methods to make specific recommendations for change. Bogdan and Biklen cited numerous action research examples, which included studies designed to change the negative ways females are depicted in texts used by schools, advocating for the rights of disabled students, exposing negative conditions and practices at government institutions for ethnic minority clients, and unethical treatment of prisoners.

Even though action research may identify practical needs and their solutions, Bogdan & Biklen (1982) explained that it is frequently considered unacceptable because it violates two assumptions some discovery-paradigm scholars hold dear: (1) Researchers should be academically trained only and should not conduct research in applied contexts; and (2) research should always be nonpartisan (p. 214). Because action research goes beyond purely explanatory and predictive claims, it has been negatively evaluated by some scholars. But research that blurs paradigm boundaries is often research that engages us creatively and constructively, as you will see in many instances throughout the book.

The second area of boundary fuzziness has to do with the types of claims associated with rhetorical criticism. As we have shown in earlier sections of this chapter, many methods of rhetorical criticism and critical studies make use of interpretive, evaluative, and reformist claims. And for the most part, the ability to construct explanatory and predictive claims in causal arguments is a major characteristic of empirical science from the discovery paradigm. However, if you were interested in certain methods of rhetorical criticism, you could also identify your work as explanatory and even predictive. Andrews, Leff, & Terrill (1998), three contemporary rhetorical critics, claimed that rhetorical theories help us to understand patterns or principles that "explain a complex set of facts or phenomena":

> The more we learn about what happened in one particular situation—that is, the more information bits that can be adduced—the better able we will be to generalize a pattern of rhetorical behavior. As these patterns are formed, and compared and contrasted with other patterns, a basis for predicting what will happen in similar cases is established. (pp. 19–20)

Neoclassical rhetorical scholars from the discovery paradigm use explanation in at least two ways (S. K. Foss, 2004, pp. 16–19). First, they must accurately explain communication texts or messages when they give overviews or summaries of the main features or elements of the text they have selected to study. Second, explanation occurs whenever the rhetorical critic makes a rational and sometimes causal argument for rhetorical outcomes based on inherent rhetorical components. We will discuss these in more detail in Chapter 9 on *Rhetorical Criticism*. Andrews et al. also warned that not all rhetorical criticism is explanatory and predictive; that is, your intention may be not to develop a set of generalizations that allow future critics to predict certain sets of results. Rather, you may be more concerned with simply illuminating a particular speaker's motive or situational constraints to increase our understanding of existing rhetorical texts or acts. If this is your general purpose, your claims are likely to be more interpretive than explanatory. Or your goal may be to reveal the negative consequences of a communicative practice and urge social change. In this case, your claims will be more evaluative and reformist than simply focusing on explanations and predictions. Whether you are engaged in action research or practice nonempirically based rhetorical explanations and predictions, we encourage you to consider carefully your own and others' assumptions about the purpose of research in understanding the types of claims constructed for a study.

Summary

In this chapter, we have defined and applied the first component of our research-as-argument model, the *claim*. The

Table 4.5 Claims Summary Table

Discovery Paradigm	Interpretive Paradigm	Critical Paradigm
Explanatory claims Predictive claims	Interpretive claims	Evaluative claims Reformist claims

claim refers to the central assertion on which a specific analysis is based. There are five different types of claims: interpretive, evaluative, reformist, explanatory, and predictive. We showed how each of these types is illustrated by applying a variety of methodologies spanning the three epistemological paradigms we discussed in Chapter 2. This illustration appears in Table 4.5.

How we as researchers understand the types of claims we construct depends in a large part on the paradigmatic assumptions we make when we engage in the research process. So, for example, it is very likely that you would find explanatory and predictive claims presented together in discovery research, and evaluative and reformist claims appear just as frequently in combination when investigating critical research. Many empirical researchers who see their studies as explanatory and predictive do not share the same goals of or assumptions about research with rhetorical critics who see their analyses as interpretive, evaluative, and reformist. We do not present these differences here to make you take sides but to help you understand why they exist as you begin to read through the many different types of studies in our field. You will have an opportunity to explore the differences in assumptions and goals in the later chapters and in the activities that follow at the end of this and other chapters.

Key Terms

Action research
Associative claim
Causal claim
Claim
Conditions of causality: time order, association, ruling out competing claims
Deductive Reasoning

Dependent variable
Evaluative claims
Explanatory and predictive claims
Grounded-theory approach
Hermeneutic circle
Hypotheses
Independent variable

Inductive reasoning
Interpretive claims
Principle of covariation
Reformist claims
Research questions
Taxonomy

Discussion Questions

1. What assumptions are made in the discovery paradigm that make explanatory and predictive claims more likely than interpretive or evaluative claims?
2. In what ways are evaluative and reformist claims different than interpretive claims?

"Try It!" Activities

1. Watch a persuasive speech from *TedTalks* and identify the claim(s) made by the speaker. After listening to the entire argument, how would you classify the claims? Do they seem to serve an explanatory and predictive function? Do they seem more interpretive? Are they evaluative or imply the need for social reform?
2. For interpretive claims, find an article similar to Monto, Machalek, & Anderson's (2013) study of male graffiti artists or Tracy, Myers, & Scott's (2006) study of the role of humor in organizations. Discuss how the claims of your study illustrate the ways that communicators socially construct meanings and accomplish purposeful action together.
3. To explore evaluative and reformist claims, select an article like Arnold and Doran's (2007) study of eating disorders or Forman's (2013) study of 'Hood workers. Discuss how claims from your study negatively evaluate some form of current social practice and indicate whether the authors also argue for social change or reform.
4. As an application of explanatory and predictive claims, select an article like the example of Hmielowski, Holbert, & Lee's (2011) study of political satire, finding one with independent and dependent variables. Using the variables, explain the causal argument that your study's researchers are making. What causes have they identified and what predictions do they make about their effects in their claims?

5 What Counts as Communication Data?

Introduction

In this chapter, you will learn about the second element of the research-as-argument model, the data. We first outline some typical sources, settings, and strategies for collecting communication data, emphasizing the relative value of each of these for supporting particular types of research claims. We then introduce the ideas of measurement, research design, and triangulation (including mixed methods research); we focus on how each of those processes is used somewhat differently by discovery, interpretive, and critical researchers.

Learning Outcomes

After completing this chapter, you should be able to:

» Identify the type of data source(s), the setting, and data collection strategies used in published communication research reports and critical essays.

» Propose effective data sources, setting(s), and data collection strategies to investigate a given claim (perhaps one that you intend to explore in a study you conduct).

» Articulate the ethical dilemmas associated with particular data sources, settings, and collection strategies.

» Reasonably defend your plans to protect human research participants' rights to freely choose participation, have privacy, and be treated honestly in research.

Outline

Data Collection Sources
» Texts
» Direct Observations of Communicative Behaviors
» Self-Reports of Communicative Behaviors, Beliefs, and Characteristics
» Other-Reports of Communicative Behaviors, Beliefs, and Characteristics

Data Collection Settings

Data Collection Strategies
» Selecting Data Sources
» Random Selection Methods
» Nonrandom Selection Methods
» Selection in Critical Studies

Capturing Observed Behaviors

This chapter deals with the second component of the research-as-argument model, the data or evidence. You will learn about a variety of sources for communication data, settings in which data are collected, and strategies that you can use to collect data. In addition, we introduce you to research design and triangulation, including mixed methods research: Understanding these ideas will help you to evaluate research from all three paradigms and develop your own research studies, whether you are working in the interpretive, discovery, or critical paradigm.

In Parts 2 and 3 of this book, you will learn more about *how* to select particular data sources and settings and why certain data collection and analytic strategies are preferred in particular research methodologies. For now, let's start with some basic definitions and examples of communication data sources, settings, and strategies.

Data Collection Sources

By data collection sources, we mean the points from which data originate; the data are evidence collected to explore a specific research claim. We do not mean the previously published theoretic essays and research studies used in a literature review. Those sources justify the need for, or the importance of, a research project. But most researchers don't think of them as data. Instead, data can originate from four possible points: (1) existing texts; (2) direct observations of communicative behaviors; (3) self-reports of communicative behaviors, beliefs, and/or characteristics; and (4) other-reports of behaviors, beliefs, and/or characteristics. Let's briefly differentiate

each data source before we move on to consider the settings where these sources can be collected and the means used to capture each source so that it can be used systematically in a research project.

Texts

You probably think of texts as written or spoken words, as we do! However, when you think of textual data for communication research studies, you must also include texts that are symbolic, performed, and purely visual or pictorial (Bowman, 1996; Jarmon, 1996; Phillips, 2012). It is true that all researchers use textual evidence since all researchers conduct literature reviews of the primary published sources available on their topics. You can conduct a literature review and stop there, without collecting any additional texts or other data sources. But if your research project begins with a literature review and then proceeds to include other texts collected from an archive or a field setting, and/or observations of communication behavior, self-reports, or other-reports of communicative attitudes or behaviors, then you are doing empirical research. You could adhere to the assumptions of the interpretive, critical, or discovery paradigm, since the use of empirical data to test and refute claims is part of the theory-building process in all research.

When you conduct a literature review using archival texts from the library or online databases, you must evaluate the credibility of those sources in order to frame your research argument. Table 5.1 lists some criteria you should consider when evaluating the credibility of literature review sources.

Table 5.1 Criteria for Evaluating Literature Review Sources

Key Question: "How credible is this source?"	
Criteria	**Questions to Consider**
Authorship	What can you discern about the author(s) (e.g., institutional affiliation, degrees, prior research on this topic)? Try Googling the author(s) names to find out more about their prior work and areas of expertise.
Publisher	Who published the source (i.e., journal or book)? Ask your instructor about the respective credibility of different scholarly journal publishers. Check Technorati.com for the *Top 100 Blogs* list, updated daily, and for the annual "State of the Blogosphere" report.
Peer review	Is the research report or critical essay invited, or competitively selected for publication? If competitively selected, was the manuscript peer reviewed? Were the authors' names blinded from reviewers? Were reviewers' names blinded to authors?
Currency	When was the source published? If data were collected, when did that happen? How likely is it that things have changed since either data were collected or the source was published?
References	Are the references from scholarly, peer-reviewed journals? How current are the references?

Note: Many of these criteria can be used to evaluate the credibility of Internet websites.

However, an endless variety of texts can be analyzed in order to study communication empirically. Textual data sources can include annual reports, blog entries and comments, census documents, chat room discourse, class notes, corporate balance sheets, diagrams, diaries, e-mail messages, employee records, films, financial records, journals, maps, memos, magazine and newspaper articles, photographs, poetry, prose, policy statements, production records, Tweets or other social media posts, videos, and so forth. This list does not even include symbolic texts like architecture, gestures or signs, clothing, hairstyle, jewelry, types of mobile phones, automobile or other material possessions, and so forth. As you can see from this list, the range of texts that can be studied by communication scholars is theoretically endless.

Direct Observations of Communicative Behaviors

If you collect **direct observations of communicative behaviors** between people, you may be interested in observing the verbal and nonverbal messages themselves, the communicators who construct and interpret those messages, or the channels through which interactions occur. You might choose to observe talk in interaction by collecting boardroom conversations, shop-floor humor, informants' facial expressions, or other participant observations in the settings where those interactions occur naturally. Alternately, you might observe experimental participants' behaviors in a carefully controlled research environment (i.e., laboratory setting), or in the environments where their communication usually takes place (e.g., observe website traffic or Tweets online; observe nonverbal behavior on the street, or on a city bus). Notice that observing people, even in public places, has some ethical implications for their right to choose to participate in research, as well as for respect and privacy protections.

Whatever communicative behaviors or interactions you choose to observe, you'll want to take detailed notes about what you see. Depending on your research claim, you also may want to audiotape or videotape communicative behaviors, since those methods will provide the most exact replications of the original behavior (Amidon, 1971). You can record communicative behaviors live and in real time, depending on the availability of observational equipment and trained observers—or you can employ previously recorded audiotaped or videotaped data from an archive if one is available to you. It may be useful to take photographs of people in large groups or of key **artifacts**, things made by or used by humans, in order to capture some of what your eyes can see as empirical data. For example, Phillips (2012) took photographs of protest signs in order to analyze their message content, but also their relative size, visibility, layout, and other design features. The specific decisions about what or whom to observe, how to observe, and when to observe are all important aspects of collecting observational data that you will learn more about in Part 2 of this book, especially in Chapter 7, "Ethnography."

Physiological responses, like pupil dilation and blushing, provide another way to observe communicative behavior. Early advertising researchers believed that pupil dilation indicated a desire to buy the product, and they used pupil dilation to evaluate packaging and advertising materials (Blackwell, Hensel, & Sternthal, 1970). Physiological symptoms like queasy stomach, shaky voice, and blushing have been associated with anxiety in making sales calls (Verbeke & Bagozzi, 2000); and in at least one set of nonverbal experiments, blushing has been shown to contribute to an observer's perceptions that someone who has violated a social rule is more trustworthy, and so, less responsible than someone who does not blush (de Jong, 1999). Whether you observe participants' physiological responses, collect direct observations of communicative behaviors, or use some audio- or video-tape archive, observations are an important source of data for communication researchers.

Self-Reports of Communicative Behaviors, Beliefs, and Characteristics

A third possible source of data for communication research is to ask people to **self-report**, or to disclose their own behaviors, beliefs, or characteristics related to communication. If you want to know what people feel and how they think, self-report data should be your data source. You collect self-report data in survey questionnaires and whenever you interview key informants individually, or in groups. In fact, **focus groups** often are used to get a sense of how some defined group of people feel about a given topic (e.g., voters) or product (e.g., consumers). Focus groups are also used to explore a new research topic and develop suitable survey items (e.g., Yang & Brown, 2013).

From the point of view of the discovery researcher, self-report data is subject to some standard biases or sources of error. For example, humans tend to overestimate their own positive qualities and behaviors and underestimate their negative qualities and behaviors. Depending on the research topic, their relationship with the researcher, and many other factors, people may not report all of their thoughts and feelings. Reported memories can be incomplete, inaccurate, and so on. Despite these well-known limitations, self-report data is quite prevalent in communication research. You will learn much more about how to deal with bias in self-report data collection and analysis from Chapter 6, "Warrants for Research Arguments" and in Part 3 of this book, where each chapter deals with discovery paradigm research.

Other-Reports of Communicative Behaviors, Beliefs, and Characteristics

Other-reports, collected by asking people to report their perceptions of another person's behavior, beliefs, or characteristics, are the fourth and final source of communication data. Communication researchers routinely use **other-report** data in at least three ways, each for a different purpose. The first way that other-reports are used is when a researcher wants to know how a certain communicative act affects those who receive it (i.e., people who are not the source or creator of that act). For example, studies of audience reactions to mediated messages, such as news stories, films, or websites, or to nonmediated messages like those used in public speeches, often rely on other-report data. Audience members are asked to report their reactions to the message or their perceptions of the communicator, or to rate particular message characteristics (e.g., credibility, interest level). The second way that other-report data gets used is when a researcher wants to compare self-perceptions of a communicative act with other perceptions of the same act. Here, participants are asked to report how they perceived someone else's communication behaviors (e.g., friendly, knowledgeable customer service, or supervisors' influence attempts). Oftentimes, the research claim concerns the difference between how we see our own communication and how others see our communication. For example, communication competence scholars have learned that we typically think of ourselves as more competent, attractive, and so on than others do (e.g., Spitzberg & Hecht, 1984). Finally, other-report data is sometimes used for verification purposes; almost like voting by majority rule, other-reports are used to show the truth as more than one person sees it. We'll return to this idea later in this chapter, when we talk about triangulation of data sources and investigator viewpoints.

Data Collection Settings

Data collection settings are the places where observations, self-reports, other-reports, and communicative texts or artifacts are gathered or found. The issue of a data collection setting is less relevant when an archive of textual data is used to explore a research claim. An **archive** is a preexisting collection of artifacts or other textual evidence. Examples of archives include the county clerk's office where birth and marriage certificates are recorded, museum collections, legal and policy documents, and so on. Whenever data are collected via direct and immediate observations or from people's reports, there are essentially two possible settings, either in the field or in the laboratory (Smith, 1988).

Most interpretive communication research takes place in the **field settings** where communication occurs in its usual and customary fashion. By contrast, in **laboratory settings**, the researcher selects and controls the environment for communication. In a lab setting, the researcher induces the communication phenomena of interest to occur, controlling what behaviors occur, when, for how long, and for whom. Communication research laboratories are often rooms in academic buildings that have been set up to resemble the settings where communication usually happens (e.g., classrooms, living rooms, workplace or medical waiting areas). Communication laboratories sometimes contain one-way mirrors so that behaviors can be observed without participants' knowledge. Labs may be equipped with audio- or video-recording equipment that is less obtrusive than simply placing a tape recorder or camera on a table in the middle of a room.

Laboratory settings are somewhat artificial, no matter how cleverly you set up the space and mask your data collection equipment from the research participants. For this reason, the *rigor* provided by a laboratory setting often comes at a cost: Research findings obtained in the laboratory may be less *relevant* to people operating in nonresearch settings than findings obtained in field settings. The benefit of rigor is typically to realize a higher degree of control over variables that are part of a causal argument. The degree to which research participants are aware of and change their behaviors during data collection (in the laboratory or field setting) will be of grave concern to you if you are making explanatory and predictive claims. Even in a field setting, when you claim to interpret or evaluate participants' behaviors or messages, the value of your analysis will be reduced if the participants changed their behaviors or edited their

messages because you were present, relative to the ways they interacted when no data collection was happening.

Data Collection Strategies

Data collection strategies deal with how the data for a study are gathered, whereas data sources refer to the people or messages from whom the data are sampled. Data settings refer to the physical location in which the data are actually collected. For example, self-report data can be captured using interviews, written surveys, or written diaries. Other-report data can be collected using interviews, surveys, or existing texts (e.g., written performance appraisals). Behavioral observations can be gathered by taking field notes but may also be preserved using audiotape, videotape, or photographs. Obviously, all self- and other-reports and direct observations of communication behavior can be archived, once collected, in textual form. Those archives can then be used for similar or different purposes in subsequent research projects, provided such use was approved by an IRB. Conversation analysts often maintain such collections of talk in interaction and use those databases to test claims about interaction structures or functions across a variety of contexts (e.g., The University of Texas, Austin, and the University of California, Los Angeles, both maintain sizeable archives of interaction data that are digitally accessible to a virtual, online research community).

Now that you know something about data sources and settings, let's look at how you can decide which people or messages to include in your study. Selecting sources of empirical evidence is an issue that you will approach differently, depending on your methodology. It all depends on your research claim.

Selecting Data Sources

How do you pick the people whose behavior will be observed or who will be asked to report on their own or others' behaviors, beliefs, or characteristics? Or if your data will consist of verbal and/or nonverbal messages, how should you choose the particular messages to be analyzed in your study? If you study symbolic texts, how will you pick them? These are issues of data selection.

As a general rule, random selection methods are preferred in the discovery paradigm, because randomly selecting people or messages to study helps insure that your findings will accurately represent a reality that applies to some larger group of people or messages. On the other hand, nonrandom selection methods are preferred in the interpretive paradigm, where the general purpose of research is to understand how meaning is created among particular people, or in particular message contexts. Critical researchers approach the whole issue of selection quite differently than do researchers in either the discovery or interpretive paradigm.

In the discovery paradigm, the issue of selection is referred to as data **sampling**, "the process of selecting a set of subjects for study from a larger population" (Fink & Gantz, 1996, p. 117). *Sampling* is a social scientific term that we use whenever we select a relatively smaller number of cases to represent some larger group of cases or persons. The larger group of cases or instances that you are attempting to represent is called the **population**. A research population is a "comprehensive and well-defined group (a universal set) of the elements pertinent to a given research question or hypothesis" (Smith, 1988, p. 77). For example, the population of the United States of America can be theoretically specified in a number of ways, such as all the persons who are US citizens or all the persons residing within the borders of the nation. Notice how these two different definitions of the US population would include somewhat different groups of people. Populations are always theoretically bracketed. Of course, we can choose to study every person or message if our population is very small.

In discovery research, you will try to select a sample that well represents the population in which you seek to explain communication, or about which you hope to make accurate predictions. Therefore, when you are conducting survey, experimental, or content analytic research, you will want to use **random selection methods**, procedures for selecting samples that are most likely to represent a population within the limits of chance or random error (Smith, 1988). Randomizing data selection introduces some element of chance as to the people or texts included in a study, which will help you eliminate bias, specific sources of error in selecting data.

Random Selection Methods

Using sample data to represent a population is fundamental for discovery paradigm research. In Chapter 11 you will learn how to accomplish random selection of people and messages for research projects that deal with cause-and-effect explanations. In this section, we

Table 5.2 Types of Data Sampling Methods

Random sampling methods
Simple random sampling
Systematic sampling with a random start
Stratified sampling
Nonrandom sampling methods
Convenience (or volunteer) sampling
Purposive sampling
Network or snowball sampling
Quota sampling

will introduce you to three random selection methods: (1) simple random sampling, (2) systematic sampling with a random start, and (3) stratified sampling. These methods, along with nonrandom selection methods, are listed in Table 5.2, above.

Chief among random selection methods is **simple random sampling** in which each person or message in the population has an equal chance of being selected for inclusion in a study. To do this, you will select a subset of the population randomly from a **sampling frame**, a list of all the members of the population. For example, if you are interested in obtaining a random sample of students from your university, the registrar's list of currently enrolled students is one possible sampling frame for that population. Of course, you'll have to decide whether that list should include full-time and part-time students, students on academic leave for the term, and so on. That is why we mentioned earlier that all populations have to be theoretically specified. Likewise, the telephone book used to be a common sampling frame for the population of a city, but with all the mobile phones in use today and the decline of land lines, you can see why the phone book isn't a good sampling frame for a city's population anymore, and why random digit dialing is more often used to select participants for telephone data collection. If you do use a sampling frame, it must be as complete and accurate as possible, or else the people or texts you select will not represent the population well.

The second random selection method is systematic sampling with a random start. To conduct **systematic sampling with a random start**, select the first element by chance, and select the remaining elements systematically from the total sampling frame. For example, if you are studying the population of students at your university, and your sampling frame contains 10,000 currently enrolled students from which you want a sample of 1,000 students, you could select the first student randomly (e.g., roll a dice; if it lands on "5," begin with the fifth person listed on your sampling frame; the list could by alphabetical by last name, or it could be numerical, by student ID number). You could then select every tenth student from the registrar's list for inclusion in your study. It is now fairly well established that simple random sampling and systematic sampling yield virtually identical samples, so most researchers opt for using systematic sampling as the easier of these two methods (Babbie, 2001).

However, a potential problem with systematic sampling is **periodicity**—a recurring pattern or arrangement that exists naturally in the sampling frame. For example, imagine that you want to obtain a random sample of rooms in a large dormitory on campus. The rooms might be arranged in such a way that sampling every tenth dorm room would lead to the selection of only rooms near the stairwells (adapted from Babbie, 2001). If your research is about the effect of noise on studying in the dorms, then a pattern like that could lead you to select a biased sample, not a representative one.

Our third random selection method, stratified sampling, is more refined and complex than either simple random sampling or systematic sampling with a random start. **Stratified sampling** organizes a population into subsets of similar elements; we can then select elements from each subset using systematic or simple random sampling. As in the other random sampling methods, we must first obtain an accurate sampling frame. But in this case, we know that some groups in the population share common characteristics. For example, you may know that two-thirds of your university's student population is female and one-third is male. You can *stratify* that population by separating the sampling frame into females and males and then randomly selecting a sample from each group, using the approximate proportions of the sexes that represent your university's population. Large polling companies such as Gallup frequently stratify voters on the basis of geographic location to increase sample representativeness in terms of ethnicity, social class, urban and rural differences, types of occupations, and so forth. Generally, if you are measuring a number of variables in a very large population, you are more likely to achieve representative sampling if you stratify

the population than if you use simple random or systematic sampling (Babbie, 2001).

No matter which random selection method you use, you must be concerned about sample representativeness. If your sample adequately represents its parent population, then the results of your study will be generalizable to all other members of that population. We call this ability to generalize findings to a parent population *external validity.* You will learn more about it in Chapter 6, "Warrants for Research Arguments." But for now, let's contrast random selection methods with nonrandom selection methods.

Nonrandom Selection Methods

Nonrandom selection occurs when we select people or texts in ways that do not ensure that the resulting data sample represents some theoretic population. There are at least three reasons for choosing nonrandom selection methods. First, the constraints of your data setting or research question may make random selection methods untenable or unethical, even when your purpose is to explain and predict communication in a larger population (Fink & Gantz, 1996; Stake, 1998). In such cases, you can use quota sampling, defined later in this section, as an alternative to random selection methods.

Second, you may want to represent a population but be unable to use one of the random selection methods because you lack the required time or money. In that case, use of nonrandom selection methods will weaken your ability to claim that your sampled results apply to some larger population. So you will need to acknowledge the possiblity that sample bias is a limitation in your research report.

The third and best reason for using nonrandom data selection methods is that you are relying on interpretive or critical paradigm assumptions and not on the discovery paradigm assumption of generalizability. Interpretive and critical researchers tend to prefer nonrandom selection methods because their research claims are more likely to be based on representing communicative phenomena within a specific context. If you want to preserve participants' subjective realities and richly describe a specific communication context, you are likely to prefer one of the nonrandom selection methods that we outline next. We give you some rationale for using each method as we discuss these four types of nonrandom selection: (1) convenience or volunteer sampling, (2) purposive sampling, (3) network or snowball sampling, and (4) quota sampling (listed in Table 5.2).

The first nonrandom selection method is called convenience sampling. **Convenience samples** are comprised of whatever data is convenient to the researcher (e.g., people who volunteer to fill out a questionnaire, messages that are readily available, behaviors that the researcher had already captured for other purposes, etc.). Convenience sampling is less than desirable for most research. Let's consider why by looking at two examples.

First, imagine that you are a survey researcher and that you use convenience sampling to recruit participants who are easily obtainable. In academic contexts, your participants probably will be college students, typically those enrolled in large, undergraduate introductory communication. The fact that they are college students is irrelevant, since they are not chosen for any particular reason other than their accessibility. But college students are unlikely to represent the general population in terms of their individual characteristics like age, ethnicity or socioeconomic status. Their attitudes also may differ from the attitudes of the broader population (e.g., all voters, or all consumers). Because your selection process is nonrandom, the resulting sample will not represent the population of either college students or people in general. Factors like the type of course it is, the time of day, and the geographic region of the university, along with participants' characteristics and attitudes, are all likely to introduce biases that threaten your sample's ability to represent the population of interest.

Second, imagine that you are a conversation or discourse analyst who uses convenience sampling to select messages that are readily available. Here, your problem may be the ability to represent a message population if you intend to generalize beyond those conveniently accessible messages. But if you aim to *interpret* the ways that messages are used in a particular context, then a convenient sample of messages also is likely to be inadequate. If your research question deals with particular types of people, or messages, or behaviors, then a purposive sampling strategy will be the most appropriate choice.

Purposive samples "intentionally focus on the target group to the exclusion of other groups" (Smith, 1988, p. 85). Although purposive sampling methods lack representativeness, just as do other nonrandom selection methods, randomization may not be a practical or desirable way to collect evidence for some research questions. To illustrate, Kassing and Infante (1999) asked athletes to report on their coaches' verbal and physical aggression.

They had limited access to certain types of athletes and virtually no access to their coaches. They used a purposive sample of athletes to report their perceptions of coach behavior. Purposive sampling lets you access just the right people or texts for your study when you do not have the sampling frame that would be required to use stratified random sampling.

For similar reasons, researchers often use network sampling (Lindlof, 1995). **Network sampling** is sometimes called snowball sampling because the data sample is collected in much the same way that snow is collected when you roll a snowball down a hill. Just as each snowflake picks up other snowflakes, each participant in a snowball sample solicits additional people to participate in the study. For example, in couple communication studies, the researchers sometimes ask marital partners and their friends to recommend other couples whom they know as potential participants (e.g., Bruess & Pearson, 1997; Hinkle, 1999). Snowball sampling is often purposive, as participants are selected because of one particular characteristic (e.g., being in a committed relationship). Instagram users are likely to know other Instragrammers, just as people who have any one characteristic often know others who share that characteristic. Snowball sampling is a great selection method to use when you want to study members of an underrepresented population who may only be accessible through one another's recommendations.

The fourth nonrandom selection method is called **quota sampling**, which involves dividing a population into relevant subgroups and then (conveniently or purposively) selecting the desired proportion of people or messages from each group needed to represent the whole population. Quota sampling is useful whenever your target population is relatively small, and its characteristics are well known. For example, Kirkman and Shapiro (2000) sampled employees from a Fortune 500 insurance company. They solicited participants until they achieved a demographic profile of the sample that matched the demographic profile of the entire organization. **Demographics** are the general characteristics common to any group of people, such as age, biological sex, socioeconomic status, level of education, ethnicity, and so forth. Kirkman and Shapiro were attempting to achieve a sample of voluntary participants that represented the population of the insurance company. They were interested in team members in this particular context, not all team members in every organization, or even every insurance company. As you can see from this example, quota sampling is the best alternative from our nonrandom selection methods if you do want your sample to represent a parent population.

Selection in Critical Studies

Even though published critical essays that are based on empirical evidence rarely address the selection of cases for analysis in any explicit way, critical researchers do emphasize the issue of selection when choosing a topic or a particular case to study. In critical communication studies, "topic selection usually begins with only a vague idea of some broad question or issue that may not be narrowed down until well into data collection" (J. Thomas, 1993, p. 34). The whole concept of selecting evidence is framed very differently in critical studies. Instead of selecting data to support particular claims, critical scholars engage in gathering and analyzing evidence until the questions that are most interesting emerge, as a visual figure emerges from a chaotic background. The critical scholar's very topics, not just the particular data sources to be studied, are unspecified at the outset of the research project because "the focus of attention often lies in areas at first glance unnoticeable and within data sources possessing mechanisms to conceal, rather than reveal, their secrets" (J. Thomas, 1993, p. 35).

Nevertheless, as a critical researcher you might select a case of "some typicality, but leaning toward those cases that seem to offer opportunity to learn" (Stake, 1998, p. 101). Even once you have selected a case, the sampling of persons, places, and events to observe within the case is another factor you will need to consider. At the early stages of your critical study, variety, rather than representativeness, should guide your selection decisions (Stake, 1998). For example, if you are conducting rhetorical criticism of presidential rhetoric, you will want to start by immersing yourself in as many presidential speeches, letters, and memoirs as you can, perhaps narrowing your focus to one president, and perhaps one form of rhetoric (e.g., public speeches), as you develop your purpose and claims.

Now that you have some sense of how to approach *selection* for critical studies, and an overview of random and nonrandom selection methods, let's next consider some specific data collection *strategies*, beginning with ways to collect observations of communication behavior.

Capturing Observed Behaviors

Whether you are interested in studying communication behavior as it happens in its ordinary context (i.e., field settings) or in a controlled laboratory setting, you will have to devise some means of capturing all the information you sense if you are to study those data systematically. The means of capturing communication research data are highly biased to our senses of sight and sound, although performance studies scholarship is one segment of communication research that pushes the means of capturing observed behavior well beyond visual and auditory boundaries to include touch, movement, and scent. But sight and sound are still the primary senses used to record observed communication behaviors (Lindlof, 1995).

Videotape recordings, films, websites, Tweets, and Instagrams capture both visual and linguistic data simultaneously. Sight and sound records capture communication data consistently and accurately, provide a tool for training observers, give a permanent record of the research data, increase the number of possible observers through replay and remote broadcast, and allow self-observation and analysis (Amidon, 1971). In addition, sight and sound records provide a basis for supervisory diagnoses and evaluations. For example, telephone calls often are recorded to facilitate the training and development of employees' customer service, selling, or technical support skills (see Feldman, 2012, or Pal & Buzzanell, 2013, for examples).

However, audiotaping and videotaping people's behavior require specialized equipment and facilities, and raises a host of ethical issues, too. A camera does not pick up every behavior in a context because the researcher has to choose the camera's angle and range. It's much harder to ensure participants' privacy with video data, and unobtrusive recordings should never be taken without participants' full awareness and consent. Lastly, the means of analyzing the complex data provided by sight and sound recordings are still being codified.

Capturing Self-Reports and Other-Reports

As we pointed out earlier in this chapter, two of the most frequently used ways that you might capture self-report and other-report data are by interviewing people or distributing survey questionnaires, orally or by print/digital means. For example, Lin & Tsai (2011) conducted pilot interviews with medical patients in order to create survey items for their primary study; so they used self-report data sources at both stages of their data collection. Another, less frequently used way to capture self-reports and other-reports is by asking people to complete some sort of task, such as rating behaviors, explaining observed behaviors, or sorting written records of observed behaviors into categories (e.g., coding tasks). Table 5.3 shows how particular data collection strategies may be linked to different types of research questions.

As we already mentioned, there are some aspects of communication data selection that are treated much differently in the discovery paradigm than in interpretive or critical scholarship. If you are conducting discovery paradigm research, you will need to specify both the concepts you want to study and your ways of measuring those concepts before you can collect direct observations of communicative behaviors; self-reports or other-reports of beliefs, attitudes, and values; or before you analyze the content of textual data. For this reason, we have included a short chapter on conceptualization and operationalization at the beginning of Part 3, "How to Discover Communication."

Table 5.3 Linking Data Collection Strategies to Research Questions

Data Collection Strategies	Type of Research Question
Audiotaped conversations	Meaning questions aimed at eliciting the "essence of experiences"
Written anecdotes of personal experiences	
Phenomenological literature, such as poetry	
Unstructured interviews	Questions aimed at describing group values, beliefs, and practices
Participant/observation	
Field notes	
Documents, records, photographs, maps, diagrams	
Interviews	"Process" questions involving experience over time, especially changes in phases or stages
Participant/observation	
Memoing	
Diaries	
Dialogue (audio/video recorded)	Questions regarding verbal interaction and communication behaviors
Observations	
Field notes	
Interviews	Questions about macrolevel behavior (e.g., group norms, values)
Photography	
Observations	
Field notes	

Source: Adapted from Morse (1998) and Lofland, Snow, Anderson, and Lofland (2006).

Research Design

In its broadest sense, a **research design** is the logical sequence that connects a researcher's claim, data or evidence, and warrants. But the words, *research design* are used very differently by different kinds of researchers, often without any explicit recognition of the existence of these different meanings.

Design as a Bypassing Term

Over the past forty years or so, communication scholars have greatly increased the number and variety of methods we use to conduct research, and some terms from one paradigm have come to be used in quite different ways by practitioners of other paradigms. From the discovery paradigm perspective, the term *research design* encompasses many specific strategies for carefully controlling the selection of the people or messages to be included in a study, the setting in which the data will be collected, and the strategies for capturing those data. Careful control is needed whenever you want to argue cause-and-effect sequences.

By contrast, interpretive researchers typically use the word design to indicate the emerging or unfolding process of collecting and analyzing field data. In interpretive research, design includes attention to the identification and selection of key informants, development of interview questions and perhaps observation schemes, and sampling techniques for data collection. Communication criticism is often conducted without ever using the words *research* or *design*. This, in combination with discovery and interpretive scholars' different uses of those words, makes research design an instance of bypassing because researchers use the term to mean very different things across different research paradigms. Nonetheless, in the most basic sense, a research design is your plan for exploring a research question or testing a hypothesis.

Cross-Sectional Research Designs

Cross-sectional research designs are the most simple and common form of design used in communication research. In **cross-sectional studies**, a sample of data collected at one point in time is used to draw inferences about the research question. Just as a tree stump shows a cross-section

of the tree's life, evidenced in the growth rings, a cross-sectional study gives the researcher a snapshot, one perspective on the phenomenon of interest. Whenever we select data from one point in time, the design is cross-sectional, whether those data are self- or other-reports, texts, or observed communication behaviors.

Longitudinal Research Designs

Longitudinal studies are those in which we collect data at several different points in time. Although less commonly used in communication research than cross-sectional studies, longitudinal studies are important whenever we want to explain or interpret how communication changes over time. Certain types of survey research, like television or radio program ratings, or website traffic, rely on longitudinal research designs to assess changes in audience consumption over time. But so do ethnographic studies, where the researcher needs to be immersed in a field setting over weeks or months in order to interpret participants' communication in that context. Interpretive historical critics sometimes aim to show how communication artifacts or interpretations of texts shifted over a certain period of time. In each of these cases, collecting data over time is vital to exploring the research claim. The right design for your study depends on the claim you are making!

Triangulation and Mixed Methods Research

Originally, the concept of **triangulation** came to social science research from military navigation, where using more than one reference point enabled navigators to pinpoint an object's exact location (Newman & Benz, 1998). Thus, the first uses of triangulation in research were efforts to increase the accuracy of measurement by confirming data from more than one source or setting. However, over the last century, the notion of triangulation has been elaborated to include using multiple data sources, settings, collection and analytic strategies, and investigators (Denzin, 1978; Janesick, 1998; Lindlof, 1995; Lofland et al., 2006; Miles & Huberman, 1994; Morse, 1998; Newman & Benz, 1998; Seale, 1999; Stage & Russell, 1992).

The basic assumption that discovery researchers make about triangulation is that using multiple data sources, settings, data collection strategies, and so on will compensate for the inherent weaknesses of each individual method. In this sense, triangulation contributes to verification, the attempt to accurately describe one, knowable reality (Matthison, 1988). But when we use multiple data sources, settings, and so on to support interpretive or critical research claims, triangulation is not intended to verify one true reality (Denzin & Lincoln, 1998). Rather, using more than one data source, setting, or investigator can enrich the range of subjective participant views available to us. In **mixed methods research**, inconsistencies and "contradictory findings may actually help to understand the richness of what is being studied" (Stage & Russell, 1992, p. 489). Indeed, the advantages of reading and incorporating insights from multiple studies, using different data collection sources, settings, and strategies, simply extend the idea on which triangulation is based (Miles & Huberman, 1994). Insights from the discovery, interpretive and critical research paradigms have contributed to our current understandings of and knowledge about most areas of the field, whether that means media, intercultural and interpersonal communication, or health, political, and organizational communication. In the sections following, we outline five ways that triangulation can be accomplished within a study, or across several studies, including multiple data sources, settings, collection and analytic strategies, and investigators. We will then use Y. Y. Kim, Luhan, & Dixon's (1998) ethnographic study of American Indian identities to illustrate all five types of triangulation.

Multiple Data Sources

Multiple data source triangulation means that you compare data from more than one source, such as combining self-report and other-report data, or behavioral observations with archival textual analysis (Denzin, 1978; Lindlof, 1995). This type of triangulation is quite ordinary in ethnographic research in which researchers observe behaviors over a long time in the field and analyze self-report data gained during in-depth interviews (e.g., Browning & Beyer, 1998; Covarrubias, 2007, 2008; Lindsley, 1999). If you take photos or videotape of your observations in a commuication setting where you are also a participant, you can later compare those images to other participants' reports, and to your own recall of communication in that setting (Phillips, 2012; Vignes, 2008). Or you can ask participants to take their own photos or video of what is important to them, and triangulate those data sources with your interviews or participant observations, as Druits (2009) did when she investigated eighth grade girls' use of popular media in the classroom. Alternately, you could ask participants in a focus group to discuss and analyze their meanings for interview or participant-observation data you collected from other participants, as Favero & Heath (2012) did when they asked Baby Boomer and Generation X/Y women to discuss transcripts and questionnaire data collected in two pilot studies about generational attitudes toward work and life.

Multiple Data Settings

Besides multiple data sources, another way to use triangulation is to examine a single phenomenon at multiple settings or data collection sites. Using multiple data collection sites for verification helps increase generalizability by reducing the effects of one setting (or one group of participants) on the researcher's interpretations of those phenomena (Getis, 1995; Newman & Benz, 1998). In addition, choosing underresearched groups or settings can help to counteract the unique effects of one setting and contribute to a richer description of the phenomena being studied (Frey, Botan, & Kreps, 2000; Newman & Benz, 1998). For example, Javon Johnson's (2010) comparison of slam poetry at *Da Poetry Lounge* in Hollywood, California, with the spoken word poetry typically performed in "Leimert Park, a Black, middle-class neighborhood in South Los Angeles" (p. 397) helps to show how Black masculinities are performed differently in those two settings. Using multiple data settings is a good triangulation strategy whether you adhere to the discovery, interpretive, or critical research paradigm.

Multiple Data Collection Strategies

Recall that multiple data collection strategies have to do with *how* data for a study are gathered, whereas data sources and settings refer to the people and places *from whom* or *where* the data are sampled. For example, self-report data can be collected using 1:1 or focus group interviews, written surveys, and diaries. Other-report data (i.e., perceptions about other people's behavior or attitudes) can be collected using interviews, surveys, or existing documents (e.g., performance appraisals). Behavioral observations may be collected live, face to face, but may also be preserved using audiotaped or videotaped recordings.

We think it is good practice to use several kinds of evidence to support a claim: If you are interested in verifying one knowable reality, then you might combine other-report data collected from interviews with existing documents (i.e., archival texts) and use only those reports that are confirmed by both means of data collection. If you are interested in interpreting multiple realities, then collecting self-reports using a combination of oral interviews and written diaries should help you enrich the range of interpretations you gather from members of a cultural group (Phillips, 2012). Conflicting interpretations may suggest who shares, or does not share, particular interpretations of communication in that setting.

Multiple Data Analytic Strategies

It is also possible to use more than one data analytic strategy as a form of triangulation, and doing so is probably the most widely understood use of the term mixed methods research today. Quantitative data analysis involves the use of numbers to indicate the amount, degree, or frequency of some variable(s). Simple frequency counts and percentages, along with visual charts and graphs, are always the starting point for more complex statistical analyses that involve exploring relationships and differences among variables in order to explain their causes or effects, or to predict their future occurrences. But qualitative data analysis also often starts with some simple quantification, like using the most frequently mentioned terms to infer their importance, or noticing that participants in a setting mostly use particular artifacts (e.g., iPhones vs. other mobile telephones). However, qualitative data analysis proceeds to identify key themes or patterns of meaning in the data, rather than via statistical analysis.

Multiple Investigators' Viewpoints

The last form of triangulation, multiple investigator viewpoints, is used in a particular way in discovery research, but it is also characteristic of many interpretive communication research studies.

Discovery researchers triangulate multiple investigator viewpoints in the very early stages of data analysis to insure observational validity and decrease the possibility of observer bias (Amidon, 1971; Mathison, 1988). For example, if you wanted to know whether your teacher is calling on more male students than female students, you could have several people observe whose hands are raised, and who gets called on by the teacher, over several class periods. Before you could answer your research question, you would have to first determine whether all the observers agreed about "who had a hand up?" and then, "who was called on by the teacher?" Once you verified the validity and reliability of those behavioral observations, you could then compare the frequency data for "hands up" and "called on" between male and female students in the class.

Interpretive field researchers often collaborate throughout the course of a study (i.e., planning the research, collecting and analyzing the data, writing up the report). Interpretive researchers arrange some form of collaboration among two or more researchers to "compensate for their individual biases, or shortcomings, or to exploit their specific strengths" (Douglas, 1976, as cited in Lindlof, 1995, p. 239). In our student research projects, for example, we might deploy more than one researcher in the same setting, or we might have one student researcher work with another to analyze themes from interview data. You could check the soundness of a category you have identified by talking it over with someone who was a participant in your data collection setting or someone who is a content expert on your topic (ask your professor). As you can see, team research offers several advantages for making interpretive claims.

Sometimes, more than one type of triangulation is used in a single study, as you can see if you check out Y. Y. Kim et al.'s (1998) study of American Indians' identity experiences in Oklahoma. During the *data collection* phase, the researchers employed multiple data collection strategies, sources, and settings: They conducted individual interviews with 182 American Indians at six different research sites in Oklahoma, at the same time collecting observational data and testimonials from community members. During the *data analysis* phase, they applied two coding schemes: They first grouped their interview data into thematic clusters that represented American Indians' different ways of responding to identity dilemmas, as well as their interpersonal, organizational, and mass media consumption patterns. But Y. Y. Kim et al. also applied numerical data analysis, such as measuring the participants' degree of involvement with in-group and out-group members (i.e., how many friends they reported who were Indian vs. friends who were White). Finally, the study was conducted by *multiple investigators*: "The six-member research team consisted of three members who had Indian backgrounds and were long time residents of Oklahoma. . . . The other

Table 5.4 Communication Data/Evidence in Three Paradigms

	Discovery Paradigm	Interpretive Paradigm	Critical Paradigm
Sources	Self-report and other-report surveys; categorizing behavioral observations or texts	Self-report and other-report interviews, behavioral observations, and texts	Mostly textual analysis
Settings	Laboratory and Field	Field	Archival texts, or Not Applicable
Triangulation	Used to verify one objective reality	Use to enrich understanding of multiple realities	Use to demonstrate the pervasiveness and/or stability of hegemonic realities

Note: This table identifies the data sources, settings, and uses of triangulation that typify communication research in three paradigms; exceptions do exist.

three non-Indian members were of Asian, Black, and Irish backgrounds" (Y. Y. Kim et al., 1998, p. 259). In short, the reseach team employed all five types of triangulation: multiple data sources, data settings, data collection, analytic strategies, and multiple investigator viewpoints. We hope that this example helps you think about how triangulation can be used in practice and what potential benefits triangulation or mixed methods research might offer you in designing communication research.

Summary

In this chapter, we've outlined the second element of the research-as-argument model, the data or evidence assembled in support of a research claim. We began by discussing the typical sources, settings, and strategies used by communication scholars for collecting research data. We have stressed the relative value of different data collection sources, settings, and strategies for supporting particular research claims. We hope that our approach will help you begin to appreciate some of the key differences in the communication research conducted by interpretive, critical, and discovery scholars, as each of these research paradigms contributes valuable insights to the field of communication studies. Table 5.4, above, recaps some typical uses of communication data or evidence in each paradigm. Finally, our discussion of triangulation and mixed method research should help you to think more broadly about designing your own research.

Key Terms

Archive
Artifacts
Bias
Collaborative ethnography
Cross-sectional research
　　designs
Data collection settings
Data collection sources

Data collection strategies
Focus groups
Longitudinal research designs
Mixed methods research
Observed behaviors
Other-report
Population
Research Design

Sampling
Sampling frame
Selection
Self-report
Text
Triangulation

Discussion Questions

1. Think about the settings in which you regularly participate as a communicator (e.g., classrooms, home, commuting to/from school or work, shopping malls, airports): Which of these settings are routinely videotaped? What ethical problems would you have to consider if you wanted to study the communication captured in those videotapes?

2. How might triangulation or mixed methods contribute to the worth of a research project given the different values and forms of argument used in discovery, interpretive, and critical communication research? It may help to consider this question in terms of the different forms of triangulation described in this chapter.

3. Academic research is frequently conducted using university students as participants. What research topics can be studied appropriately using random samples of college students as participants? What topics would be better explored using purposive samples, or seeking participants from outside the university setting?

"Try It!" Activities

1. Collect instances of ordinary uses of the words *data* and *evidence* from magazines and newspapers, your workplace, the Internet, or when those terms are mentioned in your other classes. What meanings of the words *data* and *evidence* are reflected by the research we do in communication? What parts of the research done by faculty members in your department are not reflected in these ordinary meanings of the word *data*? What is meant by the phrase *big data*?

2. Which of the claims following would be best studied using one of the random selection methods? Which claims would best be studied using one of the nonrandom data selection methods? Give reasons for your answers.
   (a) Family phone calls can show how family members address uncertainties associated with understanding a loved one's cancer diagnosis, treatment, and prognosis (Beach & Good, 2004).
   (b) Research question: What are undergraduate public speaking texts teaching students about communication ethics? (Pearson, Child, Mattern, & Kahl, 2006).
   (c) *Girls Gone Wild* and *Guys Gone Wild* videos use space and time differently to both critique and reinforce white, middle-class male, and female gender roles (Pitcher, 2006).
   (d) Masculinity is a cultural performance (e.g., Chicano masculinity is performed by cultural workers and represented in mediated texts like the television show, *Resurrection Blvd.;* Holling, 2006).
   (e) Affectionate communication is associated with the human body's ability to handle stress (K. Floyd, 2006).

3. Use Table 5.1 to evaluate the source credibility of any two studies cited in this chapter. Which is more credible and why? Give reasons for your answer.

6 Warrants for Research Arguments

Introduction

In this chapter, you will learn about the third element of the research-as-argument model, the warrants and backing. Warrants are the standards used to evaluate whether particular evidence is a good way to support a claim. There are inherent relationships between values, forms of argument, and the different standards used to judge research in each paradigm (i.e., interpretive, critical, and discovery communication research). We first outline the values and forms of argument preferred in each paradigm. Then we show you how to develop the warrants for each type of argument based on those values. We end this chapter by comparing three different views of truth, one for each paradigm.

Learning Outcomes

After completing this chapter, you should be able to:

» Identify and explain the values, form of argument, and standards for evaluating evidence in interpretive, critical, and discovery paradigm communication research.

» Recognize which standards the authors of a published research report or critical essay have used to evaluate the link between their claim(s) and data/evidence.

» Evaluate published research reports and critical essays based on the fit between their claims, data/evidence sources and settings and warrants.

Outline

H‌ave you ever heard someone make an assertion and wondered, "What's the evidence for that claim?" or "Where'd they get *that* idea?" The link between a claim and the evidence offered to support it is the warrant, "something that serves as an assurance, or guarantee, of some event or result" (Guralnik, 1986, p. 1602). To warrant is to give formal assurance or guarantee something. Research warrants allow us to state with confidence that our evidence or data support our research claim (Booth, Colomb, & Williams, 1995).

But the warrants that researchers in each paradigm use to link their claims to data are slightly different, because scholars in each of the paradigms for communication research have somewhat different values. Thus, we will begin each of the main sections in this chapter by first introducing you to the values embraced within that paradigm. Then we will outline the form of argument that researchers in that paradigm make. Finally, we'll define and give examples of the specific standards used to evaluate evidence in that paradigm.

Values guide all of our choices as researchers. The way we frame research problems, decide what will count as data, select the strategies we use to collect and analyze evidence, and estimate the worth of our conclusions all

depend on our values. The different paradigm values lead researchers to prioritize ethical choices in different ways. Of course, all researchers share certain ethical concerns, such as managing the risks and avoiding harm to research participants, preserving people's right of choice to participate in research, and sharing information ethically (Johannesen, 2001). But researchers operating in the three paradigms respond to those ethical issues somewhat differently.

We do not think that some paradigms are more ethical than others. In fact, we prefer all three paradigms coexisting in the world of communication inquiry, but not in one person or in one study! If you want to fully understand any communication topic, you can benefit from knowledge gained in interpretive, critical, and discovery paradigm studies. So, instead of paradigm allegiance, we prefer that you develop methodological awareness, which "can be acquired by exposure to almost any intelligent methodological discussion" (Seale, 1999, p. 465). Reading and discussing methodological ideas builds your intellectual muscles and makes you a stronger, more alert practitioner and consumer of research. Methodological awareness will serve you well in your other major courses, but also when you interact with research in your career and as a consumer. Let's begin by considering the values, form of argument, and warrants for interpretive paradigm research.

Interpretive Paradigm Warrants

As you already know from Chapter 2, "Three Paradigms of Knowing," interpretive research is rooted in philosophies that include the idea of multiple realities, equally plausible interpretations that are socially constructed through communication. These subjective realities are best understood from the standpoint of the knower. The whole purpose of interpretive research is to appreciate how meanings are created, maintained, or changed by people communicating in a certain context. That's why the warrants for interpretive communication research address your ability to capture and represent multiple realities, while you **bracket**, or set aside, your own understandings in order to privilege the participants' views: For now, we'll call this your credibility. Interpretive warrants also include your ability to help other people understand communication in that context (by providing plausible interpretations), and to understand communication in other, similar contexts (transferable findings). Before we consider each of these standards for evaluating interpretive paradigm research, let's consider the values and form of argument embraced by interpretive researchers.

Interpretive Values: Subjectivity and Rich Description

If you want to understand how people create meaning in context, you will need to prioritize subjectivity and rich description in your research project. Acting on these values starts with your choice of topics and research question (i.e., study the communication that matters to your participants). But paradigm values also influence what counts as good data collection and analysis and whether your findings are considered believable and important.

Subjectivity refers to our human ability to know using our minds based on our thoughts and feelings. It's the idea that perceptions of reality are every bit as important as, or even more important than, any reality that exists independent of human perception. Interpretive researchers have taken a stance on the side of valuing subjectivity, whereas discovery paradigm researchers prioritize objectivity (i.e., the ability to know about something outside your own perceptions, thoughts, and feelings).

One way that you can show that you value subjectivity is to privilege instances of communication as they usually occur when no research is being conducted. That's why interpretive field researchers prefer naturalistic observations and interviews, especially unstructured conversations between researchers and participants, over other ways of collecting data, like written surveys or laboratory experiments. The preference for direct observation is linked to epistemology, specifically, the belief that face-to-face participation with other humans is needed to acquire social knowledge (Lofland et al., 2006).

Interpretive rhetoricians also value subjectivity, but they enact that value somewhat differently than field researchers do (e.g., ethnographers and ethnomethodologists). For example, in a dramatistic rhetorical criticism of Illinois Governor George Ryan's statewide moratorium on capital punishment, Moore (2006) noted that Ryan faced considerable disapproval for sparing the lives of 167 death row prisoners by commuting their sentences shortly before the end of his term. Nonetheless, "people may still scorn and ridicule [Ryan], but he experienced a resolution of the inner self. After deciding to act, he said he slept well at night" (Moore, 2006, p. 325). Moore's conclusion thus privileged Ryan's subjective thoughts and feelings.

Rich description is the other value that characterizes interpretive communication research (Lofland et al., 2006; Miles & Huberman, 1994). Rich descriptions address every aspect of a social situation or text such as the setting, the participants, and their actions, relationships, and roles (Geertz, 1973). You can prioritize rich description by the kinds and amount of data you choose to collect, but also in the ways that you depict data in a research report or critical essay. Rich descriptions are best achieved when you are immersed in a social situation or in the analysis of a text over a long period of time. Being deeply immersed in the setting or with the texts serves at least two purposes: First, it allows you to understand one text or one social situation as fully as possible. Second, it helps when you want to think about how one text or social situation compares with another (transferable findings).

Rich descriptions will be important to all of your interpretive research projects, whether you are studying participants' communication behaviors in natural settings or analyzing textual evidence. In doing ethnography or ethnomethodological research, you will use rich description to capture and depict the full range of participants' meanings. In discourse analysis and rhetorical criticism, you will use rich description of messages and artifacts to elaborate your multiple readings of those texts. Prioritizing participants' subjective understandings and richly describing them will help you make arguments about the multiple interpretations of reality at play in a communication setting or situation.

Form of Argument: Demonstrating Multiple Realities

Interpretive research thus consists of making arguments that demonstrate multiple social realities. For now, you can contrast this sort of argument with the discovery researchers' arguments about association or about cause-and-effect sequences. You might also contrast an argument for multiple realities with the arguments made by critical scholars, who evaluate communication against some standard, and sometimes argue that the standards need to change (i.e., arguments for ideological change).

But interpretive paradigm philosophies emphasize that there is more than one justifiable interpretation of reality at play in any social situation. So triangulating data sources, settings, or researcher viewpoints helps interpretive researchers to see "various pictures of the same phenomenon and provide a broader view" (Trumbo, 2004, p. 420). Those same forms of triangulation also can produce "divergent results and provide a provocative analysis" (Trumbo, 2004, p. 420). These two uses of triangulation are fairly common in interpretive communication research, where triangulation contributes to surfacing multiple realities.

In the sections below, you will learn three specific standards that interpretive researchers use to evaluate the links between claims and data: researcher credibility, plausible interpretations, and transferable findings.

Researcher Credibility as a Standard for Evaluating Evidence

Researcher credibility means many things, and it is important in all research paradigms. But for interpretive communication scholars, researcher credibility is an especially important standard because the *researcher* is the primary instrument through which interpretations

are made. This is true whether gathering data via interviews and/or participant observations, or doing textual analysis (Patton, 1990). In this section, we'll help you explore three aspects of your credibility as a researcher: your training and experience, your degree of membership in the social situation under study, and your faithfulness.

Training and Experience

Interpretive methods for collecting and analyzing communication data rely on your skills and abilities to a somewhat greater degree than in discovery research, where some of the measurement can be warranted by a measuring instrument (see the sections on criterion-related and construct validity, later in this chapter). As an interpretive researcher, your main instruments are your own skills at observing, interviewing, and analyzing texts.

Consider some of the skills you will need to be a successful participant observer. You will need to be able to enter the field of observation in the least intrusive way possible. You will need to know how and when to blend in versus when to be openly in the learning role or when to appear competent in a participant role. You will need to be adept at recalling and taking notes about what you see, hear, feel, touch, and smell. And this list is really just the tip of the iceberg!

Since interpretive field researchers often triangulate their observations of communication by interviewing participants in a setting, you also will need interviewing skills. As an interviewer, you will need to develop and ask good questions; know when and how to probe for additional information; know how to recognize and interpret evasions, avoidance, and lies from participants; be experienced in using audio or video recording equipment; be familiar with the practices of transcribing taped material to written form; and so on.

A similar list of learned skills can be named for textual analysts and rhetorical critics, who must select a focus of criticism, develop a theoretical and critical vocabulary, select perspectives from which to approach their work, and so on (Brock et al., 1990). And regardless of whether you are using participant observation, interviewing, textual criticism, or some combination of these data collection and analytic methods, you will need both methodological awareness (Seale, 1999) and theoretical sensitivity (Strauss & Corbin, 1998). Both of these terms suggest highly developed knowledge of, and experience with, communication research methods and theories.

You already know a little bit about methodological awareness from the beginning of this chapter. *Theoretical sensitivity* is a similar concept except that it connotes experience with and knowledge of communication theories rather than research methods. Although interpretive researchers often enter the field of data collection without hypotheses, and sometimes without any explicit research question, they are not blank slates onto which the lived experience of participants can be written. Strauss and Corbin (1998) emphasized the "unquestionable fact (and advantage), that trained researchers are theoretically sensitized. Researchers carry into their research the sensitizing possibilities of their training, reading, and research experience, as well as explicit theories that might be useful if played against systematically gathered data" (p. 167). Theoretical sensitivity is also important for interpretive research because sometimes "the method is the theory," especially when you are interpreting and analyzing certain data (Madison, 2005, p. 18). If you triangulate multiple investigator viewpoints, then each researcher's theoretical sensitivities will contribute to your collective understandings of the communication that you study.

The more developed your awareness of method and theory, the better tuned you will be as a research instrument, and the better choices you are likely to make as you conduct research. Think about one thing that you know how to do very well: Let's say it's driving a car. When you first learned it, you probably had to concentrate more than you do now, and you probably did it more slowly at first. But once you know something very well, you do it more effectively, faster, and with less exclusive concentration. The skills associated with researcher-as-instrument are something like that: It takes some specific knowledge of procedures (which we get from training) and some practice in context (which we get from experience) to be effective. Even highly trained and experienced interpretive researchers must think about their degree of membership in a social setting to develop good claims and evidentiary support for their claims.

Degree of Membership

Well-trained, highly experienced researchers are not automatically guaranteed interpretive credibility. One way that interpretive researchers gain credibility is to study social groups to which they already belong. A researcher's **degree of membership** in a social group can provide a number of advantages. First, members can sometimes gain access to the sites of study more easily than can nonmembers (Ellingson, 1998; Lindlof, 1995). Second, members can recognize and enact a range of communicative features, patterns, and practices (and recognize blunders in the enactment of these practices) in ways that nonmembers cannot (Dollar, 1995). Third, members ask different questions about a situation than do nonmembers; but even more importantly, members understand how social relationships and actions are constructed differently than do nonmembers. For example, Ellingson (1998) described how her experience as a cancer survivor shaped her ethnographic research in an oncology clinic and how the research influenced her own understanding of her personal experiences with cancer: "I believe I was more easily trusted and was afforded greater credibility by patients who knew I had survived cancer" (Ellingson, 1998, p. 500). In addition, "I could not have understood it intellectually, I don't think, if I had not experienced it emotionally" (Rothman, 1986, p. 53, as cited in Ellingson, 1998).

However, not everyone agrees that membership status necessarily confers additional credibility on the interpretive researcher. Sometimes, a greater degree of membership can actually blind the researcher to "the peculiarities he is supposed to observe" (Newman & Benz, 1998, p. 59). In that case, using multiple observers whose degree of membership in the situation being studied varies can enrich the data collection and interpretation.

No matter whether you are an insider or an outsider in an interpretive research situation, you will need to make the familiar unfamiliar and vice versa. Fred Davis (1973) described two roles you might take toward what you are studying, the Martian and the Convert. The Martian tries to make everything strange in order to grasp it without imposing his or her own cultural knowledge, whereas the Convert tries to make it all familiar: "To ask questions of, to 'make problematic', to 'bracket' social life requires distance (Martian). To understand, to answer questions, to make sense of social life requires closeness (Convert). The sensitive investigator wishes not to be one or the other but to be *both* or *either* as the research demands" (Lofland & Lofland, 1984, p. 16).

If you have accrued adequate training and experience to be a credible researcher and you have considered the issue of your degree of membership in the situation you are studying, then you are ready to think about the third way that researcher credibility matters when connecting interpretive claims to data—faithfulness.

Faithfulness

To be faithful means to remain constant or steadfast. In interpretive research, **faithfulness** means both doing things right and doing the right things.

As an interpretive researcher, you can demonstrate faithfulness in a number of ways. First and foremost, you will need prolonged engagement in the field or topic of study. When you listen carefully to your research participants over weeks or months of observations or interviews, you are being steadfast. When you wait until participants in a setting know and trust you before choosing key informants or asking them questions, you are being faithful. Each step you take to make careful observations, document and store your field notes, and analyze all the evidence repeatedly, helps to ensure that your interpretations are believable.

A faithful researcher will steadfastly continue to do the right things, even when those things are difficult. Doing your own fieldwork, transcription, filing, coding, and writing are some specific, practical ways that you can practice faithfulness (Miller, Creswell, & Olander, 1998). In textual analysis, identifying your own assumptions about a research topic, setting, or participants at the outset of your research project, and acknowledging your own limitations honestly and forthrightly in terms of yourself as a research instrument, also show faithfulness.

Plausible Interpretations as a Standard for Evaluating Evidence

Because in interpretive research we believe that there are many potentially legitimate interpretations of any social situation, our task is to develop plausible, rather than correct or accurate, interpretations of a situation. In this section, we present three aspects of developing plausible interpretations: adequacy of evidence, coherence, and negative case analysis.

Adequacy of Evidence

Adequacy of evidence refers to the amount of data or evidence that a researcher has collected. "Adequacy is attained when sufficient data have been collected that saturation occurs and variation is both accounted for and understood" (Morse, 1998, p. 76). In interpretive research, you may need to overlap the tasks of data collection and analysis in order to make good decisions about when you have amassed adequate evidence. You will

stop collecting and analyzing interpretive research evidence when the data and interpretations you have accrued are adequate to support your claim(s). There are a couple of tests by which you can determine adequacy.

First, you may elect to exit field data collection when everything in that social situation seems routine and nothing surprises you anymore. Second, you may recognize **theoretical saturation**, when any new data that you collect adds little that is new or useful to the explanation or categories you have already generated (Snow, 1980). Lindlof (1995) advised interpretive field researchers to complete three tasks before quitting field data collection. The tasks were to check out questionable hunches, evaluate the credibility of informants, and settle any "outstanding moral and material debts to informants and others . . . leave on good terms" (Lindlof, 1995, p. 242). All of these tasks will help you to ensure that you will have collected adequate evidence to elicit plausible interpretations of participants' talk and action. The last one will help you proceed ethically when exiting a field setting.

Accordingly, if you are conducting rhetorical analysis of texts, such as a number of speeches from one political candidate, you can apply these same tests: Are your understandings of the candidate's persuasive strategies being challenged by considering any additional speeches? Does another theoretic concept add anything substantive to your analysis? If the answer to either of these questions is affirmative, then you have not yet have achieved adequacy. If you have adequate evidence, then you will need to consider the coherence of your interpretations.

Coherence

The concept of coherence, defined as internally consistent logic in interpretive research, has gradually replaced a concept that was more directly linked to discovery research, that of internal validity. In early interpretive research studies, the notion of internal validity was the way we thought about the worth of participant observations and textual criticism. It meant accuracy within one study, just as internal validity is practiced in discovery paradigm research. Gradually though, in light of their commitments to multiple realities and subjectivities, interpretive researchers have moved away from the idea of accuracy, per se, and moved toward the idea of coherence, instead. Whether you are conducting textual criticism or field interviews and observations, coherent interpretations are supported by clear, logical links between the evidence you examined and your claim(s).

Miles and Huberman (1994) identified some specific steps you might take to achieve coherent interpretations of observational or interview data including noting patterns or themes, clustering similar concepts together, making metaphors, counting, drawing comparisons, subsuming particulars into a general interpretation, and building a logical chain of evidence. Although space limitations prevent us from giving more detailed explanations of each of these techniques, we hope you can see that each one is a way of synthesizing particular bits of data into broader interpretations so that you can convey your detailed understanding of a social situation to people who have not lived in that situation, at that time, or in that place.

For interpretive rhetorical critics, coherence is achieved by presenting the totality of the text to readers and making logical connections between the elements of the evidence. For example, to achieve coherence in narrative criticism, you will need to show logical connections between your interpretations of the story's characters, setting, and plot development (W. R. Fisher, 1987). If your interpretations of the evidence are coherent and if the rhetoric is true to the rhetor (an achievement W. R. Fisher, 1987, called **fidelity**), then your interpretations will be warranted. In narrative criticism, both coherence and fidelity are important standards for evaluating whether rhetoric is socially worthwhile.

Coherence refers to the totality of your interpretive study. You need to identify a good claim, select the right kind of evidence, and give good, logical reasons for the links you are making between your evidence and claim(s). If you have collected adequate evidence and developed a coherent interpretation of the social situation or texts you are analyzing, then you are ready for one final step to ensure plausible interpretations, negative case analysis.

Negative Case Analysis

Negative case analysis is a conscientious search for counterexamples, instances of data that do not fit your categories or interpretations of a social situation or of texts (Lindlof, 1995; S. Jackson, 1986). If examples are found that do *not* fit your interpretations, then you must revise your interpretations to accommodate those data. You have to keep revising until there are no negative cases left: "Ultimately, negative case analysis results in a highly confident statement about a phenomenon" (Lindlof, 1995, p. 240). Admittedly, negative case analysis is used more for interviews and participant-observations than for rhetorical criticism.

In the normal course of interpretive scholarship, you will develop an initial claim using some inductive process. Inductive reasoning involves generalizing from particular cases, whereas deductive reasoning involves "moving from the general to the particular" (Bulmer, 1979, p. 660). In an interpretive research project, you are more likely to operate in an inductive, rather than a deductive, fashion because inductive reasoning will help you "to maintain faithfulness to the empirical data while abstracting and generalizing from a relatively small number of cases" (Bulmer, 1979, p. 661).

Discourse analysts and some rhetorical critics refer to this reasoning process as **analytic induction.** Sally Jackson (1986) outlined the method of analytic induction in her essay titled "Building a case for claims about discourse structure." Start by collecting several examples of the communication phenomena or practice that you want to study. As you gather examples, try to work from each one's specific features or properties to some more general account of them, as a set. Call this more general account your claim, or hypothesis. "The method of analytic induction requires that empirical claims be tested through active, procedurally diverse search for counter-examples. (Jackson, 1986, p. 129).

For ethnographers and ethnomethodologists, negative case analysis, the deliberate search for examples that do not fit the hypothesis, is a way to evaluate interpretations developed in the field while collecting and analyzing participant observations, interviews, and field notes. Negative case analysis helps you know when you need to collect additional data to back up or test some of your early interpretations. For discourse analysts, the search for counterexamples is a more central aspect of data analysis rather than a standard used to warrant its worth (Jacobs, 1990; Pomerantz, 1990). For interpretive rhetorical critics, negative case analysis consists of attempts to locate texts that demonstrate a different, though equally plausible interpretation, and may consist of the critic's efforts to demonstrate how different interpretations of the same text are warranted. If your interpretations are credible, and there are no negative cases that seem to threaten them, then you are ready to consider how your interpretations might shed light on communication in another setting or situation.

Transferable Findings as a Standard for Evaluating Evidence

One final test of the worth of interpretive research is its **transferability:** Can insights from one study be used to help understand communication in other settings, with other participants, or different texts? Transferability is related to, but not the same as, generalizability, a concept used in discovery paradigm research. In discovery research, a study is generalizable if the sample selected adequately represents the population of interest (Kerlinger, 1986). If a data sample well represents the population, then findings based on a small sample of participants or messages can be accurately applied to all those people or messages that were not studied but that belong to the same population. Because of the contextual nature of the communication studied by interpretive scholars, "... the move to generalize in the traditional sense is neither warranted nor particularly desirable" (Lindlof, 1995, p. 238).

Transferability, then, is less direct than generalizability. It means that an interpretive insight is heuristic, or useful in some other way, even though it cannot be directly applied to another setting or with other participants. For an interpretive insight to be of use in some other setting, or with other texts or participants, it must be both confirmable in the original study and relevant to the setting or people where you want to apply it. We describe each of these aspects of transferability in more detail below.

Confirmability

Because you will presume multiple subjective realities when doing interpretive research, you'll be seeking interpretations that are confirmable, rather than accurate, per se. Later in this chapter, you will learn much more about the discovery paradigm researcher's quest for accuracy. Here, we will introduce you to member checks and audit trails, two strategies you can use to establish confirmability in your interpretive research project.

Member checks involve allowing your research participants to review some or all of the materials that you have prepared such as field notes, interview transcripts, and narrative research reports. In this way, the participants can verify (or modify) the interpretations that you have attributed to them in the course of doing your fieldwork (Janesick, 1998; Lindlof, 1995; Miles & Huberman, 1994; Strauss & Corbin, 1998). The people who participate in member checks need not be key informants or people with whom you have had any prolonged engagement. Member checks can be informal, even spontaneous. For example, you might complete member checks with people who have been, up until that point, insiders to the culture but outsiders to the

research project (Lindlof, 1995). However, consistent with the interpretive researcher's value of subjectivity, "no participant is a dispassionate, fully informed member of his or her culture. A person's alliances and passions about certain things, and disinterest about others, surely affect what he or she can authenticate" (Lindlof, 1995, p. 241).

Carbaugh (1988) used **performance tests**, another form of member checking when he conducted participant observations and interviews at a television station and developed interpretations about how the employees there viewed themselves and their workplace. He tried out his interpretations by returning to the scene and using the categories (types of persons, like *paper-pusher*) that he had developed while talking with the employees. Then he would take note of their reactions to his usage of those terms. For example, if the employees affirmed Carbaugh's (1988) usage or if there was no indication that the employee disagreed with the terms, he considered his interpretations confirmed.

Douglas (1976) used the term **fronting** to describe participants' attempts to avoid telling the whole truth when being interviewed. Fronting includes not only telling outright lies but also half-truths, evading answering a question, and so on. The term comes from a dramatistic metaphor in which those aspects of a situation that can be seen by an audience are considered front stage. Other aspects, also important to the situation, are not seen by the audience and so are referred to as backstage (Goffman). Fronting is most likely in public settings with people who have or want power; in those situations, fronting can help participants to maintain face or accomplish ulterior motives, like to thwart or to please the researcher (Lindlof, 1995).

Obviously, fronting is a concern in performing member checks, just as it can be a concern in conducting interviews in the first place. Interview participants use fronting to deceive researchers and themselves. But fronting can give you valuable clues toward understanding the participant's world, if you see it occur (Van Maanen, 1988). So fronting is not a threat to your ability to develop plausible interpretations. Rather, fronting adds a layer of complexity in understanding your participants' subjective realities. You may detect fronting when performing member checks, or it may be just a suspicion that you log into field notes and that later develops into part of an interpretation about the communication in that setting. Such notes will be useful later only if you maintain a careful audit trail.

An **audit trail** is your best way of documenting the development and progress of your interpretive research study. It is important because of the massive quantity of data that is generated in interpretive research: Without the audit trail, you may end up with a warehouse of information of which no sense can be made. Notes from participant observations and interviews, plus expanded accounts, journal entries, analysis, and interpretation notes, all need to be retrievable as you write up your interpretive research report. You may have encountered ethical problems, for example, and want to write about your response to those problems later (Spradley, 1980). Carefully documenting the conceptual development of a project helps you retrace your steps when reporting how your interpretations were developed. You won't be able to back up your claims with evidence if you can't remember where you got a certain interpretation.

A good audit trail also provides evidence that interested parties (like your research methods teacher) can use to reconstruct the process by which you reached your conclusions. An audit trail consists of several types of documentation including (1) raw data; (2) data reduction and analysis products like category lists or classification schemes; (3) data reconstruction and synthesis products, like models or theoretic frameworks; (4) process notes related to the setting, including permission agreements with participants; (5) materials relating to your own intentions and dispositions; and (6) instrument development information such as interview guides (Y. S. Lincoln & Guba, 1985; Miles & Huberman, 1994; Morse, 1998). Your audit trail also will help you document the relevance of specific interpretations should you want to argue **transferability** (i.e., how those interpretations matter in some other setting, with other participants or texts).

Relevance

For an interpretive finding to be transferable, it must be confirmable in the original setting or text and relevant to the setting or text in which its insight is expected to contribute. This kind of relevance involves a translation of sorts: "A translation discovers the meanings in one culture and communicates them in such a way that people with another cultural tradition can understand them" (Spradley, 1980, p. 161). It is possible for you to do a good job of discovering cultural meanings but a bad job of communicating those meanings to another audience. If so, you may not be able to use the insights from your study in their own communicative worlds.

If you look back at Table 2.2, "Defining Assumptions of the Epistemological Paradigms," you can see why the warrants for each paradigm are different. Discovery paradigm arguments about cause-and-effect relationships that exist as one knowable reality rest on concerns for accurate and consistent links between claims and data (i.e., validity and reliability, respectively). Interpretive paradigm arguments about participants' multiple realities depend on the researcher's credibility to provide plausible interpretations that are relevant and are transferable to other situations, participants, or texts. Critical paradigm arguments about the value of particular rhetoric, or the need for ideological change, also assume multiple socially constructed realities. But critical scholars emphasizes how those realities are shaped by the knowers' social, political, economic, ethnic, gender, and ability standpoints. Critical scholars also view research as revelatory, revealing hidden structures of oppression and instigating social change. If you want to evaluate and change communication, based on your standpoint, then you will want to link your claims and data using the values, form of argument, and standards associated with the critical paradigm.

Critical Paradigm Warrants

The earliest critical communication studies were ideological critiques based on unobtrusively collected textual data. So the warrants for critical communication research proceed from, and add to, interpretive paradigm warrants. Today, there also are many *studies of communicative action based on ideological critique* (e.g., Bajali, 2011; de Turk, 2012; Geraghty & Velez, 2011; Groscurth, 2011). The warrants for those studies depend on the evidence you use to support your claim. Let's start with ideological critique.

In making claims of evaluation and ideological reform, your subjective evaluations and criticisms of the text (or other evidence on which your claims are based), are desirable and valuable. If other people disagree with your evaluations or ideas about what social practices ought to be changed, they are free to resist those ideas in a variety of ways or ignore them altogether. Thus, when you provide an ideological critique, you will warrant your analysis by establishing a coherent argument while acknowledging your subjective position as the researcher and other people's freedom to disagree with your point of view. You also may want to consider whether your critique will change anyone's awareness of oppression or their communicative practices.

When you conduct a study of communicative action informed by an ideological evaluation, you still have to establish a coherent argument, acknowledge your subjective position as a researcher and other people's freedom to disagree. But you also must demonstrate your credibility as a researcher, show how your interpretations are plausible, and indicate the degree to which your key findings are transferable to other groups or settings (e.g., Barge, 2004). If your critique rests on generalizable evidence from surveys or some kind of statistical data, then you may need to show that those data were accurately and consistently measured, too.

In the next sections, we'll outline some general ways to establish coherence, acknowledge subjectivity and freedom of choice, and gauge the likelihood of your study contributing to any change! When you conduct your own critical study, you probably will want to refer to the later chapters on rhetorical criticism and critical studies if you are doing ideological evaluation and critique. If you are doing a critical empirical study of communicative action, you can refer to the chapters on content analysis, ethnographic research, or discourse analysis for specific advice on how to warrant your claims. Before we consider the standards that link claims to evidence, let's look at the values and forms of argument used for critical studies.

Emancipatory Values: Voice and Liberation

Two values undergird the methodology of critical studies in communication: voice and liberation. **Voice** is related to participation and existence in a democratic society. One of the ways that we participate is by making our voice heard. If our voice is never heard, it's as though we don't exist. Because critical scholars value voice, we ask such questions as "Who can and cannot speak here? What is said and not said here? Who benefits?" (Littlejohn & Foss, 2005).

In addition to voice as an issue of democratic communication process, voice also is a way of "giving an account of oneself" (Butler, 2005). If our group has a voice in matters of public policy, or media representations, for example, then we can represent our own interests, rather than having someone else determine and represent those interests.

Thus, making our voice heard is the first step toward liberation, which can be defined as the "securing of equal social and economic rights" (Guralnik, 1986, p. 814). Instead of **liberation**, we could use the word emancipate, which means "to set free, release from bondage, or from constraint" (Guralnik, 1986, p. 455). Critical scholars aim to give voice to people who are underrepresented in the current societal discourse and to liberate those people from the bonds of ideological oppression (i.e., liberation through awareness). The claims and evidence of critical scholarship are evaluated by considering the researcher's subjective position in relation to the topic, the readers' freedom to disagree, and the coherence of the researcher's argument, and the likely impact of the critique (will anything really change). The basic form of argument used in this research is to evaluate communication, and in some cases, to argue the need for ideological change.

Form of Argument: Demonstrating Ideological Need for Change

Critical studies emphasize evaluative and reformist claims. So the basic argument made in critical studies is to evaluate some communication practice or structure, and sometimes, argue the need to change an existing ideology. **Ideology** is "a set of ideas that structure a group's reality . . . a code of meanings governing how individuals and groups see the world" (Littlejohn & Foss, 2005, p. 318). Ideologies greatly influence communication practices and structures, after all. Awareness of a need to change, or perhaps dissatisfaction with some present view or circumstance, is the first precursor to change itself. In critical cultural studies, ideological change often begins with efforts to raise awareness of unjust power relations (e.g., Nakayama & Martin, 1999; Pearce, 1998; Puhl, Luedicke, & Heuer, 2013; Trethewey, 2001).

Hegemony occurs "when events or texts are interpreted in a way that promotes the interests of one group over those of another" (Littlejohn & Foss, 2005, p. 319). Thus, the basic form of argument for critical communication research is to demonstrate the ideological need for change, due to hegemonic oppression, and to assert that all members of a society should share equal rights and privileges (Gramsci, 1971; Lears, 1985). To argue the need for ideological change, critical scholars highlight such factors as the stability of the dominant ideology. If the dominant code of meanings (or worldview) is very stable, then power relations are heavily entrenched and resistant to change. If there are already competing ideologies at work in a social situation, then multiple interpretations of power relations, and change, may be more likely (see deTurk, 2011, or Johnson, 2010 for examples of this line of argument).

In fact, *ideological critique* works to surface conflicts of interest within a particular ideology and may destabilize that ideology (Deetz, 2005). Nakayama and Martin's (1999) book, *Whitensss: The communication of social identity* is one such critique, as is M. S. Kim's (1999) critique of the Western view of communication avoidance as a deficiency in communication competence. Nakayama and Martin's critique raised awareness of white privilege, whereas M. S. Kim's essay raised awareness of oppression based on White, Western norms. Both essays encouraged change in a familiar and relatively stable ideology among US Americans. To elaborate, M. S. Kim pointed out that the motivation to approach, rather than avoid, communicating with others (and thus asserting oneself), has been privileged by Western theorizing and research due to a philosophical bias toward individualism. That bias privileges assertiveness over avoidance. For instance, students in US classrooms are taught that they must speak up to get what they need and that if they do not speak out, then the fact that their needs may be overlooked is, at least in part, their own fault (Bolkan & Goodboy, 2013). That advice privileges individualist cultural norms and may oppress speakers whose practices are more collectivist.

Coherence as a Standard for Evaluating Evidence

Arguing the need for ideological change requires you to show that there is a stable, dominant ideology at work in a particular context. You will have to make clear and logical connections between the social situation and your claims, just as you would do in interpretive research. You must show how that particular ideology privileges some people in the context and disadvantages others, or how people in that context are willingly adopting behaviors that violate their own self-interests (i.e., hegemonic relations). Thus, the first standard by which your critical study will be evaluated is **coherence**, the degree to which your arguments are logical, consistent, and intelligible to others.

In this sense, coherence serves to warrant all communication research. But the ways that we demonstrate coherence depend on our claims. For example, if you are using numerical data to argue that a particular ideology is dominant and stable (e.g., national average

salary differences between male and female workers in a particular industry; retention or graduation rates for students from different racial or socioeconomic groups), then you must be sure that the numbers you cite were measured accurately and consistently (discovery paradigm warrants). If your evidence for ideological domination comes from the subjective views of people in a particular time, place, and social group, then you must show that you have the credibility to represent those views well, how those interpretations are plausible, and how they might provide useful insights for other similar cases (interpretive paradigm warrants).

However, there is one important difference in the way we evaluate coherence for interpretive and critical studies. Interpretive researchers focus on making consistent, thought through links between their evidence and claims. But critical researchers always ask, "Consistent for *whom*?" Critical paradigm thinking begins with evaluation, the assumptions of hegemony, power relations at work; so critical scholars assume that what is coherent to the dominant group members will be different than what appears most apparent, reasonable, or logical to members of a marginalized group (Lears, 1985).

Let's consider how you can achieve coherence in your critical study, depending on whether you are conducting ideological critique as an end in itself or whether you are offering an ideological critique in conjunction with an empirical study of communicative action.

If you are conducting an ideological critique based exclusively on a review of previously published research and application of a theory to a specific social situation or case, then you will be presenting your own view as a researcher rather than the perspective of the people in that social situation. You will need to make clear connections between the studies you review and the theoretic concepts you believe best describe that situation. If your description or evaluation of the previous research, the theory, or the social situation you aim to critique is unclear, others will not be able to recognize your argument. If your argument is clear but filled with internal contradictions, others will not be persuaded by your argument. If you make a clear and logical argument about how prior research and theory can be used to describe or evaluate ideology in a situation, others are of course, "free to accept or reject the argument" (Fink & Gantz, 1996, p. 119).

Sometimes, your critical study will aim to critique an existing ideology using empirical evidence of communicative action in a specific context. In that case, you may be a member in that social setting, and/or you may use participant observations and member interviews, artifact analysis, or even survey data to inform your argument about hegemonic relations. If you use empirical evidence of communicative action to show how a dominant, stable ideology privileges some members and disadvantages other members in the situation, then you can apply the warrants from the interpretive or discovery paradigm as standards for evaluating how well your evidence supports or refutes your claims. If you used participant observations or interviews with members, then you will want to outline your membership in the context you studied and/or how your participation in that situation over a long period of time makes you able to legitimately represent those participants' perspectives. You may also want to show how the phrasing and vocabulary used by members of different groups in that context privileges the values or ends of one group over another. If you use survey data to show how an ideology privileges a certain portion of the people (e.g., demographic information comparing salaries for men and women in a given industry), then you'll need to be sure that the variables were accurately and consistently measured and that the sample represented the population to which you wish to generalize those findings.

Whether your critical study represents your own views or the views of people in a particular social situation, your position as a researcher is another important standard for evaluating the worth of your study. Let's consider that standard next.

Researcher Positionality as a Standard for Evaluating Evidence

Because critical scholars value voice and liberation, they place great emphasis on their own subjective positions in relation to the topics that they elect to study. We use the term **researcher positionality** to include both the researcher's standpoint and his or her reflexivity. Let's next consider each of these terms.

Standpoint theory "argues that the material, social, and symbolic circumstances of a social group shape what members of that group experience, as well as how they think, act, and feel" (Wood, 1997, p. 384). Your standpoint as a researcher will affect the topics you believe are worthy of study, the views of a topic you elect to present or to ignore, and the kinds of evaluation you offer, or the reforms you want to effect. Our standpoints depend on our membership in various social groups

because what we see of the world depends on where we are standing as we view it. For example, "standpoint logic would suggest that whites are less likely than people of color to recognize the continuing legacy of racism and discrimination" because people of color have conscious experiences of being discriminated against, whereas White people living in the United States have likely benefited from racism in ways that are invisible, or unexamined (Wood, 1997, p. 255).

Yep's (1997) essay, "My Three Cultures: Navigating the Multicultural Identity Landscape," described his standpoint as an "Asianlatinoamerican":

> Although I have never been to China, I am racially what my parents describe as "100% pure Chinese." During my formative years, we lived in Peru, South America and later moved to the United States. . . . I am trilingual (English, Spanish, Chinese), and I speak all three languages with a slight accent. I used to be concerned about the accent in my speech, but in recent years I have adopted a different attitude: My accent might simply be an indication that I probably speak more languages than my conversational partner. (p. 43)

All three of Yep's (1997) cultural memberships, "Asianlatinoamerican," contribute to his standpoint, which he views as connected and unified, although not "necessarily harmonious and free of tension" (p. 54). Yep's (1997) awareness of how each culture contributes to his thoughts, actions, and feelings in communicating with others, and to his scholarship, is called reflexivity.

Reflexivity is the process by which researchers recognize that they are inseparable from the settings, contexts, and cultures they are attempting to evaluate and/or change. Critical scholars use reflexivity to question their own interpretations and representations of social situations (e.g., Groscurth, 2011; May & Pattillo-McCoy, 2000; Nakayama & Krizek, 1995).

Quite often, critical scholars will consider one particular social situation or one case in which they have some intrinsic interest. "Perhaps the simplest rule for method in qualitative casework is this: Place the best brains available into the thick of what is going on. The brainwork ostensibly is observational, but more basically, reflective" (Stake, 1998, p. 99). If you are considering a particular case in which you have some interest, reflexivity becomes very important. For instance, you might select a case of "some typicality, but leaning toward those cases that seem to offer *opportunity to learn*" (Stake, 1998, p. 101). Once you select a particular case to study, sampling people, places, and events to observe within that case is also a factor on which you should reflect. Here, variety, rather than representativeness per se, should guide your selection decisions. The primary criterion is the opportunity to learn (Frey, 1994a; Stake, 1998). For example, Frey (1994a) urged communication researchers to study underresearched populations and groups because they offer an opportunity to learn something that is not represented in existing published communication research.

In fact, during the end of the last century, some communication researchers actually referred to their work as *critical-interpretive* research (e.g., Deetz, 1982; Scheibel, 1994, 1996, 1999). Today, it is not uncommon to see published studies labeled "critical discourse analysis" or "critical ethnography," where the word "critical" suggests that the work bridges the assumptions and warrants of the critical and interpretive paradigms. You will learn more about rhetorical and critical studies in Chapters 9 and 10.

Change in Awareness and Praxis as a Standard for Evaluating Evidence

Providing coherent arguments about hegemonic realities, arguments that are reflexively linked to your standpoint, will help make others aware of ineffective communication and/or oppression, and can help to establish the need for social change. In fact, some early critical paradigm studies, especially those from the Frankfort School in Germany after World War II, were based on the hope that describing and evaluating oppressive ideologies would reduce their power. The idea was that people who were formerly unaware of their privilege or oppression would, once made aware, begin to make different, more equitable choices. But in fact, raising awareness of hegemonic realities sometimes has the opposite effect: Awareness can make people in the dominant group dig in to preserve their power! For example, awareness of gender and racial oppression has led to terms like political correctness becoming part of ordinary language use in the United States. Speakers who are accused of being "PC" are charged with acting more respectful of someone else's social category memberships than they really feel inside. They may act respectful as a strategy for preserving their own power.

The 2008 meeting of the International Association for Communication (ICA) was organized around the theme of *Communicating for Social Impact*, which then-President Patrice Buzzanell intended to represent ". . . the ways in which many ICA members questioned how we, as a discipline, meet society's most significant challenges" (Buzzanell, 2009, p. vii). Those challenges include designing and delivering equitable health care, creating "technologies and virtual communication processes that enhance collaboration among nations and multinational and multidisciplinary teams," (p. viii), improving learning in science, technology, engineering, and math (STEM) education, and understanding human impacts on climate change, among others.

The fact that dominant power holders can entrench themselves further as awareness of their power grows, and our field's increased attention to communicating for social impact led us to emphasize changes in *awareness and praxis* as a standard for evaluating critical studies. Praxis is one of the three types of knowledge described by Aristotle. **Praxis** deals with the use of theoretical knowledge in social action. If a critical study changes how you think about an oppressive ideology, that's one level of success. But if research contributes to people communicating differently or acting in ways that contribute to a more just world for all, then it may be even more valuable. "Deconstruction of everyday and societal discourses can inform the reconstruction of more appropriate and feasible changes" (Buzzanell, 2009, p. ix).

Desire for change in praxis drives some critically minded scholars to prioritize activist work over publishing in academic journals or presenting at professional association meetings. Of course, some people combine activist and scholarly projects (see Frey & Carragee, 2007, for examples). Those combined efforts contribute to academic knowledge. But their main focus is on helping people in particular contexts to use theoretic knowledge to accomplish actions that change social structures, laws and policies, and norms of interaction. Service learning projects and volunteering are two ways that you can participate in changing both awareness and praxis. If you are writing an ideological critique or a critical empirical essay, then you can help establish changes in praxis by suggesting ways that your readers can use what they learn from your study to communicate differently, and to resist hegemonic structures, policies, and norms. Efforts to change oppressive ideologies "work between a focus on individual-level change and shifts in social structures" (Dutta & Harter, 2009, p. 4). So your suggestions may also address how people can work together to change broad social structures through their collective actions.

Discovery Paradigm Warrants

Recall from Chapter 2 that the discovery paradigm has its origins in the philosophical traditions of rationalism and empiricism (Corman, 2005). Rationalism emphasizes "a common reality on which people can agree" (Newman & Benz, 1998, p. 2), whereas empiricism is about knowing and explaining using sensory data. Therefore, the warrants for discovery paradigm studies necessarily address issues of agreement and the values of precision and accuracy. In the next section, we describe and illustrate three scientific values. We will then show you the basic form of scientific argument, the attempt to demonstrate causality. Finally, we'll conclude this chapter by outlining two standards for evaluating evidence in discovery research, namely, validity and reliability.

Scientific Values: Precision, Power, and Parsimony

You can use alliteration to remember the scientific values embraced within the discovery paradigm. Just remember the three *P*s—precision, power, and parsimony. These values will guide your discovery research project from start to finish, starting with the way that you frame research questions and hypotheses, to the type of data and how you collect it, the strategies you use to analyze those data, and of course, the procedures you use to estimate how well that data supports the research claim.

Precision refers to detailed accuracy in defining and measuring communication variables. Precise definitions specify what the concept is and what it is not. Precise measurements are informative because they show how a variable can be differentiated from other variables. Precision also connotes agreement. For example, you may think that your research methods teacher talks too fast during class lectures. But what does that mean, precisely? A rate of speaking that is too fast for one student may be perfectly acceptable to another student. You could count the number of words your teacher speaks in 60 seconds: A teacher who speaks 80 words per minute is speaking faster than a teacher who speaks 50 words per minute. A group of 40 students could probably agree on a range of words per minute that is too fast for comprehension or for note-taking purposes. Of course, a number of other factors would be relevant to this evaluation of speaking rate, such as clear enunciation by the

teacher and the listeners' prior exposure to the topics, as well as listener motivation and skill levels. The point is that discovery communication research aims for descriptions that are precise and that are likely to be agreed on by more than one person. In discovery research, we also value precision because we use numerical data; math demands precision.

The second value embraced in discovery communication research is power. In statistical analyses, **power** refers to the ability of a test to detect effects, if they exist. Statistical power is related to, but much more specific than, the discovery paradigm value of power. As a value, power refers to discovery researchers' preference for broadly applicable definitions, data selection techniques, and research findings. The analogy of a flashlight provides a good way to start thinking about this value.

A flashlight is more powerful when it shines a brighter light on a larger area of darkness. In the same way, conceptual and operational definitions are more powerful when they capture more detail or the broadest aspects of a concept than when they capture less detail or only very narrow aspects of a concept. Likewise, data selection techniques that better represent the population under study are considered more powerful because they allow us to generalize from the people or messages we studied to those we did not include in our study. In this way, we can offer a more powerful explanation or description of communication because our account will apply to more people.

The flashlight analogy also helps us to understand the idea behind statistical power by asking, "How likely are we to mistake what we see when we point our flashlight into a dark place?" Under the beam of a weak flashlight, a dusty floor may be mistaken for a clean floor, so if we're looking for dust, the weak flashlight will not be able to detect it! In the same way, when we use a low-power statistical test in discovery research, a small effect may be mistaken for no effect. This mistake is called a type II error, and you will learn much more about in it Chapter 16, "Descriptive Statistics and Hypothesis Testing."

Finally, **parsimony**—the combination of precision and power—is highly valued in discovery research. A parsimonious study of communication is both accurate in detail and covers a broad or important concept. In other words, a parsimonious explanation of communicative behavior or processes offers a bright light in a dark area. Discovery paradigm adherents appreciate data collection and analytic strategies and research studies that say a lot in a succinct way (i.e., that are parsimonious). Likewise, statistical techniques that deal with cause-and-effect explanations of several variables at once (called *multivariate statistics*) are valued in discovery research because they are more powerful and elegant than data analytic techniques that deal with only two or a few variables. This idea of succinctness, or simple elegance, goes beyond our flashlight analogy of making bright a dark area, to privileging succinct descriptions and explanations of many variables and the relationships among them.

Form of Argument: Demonstrating Causality

Causal arguments are the basis of discovery research. However, not all discovery research studies offer full causal accounts of communication phenomena. Most survey researchers only argue that variables are associated with one another. But even those studies are concerned, at least in part, with cause-and-effect reasoning.

In scientific notation, X is used to denote the cause, and Y is used to denote the effect. Three types of evidence are needed to support a causal argument, the idea that "X causes Y." The three types of evidence are (1) time order, (2) covariation, and (3) control over rival hypotheses. All three are required to demonstrate causality (Cook & Campbell, 1979). Table 6.1 defines each type of evidence.

The best way to demonstrate causality is to use a true experimental design, a strategy that you will learn about in Chapter 14, "Experimental Research." Experimental designs provide evidence that can be used to test the claim "X causes Y." In experimental research, we want to show that variable X, and not some other factor, is the best possible explanation for variable Y. So the main function of an experimental design is to control for extraneous influences on X, the hypothesized causal variable.

Table 6.1 Evidence Needed to Support a Causal Argument

Time order: X changed (or occurred) before Y changed (or occurred).

Covariation: When X changed (or occurred), Y also changed (or occurred).

Control over rival hypotheses: Change in (or occurrence of) X is the best possible explanation for the change in (or occurrence of) Y.

Note: All three types of evidence are required to argue causality.

Experimental research designs address standard rival hypotheses, which are competing explanations about the cause of Y. You will learn much more about rival hypotheses in Chapter 14. Thus, experimental research fits well the values of the discovery paradigm. When you conduct an experiment, you are not interested in developing your subjective interpretations of an event, nor do you offer evaluations of communicative practices. Instead, careful explanation and prediction are your goals in doing communication research.

Causal claims are constructed in the form of hypotheses and research questions. As you know from Chapter 4, "Making Claims," hypotheses are declarative statements that predict what effects a causal variable will have if that variable is manipulated. Research questions, worded in interrogative form, are concerned with how variables can be classified or with covariation between variables, which is one part of making a causal argument. There are two basic conditions for causal explanations—necessity and sufficiency. Let's look at each of these conditions next.

A cause is necessary if the effect that occurs when it is present cannot occur when it is absent. Necessary conditions *must* be present for the effect to occur. As the old saying goes, you can't win the lottery if you don't buy a ticket! Buying a ticket is a necessary condition for winning the lottery. However, a cause is sufficient when it is the best possible explanation for the effect under study. Buying a ticket is a necessary, but in most cases insufficient, condition for winning the lottery. For discovery researchers, it is most satisfying to discover a cause that is both necessary *and* sufficient, although it is satisfying to show that a cause is either sufficient or necessary to produce the hypothesized effect.

We evaluate the merit of causal and associative arguments using two standards of evidence: **validity** (accuracy) and **reliability** (consistency). We will define and illustrate each of these standards in the next two sections.

Validity as a Standard for Evaluating Evidence

The discovery researcher's quest for accuracy, or valid research findings, rests on the assumption of *one* observable reality. Just as consistent measurement within each study (and replication across studies), is prized in discovery research, so too are discovery researchers concerned with validity in each study, and across studies. Efforts to assure **internal validity** warrant the precise and factually accurate measurement of variables within one research study. Efforts to assure **external validity** warrant the precision and accuracy of applying conclusions from one study to other people or messages or in another setting.

Valid measurement is accurate, so valid measuring instruments measure precisely what they claim to measure. A valid household scales will report the weight of that 5-pound bag of flour at precisely 5 pounds, not 5.1 pounds or 4.9 pounds. If the scale is both valid and reliable, it will register precisely 5 pounds every time that same bag of flour is placed on the scale. Good measuring instruments have to be both valid and reliable, both accurate and consistent. But it is possible for a measuring instrument to be consistently inaccurate (i.e., reliable, not valid). If a measuring instrument is accurate, it should also be consistent.

Before we look at the different ways to demonstrate internal and external validity, let's consider the problem of inaccurate measurement caused by bias.

Bias: A Threat to Accurate Measurement

Bias is a constant source of error in measurement. When bias is present, it is impossible to accurately measure anything. You are probably familiar with the idea of bias. You may have thought, for example, "My math teacher is biased against communication majors." Your math teacher may be unable to accurately measure your performance in class if he or she is biased against communication majors. In the same way, measuring instruments that are contaminated by bias do not accurately measure communication variables. In discovery research, we are trained to guard against several standard biases, which we sometimes refer to collectively as *rival hypotheses*. For example, biased findings may result from selecting only a particular type of research participants. Or bias may result from participants reacting to the researcher's personal attributes (e.g., age, race, sex). As we mentioned earlier in this chapter, you will learn about a number of rival hypotheses in Chapter 14, "Experimental Research." For now, it is enough to know that bias, or systematic patterns of constant error, threaten accuracy of measurement. Let's consider some ways that you can ensure that your measurements are accurate, or free from bias.

Types of Measurement Validity

Measurement validity refers only to the accuracy of measurement within one study. In this section, we introduce you to four types of measurement validity:

(1) content validity, (2) face validity, (3) criterion-related validity, and (4) construct validity.

Content validity. The most basic form of measurement accuracy is content validity, which means that the items that make up a measuring instrument cover "a representative sample of the behavior domain to be measured" (Anastasi, 1976, p. 135). If you created a measure of teachers' persuasive strategies, for example, and you only included antisocial strategies like threats, punishment, and embarrassment, your measure would lack content validity because it would not represent the prosocial persuasive strategies teachers sometimes use such as praise, encouragement, and rewards. A measuring instrument with high content validity precisely captures the full richness of the concept it was designed to measure. Instruments that capture more inclusively the broadest meanings of a concept are considered richer and more powerful in discovery research. And, as we mentioned earlier in this chapter, statistical power helps us to locate and explain even weak effects of X on Y. But conceptual power attained via high content validity allows us to fully capture the complete nature of a variable, which might enable us to explain a range of weak and strong effects on other variables.

One way to make a strong case for content validity is to ask people with considerable training and expertise in your topic area to examine the content of your measure. You might even submit your measure to a **panel of judges**, as Bradford, Meyers, and Kane (1999) did when they asked Latino focus groups to define communication competence from their particularly knowledgeable cultural perspective. Bradford et al. asked the focus group members open-ended questions so that they would define communication competence in their own terms. If Bradford et al. had then created a quantitative measuring instrument on the basis of those focus group discussions they would have made a strong case for having a content-valid measure of communication competence from a Latino cultural perspective.

Face validity. Content validity is closely related to, but not the same thing as, face validity. Whereas content validity refers to what a test *actually* measures, face validity addresses what the test *appears* to measure (Anastasi, 1976). Face validity answers the question, "Does this test *look* valid?" For instance, a measure designed to assess ethnocentricity in young children might work just as well with adults, but if the items appear irrelevant or in sappropriate to the people asked to take the test, the administrators who permit the data collection, or other technically untrained observers, then the measure lacks face validity for use with adults, even though it has good content validity (Anastasi, 1976). Since "a test is valid only for some specific functions with specific groups under specific conditions" (Nunnally, 1972, p. 21), you should assess content and face validity of measurement in every study, not simply report that your measure has been shown valid in previous studies.

It is possible and desirable to establish measurement accuracy in ways that go beyond content and face validity. But the next two types of measurement validity are more complex, and they are not assessed in most discovery research studies. Instead, criterion-related and construct validity typically are considered only when developing a new survey instrument to measure people's attitudes or beliefs. We'll explain what each one is, and give you some examples to show how they work.

Criterion-related validity. If your measure is deemed representative in its content, and appears worthwhile to users, then you might want to ascertain its **criterion-related validity**, that is, its ability "to predict an individual's behavior in certain situations" (Anastasi, 1972, p. 140). If you want to predict attitudinal or behavioral change, then criterion-related validity will strengthen your argument that the data are related to your claim (whether those data support your claim or not). With criterion validity, you will be able to show that your measure accurately predicts participants' scores on another measure, the criterion. Anastasi (1976) pointed out that a "test may be validated against as many criteria as there are specific uses for it" (p. 142). For example, a measure of empathy might be validated against a listening skills test to assess graduating seniors' communication competence; later, the empathy scores could be related to successful job performance as a customer service representative, or to a two-week observational assessment of parenting skills. The same empathy measure could then be validated as a predictor of three different criteria (i.e., communication competence at graduation, in performance of customer service tasks, and in parenting children). These examples show how valuable criterion-related validity can be in proprietary research (i.e., what makes people listen to a certain format of news program or enjoy particular films?).

To assess criterion-related validity, we administer two measuring instruments and use the correlation statistic to assess the degree to which people's scores on the first measure were related to their scores on the second measure, the criterion. If we ask people to respond to the predictor and criterion measures at the same time, we are trying to establish concurrent validity. This is appropriate if we want to diagnose existing trait status (e.g., "Is this person anxious about giving a speech?"). When we administer the predictor measure first, and the criterion measure at a later date, we are trying to establish predictive validity. This is appropriate when we want to predict a future outcome (e.g., "Is this person likely to give a poor speech due to anxiety about the situation?"). It's important to note that the criterion measure against which our new instruments' scores are to be validated must be already established as valid and reliable. The criterion measure could be a self-report, other-report, or behavioral observation measure. Let's briefly consider an example of each type of criterion-related validity from published communication research.

Krcmar and Valkenburg (1999) attempted to establish the *concurrent validity* of two measures of children's moral reasoning. They compared children's responses on a new measure, the Moral Interpretation of Interpersonal Violence Scale, with the responses to a short form of another instrument called the Sociomoral Reflection Measure. Ostensibly, both instruments measure children's moral reasoning. If the results from Krcmar and Valkenburg's new measure had shown a pattern similar to the results from the other test, the new measure would have been established as accurate. Unfortunately, Krcmar and Valkenburg (1999) could only validate portions of the new scale, and they argued that it is likely that the conceptual territories of the two measures have areas that do not overlap.

Practically speaking, when you set out to establish *predictive validity* for a new measure, you'll want to find some way of identifying the communication behaviors or attitudes that are associated with people who are likely to score at the high end of your scale and with people who are likely to score at the low end of your scale. For example, Burgoon, Johnson, and Koch (1998) asked some college students to compare a set of statements that were constructed to reflect a dominance-submission continuum to the one, most dominant person in their circle of friends. Burgoon et al. (1998) then asked a second group of college students to compare the same statements to the one least dominant person in their circle of friends. Ideally, Burgoon et al.'s (1998) measuring instrument should discriminate between the two sets of friends (i.e., people at either end of the dominance-submission continuum). This way of assessing predictive validity is sometimes also called the *known-groups method* because the scales are validated by groups of people known to already possess the construct's characteristics (Smith, 1988, p. 49).

Construct validity. The fourth type of measurement validity is construct validity, which refers to "the extent to which the test may be said to measure a theoretical construct or trait" (Anastasi, 1976, p. 151). A construct is any concept that can be measured using numbers—for example, verbal aggression or communication apprehension. Constructs "do not exist as visible events in daily life. . . . Rather, they represent devices employed to explain forms of behavior" (Nunnally, 1972, p. 31). Traits are psychological predispositions, or ways of thinking, feeling, or behaving that tend to remain the same across time and across different situations.

Construct validity is the strongest way to demonstrate measurement accuracy, and it is the most difficult sort of validity to establish because it includes face, content, and criterion-related validity. "In order to demonstrate construct validity we must show that a test correlates highly with other variables with which it should theoretically correlate, but also that it does not correlate significantly with variables from which it should differ" (Campbell, 1960, as cited by Anastasi, 1976, p. 156). Thus, the processes of convergence and divergence are used to establish construct validity (Anastasi, 1976; Nunnally, 1972). If two concepts are thought to be theoretically related, then the scores obtained from those two measuring instruments should converge, or covary. Likewise, when two things are unrelated in theory, the scores obtained from measuring those concepts should diverge; they should be unrelated. Together, the processes of convergence and divergence provide a thorough conceptual analysis that Campbell and Fiske (1959) called a "multitrait, multimethod matrix": Two or more variables are assessed at the same time, using two or more methods—for example, verbal aggression and communication anxiety can be assessed, each by self-report and by other-report measures. The self-report and other-report measures for each variable should converge, but the ratings for aggression and anxiety should diverge, whether by self-report or other-report. Assessing these complementary processes of convergence and divergence is sometimes called discriminant validity.

Because the process of establishing construct validity is complex and difficult, and because many communication researchers have moved away from the study of psychological traits, we do not often see attempts to establish construct validity in communication journals. For that reason, we only define construct validity here. We suggest that you ask your instructor for resources if you need to learn more about it, or if you are trying to establish construct validity for your own trait measure.

All four ways of establishing internal validity (content, face, criterion, and construct validity) refer to the accuracy of measurement within a single research study. If you measure variables accurately, and you want to generalize your findings to a population of people or messages that goes beyond your sampled data, then you'll need to confirm that your study also has external validity. External validity is the topic of the next section.

External Validity

External validity refers to the accuracy of applying conclusions from one research study to another setting, another group of people, or other messages. The most common way this happens in discovery communication research is when we want to apply the results from one sample of people or messages to an entire population. For example, election pollsters survey a few hundred people to predict the likely voter behavior of millions of people. When you want to generalize from a data sample to the whole population, external validity is a very important concern.

But researchers also sometimes wonder about **ecological validity**, the degree to which it is accurate to apply the results from one study to the same people in a different setting (e.g., politeness at work, school, home). Ecological validity is a special form of external validity that is of most concern in laboratory research because we know that participants may behave differently in the laboratory setting than they behave when they are not participating in a research study. The laboratory offers the researcher control over important features of the setting and communication situation, but that control can reduce ecological validity.

As a general rule, tighter control over the variables of interest increases internal validity, but that usually comes at the cost of external validity. So even though a study may have excellent internal validity, it could be inaccurate to apply the conclusions from that study to people, messages, or settings beyond those included in the study. If the data for a study do not represent the larger population because there was some form of bias in the selection of research participants or messages, then external validity will be threatened. If the setting in which the data were collected somehow biased the participants' responses, then ecological validity is similarly threatened. In either case, the findings from that study may be accurate, but it would not be accurate to apply those findings elsewhere.

Now that you know four ways to establish measurement validity, let's consider the standard of consistency, or reliability.

Reliability as a Standard for Evaluating Evidence

Discovery paradigm researchers value studies that are replicable: Their procedures and findings can be verified when the study is repeated by another researcher or with different participants in a different setting. If your study is to be replicable, then your measurements must be reliable.

Measurement reliability refers to consistency of measurement over time, across settings and participants. Reliable measuring instruments are free from random variations. Remember that 5-pound bag of flour we mentioned earlier? If you have access to a reliable household scale, weigh a 5-pound bag of flour. It should register 5 pounds (accuracy) and it should weigh 5 pounds every single time you weigh it, assuming you don't add or remove any flour. Good measurement is both accurate and consistent, valid and reliable. But on an unreliable household scale, your 5-pound bag of flour may register 4.5 pounds the first time you weigh it, and 4.3 pounds the next time you weigh it. If your household scale is so unreliable, you should never believe the results when you weigh yourself! Likewise, in discovery research, if a measuring instrument does not yield consistent results over time, settings, or participants, then we should not believe the conclusions that instrument leads us to make regarding its relationships with other communication behaviors or attitudes.

Reliability is an ideal in measurement. In practice, we never achieve perfectly consistent measurement because it is impossible to completely eliminate random errors of measurement. Before we spell out all the different ways to show measurement reliability, let's take a closer look at the problem of inconsistent measurement, a problem caused by random sources of error.

Noise: A Threat to Consistent Measurement

Random errors in measurement are sometimes called *noise* because they attenuate measurement reliability the

way that static noise attenuates a radio or telephone signal. When there is too much static noise on your phone, you have trouble hearing the voice of the person you're trying to speak with. Just so, when there are too many random errors in measurement, you'll have trouble capturing the variable you are trying to measure.

Three sources of random error contribute to inconsistent measurement: (1) random individual differences, (2) lack of instrument clarity, and (3) errors in data processing (Smith, 1988). Random individual or situational differences simply mean that every person and situation is unique. People experience transient states of being, such as mood swings, illness, or fatigue. Situational characteristics also vary, such as lighting, temperature, and so on. Since random individual and situational differences cannot be entirely controlled, they threaten our ability to consistently measure a behavior or attitude across different people or situations.

Random measurement errors caused by lack of instrument clarity can come from ambiguously worded questions on a survey questionnaire or in an interview or from unclear instructions to research participants. Either ambiguous questions or unclear instructions might lead participants to respond inconsistently.

Finally, errors in data processing occur when data are being translated from one form to another, usually by human effort. For instance, an error may be committed when entering data from a survey questionnaire into a computer spreadsheet, or when transcribing interview responses from audiotape using a word processor.

All three of these problems—individual or situational differences, lack of instrument clarity, and errors in data processing—result in inconsistent measurement (i.e., they all lower measurement reliability). Now that you know how noise can threaten reliable measurement, let's look at some specific ways that you can assess measurement reliability.

Types of Measurement Reliability

Measurement reliability is estimated in different ways depending on the type of consistency you are trying to achieve (i.e., consistency over time, across participants and settings, between two measures, and across scorers). In this section, we introduce you to four ways of assessing measurement reliability: (1) test-retest method, (2) internal consistency, (3) alternate-forms method, and (4) scorer reliability (Anastasi, 1976; Nunnally, 1972).

Stability of measurement over time is assessed using the **test-retest method**. Stability means that the results obtained by one measuring instrument remain consistent when administered to the same group of participants at a later date. Measures with high test-retest reliability are less susceptible to variations caused by random individual or situational differences (Anastasi, 1976). If you want to assess test-retest reliability, you must carefully consider the time interval between the first and second test administration: Think about the experiences participants have had between tests. Have they "really" changed since the first test? If so, inconsistent scores will be due to their changed attitudes or behaviors rather than to a problem with the measuring instrument itself. Test-retest reliability is used to assess the consistency of behavioral observations and self-report data. It is most appropriate for sensory discrimination and motor skills tests and less appropriate for psychological trait measures because participants taking the test for a second time might simply recall the answer they gave earlier (Anastasi, 1976).

The second form of measurement reliability is **internal consistency** (a.k.a. homogeneity). When we say that a measuring instrument has a high degree of internal consistency, we mean that all of the items used to measure the concept yield consistent responses from research participants. The way to make that happen is to have each item in the measuring instrument refer to the same underlying concept. Internal consistency is demonstrated when scores on one self-report item are similar to scores on the other self-report items that make up a single measuring instrument. Look at Table 11.4, for example: To show the internal consistency of a unidimensional instrument such as the Verbal Aggressiveness Scale, you can evaluate whether participants' responses to Item 1 are similar to their responses for Items 2 and 5 (indicating presence of verbal aggression) and whether responses for Items 3 and 4 are consistent (indicating a lack of verbal aggression). Notice how a lack of instrument clarity, due to ambiguous items or unclear instructions, will threaten internal consistency.

Another way to show internal consistency is to see whether research participants whose scores place them at one end of a variable continuum score similarly to one another, but differently from people at the other end of that same continuum. For example, McCroskey's (1982) Personal Report of Communication Apprehension (PRCA) has been shown to have a high degree of internal consistency across participants and settings: People who are highly anxious tend to respond similarly to one another on each item and differently from people who

are only slightly anxious. Internal consistency is a good way to check the reliability of measurement for self-report and other-report data, especially when we want to measure communicative attitudes and beliefs (a.k.a. psychological trait measures).

The third way to assess measurement reliability is to use the **alternate forms method**, which simply means that we administer two different measuring instruments to the same research participants at the same time, and those two measures yield similar sets of scores. The alternate forms method is sometimes called equivalence, and it is another way to demonstrate the reliability of self-report and other-report data. Both forms of the measuring instrument should be comparable; for instance, they should be about the same difficulty level, have similar time limits and formats (Anastasi, 1972). Alternate forms reliability is most often used by communication researchers when we want to find out whether a shorter version of a test will produce results that are consistent with the longer version of the test. For example, the 24-item PRCA can be compared to a 12-item version of the same test. If the same people are identified as highly anxious (or minimally anxious) on both tests, then we will feel confident using the shorter, more parsimonious version in our research.

Just as we can assess self-report and other-report data for its consistency across time, across participants, and across different measuring instruments, we can also assess scorer reliability, or the consistency of people's judgments about behavioral observations. This kind of reliability is important whenever a test "leaves a good deal to the judgment of the scorer" (Anastasi, 1972, p. 119). So when we categorize participant behaviors that we observe in a field setting, or messages that participants provide to us in open-ended items on a survey questionnaire, we need to verify the consistency of our judgments by having two people independently rate the behaviors (or categorize the messages), correlate those scores, and estimate the degree of error due to different scorer judgments. You can encounter three specific versions of scorer reliability when you read published communication research: (1) interrater reliability, (2) intercoder reliability, and (3) intertranscriber reliability.

Interrater reliability concerns the agreement among either research participants or researchers who rate communication characteristics of a single target (e.g., asking people to rate a person's amount of eye contact as "too little," "about right," or "too much"). *Intercoder reliability* concerns the agreement among two or more researchers who are categorizing messages (e.g., types of compliments). You will learn more about these two specific forms of scorer reliability in Chapters 8 and 12. Finally, *intertranscriber reliability* is demonstrated when two independent transcribers agree about the content of a source audiotape or videotape (Patterson et al., 1996). You will have a chance to practice conducting this kind of reliability assessment in the "Try It!" Activities included with Chapter 8, "Conversation and Discourse Analysis: How to Explain and Interpret Talk."

In the last section of this chapter, we present three views of the truth, as seen by adherents to the interpretive, critical, and discovery paradigm, respectively.

Three Views of Truth

So far in this chapter, we have looked at the values, forms of argument, and standards for evaluating evidence in three paradigms. In a research-as-argument model, the values, form of argument, and standards for evaluating evidence all work together to warrant research. Each paradigm has different warrants, in part, because the very nature of truth itself is viewed differently in each paradigm. Perhaps you already find yourself strongly identifying with one paradigm's view of truth and wanting to reject the other views of truth. We want to present all three paradigms evenhandedly. So we will let the views of truth be represented by authors of published research in each paradigm, starting with the interpretative researchers' view.

Interpretive Paradigm

From the interpretive paradigm perspective, truth is viewed as subjective, although not wholly individual. Rather, some collective truths can be ascertained by social agreement, which may be relatively stable or unstable. Truth is therefore subject to the interpretations of human actors who participate in *and* who conduct academic research. This is one reason interpretive scholars make every effort to include multiple perspectives in their research. As Strauss and Corbin (1998) pointed out, "Perhaps not every actor's perspectives can be discovered, or need be, but those of actors who sooner or later are judged to be significantly relevant must be incorporated" (p. 172).

May and Pattillo-McCoy (2000) addressed this interpretive view of *truth* in their collaborative ethnographic study of a neighborhood community center. "Indeed, most academic writing (primarily journals and books) requires that there be some suggestion that the author is offering the 'truth' about the field he or she studied. What our experience taught us was that there is neither one truth nor one reality" (May & Pattillo-McCoy, 2000, p. 67). These authors emphasized that collaborative ethnography offered them several advantages, such as increasing the amount of detail in their field notes, pointing out inconsistencies, and revealing the subjectivity of each researcher due to background, experience, race, class, gender, and so on. Yet May and Pattillo-McCoy cautioned, "We do not believe that if we just had enough people in the field, then we might have got at some reality that is more true than the one we recorded" (p. 84). Because interpretive researchers view truth as a matter of some social agreement, more agreement does not necessarily equal more truth. Furthermore, what any one researcher or participant sees, at any one moment, in any social setting is bound to look slightly different at another moment in that same setting.

The provisional, temporal nature of interpretive truths is as relevant in rhetorical criticism as it is in field research. For example, Brock et al. (1990) allowed that rhetorical critics adhere to authority and tradition as criteria for evaluating the effectiveness of persuasive appeals *because* the dictates of authority and tradition have already shown themselves to be logical and coherent. Even if a rhetorical scholar rejects a tradition, "she or he will probably do so either because it fails to do what it promises or because the critic appeals to standards that are outside the tradition" (Brock et al., 1990, p. 19). In either case, accepting authority and tradition as guidelines, or rejecting those guidelines for criticism, involves an appeal to subjective truths. So an interpretive paradigm view of truth is one grounded in social agreement at particular times and places.

Critical Paradigm

Communication researchers who embrace the critical and interpretive paradigms tend to agree that no one thing is true for all people, at all times, in all places. However, critical paradigm researchers are more likely to emphasize the idea that truths are subjective and political, or power related. Thus, critical paradigm scholars share with interpretive scholars an acknowledgement of subjectivities. But in critical scholarship, subjectivities always implicate power relationships, privileging some participants and oppressing others (Strauss & Corbin, 1998).

Denzin and Lincoln (1998a) called the idea that there is no one knowable truth a "postmodern sensibility" (p. 9). However, the debate over *truth* is more specific and discrete than whether one knowable truth exists or more than one. S. Thomas (1994) pointed out that the contested meanings in content analysis are not about which messages fit into which categories as warranted by estimates of intercoder reliability. "For instance, if there is a count of words or a coding of characters' hair color, or even noting violent acts (as explicitly defined), few would argue that these measurements alone are sites of contested meaning" (S. Thomas, 1994, p. 693). Rather, what is likely to be contested is whether particular categories should even be counted in a study or whether the distribution of categories means what the researcher thinks it means.

Discovery Paradigm

Adherents to the discovery paradigm agree that truths exist that can be objectively verified. Standard ways of designing research and controlling for rival hypotheses (which are the focus of Chapter 14, "Experimental Research") link discovery research questions and evidence to their truth values (Newman & Benz, 1998). As you already know, validity means that the researcher accurately measures variables and makes appropriate attempts to generalize findings from one study to another setting, group of participants, or messages. To the degree that variables are validly and reliably measured, findings are empirically verified, or confirmed as *true*. So, for discovery researchers, truth is objectively verifiable. It is achieved by accurate, consistent measurement of variables and appropriate, ethical attempts to generalize findings.

Newman and Benz (1998) asserted that "science, as reflected in the scientific method, is the only defensible way of locating and verifying truth" (p. 10). However, science has been the subject of some backlash in recent years. Robert Abelson, a statistics professor at Yale for 42 years, wrote that most of us distrust statistics because someone, probably via the media, has tried to deceive us with statistical claims: "Suspicion of false advertising is fair enough, but to blame the problem on statistics is unreasonable. . . . Rather than mindlessly trashing any and all statements with numbers in them, a more mature response is to learn enough about statistics to distinguish

honest, useful conclusions from skullduggery or foolishness" (Abelson, 1995, p. 1).

The three views of truth that we have outlined in this section correspond to the interpretive, critical, and discovery research paradigms, respectively. The standards for evaluating evidence in each paradigm serve to link evidence to claims, and to assure the audience for research of its worth, given particular values and forms of argument. When we seek to explain the causes and effects of communication attitudes or behaviors, it makes sense that we would value precision, power, and parsimony and that we would warrant our research by demonstrating reliable and valid measurement of variables and by showing how generalization of our findings to a broader population is warranted. In the same way, when we seek to demonstrate multiple realities from the viewpoint of members in a particular social situation, it is practical to value those members' rich, subjective descriptions, to emphasize our credibility as researchers, and to call attention to the plausibility and the transferability of our interpretations as measures of their worth. Likewise, when we aim to evaluate and reform ideologies, valuing voice and liberation, and warranting our coherence and positionality, are important and sensible ways to estimate the worth of our scholarship. No matter what paradigm your research fits into, you must continue to protect the rights of research participants and the community in the process of warranting your communication research.

Summary

In this chapter, we have outlined the third element of the research-as-argument model, the warrants and backing. We cannot begin to include all the backing (i.e., social, cultural, and procedural rules and knowledge) that experienced researchers bring to bear on their assessments of a study's merit. Knowing this, we elected to begin the description of warrants for each epistemological paradigm by presenting some of the values embraced by researchers in that paradigm. We also presented a basic form of argument for each paradigm. Interpretive researchers typically seek to demonstrate multiple realities. Critical researchers seek to evaluate communication and perhaps, to argue the ideological need for change. Discovery researchers typically seek to demonstrate causality, or at least associations between variables.

For each of these three paradigms, we have presented some of the standards by which you can assure the value of your data collection and analytic sources, strategies, and settings. The standards link research claims to evidence, given particular values and forms of argument. Table 6.2, following, summarizes the elements of research warrants in each paradigm.

As you can see by reviewing Table 6.2, in interpretive research, the warrants assure the researcher's credibility as an interpreter of the data, and they also specify when it is and is not appropriate to transfer the results of data analysis from one setting to another. In the critical paradigm, warrants establish the coherence of an ideological critique and reveal the positionality of the researchers, both their standpoint and the degree to which they are reflexive (i.e., aware of their own position as it influences their evaluations). Revealing your own position will allow others to more freely consider the source

and choose to accept or to reject your ideas. Critical paradigm research also may be warranted by the likelihood of changes in awareness or praxis. Finally, in the discovery paradigm, warrants ensure consistent and accurate measurement of variables and accurate attempts to apply the results of data analysis from one study to another group of people or messages.

As we said in Chapter 2, "Three Paradigms of Knowing," backing for any argument rests on a large body of information that clarifies how the warrants are to be understood, applied, and relied upon. Ultimately, the backing or support for any warrant depends on the researcher's conceptualization of truth. That's why we compared three possible views of truth in this chapter and argued that these views are associated with our three ways of knowing about communication.

Table 6.2 Warrants and Backing: Values, Form of Argument, and Standards for Evaluating Evidence

	Interpretive Paradigm	**Critical Paradigm**	**Discovery Paradigm**
Values	Subjectivity Rich Description	Voice Liberation	Precision Power Parsimony
Form of Argument	Multiple realities	Evaluate communication and sometimes, the need for ideological change	Causality (or at least association)
Standards for Evaluating Evidence	Researcher credibility Plausible interpretations Transferable findings	Coherence Researcher positionality Change in awareness or praxis	Measurement validity Measurement reliability External validity

Key Terms

Adequacy
Alternate forms method
Analytic induction
Audit trail
Bracket
Coherence
Concurrent validity
Construct validity
Content validity
Criterion validity
Degree of membership
Ecological validity

External validity
Face validity
Faithfulness
Fidelity
Fronting
Generalizability
Hegemony
Homogeneity
Ideology
Internal consistency
Internal validity
Liberation

Measurement reliability
Member checks
Negative case analysis
Panel of judges
Parsimony
Performance tests
Power
Praxis
Precision
Predictive validity
Reflexivity
Reliability

Researcher positionality	Subjectivity	Transferability
Rich description	Test-retest method	Validity
Standpoint	Theoretical saturation	Voice

Discussion Questions

1. Think back to the one thing you said you knew for sure, when you first read Chapter 4. We asked you to make some argument for how you knew that thing. Was your argument an argument about your own (or another person's) subjective reality? Was it an argument about something that needs to be changed? Or was it a causal argument?

2. Why would a research study be more believable if the researcher demonstrated more than one standard for evaluating evidence (e.g., researcher credibility and member checks for interpretive research; coherence, positionality, and increasing awareness of the need for change in critical research; or several different forms of internal validity for discovery research)?

3. Pick one communication research topic (e.g., media influence; interpersonal violence): How can research from each paradigm inform our understandings of that topic?

4. Consider your own level of *theoretical sensitivity* and *methodological awareness*: What communication theories have you learned about in the classes you have already completed for your major? What research reports and critical essays have you read in those classes? Given those experiences, which paradigms are most familiar to you?

5. Go back to the section on "researcher credibility" in this chapter, and use the lists of skills needed for effective participant-observation, interviewing, and textual analysis to evaluate your credibility as a researcher: Which of these skills are already strengths for you, and where did you gain those skills? Which are skills you would need to grow if you are to do credible interpretive paradigm research?

"Try It!" Activities

1. Find one instance of a research study being cited in a print/Internet/broadcast news story. Try to articulate the link between the story's main claim and the data or evidence given to support it, using at least one of the standards for evaluating evidence discussed in this chapter. Do you think that the research mentioned in your news story was most likely done from an interpretive, critical, or discovery paradigm perspective?

2. Look up three academic studies mentioned in this chapter: Bolkan and Goodboy (2012); DeTurk (2012); May and Patillo-McCoy (2000). Read each study and answer the questions below about each one. Give reasons for your answers:

    (a) Considering the values described in this chapter for each paradigm, what do the authors of this study seem to value most (i.e., subjectivity and rich description; voice and liberation; or precision, power, and parsimony)?

    (b) What basic argument are the authors making in each study (i.e., multiple realities; evaluating communication and possibly changing it; or some cause-and-effect sequence)?

    (c) What standards did the authors use to link their claims to the evidence? (i.e., researcher credibility, plausible and/or transferable interpretations, coherence, researcher positionality, changes in awareness and praxis, internal validity, and/or reliability, external validity).

Part 2

How to Interpret
and Critique Communication

7 Ethnography: How to Interpret Participants' Realities

Introduction

After completing Part I of this book, you know some things about communication research paradigms and their arguments based on the claim-data-warrant model, In Parts II and III of this book you will learn how to do your own research projects, starting with the interpretive paradigm methods of ethnography. We will first introduce you to ethnomethodology (Garfinkel, 1967), the sociological tradition from which interpretive field methods for studying communication emerged. Interpretive field methods are now sometimes referred to Language and Social Interaction (LSI) research, which includes ethnography, as well as conversation analysis (CA) and discourse analysis (DA). You will learn about CA/DA in Chapter 8. All of the LSI methods emphasize the ways that people use language and construct meanings through interaction. In this chapter, you will learn to identify and select ethnographic data sources using participant observation, interviews, archival texts, and artifacts. You also will learn how to conduct those participant observations and interviews with key informants, how to record and organize your field notes, and how to analyze your data to develop claims of interpretation, evaluation, and reform. In the last section of this chapter, you will learn how to apply the warrants of the interpretive paradigm to your ethnographic research project: Specifically, how can you prioritize the values of subjectivity and rich description? How can you demonstrate your own credibility as a researcher, the plausibility of your interpretations, and the transferability of your findings?

Learning Outcomes

After completing this chapter, you should be able to:

» Explain the three principles of ethnomethodology and link each one to interpretive paradigm assumptions;

» Identify communication field settings where your group and cultural memberships facilitate access to credible participant-observations and might help you identify key informants, archival texts and artifacts to supplement those observations and/or interviews;

» Conduct initial participant-observations in a field setting, take notes, and articulate tentative topics or purposes for an ethnographic research project;

» Conduct an oral history, personal, or topical interview with one key informant; transcribe the interview (verbatim) to a digital file; make notes about your early interpretations or reactions to the interview;

» Analyze the above observations and interview for common themes relevant to your topic or purpose (claim);
» Evaluate your own credibility, as well as the plausibility and transferability of your interpretations.

Outline

Imagine that you enter an elevator and find that the other three people already on board are facing the back of the elevator and are staring at the floor. If you see that there is an interesting bug on the floor at the back of the elevator, you will be able to account for their behavior and *go on* as though nothing out of the ordinary has occurred. If you don't notice anything out of the ordinary by just observing, you might ask one of those three people a question, like, "What's going on?" You might just cock your head to one side and raise an eyebrow, as a way of asking, "What's up here?" In all likelihood, one of the persons facing the back, seeing your expression, might *answer* your question and

explain what was happening. But until you find some sensible explanation for this unusual elevator behavior, you probably will feel that you cannot just proceed as usual. You may feel that you are in a different culture or that these three people are "from somewhere else." You might think, "That's strange." Chances are, if you have lived in more than one culture or in a multicultural setting, you have experienced the process of having to actively make sense of a social situation in order to go on with mundane, everyday life experiences.

We hope that this somewhat silly example will help you start thinking about how you might study everyday communication in context and how that kind of research differs from some of the methods you will learn about in Part III this book (i.e., conducting surveys, experiments, or content analyses).

Research methods for ethnography, conversation and discourse analysis arose over the past 45 years from the historical precedent of ethnomethodology (Bode, 1990; Garfinkel, 1967; Maynard & Clayman, 1991; O'Keefe, 1980; Wooffitt, 2005). **Ethnomethodology** is a sociological tradition that aims to explain and interpret how members engaged in social situations go about making sense of their own and other people's behaviors.

In the last 25 years or so, communication scholars began using the phrase Language and Social Interaction (LSI) to collectively refer to

> Studies of speech, language, and gesture in human communication; studies of discourse processes, face-to-face interaction, communication competence, and cognitive processing; conversation analytic, ethnographic, microethnographic, ethnomethodological, and sociolinguistic work; dialect and attitude studies, speech act theory, and pragmatics. (LeBaron, Mandelbaum, & Glenn, 2003, p. 2)

Like ethnomethodology, LSI emphasizes the study of everyday social situations and participants' common sense, or taken-for-granted, realities (Hopper, 1999; Tracy & Haspel, 2004). However, more so than sociologists, LSI researchers orient explicitly to social life as a communicative accomplishment (i.e., language use is *the* aspect of interest to the researcher, not just *one* aspect of the social situation).

In the first section of this chapter, we give you an overview of some of the main ideas of ethnomethodology because LSI research developed from that tradition (Hopper, 1999; Tracy & Haspel, 2004). Specifically, you will learn what ethnomethodology has in common with LSI research. It's important to acknowledge here that ethnography also has roots in anthropology, a connection we will return to shortly.

The Roots of Interpretive Field Research in Ethnomethodology

Ethnomethodology literally means "the people's practices" (Garfinkel, 1967), and ethnomethodologists assume that people are constantly trying to make enough sense out of a social situation to produce their own appropriate behaviors. In all situations, we have to sort out who we are being, to whom we are speaking, and the topic in order to produce seamless interactions (Potter & Wetherall, 1987).

Ethnomethodology relies on three principles: (1) People assume things are as they appear to be unless there is a good reason to believe otherwise; (2) the knowledge held by people is typically incomplete; and (3) whenever people engage in coordinated actions with others, they usually assume that others see things as they do (Schutz, 1967). **Breaching**, or deviating from these three principles, disturbs everyday life, even though some deviations can be interpreted as meaningful (Garfinkel, 1967), as in the elevator example you read about at the beginning of this chapter.

Just as you might be able to *go on* once you made some sense of the people facing the wrong way on the elevator, we all *go on,* or coordinate our everyday actions, because social situations are constrained by rules systems, even when those rules are unspoken, or violated. Rules are general prescriptions for behavior that must be elaborated in context if they are to be applied (Garfinkel, 1967). Because we sometimes deviate from the rules, our accounts, the reasons we give for such deviations, are one important research topic for LSI scholars (e.g., Bolden & Robinson, 2011; Buttny, 1987, 1993; Hewitt & Stokes, 1975; Mongeau, Hale, & Alles, 1994).

Ethnography does not have one universal definition, perhaps because there are several different forms of ethnographic research (Denzin & Lincoln, 2003; Duranti, 1997; Stewart, 1998). In general, **ethnography** is a method for grasping "the native's point of view" (Malinowski, 1922, p. 25), and "it is the trademark of cultural anthropology" (Schwartzman, 1993). Notice that interpretive field research has roots in both sociology (ethnomethodology), and in anthropology (ethnography). Communication scholars tend to differentiate those research traditions from four forms of ethnographic research practiced in our field: Autoethnography, ethnography of speaking, ethnography of communication, and performance ethnography.

One good place for you to start sorting out different ethnographic forms is to distinguish between **macroethnography** and **microethnography** (Spradley, 1980). Macroethnography involves years of field research, sometimes by numerous ethnographers, whereas microethnography refers to studies of much shorter duration, usually focused on a single social situation and conducted by one researcher. You won't be able to conduct your own macroethnographic study in a research methods class. You may be able to do a microethnographic project that is "no less sophisticated, but only more limited in scope" (Spradley, 1980, p. 47). Your general purpose will be the same, to "discover the cultural knowledge people are using to organize their behavior and interpret their experience" (Spradley, 1980, p. 31). Notice how that general purpose echoes the interpretive paradigm assumptions we outlined in Chapter 2 (Table 2.2): There are multiple plausible realities that are socially constructed (e.g., Vignes, 2008). Subjective knowledge is prized, so the context and the knower's standpoint both matter, and participants' understandings matter more than the researcher's understandings of the situation.

It is a very short step from interpreting behavior and experiences, to evaluating them or thinking about how they might be reformed. For that reason, ethnographic research can bridge the interpretive and critical paradigms in communication scholarship.

Whether they are conducting autoethnography, ethnography of speaking, ethnography of communication, or performance ethnography, ethnographic researchers often rely on grounded theory (Glaser & Strauss, 1967; Strauss & Corbin, 1998) and/or naturalistic inquiry (Frey, 1994b; Frey, Botan, et al., 2000; Y. S. Lincoln & Guba, 1985). So before we differentiate those types of ethnographic research, let's look at these two broad terms for field research.

Grounded theory is a way of developing theories by systematically gathering and analyzing field data. Remember that in Chapter 1 we said that theories are stories about how things work or how they should work. Rather than imagining how a communicative process *might* work in practice, grounded theory "evolves during actual research, and it does this through continuous interplay between analysis and data collection" (Strauss & Corbin, 1998, p. 158). For example, Stamp (1999) examined 288 interpersonal communication research studies published in *Human Communication Research* between 1974 and 1999 and used constant comparison to place those articles into a 17-part category system (e.g., cognition, nonverbal communication, compliance gaining, etc.). By examining the categories in relationship to one another, Stamp developed a theoretic model of interpersonal communication. Thus, grounded theory begins with observed evidence, whereas other kinds of theories begin with researchers' ideas about how communication happens, ideas that may be tested in subsequent data collection and analysis

or through logical argument and reasoning. Stamp's (1999) study shows us that grounded theory can be used in ways that are quite distinct from the purpose of ethnography (i.e., grasping the participant's point of view about how meaning is created in a social situation). Yet ethnography shares with grounded theory the preference for starting with field data: "The analysis must be made on the ground. We must know what patterns are available in what contexts, and how, where, and when they come into play" (Hymes, 1962, p. 20).

In the same way, naturalistic inquiry complements, but is somewhat different from, ethnographic research. **Naturalistic inquiry** is "the study of how people behave when they are absorbed in genuine life experiences in natural settings" (Frey, Botan, et al., 2000, p. 427). Both grounded theory and naturalistic inquiry are inductive reasoning models that are more local than general. They both begin with cases or specific instances of communication. They both explore how participants interpret behaviors, roles, and situations. One difference between grounded theory and naturalistic inquiry is that naturalistic inquiry can be used to test communication theories, but it is not necessarily meant for developing theories. Ethnographic researchers usually view grounded theory and naturalistic inquiry as complementary rather than competitive (Strauss & Corbin, 1998).

Let's turn now to the four forms of ethnographic research we mentioned earlier. We'll start by defining ethnography of speaking because that was the first ethnographic form to be used extensively by communication scholars. You will see that each of these four ethnographic forms builds on or extends the work that emerged before it in our field.

Ethnography of speaking (EOS) is a specific method for describing and explaining culturally distinct communication patterns and practices using the sociolinguist Dell Hymes's (1962) SPEAKING acronym as a theoretic framework. You'll learn more about the SPEAKING framework in the claims section of this chapter (and the SPEAKING framework is depicted there in Table 7.1). For years, EOS studies have been most closely associated with Philipsen (1975, 1976, 1989, and 1992) and his colleagues from the University of Washington. However, Zand-Vakili, Kashani, & Tabandeh's (2012) EOS of the television series *Friends* suggests that the SPEAKING framework can be used to improve intercultural teaching, by helping teachers and students to focus on the specific norms, genres, and speech events of another cultural group. Pal and Buzzanell's (2013) post-colonial analysis of Indian call centers reported, for example, that workers were advised to watch *Friends* in order to learn how to mimic American cultural norms during interactions with US-based telephone clients.

Ethnographers of communication (EOC) focus on how members of particular speech communities constitute their place and positions in particular settings or situations (Witteborn, Milburn & Ho, 2013). EOC researchers assume that "the effective communicative resources for creating shared meaning and coordinating action vary across social groups" (Philipsen, 1989, p. 258). They assume that there is more than one effective way to communicate in any social group, because there are multiple plausible realities. Instead of one shared reality, "there are moments of communicative effectiveness" in which participants "act as if they express a common sense" (Philipsen, 1989, p. 258). For the interpretive researcher, these moments of acting as if meaning is truly shared suggest ways that participants are able to coordinate their actions and go on with their everyday lives.

Furthermore, since interpretive paradigm scholars view truth as subjective, they take participants' coordinated actions as evidence of their common sense of a situation. In this way, ethnographers share with other LSI scholars a view of social life as a communicative accomplishment, or a social construction.

Coordinating actions and creating harmonious perceptions of what is going on in a social situation is particular to a culture or group (Phillipsen, 1989). There is a "community-specific system of resources for making shared sense and for organizing coordinated action" (Philipsen, 1989, p. 260). As you can see from this description, the main difference between EOS and EOC is that EOC does not make specific use of Hymes' (1962) SPEAKING framework. Instead of the SPEAKING acronym, EOC researchers use a more general term, communication codes. Within a particular speech community, the **communication code** is a set of rules for speaking and interpreting others' speech (Carbaugh, 1993; Dollar, 1999; Philipsen, 1992, 1997). Hymes' (1962) SPEAKING framework is one way to articulate the elements of a communication code.

In the past decade, there has been a growing use of **autoethnography**, the analysis of a social setting or situation that connects "the personal to the cultural" (C. Ellis & Bochner, 2003). Like EOS and EOC,

autoethnography relies on systematic gathering and analysis of field data from people involved in genuine life experiences, whether at the microethnographic or macroethnographic level. But autoethnography extends the interpretive paradigm values of subjectivity and rich description to include the researcher's own lived experiences. Autoethnography also extends the ethnographer's focus on degree of membership to describing and interpreting one's own sense-making in a cultural situation or setting. In autoethnographic research, the key informant is the researcher himself or herself (e.g., Crawford, 1996; Griffin, 2012; A. F. Wood & Fassett, 2003).

Autoethnographic writing is different from the interpretive research reports typically found for EOS and EOC studies: "Usually written in first-person voice, autoethnographic texts appear in a variety of forms—short stories, poetry, fiction, novels, photographic essays, personal essays, journals, fragmented and layered writing, and social science prose" (C. Ellis & Bochner, 2003, p. 209). For example, here are the first few lines from Rachel Griffin's (2012) autoethnographic essay, entitled, "I am an angry black woman; Black feminist autoethnography, voice and resistance": "I AM an Angry Black Woman. Unapologetically, rationally, and rightfully so. I am blistering mad! I am frustrated and enraged! I am devastated, and my blood is boiling at a temperature so hot that I think my heart might stop beating at any given moment!" You can see how Griffin's use of first-person voice, exclamation marks, and sentence fragments differs from the writing in most scholarly journals. You might scan issues of *Text & Performance Quarterly*, published by the National Communication Association, to see other examples of autoethnographic and performative writing (e.g., Kilgard, 2011; Moreman & Non-Grata, 2011).

Autoethnography can be used in ways that fit the assumptions of the interpretive and/or critical paradigms. Critical autoethnographers document their own experiences of coming to question and resist larger social structures, like capitalism, religion, family, culture, or history as those structures are commonly defined and understood (Denzin, 2003).

Performance ethnography builds on EOS, EOC, and autoethnography as ways of studying culture and communication by systematically gathering and analyzing field data (Denzin, 2003; Warren, 2006). Performance ethnography is "often contradicted and contested" (Warren, 2006, p. 318). In paradigmatic terms, it is an explicitly critical method, because it goes beyond interpreting participants' cultural meanings and representing them in public performances and performative writings, to evaluating those meanings and working to "make sites of oppression visible" (Denzin, 2003, p. 14). In other words, performance ethnography makes explicitly evaluative and reformist claims. Thus, "performance ethnography enters a gendered culture in which nearly invisible boundaries separate everyday theatrical performances from formal theater, dance, music, MTV, video, and film" (Denzin, 2003, p. x).

As you read the rest of this chapter, we will provide you with some examples from published EOS, EOC, autoethnography, and performance ethnography scholarship. It's important to point out that ethnography is an inductive research method (i.e., ethnography begins with data collection, where specific topics or purposes emerge; data collection and analysis are cyclical processes used to develop interpretations of multiple realities). Nonetheless, we will start this chapter by considering the claims you can explore with ethnographic research.

Ethnographic Claims

As a novice ethnographer, you should first select a research topic that you sincerely care about. After all, you will be immersed in collecting and analyzing field data over an extended period of time, and possibly creating performances with those data. That time could be weeks or months for microethnography, but it might be years for a macroethnographic project. For example, Barker's (1993) ethnographic analysis of self-managing teams at a CO circuit board manufacturer was based on participant-observations, interviews, and textual analysis over a period of more than 2 years. Conquergood's classic ethnographic studies of Chicago gang members' experiences were the result of his immersion with those participants over years. Many of the studies you read about in this chapter rely on the researcher being immersed in a field setting over similar periods of time. You simply cannot do justice to a full-scale ethnographic project in one school term.

But let's start where you are now. Think about your personal circumstances, both in terms of your current involvements and activities, and those situations to which you are related because of your personal history (Lofland & Lofland, 1995; Morse, 1998). As a student, perhaps working full- or part-time to help pay your college expenses,

you may be employed as a waitperson in the food service industry, or a sales representative, or a customer service representative in a retail environment. You are a member of particular cultural or familial structures, and from those experiences you know about particular stories, rituals, or social dramas (Turner, 1986).

Ethnographers often "'make problematic' that which is problematic in our lives" (Lofland & Lofland, 1995, p. 13). What situation in your life most stands out as you consider moments of communicative effectiveness or ineffectiveness (Philipsen, 1989)? When you think about the cultural knowledge you use to make sense of your day-to-day experiences and to coordinate actions, what situations come to mind? Which of your activities or stories would probably mean something different to people who do not share your personal history? Choosing a topic that you already know and care about will help you to enter the inductive reasoning process more competently, because you already have subjective knowledge that will make you more credible in that topic area.

Because interpretive ethnographers value subjectivity and aim to privilege participants' views of their own lived experiences, you will use an inductive approach to frame your research claim. This means that you will never pose a formal hypothesis. You probably won't even know your exact research question at the start of your ethnographic project. Instead, you might begin with only a social setting or a situation that you want to explore. You will collect some initial field data, but without articulating specific research questions in advance, because you will need to know something about the nature and quality of the relationships in a social context in order to know which questions you can effectively pursue there (Katriel, 1995). For instance, will it be acceptable for outsiders to observe and ask questions in that setting? How might the presence of an outside observer change people's behaviors or sense-making practices in that situation? Of course, if you are doing autoethnographic research, you already know a great deal about the nature and quality of relationships in the setting or situation that you intend to study, ones from your own experiences. But you may not know exactly what it is that you hope to represent, or even perform, about that situation.

After you have selected a communication topic, and perhaps collected some initial participant observations, texts, or informal interviews, you can start thinking more specifically about your research questions. Start writing down some general research questions as early as possible in your ethnographic project. As you write your questions down and review them, you will be making your theoretical and methodological assumptions more clear. Keeping detailed notes about those ideas will help you figure out the choices you should be making in your data collection and analysis (and performances, if applicable). At this stage, you should be reading other published studies about your topic, too. We believe it will be useful for you to read discovery, interpretive, and critical paradigm studies on your topic, because all of those perspectives will inform your thinking, and because understanding those multiple views is consistent with an interpretive paradigm view about the nature of reality (i.e., multiple plausible truths exist).

When you have a list of potential research questions about the situation or the setting that you intend to examine, and after you have conducted an initial literature review, try writing the questions on note cards and sorting them in different ways to see how a structured set of interview questions might emerge. If you have more than four or five questions, you might try grouping them into major questions and subquestions. "Drafting and iterating a set of six or seven general research questions should take at least 2 or 3 hours" (Miles & Huberman, 1994, p. 25). Your questions are likely to improve if you do this work in more than one sitting.

Ethnographic research is used primarily to explore claims of interpretation. Critical ethnographies also put forward claims of evaluation and reform. In the following sections, you will learn how to develop each type of claim whether you are conducting EOS, EOC, autoethnography, or performance ethnography.

Interpretive Claims

In doing ethnography, we seek to understand how people in a particular group or culture *interpret* communication norms and practices (Philipsen, 1989). In the next chapter, "Conversation and Discourse Analysis," you will learn more about norms and practice. Here, we will briefly define the terms group and culture. A **group** is a set of "3–12 people who interact regularly over a period of time and conceive of themselves as a social entity" (Lofland & Lofland, 1995, p. 107). By contrast, a **culture** is defined as a system of shared meanings, or *webs of significance,* held in common by group members (Geertz, 1973).

EOS describes the ways that members of a culture name their speech events, the components of those speech events (e.g., senders, receivers, message forms, channels, etc.), and the functions of speech events (i.e., what is being accomplished by that speech event?). To conduct EOS, we use the SPEAKING framework developed by sociolinguist Dell Hymes (1962). Table 7.1 lists the elements of the SPEAKING framework.

The elements of the SPEAKING framework are used to *describe* "what a child internalizes about speaking, beyond rules of grammar and a dictionary, while becoming a full-fledged member of its speech community. Or, it is a question of what a foreigner must learn about a group's verbal behavior in order to participate appropriately and effectively in its activities" (Hymes, 1962, p. 16). Table 7.2 contains several examples of interpretive ethnographic claims from published studies.

A **speech community** is a group of people who share rules for using and interpreting speech (Romaine, 1982). Some of the speech communities that have been represented in early EOS and EOC research include street youth (Dollar & Zimmers, 1998), a charismatic church (Sequeira, 1993), a regional symphony (Ruud, 1995), organizational groups in a television station (Carbaugh, 1988), and a group of Vietnam veterans (Braithwaite, 1997c). More recently, for example, EOC researchers have explored Latino/Latina (e.g., Aoki, 2000; Moreman & Non Grata, 2011; Witteborn et al., 2013) and Native American speech communities (Covarrubias, 2007, 2008). Each of these studies interprets the culturally distinct knowledge used by members of a social group to speak and be understood by others. Of course, you also could use autoethnography to describe the communication code used in your own speech community (e.g., Griffin, 2012; Johnson, 2003; Pelias, 2004). At its broadest level, the interpretive ethnographic claim addresses how culture creates communication and vice versa.

Table 7.1 Hymes' (1962) SPEAKING Framework

> **S**cene and setting (from the perspective of members)
> **P**articipants (age, role, gender, ethnicity, etc.)
> **E**nds (goals of the participants and actual outcomes of the event)
> **A**ct sequence (structure and topic of the messages)
> **K**ey (tone or manner of the communication)
> **I**nstrumentalities (channels of communication, jargon, dialects, etc.)
> **N**orms of interaction (how to do communication) and interpretation (how to make sense of messages)
> **G**enre (categories like poetry, myth, jokes, etc.)

Table 7.2 Interpretive Ethnographic Claims

Ethnography of Speaking and/or Ethnography of Communication:
What are the scenes, participants, ends, act sequences, key, instrumentalities, norms, and genres for speaking in a given cultural context?
1. What speech events and cultural norms are most frequently presented in media discourse as characteristic of a friendly relationship? (Zand-Vakili, Kashani, & Tabandeh, 2012, EOS analysis of the TV show *Friends*).

How are communication resources or shared knowledge used by members of a group or culture to interpret and organize action?
1. "Silence, like other communicative resources, if not "invisible" to Whites (McIntosh, 1992) can be more difficult to detect even though for people of color, racialized silence is seldom invisible or inaudible. On the contrary, silences reveal themselves in plain sight and are loudly heard by those to whom discriminatory silences are aimed" (Covarrubias, 2008, p. 229).
2. The Finnish communication code "structures some cultural scenes as occasions for positive silence," and uses the term quietude (hiljaisuus in Finnish) to embody "a model of personhood for which this is a valued, respected, and natural practice" (Carbaugh, Berry, & Nurmikari-Berry, 2006, p. 203).

How does the use of communication resources or knowledge vary within a culture or group?
1. "The present analysis first explores variations in the identity experiences of Oklahoma Indians.... Additional analyses test the linkages between ... participation in communicative relationships outside one's own ethnic community ... participation in communication relationships with other Indians ... [and] development of intercultural identity" (Y. Y. Kim et al., 1998, p. 259).
2. "Instances of morphophonemic variation ... may express a number of various meanings that express, reflect, and reproduce speakers' life experiences. The analysis also enables us to develop a set of theoretical statements that explain the motivations of workers' selections of a low prestige variant and why workers' reliance on a low prestige variant persists" (Huspek, 1986, p. 149, on ing/in' variation in North American workers' speech).

What is the relationship between culture and communication?
1. Within a given cultural context, silence may be viewed negatively (consumptive silence) or positively (generative silence): "In consumptive silence interactants are seen to expend key resources of a communication event (i.e., time and symbols) for negative or relatively unproductive outcomes.... In generative silence interactants are seen to engage in a fertile communication activity wherein people affirm the self and each other personally, interpersonally, culturally, and even metaphysically" (Covarrubias, 2007, p. 268).
2. How do bilingual teachers use codeswitching to manage their identities? (see Chien, 1996, on how teachers in Taiwan embed English words or sentences in Chinese-based interactions to either show solidarity or establish social distance in Taiwanese classrooms; or Jaffe, 2007, on how bilingual teachers in Corsica switch between French and Corsican to display their own stance toward "the content and the form of their utterances," p. 53).

What is the communal function of communication?
1. In the Chicago suburb he called Teamsterville, "speaking like a man" helps to create and affirm the shared identity of blue-collar workers (Philipsen, 1975).
2. Latin American mojado festivals help to teach non-Latino/a people about La Raza culture (Murillo, 1996).
3. "This paper attempts to show how people use narratives in the process of self-definition based on locale" (Schely-Newman, 1997, p. 401).
4. The themes of hard work, family, and religion "serve as unifying forces despite the economic struggles" of Mexican-American families in Biola, California (Aoki, 2000, p. 207).

Autoethnography:
"The experience of teaching in the days following the Texas A&M University 'bonfire' collapse in November of 1999 is examined ... by considering the intense experience of emotions and the struggle to balance the needs of students with the need to cover course material" (K. Miller, 2002, p. 571).

Performance Ethnography:
1. "This interpretive ethnography describes the barbershop in a Black community as a cultural site" and "a centralized occasion within a cultural community that ... meets at the intersection of culture and performance" (Alexander, 2003, p. 105).
2. "I decided Menopause and Desire would be composed of interconnected prose poems and scenes dealing with such topics as sexuality in middle age, how to admire the postmastectomy body, and whether or not it is possible to learn anything about love, even if you live to be a hundred" (Jenkins, 2005, p. 254).

You can also use ethnographic methods to support an interpretive claim about more specific relationships between culture and communication. A specific relationship that you might study with EOC, autoethnography, or performance ethnography is the **communal function of communication**—the ways that communication is used to create and affirm shared identities (Philipsen, 1992). Table 7.2 includes sample claims about the communal function of communication. Notice that communication can serve a different communal function for cultural insiders (e.g., Philipsen, 1975; Schely-Newman, 1997) than for outsiders (e.g., Murillo, 1996).

Codeswitching, mixing the rules of one speech community with the rules of another, also can be studied with ethnographic methods. Studies of codeswitching are especially relevant for intercultural communication research. To study codeswitching, you'll need to be fluent in both (or all) of the codes you want to study. We will say more about your degree of membership as a researcher in the warrants section of this chapter.

When you study the communal function of communication or codeswitching in a cross-cultural setting, you might make a claim of evaluation and reform that goes beyond interpretation (i.e., you might be doing critical ethnography). Interpretive ethnographic research stops just short of evaluating participants' cultural communication. But critical ethnography is used to support claims of evaluation. Critical ethnographers may go so far as to suggest how society should be reformed in order to give voice to a cultural group or to liberate some oppressed group of people. Let's consider those claims next.

Evaluative and Reformist Claims

Claims of evaluation are advanced when you judge the worth or value of the communicative practices or messages that you are studying. As we pointed out in the first part of this book, evaluative claims are quickly put to use in support of changing communication practices in particular groups or cultural contexts. Perhaps you, the researcher, will decide what changes are needed, or you may give the results of your analysis to another person or group who will then decide what changes to attempt (see Dorazio & Stovall, 1997, or Witteborn et al., 2013 for thoughtful discussions of this point). Either way, it is a short step from evaluating communication practices to thinking about how to change them.

Around 1990, critical ethnographies (i.e., EOC, autoethnography, or performance ethnography) began to focus on showing how norms of communication and power usage privileged some group members and oppressed others (e.g., Ang, 1990; Conquergood, 1992, 1994; Crawford, 1996; Gordon, 2002; Trujillo, 1993; Witmer, 1997). Critical ethnographers go beyond interpreting and evaluating cultural variations in speech codes when they "attempt to take action against the social inequalities exposed in their research, action aimed at challenging the status quo and calling for a rebalancing of power" (Dollar & Merrigan, 2002, p. 62).

Perhaps the earliest and most well-known proponent of critical ethnography in communication is Dwight Conquergood (1983, 1991, 1992, 1994, and 1995). Conquergood's participatory research with a Chicago Latino gang included actions aimed at helping gang members stay out of jail, learn to read and write, and gain a more empathic voice in the media (Conquergood & Seigel, 1990). Conquergood's (1992, 1994) attempts to understand this cultural group moved well beyond interpretation for its own sake or for the sake of developing theory. An equally important goal of his research was the attempt to redress power imbalances experienced by members of the culture (Conquergood & Seigel, 1990).

As you read critical ethnographic studies and conduct those studies yourself, you may notice a blurry line between making claims with ethnography and writing about or performing a culture. Goodall (2000) argued that critical ethnographers approach *writing as inquiry*. In critiquing power relations within a culture, or between cultural groups, writing is not merely something you do after the research is conducted. Instead, writing is *the* manner of interrogating and exposing power relations within the social situation. It may even be a way of interrogating your own beliefs and participation in an oppressive social system, especially if you use autoethnographic writing or if you participate in collaborative writing (Trujillo, 1999). Table 7.3 contains several examples of evaluation and reform claims from published ethnographic research.

Furthermore, performance ethnographers use their participant observations, interviews, and textual analyses to create public performances that evaluate cultural communication norms and practices, and suggest how they might be changed (e.g., Jenkins, 1999, 2000; Vignes, 2008). As such, performance ethnographers are always consuming and producing texts, and since both consumption and production are power-laden, both activities require reflexivity (Bowman & Kirstenberg, 1992). Table 7.3 contains one such sample claim (Rusted, 2006). Jenkins' (2000) play, *A Credit to Her Country*, provides another example: The play is about gays and lesbians who served in the US military, and it was based on Jenkins' ethnographic oral history interviews with men and women who were discharged from military service because of their sexual orientation. In a later play titled, *Menopause and Desire*, Jenkins explored intersections of age, cancer survivorship, and sexuality. The use of ethnographic data in performance studies has expanded significantly in the past decade.

Now that you have some sense of the range of ethnographic claims, let's turn our attention to the sources, settings, and strategies for ethnographic data collection and analysis.

Ethnographic Data

In this section, you will learn more about the major sources for ethnographic data collection, including participant observations, interviews, and analysis of archival documents and cultural artifacts. We help you consider the procedures you can use to collect these data, from gaining access to selecting key informants, taking field notes, and exiting the field. Finally, you'll learn more about how to analyze ethnographic data, including transcribing interviews, coding and reducing data, applying descriptive frameworks to analyze communication norms and rules of interaction, and writing case studies. All of these ideas will build on the concepts you learned in Chapter 5, "What Counts as Communication Data?"

Table 7.3 Evaluative and Reformist Ethnographic Claims

Ethnography of Speaking and/or Ethnography of Communication:
How do members' use of communication resources or knowledge deal with power, or privilege some members' interests at the expense of others members' interests?

1. "The Internet is not a placeless cyberspace that is distinct and separate from the real world. . . . People in Cybercity are investing as much effort in maintaining relationships in cyberspace as in other social spaces" and "are widening their relationships, not weakening them" (Carter, 2005, p. 148).

2. "Our findings suggest that grammar and language instruction needs to be reconceptualized in order to promote language ideologies that are reflective of current research in linguistics, that help students become more proficient in written Standard English, and that build upon students' linguistic experiences in positive ways" (Godley, Carpenter, & Werner, 2007, p. 123).

3. "Invisibility shapes (and is shaped by) processes of stigmatization, 'street smarts' as enacted by youth, and 'Mayberry' and 'not in my backyard' community discourses. . . . The disappearance of youth without homes simultaneously serves and undermines various stakeholders" (Harter, Berquist, Titsworth, Novak, & Brokaw, 2005, p. 305).

Autoethnography:

1. "This article illuminates the omnipresence of oppression in the lives of Black women in general and in my own life as a biracial Black female academic in particular" (Griffin, 2012, p. 139).

2. "Inferential sexism and racism are endemic to U.S. higher education and classrooms and are as dangerous as overt forms of sexism and racism because they are harder to identify, and more naturalized and acceptable" (Patton, 2004, p. 60).

3. Autoethnographic research "highlights the need among practitioners to correct ourselves, as much or more than the need for us to correct them (offenders)" (Williams, 2006, p. 23).

Performance Ethnography:

1. "Artwork themed on the activities of the North American cowboy and the North American west has a marginal status in contemporary art worlds despite its iconic place in popular culture. The expression of such a social distinction is embodied in the performative practices of institutions that collect, legitimate, or exhibit such work" (Rusted, 2006, p. 115).

2. Public performances of interview data from uninsured or underinsured California workers can "engage readers, the public, and policymakers to address difficult issues associated with the lack of health insurance" (Saunders, 2008, p. 528).

3. "Stories of home are how and where I make sense of my own life and the importance of the human experience. I know who I am through the stories of my family and my native region" (performance autoethnography, Vignes, 2008, p. 345).

Sources for Data Collection

The defining characteristics of ethnographic research are that "the investigator goes into the field, instead of bringing the field to the investigator" (Schwartzman, 1993, p. 3) and that data are represented from the view of the participants (Stablein, 1996). Thus, **participant observation** is the process of watching and learning about the setting and people while you are participating in the daily realities you are studying (Lofland & Lofland, 1995; Spradley, 1980). **Interviews** with key informants are interactions between you, the researcher, and informed, articulate members of the culture or group that you want to understand. If any of the key informants are the researchers, then the work is at least partially autoethnographic. **Archival documents** are written or symbolic records of cultural communication such as letters, newspapers, websites, instant messages, billboards, or memos. **Artifacts** are objects used by group or cultural members, such as clothing, jewelry, buildings, tools, or toys.

In doing ethnography, you probably will triangulate two or more data sources. For example, you may follow a period of document analysis and participant observations with some interviews, and then do some more observations (a.k.a., iterative cycles of data collection and analysis). Your ethnographic account is likely to proceed from making broad observations to making increasingly more selective and focused observations (Spradley, 1980). Let's look at how you can collect each of the four sources of ethnographic data, starting with participant observations.

Participant Observation

As an ethnographer, your involvement in the communication you choose to study may be somewhat detached (i.e., you are just there to observe). Or you may be an active participant, helping to create the communication in that cultural setting or situation. Your degree of participation will depend on your purpose, and the kind of access you have to the field setting. For example, Braithwaite's (1997b) ethnography of Navajo educational communication practices was based on 8 months of participant observation, during which Braithwaite (1997b) lived in a dormitory at Navajo Community College in Tsaile, Arizona. As he observed over 100 hours of classroom interactions, Braithwaite (1997b) collected more than 300 pages of field notes, including descriptions of class content and specific verbal

and nonverbal speech events. In this setting, Braithwaite (1997b) was a participant in the sense that he resided in the dormitory with the Navajo students. But he was an observer, since he was faculty member rather than a student, and because he is not of Navajo descent. Compare Braithwaite's standpoint with Vignes's (2008) *complete participation* in developing the peformance, "Hang It Out to Dry," a solo show about the "washed away community and spun tales of Chalmette, Louisiana, in the wake of Hurricane Katrina" (p. 349). Vignes interviewed family members and friends, and she "witnessed and dealt with the aftermath of Katrina on an everyday basis as a participant and as an observer; therefore, I can tell the story" (p. 349).

In another ethnographic study, this one about baseball, Nick Trujillo (1992) used participant observation and interviews to gather data over two years and 500 hours of fieldwork at a major league baseball stadium. His participant observations included a variety of roles and settings. Trujillo (1992) began the process of data collection by observing numerous off season, "luncheons, banquets, autograph appearances, and speaking engagements" (p. 353). Then, during the two seasons under study, Trujillo (1992) "attended a total of 67 home games" (p. 353) where he participated as a *fan, invited observer,* and *ballpark wanderer,* observing and conducting brief interviews in many locales. During these interviews and observations, he took extensive field notes to reconstruct the communicative actions of workers. In all of these interactions, Trujillo participated as a fan and a researcher, but he never participated as a player or team employee. He observed those roles, and used interview and textual data sources to inform his interpretations of their communication.

Whatever your degree of participation during observations, it is important that you develop and maintain trusting relationships with the group members that you study. Your access to participants' knowledge is relative to the kinds of relationships you establish with group members. The roles that your key informants play in their local networks, and their goals in relating to you, influence your degree of participation and the observations you are able to collect. As a case in point, Schely-Newman (1997) observed instances of codeswitching when she interviewed members of her family and friends who all lived in an Israeli *moshav* or cooperative community. She noted that her participants spoke a variety of languages (Arabic, French, Hebrew), "with varying degrees of fluency" (p. 405). Speakers would sometimes switch languages for particular reasons, including the

"the subject discussed (Israeli politics are discussed in Hebrew; the concerns of women and children, in Arabic), or the image being presented by the narrator (sophistication is marked by French)" (p. 405). She observed that in formal events with a mix of different language speakers, codeswitching happened less often. Such an observation could be made only if she selected informants capable of performing multiple language codes and if her relationship to the informants allowed them to share stories with her, during which codeswitching occurred naturally because she was a family member.

As these three example studies suggest, you will need to possess or develop certain skills and attitudes to be an effective participant observer: You will need to be good at recognizing and performing the communication as it is done in the social group that you are studying (Dollar, 1995; Lindlof, 1995). You also will need to be good at "creating sharp, detailed, and theoretically informed descriptions" (Lindlof, 1995, p. 135). For that, you will have to become skilled at writing, organizing, filing, and synthesizing field notes. Those skills can be learned if you do not already possess them. Ask your instructor for tips on organizing and synthesizing your field notes.

Finally, to be an effective participant observer, you will need to possess certain attitudes and sensitivities. For instance, you will need to be capable of and comfortable with fading into the background of a social situation—what Lindlof (1995) called a tolerance for marginality. You also will need to be sensitive to all the verbal and nonverbal communication cues that are available in a social setting, not just the visual and auditory cues. Ethnographers must "open up our sensing to the tastes, smells, tempers, touches, colors, lights, shapes, and textures of the cultures we study" (Lindlof, 1995, p. 138). Finally, to be an effective participant observer, you will need to be good at "giving people the benefit of the doubt, getting along by going along, and not being overly querulous or contentious" (Fine, 1993, as cited in Lindlof, 1995, p. 139). If you are observing yourself, you will need to use all of the skills we just mentioned, and you will need to develop *reflexivity*. "A researcher must reflect on their own experiences in order to discern how they are both product and producer of a given cultural phenomenon" (A. F. Wood & Fassett, 2003, p. 288).

Participant observation will allow you to see what members do and say in their setting. Interviews with key informants will help you see what members *report*

that they do and say, or what sense members make of those actions and interactions. Notice that these two data sources provide slightly different windows into participants' realities. For example, you may observe the stories that participants tell, to whom those stories are told, where, with what structures, forms of elaboration, and so on. The stories participants tell one another in their natural settings may be quite different than the stories they relate to you, the researcher, in the context of an interview. Thus, observations give a different view of the participants' worlds than participants' talk about their worlds. Interviews with key informants are one of the ethnographer's methods for uncovering participants' talk about their world.

Interviews with Key Informants

The **ethnographic interview** is "the most informal, conversational, and spontaneous form of interview" (Lindlof, 1995, p. 170). Ethnographic interviews take the forms of conversations and storytelling between participants and researchers. You will learn more about formal interviews in Chapter 14, "Survey Research." But interviewing, whether formal or informal, is a way to find out things that you cannot directly observe (Newman & Benz, 1998; Patton, 1990). Interpretive researchers often use interviews because they value the subjectivity and rich description that participant interviews provide.

Just as selecting participants to interview is critical to your participation in and observation of a setting, establishing rapport with key informants is essential if you are to collect good interview data. **Rapport** means that the people you interview and observe feel comfortable with you and trust you. They do not see you as naïve, "or an easy target for deception" (Madison, 2005, p. 32). Your demeanor and appearance, your listening skills, and your nonverbal style all contribute to your effectiveness as a human research instrument during the interview process.

There are three main forms of ethnographic interview: (1) "*oral history* which is a recounting of a social historical moment reflected in the life or lives of individuals who remember them and/or experienced them"; (2) "*personal narrative*, which is an individual perspective and expression of an event, experience, or point of view"; and (3) "*topical interview*, the point of view given to a particular subject, such as a program, an issue, or a process . . . each type will often and necessarily overlap with the others" (Madison, 2005, p. 26). Each of these types of interview can be conversational or more formally structured (Spradley, 1980). Survey research interviews are more formally structured than ethnographic interviews. In survey research, you will use a written schedule of questions to ensure that each of your questions, and the overall organizational pattern, is consistent, or reliable across interviews. But your ethnographic interview is likely to be quite informal or conversational, so you may have only a few key topics that you want to discuss before you began the interview itself. Quite probably, the participants' actions will indicate to you what questions are important to ask (Schwartzman, 1993; Spradley, 1980). For that reason, it's a good idea to conduct some participant observations before you determine whom you want to interview.

Also before you conduct your first interview with an informant, you will need to develop face sheets and postinterview comment sheets. Both of these items will help you develop an audit trail, a record of all the data you collect (Lofland & Lofland, 1995). **Face sheets** include details about the interview, such as a code or name for the participant; the date, place, and time of the interviews; and any relevant demographic information about the interviewee. **Comment sheets** are for you to jot down notes after your interviews, perhaps concerning the emotional tone of the interview, your insights and reflections about any difficulties you encountered during the interview, and your initial interpretations of, or additional questions about, the participants' communication.

In addition to creating face sheets and comment sheets, you will need to develop an introduction to the interview. What will you say to a participant before you begin the interview? You will probably want to tape record interviews, so you can think and talk and not be occupied with field notes during the interview (Lofland & Lofland, 1995). But you should take a few notes while the tape is running just to help you pay attention.

As a novice ethnographer, never enter the interview scene without some interview guide. Your guide might be a page of one-word notes about themes, symbols, and patterns observed in artifacts or other data, but it would never be a strict schedule of questions. If you are doing ethnography of speaking, you may want to have a copy of Hymes's (1974a) SPEAKING mnemonic with you during observations or interviews. You can use it to remind you to notice things about the participants, events, acts, and so forth. If you are doing performance ethnography, you may want to have with you some

outline of the scenes that you intend to develop from your data collection (Denzin, 2003; Madison, 2005). The important thing is to give yourself enough of a guide to focus your interviews but not so much as to override the direction your key informant suggests for your conversation.

In some cases, you may want to combine participant observations and/or interviewing key informants with analysis of archival documents or cultural artifacts (i.e., texts). Let's consider each of these sources of ethnographic evidence next.

Archival Documents

The archival texts used for ethnographic research are usually written documents you encounter in field settings. Archival documents are sometimes implicated in the talk or actions of the participants you are observing (e.g., in Barker's 1993 study, the manufacturing workers posted their own attendance records prominently in their work area, as a way of enforcing their own rule about timely attendance by team members. Barker described that artifact in his research report, as part of his account of concertive control among self-managing teams). Some archival texts won't come up in the interview, but you might search them out for background information that you need to reconstruct past events or processes which are not available for you to observe (see Witteborn et al., 2013, and Covarrubias, 2008, for examples). Finally, library or Internet research about a setting or situation, including conducting a literature review on the topic that you are studying, makes use of archival documents. In this section, however, we will refer more to the documents you are likely to encounter during field data collection, such as participant diaries, memos, email messages, newsletters, signs, and newspaper clippings. For instance, in her ethnography of Far End Design, Markham (1996) analyzed official company literature and diaries kept by employees, along with her field notes from observations and interview transcripts. By considering not only the content of those documents but also their format characteristics, origins, uses, circulation, and so on, in conjunction with her other evidence, she identified some of the ambiguities and contradictions experienced by those employees. We hope this example helps you see how archival documents can supplement your interview and/or participant observations, and help you understand how participants are making sense of their situation.

You may also want to incorporate visual media, such as film, video, or still photography, in your ethnographic project (e.g., Vignes, 2008). If so, then those visual media also become *texts* for analysis. In Chapter 10, "How to Critique Texts," we consider some examples of entire research projects based on textual interpretation and evaluation of media sources. But for ethnography, visual media are most often used to triangulate evidence gained from self-report interviews and/or observations with participants.

Artifacts

Ethnographers examine the actual objects used by participants in the settings they study, in order to understand participants' communication rules, meanings, or behaviors. Sample artifacts could include the participants' costumes and dress; items used in routine activities like eating, cooking, bathing, meetings, or interacting with other participants, and so on. As we just mentioned, artifacts typically support other kinds of ethnographic evidence. This is a good time to point out that artifact analysis plays a much more central role in rhetorical criticism and critical studies (see Chapters 9 and 10 for examples from published communication research).

Strategies for Data Collection

In this section, you will learn some additional procedures for collecting ethnographic research data. As we already mentioned, you probably will start your ethnographic project by collecting participant observations in a field setting. You might conduct some interviews after those initial observations, or you might move next to analyzing archival documents or artifacts, before you do any interviews. If you are doing a macroethnographic project, you probably will collect all four kinds of evidence over time, and the sequence in which you collect those types of data may vary, depending on your research claim (Philipsen, 1982). Ethnographers normally go through several cycles of data collection and analysis, until they reach theoretical saturation and have coherent, plausible interpretations of the communication in a cultural setting or situation.

Because there's a lot of evidence, over a long time, you need to think about the issue of time management at the beginning of your ethnographic project. You will have to allow extra time to develop skills you do not already have, since things go more slowly the first few times,

whether it's interviewing, taking field notes, coding data, writing reports, or whatever. As you think about the amount of time needed for your project, consider some of the tasks you will have to accomplish. You will be entering a site of data collection; conducting a literature review; spending days, weeks, or months at the site; writing up and coding interview transcripts; analyzing data within and across cases; writing up notes from site visits and interviews; holding weekly meetings with other researchers, if applicable; and writing interim and final reports. Miles and Huberman (1994) estimated 185 days for such a task list, which is probably a conservative estimate. Trujillo's 2-year study of baseball culture involved over 500 hours, or over 60 workdays, 8 hours a day, in just the fieldwork tasks! "Time plans usually suffer from excessive optimism. Get a cynical skeptic to critique them" (Miles & Huberman, 1994, p. 47). One issue in planning your timeline is gaining access to the field.

Gaining Access to the Setting

"Stepping into a setting for the first time is probably the most significant phase of the entire ethnographic process" (Schwartzman, 1993, p. 49). "Everything counts" (Goodall, 1989, p. xv, as cited in Schwartzman, 1993). Ethnographers call the process of getting participants' permissions and approvals for doing research in a particular setting gaining access or entry (Lindlof, 1995; Spradley, 1980). You can elect different roles at this point, depending on the degree of participation you desire in the setting, ranging from pure or even covert observer, to full, overt participant, or somewhere in between these two.

In ethnography, we sometimes refer to the period prior to gaining access as "casing the scene" (Lindlof, 1995). While casing the scene, you can collect some initial impressions of the setting and participants, and consider, "Is *this* the right project *now, for me*" (Lindlof, 1995, p. 82). Go into those places, "looking, listening, touching, and smelling—*hanging out*" (Lindlof, 1995, p. 82). Of course, you will already have some idea that this setting and your timing are appropriate. But your initial observations may change your idea of whether the study you have in mind is actually feasible or not. For example, can you devote the amount of time needed to adequately study communication in this setting? What expenses or risks might you incur for traveling to and/or participating as a group member in this setting? Finally, are you competent enough in the cultural communication codes needed in order to function effectively as a researcher and participant in this setting (Lindlof, 1995; Philipsen, 1997; Spradley, 1980)?

One debatable topic among ethnographers is the issue of your membership in the culture you study. Some ethnographers feel it is essential that you be a member of the culture in order to understand how members interpret their realities. Other ethnographers acknowledge that degrees of membership are possible and helpful in data collection and interpretation, especially in gaining access to the setting (Ellingson, 1998; Lindsley, 1999).Your degree of cultural membership impacts your ability to enter the setting, to choose which concepts to attend to, and the interpretations you are able to make about the data (Dollar, 1995; Dollar & Merrigan, 2002; Spradley, 1980).

Not only can you gain access to the setting more easily as a cultural insider, but membership also allows you to recognize features of meaning that would be unrecognized by a nonmember. For example, Dollar and Zimmers's (1998) use of the term *houseless,* rather than *homeless,* youth stemmed from Zimmers's 5-year participation as a job placement coordinator in that community. Zimmers recognized that the youth in this study intentionally used the term *houseless* to mean something different than homeless. They constructed themselves as being without a house (i.e., the building), but as having homes in the places they hung out, ate, and slept. Your degree of membership and the roles you can enact in a setting will influence your selection of key informants for ethnographic interviews.

Selecting Key Informants

Our ethnographic observations rely on and are influenced by our identification of **key informants**, group members who either are highly articulate, or are especially helpful and wise, relative to other participants in that setting (Lofland & Lofland, 1995). Key informants provide information about the relationships, groups, and cultures you seek to interpret and/or evaluate and reform.

One good way to identify key informants in your setting is to look for **gatekeepers**, the participants who have power to grant or deny your access to the setting. In addition, you might want to identify sponsors. A **sponsor** is a participant who "takes an active interest in the project, vouches for its goals, and sometimes helps the researcher locate informants or move into participation roles" (Lindlof, 1995, p. 109).

You might purposively select informants who can represent different qualities that are present in the setting or situation that you study, a process called maximum variation sampling (Y. S. Lincoln & Guba, 1985). For example, Barker (1993) interviewed team members at the circuit board manufacturing plant, and he made sure to interview men and women, as well as workers from different ethnicities and different teams, so that his interpretations could account for their different perspectives. Another strategy you could use is to ask key informants to suggest other people that you might interview or observe (i.e., use the network or snowball selection method). Of course, you can also use convenience or volunteer sampling. But those methods may not be as effective as purposive or snowball selection methods, in terms of maximizing coherent and plausible interpretations of communication in the setting.

Finally, if you are conducting grounded theory, you may want to use **theoretical sampling**, a process of collecting the additional data specifically needed to fill out one part of an emerging theory (Glaser & Strauss, 1967; Janesick, 1998). That additional data will give you a way to check the adequacy of emerging categories and the relationships you are theorizing among those categories. In addition, you might use **deviant case sampling**, the deliberate search for cases that are different from those you have already collected to sort out contradictions or inconsistencies in your initial interpretations (Janesick, 1998; May & Pattillo-McCoy, 2000).

Once you have some sense of your key informants, you can think about how many contacts, or interview opportunities, you will need, and what will be the duration of those contacts (e.g., how long will you observe in the setting, and how many interviews, of what length, will you need to complete with members). Using Barker's (1993) study again, observations occurred once a week, for 4 hours, over a period of 2 years. Barker interviewed volunteers at first. But later, he sought out informants that would help him to represent all workers' subgroups (e.g., full-time and part-time employees, members of different teams, males and females, etc.). The exact answers to all of these questions will emerge over the course of your study (i.e., inductive reasoning process). But it's important to give these questions some thought at the outset of your project.

The next step in preparing for participant observations or interviews will be to think about how you will record and organize your field notes.

Taking Field Notes

Since ethnographic research depends on your prolonged immersion in and observations of the field setting and its participants, keeping good field notes is a crucial aspect of ethnographic data collection. Start by keeping an informal log of problems or questions you encounter as you plan your study. Then add to that log as you begin to collect and analyze data. Your research log will be immensely useful when you are writing up your study (Lofland & Lofland, 1995; Miles & Huberman, 1994; Miller, Creswell, & Olander, 1998). It can be used for recording "experiences, ideas, fears, mistakes, confusions, breakthroughs, and problems that arise during fieldwork" (Spradley, 1980, p. 71). All of your log entries should be dated, as they will be "an important source of data" when you start writing up your study (Spradley, 1980, p. 71).

It is sometimes feasible to make notes quite openly during participant observations. At times, you can incorporate note taking into the roles you are already playing in the field, by disguising note taking as some other situationally appropriate behavior, like doing homework in an educational setting or working on a report in an organizational context (Lindlof, 1995). Trujillo (1992) sometimes posed as a "reporter" while taking notes in the pregame dugout and in the baseball locker rooms. As a "fan," Trujillo carried his notebook inside a game program, where he made brief notes as he observed ballpark employees; he elaborated these notes during lulls in ballpark action and he dictated additional ideas into a tape recorder as he drove home from the games. Of course, mobile phones could make note taking less obtrusive than pen-and-paper methods, if you can record some notes into your phone while appearing to have a conversation or text with someone else.

When there is no situationally appropriate ploy for taking notes, you can withdraw or be shielded for moments to record your notes. You might retreat to a bathroom, your car, or just around the corner (Lofland & Lofland, 1995). Tardy and Hale's (1998) participant observations of mother-toddler playgroup meetings were collected when "the attending researcher sat as unobtrusively as possible near sites of conversations, and essentially, 'eavesdropped'" (p. 342). The key problems with eavesdropping are the ethics of deception and whether participants will change their communication when they sense they are being observed (see the ethics section later in this chapter for more).

Data logging is the ethnographic term for carefully recording various forms of data, including field notes from participant observations, write-ups from interviews, maps, photography, sound recordings, document collections, and so on (Lofland & Lofland, 1995, p. 66). The researcher who boasts, "I didn't take notes because nothing important happened" is either being arrogant or naïve. Your ability and motivation to record detailed notes during or shortly after interactions with participants, and to organize your notes effectively so as to later make sense of them, is vital to doing good ethnographic research. We will talk about this aspect of faithfulness later in the warrants section of this chapter.

Exiting the Field

As you can see by now, ethnographers are sometimes involved with the members of a group or culture over months, or even years. You are likely to develop a variety of relationships with group members if you did not already have those relationships prior to beginning your study. So the idea of *exiting the field,* as it has been traditionally called in anthropological research, is more complicated than just closing your notebook after writing your last field note and then not returning for any additional observations or interviews.

Of course, you could just leave the field of data collection, but more likely, you will have some process of disengagement over time. For example, your official observations may cease by agreement between you and your key informants, but unofficial reflections may come to you in the setting long afterward. Perhaps you will continue to interact with participants on topics unrelated to your research project. Or you may invite group members to read and respond to your interview transcripts, a report of your interpretations of the group's communication practices, or some prose or poetry based on your data collection in that setting (see the warrants section of this chapter for more on member checks and performance checks). In any case, exiting the field of human communication relationships is every bit as delicate and important an issue as entering that field. For ethnographic researchers, both access and exit require serious attention and ethical care. Morse (1998) advised that it is time to exit the field when one of two things happens: Either you recognize that you are putting other goals ahead of the research, or you realize you have reached theoretical saturation. Of course, you will need to be continually analyzing your data to know when you've reached the theoretical saturation point. So this is a good place to consider your strategies for analyzing ethnographic data.

Strategies for Data Analysis

For the ethnographic researcher, "The analysis of data begins shortly after the data collection commences and continues during data collection and beyond" (Morse, 1998, p. 75). You will amass field notes from observations, interviews, archival texts, and artifacts. At some point, you will have to face the daunting task of somehow reducing and analyzing those large amounts of data, then reporting, performing, or otherwise representing the whole process.

You will begin analyzing ethnographic interviews by doing some kind of transcription, translating audiotaped or videotaped recordings of interview conversations with key informants into written form. You will need to integrate the transcript data with your field notes, including your observations of and reflections about participants, the setting, relevant artifacts, and so on.

One way to integrate multiple data sources and multiple kinds of inferences is to reduce specific observations into themes or categories. We call this process **coding** the data. Sometimes, you will apply a descriptive framework that consists of predetermined categories, such as the SPEAKING mnemonic used by ethnographers of speaking and presented earlier in this chapter. At other times, you might generate your own themes or categories to describe the data (e.g., you might try to identify the most frequent, or the most intense sorts of responses found in your interviews and observations). Another way to pull together interpretations from different data sources is to write a **case study,** a narrative account of the communication practices in a particular setting and among specific participants (Philipsen, 1982; Witteborn, et al., 2013). Each of these data analytic processes is outlined in more detail below.

Transcribing Interviews

At some point during or after field observations, you will need to produce written transcripts of your interviews with key informants. At the very least, your transcripts will reproduce the verbatim verbal interaction between you and the informant. But your transcripts also may contain paraverbal indicators such as pause length, word stress, interruptions, and so on. Plan to spend "as much time *immediately* studying and analyzing the interview material as you spent in the interview itself" (Lofland & Lofland, 1995, p. 87). This means studying transcripts *as you go along,* so that you will *know* when you need to collect more data; where to classify and file observations, field notes, and so on. Doing your own transcription is a chore! But it is also an activity of enormous value to you as an interpretive researcher, because it keeps you close to your data. You will be making interpretations as you listen to or watch the tapes many times.

Ethnographers' transcripts range from verbatim texts of verbal and nonverbal interactions to summaries of what was said at what point, combined with your own tentative ideas, early bits of analysis, and notes on methodological difficulties. You will learn more about formatting transcripts and some conventions for notating paraverbal interaction cues in the next chapter, "Conversation and Discourse Analysis." Now, let's look at the steps you can take to make sense of your collected field notes.

Coding and Reducing Field Notes

Feldman (1995) described the problem of working through massive quantities of field data, commenting that the complexity and ambiguity were at times overwhelming: "The task at hand is to create an interpretation of the setting or some feature of it that will allow people who have not directly observed the phenomena to have a deeper understanding" (p. 2). Ethnographers create interpretations based on participants' meanings. To do so, you have to somehow get away from two kinds of prepackaged interpretations. First, you must avoid creating interpretations that are based only on what you knew about the setting before you began collecting data. Second, you must avoid creating interpretations that are based only on what you know about other similar settings. In other words, your interpretations need to come from your field notes.

For that reason, you will be reducing and coding data as you form interpretations and develop theoretic propositions about relationships between concepts in the setting you study. You may impose coding categories onto your data from the outset, as is the case when ethnographers of speaking apply the SPEAKING framework. If you are planning to "perform or adapt the data for the stage, you may also code with scenes for your performance in your mind" (Madison, 2005, p. 37).

Alternatively, you could induce categories for coding data after considerable immersion in the setting as is the case when you use constant comparisons to develop a grounded theory (Glaser & Strauss, 1967) or when you use analytic induction (Goetz & LeCompte, 1984). For example, Lindsley (1999) used inductive reasoning to categorize different types of misunderstandings and conflicts encountered by US American and Mexican employees at a maquiladora (i.e., a US-owned assembly plant located in Mexico). Based on data collected in interviews, nonparticipant observations, and written periodicals on the maquiladora industry, Lindsley used constant comparison to group problematic interactions into three categories (e.g., negatively stereotyped identities).

Another way that you can begin to analyze a culture or group is to identify and describe the participants' rules for interaction. **Rules** are prescriptions for who can speak, on what topics, in what settings, and how speaking by others is to be interpreted. One form that a communication rule can take is "Do *X* in order to be seen as *Y*." College students know many such rules, such as "Show up for class on time to be seen as a serious, motivated student." Rules are followable, prescribed, contextual (Shimanoff, 1980, 1985). Therefore, rule-governed behavior is controllable, criticizable, and contextual (Dollar & Beck, 1997). All of these characteristics suggest strategies that you can use to describe and evaluate the rules for conduct within a culture or group. For example, you can look for *breaches*—instances when members violate rules and are called to account for their behavior; you can try to analyze what rule has been violated in that case. Notice that rules and breaching are concepts from ethnomethodology (Garfinkel, 1967).

Applying Descriptive Frameworks

Frameworks are favored by some ethnographers who believe that it is impossible to enter a social scene completely free of any interpretive categories (Philipsen, 1992). A variety of descriptive frameworks may be used to analyze communication within a group or culture. As we've mentioned several times, Hymes's (1962) SPEAKING framework has been used by ethnographers of speaking to analyze a variety of cultural groups (e.g., Dollar, 1999; Katriel & Philipsen, 1981; Philipsen, 1975, 1992; Ruud, 1995; Sequeira, 1993). One of the benefits of using the same descriptive framework across many groups is the ability to compare interpretations across multiple groups or cultures. If your interest is in comparing groups or cultures, you will probably tend to see a description of any one social setting as a case study.

Writing Case Studies

C. J. Mitchell (1983) and Philipsen (1982) have argued that theoretically plausible interpretations can be made from one good case (e.g., Bastien & Hostager, 1992; Braithwaite, 1997a; Eisenberg, Murphy, & Andrews, 1998; B. J. Hall & Noguchi, 1993; M. Miller, 1995). A typical case is one instance of communicative behavior or practice that "is similar in *relevant* characteristics to other cases of the same type" (C. J. Mitchell, 1983, p. 189). Philipsen (1977, 1982) has advocated that researchers scan a number of cases for familiar concepts that can be analyzed and to hypothesize links between those cases and particular theories. The data for comparing cases can be gained from participant observations, interviews, archival documents, artifacts, or some combination of these data sources. Witteborn et al. (2013) used three EOC case studies from organizational, health, and institutional communication to show how ethnography can be used as an applied research method if the researchers yield their own purposes to the purposes of the communities they study. Let's consider one published EOC case study in more detail.

Braithwaite's (1997a) ethnography of interaction management rules in naturally occurring conversations at a blood plasma donation center well illustrates the value of a single case study. Braithwaite (1997a) donated plasma 16 times over a 2-month period to observe conversations between other donors and the technicians who worked at the center. He discovered that conversational rules that are *normal* in other settings were consistently violated at the plasma donor center. His analysis showed how task requirements in that setting took precedence over the usual rules for interaction management. But Braithwaite (1997a) also showed how the normal rules for conversation management applied in this setting, even though they were routinely violated whenever "successfully accomplishing a task takes precedence over a 'normal' conversation" (p. 70). Braithwaite (1997a) gave several examples from other settings in which participants prioritize task requirements over following normal conversational rules, such as parents conversing together while watching their children play in a park or professors trying to get to their next class while engaging in a hallway conversation with a student. Consistent with the interpretive paradigm's view of truth as subjective and comprised of multiple realities, incongruencies among cases will likely be seen as illustrative, rather than problematic, by the interpretive researcher. But while we are thinking about contradictions, let's look at some of the ethical issues you will need to consider in your ethnographic data collection and analysis.

Ethical Issues for Ethnographers

Recall from Chapter 3, "Ethics and Research," the four rights of research participants: to freely choose their participation in research, to privacy, to be treated with honesty, and to be kept free from harm. It is your obligation as a researcher to protect these rights for your participants. But doing so in the field, over a long time, perhaps with a team of researchers, is different than doing so in a one-shot experiment or a survey questionnaire study (Tinney, 2008). The same is true for representing other people's communication in public performances (Denzin, 2003).

In this section, we stress some of the ethical choices you will make when doing ethnographic research. If you want to look at a professional code of ethics that was developed with ethnographic research in mind, you might check out the codes of ethics posted by the American Anthropological Association, or the American Folklore Association, on their respective websites (Madison, 2005).

As you conduct your initial participant observations in the field setting, think about how you might be open and transparent with those participants about your ethnographic project (Madison, 2005). We mentioned eavesdropping earlier: In what circumstances would you find eavesdropping on other people's communication an acceptable practice? If you were eavesdropping during an initial field observation, for example, at what point would you share your motivations for selecting that setting with those informants? If your study was funded, would you let participants know? Would you use some of your funding to benefit participants, such as paying them for interviews or buying food for homeless informants (Dollar & Zimmers, 1998)? How will your interactions with those participants, or your departure from those relationships once you finish data collection, affect them (Tinney, 2008)? If you create performances based on your observations and interviews, how will you take responsibility for your "interpretations of the life experiences of others" (Denzin, 2003, p. 53)? Specifically, how will you decide what to perform, from whose point of view, as well as what to reveal, conceal, or overlook? Will you fictionalize any part of the performance? If so, will that be revealed to your audience?

Conquergood (1985) identified four ethical problems that we should anticipate and avoid if we are to ethically represent other people's actions in writing or on stage. First, the **custodian's rip-off** happens when we look for *good* texts to study and perform, often "denigrating family members or cultural groups" in the process (Denzin, 2003, p. 55). You can avoid this pitfall by preserving other people's freedom to consent to participate in research. You can take steps to preserve their privacy (e.g., use pseudonyms, or codenames), if the participants feel comfortable with that strategy (Covarrubias, 2008). Finally, you can use member checks to see if they approve of your interpretations or performance choices.

The second problem, the *enthusiast's infatuation*, happens when an ethnographer trivializes other people's experiences by presenting surface interpretations or stereotyped representations of things she or he does not understand well (see Johnson, 2003, for more). You can avoid this problem by being immersed in a field setting over a long time, taking faithful field notes during observations and interviews, and honing your research skills (e.g., listening, fading into the background, asking questions, conducting performance checks, etc.). Be especially wary of this problem if you do a microethnographic project in a single school term. It is extremely difficult to immerse yourself deeply into a cultural setting with a timeline of only 10–15 weeks.

Conquergood's third problem, the *curator's exhibitionism*, happens when a researcher or performer "sensationalizes the cultural experiences that supposedly define the cultural world of the other" (Denzin, 2003, p. 55). The main thing you can do to avoid this ethical problem is to become more self-reflexive. Notice when you are feeling tempted to overstate or exaggerate a participant's interpretation (e.g., because you want to get other people's attention focused on their world). Are you privileging the participants' interpretations? Or has your own subjectivity become more important?

Finally, you can avoid the *skeptic's cop-out*, "detachment and a cynical viewpoint" (Denzin, 2003, p. 55) by being honest with yourself, your readers, or your audience members about why you chose to study a particular topic and how you came to particular interpretations of communication in that setting or situation. As you write up your ethnographic study, and/or prepare public performances based on field data collection, you will need to think very carefully about how to avoid harming the people with whom you've worked and the places and materials that you studied (Madison, 2005, Miller et al., 1998). What impact will your manuscript or your performances have on their safety, dignity, or privacy? Will you offer them any assistance, or reciprocal use of your time, in exchange for their assistance in data collection? It is not uncommon for communication researchers to offer training workshops, or simply volunteer in the community of their ethnographic projects, in order to benefit their participants and as a way of compensating participants for their contributions to the ethnographic research.

More and more ethnographic data collection is occurring over the Internet (e.g., Bakardjieva & Smith, 2001; Cezec-Kecmanovic, Treleaven, & Moodie, 2000; Gillen & Merchant, 2013; LaRose & Whitten, 2000), which raises specific ethical issues, whether the data come from a chat room, email messages, social media posts, or other sources. Computer-mediated interactions are more readily observed in covert fashion, and there are still vast "unsettled distinctions between 'public' and 'private' behavior across a range of cyberspace contexts" (Lindlof & Schatzer, 1998, p. 186). The processes of gaining participants' informed consent, disclosing research procedures, making agreements with participants, negotiating access, and so on are all impacted by differences between virtual and embodied communities. Finally, because the data for such research projects already exists in digital form, the storage and later use of those data must be approached with particular attention to maintaining participant privacy and assuring freedom from harm.

In fact, deciding when to pursue institutional review board (IRB) approval for your ethnographic project is an ethical matter. On most campuses, you must get IRB approval before you interview participants. But you may want to do some initial participant observations in a setting before you know whom to interview, let alone what questions you might ask. If you are observing legally competent adults, in a public setting, you can conduct your initial observations before pursuing IRB approval of your project. But you must realize that simply securing a signature on an informed consent document is not the same as demonstrating respect for a person; likewise, justice is more than selecting the right participants and distributing outcomes evenly (Denzin, 2003). The fact that some university's IRBs do not review ethnographic or performance scholarship does not exempt you from carefully considering how to demonstrate respect, justice, and beneficence in your ethnographic project.

Finally, reform claims pose particular ethical dilemmas for ethnographic researchers (Denzen, 2003; Madison, 2005). Namely, your presence affects the lives of your research participants for better or worse. "Just as there are many political ideals which can claim the allegiance of persons of good will, so ethnography leads you to the careful study and appreciation of many discourses, including, on occasions, discourses of power" (Philipsen, 1992, p. 329). With these sobering thoughts in mind, we turn to the warrants for ethnographic research.

Ethnographic Warrants

In this section, we reiterate some of the ideas that we first presented in Chapter 6, "Warrants for Research Arguments"—ideas about the standards for what counts as good interpretive and critical research. You already know that interpretive researchers illuminate multiple realities by valuing subjectivity and rich description at every stage of their research project. In this chapter, we show you how to demonstrate that you are a credible ethnographic researcher, that your interpretations of the field data you collect are plausible, and that the insights you gained in a particular setting or situation are transferable (i.e., that they are heuristic, or thought provoking to those interested in culture and communication, not that they are generalizable in the discovery paradigm sense).

If your ethnographic project includes claims of evaluation and reform, then you also will need to draw on the critical paradigm values and standards to warrant your project. To make a coherent argument about the worth or value of communication, and perhaps the need for ideological change, your critical ethnographic research (most likely autoethnography or performance ethnography) should include elements from the interpretive and critical paradigm warrants outlined in Chapter 6. In the sections following, we bring into play the values of voice and liberation and the standards of coherence and researcher positionality, as those are relevant to critical ethnography.

Let's start by considering how the interpretive values of subjectivity and rich description are enacted in ethnographic research.

Valuing Subjectivity and Rich Description

Subjectivity refers to your ability to know using your own mind, your thoughts, feelings, and reasoning processes. Your perceptions of the social situation you study, and your ability to represent participants' perceptions of communication in that situation, are as important in ethnographic research as is any objective reality that exists independent of your perceptions or the participants' perceptions.

Interpretive researchers champion the value of subjective knowledge. In doing ethnographic research, you will act on this value by privileging your participants' views, and by using field settings for data collection. If you are doing autoethnography, you will privilege your own experiences and feelings in data collection and analysis. But you will need to be rigorous and reflexive about your own standpoint (Pelias, 2003). The kinds of ethnographic data you collect, the time you spend immersed in the group or culture, and the detail level of your interviews and field notes will allow you to richly describe that situation, its participants, their actions, and relationships. Ultimately, you will be presenting your subjective understanding of those participants' meanings.

Triangulation is customary in ethnographic research because triangulating data sources, settings, collection and analytic strategies, or even researcher perspectives enriches our descriptions of communication and helps to flesh out multiple plausible interpretations. **Collaborative ethnography,** the use of more than one researcher to provide multiple viewpoints on a setting, or on similar settings, can actually help you warrant your ethnographic project (Denzin & Lincoln, 2003; Duranti, 1997). As a case in point, May and Pattillo-McCoy (2000) conducted a collaborative ethnography of Chicago neighborhood recreation centers. May and Pattillo-McCoy recorded their observations separately and then photocopied their field notes and examined points of similarity and difference in their written observations. May and Pattillo-McCoy found that their combined field notes contained more details than either researcher's notes alone, and their combined notes brought out points of inconsistency in their individually recorded observations, which they resolved through discussion during team meetings or informal conversations.

May and Pattillo-McCoy (2000) advocated that ethnographers intentionally induce diversity into their research teams, such as having researchers from different age groups, races, cultural backgrounds, or disciplines,

and that "collaborative ethnography can be useful for providing a richer description, highlighting perceptual inconsistencies, and recognizing the influence of the ethnographers' personal and intellectual backgrounds on the collection and recording of data" (p. 65). Notice how this use of collaboration is similar to the federal requirement for diverse IRB memberships, which are thought to increase the likelihood of representing different perspectives on the potential harms and benefits associated with particular research projects.

Another way of doing collaborative ethnography is to have several researchers gather data on the same social phenomenon but in different settings (e.g., Communication Studies 298, 1999; Gillen & Merchant, 2013; Trujillo, 1999). For example, Gillen and Merchant (2013) used collaborative autoethnography to examine *Twitter* as sociolinguistic practice, and to think about "how communication using web 2.0 technologies can best be described" (p. 48). At a professional association meeting, the authors realized their shared interest in media literacy and the fact that they both tweeted. Between May 2010 and May 2011, they shared "screenshots of each others' Twitter streams, contextualised through lengthy discussions" (p. 48). Their analysis identified the different kinds of Tweets (e.g., citizen journalism, political activism, crowd sourcing), key message conventions, and the data shown on the tweeter's homepage, but also how users interpreted terms like "follow," and why only "newbies" address Twitter's intended prompt (i.e., "what's happening?").

Whether you work with a research team in one setting, or collaborate with another researcher to study phenomenon from different points of view, collaborative ethnography complicates data collection and analysis. It adds an extra layer of coordinating activities and interpretations with other researchers. "Team members must be able to brainstorm together frequently, preferably every day; members must have respect for the contributions of others; and relationships among team members must be excellent and egalitarian" (Morse, 1998, p. 75). Even when you are doing solo ethnography, your role as an observer is often partly participant. So collaboration may refer to your collaboration with those participants (Denzin & Lincoln, 2003, p. 111). Studying communication with other researchers and privileging participants' views will help you to enact the values of subjectivity and rich description.

Valuing subjectivity doesn't mean "anything goes," though. Some ethnographic interpretations will be more credible, plausible and transferable than others. Let's look at how you can develop good ethnographic interpretations by considering your training and experience; your degree of membership in the situation you are studying; and your faithfulness in collecting, analyzing, and reporting evidence.

Researcher Credibility

In Chapter 6, "Warrants for Research Arguments," we mentioned that **researcher credibility** is important in all three paradigms. But credibility is an explicit standard for evaluating interpretive research because you, the researcher, *are* the instrument through which subjective interpretations are made, whether you collect and analyze interviews and participant observations, conversational transcripts, or rhetorical texts and artifacts.

In all likelihood, you are reading this book as part of your initial training as a researcher, so you probably don't have experience collecting and analyzing field data. You may have some theoretic knowledge that sensitizes you to noticing things about culture and communication in a field setting. In addition, you should have at least some experience with the group or culture that you intend to study. In this section, we will help you consider two issues related to your credibility as an ethnographic researcher. First, we help you think about your own and your key informants' *degree of membership* in the culture or group you intend to study. Second, we show you how the issue of **faithfulness**—the steadfastness with which you engage in data collection, analysis, and reporting—contributes to the credibility of your ethnographic project.

Degree of Membership

Your credibility as a human measuring instrument in the field is closely related to your degree of membership in the culture or group you seek to understand (Dollar, 1995; Fitch, 1994). You should be "deeply involved and closely connected to the scene, activity, or group being studied," but you should also "achieve enough distance from the phenomenon to allow for recording of action and interactions relatively uncolored by what [you] might have had at stake" (Fitch, 1994, p. 36).

You may recognize these two requirements as a sort of dialectic tension. Your ability to become deeply involved in a social situation is enhanced by membership, whereas your ability to distance yourself from interactions you observe, or in which you participate, may be inhibited by being a member. Remember the Martian and the Convert roles (F. Davis, 1973) that we described

in Chapter 6? The Convert makes unfamiliar actions and situations familiar by becoming deeply involved, whereas the Martian tries to make everything strange or unfamiliar, so as not to impose his or her own cultural knowledge on the situation. In any given study, you will want to be "both or either" of these roles (Lofland & Lofland, 1995, p. 23). Don't expect to always be the Convert or always be the Martian.

Membership is partly a matter of knowing the cultural rules of the situation that you intend to study: If you are a member, you may already know those rules before you begin the study; or you may intend to learn as you go if you are an outsider. Anthropologists call these emic and etic views of culture, respectively (J. A. Anderson, 1987). An **emic view** holds that the participants' understanding of what they are doing in the situation is the most useful or important. An **etic view** prefers the patterns of behavior that are available to the outside observer.

Think back to Y. Y. Kim et al.'s (1998) analysis of identity among American Indians in Oklahoma (from Chapter 5, "What Counts as Communication Data"). Y. Y. Kim et al. combined the emic and etic perspectives. Their six-member research team consisted of "three members who had Indian backgrounds and were long-time residents of Oklahoma. One of the three was an active, full-blooded Kiowa. The other three non-Indian members were of Asian, Black, and Irish backgrounds" (Y. Y. Kim et al., p. 259). In addition to the research team, 26 Indian students served as interviewers and coders, and 17 Indian residents served as community informants.

If your research claim concerns the rules that participants in a social situation use to construct and interpret their own and others' behaviors, then the emic, or insider perspective, may be your best bet for studying culture and communication. After all, insiders possess at least two kinds of cultural knowledge: Explicit cultural knowledge is used to interpret experience, or to read cultural artifacts, physical environments, and behavior and events (Spradley, 1980). Tacit cultural knowledge is used to generate behavior in culturally intended ways including taking actions, feeling, and using cultural artifacts (e.g., what to wear, buy, eat, etc.).

The concepts of emic and etic perspectives, and explicit and tacit cultural knowledge, should help you see why many ethnographers feel that the researcher who is more of a cultural insider is more credible. Regardless of your own degree of membership, you will need to evaluate the credibility of your key informants. The people with whom you interact as well as those you observe and interview must be good representatives of their group or culture. They should represent different types of participants in that setting (i.e., different roles) if you are to capture the full range of subjective meanings available to members.

Both you and your informants enact your degree of membership when you competently recognize and perform culturally appropriate communication (Dollar, 1995, 1999). Your abilities to recognize and perform a range of communicative practices, to avoid making blunders or mistakes in communication and to recognize violations when they occur, as well as to be playful with cultural language (e.g., jokes, teasing) all demonstrate your degree of membership (Dollar, 1995, 1999). Of course, recognizing these communicative patterns is different from being able to *perform* culturally competent communication such as interacting competently with members you do not already know or making a joke others in the culture will recognize and appreciate. Those competencies will be especially relevant if you are conducting performance ethnography since you will be trying to recreate and embody verbal and nonverbal elements of communicative acts and events that you witnessed in the field, later, in your public performance(s). If you or your key informants cannot recognize or perform the subtle variations in cultural communication, then the plausibility of your interpretations and performances will be threatened.

Being honest about your own degree of membership and working to locate and build relationships with credible key informants are both related to your faithfulness as an interpretive field researcher. Even if you and your key informants are members of the culture you study, lack of faithfulness can threaten your credibility. So let's take a look at what you can do to be a faithful ethnographer.

Faithfulness

No matter how much training and experience you have as a researcher, no matter what your degree of cultural membership, inevitably there will be limits to your credibility. As the measuring instrument during field data collection, your memory, hearing, and recognition skills will all influence the credibility of the data you collect and the interpretations you make of those data. Even though some of these limits on your credibility are physiological (such as memory or hearing), some are limits of faithfulness, your steadfast commitment to represent the participants' (or your own) meanings fully and fairly. Recognizing and

acknowledging these sorts of limitations is part of operating faithfully as an ethnographer.

Faithfulness is further achieved by spending enough time in the field, going over field notes many (rather than a few) times, maintaining close and trusting relationships with key informants, and searching for additional sources of data to corroborate those already considered (Lofland & Lofland, 1995; Miles & Huberman, 1994; Spradley, 1980). Your faithfulness paves the way for you to make plausible interpretations.

Plausible Interpretations

Recall that plausible interpretations are reasonable and likely truths—they are not necessarily *valid,* in the discovery paradigm sense, as objectively verifiable truths. After reading this much of the chapter, you should already be able to articulate some ways that ethnographers work to develop plausible interpretations.

First, due to membership and sustained participant observation, you can refine your ethnographic interpretations over time, allowing them to benefit from insights you gain in additional data collection or analysis. Second, in your interviews with key informants, you will use participants' phrasing and vocabulary whenever possible, thus increasing your chances of tapping into the emic view of the situation and decreasing your chances of being misinterpreted by participants. Third, the everyday settings within which your participant observations occur should increase the relevance of the behaviors you observe, relative to more contrived settings such as an experimental laboratory. Fourth, your self-monitoring process during data analysis requires you to continually question the data and your interpretations of it. All four of these advantages of ethnographic research were pointed out by LeCompte and Goetz (1982, p. 43) when they argued that ethnographic research had superior internal validity, relative to survey or experimental research methods.

In conducting ethnography, you probably will triangulate data as another way to ensure plausible interpretations so that you can compare interpretations of what things mean across more than one data source (e.g., self-reports and other-reports, behavioral observations, archival texts, or cultural artifacts). Interviews with key informants and participant observations will provide you with instances of verbal and nonverbal communication as practiced in the speech community; archival documents might also provide such instances but in ways that are more public and verifiable. Artifacts provide additional sources from which you can triangulate interpretations about participant meanings. Artifacts also suggest concepts that you should analyze because they seem important to participants.

When you embrace the idea of multiple subjective realities, you have to consider whether the interpretations you are making are believable or can be supported with arguments and reasoning (Dollar, 1995; Fitch, 1994). In the remainder of this section, we show you how to make two kinds of arguments about the plausibility of your interpretations: The first is that you have adequate and coherent evidence for making those interpretations; the second is showing that you've thought about alternative interpretations, in other words, that you can address counterclaims.

Adequacy and Coherence of Evidence

You need to base the evidence you present in support of an ethnographic claim on an adequate selection of the total corpus of data (Fitch, 1994). You will be arguing from the examples that you amassed in interviews, observations, and field notes, but having some part of your ethnographic data come from publicly accessible observation records will help you to bolster the plausibility of your interpretations because it will allow other people to check your subjective interpretations of the data against their own. In addition, you will need to include your consideration of "inferences and interpretations as well as concrete phenomena" when you report your data analysis (Fitch, 1994, p. 36). For example, when you present examples from interview transcripts as evidence of an interpretation that you are making, you will be allowing the reader of your manuscript to see the communicative phenomenon of interest, how that event was represented in the data set, and your analytical inferences. That will allow your readers to "decide for themselves whether or not to believe [your] account of what it is that a particular group of people are doing at any given time (McDermott, Gospodinoff, & Aron, 1978, p. 245).

Philipsen (1977) suggested three questions that you can ask yourself to test "the adequacy of statements which purport to represent the native's view" (p. 49):

> First, does the report use the native's own terms or verbatim description? Second, and failing the first test, do the ethnographer's terms or descriptions refer to something that the native agrees is a recognizable feature of his social world, and if so, can the native person give it a

name? Third, does the native person agree that the ethnographer's insight enables him (the native) to better understand his own social world? (p. 49)

Of course, ethnographers always allow room for more than one plausible interpretation of a situation or phenomenon. Paying attention to other possibly valid interpretations is another way to ensure that your interpretations of ethnographic data are plausible.

Negative Case Analysis

Negative case analysis is a way to ensure plausible interpretations by considering possible **counterclaims**— other interpretations that might be supportable with your data. Thinking about counterclaims is especially relevant whenever you are coding or reducing data into categories or themes. As you organize instances of talk into categories, consider all the instances of talk that don't fit into any one of your categories. If there are too many of those instances, then perhaps your overall data set does not support that interpretation adequately. Perhaps some other interpretation will make better use of the data (Agar, 1983). You might try playing with more than one category scheme to see which one better fits your total corpus of data.

You also should search out disconfirming observations, if they do not already appear in your data, in order to insure that your interpretations are plausible. Refer back to our discussion of negative case analysis in Chapter 6, "Warrants for Research Arguments." Consider whether you need to collect some more observations using deviant case sampling (Patton, 1990), that is, returning to the field and trying to find instances of data that do not fit the interpretations you have tentatively identified so far. To the degree that no such instances of communicative data can be located, your interpretations are warranted as plausible.

Now that you have some idea how you might demonstrate the plausibility of your interpretations, you will want to think about the degree to which your findings are transferable, the last warrant for interpretive ethnography.

Transferable Findings

Interpretive researchers have as their goal "producing meaning-centered investigations of social life that can be coherently tied to other such investigations" (Fitch, 1994, p. 36). In this section, we want to help you think about whether, and how, the insights from your ethnographic study might transfer, or be applicable to, some other group or culture. In addition, we will consider how insights from your study might transfer to public performances for performance ethnography.

The confirmability and relevance of your interpretations and inferences all contribute to transferability. Let's look at each of these concepts in turn.

Confirmability means that the findings you put forward, based on your analysis of data, could be substantiated by another person who had similar access to the same data or evidence. This is somewhat akin to *agreement among judges,* a form of content validity that we outlined in Chapter 6, and which is used by discovery researchers. Fitch's (1994) argument that researchers ought to try to make claims for which at least part of the data come from publicly accessible observation records comes in part from the desire for confirmability. You can use Carbaugh's (1988) *performance tests* (which we mentioned in Chapter 6, "Warrants for Research Arguments") to establish confirmability. To do so, you will need to return to your data collection setting and ask members to explicitly confirm the terms, forms of address, or other interpretations you have developed from the data (Barker, 1993, also used this strategy, a.k.a., member checks). Alternatively, you can simply try out those interpretations in conversation with members; if they seem to understand your performance, or do not show any signs of objecting to your performance, then you have some evidence that your findings are confirmable.

Relevance means that your interpretations matter to the participants. You should be able to show how participants orient to and signal others about the communication practices that you are describing, interpreting, or evaluating (McDermott et al., 1978). Perhaps members reference the context for their own behaviors; they may hold one another accountable to proceed in contextually appropriate ways, or their collective positioning and actions may indicate what they are trying to accomplish together. Your ability to represent these matters in your manuscript or performance will make your interpretations relevant, and more likely transferable. For example, if you can show how one participant orients to the immediately preceding action of another member, as a way of making sense of culturally situated behaviors, then your insight may be relevant to a conversation analyst who is working at a microlevel to understand that particular bit of *sequence organization* (Schlegoff, 2006).

Coherence and Researcher Positionality for Critical Ethnographic Research

As we mentioned at the start of this chapter, ethnographic research in communication bridges the interpretive and critical paradigms: EOS and EOC studies nearly always follow interpretive paradigm assumptions and values, but autoethnography and performance ethnography can correspond to either the interpretive or critical paradigm.

If your ethnographic project includes claims of evaluation and reform, you should integrate the values and standards of the interpretive and critical paradigms. In this section, we give you some examples from published works to show you how the critical paradigm warrants of coherence and researcher positionality can be demonstrated in critical ethnographic research.

Coherence

When you conduct a critical empirical study of communicative action using ethnographic methods, you evaluate communication and suggest how it might be changed to interrupt hegemonic power relations. In that case, you will need to show clear and logical connections between the data you analyzed (participant observations, interviews, texts) and the power relations you aim to change. A theoretic perspective may help you to make those connections. For example, Y. Y. Kim et al. (1998) began their analysis of communication among Oklahoma Indians with two broad categories of identity, Berry's (1990) identity modes and Kim's (1995a, 1995b) cultural-intercultural continuum. Similarly, Mayer's (2005) essay on the role of whiteness as a concept absent from most ethnographic audience research used poststructuralist theories (see Chapter 10 for more on poststructuralism) to argue that ethnographers have essentialized whiteness as either a form of structural dominance or as an individual vulnerability. If you read Y. Y. Kim et al. (1998) or Mayer (2005) in full, you will get a better idea how using one or more previously developed theories could help you to establish clear and logical relationships among different forms of evidence in your ethnographic project. Of course, as a critical researcher, you will have to ask yourself, *"For who is my narrative coherent?"* A critical essay or a piece of performative writing (e.g., a song lyric or a poem) will be more coherent for some audiences than for others.

Researcher Positionality

Carolyn Ellis (2004) is one well-known autoethnographic researcher in communication studies. Her book, *The Ethnographic I: The Methodological Novel About Autoethnography*, exemplifies the standard of researcher positionality as a warrant for ethnographic research. C. Ellis has been applauded and chastised for revealing a great deal about herself in her autoethnographic writing, for making friends with the people she studies, and for fictionalizing characters in the novel based on some of the students in her autoethnography course at the University of South Florida. Each of those choices, and other researchers' freedom to disagree with them, make C. Ellis's position as a researcher explicitly relevant in her writing and underscore critical researchers' values of voice and liberation.

In fact, autoethnography demands that you make your positionality as a researcher explicitly available to those who read your critical essay or attend performances based on your data collection and analysis (Pelias, 2003). So even if your autoethnographic claims do not include explicit evaluations or suggest reforms of communication, you should disclose your standpoint (i.e., your material, social, and symbolic roles in the situation or group you are studying). For example, A. F. Wood and Fassett's (2003) autoethnography of identity, power, and technology in communication classrooms included quotes from student emails, as well as italicized reflections of the authors' thoughts and feelings, in the published research report.

In addition to disclosing your standpoint as a researcher, you may want to disclose your reasons for doing a critical ethnographic project as a way of warranting your researcher positionality. Crawford's (1996) essay on personal ethnography provides an illustration: He recounts a swimming game among five Peace Corps volunteers in Africa that ended in the death of one volunteer, who was eaten by a crocodile. That experience made Crawford "take the ethnographic turn" as a researcher (p. 161).

Finally, your ability and willingness to articulate your standpoint will demonstrate your reflexivity as a critical ethnographer. For instance, what has led you to collect particular kinds of evidence or to favor specific interpretations of the data? Obviously, a good *audit trail* and faithful, detailed field notes will help you to recover these concepts and represent them in your critical essay or performative writing.

Table 7.4, below, summarizes the paradigm relationships, claims, data, warrants and manuscript forms typically used in ethnographic research.

Table 7.4 Ethnographic Research Summary Table

Paradigm	Claims	Data	Warrants	Manuscript Format
Interpretive (EOS, EOC, some autoethnographies)	Describe and interpret how cultural groups coordinate social actions and accomplish shared meaning	Participant observations, interviews with key informants, and texts/artifacts collected in a social setting or situation	Researcher credibility, plausible interpretations, transferable findings	Research report (including selected quotes from key informants, drawings or representations of artifacts, etc.)
Critical (Some autoethnographies, performance ethnography)	Describe and evaluate how cultural variations in speech codes implicate power relations and suggest how those relations should be reformed	Participant observations, interviews with key informants, and texts/artifacts collected in a social setting or situation	Coherence, researcher positionality (i.e., standpoint + reflexivity), change in awareness or praxis	Critical essay (i.e., empirical study of communicative action based on ideological critique), or performative writing (i.e., poetry, spoken word, etc.)

Key Terms

Archival documents
Artifacts
Autoethnography
Breaching
Case study
Coding
Codeswitching
Collaborative ethnography
Comment sheets
Communal function of
    communication
Communication code
Confirmability
Counterclaims
Culture
Data logging

Deviant case sampling
Emic view of culture
Ethnographic interviews
Ethnography
Ethnography
    of communication
Ethnography of speaking
Ethnomethodology
Etic view of culture
Explicit cultural knowledge
Explicit vs. tacit cultural
    knowledge
Face sheets
Faithfulness
Gatekeepers
Grounded theory

Group
Interviewer training
Key informants
Macroethnography (vs.
    microethnography)
Naturalistic inquiry
Participant observation
Performance ethnography
Rapport
Relevance
Researcher credibility
Rules
Speech community
Sponsors
Tacit cultural knowledge
Transferability

Discussion Questions

1. How do the three principles of ethnomethodology apply to the elevator example at the beginning of this chapter? Think of your own example of an everyday social situation where *breaching* occurs: How do interactants make sense of that reality? What *rules* and *accounts* might you study in that situation?

2. Think about the cultures to which you belong. What interpretations are *common sense* for most members of those cultures? What are some of your familiar ways of interacting that might be "made strange" for ethnographic analysis? Make a list of the speech communities to which you belong. What are some of the rules for speaking and interpreting the speech of others in one of these communities? Compare your list with those of your classmates. Do you see any commonalities?

3. If you are a bilingual speaker, share with classmates your experiences of codeswitching (i.e., when you use each language and why). Then discuss how codeswitching occurs within a single language group of speakers: For example, while speaking only in English, you may switch codes as you participate in and communicate with different groups (e.g., in the classroom, while socializing with peers, at home, at work). How frequently does codeswitching occur in your groups? When do members switch from one way of speaking to another? Why do they switch codes, or what does codeswitching accomplish?

4. Write a short essay describing the communication practices in your family of origin. Use the warrants described in this chapter (i.e., credibility, plausibility, and transferability) to evaluate your description. Is it adequate? Think about the ethics of representing your family in this essay: If you shared or performed the essay, would you "do harm" to anyone in your family? What did you choose to reveal? What did you choose to conceal, or overlook, about your family's communication? Would your family members permit you to share this story if you asked them?

"Try It!" Activities

1. Spend 2 or 3 hours visiting one of the social situations that you are considering for your ethnographic research (Spradley, 1980).
   (a) Try to identify one or two people that you suspect might be *key informants* in that setting and describe what led you to identify these people.
   (b) What initial topics or questions might you want to talk about with these key informants?
   (c) What artifacts or archival documents might you be able to use to triangulate your interviews with and/or observations of key informants?
   (d) What would you need to do to gain access to this setting?
2. Participate in and/or observe a group or cultural scene for about 30 minutes.
   (a) Write down three topics or research questions that you think might be investigated about the communication in this social situation (Spradley, 1980).
   (b) If you are a member of this group or culture, note what communication patterns or processes are most likely to be misunderstood by an outsider to this situation.
   (c) If you are an outsider to this group or culture, try to notice what you do *not* understand in this setting.
3. With one of your classmates, take separate field notes in the same setting and then compare your notes with one another: What different observations did you record? How did those differences affect your interpretations of the situation? You might read Trujillo's (1999) "teaching ethnography with collaborative learning" for more on this.
4. Select one of the three ethnographic interview types (i.e., oral history, personal interview, topical interview) for this activity:
   (a) Jot down three to four things you would talk with an informant about during an informal interview of that sort.
   (b) Create a face page for the interview: What information will you need to record about each informant in order to create a good audit trail (e.g., date, time, place, informant membership role, other demographic information).
   (c) Create an introduction: What will you say to the informant when you request his or her permission to do the interview? What will you say about your purpose for doing the interview? Will you be using an informed consent document, and if so, how will you talk about it with the informant?
   (d) Conduct the interview.
   (e) Within 24 hours after you do the interview, use a comment sheet to make notes about your impressions: Did the interview go well, in your opinion? What communication cues contribute to your evaluation of the interview? How do this informant's responses connect to your participant-observations so far? What additional questions do you have about communication in this setting or situation, based on the interview you just conducted?
5. After you have collected some ethnographic evidence and begun analyzing your data, select one key interpretation that you are making of the situation or setting for this activity. See if you can complete these questions regarding that interpretation:
   (a) Regarding Philipsen's (1977) tests of adequacy: Does your report or performance of this interpretation use the participants' own terms and mannerisms, or verbatim descriptions, of the communicative event or act you are interpreting? If not, would the participant(s) at least recognize your terms or performance or descriptions as referring to something they recognize in their social world? What might happen if you used a member check or a performance check to test your interpretations with other members of this culture or group?

(b) Are there examples or instances in your entire data set that support very different interpretations than the one you have chosen for this exercise? If so, how might you account for those alternate examples (or counterclaims) in your research report or performance?

6. Based on the above activities, write a short essay detailing your responses to the questions identified in this chapter's, "Ethical Issues" section. Articulate and reasonably defend your strategies for protecting participants' free choice to participate in research, be treated honestly, maintain privacy, and be kept free from harm. Read Vignes (2008) for a good discussion of how she wrestled with some of these ethical dilmemnas during her ethnographic research and performance work about Hurricane Katrina.

8 Conversation and Discourse Analysis: How to Explain and Interpret Talk

Introduction

In this chapter, you will learn how to analyze talk closely to support claims of explanation and interpretation. Specifically, you will learn to develop explanatory claims about how conversations are sequentially organized with conversation analysis (CA), and how to develop interpretive claims about the ways we use language to construct meanings with discourse analysis (DA). We will help you build on what you already know from Chapter 7, "Ethnography," in terms of collecting, transcribing, categorizing, and analyzing textual data. You will learn more about how you can protect participants' rights to informed consent and privacy when you study their talk. Finally, you will learn to apply the standards for conducting good CA and DA studies. CA fits the assumptions of the discovery paradigm, so you will need to show that your conversational transcriptions are valid and reliable, and that you analyzed ordinary talk-in-interaction, which is a way of establishing external validity for conversation analysis. DA better fits the assumptions of the interpretive paradigm. So the warrants for your DA study will include your credibility as a researcher, the plausibility of your interpretations, and the degree to which your findings are transferable.

Learning Outcomes

After completing this chapter, you should be able to:

» Compare and contrast conversation and discourse analytic studies to show at least two ways in which conversation analytic studies best fit the assumptions and values of the discovery paradigm, whereas discourse analytic studies best fit the assumptions and values of the interpretive or critical paradigm.

» Evaluate and reasonably defend your position relative to the ethical dilemmas of analyzing publically available discourse.

» Given a small sample of talk, identify features that could be used to explain its form or sequence, or features that can be used to interpret its meanings.

» Explain how conversation and discourse analysis can be used to explain and interpret talk for practical purposes in business and industry.

Outline

Think for a minute about all the ways you use language to communicate with other people. Only some of those ways involve unscripted or naturally occurring talk, which is the focus of conversation analysis (CA). All of the other ways that we use language to make meaning can be explored with discourse analysis (DA).

Along with ethnography, CA and DA are useful methods for exploring language in use, since they both rely on textual data sources. But their paradigm assumptions and approaches are different: As we mentioned already, CA studies deal with the sequential organization and function of language as it is used during conversation. But in DA, "the question of how things work is replaced by the question of what things mean . . . ; we are interested in how and why the social world comes to have the meanings that it does" (Phillips & Hardy, 2002, pp. 13–14). Before we define each method further, let's look at a recent example that shows the advantages of studying everyday talk.

Heidi Feldman (2012) collected 500 service calls to a camera repair shop in order to explain how customer service representatives and customers cocreated service inquiries during the calls. She selected 56 calls that were "uncomplicated by elaborate complaints or problems" (p. 16), and she transcribed them using Jefferson's transcription system as shown in Table 8.4, later in this chapter. Each customer telephoned the shop's onsite call center to inquire about the status of their equipment repair. The representatives who staffed the call center were trained to respond to calls with two steps: First, confirm that the equipment was in line for repair by checking a computer-tracking system. Second, estimate the date when the repair would be completed by checking a whiteboard on the wall that showed the average number of days the shop's technicians were spending to repair different types of equipment. Feldman showed how both customers and service representatives mutually oriented to those two steps: "In 59% of the cases

(33 of the 56 calls), representatives designed their responses to include both the current repair status and the repair completion time as a single response" (Feldman, 2012, p. 18). When the customer service representative did not provide both parts of the response, customers used "continuers" (like "Mm-hm") to indicate that the response was not yet complete, or they directly asked for the second part (e.g., "When will my camera be fixed?"). Feldman described micro-level features like "continuers," direct questions and closing sequences, to explain how customers and service reps participated together in structuring an everyday institutional interaction, the customer service inquiry. Feldman's study gives you some idea of the precision and detail level that's required to explain the sequence organization and function of ordinary talk.

Conversation analysis (CA), then, is a scientific method for explaining the structure and functions of talk. **Conversation**, or interactive discourse, usually refers to telephone or face-to-face interactions between two or more participants (Wooffitt, 2005). CA researchers explain how participants accomplish social actions and events by collaboratively organizing sequences of talk-in-interaction (Schegloff, 2006; Hopper, Koch, & Mandelbaum, 1986). For example, Harvey Sacks' early studies of telephone calls to a suicide hotline in Los Angeles showed that if a call center worker gave a suicidal caller his name, the caller would likely reciprocate. Having the caller's name gave workers a way to keep the callers on the phone, increasing the chance of getting them professional help.

Today, CA research is actually increasing among practitioners in healthcare (e.g., Beach, 2003a, 2003b; Denman & Wilkinson, 2011; Robinson & Turner, 2011; White, 2012) and in business (e.g., see Clifton, 2012; Garcia, 2012; Nielson, 2013). CA still is used in applied linguistics, linguistic anthropology, social psychology and sociology, as well as in some communication departments. CA studies have helped scholars theorize about how people accomplish routine sequences of interaction more or less successfully (like starting or ending a conversation, or a meeting). But CA research has helped all of us solve practical problems in talk, whether that means how to apologize or deliver a compliment effectively, or how to repair the situation when offense and misunderstandings arise.

Discourse analysis (DA) is an interpretive method for studying talk and language in use. DA studies may include ordinary talk, but also can deal with narrative discourse, such as blogs, films, advertisements, and so forth. DA researchers embrace social constructionist epistemology, the idea that everything we know is made real through language (Berger & Luckmann, 1967; Schutz, 1967; Wittgenstein, 1953). DA is a way of examining both interactive and narrative discourse for the sake of understanding participants' meanings and experiences, rather than to explain the structure or functions of language use. DA research has become increasingly common in communication, but also in anthropology, applied linguistics, discursive psychology, and sociology (LeBaron et al., 2003; Van Dijk, 1997; Wooffitt, 2005). Instead of a conversation, in DA, we speak of discourse. **Discourse** refers to "an interrelated set of texts, and the practices of their production, dissemination, and reception, that brings an object into being" (Parker, 1992, as cited in N. Phillips & Hardy, 2002, p. 3).

For example, you are a college student. What "interrelated set of texts" (written or spoken words, performances, and visual/pictorial symbols) contribute to the social reality of being a *college student* in the United States at the beginning of this century? How are those texts produced, disseminated, and received? What might it have meant to be a *college student* in the United States in 1914 rather than in 2014? These are the kinds of research questions that you can explore using DA. In other words, you can use DA to support claims that interpret how we construct and maintain our social realities over time through language.

Alternatively, you might be interested in evaluating social realities constructed and displayed through language use. If your claim about *college students* focuses more on hegemony and emancipation, that is, if you are concerned primarily with unequal power relations in the reality of *college students* at a particular time in history, or in a particular geographical, socioeconomic, or other location, then critical discourse analysis probably will be a more suitable method for your study. **Critical discourse analysis (CDA)** is "a form of intervention in social practice and social relationships" (Fairclough & Wodak, 1997, p. 258). CDA studies aim to evaluate the social construction of reality and to suggest how discursive texts and practices should be reformed (Fairclough & Wodak, 1997). If you want to conduct CDA, you also should read Chapter 10, "How to Critique Texts and Social Realities."

It's worth mentioning here that ethnomethodology, CA, and DA scholarship exists in Japanese, Russian, Cantonese, French, Spanish, German, and Italian, among other languages. But usually, those studies deal with a single language. Linguistic and cultural limitations prevent most researchers from analyzing talk and social realities across more than one language or culture (Van Dijk, 1997). Recently though, there are more scholars who explicitly aim to "advance the agenda of culturally-inclusive discourse research" (Scolo, 2011; Wei, 2002). Some of those studies use bilingual texts and focus on codeswitching between participants who are bilingual speakers (e.g., Cheng & Powers, 2012; Wei, 2002). Other researchers emphasize "non-Western data and methods, marginalized, disadvantaged, and developing discourse communities, with a particular focus on Asian, African, and Latin American cultures" (see Scolo, 2011, for more on this line of research, which uses Donal Carbaugh's Cultural Discourse Theory to interpret talk).

In the first section of this chapter, we will outline three key differences between CA and DA. The rest of the chapter is organized using the claim-data-warrants model. Within each of those sections, however, we will point out places where the differences between CA and DA research matter most. To get started, let's look at the differences between CA and DA research, namely, their respective (1) paradigm affiliations, (2) levels of analysis, and (3) emphasis on context.

Key Differences Between CA and DA

Paradigm Affiliations

CA and DA have come to be affiliated with different epistemological paradigms. CA and DA paradigm differences are most apparent when we compare their respective assumptions, data sources, and selection methods.

CA is a discovery paradigm method, often spoken of as a science. "What differentiates conversation analysis from other approaches to language is the assumption, 'that all aspects of social action can be found to exhibit organized patterns of stable, recurrent structural features'" (Feldman, 2012, p. 17, citing Atkinson & Heritage, 1984, p. 241). CA's reliance on one knowable reality, available to any knower who carefully scrutinizes a detailed conversational transcript, for the purpose of accurately representing how participants orient to one another's actions, makes it a good fit for the discovery paradigm. CA researchers attempt to draw conclusions about their observations using careful, systematic, and repetitive procedures, and they endorse the discovery paradigm assumption that any researcher who uses the

same definitions and the same procedures will be able to observe the same pattern of results in sampled conversational data. In fact, CA researchers in the same department or campus, or at annual professional association meetings, work cooperatively in data sessions where they listen to audiotapes or watch videotapes together and triangulate multiple investigator viewpoints. Some CA researchers randomly sample conversations to support their arguments that certain interactional practices are organized in generalizable ways across contexts (i.e., settings, relationships, participants).

By contrast, DA is most often associated with the interpretive paradigm. DA researchers are much more likely to embrace their own subjective interpretations of textual data. DA researchers assume that there are multiple plausible interpretations of participants' language use (Van Dijk, 1997; Wooffitt, 2005). DA studies may include naturally occurring talk-in-interaction (i.e., conversational data) but also include participant observations; interviews and texts gained from films, novels, or other print media; as well as pictures or other kinds of symbolic artifacts (i.e., triangulation of multiple data sources). The texts used in DA are purposively selected for their utility in exploring particular research claims.

Finally, CDA is a critical method for evaluating texts (Wooffitt, 2005). Like DA studies, CDA research begins with the assumption of multiple social realities that are constructed in interaction, and which are interpreted from an individual's standpoint. But CDA also begins with the assumption that texts have hidden or contradictory meanings, and that those meanings impact social groups differently. Thus, CDA studies aim to reveal how certain interpretations are likely to benefit particular groups of people, and oppress others. CDA researchers select texts purposively, often selecting texts that "produce information on subjects that have been accidentally or deliberately excluded ... from traditional studies of human behavior" (Halberstram, 1998, p. 13, as cited by Yep, Olzman, & Conkle, 2013, on p. 126). You will learn much more about CDA in Chapter 10, "How to Critique Texts and Social Realties."

Levels of Analysis

A second important difference between CA and DA is that they work at different levels of analysis. CA studies describe and explain **sequence organization**, "the ways in which turns-at-talk are ordered and combined to make actions take place in conversation, such as requests, offers, complaints, and announcements" (Schegloff, 2006, p. 1). Thus, CA emphasizes microlevel organization in conversation, usually between two individual speakers, based on close analysis of transcripts and their audiotaped or videotaped sources. Of course, CA can focus on embodied communication behaviors other than talk, such as vocalic rate and intonation, kinesthetic movements, bodily position, or gestures (e.g., M. H. Goodwin & Goodwin, 1986; Sacks, Schegloff, & Jefferson, 1974; Schegloff, 2006). Even when CA studies highlight nonlinguistic behaviors like these, the focus is still micro-level, analyzing how small changes in behavior help the participants orient to one another and coordinate their actions.

By contrast, DA emphasizes macro-level social organization, because DA studies include social practices and the ideological structures evident in those practices (Duranti, 1997; Van Dijk, 1997; Wooffitt, 2005). Both social practices and ideology get at some larger social reality than a single conversation.

First, social practices are broader than the actions or events that we accomplish through talk-in-interaction, even though they might include talk. Take debate, for example. The social practice we call debate is key to participating in a democratic society. Debate is a form of discourse that is used in classrooms, in courtrooms, and in politics. Debate has social, political, and cultural functions (Van Dijk, 1997). But few of us would call a debate a "conversation," even though both debate and conversation are both interactive. If you want to study how ideas are debated, you might include texts like newspaper editorials and letters to the editor, discursive texts that are not interactive. DA studies operate at a macro-level of analysis, because they deal with larger social practices (perhaps including conversation).

Second, DA deals with ideological structures. We introduced the word ideology in Part I of this book, as a group's system of beliefs and values. Think about debate as a social practice: Can you name some of the ideological beliefs and values evident in debate? For example, debate is prized in a democratic society because participation by all members is valued (free speech). Debate also privileges competition as a way of vetting ideas and arguments. Valuing participation and believing that "the best ideas will win out" are ideological structures that undergird debate. We cannot really understand a debate without understanding those values and beliefs. We have to consider the macro-level social practice and its ideological underpinnings to make sense of debate!

To get to both social practices and ideologies, DA researchers cannot focus on one single source of textual data, such as a conversational transcript (Wooffitt, 2005). Instead, DA "must refer to *bodies* of texts because it is the interrelations between texts, changes in texts, new textual forms, and new systems of distributing texts that constitute a discourse over time" (N. Phillips & Hardy, 2002, p. 5).

CA and DA scholars share the belief that humans create social realities though our use of language (Berger & Luckmann, 1967); but CA and DA scholars disagree on how much of an impact talk itself is likely to have on macrolevel social order. DA scholars focus on discourses, at the macrolevel, as the best explanation for social structures. But CA scholars prioritize talk-in-interaction, per se, as the fundamental way we accomplish social order, moment by moment, and turn by turn. These different levels of analysis mean that CA and DA scholars (and ethnographers) sometimes disagree on the role that context factors should play in data analysis (c.f., Billig & Schegloff, 1999; Hymes, 1974a; Schegloff, 1997).

Emphasis on Context in Analysis

Both CA and DA researchers frame text and context hierarchically. But they disagree about whether the text itself, or the text in context, is the best way to explain and interpret talk (c.f., Billig, 1999; LeBaron et al., 1997; Schegloff, 1997 1999a 1999b; ten Have, 1999).

Conversation analysts follow the **strict empirical requirement**, which means that they rely on conversation transcripts, and their audio- or videotaped sources, as evidence for their claims. In conducting CA, you will not orient to local context details, such as the speakers' social category memberships, or their relationships to one another, unless the conversational participants explicitly do so in their talk (Schegloff, 1997, 1999a 1999b, 2006). Of course, your knowledge of the settings and situations you are analyzing will help you to provide a more nuanced account of the interactional practices you are investigating (Maynard, 2003).

Conversely, discourse analysts always emphasize contextual constraints on language use (Van Dijk, 1997). DA researchers attend to the **institutional frame** in which a discourse exists (e.g., a discourse may be framed in legal, journalistic, medical or educational terms). DA researchers also analyze participants' memberships in social categories or groups as a way to include context in their analyses (e.g., age, ethnicity, social class). An easy way to think about context is to ask yourself, "when, where, as whom, and why people speak" (Sillince, 2007, p. 363). DA shares with ethnographic studies this attention to participants' social category memberships, social networks and how setting or situation constrain people's options for what can be done with language.

In the remainder of this chapter, you will learn to apply the research-as-argument model to the methods of CA and DA. We start with CA claims that explain sequence organization in ordinary conversations and institutional contexts (Drew & Heritage, 1992; Maynard, 2003; Schegloff, 2006).

Conversation Analytic Claims

Because CA researchers make arguments about the sequence or functions of talk using actual bits of conversation as examples, they usually start by noticing something interesting in a conversation. It might be a certain accomplishment, like a happy customer completing a service or medical interaction; or, it might be a troublesome sequence, like a person feeling insulted or disrespected.

In doing CA, your claims will explain what one utterance *does,* or accomplishes, in relation to the utterances that precede it and that follow it. You will take each speaker's next turn at talk as evidence that that speaker is oriented to the previous speaker's turn, and so on (Hutchby & Wooffitt, 1998; Schegloff, 2006). To determine how utterances are sequentially related, you will focus first on "turn-taking in conversation—how people get to talk and for how long and with what consequences" (Schegloff, 2006, p. ix).

In addition to studying everyday talk-in-interaction, you may want to show how sequence organization works in an institutional context, like medical or journalistic interviews, courtroom interrogations, or classroom situations. Table 8.1 illustrates some different types of CA claims. CA research is helping to improve communication practice in business and institutional settings by explaining interaction sequences (e.g., Nielson, 2013 on opening and closing department meetings; White, 2012, on closing surgeon-patient consultations) and functions (e.g., Denman & Wilkinson, 2011, how individuals with traumatic brain injury use touch to communicate; Garcia, 2012, on advice-giving in Ωdivorce mediation sessions).

You might start your CA project by *describing* some conversational **units of analysis**, whether those units

are utterances, sentences, a speaking turn, or some larger sequence of talk (Heritage & Sorjonen, 1994; Maynard, 1997; Raymond, 2000; Sacks et al., 1974; Schegloff, 2006). The whole endeavor of CA begins with a focus on turn taking.

Turn Taking

All sequence organizations that are "accomplished by talking get done in turns-at-talk" (Schegloff, 2006, p. 3). Turns are fashioned out of two related components, the turn-construction unit (TCU) and the turn-allocation unit (TAU; Sacks et al., 1974). The first component, the turn construction unit, specifies what counts as a speaking turn. The second, a turn-allocation unit specifies who gets to speak and when.

In ordinary conversation, grammar and vocal intonation help speakers negotiate TCUs (Schegloff, 2006). For example, native speakers of a language learn to competently recognize when a word, phrase, sentence, or coherent thought unit counts as a *turn.* We use rules of grammar and paraverbal cues like rising or falling intonation, along with eye gaze, or other cues, to recognize when another person's turn is ending, and to competently perform turn endings ourselves. In this way, turn taking is "context independent, because it does not rely on particulars of the circumstance to operate" (Wooffitt, 2005, p. 29).

Turn-allocation units (TAUs) may be negotiated between people, as when one speaker *recognizes* the next speaker's turn using words ("I yield to the Senator from Ohio"), or visual cues (e.g., eye gaze) or vocal cues (e.g., a brief pause). However, TAUs depend more on the interactional context or situation. For instance, in your college classes, you have some idea of who gets to talk more (usually the instructor) and when to talk (e.g., when invited by the teacher or during group work). Especially in institutional contexts, TAUs may be specified before the interaction even begins! For example, in a courtroom trial, the order of speakers and even some turn lengths are known at the outset of interaction (Drew, 1992). Interviews, debates, and press conferences are examples of institutional contexts in which TCUs and TAUs are enacted differently than they are in ordinary conversation (Duranti, 1997). Likewise, in a work setting, the people at the top of the hierarchy often are allocated the first and last speaking turns. Once you orient to turn taking, you can begin to notice how sequence is being organized from one speaker to the next.

Table 8.1 Conversation Analytic Claims

I. Explaining sequence organization in ordinary conversations

---

A. How do interactants accomplish turn taking? (Sacks, Schegloff, & Jefferson, 1974; C. West & Zimmerman, 1983)

B. How do adjacency pairs work?

1. Question-answer (e.g., Boyd & Heritage, 2004; Clayman, 1993; Clayman & Heritage, 2002, 2003; Drew, 1998; Heritage, 2002; Heritage & Roth, 1995; Houtkoop-Steenstra & Antuki, 1997; Leon, 1994; Raymond, 2000; Stivers & Heritage, 2001).

2. Compliment-response (e.g., Pomerantz, 1978; Valdes & Pino, 1981)

3. Greeting-return greeting

C. How do interactants insert utterances before, during, and after adjacency pair parts to do things with talk? For example, see Schegloff, 2006, on pre-sequences (e.g., pre-invitations, pre-offers, pre-announcements).

D. How is a longer action sequence constructed on a turn-by-turn basis?

1. How are telephone calls sequenced? (Godard, 1977; Hopper, 1992; Hopper, Doany, Johnson, & Drummond, 1990; Lindstrom, 1994; Park, 2002; Schegloff, 1979)

2. How do speakers use quasi-lexical objects to manage interaction? (e.g., Heritage, 1984, 1998, on "oh"; Jefferson, 1983, on "yeah" and "mm-hm"; Schegloff, 1982, on "uh-huh"; Wong, 2000 on "yeah" in nonnative speakers' English conversations)

3. How are honesty phrases used in telephone calls and police interrogations to express a speaker's stance on a particular bit of talk-in-interaction? (Edwards & Fasulo, 2006)

4. How do speakers integrate vocal and nonvocal activities? (e.g., C. Goodwin, 1980, on achieving mutual eye gaze in turn-beginnings; M. H. Goodwin & Goodwin, 1986, on searching for a word; Goodwin & Goodwin, 2012, on integrating visual information in interaction in a moving vehicle; Holtz, 2012, on laughter; Denman & Wilkinson, 2011, on touch)

5. How is conversational repair initiated and accomplished? (e.g., Drew, 1997; Robinson, 2006; Schegloff, Jefferson, & Sacks, 1977)

II. Explaining sequential structures in institutional contexts (see Drew & Heritage, 1992; Heritage & Maynard, 2006)

A. How are physician-patient interactions sequenced? (Boyd & Heritage, 2004; Heritage & Robinson, 2006; Robinson, 1998, 2003; Robinson & Stivers, 2001; Robinson et al., 2011; White, 2012)

B. How are calls for help sequenced? (Whalen & Zimmerman, 1987)

C. How are ordinary interactions sequenced? (Atkinson & Drew, 1979, courtrooms; Feldman, 2012, customer service inquiries)

D. How are department meetings opened and closed? (Nielson, 2013)

E. How do participants accomplish conversation sequence & function when faced with disease or injury? (e.g., Griffiths, et al., 2011, on Parkinson's disease; Denman & Wilkinson, 2011, traumatic brain injury)

F. "How do lay persons exhibit understandings of technical/medical procedures?" (Beach & Good, 2004, p. 8)

Source: Adapted from Adler, Adler, & Fontana (1987).

Adjacency Pairs

You may have noticed that some turn-taking happens with a simple two-step sequence. A compliment demands a response. Questions call for answers. Greetings invite return greetings. The two-turn sequence is arguably the unit on which all other conversational sequences are built (Schegloff, 2006). **Adjacency pairs** are two-part conversational structures in which the first turn calls for, or invites, the second turn. The question-answer, compliment-response, greeting-return greeting, complaint-apology/justification, or invitation-accept/decline sequences are all adjacency pairs. There is a sizeable body of CA research about adjacency pairs, most of it based on explanatory claims, such as "How do speakers construct the two parts of the adjacency pair?" Table 8.1 shows you quite a variety of CA claims that explain interaction sequence in ordinary conversation and in institutional settings, starting with turn taking and the adjacency pair.

But to competently converse with another person, it's not enough to know how to construct the two parts of an adjacency pair. We also need to know "What is the preferred second turn for a particular first turn in an adjacency pair?" Explaining preferred interaction sequence organization is the next important claim in CA research.

Preference

Any time we have choices about how to go on with a conversation the notion of preference becomes important (Atkinson &Heritage, 1984). For example, the preferred response to a compliment is modest acceptance (Pomerantz, 1978). The preferred response to a greeting is a return-greeting, and so on.

Claims of **preference organization** deal with the possible ways that speakers can respond to previous speakers' turns at talk. In many situations, there is a contextual standard for behavior. For example, in the case of questioning, the basic standard is to answer a question truthfully and briefly, yet without leaving out relevant details (Grice, 1975). Think about your teacher's response to student questions, or a politician's response to questions in a press conference: In either case, there is a preferred way to answer questions. Conversation analytic studies of preferred and dispreferred interaction sequences explain why some action, like complimenting, is accomplished in a particular way (e.g., *X* happens because *Y* culture prefers that behavior).

As speakers, we sometimes deviate from what we know is a preferred response, such as when we reject an offer or disagree with another person's assessment of the situation. When asked a question, we may try to dodge it by changing the subject, or we might provide a partial answer. Studying ". . . both *preferred* and *dispreferred* replies to questions and other first pair parts can give us a sense not only of what social actions actors are after, but also of what is considered to be normal or expected in any given situation (Duranti, 1997, p. 260). So your CA claim might address what responses are preferred or how preferred and dispreferred choices are enacted, as well as what happens to sequence organization when a dispreferred response occurs.

Breaching, violating a preferred organization sequence, can lead to conversational trouble because it interrupts an expected sequence of interaction and causes problems of understanding or offense (Schegloff, Jefferson, & Sacks, 1977). In those cases, your CA research can explain the conversational repair process.

Repair

A large number of CA studies that deal with the preference organization also address **repair**, interactants' attempts to resolve conversational trouble (e.g., Drew, 1997, Robinson, 2006; Schegloff, Jefferson, & Sacks, 1977). **Conversational trouble** usually means that at least one speaker did not orient to or accommodate the other speaker's preferences. Such trouble might come from a lack of understanding (e.g., one speaker cannot hear the other speaker, does not know the meaning of the other speaker's words, or knows more than one meaning but doesn't know to which one the first speaker is referring). For problems of understanding, repairs might involve restating, rephrasing, or explaining in more detail. However, conversational trouble also can arise when a speaker is offended (e.g., if one speaker thinks that another speaker is being impolite, irrelevant, or untruthful). When the trouble is about being offended, the repair might include an apology or an excuse. In all of these cases, CA studies help to explain when trouble arises, who initiates the need for repair (self- or other-initiated), how repairs are sequentially accomplished, and how conversation goes on following successful repair work (e.g., Robinson, 2004). Notice that the concepts of breaching (violating rules) and *going on* (proceeding with interaction when trouble arises) link CA to the traditions of ethnomethodology and LSI research more broadly.

Action Sequences

As we mentioned earlier, adjacency pairs may be the most basic unit of all sequence organization in conversations (Schegloff, 2006). Of course, conversational participants expand on those two-turn sequences before, during, and after the turns that comprise the adjacency pair (Schegloff, 2006). Those expansions are sometimes called preexpansions, insert-expansions, and postexpansions, respectively. For instance, you probably have had the experience of recognizing in advance that another person was about to invite you to do something (preinvitation), offer you something (preoffer), or tell you something (preannouncement; Schegloff, 2006).

By combining adjacency pairs with preexpansions, postexpansions, and/or insert-expansions, you may be able to explain longer conversation sequences that accomplish some action, like "disagreeing, offering, contesting, requesting, teasing, finessing, complying, performing, noticing, promising, and so forth" (Schegloff, 2006, p. 23). A myriad of actions are performed in this way. For example, when physicians and patients move from the diagnostic interview to the actual medical examination, there is a predictable sequence organization (Robinson & Stivers, 2004).

You've already seen, from Feldman's (2012) study at the beginning of this chapter, how claims about sequence organization can be based upon vocal speaking turns. But sequence claims also can be based on nonvocal conversational behaviors. For example, Robinson's (1998) study of doctor-patient visits in a British health clinic relied on nonverbal cues to explain how those conversations were sequenced. Robinson analyzed 86 audio and videotaped doctor-patient consultations, and he focused specifically on the openings of these visits. His study explained how "doctors used eye gaze and body orientation to communicate that they are preparing but are not yet ready to deal with" patient complaints (p. 97). Robinson characterized these openings as being marked by interactional asymmetry, since doctors, and not patients, routinely opened the conversations (see Schegloff & Sacks, 1973, for work on sequence closings). Robinson explained that doctors may nonverbally control the opening of those interactions because they are reproducing social power relationships in which "doctors are powerful and patients subordinate" (Robinson, 1998, p. 115). But the interactions may have been asymmetrical because "patients are unlikely to know exactly when doctors are ready to deal with the chief complaint and thus wait for and allow doctors to solicit the chief complaint" (Robinson, 1998, p. 115). Chances are good that you know when to speak and not speak in class, based on similar nonverbal behaviors.

We hope that you can see from this section how CA research is used to explain interaction functions like turn taking, preference, and repair, and the sequence organization of interactions, including turns, adjacency pairs and the larger action sequences of which they are a part. Now let's consider the interpretive claims of discourse analysis.

Discourse Analytic Claims

DA researchers readily acknowledge that their interpretations of language in use are subjective. They view discourse as socially constructed within particular times, places, and cultures. So DA fits the assumptions of the interpretive paradigm (Heritage, 1985; Phillips & Hardy, 2002; Wooffitt, 2005). DA research takes a broader approach to the study of talk than CA, so DA scholars incorporate whole bodies of texts, called discourses. To start thinking about your own DA claims, you might start by asking questions such as the following:

- What texts are most important in constructing the object of analysis?
- What texts are produced by the most powerful actors, transmitted through the most effective channels, and interpreted by the most recipients?
- Which of the preceding texts are available for analysis? (Phillips & Hardy, 2002, p. 75)

Questions like these should help you focus on the social construction of the reality you aim to describe and interpret. The texts that are produced by powerful actors and transmitted to many recipients are more likely to change participants' realities than are texts produced and transmitted by weak actors through ineffective channels. Of course, not all texts are available for analysis. There may be ethical and practical reasons not to analyze some texts.

In this section, we will show you how to use DA to investigate claims about interactional accomplishments, and how discourses make up social practices and entities. Then we will show you how to use DA to interpret social practices and entities at a broader level of analysis, beyond individual interactions. Table 8.2 contains sample claims from each of these kinds of DA studies.

An endless variety of interactional accomplishments can be studied. Here, we will use facework and identity performances to illustrate these two sorts of DA claims.

Interpreting Interactional Accomplishments

Both CA and DA are useful methods if you want to explore how communication functions get accomplished in interaction. For example, how do people perform particular roles? How do we display our social identities? But CA and DA approach the study of function at different levels of analysis: CA studies explain why speakers construct utterances and place them within a certain speaking turn. However, DA studies interpret how language use accomplishes something in a broader sense. "This does not mean that discourse analysts are uninterested in specific conversational activities, or

Table 8.2 Discourse Analytic Claims

I. Interpreting facework
A. How do speakers negotiate power relations in interaction using interruptions, leading questions, and challenges? (e.g., C. West, 1982; C. West & Zimmerman, 1983) B. How do speakers negotiate politeness norms and do facework? (Beck, 1996; Clifton, 2012)
II. Interpreting role/identity performances
A. How do speakers display their social identities and membership in various speech communities by code switching? (e.g., Scotton, 1985; Valdes & Pino, 1981) B. How does identity performance work in online fan communities (Whiteman, 2009) C. How do speakers negotiate gender rules and do gender identities? (Ashcraft & Mumby, 2004; Leidner, 1987) D. How do speakers produce, maintain, or resist heteronormativity in talk-in-interaction? (Kitzinger, 2005; Speer & Potter, 2000) E. How do business coaches construct and display competence & professionalism in interactions? (Rettinger, 2011; see also, Carbaugh, 2007) F. "Who has suicidal thoughts? What triggers suicidal thoughts? What is it like to feel suicidal?" (Dodemaide & Crisp, 2012, p. 308)
III. Interpreting social practices and entities
A. Speed-dating (Turowetz & Hollander, 2012) B. Family communication: Marriage (Lawes,1999); working motherhood (Buzzanell, Waymer, Paz Tagle, & Liu, 2007); adoption letters (Baxter & Norwood, 2011) C. College students' communication competence (Almeida, 2004) D. Advice-giving in mediation sessions (Garcia, 2012) E. Whale watching (Lawrence, Phillips, & Hardy, 1999)

their sequential contexts; rather, their interest is not restricted to that level of action" (Wooffitt, 2005, p. 44).

Studies of communicative function based on CA and DA sometimes overlap, since "storytelling may be constitutive of corporate culture, argumentation and rhetoric in parliament may be an inherent part of legislation, and educational discourse may define the social process of schooling" (Van Dijk, 1997, p. 21). CA researchers are most likely to get at the unfolding of stories, arguments, and classroom talk. DA researchers are more likely to make claims about how corporate culture, legislation, or schooling are socially constructed in a particular time and place.

In the first part of this section, we show you how to use DA to describe and interpret interactional accomplishments. Although we use facework and identity performances as examples, there are many other functions that people accomplish using talk-in-interaction (see Valdes & Pino, 1981, on code switching, or Scotton, 1985, on style shifting, for two additional examples).

Facework

How do you show that you are being polite, respecting others, or trying not to intrude on another individual's personal space? These are interactional accomplishments of politeness behavior (Brown & Levinson, 1987; see also, Goffman, 1967). Politeness strategies are used to save and give face (i.e., to show respect for and avoid offending other people). Notice how these accomplishments might vary in different institutional contexts, different settings, or different situations.

DA is an excellent way to study the interactional accomplishment of facework, actions taken to save or give face. Facework happens whenever we use politeness behaviors to show respect for and to avoid offending other people. K. Tracy and Tracy's (1998) analysis of two telephone calls by citizens in a large city to a 911 emergency call center will serve as a brief example. By comparing the discourse in these two calls with the existing published literature on facework, Tracy and Tracy (1998) showed "the subtle and blatant ways in which vocal delivery, substance and type of selected speech acts, second pair parts, and selected stance indicators do face attack" (p. 225).

Recently, communication studies of how people manage their privacy boundaries in interaction have used DA to show how people accomplish autonomy when talking with others about what may be seen as private topics. For example, Bute (2013) studied how women who have experienced fertility problems accomplished disclosure of those problems, or avoided disclosing the problems, during interactions. Bute "recruited participants through advertisements in an electronic newsletter" (p. 169) and then conducted in-depth interviews with 23 such women, which she recorded and transcribed verbatim. Bute used the interview data to build an argument about how the topic of infertility comes up in conversations (i.e., initiated by the discloser; brought on by the "textual momentum of the conversation," p. 173; or in response to a request for information made to the discloser). Bute also identified some dilemmas the women faced when they were deciding to disclose or avoid disclosing their fertility problems (e.g., disclosing a fertility problem could help educate another person, but it might lead to the other person offering unhelpful support, which would make avoiding disclosure look like a better option). In other words, Bute (2013) closely analyzed multiple instances of fertility discourse, and then constructed a general account of "when where, as whom, and why" women spoke or kept silent about their experiences with fertility problems. Her analysis links the discourses of family, motherhood, and medical institutions, as well as privacy discourse.

This is a good point at which to stress that DA researchers often start with a theory or concept that can be applied to discourse, whereas CA research is data driven. CA begins with the talk itself and then the analyst tries to figure out what concepts or structures the participants are oriented to as they accomplish conversations (Clifton, 2012). The way that we perform particular roles, or display our social identities, is another interactional accomplishment you might use as a starting point for your DA project.

Role and Identity Performances

DA can describe and interpret how people use language behavior to perform roles, as in the case of a group of students working together on a class project. The leader of the group may be identified by his or her

performance of the leader's role during the group's interaction, as much as by any title or authority designated to him or her before the interactions began. Even when there is a designated leader, some other group member may lead at a particular moment in the interaction by producing certain behaviors. Similarly, the formally designated task leader may adopt the interactional role of a group member for certain moments within an egalitarian group. In the same way, we perform roles such as "parent," "significant other," or "friend" through our discourse. So you can use DA to describe and interpret those performances. In fact, performance studies scholars often use DA to develop their embodied representations of communication (e.g., Vignes, 2008).

A great deal of research has been published in communication, discursive psychology, linguistics, and sociology on the performance of identities, or how people display social category memberships through language and social interaction (Phillips & Hardy, 2002). Some of the identities you might explore with DA include cultural membership categories, like race/ethnicity, socioeconomic class, gender, or even gender roles (e.g., see Buzzanell, Waymer, Paz Tagle, and Liu's, 2007, study of transitions to working motherhood in Asian, Hispanic, and African American women's discourse).

Of course, DA can be used to describe and interpret any of these identity performances in a specific social or historical context. For example, Dodemaide and Crisp's (2013) study of online forum posts from people living with suicidal thoughts explored how the "dominant understandings of suicide have privileged the professional observations of health professionals" over the perspectives of the people who have those thoughts (p. 308). Norwood and Baxter's (2011) study of online adoption ads, letters to birth mothers from parents seeking to adopt a child, are making adoption a more open topic, and a business proposition.

But let's take an example you know a great deal more about. How do you perform *good student* with your university instructors? How might such a performance have been different at your university 20 or 30 years ago? (Hint: It wasn't all about the mobile phone). What texts have contributed to your current ways of performing the *good student* identity? Think about books you have read, movies, television portrayals, or songs that you know of that portray students: Which texts contributed to your ideas about what *good students* do, how they talk, or what things mean to them? How were those important texts produced? How were they distributed? This is just one very simplified example. But there is a vast range of identity performances that you might explore using DA and an endless array of texts you could use to interpret those identity performances.

Interpreting Social Practices and Entities

You also can use DA to interpret social practices and entities as well as to trace how those phenomena came to exist at all, and how they are maintained or change (Phillips & Hardy, 2002). Earlier in this chapter, we mentioned debate as one example of a *social practice,* but we could add examples like dating, managing, texting, blogging (Boicu, 2011), storytelling, arguing, spamming, or campaigning to our list of potential social and communicative practices (see also, Carbaugh, Gibson, & Milburn, 1997). You could study social practices in a specific context, whether organizational (i.e., business practices), health care (i.e., diagnostic practices), or judicial (i.e., legal practices). Of course, your DA claim would interpret how participant meanings are constructed in those contexts, whereas a CA study of institutional discourse would probably focus more on how conversations are structured, or how they operate, in those settings.

Entities are things, objects, or articles. Some of the entities you might interpret using DA could include iPads, personal shoppers, group projects, board shorts, or insurgents. Any of these entities could be described and interpreted using DA because DA "connects texts to discourses, locating them in a social and historical context" (Phillips & Hardy, 2002, p. 4). Your claim should describe a social practice or entity that is meaningful for the participants, and you should aim to show how "incomplete, ambiguous, and contradictory discourses . . . produce a social reality that we experience as solid and real" (Phillips & Hardy, 2002, pp. 1–2).

If you are looking for the claim in a published DA study, try looking for the author's indication of purpose, or central assertion. This can usually be found first in the abstract, and elaborated in the introduction to the study.

Now that you have some understanding of the range of claims you can explore with CA and DA, let's consider the evidence you will need to support those claims, the data.

Conversation and Discourse Analytic Data

We begin this section by outlining the procedures for collecting and transcribing talk-in-interaction, since that data source is fundamental to CA and is sometimes used in DA studies, too. Next, we elaborate on the other ways that you can purposively select narrative discourse for DA. Then we turn to data analytic strategies, including how to determine the unit of analysis for your study, and how to make sense of discursive evidence that starts with particular cases and moves toward a general conclusion. Before we take up the procedures for collecting and transcribing conversations, though, let's compare the basic sequence for conducting CA and DA, outlined in Table 8.3.

The procedures for collecting and transcribing talk-in-interaction are important for both CA and DA researchers. So let's start by thinking about those data sources and collection strategies.

Collecting Interactive Discourse

To describe *sequence organization* (Schegloff, 2006) in conversation, you will need to accumulate multiple instances of a particular conversational practice, and examine each instance as an individual case (Maynard & Heritage, 2005; Wooffitt, 2005). You probably will consider how the words themselves are integrated with other vocal (e.g., laughter, intonation) and nonvocal cues (e.g., pauses, conversational overlaps). Usually, the interactions that comprise CA data are captured in real time, in ordinary settings, either by audiotaping or videotaping. Then, those interactions are transcribed to written or digital form by the researcher (C. Goodwin, 1993; Schegloff, 2006; ten Have, 1999). Transcribing your own data actually jumpstarts the analytic process, because you are becoming intimately familiar with conversational details as you produce the written transcript.

A wide range of conversational circumstances have been studied, including home and work settings, situations varying from meals to arrests, from sales to therapy, from health care diagnostics to treatment interactions. The data for these studies has been collected over the telephone and intercom, on hidden and open microphones, on the Internet, via participant observation and field notes, and so on.

Table 8.3 Comparing the Basic Steps for Doing Conversation and Discourse Analysis

Basic Steps for Conducting CA	Basic Steps for Conducting DA
1. First, you will need to access a sample of naturally-occurring conversation, either by audio- or video-taping talk, or by accessing a conversational database.	1. Identify the interactional accomplishment, social practice, or entity that you want to interpret. It should be a "significant, recurring, meaningful" accomplishment, practice, or entity.
2. If you record new conversations, transcribe them at the level of detail required for your analysis.	2. Purposively select and collect multiple instances of the interactional accomplishment, social practice or entity using spoken discourse gained from interviews or participant observations (you will need to transcribe these), or obtain written texts from media and/or archived sources.
3. Start analysis by noticing something interesting about one single instance of talk, "for example, a sequence of turns which seems to display some interesting properties" (Wooffitt, 2005, p. 41).	3. Determine the unit of talk you will analyze (e.g., sentences, paragraphs, stories, whole conversations or interviews, etc.)
4. Analyze that one case in as much detail as you can: What details can you notice about TCU/TAUs, adjacency, preference, etc.?	4. Analyze each unit of discourse in your sample in terms of its source credibility, structure, and specific language choices.
5. Collect other, similar instances of talk, perhaps from a corpus of archived conversational data. All of your cases need to be at the same level of analysis (e.g., single lexical behaviors like laughter or eye gaze, one speaker's turn at talk, spoken adjacency pairs, or larger sequences of conversation).	5. Next, look for and interpret broad similarities or patterns in the cases you have analyzed. If there are frequent similarities, or patterns, take them at face value, that is, as accurate accounts of what is really going on for the participants in this setting or context.
6. Develop your formal, detailed account of how the cases you analyzed are sequentially organized (Wooffitt, 2005).	6. Construct a generalized version of what is going on, and present this account as your analytic conclusions (Gilbert & Mulkay, 1984, p. 5, as cited in Wootfitt, 2005, p. 16).

Note: TCU = turn-construction unit; TAU = turn-allocation unit.

The focus on ordinary conversations and interaction settings is a key aspect of data collection for CA. If you are new to CA, you will be amazed at the lengths to which researchers go to document how talk is organized. For instance, C. Goodwin (1979) analyzed over 50 hours of "videotapes of actual conversations recorded in a range of natural settings" (p. 113) and her essay showed how one sentence "can be shaped and reformed in the process of its utterance" (p. 97). For C. Goodwin (1979), a sentence was much more than a mere linguistic unit of analysis, the words that appeared between a capital letter at the beginning and a period or similar punctuation mark at the end. Instead, C. Goodwin (1979) showed how a sentence must be interpreted in the context of its situated production. To put it differently, the length and meaning of a sentence emerge as products of a dynamic process, the interaction between speaker and hearer.

C. Goodwin's (1979) essay focused on a sentence taken from a videotaped conversation that happened during "dinner in the home of John and Beth, attended by their friends Ann and Don" (p. 98). John stated that he gave up smoking cigarettes a week earlier. C. Goodwin (1979) showed how John used eye gaze to accomplish the function of "who is being addressed?" John oriented to the relationship between himself and the hearers by adding "A week ago today, actually," as he looked at his wife, Beth. Since the dinner guests, Ann and Don, had only learned of John's decision to quit smoking when he announced it that night, John did not need to add the words "A week ago today, actually," until his gaze moved to his wife, Beth. Beth was a hearer who knew the precise timing of John's decision to give up cigarettes. In other words, John's turn at talk was mutually constructed between himself and his hearers. We hope that this example helps to show you how important the use of verbatim conversations from natural settings is to doing CA research. Without the videotaped dinner table talk, C. Goodwin (1979) may never have been able to show how sentences are constructed and understood as a joint production of situation, speaker, and hearer(s).

Naturally occurring conversations from ordinary settings are crucial for CA. Conversations include the elements of simultaneous talk, and the potential for overlap, interruption, and forms of participation that are facilitated by face-to-face or telephone interactions. Conversations are sometimes the focus of DA research (e.g., Licoppe & Morel's 2012 study of how Skype video calls are sequenced). But DA scholars often collect interactive discourse that is not conversation. For example, DA research can employ interactions gained from informal interviews (Bute, 2013), as well as a variety of interactive media discourse, like blogs, Internet chatrooms, film dialog, etc. If your CA or DA study includes interactive data, chances are that you will need to capture that data by audio- or videotape recording. The next two sections give you some recording tips and some advice for collecting interactive talk in an ethical manner.

Recording Techniques

Audiotapes have been used most to capture interactive discourse for analysis, and that is probably still the easiest and most practical method of recording ordinary conversations (Goodwin, 1993). However, videotaping can capture nonverbal aspects of conversation and may be preferable, depending on your research question, equipment availability, and expertise (Manusov & Trees, 2002; M. L. McLaughlin, 1984). Of course, the prevalence of digital video technology has greatly increased the potential for CA researchers to study embodied interactions (LeBaron et al., 2003); videotaping can help you to incorporate how talk is integrated with "the physical environment, the use of objects, technological artifacts, and/or the body or bodies of one or more of the participants (ten Have, 1999, p. 52).

However, videotaping is complicated by intricacies of lighting, camera angles, and so on. It can be more expensive, less readily accessible to most researchers, and in most settings, more intrusive than audiotape recording.

It is very likely that videotaping will compromise the naturalness of the conversational data you collect, unless the setting is one in which videotaping is already routine prior to your study (e.g., in some hospitals and medical offices today, interactions are routinely videotaped for research purposes, just as some employees are routinely videotaped for security and training purposes). If videotaping is not part of the participants' usual and customary way of conversing, then the nature of video cameras and recording equipment will be very intrusive (Wiemann, 1981).

Audiotape recorders typically are smaller and less intrusive, yet still produce excellent sound quality, which enhances their fit with the requirement of naturalness in conversational data acquisition. Of course, recent increases in video surveillance in public locations in the United States—along with many people's increasing familiarity and ease with video cameras and innovations in ever-smaller and more powerful video cameras—are rapidly changing the potential of videotaped interaction observations in social settings. The ease of capturing field data with phone/notebook/tablet technologies brings us abruptly to the ethical dilemmas of studying people's everyday language use.

Ethical Issues

Both audiotaping and videotaping require you to carefully consider your research participants' rights to privacy, honesty, and choosing whether to participate in research. Before you begin a CA or DA study, your research protocol must be reviewed by an institutional review board who will determine whether your procedures adequately protect those rights of participants. Of particular concern for CA researchers is whether participants will permit their conversations to be used in future research (i.e., to become part of a data archive from which other CA researchers can sample instances of talk). It's one thing to provide anonymous survey data but quite another to be audiotaped or videotaped in conversation, knowing that those sounds or images could be published in a research report, shown at a professional association meeting, and/or heard and seen by other researchers, sometimes years after the original interaction (ten Have, 1999). In any case, if you intend to study interactive discourse, you will want to convert tape-recorded conversations into digital or print representations. Let's look at some basic procedures for transcription next.

Transcribing Interactive Discourse

Transcription is the process of converting audiotaped or videotaped interactions into digital or print form. Speech act theorist, Gail Jefferson developed the means of notating and formatting conversational transcripts that most CA researchers still view as standard today (Jefferson, 1983, 1985, 1996, 2004; see also Ochs, 1979; Psathas &Anderson, 1987; Bucholtz, 2000).

Notating Transcripts

The standard notation conventions for transcribing natural conversations aim to provide vocalic details of emphasis, intonation, and so on, in addition to the exact words of the speakers. Table 8.4 shows Jefferson's (2004) glossary of transcription symbols. You will need additional conventions for transcribing the nonverbal aspects of videotaped interactions (for help, see C. Goodwin, 1981; Gumperz & Field, 1995; Manusov & Trees, 2002). Online instructional resources for the use of transcription symbols also can be found at http://www.sscnet .ucla.edu/ soc/faculty/schegloff/TranscriptionProject/ index.html and at http://www.paultenhave.nl/resource. htm. Of course, the level of detail you will need to transcribe depends (for the most part) on your claim.

A big issue in doing CA is time. Most introductory students of CA are shocked at how slow and tedious it is to transcribe conversation. C. West and Zimmerman (1983) estimated that it takes an experienced transcriber 8 to 10 hours to transcribe 1 hour of audiotape. The required time would be even more for videotape. Another study estimated a 30:1 ratio for transcription to tape time (Patterson et al., 1996). Of course, these estimates depend on what level of detail you need to produce to satisfactorily answer your research question, but it's usually the case that CA will require more details (e.g., paraverbal and phonetic cues) than DA. Patterson et al. (1996) found that reliable transcription of verbal content was easier to achieve than paraverbal content (except for pause length). To transcribe pause length, try using a stopwatch to time the pause at least three times and then record the average time on your transcript.

It may be tempting to hire someone more experienced than you to transcribe your taped conversations. But, given the preceding estimates, paid transcription for a 10-minute conversation, at a rate of about $25 per hour, will be expensive! More importantly, your initial ideas about what is going on in a segment of interaction will probably occur to you as you transcribe the data,

listening to or viewing the tapes many times, and typing out the words and paraverbal behaviors of the speakers (Patterson et al., 1996; Sigman et al., 1988). Even if/when technology permits transcription of spoken words to digital form using software, you will still have to decide whether and how to notate paraverbal content. Staying close to your data is advisable no matter what paradigm your research fits into and no matter what other methodological choices you make.

The detail level you elect to include in your conversation transcript could depend on your anticipated future uses of the data as well as your current research question. First, think about your research question: Will the words by themselves be enough to satisfactorily answer your question, or will you need to include paraverbal cues like pause length, interruptions, or overlapping segments of talk (aka talk-overs)?

Second, consider the uses to which you anticipate putting your data: If you are the only person who will ever use these data, and only for this one study, you can transcribe just as much detail as your current research question demands. If you think you will be conducting future studies with these data, or if you would like to share your data with other researchers, then you may want to anticipate those needs in your current transcription (Preston, 1982). For example, you may transcribe paraverbal details, even though they are not the focus of your current research question, so that your transcripts can be used to answer other research questions in the future. Another option is to keep your tapes and enter your discourse into a computer software program so that you can revise your transcripts later according to your needs. Your understanding of the data probably will change over time. So you may want to revise your transcripts later, even at the original level of detail (Duranti, 1997). You probably will not know in advance just how much transcription detail you are going to need. So it's a good idea to get advice from a more experienced colleague on this issue, at least for your first CA or DA study.

Never attempt to fix participants' talk, such as correcting their grammar, or spelling words incorrectly to "capture the flavor" of a participant's speech (Preston, 2000, p. 614). Attempts to fix participants' talk invariably make them seem less intelligent and could even mask their social practices from analysis (Preston, 2000). Whether you are a CA researcher explaining sequence organization or a DA scholar who wants to interpret participants' social realities, you must protect the integrity of the discourse, precisely as it was spoken or written.

Table 8.4 Jefferson's (2004) Glossary of Transcript Symbols (with revisions for computer)

[	A left bracket indicates the point of overlap onset Kalm: uhv never do anything (.) imprope[r? Ehrl: [Su:re.
]	A right bracket indicates the point at which an utterance or utterance-part terminates vis-a-vis another. Kalm: en uh [g o for]ward, Ehrl: [Mmhm,]

=	Equal signs indicate no break or gap.
	A pair of equal signs, one at the end of one line and one at the beginning of a next, indicates no break between the two lines.
	Kalm: Hi:.=
	Ehrl: =How'r you:.
	A single equal sign shows no break in an ongoing piece of talk where one might otherwise expect it.
	     Ehrl: A:nd uh so I said I jis' fi nd that hard to ima↓gine.=Now
	                    (0.4) .p ↑since ↓then I've retained coun↓sel.

(0.0)	Numbers in parentheses indicate elapsed time by tenths of seconds. Kalm: kin I git in: dih see you duhmorrow before I go: (.) in there et two?
(0.8)	 Ehrl: If you wan' to
(.)	A dot in parentheses indicates a tiny 'gap' within or between utterances. It is probably of no more than one-tenth of a second's duration. Kalm: Ehm: I:'m uh scheduled fċr ↑two duhmorrow afternoo:n. (.) Ehrl: Aah:: whe:re.
_____ | (0.0) —|—	Numbers in parentheses bracketing several lines of transcript indicate time elapsed between the end of the utterance or sound in the fi rst bracketed line and the start of the utterance or sound in the last bracketed line. Kalm: He i↓:[s. Ehrl: _____ [Ya:h. | (0.6) Ehrl: (1.3) .p.k | (0.3) Kalm: _|_ °hHe is.° In this case, then, one and three-tenths second elapses between Ehrlichman's "Ya:h." and Kalmbach's "°hHe is.°".Underscoring indicates some form of stress, via pitch and/or amplitude. A short underscore indicates lighter stress than does a long underscore. Ehrl: Well Dean has: uh:,h totally coop'rated with the US Attorney.
::	Colons indicate prolongation of the immediately prior sound. The longer the colon row, the longer the prolongation. Kalm: The who:::le (.) enchilada?
::__	Combinations of underscore and colons indicate intonation contours. Basically, the underscore "punches up" the sound it occurs beneath. wo:rd If a letter preceding a colon is underscored, the letter is "punched up," i.e., the underscored-letter-followed-by-colon combination indicates an "up-to-down" contour. Kalm: Hi:.= Ehrl: =How'r you:. wo:rd If the colon is underscored, then the colon is "punched up," i.e., the letter-followed-by-underscored-colon combination indicates a "down-to-up" contour. Ehrl: He tell yih 'bout Dea:n? (0.4) Kalm: No: pe? wo:rd If underscoring occurs prior to the vowel preceding the colon, then the entire word is "punched up," i.e., there is no mid-word shift in pitch.

Kalm: he said the ↑rea:son thet wuz: ü-fer the <u>ca</u>:ll wz La<u>Ru</u>e
ed (.) tol:d *hi*:m . . .

In this case, the entire word "<u>rea</u>:son" is punched up, in contrast to the words "<u>ca</u>:ll" and "*hi*:m" in which pitch drops at the colon.

This also holds for <u>multi-syllabic words</u>.

Ehrl: [He said] ë-I came dih you:,hh fr'm M*i*tchell,hh en I sai:d*,h uh↓: M*i*tchell needs <u>m</u>oney?

Here, the first mention of "<u>M</u>itchell," with only the initial consonant underscored, is produced with the entire word punched up, while in the second mention, "M<u>i</u>tchell," with the underscored vowel, pitch drops at the second syllable. Likewise, the entire word "<u>m</u>oney" with only the initial "m" underscored, is punched up.

↑↓   Arrows indicate shifts into especially high or low pitch.

Ehrl: A:nd uh so I said I jis' fi nd that hard do ima↓gine.=Now (0.4) .p ↓since ↓then I've retained coun↑sel.

. , ? ?   <u>Punctuation markers</u> are used to indicate <u>intonation</u>. (The italicized question-mark [?], substituting for the questionmark/ comma of my typewritten transcripts, indicates a stronger rise than a comma but weaker than a question-mark.) These symbols massively occur at appropriate syntactical points, but occasionally there are such displays as the following (an old favorite, not from the Watergate materials):

Marge: Oh I'd say he's about what.=five three enna ha:lf?=aren'tchu Ronald,

WORD   <u>Upper case</u> indicates especially loud sounds relative to the surrounding talk.

Kalm: I returned it 'n went over the:re (.) tih_da:y, (0.5) A::ND uh (0.8) he said the _rea:son thet . . .

t*,d*   <u>An asterisk following a consonant</u> replaces the single sub- or superimposed dot which serves as a "hardener" in my typewritten transcripts.

Kalm: I w' jist (.) understa:nd thet* uh: you en I are deh- abs'ooly dihgether on tha:t,

Ehrl: No question about it*?=uh hHerb

In this case, while Kalmbach produces "jist" and "tha:t," with the American- standard, soft 't', the 't' in "thet*" and in Ehrlichman's "it*?" are crisp, dentalized, i.e., "hard."

ä,ë,ï   <u>Two dots (trema, diaeresis, umlaut) over a vowel</u> replace the single sub- or superimposed dot which, as well as a "hardener," serves as a "shortener" in my typewritten transcripts.

Ehrl: ä-he:: told me::? . . . an:d uh,h ï-he sid we:ll? (.) that _does it,

Here, while conceivably the "e-' in "e-he" and the 'i-' in "i-he" could be read as long sounds, "ee" and "eye," the diaeresis confi rms that they are short. I don't show them as "eh" and "ih" because they are more fl eeting than those spellings indicate. The diaeresis does an additional job in transcripts where I'm using non-standard orthography. Many words get a range of oddball spellings, in keeping with the range of pronunciations they are subject to. On occasion such a word appears in its standard spelling. If that word carries a diaeresis, this means that while such a spelling could be the result of a lapse of transcriber concentration, in this case it does indicate the way the word was pronounced.

1   Kalm: Ehm: I:'m uh scheduled fċr ↑two duhmorrow afternoo:n.

.   .

.   .

17   Kalm: he said the ↑rea:son thet wuz: ü-fer the ca:ll ez LaRue ed (.)
18   tol:d hi:m . . .

In this case, while Kalmbach is shown at line 17 pronouncing the word "for" as "fer," the diaeresis in "for" at line l indicates that it's not that the transcriber at that point simply wrote the word in its standard orthography, but that it is there pronounced as "for."

(b)   <u>A parenthesized italicized</u> letter replaces the parenthesized letter with a sub- or superscribed degree sign which, in my typewritten transcripts, indicates an "incipient sound."

Ehrl: But they- (.) thä(*p*) the point is . . .

Here, after an initial "the," Ehrlichman is about to produce something beginning with a 'p' which remains unvoiced (perhaps 'point', perhaps not), and then starts again with "the" and goes on with "the point is . . . ".

when   *an italicized "h" appearing in such a word as "which," "where," "what," "when," "whether," etc.,* indicates that while such words are often produced with the "h" silent (as if they were the words "witch," "wear," "wen," "weather," etc.), in this case the "h" was sounded.

Ehrl: En I said well Joh:n *w*hat 'n the world er yih talking ↑about*.

.

.

Ehrl: See ↑*w*hat they've said duh Dean is thet he gets no consideration

	from the:m, unless they c'n corrobor↓ate.
	In this case, while at one point in the conversation (3:8) Ehrlichman pronounces the word "what" with the "h" sounded, at another point (6:15) the "h" in "what" is silent.
no*pe*	An italicized letter replaces the sub-or superscribed degree sign which, in my typewritten transcripts, indicates unvioiced production.
	Ehrl: He said We:ll?=hmhh ä-I came dih you:,hh fr'm Mitchell,hh en I sai:d*,h uh↓: Mitchell needs money? (0.6)=
	(Kalm): (°°Right°°)
	Ehrl: =(0.6) Uh::: could*=uh we::: ca::ll Herb Kalmbach en ask im duh raise ↓some.
	Kalm: °°Yeah.°°
<	<u>A pre-positioned left carat</u> is a "left push," indicating a hurried start; in effect, an utterance trying to start a bit sooner then it actually did. A common locus of this phenomenon is "self-repair" (not from Watergate materials):
	Ruth: Monday nights we play, (0.3) <I mean we go to ceramics,
	---
	Polly: y'see it's diff 'rent f'me:. <eh f' (.) the othuh boy:s
	A post-positioned left carat indicates that while a word is fully completed, it seems to stop suddenly:
	Meier: Uh well I fel' like my lef' side of my (.) chest I c'd (.) mah had a k- cramp<
-	<u>A dash</u> indicates a cut-off .
	Ehrl: An' I said (0.2) 'n dee- uh Dean said t'me . . .
> <	<u>Right/left carats</u> bracketing an utterance or utterance-part indicate speeding up.
> <	<u>Left/right carats</u> bracketing an utterance or utterance-part indicate slowing down.
.hhh	<u>A dot-prefixed row of h's</u> indicates an in breath. Without the dot, the h's indicate an out breath.
wo*hh*rd	<u>A row of h's within a word</u> indicates breathiness.
(h)	<u>A parenthesized 'h'</u> indicates explosiveness. This can be associated with laughter, crying, breathlessness, etc.
£	<u>The pound-sterling sign</u> indicates a certain quality of voice which conveys "suppressed laughter."
w*gh*ord	<u>An italicized "gh" stuck into a word</u> indicates gutturalness.
( )	<u>Empty parentheses</u> indicate that the transcriber was unable to get what was said. The length of the parenthesized space refl ects the length of the un-gotten talk. If possible, nonsense syllables are provided to give at least an indication of various features of the un-gotten material.
	In the speaker-designation column, the empty parentheses indicate transcriber's inability to identify a speaker.
(word)	<u>Parenthesized words</u> are especially dubious hearings or speaker-identifi cations.
(ø)	<u>A null sign</u> indicates that there may or may not be talk occurring in the designated space. What is being heard as possibly talk might also be ambient noise.
(( ))	<u>Doubled parentheses</u> contain transcriber's descriptions
End glossary	

Formatting Transcripts

The page layout you use in transcription should ease the tasks of reading your transcript and locating information within it. The way you visually represent verbal and nonverbal interactions on a page or screen is important to consider because "transcription is a selective process reflecting theoretical goals and definitions" (Ochs, 1979, p. 44). Transcription also has political implications because the way you interpret and represent discourse can enable certain interpretations, advance particular interests, and favor specific speakers (Bucholtz, 2000).

One artifact of page layout is that how you format your transcript will influence what your readers notice and interpret about an interaction. If you place Speaker G's turn at talk just below Speaker C's turn at talk, readers are likely to view those two utterances as contingent on one another, or at least sequential, which may not have been the case. Ochs (1979) pointed out that certain formats encourage readers to link adjacent utterances, and she argued that such a move would likely be more appropriate when transcribing adult Western speech than when transcribing the speech of language-cquiring children.

So as transcript readers analyzing interactions, we are likely view adjacent utterances as related to one another. We also make meaning of the way pages are spatially organized (Ochs, 1979). In the English language, we bring a top-to-bottom bias and a left-to-right bias, so that things at the top left are attended to first. Given these cautions about formatting pages and cultural biases, it is nonetheless common practice in this country to format transcripts so that turns at talk follow one another in sequence, with notation for overlaps, interruptions, and the like. It is also standard practice to number each line of a transcript (i.e., each line on a page), so that the location of an utterance in the total transcript can be shown (e.g., "page 42, line 37").

Be sure that you always include in your transcript the time, date, and place of the original recording (ten Have, 1999). You will want to be as explicit as possible in your research report about the conventions you used to notate and format your transcripts (Duranti, 1997).

Transcription Programs

As a beginner in CA/DA, you probably will work with two different programs to download and transcribe conversation data. The easiest way is to use one program to *play* the audio or video file (e.g., Audacity, Quicktime, or Windows Media Player) and another program to *transcribe* the audio or video file, such as MS-Word. However, some conversation and discourse analysts use specialized transcription software that combines an audio/video player and a text editor to transcribe conversations. A combined software program can control playback in ways that ease the task of transcription (e.g., keyboard shortcuts allow the user to play, pause, or rewind the conversation while typing and without looking away from the computer screen). Some software also produces the **spectrogram**, a visual description of data that shows speakers' vocal volumes and/or pitch range. Various software programs are available, although some are expensive. Of course, they all require time and practice to learn.

Two free programs you may want to try include ELAN and CLAN. Both are under constant development by their respective user communities. Both run on PCs, Mac, and Linux operating systems, and both produce transcription files (e.g., transcripts, audio, video, JPEG, and field notes) that can be exchanged between platforms. You can learn more about these programs and download a selection of CA transcripts from www .conversation-analysis.net.

Collecting Narrative Discourse

Because DA begins with a focus on particular interactional accomplishments, social practices, or entities, interactive and narrative discourse are purposively selected for their ability to shed light on what certain social realities mean, how they came to have those meanings, and how those meanings are maintained or changed. As we mentioned earlier, DA research can use interactive data that is not conversational in the traditional sense (e.g., blogs, interviews, focus group and chatroom interactions, SMS messages). DA researchers also employ narrative and archived text sources (e.g., cartoons, films, diaries, articles, letters, novels, speeches, Tweets).

By triangulating more than one discursive data source, you can construct a case study, a narrative account of communicative behavior in some social situation or setting. A case study allows you to richly describe and interpret how participants understand interactional accomplishments, social practices, or entities. Let's look at one example in some detail.

Lyu (2012) used a combination of discourse analysis and content analysis to examine two companies' crisis communication strategies (CCS) during a melamine-tainted milk scandal in Mainland China and Taiwan during 2008. She used DA to "examine how distinct political and media systems contributed to the difference of CCS selection between Sanlu and KingCar" the two companies who produced and distributed the tainted milk (p. 782). She used content analysis to compare the range and frequency of use for crisis communication strategies between those two companies (see Chapter 13 for more about content analysis).

The first two pages of Lyu's research report presented case details about the two dairies (Sanlu and King Car) and about the two countries' political systems (Mainland China & Taiwan). Both the company and country differences contributed to Lyu's analysis of how context constrained those company leaders' options for responding to a crisis. Lyu's DA data came from newspaper stories about the crisis, and she purposely selected three "newspapers with the highest circulation and . . . the most coverage on Sanlu Crisis in Beijing, Shanghai and Guangzhou, respectively" (p. 784). Together, those newspapers included 216 news stories about the crisis. Lyu found that these two organizations, one in China, the other in Taiwan, used mostly the same crisis communication strategies, but Sanlu's responses "moved from defensive to accommodative. . . as time went by whereas, in contrast, KingCar started with accommodative strategies and moved towards the defensive" ones (p. 779). We hope Lyu's study helps you understand how DA can be used to interpret social (crisis communication) practices, using narrative discourse (newspaper stories) that is purposely selected to represent a certain time and place (Mainland China & Taiwan during 2008).

Once you have collected an initial sample of discursive texts, you will need to select the unit of talk that will be the focus of your analysis.

Determining the Unit of Analysis

For many research methods students, the most difficult step in analyzing discourse is determining the unit of analysis. Many different units of talk have been identified and studied in CA and DA, including utterances, turns, acts, moves, stories, lists, descriptions, and so on (Ford, 2004; Sacks et al., 1974). Some contexts, like interviews or conversations, can themselves be considered units of analysis (Schiffrin, 1997). For example, Mandelbaum (1987) published a conversation analytic study of couple's shared stories, a relatively large unit of analysis compared to Sacks et al.'s (1974) study of turn taking in conversations. Of course, your unit of analysis will depend on your research question.

Until you know your exact research question, one good place to begin determining your unit of analysis is to decide whether the discursive units that you wish to study are larger or smaller than one sentence. The units typically studied in CA vary from a single lexical unit (e.g., saying "uhm," or laughing), to a sentence, a single speaker's turn at talk, or sequential action chains across two or more speakers' turns (Schegloff, 2006).

The function(s) and structure of talk that you want to describe also will help you to decide what unit of analysis to examine in your transcripts. A single utterance may serve more than one function. Because CA and DA are performed in iterations (i.e., repeated sequences or cycles of action), it is okay to make an initial decision and then revise your unit of analysis as you work through the transcription and analytic processes.

Once you know what your unit of analysis is, you may find that you want to examine particular types of utterances across many conversations or discourse transcripts. If you are interested in the apology-accept/decline adjacency pair, for example, you may have some instances of apologies, or you may be able to find them in a corpus of existing conversation data. There are many online resources of sound/video and transcripts, including "TalkBank" (http://talkbank.org/), the CHILDES database (http://childes.psy.cmu.edu/data/), and the Santa Barbara Corpus of American Spoken English (http://www.linguistics.ucsb.edu/research/sbcorpus_obtaining.html). Once you have accrued an adequate sample of your selected conversational units, you are ready to describe and explain their sequence organization (for CA) and/or interpret their functions (for CA or DA).

The placement of talk in a sequence of interaction is one example of the type of evidence that might be selected from a conversational transcript to support an interpretation of function. For instance, saying, "Well, I need to go now," signals the imminent "Buh-bye," that ends a telephone conversation (Hopper, 1992). But placement of talk is not the only type of evidence that may be used to support a claim of function. You may also use nonspoken, or embodied, actions that are available in the audiotapes or videotapes and transcripts to resolve a problem of hearing and interpretation in the interaction. For example, in response to one interactant's words, "This dish needs more salt," another interactant passes the salt shaker. The second interactant's embodied action, passing the salt, might be interpreted as a response to the first speaker's functional request, depending on where it occurs in the meal time—at the beginning, middle, or end, and on who says it—the cook or a guest eating it. If a guest says, "This dish needs more salt," it may be followed with some conversational repair, either because the cook has prepared the dish badly or because the guest has insulted the cook.

In terms of interaction sequences, one speaker alone cannot control a sequence. We can initiate what we think is the first part of a sequence, but our interactional partner's response will have as much to do with the coordination of how subsequent talk is sequenced as will our original utterance. For example, Harry may want to compliment Kate on her new haircut:

Harry: "Hey, Kate. Did you get your hair cut? It looks terrific!"
Kate: "Are you saying my hair looked terrible before?"

Harry may think he has given Kate a compliment. But the interaction can take the direction of a face-threatening incident or even an argument. It is likely that some sort of repair sequence needs to ensue with the next turn at talk.

Analytic Induction

Both CA and DA researchers argue from example. Data analysis for both methods begins with a single instance of talk. The researchers then use additional instances of similar talk to build an argument about how the talk functions, or how it is sequenced, or what it means to a group of people. You can use the questions in Table 8.5, below, to start thinking about how particular texts or images function, in terms of their source credibility, structure, or other specific elements. *Analytic induction* is the name we use for arguments that are based on a

Table 8.5 How to Analyze Linguistic Texts and Visual Images

Linguistic Texts	1. First, evaluate the source credibility:
	a. Who created the text?
	b. What can you tell from the text about the author's ethos (i.e., his or her expertise, honesty or fairness)?
	c. Where else might you look for evidence that would help you evaluate the source credibility of this text?
	2. Then, consider the structure of the text next:
	a. Does the text contain any identifiable introduction? Conclusion?
	b. Does the text contain any kind of internal sign-posting (i.e., cues to the main ideas, or transitions)?
	c. What is the main idea?
	3. Next, evaluate the specific language choices in the text:
	a. How would you describe the cultural context where you found this text?
	b. What language or dialect does the author use?
	c. Note any instances of code-switching in the text (i.e., change from one language to another, or one way of speaking to another way of speaking).
	d. Look for intertextuality: Does the author refer to or directly quote any other texts or speakers? If so, what is the purpose and effect of doing so?
	e. What cultural knowledge does the author seem to take for granted? What things are left out of the text because they are assumed to be understood in this context?
	f. What do the author's language choices suggest about his/her nationality, ethnicity or race, socioeconomic class, gender or sexual identity, [dis]ability, religious beliefs, group memberships, education level, etc.?
	g. What do the author's language choices suggest about his or her intended audience?
	4. If applicable, consider how theoretic concepts are relevant to the text. Revisit the sample research questions in Table 10.1 and 10.2 for this part of your analysis.
Visual Images	1. First, evaluate the source credibility of the image:
	a. Where did you locate the image?
	b. Who created this visual image?
	2. What seems to be the main purpose of the image (e.g., to inform, entertain, persuade)?
	3. Now evaluate the content of the visual text:
	a. Describe the contents using words. Note any recognizable people, shapes, or parts and their relationship to one another.
	b. What do these elements mean to you?
	4. Now consider the image elements or parts:
	a. How would you describe the emotional mood of the image?
	b. How large is the image?
	c. How much of the image is "background" or blank space?
	d. If the image appears with linguistic text, how much space is devoted to the image, relative to the linguistic text? Which one is more prominent, and why (e.g., size, use of color, bold/italic font, etc.)?
	e. How would this image convey a different meaning if any of these elements were different (i.e., size, background space, use of color, etc.).

Source: Adapted from Kirszner & Mandell (2010), The Brief Wadsworth Handbook, and Gee (2011), How to do discourse analysis: A toolkit.

collection of examples, and in some cases, counterexamples, too (Jackson, 1986).

CA researchers use sequences of naturally occurring talk to show how participants orient to one another's actions on a turn-by-turn basis. DA researchers unpack the meanings that participants in certain contexts have for terms, phrases, or ways of speaking, and how language is used to accomplish actions, or to construct social practices or entities. For both CA and DA research, data analysis starts by noticing something interesting, one particular example, or one bit of data that intrigues the researcher. The approach is inductive. It's just the opposite of the deductive approach we use to analyze survey data, or to support claims about the relative frequency of particular messages in a content analytic study. You will learn about the deductive approach to data analysis in Part 3 of this book.

Arguing from examples should be systematic and careful work (Cappella, 1990; Heritage, 1984; ten Have, 1999). Cooperative data sessions, like the ones that happen at professional association meetings, allow CA researchers to work as a team to elaborate patterns they see in their data. They brainstorm potential interpretations of the structure and function of particular segments of talk, and they sometimes perform the conversations aloud, as a resource for understanding what participants are doing in their talk (Jarmon, 1996). During the brainstorming portion, researchers will watch a particular segment of talk on video, or listen to an audiotape of the talk, at least 10 or 20 times. They take turns offering potential explanations for why turns unfolded as they did. They often argue about different explanations and try to think of cases where things work the same, or work differently. Data sessions are terrific training grounds for CA and DA scholars (ten Have, 1999). One of the *"Try It!" Activities* at the end of this chapter will give you and your classmates a chance to practice a conversation data session.

In data sessions or working alone, you will try to find and present examples from the data that support your claims. You might start by reading through a transcript alone and writing brief a data memo about your initial impressions of the text (i.e., what you notice first about the conversation structure or functions of talk, or what particular terms or phrases seem to mean to participants). Later you can compare the examples you collect, and try to see what they have in common, or how they are different from one another. You might notice some theme that connects some of your examples with

other ones. You will keep going back and forth, from the data, to your memos, and then back to the data, until you can account for all the plausible meanings (with DA), or until you determine which explanation of conversational structure or function your data can best support (for CA).

But you also will actively seek out counterexamples when doing CA and DA! **Counter examples** are instances of data that do not fit your claim and that might support a competing explanation or interpretation of the talk. Here, you may want to review the concept of *negative case analysis* from Chapter 7, "Ethnographic Research"). Using counterexamples also helps to assure that your examples really do support your claim, because your explanation about the conversational structure or function is generalizable to other conversations between other people. Using counterexamples helps to support your DA claim of interpretation by showing how participants sort out meanings when there is more than one plausible interpretation for some textual data.

Review the basic steps for DA that we presented in Table 8.3, earlier in this chapter. As you argue from examples of discourse, you will try to describe patterns of similar meanings across settings, participants, or texts: It is important that you privilege the emic perspective by using categories that members apply to themselves rather than imposing categories onto your data (Phillips & Hardy, 2002; ten Have, 1999; Van Dijk, 1997).

Next, let's consider the warrants for conversation and discourse analysis.

Conversation Analytic Warrants

Conversation analyses are warranted using discovery paradigm standards as outlined in Chapter 6. The first two warrants we develop in this section, transcription veracity and detail level clearly reflect discovery paradigm assumptions and the values of precision, parsimony, and power. Your CA data sample has to represent the population of conversations you seek to explain (external validity). The conversations you analyze have to be transcribed accurately and with the right amount of detail, without compromising sample naturalness (internal validity).

However, it is important to notice that CA researchers make arguments of association and not full causality. CA scholars recognize that there are so many interactional choices in practice that a researcher cannot predict what people will do in any given conversational turn. Therefore, rather than predicting that some conversational move will happen, CA researchers look to see what actually happens and then try to explain it by examining its featured regularities. Of course, you will also warrant your inferences about a conversational transcript using your own cultural knowledge of, or experience with, the kinds of conversations that you are analyzing (Stokoe & Smithson, 2001).

Like the ethnographer, CA researchers have to hone their skills at observing detail very closely, describing what they observe, and systematically making sense of a myriad of detailed observations (Hutchby & Wooffitt, 1998). For now, let's consider two strategies that are particular to CA: How you can demonstrate transcription veracity and detail level? How you can assure that the conversations you study are ordinary, or naturally occurring?

Transcription Veracity

Transcription veracity refers to the degree of correspondence between the words typed in a computer file and those recorded on a segment of audio- or videotape. Veracity is typically judged as a matter of agreement. So if two people wrote down the same words after listening to one bit of taped interaction, the transcript is considered to have high veracity. Obviously, this concern is closely linked to internal validity.

Patterson et al. (1996) wondered whether high veracity transcripts could be produced by college students who had only about one-half hour's training and who used their own familiar recording and word-processing equipment. So Patterson et al. (1996) conducted an experiment that measured intertranscriber reliability. Remember, reliability means consistency in measurement. So intertranscriber reliability just means that two or more people accomplish consistent transcription of conversation (Roberts & Robinson, 2004). Based on the results of their experiment, Patterson et al. (1996) concluded that "with a minimum of training, multiple independent transcribers are capable of producing similar transcripts from the same source tape" (p. 87). And even though notation *agreement* does not guarantee the *accuracy* of transcription, they wrote, "It does provide corroboration and a greater likelihood of accuracy" (p. 81).

As you might expect, the agreement rates achieved in Patterson et al.'s (1996) experiment were different, depending on the type of communication being transcribed. The highest level of agreement among the college student transcribers was for verbal content (94% agreement rate). Reliable transcription was slightly lower for notating areas of overlapping talk among two or more speakers (86% agreement rate) and for documenting rising and falling intonations (82% agreement rate). The hardest thing to transcribe reliably was pause length (49% agreement rate). Most of the disagreements Patterson et al. (1996) discovered happened when one student failed to transcribe something that other students did transcribe (i.e., error by omission).

Most of the published CA studies that you read will not use multiple people to transcribe a tape. Typically, conversation analysts either transcribe their own tapes or hire a person to transcribe the words on the tape and then add details of paraverbal cues themselves. Most published CA studies do not assess or report intertranscriber reliability, although conversational databases allow other researchers to examine the recorded conversations to verify that the transcript is indeed accurate and that they agree with the analysis of what is going on. If you are new to CA/DA research and you are not using any software program for data analysis, it may be a good idea to verify your transcription with another person, especially if your research question deals with paraverbal interaction features like pause length.

Detail Level

For CA and DA, both the tape-recorded interactions and the written transcripts constitute data sources (Patterson et al., 1996; Sigman et al., 1988). "It is, after all, because we can review the recordings and study the transcripts endlessly that we come to see the details of conversational organization hidden by real time and ordinary sensibilities" (Schenkein, 1978, p. 3). One warrant for the worth of your CA/DA argument is to demonstrate that you have recorded and transcribed the appropriate level of detail needed to answer your research question. If your claim is to explain interruption behavior in a cross-cultural situation, you will need to demonstrate that your transcription of pause length is sufficiently detailed and accurate before you start interpreting the function of particular instances of overlapping talk. You may also want to ensure that those who produce the written transcripts from audio- or videotapes are members of the culture being studied. (See our discussion of degree of membership in Chapters 6 and 7 for more on this issue.)

Sample Representativeness

When considering any given CA study, nearly endless philosophical arguments may be raised about how natural was a certain sample of conversational behavior. We do not want to raise such philosophical debates here. Instead, we hope to point out a basic general principle: The sample talk that you select for CA should, insofar as possible, represent talk *as it would have occurred* if no research project were being conducted. To the extent that talk is contrived or influenced by your presence as a researcher, or your recording equipment, then sample naturalness will be threatened. Without sample representativeness, all claims to explain ordinary conversational behavior and sense making will be suspect, because your study will lack external validity.

For example, Nielson's (2013) study of how meetings are opened and closed was based on audio- and videorecordings of 17 meetings at four Danish companies and a national trade union. In the published research report, Nielson wrote that, ". . . all recorders were set up and switched on before the first participant entered the meeting room and only turned off after all participants had left the room" (p. 39). Nielson's consistent recording practice for each meeting helped her to establish reliability. But we don't know how much the presence of video cameras in those meetings may have affected the participants' talk (i.e., validity).

Discourse Analytic Warrants

Discourse analyses and ethnomethodological research are warranted using standards from the interpretive paradigm, as outlined in Chapter 6. Given the interpretive paradigm values of subjectivity and rich description, and the processes of triangulation, DA scholars have various ways of demonstrating their credibility as researchers, the plausibility of their interpretations, and the transferability of their findings. Since you may triangulate evidence from informant interviews or participant observations with archival texts to warrant your interpretations of what is going on in a social situation, you may want to review Chapter 7, "Ethnography" if your DA project includes texts you gained in observation or interviews.

Researcher Credibility

If you want to analyze the discourse of college students from a cultural insider's perspective, you should be prepared to demonstrate both that you are a member of that culture yourself, *and* that the talk you analyze is produced by members of that culture. If you hope to interpret communicative accomplishments, social practices, or entities that matter to college students, you will need to be able to recognize what activities students are engaging in when they interact (Hutchby & Wooffitt, 1998). Interpretive researchers call this work *building a case* for particular interpretations (S. Jackson, 1986).

Remember that cultural insiders and outsiders make different sense of situations, so degree of membership does not guarantee credible DA analysis. Keep in mind the advice we gave you in Chapter 6, "Warrants for Research Arguments," about faithfulness and theoretical sensitivity. The credibility of your DA study depends greatly on you being a good interviewer or participant observer (if you use those strategies to collect discourse). Your dedication to logging detailed field notes and data memos during your data analysis also contributes to you writing a credible research report. A clear audit trail will help you specify where and when and how you arrived at a particular interpretation of the evidence you analyzed.

Plausible Interpretations

We have already stressed that interpretive research often relies on triangulating multiple data sources, data settings, and data collection strategies, as well as researcher viewpoints. Triangulating data sources, settings, and researcher viewpoints helps to ensure plausible interpretations. Your training and experience with purposively sampling textual data, and your grasp of different theoretic concepts, also will help you to create a *coherent* narrative about the categories or patterns that you observe in discourse. You also may want to use participants' explicit understandings of a situation in order to show that your interpretations are plausible.

As a case in point, Bastien and Hostager (1992) used a combination of participant observations, interviews, and transcript analysis to examine how jazz musicians cooperatively accomplished the organization of an improvisational concert performance. Their claim was one of communicative function. How is the structure of an improvised jazz performance organized by the performers' verbal and nonverbal discourse?

Briefly, Bastien and Hostager (1992) first observed and videotaped a jazz performance. Then they analyzed the videotape and transcribed the spoken and embodied actions of all the participants. They interviewed one participant while watching the videotape and elicited a blow-by-blow description of all the turns in the interaction. Using their observations, the videotape, the transcript of the concert, and the transcript of the interview, Bastien and Hostager interpreted how these jazz musicians accomplished organizing. Bastien and Hostager's (1992) study was similar to Eisenberg's (1990) examination of how basketball players organize improvisational "pickup" games. In both studies, the research question might be phrased this way: "How do strangers, who know the rules for a social situation but do not know each other, or have assigned roles in their performance of the situation, structure their interactions in ways that accomplish sense making?" Notice that both jazz improvisation and pickup basketball games are social realities, that is, historically and socially situated interactional accomplishments.

You will need to be cautious about some potential problems with informant data (Sigman et al., 1988; Stokoe & Smithson, 2001). The perspective offered in an interview may not be exactly the perspective participants actually employ when they are engaged in interaction, for at least three reasons: First, interviews often allow more time for reflection about behavior than real-time interactions permit. Second, interviews encourage face-saving interpretations of participants' communication competence. Third, interview questions are likely to structure what participants do (and do not) reveal to you about a social situation (i.e., demand characteristics; see Chapter 15 for more). Questions invite answers, and interview data are always subject to the limitations of questions asked and unasked by the researcher. Whether you are conducting DA yourself, or evaluating a published DA study, think about how the data source might impact the plausibility of interpretations, especially if the data were gained during observation or through interviews.

Another way to think about plausible interpretations of discourse is to look for theoretical saturation, the sense that you understand everything important about the social situation and that analyzing more textual data would not add anything important. This does not mean that you will resolve different, competing categories of meaning—in fact, you will allow "different voices to pervade" your DA research report

(Phillips & Hardy, 2002, p. 85). In fact, you should customize your DA research report, and not just rely on conventional procedures, because you are helping to constitute the phenomena you study as you write your research report (Duranti, 1997; Van Dijk, 1997). You will need to be reflexive about "word choice, writing style, and presentation of data, recognizing that these are in part constitutive of the social phenomena under investigation" (LeBaron et al., 2003, p. 11). As a reader of such reports, you might think about how the author's word choice, writing style, or presentation of evidence helps you understand that communicative accomplishment or social practice, too.

Transferable Findings

As you know from Chapter 6, transferability means that insights from one study can shed light on communicaton in other settings, among other participants, or on the meaning of another discourse. For instance, LSI research contributes to performance studies scholarship in several ways because LSI studies "invite noticing of poetic and performative features of everyday interaction" (LeBaron et al., 2003, p. 10). First, the findings of CA and DA research can be performed directly, or used to create fictional performances (e.g., plays, novels, films) that more closely resemble everyday life performances, especially when those studies focused on ordinary talk and included embodied interactions. The transcription conventions developed by Gail Jefferson (2004) made it possible for CA research to contain detailed descriptions of vocal inflection, overlapping talk, and pausing that would help creative writers produce dialogue that more closely resembles the way people really speak (Stuckey & Daughton, 2003; see also, Jefferson, 1996).

Second, conversational or other everyday life performances (Hopper, 1993; Stuckey & Daughton, 2003) can be used to help practitioners in many endeavors to learn about their contexts, roles, or expected identities. For example, those who train people to do interviews in the medical context, or to provide customer service on the telephone, can use CA and DA findings from those settings to construct relevant training scenarios and to train people how to perform those service roles (Feldman, 2012; Robinson & Turner, 2011; ten Have, 1999). This does not mean that CA and DA findings are generalizable, in the sense that they apply to a whole population of people or messages. Rather, the insights from CA and DA studies may be of benefit to people who are trying to become competent communicators in those contexts or roles. Pal and Buzzanell (2008) noted, for example, that workers in an Indian call center were instructed to watch episodes of *Friends* in order to learn how to interact as if they were US Americans during customer service calls with US residents.

One way that you can make your CA or DA research project more transferable is to anticipate in your IRB process how others might be able to access your tapes and transcripts since those are not usually included in a research report. Your research report also might specify contexts or roles for which your study provides transferable insight.

More Ethical Issues in CA/DA Research

In the section on collecting interactive discourse for CA and DA, earlier in this chapter, we stressed that audiotaping and videotaping talk-in-interaction requires you to carefully protect people's rights to privacy, honesty, and autonomous consent to participate in research. Similarly, if you are considering the use of video surveillance data for your CA/DA study, you need to remember that the opportunity for informed consent is compromised and that this puts an even greater ethical burden on you, the researcher. At this point, you should be able to articulate some of the choices that you might make to protect participants' rights during data collection, transcription, and analysis, as well as in the ways that you can ethically you store data after your study is completed, and report CA/DA research ethically. But there is more to being an ethical CA/DA researcher than protecting participant rights. In this section, we briefly outline two ethical responsibilities for the CA/DA researcher that go beyond protecting participant rights per se.

First, you already know that CA and DA researchers adhere to somewhat different paradigm assumptions (i.e., discovery and interpretive/critical

paradigms, respectively). Given our definition of ethics in Chapter 2, as translating values into social action, you can be most ethical in your research if you identify your paradigm assumptions and stick to them during the course of any one study. For example, in DA research, the idea of reflexivity includes allowing different voices to pervade the text and acknowledging that all possible voices are not represented in the text (Phillips & Hardy, 2002); allowing different voices is consistent with the interpretive paradigm focus on multiple plausible realities and with the critical paradigm warrant of researcher positionality (including standpoint and reflexivity).

Second, there is ethical danger in valuing expediency over beneficence, respect, and justice when you are selecting or analyzing messages. You should know that simply categorizing messages in your CA/DA data set does not, by itself, constitute *analysis*, for "... that is a taxonomic act, not an analytic one" (Schegloff, 2006, p. 268). It is one thing to recognize what function a bit of talk is serving (e.g., small talk) or what role a person is performing (e.g., good student). It is another thing to be able to explain and interpret *how* that function works or *why* role performances look and sound the way they do in a given setting or situation. Analysis involves both naming it and explaining it!

You can be most ethical by recognizing when you are valuing expedience over beneficence, respect, or justice, at every stage of your research project (i.e., choosing what to study or not study, designing the study, collecting and analyzing data, and reporting the results of your investigations). When you catch yourself just wanting to finish the project, ask yourself, "What might I do differently to benefit participants, or to show them respect and treat them justly, even if it means that my project will take longer to complete?"

Table 8.6, on the next page, summarizes the claims, data, warrants and manuscript form typically used for conversation analyses.

Table 8.7, on the next page, summarizes the claims, data, warrants and manuscript form typically used for discourse analyses.

Table 8.6 Conversation Analysis Summary Table

Paradigm	Claims	Data	Warrants	Manuscript Format
Discovery	Explain sequence organization and/or communicative functions in ordinary talk	Audiotapes, videotapes and transcriptions of samples of naturally occurring talk-in-interaction; strict empirical analysis (i.e., evidence located within the transcript itself)	Transcription veracity, content validity of coding scheme (including detail level), and sample naturalness	Research report

Table 8.7 Discourse Analysis Summary Table

Paradigm	Claims	Data	Warrants	Manuscript Format
Interpretive	Interpret the ways that a discourse constructs social realities over time; what discourse means to participants, how those meanings come to exist or are changed.	Purposive samples of discursive texts, including audio- and videotapes with transcriptions, or archival texs; analysis combines empirical data with researchers' subjective understandings of talk.	Researcher credibility (including degree of membership), plausible interpretations, and transferable findings.	Research report *

*See Chapter 10 for advice about Critical Discourse Analysis claims, data, warrants, and essay preparation.

Key Terms

Accounts
Adjacency pairs
Breaching
Counterexamples
Conversation
Conversation Analysis (CA)
Conversational trouble

Critical Discourse Analysis (CDA)
Discourse
Discourse Analysis (DA)
Facework
Institutional frame
Preference organization
Repair

Sequence organization
Strict empirical requirement
Style shifting
Transcription
Transcription veracity
Transcripts
Units of analysis

Discussion Questions

1. Make a list of your identities (e.g., generation, social class, ethnicity, geographic location, etc.). What bodies of texts could you draw from to interpret how the identities you listed are performed or accomplished in interacting with other people? How would your data sampling strategy change if you wanted to explain how one of your identities came to exist, or is maintained, rather than to describe how that identity is accomplished in interaction?

2. What are the ethical implications of studying people's ordinary conversations? Identify at least two ethical dilemmas that might arise, and describe exactly what you would do to resolve those dilemmas. How would your approach affect the warrants for your CA or DA study?

3. Do you agree or disagree with the strict empirical requirement of CA? Remember, this means that claims can be supported by transcripts and recordings only, without relying on other cultural knowledge of the situation gained from participant-observations, interviews, or other data sources.

"Try It!" Activities for CA

1. Locate and analyze one instance of conversational trouble in a movie, fictional story, or entertainment television show. Answer the following questions about the interaction you selected:
   (a) Was the trouble caused by a lack of *understanding* or by *offense*?
   (b) If offense, how did one of the speakers violate a preferred interaction sequence?
   (c) What happened to repair the trouble?
   (d) Who initiated the repair?
   (e) What practical value could come from diagnosing **conversational trouble, preferences**, and **repair** strategies?
2. Record 5 minutes of any multi-party news, talk show, or post-game sports broadcast. Watch the tape with your classmates and try to articulate the TCUs and TAUs for the show: What counts as a speaking turn? Who can speak, and when? Are there any consequences for failure to recognize or follow these conversational rules?
3. Practice collecting conversational data and running a **data session** with your classmates: First, audio- or videotape a brief conversation (i.e., 5 minutes or less) from your daily interactions. Be sure you get permission from everyone involved in the interaction, either before or after the recording takes place.
   (a) Transcribe your conversation using the conventions developed by Jefferson (2004) and outlined in Table 8.4. You might work with a small group of students from your research methods class so that each person transcribes 1 minute of the conversation.
   (b) Listen to the audio or videotape of the conversation several times together, while looking at your (collective) transcript. Talk about potential explanations you each have for why participants behaved as they did during a particular turn at talk.
   (c) See if your group can support one explanation of "what is happening in that turn" better than other explanations offered by group members. Are there any other instances of talk in your conversation sample (or in other conversations your classmates collected) where conversation turns *work* in a similar way?
   (d) How might you build a larger sample of cases that fit your argument?
   (e) Where would you look for examples that may not fit your explanation of this conversational structure or function?
   (f) What did you learn from this activity?
4. Have another student in your class transcribe the same conversation (or portion of a conversation) that you transcribed in the previous activity. Compare your written transcripts. What differences and similarities do you notice? How would you evaluate your own transcription veracity?

"Try It!" Activities for DA

1. Choose one *discourse* (e.g., personal ads, yellow pages, grafitti, Tweets). Remember that a discourse is an interrelated set of texts that includes information about how the texts are produced, disseminated, and received. Write a short *data memo* that outlines some of your initial thoughts about these research questions:
   (a) What texts would you include to describe this discourse?
   (b) How are those texts interrelated?
   (c) How has this type of discourse changed over the past 10, 50, or 100 years?

(d) Are there new forms of texts that are relevant to this discourse (e.g., SMS messages, Instagram pages, Snap Chat messages or other social media outlets)?

(e) Are any new systems for distributing texts helping to reconstitute this discourse (e.g., smart televisions that allow online participation during televised broadcasts, ala *The Voice* or political campaign debates)?

2. Follow one major corporation's blog (or any customer or fan comment page) for two weeks. Use screen capture to collect digital records of the messages posted there each day, since they may change often. Conduct the following analysis of the messages you collected:

(a) Is this textual data narrative discourse or intearctive discourse?

(b) What communicative accomplishment, social practice, or entity does your discourse represent?

(c) Use the questions in Table 8.7 to closely analyze each comment or post (including visual images, such as photos or video clips in the blog). What does your analysis of the source credibility, structure, and language choices tell you about how to interpret this discourse?

(d) How do your group memberships inform your understanding of this discourse (e.g., are you a customer or fan of this company yourself)? How does your degree of membership help you to interpret this discourse? Can you identify more than one plausible interpretation?

(e) Think about other similar types of discourse, perhaps talk found in other comment pages or blogs: What larger societal discourse(s) are related to the texts you analyzed? (This will help you consider whether your findings are transferable.) What social realities are being created, maintained, or changed over time through the use of this discourse?

3. Collect a set of five short sequences of interaction (less than 1 minute each) or five segments of narrative discourse, all on the same topic (e.g., amount of homework in a class, qualities of a good teacher, sports talk). If you want, you can look for samples of talk on www.TalkBank.org. For each discourse sample, analyze "who, where, as whom, and why" the speaker says what she or he says. After analyzing all five bits of talk, what general account can you offer about this kind of discourse? What institutional or cultural discourses are connected to these bits of talk? It may help to look at Norwood and Baxter's (2011) discussion of how online adoption letters to birth mothers are linked to larger cultural discourses of adoption in general, and to readers' stereotypes of birth mothers (p. 203).

9 Rhetorical Criticism: How to Interpret Persuasive Texts and Artifacts

Introduction

In this chapter, you will learn about the distinction between rhetorical theory and methods of rhetorical criticism. You will explore methodological connections to the discovery and interpretive paradigms and those that bridge to the critical paradigm. Methods first associated with the discovery paradigm include neoclassical and genre criticism. Methods from the interpretive paradigm include metaphoric analysis, dramatism, and narrative criticism. New developments in rhetorical criticism include reconsiderations of text and recasting the audience in the "public sphere." As part of a historical overview of these methods, we discuss the types of claims you would be likely to assert with each method and the different sorts of texts that provide the data or evidentiary sources for these analyses. For each method, you will learn to apply the warrants of traditional and interpretive approaches to rhetorical criticism, including accuracy and logical consistency, adequacy of evidence, and the plausibility of interpretations through coherence and fidelity. We end with several ethical concerns in contemporary rhetorical criticism.

Learning Outcomes

After completing this chapter, you should be able to:

» Identify and apply essential elements of neoclassical and genre rhetorical criticism to the analysis of a text.

» Identify and apply to a rhetorical text the unique steps in the interpretive methodologies of rhetorical criticism: metaphoric, dramatistic, and narrative criticism.

» Explain the paradigm assumptions affiliated with each rhetorical method and discuss the trends toward critical paradigm assumptions.

» Discuss changes in the conceptions of the traditional elements of context and audience as public.

» Discuss the central ethical concerns in contemporary rhetorical criticism.

Outline

If you have come across the term *rhetoric* outside of class before, it was very likely to be a comment on the pompous speech or slick doublespeak of a politician, and the "oh, that's just rhetoric" comment made in that context equated the term with empty or insincere speech. Or you may have heard a teacher refer to asking rhetorical questions, which are designed to make you think but aren't really meant to be answered. These two common usages of the term give a confusing picture of what rhetoric is and explain even less about how it might be used as a method. They do not provide a hint about why we would want to study rhetoric or how it is a useful process that can be applied to our everyday lives. We will begin this chapter by exploring the basic concept of rhetoric, distinguishing between rhetorical theory and rhetorical criticism, and then spend the remainder of the chapter demonstrating the methods of rhetorical criticism from the discovery and interpretive paradigms. Chapter 10, "How to Critique Texts" will deal with critical studies of communication, including both ideological critique and critical empirical studies of communicative action.

Rhetorical Theory and Rhetorical Criticism

For those of you who have taken a class in public speaking, you may have learned that *rhetoric* is about learning to identify and use the skills of speaking persuasively. If you were to take a course in rhetorical theory, you would be learning about the various ways in which we define and explain what rhetoric means; courses in rhetorical criticism focus on the application of those definitions and explanations. You can see the fundamental connection between communication and rhetoric in each of these contexts; in fact, rhetoric, practiced as a discipline, was the first study of communication.

As we have explored in other chapters, the idea of what constitutes communication has radically changed from its classical origins of spoken words to texts and artifacts that would include books, films, TV episodes, broadcast/online/print news, music, websites, statues in public parks, events, and even social movements. Look around you. Political campaigning, marketing and advertising, images on *Facebook* pages, the interior of your room: Any communication message expressing meaning can be interpreted as a rhetorical text. Foss (2009) defines **rhetoric** in this broader sense, as "the human use of symbols to communicate," asserting that this definition focuses on three dimensions: "1) humans as the creators of rhetoric; 2) symbols as the medium of rhetoric; and 3) communication as the purpose of rhetoric" (p. 3). Other authors identify definitions with more persuasive *intent* by stating that you engage in rhetoric whenever you communicate to another person or persons your intention to get something done (Keith & Lundberg, 2008).

From Foss's definition, you can see an emphasis on rhetoric as the interpretation of symbols in human communication. All communication involves symbolic representation, which means that the messages we use to represent our relationships with people, objects, actions, or events are ones we construct and infuse with meanings embedded within these messages. This is a tough abstraction to understand in its full significance but think about some of our examples: What meanings have you conveyed about yourself on your Facebook pages? What does the way you have decorated your room say about you? When you become a rhetorical critic, you begin to look at all messages, verbal and nonverbal, as carrying some potential to influence others. Rhetorical critics develop ideas and theories about understanding the meanings of messages and acquire methods for, as Brummett identifies the process, taking a close reading of texts (2010). Learning to explore messages and their deeper more implicit meanings is a lifelong skill that you will undoubtedly be able to employ in your relationships, professionally and interpersonally.

Rhetorical theories, then, refer to the explanations and interpretations of the ways in which messages or texts are persuasive; **rhetorical criticism** refers to the systematic application of theory to persuasive communication. Burke's dramatistic theory and Fisher's narrative theory are two accounts about the nature of persuasive messages. When you apply a theory like these to the interpretation and evaluation of a message or text, you are engaged in the process of rhetorical criticism.

You will see in the various methods we apply in this chapter that rhetorical theories and how these are critically applied has changed from classical to contemporary times. As our ideas of rhetoric change, so do our criticism methods. Regardless of the changes, however, you will be able to see three characteristics of rhetorical criticism throughout: (1) inductive analysis of persuasive communication, (2) messages in the broadest sense as the focus of analysis, and (3) interpreting and understanding the rhetorical processes as the purpose of criticism (adapted from Foss, 2009, p. 6). Because criticism is systematic, we will explore the same basic steps with each rhetorical theory: the selection of the message or text, formulating the central claim, and the analysis through applying the theoretic framework. Until this chapter, we have used the terms interpretive and critical to apply distinctively to paradigm characteristics. But by these characteristics, any method of rhetorical criticism must be considered interpretive and critical. The theoretic framework is interpreted and applied to a persuasive message as a fundamental part of the analysis.

In the process of doing rhetorical criticism, the aim of your criticism is to contribute to rhetorical theory by illustrating and often expanding the theory's explanation. The method you choose will result in a critical essay, reflecting the steps of your criticism. The steps are detailed in Table 9.1: (1) an introduction, in which you will identify your central claim along with its significance, (2) a description of the persuasive message or text you have selected with a rationale or context for your

Table 9.1 Components of Rhetorical Critical Essays

Introduction	Identify central claim and its significance
Message or Text Selection	Explain selection of message and its rationale or context for interpretation
Theoretic Framework	Explanation of the theoretic framework used in the analysis
Findings or conclusions	Report of the findings or conclusions reached by application of the theoretic framework
Theory development	Discussion of the ways in which the study contributed to the rhetorical theory.

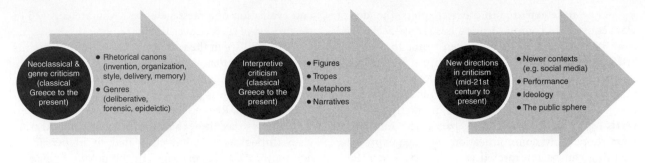

Figure 9.1 Rhetorical critical methods over time

selection, (3) the explanation of your theoretic framework, (4) a report of your findings through interpretation and application of theory, and (5) the contribution of the analysis to the development of theory (Foss, 2009, p. 13).

We have organized the many forms of rhetorical criticism methods in this chapter roughly as they emerged over time in our field. The historical timeline is represented in Figure 9.1. For comparison, you can begin by examining the sample claims from each of the three paradigms within rhetorical criticism in Table 9.2 and then refer back to those sample claims throughout this chapter as we move from one method to another. In the first part of the chapter, you will learn about neoclassical and generic criticism. Then you will be introduced to interpretive methods of criticism that challenged traditional perspectives. In the final section, you will see how neoclassical and interpretive methods have undergone a major transformation the field of rhetorical criticism, revisiting the basic concepts of communication in the nature of the public sphere, in performance and ideology, and as the impetus for social change.

Neoclassical and Genre Rhetorical Criticism

In ancient Greece, the role of public speaking (oratory) was critical to the formation of a new form of government slowly emerging from a collective state to a democracy, or rule by the citizens of the city states. They formed social practices and institutions to support this new form of government, such as the senate for legislative practices and a court system to determine how justice would be applied. It was critical that citizens learned to speak effectively in order to influence their peers in open forums in which the issues of the day were discussed and debated. There were no lawyers that citizens could employ to argue on their behalf.

Among the first theorists and teachers of rhetoric were the Sophists, whose popularity grew as citizens began to grasp the significance of speaking well. Crick (2010) has argued that the teachings and role of the Sophists promoted the democratic process by exploring effective argument and the art or technique of persuasion. Later, philosophers such as Aristotle, Cicero, and Quintilian were primarily concerned with classifying the fundamental components of speech for their students and applying these critically to orators of the day. It was from these classical origins that the canons of rhetoric and types of speaking as genres emerged and are still employed today in rhetorical criticism.

Historically, the contemporary origins of our communication field stem from the neoclassical rhetorical critics from early twentieth century to the 1960s. Rhetorical criticism of this period echoed the writings of the Greek and Roman philosophers as the foundation of rhetoric (Bryant, 1953; Kennedy, 1963). The methods that emerged share a number of characteristic assumptions made about Greek and Roman conceptions of rhetoric (Haskins, 2006, pp. 195–196):

1. The classical writings about rhetoric provide a "single, monolithic paradigm" of a rational and empirical system for constructing and analyzing persuasive arguments.
2. Rhetorical principles are "atemporal," permitting classical analyses to be mapped onto other cultures and time periods.
3. The practice of rhetoric is essentially neutral (value-free), used equally for good or evil.

Table 9.2 Sample Claims from Rhetorical Critical Methods

Paradigm	Method	Claim
Discovery	Neoclassical	How well did Nixon and his advisors choose among the available means of persuasion for this situation? In choice and arrangement of the means of persuasion, for this situation this message is by and large a considerable success (Hill in S.K. Foss, 2004, p. 39)
Discovery	Genre	This essay argues that the secular American jeremiad emerges prominently in Steven Spielberg's film, *Saving Private Ryan*. Through a close reading... I argue that the film operates, in part, as a rhetorically skillful response to the post-Vietnam crisis of national identity (Owen, 2002, p. 249).
Interpretive	Metaphoric	By using movement metaphors—particularly the journey metaphor—Obama attempted to create an image of order amid chaos. The collapse of the economy was framed as a speed bump, slowing—but not halting—the nation's progress towards its destiny (Cox, 2012, p. 11).
Interpretive	Dramatism	More specifically, we argue that journalists, commentators, and ESPN's anchors, in seeking to heal the nation and "move on" past images of post-Katrina ruin, never escaped a basic irony of purification bound up in Kenneth Burke's "paradox of purity": the harder one tries to purge dirt, the more dirt has to be introduced as a dramatic antithesis in the ritual (Grano & Zagacki, 2011, p. 202).
Interpretive	Narrative	This film [*The Matrix*] is shown to be a powerful myth for alienated and disempowered individuals in technologically driven communities, with potentially troubling consequences due to its theme of "solitary enlightenment" (Stroud, 2001, p. 416).
Critical bridge	Ideologic	Emphasizing images of women, I argue that these representations participate in the more general category of "the clash of civilizations," which constitutes a verbal and a visual ideograph linked to the idea of the "white man's burden" (Cloud, 2004, p. 285).
Critical bridge	Public Sphere	The author argues that the Pope's concern with injecting the Christian voice into the public discourse fails to address other religious voices. Benedict's model of the European public sphere incorporates Christian rationality into public reason, yet reproduces an asymmetry between Christians and other believers parallel to that which the liberal state has created between secular and religious citizens (Garcia, 2010, p. 87).

The emphasis on a common, atemporal, and neutral "objective" set of principles to be applied in the analysis of rhetorical discourse is at the core of the discovery paradigm. We call these methods traditional because they were the earliest of the more contemporary approaches.

Neoclassical Criticism

Early in the twentieth century, rhetorical critics depended on the classical methods of analyzing speeches to provide legitimate sources of teaching effective persuasive speaking in contemporary college courses (Lucaites, Condit, & Caudill, 1999, p. 8). The approach was exemplified in Herbert Wichelns' (1925) essay, "The Literary Criticism of Oratory," in which he identified rhetorical criticism's central purpose as effective persuasive speaking. Wichelns outlined in some detail the methodological approach the critic should use. Other scholars in the field, such as Hochmuth Nichols (1955) and Thonssen and Baird (1948), elaborated on his general approach. During this period, neoclassical criticism was greatly influenced by *modernism*, a philosophical perspective with a central reliance on objectivism and the pursuit of universal truths. Serving as a foundational base for the discovery paradigm, neoclassical criticism was the epitome of the modernist perspective, stressing the goals of empiricism and an amoral detachment. "To the degree that a speech employed all of the means available to it, it was judged to be a good speech," and the critic was expected to "maintain objective distance from the critical object" (Lucaites et al., 1999, p. 11).

The essential components of rhetoric were identical to those introduced in Greek and Roman societies: the speaker, the speech, the audience, and the context. Aristotle classified three contexts for speeches, the senate, courts, and forums, demonstrating how these would influence how the speaker should attempt to influence the different audiences for each. We will discuss this classification system in more detail when we explore genre criticism. Rhetorical critics either selected a speech of the day or one of historical importance, such as Lincoln's Gettysburg address. The speech was judged effective by its intended effect on the audience. As a much-cited example, Hill's (1972) analysis of Nixon's Vietnam speech text in 1969 required describing Nixon's character, the context, and characteristics of Nixon's audience. Hill then explained the effectiveness of Nixon's argument in terms of the evidence he used for persuasion; and finally, he explained the effects of the speech on the targeted audience. Four critical elements were included: the speaker, situation, speech, and audience effects.

Claims and Data

The claims in neoclassical approaches were originally explanatory and evaluative. The purpose was to accurately explain how the speaker used various persuasive devices defined by the classical philosophers and to evaluate how effective the argument appeared to be based rationally on principles of argument and empirically on the observed reactions of the targeted audiences. Because this type of criticism focused on the features of the speech and the intended effects on the audience, it was not traditionally applied to written or nondiscursive symbols (e.g., visual imagery). You can see how this constitutes a major drawback today, given the multiple and mediated forms of communication in our contemporary lifestyles. However, to dismiss this method as irrelevant would mean overlooking ways in which "empowered speakers still present reasoned, verbal arguments in carefully crafted addresses to attentive audiences. Those moments would certainly include nearly the whole of our legal system, much of the communication in places of worship, educational and technical instruction" including the typical means instructors uses to deliver course content! (Brummett, 2011, p. 66). Speeches in public forums typically comprised the data of neoclassical critics. As a

neoclassical critic today, you can use transcripts plus audio and video recordings of the speech text as well as any documentation or evidence that will help you to identify additional analytic evidence such as historical records, letters, or other accounts from eyewitnesses.

As a neoclassical critic, you will conduct your investigation over three phases: (1) reconstructing the context, (2) analyzing the speech, and (3) assessing its effects (S. K. Foss, 2009, pp. 24–28); these are illustrated briefly in Table 9.3. You will begin by situating the speech historically in time and place and by identifying as part of the context any notable characteristics of the intended audience.

Classical approaches to understanding how the situation contributed to the persuasiveness of the message resulted in attempts to classify situations and the messages that were most appropriate within specific contexts. Lloyd Bitzer (1968) expanded the classical conceptions of the **rhetorical situation** to include three components: exigence, audience, and constraints. At the basis of every rhetorical situation is the **exigence** or problem that requires change. The audience is the group of people the rhetor wishes to persuade to change, and the constraints are the obstacles that stand in the way of solving the problem. For example, as a member of your campus community, you might try to persuade students you know to help you organize a campaign to make your campus more sustainable. In order to be successful in this rhetorical situation, you would need to identify the obstacles you and your friends would be likely to encounter in promoting campus change. In his analysis of Nixon's speech, Hill (1972) illustrated how the situation and Nixon's targeted audience set the stage for the speech itself, a point Hill returned to in determining the speaker's effectiveness in the final stage.

During the second phase, we examine the speech text in terms of invention, organization, style, delivery, and memory. From classical Greek and Roman writings,

Table 9.3 Phases in Conducting Neoclassical Criticism

Phase 1	Reconstruct the historical context in which the speech occurred and advance claims.
Phase 2	Analyze the speech by applying classical elements (e.g., a canon).
Phase 3	Assess the effects of the speech on the audience.

Table 9.4 Five Canons of Rhetoric

Five Canons of Rhetoric	
Invention	The speaker's major ideas, lines of argument, or content.
Organization	Arrangement; the structure or general pattern of the various components in a rhetorical speech.
Style	The language the speaker uses.
Delivery	The mode of presentation adopted by the speaker, including vocal and nonverbal behavior.
Memory	The devices speakers use to help them remember significant ideas and illustrations throughout their speeches.

these elements comprise the **canons of rhetoric** (refer to Table 9.4). The canons originated in Aristotle's conception of rhetoric, defined as "an ability, in each particular case, to see the available means of persuasion" (Aristotle, trans. by Kennedy, 1991, 1.2.1). In this definition, you will find Aristotle's reliance on practice and teaching (*techne*), on empiricism, on the central elements (speaker, audience, situation, issue, time), and on the available means of persuasion (*pisteis*) (from *Rhetoric Glossary of Terms*). His conceptions provided the foundation for the five canons, and these you may recall from your public speaking or rhetorical theory course.

Invention. Because of the centrality of the argument to persuasive messages, many neoclassical critics focused their attention on this canon. **Invention** has been defined as "the speaker's major ideas, lines of argument, or content" (S. K. Foss, 2009, p. 26). As the critic, you would explore how the speaker's argument is supported by two types of evidence or proofs: inartistic and artistic. **Inartistic proofs** are external forms such as testimony from witnesses or key documents. **Artistic proofs,** Aristotle's conception of *pisteis*, are internal constructions of the speaker and include *logos, ethos,* and *pathos.*

The term *logos* refers to the logical or rational appeals a speaker makes by identifying the central claims made and the evidence used to support them. Aristotle listed several major logical devices or strategies applied through inductive and deductive reasoning. For example, a speaker employs *logos* when reasoning is used to show the apparent truth of conclusions drawn from the speaker's premises. Your role as critic would be to illuminate how

these devices were used to effectively persuade the audience. Hill's (1972) analysis of Nixon's speech showed how Nixon engaged his audience through deductive reasoning using a device called an *enthymeme,* a type of syllogism or reasoning from premise to conclusion.

The second form of artistic proof is called *ethos.* It refers to three basic components: moral character, intelligence, and goodwill. Moral character refers to the speaker's perceived integrity or honesty; the intelligence of the speaker "has more to do with practical wisdom and shared values" than it does with intellectual training or knowledge. The speaker's goodwill rests in the perception that the speaker regards the audience positively and will act in their best interests (Griffin, 2000, p. 279). In the analysis of Nixon's "Vietnamization" speech, Hill claimed that Nixon appealed to the audience on the basis of his moral decisions. Nixon was compelled to "tell the truth" of the Vietnam situation as a means of establishing the needed military support even though deciding to keep American troops in Vietnam was unpopular; he chose "the right way, not the easy way" to convey his ethos (as cited in S. K. Foss, 2009, p. 38).

The third and final form of artistic proof is *pathos,* or emotional appeal. The critic discovered what emotions were aroused by the speaker and how effective they were in facilitating the audience's acceptance of the speaker's claims (S. K. Foss, 2009, pp. 26–27). Hill (1972) claimed that once Nixon had established his logical premises and proper moral character, he concentrated on making an impassioned plea; by appealing to the need for strong patriotism to stand firm, he polarized dissent as disloyal and un-American.

Organization. The second canon of rhetoric is called organization (S. K. Foss, 2009, p. 27) or sometimes arrangement (Brock et al., 1990). It refers to the structure or general pattern of the various components in a rhetorical text. Your role as critic would be to try to determine whether the order or placement of the main claim, as well as the major evidence and warrants used to support them, change the effectiveness of the rhetor's argument. Hill (1972) argued that the way the premises of the enthymemes were placed, the establishment of ethos, and Nixon's epilogue allowed him to build a two-sided argument and refute his harshest critics.

Style. The neoclassical critic should also consider style, the third canon of rhetoric. Style is often equated with the language the speaker uses. The task of the critic is to evaluate "how particular kinds of words or other symbols are used by the rhetor to create varying effects" and "whether the language style contributes to the accomplishment of the rhetor's goal and helps to create the intended response" (S. K. Foss, 2009, p. 27). Hill's (1972) analysis of Nixon's style was designed to convey "clarity and forthrightness," which shifted about two-thirds of the way through his speech to emphasize a new sense of "gravity and impressiveness" (as cited in S. K. Foss, 2009, p. 39). It helped to underscore the importance and seriousness of Nixon's decision to keep military forces in Vietnam in the face of increasing demands by the American public for immediate withdrawal. We will return to this canon when we consider tropes as elements of style later on in metaphoric analysis.

Delivery. The fourth canon of rhetoric is delivery, referring to the rhetor's mode of presentation. Traditional modes included those you would probably find in an introductory public speaking text: impromptu speaking, speaking extemporaneously from an outline, or orally presenting a written manuscript of a speech manuscript as well as the speaker's nonverbal and vocal behaviors such as gestures, appearance, and vocal resonance. One of the difficulties Nixon faced generally with his audiences was his apparent "stiffness" and lack of charisma; delivery often enhances interest and influence but it can also interfere.

Memory. The last canon of rhetoric, memory, refers to the devices speakers use to help them remember significant ideas and illustrations throughout their speeches. Aristotle did not address memory specifically, and often neoclassical critics omitted it as well. It was included in classical writings as a series of techniques speakers would use to remember the progression of ideas within a speech. Such techniques were employed because classical societies relied primarily on oral messages. With the advent of print, memory was a neglected canon. However, recent changes in technology and advances in cognitive science about information processing have renewed critics' interest in this final canon.

Once you have completed the first two steps of neoclassical analysis by reconstructing the context and analyzing the speech using one or more of the canons, the last step is the assessment of the effects of the rhetorical act on the audience (S. K. Foss, 2009, p. 28). As the critic, you would assume the rhetor had a purpose in speaking to the audience. Your task is to determine whether the rhetor achieved that purpose.

In the analysis of Nixon's speech, Hill (1972) argued that Nixon and his advisors had judged the situation and audience appropriately in crafting the elements of his speech. Because of the crisis of Vietnam, Nixon effectively appealed to American values—life, political freedom, peace, and self-confidence—for an audience "not ideologically overcommitted either to victory over Communism or to peace in any case while frustrated with a prolonged war" (S. K. Foss, 2009, p. 39). To evaluate the outcome of the speech, you would look for evidence that the outcome had or had not been successful; then you would apply several standards of evaluation in determining the strength or worth of the evidence as warrants.

Warrants: Standards for Evaluating Rhetorical Effectiveness

As you explore the effects of a speech on an audience, it is important to consider how the basic assumptions from this discovery paradigm perspective can be applied to the two standard warrants of validity and reliability. Rhetorical critics do not use the terms validity and reliability. However, in neoclassical criticism, the emphasis on accuracy and logical consistency conveys the same concerns in applying these standards of evaluation. One of the underlying assumptions of neoclassical methodology is that the rhetorical principles and components will remain the same throughout history. The canons of rhetoric can be applied rationally and objectively to assess whatever is there in the text but also to explain its effects on an audience. Your goal as the critic is to first reconstruct the speech so that it is an accurate representation of the original rhetorical act. This approach requires careful attention to and exploration of the key elements: the situation in terms of the issue or problem at hand, the larger context, the particular audience, and the characteristics of the speech itself analyzed by the application of the canons (Brummett, 2011, pp. 66–67).

Your second goal is to accurately apply one or more of the rhetorical canons to demonstrate the strengths (or weaknesses) of the rhetor's skillfulness. The last goal is to assess the speech effects by reconstructing them historically. As noted by Brock et al. (1990), "If critics strive for objectivity and believe that rhetorical principles reflect a relatively stable reality, it follows that an accurate reconstruction of history is their goal" (p. 28). The concern for accuracy and truthfulness is underscored as the standard evaluation for discovery research, as we have noted in previous chapters.

As a neoclassical critic, you will also assess the level of logical consistency in the argument presented by the rhetor. The evidence presented should not be contradictory in any way but should be "sufficient, representative, relevant, and clear" (Rybacki & Rybacki, 1991, p. 58). Consistency is also frequently extended to mean that the argument used was appropriately situated in its historical context to withstand the temporal test of *reliability* (Rybacki & Rybacki, 1991), a warrant we have described in earlier chapters. As the critic, you should evaluate whether the rhetor has made consistent and valid choices in the application of the evidence in support of the speech's central claim. The emphasis is also on the consistency or reliability of the analysis over time, a function made more possible by situating rhetorical speeches within their historical contexts.

The neoclassical approach to rhetorical criticism using discovery paradigm assumptions is rarely found in our current scholarly journals. The approach was faulted for being too rational and too focused on the speaker/ speech/situation/audience effects model of communication. It could be effectively applied to only one speech at a time, concentrating on the act as discursive (S. K. Foss, 2009, p. 24; Lucaites et al., 1999). It certainly provided a classical foundation that we continue to return to even from more interpretive and critical frames.

New Directions in Neoclassical Criticism

The canons of rhetoric, forms of proofs, and other classical elements of rhetoric are easily found in our research literature; however, these critical methods are embedded in many of the assumptions shared between interpretive and critical paradigms. While neoclassical critics were engaged in rational and empirical analysis, rhetorical theories from philosophers and critics such as Kenneth Burke, Jurgen Habermas, and Michael McGee reframed our concepts of even the basic elements of rhetoric: rhetors, messages, audiences, and situations. From their perspectives, challenges of contemporary society have changed the way that we think about identity and power communicated rhetorically through multiple and complex messages that include visual and material symbols within public contexts that require abandoning our earlier conceptions of audiences and rhetorical situations (Keith & Lundberg, 2008, pp. 9–10). We will have much more to say about each of these theorists later in the chapter. At this point, we will acknowledge the ways in which technology and media have transformed our understanding of rhetorical texts and artifacts, and how this transformation has changed how we can understand and apply the canons.

In reconsidering the canons, Smith (2007) claimed that enthymemes, a logical construction as part of *invention*, could be applied to show engagement with *visual* argument. The mode of *delivery* must also be redefined with advances in various technologies. In fact, Condit (2006) argued that the canon of delivery has had to survive a "radical revision," as the modes have expanded to include a "swamp of billboards, radiowaves, fiber optic cables, blogs, pop-ups, t-shirts, blimps, television stations, film conglomerates, and cellphonetextmessagingvideosportsdownloadgamers" (p. 369). New studies of social movements require rethinking the canon of *organization*. Whereas various rhetorical artifacts or messages may not share whole patterns of connected ideas, common elements such as "ideographs, metaphors, and narratives" may be shared across the fragmented "textscape" of contemporary society (Condit, 2006, p. 369). And in terms of memory, advances in cognitive science/linguistics and cultural studies have meant revisiting the canon conceptually to include "issues of archiving, secrecy, and forced forgetting" (Condit, 2006, p. 369). Stormer (2013) provided a more recent "repurposing" of the canons by exploring how they have been conceptualized in the act of criticism in terms of what counts as discursive (language) and nondiscursive actions. In the final section of this chapter, we will also consider how new critical perspectives have resulted in reconceptualizing the basic concepts of communication as the public sphere, in performance and ideology, and as the impetus for social change. But first we explore generic criticism, another classical form of rhetorical criticism that has served as a bridge to interpretive and critical paradigms perspectives.

Genre Criticism

Our rationale for placing genre criticism in the traditional perspectives is that it represents one of the earlier approaches to rhetorical criticism in our field. Genre criticism also shares with those methods its origins in Greek and Roman rhetoric (Bitzer, 1968; Black, 1978). Generally, generic criticism is the attempt to find a genre, a common pattern in rhetorical texts across similar types of contexts. It represents a classical way of thinking about situations, which means that situations, by their very nature, require a certain kind of speech as a response. So, for example, when people are accused of crimes, they will need to determine how to argue most effectively in defense of their innocence. When a respected public figure dies, we are expected to praise their accomplishments. S. K. Foss (2009) identified the central assumption of generic criticism as the belief that "certain types of situations provoke similar needs and expectations among audiences and thus call for particular kinds of rhetoric" (p. 137).

In classical times and in our contemporary methods, the role of the generic critic includes identifying the rhetorical situation and then classifying or categorizing specific types of rhetoric that would be most effective given the constraints of the situation. You know from Chapter 3 on paradigms that a key feature of the discovery paradigm is the development of classification systems that order our social realities. Recently, the concept of genre has become a more complex conception leading to new treatments. You will learn about these in the sections that follow.

Traditional Aristotelian Genre

Genre critics have made use of Aristotle's identification of three types of oratory listed here and in Table 9.5: deliberative, forensic, and epideictic. **Deliberative rhetoric** was political discourse, speeches given on the floor of the legislative assembly for the purpose of establishing or changing a law. Because of the nature of the context, this type of speech is oriented toward the future; that is, it concerns actions that will address unmet social needs (Gill, 1994). The goal of this type of oratory was identifying the expedience (advantage) or nonexpedience (harm) in accepting a policy, achieved through the strategies of identifying the benefits and drawbacks of adopting a particular policy (S. K. Foss, 2009; Hauser, 1991).

Table 9.5 Traditional Generic Forms of Rhetoric

Traditional Genres	
Deliberative rhetoric	Political discourse; speeches given on the floor of the legislative assembly for the purpose of establishing or changing a law.
Forensic rhetoric	Legal discourse of courtroom proceedings.
Epideictic rhetoric	Ceremonial speeches given on special occasions to praise or blame another's actions, to uphold an individual as virtuous, or condemn an individual as corrupt.

The second type of rhetoric was identified as **forensic**. This genre was characterized by the legal discourse of courtroom proceedings. As we noted earlier, the people of Athens in ancient Greece did not have professional lawyers to defend them. Aristotle's conception of rhetoric was meant to teach ordinary citizens how to construct the type of speeches they would need to make when seeking justice in the courtroom, by employing strategies of accusation and defense (S. K. Foss, 2009; Hauser, 1991). Because of the nature of the context, this type of speech is oriented in the past; that is, it concerns the accounts of actions already committed (Gill, 1994).

A study by D. Johnson and Sellnow (1995) may help to distinguish between deliberative and forensic rhetoric. They investigated the rhetoric surrounding the Exxon tanker, Valdez, and the 1989 oil spill into Alaska's Prince William Sound. In the first phase of such a crisis, much of the rhetoric was devoted to discovering who was at fault and how blame should be assigned. In this phase of accusation and defense, the rhetoric was decidedly forensic; it was focused on past events. During the second phase of the crisis, the rhetoric shifted to establishing policies to prevent the problems and ensuing crisis in the future. The rhetoric of this phase was then classified as deliberative because of its forward emphasis on creating policy.

Aristotle listed a third type of rhetoric as **epideictic**. This genre refers to ceremonial speeches given on special occasions to praise or blame another's actions, to uphold an individual as virtuous, or condemn an individual as corrupt. This type of rhetoric is oriented to the present (Gill, 1994). As D. Johnson and Sellnow (1995) pointed out in the preceding example, there are elements of the epideictic genre in both phases because the castigation of Exxon and the organization's responses involved blaming and defending the integrity or character of the organizational leadership. If you listen to any news or talk broadcast, you probably will be able to identify your own examples of deliberative, forensic, and epideictic rhetoric. Regardless of the type of rhetoric, generic analysis follows the same methodological patterns as neoclassical criticism: select a rhetorical message or text, construct claims, and apply analytic framework. Let's take a look at what kinds of claims are advanced in current genre criticism and what constitutes a rhetorical message or text for those studies.

Claims and Data

The claims of generic criticism are primarily explanatory in the classification process and in the use of inductive or deductive reasoning to explain the significance of the classification. If you are conducting generic criticism, you will choose a claim from one of several options. In establishing a new genre, you would first analyze several rhetorical messages or texts to determine inductively whether a genre exists by any emerging characteristics of this kind of rhetoric (K. K. Campbell & Jamieson, 1978; S. K. Foss, 2009). So, for example, you might argue that the film Feig's *Brides-maids* constitutes a new genre of humorous films in which females are characterized in funny but nontraditional ways S. K. Foss (2009) termed this approach **generic description**. The second option is called **generic participation**, a deductive process of comparison in which you would compare the characteristics of a rhetorical text with the characteristics of a genre constructed from a previous set of studies. Your purpose would explore the known characteristics of the genre. In this case, you might select a film like Tarantino's *Django Unchained* and argue that it belongs in the genre classification of Westerns because of a number of characteristics that identify it as belonging to this genre (e.g., gun-toting bounty hunters, "old West" attire and props, etc.). The final option, **generic application**, occurs when you deductively explain how the characteristics of a genre should be applied to a specific rhetorical text to assess whether it is a good or poor fit (S. K. Foss, 2009, pp. 140–144).

In this case, you could argue that the same film *Django Unchained* was rhetorically very interesting because it didn't share some common characteristics of typical Westerns (e.g., historically occurs in pre-Civil War South; race as a predominant theme, etc.). These three terms, generic description, participation and application, identify three different approaches to generic criticism depending on the type of genre you are observing and analyzing; they appear in Table 9.6. Confusion about what constitutes a good fit as well as the recognition that Aristotle's classifications were incomplete has led to reconceptualizing this methodological approach and to the emergence of new genres, beyond forensic, deliberative, and epideictic (K. K. Campbell & Jamieson, 1978; Jamieson & Campbell, 1982).

New Approaches to Genre Studies

Generic critics have been quick to point out that the process of identifying a genre and/or applying it to a rhetorical artifact is not a clean and easy set of classifying procedures, so much as it is an act of interpretation. One of the difficulties is in deciding what constitutes a genre. The genres that Aristotle identified were those most common to his experience, and confined specifically to oratory (people speaking in a one-to-many, face-to-face context). Early contemporary studies have considerably expanded Aristotle's list of genres. Among the first in our field, genre studies included diatribes (Windt, 1972), papal encyclicals (Jamieson, 1973), doctrinal rhetoric (Hart, 1971), women's rights rhetoric (K. K. Campbell, 1973), eulogies (Jamieson & Campbell, 1982), jeremiads (Ritter, 1980), and apologias (Ware & Linkugel, 1973). This list is certainly not exhaustive but provides a sample of early genre criticism.

After investigating a number of genre studies, Jamieson and Campbell (1982; K. K. Campbell & Jamieson, 1978) argued that generic criticism could not be considered a simple classification procedure by assigning texts to an exclusive genre category. They pointed out that, in several cases, there were elements from several genres in one rhetorical text. By analyzing eulogies (funeral speeches) for Senator Robert Kennedy, for example, Jamieson and Campbell showed that eulogies are a distinct genre by themselves, but contained deliberative elements from the Aristotelian classification system. Furthermore, they found connections to Kenneth Burke's dramatization of rhetorical acts embedded within social contexts. Their description of the function of the genre signaled a

Table 9.6 Steps in Conducting Generic Criticism

Three Different Approaches to Generic Criticism*	
Generic Description (testing to see whether a new genre exists): 4 steps	1. Observe similarities in rhetorical responses to particular situations. 2. Collect rhetorical messages/texts occurring in similar situations. 3. Analyze the messages/texts to discover if they share characteristics. 4. Formulate the organizing principle of the genre.
Warranting generic description (standards for substantiating the existence of a new genre)	1. Can rules be named with which other critics can concur in identifying the genre's characteristics using the same examples? 2. Are the similarities in characteristics firmly rooted in the situations in which they were generated? 3. Would the absence of the characteristic change the nature of the message or text? 4. Does the characteristic contribute to insight about a type of rhetoric or simply lead to the development of a classification system?
Generic participation (testing to place messages or texts in genres): 3 steps	1. Describe the perceived situational requirements, substantive and stylistic characteristics, and organizing principle of the **genre**. 2. Describe the perceived situational requirements, substantive and stylistic characteristics, and organizing principle of the **message/text.** 3. Compare the characteristics of the message/text with those of the genre to see if the message/text belongs in that genre.
Generic application (testing to evaluate the effectiveness of the text/ message in fulfilling the genre characteristics): 4 steps	1. Describe the perceived situational requirements, substantive and stylistic characteristics, and organizing principle of the **genre**. 2. Describe the perceived situational requirements, substantive and stylistic characteristics, and organizing principle of the **message/text** that is representative of that genre. 3. Compare the characteristics of the message/text with those of the genre. 4. Evaluate the message/text according to its success in fulfilling the required characteristics of the genre.

*from S.K. Foss, 2009, pp. 141–145.

shift from the classical, discovery paradigm perspective to a more interpretive framework.

Two additional contributors also helped to change the concept of genre. Edwin Black (1978) was the first to use the term, generic criticism, in the 1960s when revisiting the Aristotelian types of speech contexts. He proposed that the list should be broadened to include more than Aristotle's three, but still confined it to a limited number of situations. These should prompt a narrowed set of responses from any rhetor. The recurrence of these various situational types or genres and rhetors' responses throughout history would provide the critics with opportunities to discover their common characteristics. Additionally, Mikhail Bakhtin (1987), a literary philosopher, believed that narratives and speeches consisted of many genres. Even in everyday speech, the genres of greetings, invitations, and requests for information all form a series of speech genres whose forms reveal a consistency in patterning.

Not only were generic studies becoming more interpretive, but some studies provided a critical stance as well, a point that we will return to in the last section of this chapter. If you have already read Chapter 7, "Ethnography" and Chapter 8, "Conversation and Discourse Analysis," you may recognize connections between Bakhtin's literary criticism and those ways of analyzing language use in social interactions. These examples point out the fuzzy boundaries between methodologies (e.g., rhetorical criticism, discourse analysis, and literary criticism).

There are several current examples of studies that have illustrated how generic criticism encompasses a broader application of the term, *genre,* and how various forms can be used for social change. A *jeremiad* is a rhetorical act in which there is a public accusation of wrongdoing along with the exhortation to change. In a recent essay, Wolfe (2008) used generic application to claim that *The Lorax* is a highly successful cautionary tale in the guise of a children's book, a jeremiad warning of ecological devastation to come. Theodore Geisel (Dr. Seuss) identified the story as one of his favorite, one that he had written to protest the actions of those polluting the environment. He had been involved in politics from the start of his career, taking a break from writing children's books to work as a political cartoonist during World War II. Wolfe argued that the story very effectively "extends the alarm and activism of early environmentalism, including the tendency for strong, even apocalyptic, rhetoric" (p. 12). The jeremiadic form of the story also offers a clear appeal to correct the action and avert disaster.

In another broad application of generic criticism, Mazer (2013) identified *apologia* as the genre under investigation and explored its characteristic elements based on Benoit's (1995) image restoration concept, the attempt of an orator to restore "face" after admitting some failure publicly. He used Dan Rather's apology on the CBS Evening news as a generic application. Rather had criticized President George W. Bush's service in the Texas Air National Guard based on sources that later were found to be fabricated. Mazer used the characteristics of apologias, which include direct acknowledgement of personal responsibility, to show why Rather was unsuccessful in restoring his image and the public's trust in him as a news anchor.

Reconceptualizing generic criticism has helped critics to gain greater understanding of this methodological approach. How it is defined and applied impacts the warrants, or the standards used to evaluate its claims in light of the evidence offered to support them. Along with the standards of accuracy and consistency, the newer studies and criticisms of the methodology itself suggest that interpretive and critical standards of evaluation may be ultimately more useful.

Warrants

The earliest studies in generic criticism shared a concern for accurately describing the characteristics of a genre as well as its situational constraints. Those studies also emphasized consistency in deciding how specific rhetorical artifacts should be placed within a genre (refer to Table 9.6). Notice that those standards, accuracy (or validity) and consistency (or reliability), are warrants of the discovery paradigm. The form of argument used in generic criticism relies on logical reasoning processes,

which we described as central to the discovery paradigm in Chapter 3.

Evaluators of generic criticism have recently added a new standard to accuracy and consistency, the failure to adequately establish a genre. C. R. Miller (1998) claimed that failure to establish a genre or how it is applied might happen in three ways, the first two of which implicate accuracy and/or consistency; but the third approach moves beyond the discovery paradigm. Let's consider each failure in turn: The first failure may result from the critic's inability to determine any recurring significant substantive or stylistic similarities *across several rhetorical texts from similar situations*. This is still largely a problem of accuracy and consistency in the inductive process. C. R. Miller noted, however, that generic claims without this level of evidence are rarely made.

The second type of failure is that *all of the elements in a particular genre are not clearly identified and/or applied*. The studies of the *apologia* and the *jeremiad* cited earlier illustrated the difficulties of accurate application when some features of a genre were present but others were not. Jamieson and Campbell's (1982) study of Kennedy's eulogies showed that added characteristics not included in the categorization of the genre did not diminish message effectiveness; the rhetors had strategically transformed the messages into their oratorical advantage. C. R. Miller (1998) argued that traditional classifications of genres were highly susceptible to redefinition and the addition of new characteristics because the original schema was deficient for contemporary rhetorical situations, a problem primarily related to accuracy and consistency in the definition of specific genre.

The third failure posited by C. R. Miller (1998) takes generic criticism in a very different direction, one that points the way to alternate paradigms. C. R. Miller argued that a generic claim must also be a pragmatic one, *that a genre should be considered a form of social action*. A critic must be able to find a "rational fusion of elements" across similar types of rhetorical texts to consider these a genre. C. R. Miller's analysis of "Environmental Impact Statements" led her to conclude that the documents were similar in substantive and stylistic elements and as situational or episodic responses. But one of the reasons they did not form a coherent genre is because "the cultural forms in which they were embedded provided conflicting interpretive contexts" (C. R. Miller, 1998, p. 137). With this criticism, C. R. Miller challenged the assumptions and warrants that underlie genre criticism as a discovery paradigm perspective. As you have learned in earlier chapters, accepting multiple interpretations of a rhetorical act and exploring its function in instigating social change are underlying assumptions of the interpretive and critical paradigms. Moreover, emphasizing coherence (instead of validity and reliability) is one warrant you use to evaluate interpretive claims. Other methods of rhetorical criticism from the interpretive paradigm share these same distinctions. In the next section, you will learn about three main approaches from the interpretive paradigm.

Interpretive Rhetorical Criticism

Just as we organized the last section, the methods of rhetorical criticism examined in this section have unique elements and procedures for applying them. Because of these distinctions, we explore each method separately. Be mindful, however, that at the broadest level, all three perspectives share the interpretive paradigm assumptions about what constitutes a claim, how it can be made and supported with data or evidence, and how it should be evaluated through the warranting process. Interpretive methods begin with the assumption that reality is socially constructed out of many possible interpretations, and understanding rhetorical acts from these interpretive stances is the overarching goal.

For each of the three methods described in this section, the steps you would complete in your analysis as critic will include the steps we first identified in the beginning of this chapter: select a rhetorical message/text, analyze the message/text, formulate your claim, and write the essay. Through your analysis, you will show that the rhetorical texts you selected will be better understood by the application of the interpretive framework or method you have chosen. Next is the articulation of your claim(s) by application of the method to your selected artifacts as data analysis. Finally, you will establish warrants for your claims based on the strengths of your evidence. The three interpretive frameworks or methods described in this section include metaphoric criticism, dramatism, and narrative analysis. Once again, we have combined claims and data into one section for each method followed by how to apply the warrants for that method.

Metaphoric Criticism

The use of the **metaphor** as a rhetorical form comes to us originally from Greece. Recall our discussion of *style* as one of the five canons of rhetoric. Keith and Lundberg

(2008) identified two classical categories of language used in persuasive messages: figures and tropes. **Figures** were "creative arrangements of words in phrases or sentences that catch the audience's attention and focus it on your key ideas" (p. 62). Examples of figures include repetition of sounds, words, or phrases for dramatic effect to engage listeners more effectively; for example, a "government of the people, by the people and for the people" is a form of repetition called *antistrophe*. Other figures included antithesis (opposites such as "one small step for man; one giant leap for mankind") and rhetorical questions, ones that do not expect literal answers.

The other stylistic form of language was the class of tropes. A **trope** is "a substitution of a word or phrase by a less literal word or phrase" (Keith & Lundberg, 2008, p. 66). Several of the more common tropes include *metonymy* (e.g., referring to the government as "Washington," or the movie industry as "Hollywood, physical locations central to these institutions), and *synecdoche* (e.g., referring to parts of bodies or objects to denote the whole person or thing, such as "wheels" for transportation or "hired hands" for employees). The most common form is the metaphor, which "carries or bears another meaning beyond its literal one" (Keith & Lundberg, p. 68). Aristotle distinguished between a word with its "proper" meaning and a metaphor that creates an association to an unusual meaning for the purposes of adding a more vivid and colorful dimension to the description of a term. To say that registering for classes is a zoo is an example of a metaphor. It creates an analogy between class registration and the zoo. The ability to see analogies between words that would otherwise not be connected was considered a sign of mastery in literary style, a talent not all people possessed (Kennedy, 1963).

From the discovery paradigm of classical and neoclassical perspectives where rationalism was privileged, tropes were often dismissed as unnecessary ornament or even misleading, obscuring the clear and direct argument within the message. However, rhetorical critics like Kenneth Burke thought that tropes were at the heart of rhetoric believing that no language was truly objective or rational and that the persuasion that goes unnoticed is most powerful, since it cannot be resisted (Gill, 1994). Cassirer and I.A. Richards believed all language and thought was metaphorical because language was, by its nature, symbolic and therefore representational (as cited in Gill, 1994, pp. 61–62). Later theorists, like Burke and Grassi, attributed creating meaning to metaphors used by everyone in common, ordinary language. Burke

(1989) introduced the concept of terministic screens to describe the metaphoric importance of language. **Terministic screens** represent the language choices that you make to describe any event. Choices vary by the individuals' conceptions of realities, which shape and are shaped by language as the screen: "We must use terministic screens, since we can't say anything without the use of terms; whatever terms we use, they necessarily constitute a corresponding kind of screen; and any such screen necessarily directs the attention to one field rather than another" (p. 121).

If you start listening for metaphors in your conversations, you will probably be surprised to hear how many there are. Metaphors work very well to vividly portray our experiences; referring to the leg of a table and using terms of battle to describe fighting a disease are two common examples. The linguists, Lakoff and Johnson (1980), extended the idea of metaphor to understanding culture as well as the way you define your personal reality. Gill (1994) described this process as constructing our cultural coherence:

> Metaphor constitutes a primordial activity that reveals or unconceals the deep structures of reality as experienced by humans. These deep structures do not exist in nature but in humans. Each of us, as makers of metaphor, whether intentional or unwitting, thereby participates in the societal creation of meaning. (p. 71)

The idea that we all participate in making meanings, as well as an emphasis on interpreting our perspectives as meaning-makers, puts metaphoric criticism firmly in the realm of knowing by interpretation. Metaphor serves a rhetorical function that is fundamental to the way you define and experience reality personally and socially. When you become a metaphoric critic, you develop a sense of how to apply metaphors at deeper levels of meaning.

Claims and Data

In metaphor criticism, your claims will be primarily interpretive, illustrating how meaning is created in audience members through the use of metaphor. Your data may refer to any type of rhetorical texts including speeches, *YouTube* video clips, books, films, paintings, modes of attire, and songs. In fact, you will find that some critics are analyzing visual metaphors in advertising for their discursive or language-bearing properties. Levin and Behrens (2003) analysis of the Nike *swoosh* is one such example. Frequently, in metaphoric analysis, you will choose multiple messages from a single source, such as presidential rhetoric, or multiple messages from multiple sources, such as the news media, to explore and identify various themes among the metaphors. You could examine the frequency of metaphors in various texts using a technique called cluster analysis that we will describe in the next section. Or you could search for an archetypal metaphor. An **archetypal or root metaphor** is assumed to be so primal any individual in any context could understand its meaning (Osborn, 1967). You would follow the steps for your critique outlined in Table 9.7 in selecting rhetorical texts, advancing claims, identifying metaphoric language, and analyzing its significance in terms of rhetorical impact on audiences.

Metaphors abound in political communication. Littlefield and Quenette (2007) argued that metaphors in political discourse serve the dual purposes of persuading "audience members to 'focus on one aspect of a concept' while keeping them from 'focusing on other aspects of the concept that are inconsistent with that metaphor'" (p. 4). In other words, metaphors function as terministic screens that help individuals make sense out of a crisis. For example, Cox (2012) claimed that President Obama continuously used journey or movement metaphors in his speeches following the economic collapse of 2008 to help

Table 9.7 Steps in Conducting Metaphoric Criticism

Step 1	Select rhetorical texts or messages.
Step 2	Advance claims based on text and analytic framework.

Step 3	Analyze the occurrence of metaphoric language within the texts:
	  a. through cluster analysis by examining the frequency with which various metaphor themes occur; and/or
	  b. through identification of archetypal or root metaphors with strong significance for general audiences.

Step 4	Assess the significance of the metaphor choices in creating meaning for audiences.

steer audiences toward their belief in recovery. Similarly, M. West and Carey (2006) analyzed the frontier metaphors that became increasingly frequent in President Bush's and Vice President Cheney's post-9/11 speeches. By using cowboy speech of the Old West, Bush and Cheney identified America's war on terrorism as the "Wanted Dead or Alive" campaign, reinforcing this image with other, equally Western motifs: "It's an enemy that likes to hide and burrow in. . . . But we're going to smoke them out" (M. West & Carey, 2006, p. 386). By using this basic metaphor, the president/vice president team had characterized the search for "American justice."

A review of metaphoric criticism will also reveal more recent trends toward ideological and reformist claims. A number of analyses identify ideological stances either implicitly or explicitly in evaluative claims and may even suggest the need for reform through social action. For example, Littlefield and Quenette (2007) demonstrated that the media's coverage of Hurricane Katrina moved audiences to view the role of the president ("prying him away from his vacation" and "dipping below the clouds") and the government as ineffective ("turning a deaf ear") in response to the devastation in the aftermath. The authors claimed that the media "stepped outside of their role of objective observer and assumed a privileged position to point blame toward those with legitimate authority" (p. 26). Media's empowerment gave them an evaluative role that could change the authorities' responses to the crisis. In another example, Prividera and Howard (2007) illustrated how race, gender, and nationalism intersected in the media coverage of Operation Iraqi Freedom. Their contention was that by using metaphors of "warrior" and "hero," as well as many other metaphors associated with warrior behavior, media representations of Jessica Lynch, Lori Piestewa, and Shoshona Johnson, three female soldiers, were masculinized and marginalized. This example demonstrated how metaphors can be used as powerful symbols of race, ethnicity, gender, and class, bridging between interpretive and critical paradigms. As you have learned throughout each chapter, the ways that we evaluate claim-data relationships depend on the paradigmatic view we have. In this section, we show how various claims of metaphoric criticism demand different standards of evaluation than those from the discovery paradigm.

Warrants

In Chapter 6, "Warrants for Research Arguments," we identified various standards for judging the plausibility of interpretations. We examine two standards here: adequacy of evidence and coherence. *Adequacy of evidence* refers to evaluating whether the critics reviewed enough relevant material so that a sufficient or a legitimate judgment could be made. For example, in a metaphoric analysis of Bush's and Cheney's post-9/11 rhetoric, M. West and Carey (2006) reviewed the whole first term of the Bush-Cheney administration, focusing on a period from mid-September to mid-December 2001, and then a 2-year period from Fall 2002 (just before the onset of the war) through the reelection in late Fall 2004. M. West and Carey collected an extensive database of "frontier" metaphors. Littlefield and Quenette (2007) used 52 articles about Hurricane Katrina during the first week following the disaster in one national newsprint source (*New York Times*) and one primary location source (the *Times-Picayune* of New Orleans). Though the inclusion was not exhaustive, the authors argued that these two sources were particularly credible for both large and focused readership. Collecting all of the articles for one week provided the initial reactions of the media.

Prividera and Howard (2007) also collected an extensive amount of evidence. They used the *LexisNexis* news database to retrieve transcripts of all stories about the 507th Maintenance Company that aired on ABC, NBC, and CBS over a 10-month period, plus they used articles from *Newsweek, US News and World Report,* and *Time,* totaling 218 stories and 439 pages of text. Certainly, Prividera and Howard provided ample evidence that the metaphors they described were clearly present in the relevant rhetorical texts they examined.

The second standard or warrant relevant in metaphoric criticism is *coherence.* Coherence refers to whether our interpretations fit together or make sense. As noted in Chapter 6, "Warrants for Research Arguments," one of the ways to establish coherence is by noting recurring patterns or themes. Analyzing metaphors helps us achieve this goal. In fact, Miles and Huberman (1994) specifically stated that metaphors are "pattern-making devices" and that their investigation can help us determine the significance of our interpretations (p. 252). Uses of the metaphors of the Western frontier in one study and warrior heroes in another helped us make more sense out of the experiences they represented. For example, Prividera and Howard argued that metaphors of gender tend to be powerful and *archetypal.* If the appeal to understanding is made on the basis of their archetypal nature, then *quantity* of evidence is not as important as identifying the significance of these central metaphors in building coherence across the debate of two opposing camps. In summary, metaphors are powerful discursive tools in which to frame meaning, and in some cases, move audiences to action. In the next two sections, you will see that dramatism and narrative are equally powerful interpretive theoretical frameworks that can be applied critically.

Dramatism

There are several theories of criticism that use "drama" as a centralizing theme of rhetorical criticism but none so robust and frequent as the source as Kenneth Burke's (1969a, 1969b) dramatism. Burke (1969a, 1969b) developed an extensive theory of rhetoric based on his conception of dramatistic form, but he wrote on language and symbolism, human motivation, religion, social structure, and many other subjects as well. His work revolutionized our conceptions of rhetoric by challenging the classical traditions steeped in rationalism which situated persuasion as civic practice. From Burke's perspective, humans are immersed in language, symbol creators and users, and consequently, every thought, every word, and every action is rhetorical. We have already considered Burke's concept of *terministic screens* in understanding metaphors. In this section, we will explore the claims and data of dramatism, focusing on Burke's concepts of identification and redemption, cluster analysis, and the pentad (Brock, 1990; Brummett, 1994; S. K. Foss, 2009).

Claims and Data

The claims of dramatism are primarily interpretive but also may be evaluative. Burke's own assumptions about the nature of language and human interaction as symbolic place him centrally in the interpretive paradigm. By applying Burke's dramatistic concepts, the purpose of your research will be to understand how meaning is created in the texts you have selected for analysis. To understand these concepts, you will need to learn about several of Burke's beliefs. In classical rhetoric, persuasion was conceived of in the context of rational argument. But Burke described our society as dramatistic, in which our values and emotions are central contributors the process of creating meaning.

Burke believed the essential drama of our society was its hierarchy. According to Burke, its members associate social structure with order and value. The hierarchy is the foundation for the valuing process, motivating us to make choices about virtually every aspect of our lives, (our relationships, our careers, the material objects we desire). Individuals can either accept or reject this hierarchy of valuing and their relative positions within it. Acceptance of the hierarchy leads to identification and order, whereas rejection leads to alienation and disorder (Brock, 1990). The nature of hierarchy at any level of society is simultaneously the source of identification and pollution, two terms that we explain here in more detail.

From a Burkean perspective, the groups, organizations, and institutions that we belong to have established sets of rules and principles, and by following these rules, individuals can find common ground and a means to act in concert with others. Finding common ground is the essence of Burke's concept of **identification** (Burke, 1969b). We all belong to multiple organizations, each with a different hierarchy, each establishing a different kind of common ground with a different set of rules and a different set of values. People do not follow the rules all of the time for a variety of reasons. Several hierarchical rule sets may be in conflict; for example, the rules established by your church may conflict with requirements imposed at your workplace. When people reject any hierarchical order, they "fall" metaphorically; that is, they have become **polluted** or have acted out of synch with their surroundings. Any violation of the rules is also accompanied by feelings of guilt because through their disobedience, individuals become alienated; they are no longer unified through identification. The only means of correcting this condition is through purification.

Purification can be accomplished in one of three ways (Burke, 1970; Brummett, 1994). By **mortification**, the person's act of self-sacrifice expiates the guilt and is redeeming. Refraining from an extramarital affair redeems one from the guilt of desire. Relief from guilt can also be accomplished by **victimage**, which happens when a scapegoat suffers so that society can be redeemed. Whenever genocide is committed by one group on another group of people, the victims have been scapegoated by their murderers. Hitler scapegoated the Jews in Nazi Germany as the source of the country's economic devastation. French and Brown (2011) argued that our linguistic framing of obesity and date rape tend to place blame on women for the sins of appetite and desire. Once society is redeemed, hierarchical order is restored. The third way that purification is accomplished is through transcendence. In **transcendence**, rule violation is mandated by moral necessity (a higher order). For example, Milford's (2012) study of Jesse Owens, an Olympic gold medalist

Table 9.8 Steps in Applying Burke's Redemptive Cycle

Step 1	Select social dramas depicted in rhetorical texts such as the narratives of books, films, series of events, etc. and identify claim that links the text to the analytic framework.
Step 2	Analyze the rhetorical texts by application of the redemptive cycle in the required sequence: a. pollution through social transgression b. experience of guilt c. redemption through purification (mortification, scapegoating, transcendence).
Step 3	Assess the significance of the redemptive cycle application in deepening the understanding of the rhetorical texts for society.

and African American, described his significance as a transcendent hero competing in the games in Nazi Germany during the 1930s games. Thus, order, pollution, guilt, purification, and redemption are the necessary stages of Burke's **redemptive cycle** as the *drama* of modern life (Burke, 1970; Rueckert, 1982. The redemptive cycle is at the heart of the literary genres, tragedy and comedy, and as a theoretic explanation of how we manage guilt.

In a study of dramatism, Messner (1996) used Burke's redemptive cycle to explain the social significance and effectiveness of 12-step recovery program as a therapy intervention for alcoholics and drug addicts. Messner contended that the program introduces codependency, and the recovery process as closely aligned with Burke's key terms—pollution, purification, and redemption. Messner identified the codependency process as a two-act drama. In the first act, codependent persons are encouraged to admit their "polluted" actions of addiction. The second act is marked by two stages: purification and redemption. Codependents purify themselves by mortification (admitting that they are powerless) and are redeemed (turning their lives over to God). The data, or rhetorical texts, in this analysis were four key books produced from 1987 to 1990, three of which made the *New York Times* Best Seller List. Considering the widespread popularity of the 12-step recovery programs, Messner (1996) concluded, "it is rhetorically compelling and highly successful" (p. 120). Burke's redemptive cycle was also the basis for Grano and Zagacki's (2011) analysis of race and class following Hurricane Katrina. The authors contrasted the "Superdome Hell" of the disaster's evacuees as visual and metaphorical pollution, the "remainder of American structural racism" when the Superdome became home to 30,000 of New Orleans' poorest residents. The complexities of guilt that followed

were visually cleansed (purified) through the ritualistic dedication and reopening of the Superdome for the Saints on *Monday Night Football*. In this study, the interpretive and critical paradigms are clearly bridged in claims that are both interpretive and evaluative. A summary of the redemptive cycle as steps in rhetorical criticism is provided in Table 9.8.

Burke (1973, 1970, 1969a, 1969b) identified two specific forms of data analysis: *cluster analysis* and *pentadic analysis*. As a means of exploring the concepts of identification and redemption, Burke introduced the method of **cluster analysis** (Burke, 1969a, 1973). Burke believed that the language that speakers use reveals the speakers' meanings, attitudes, and motives. As a critic using cluster analysis, your goal would be to find these sources of identification by examining key terms used by the rhetor; then groupings or categories of strategies linked to those key terms; and finally whole patterns reflecting the rhetor's meanings, motives, and attitudes (S. K. Foss, 2009, pp. 63–70). Accordingly, the patterns you uncover should reflect the speakers' attempts to identify with or alienate their audiences (Brock, 1990).

As a form of *cluster analysis*, Kenny (2000) identified central themes in the vocabulary used by Dr. Jack Kevorkian, also known as "Dr. Death," a medical pathologist who assisted several people in committing suicide. Kenny's main claim was that Kevorkian's rhetorical intent or motive was distinctly different from the rhetorical situation or scene to which he was often assigned, that is, the moral dilemma of physician-assisted suicide. Kenny based his claim on the analysis of texts either written by or spoken by Kevorkian throughout the course of his career as a pathologist. Kenny showed that Kevorkian's vocabulary revealed an "occupational psychosis," another of Burke's concepts that explained what happened when

Table 9.9 Burkean Pentad

Act	Identification of the thought or behavior around which the drama occurs.
Agent	The person or persons who commit an act.
Agency	The means by which an act is carried out.
Scene	The setting or situation in which an act occurred.
Motive	The reason for the action that the agent can readily provide for the act.

the vocabulary associated with one's profession became so dominant that it obscured an individual's identification with any other social aspect of life. Kevorkian's motive was revealed as a preoccupation with death for the purposes of "experimentation, organ harvesting, and termination" where "the focus is not the person, but the experimental research" (Kenney, 2000, pp. 390–391). Kevorkian's motive then, as revealed by Kenny's analysis, placed him squarely outside of the humanitarian debate regarding "quality of life" issues.

Just as cluster analysis is a method Burke (1969a, 1969b, 1970) described in analyzing the grounds for identification, Burke's pentad was a method for exploring the general motivation for rhetorical acts. In conducting a **pentadic criticism**, you would apply the elements of drama to any symbolic act or text to understand its underlying persuasive function. The elements of the pentad include act, scene, agent, agency, and purpose described here and in Table 9.9. The relationships among these various elements reveal these an even deeper understanding of the rhetorical context.

Act. The **act** names or identifies the thought or behavior around which the drama occurs. To name an act gives it a particular identity. For example, Kaylor (2011) used pentadic analysis to contrast two different speech acts, Mitt Romney's "Faith in America" speech and John F. Kennedy's address to the Greater Houston Ministerial Alliance. The acts are interpreted by agent and scene, and then agency and purpose to show how the two speeches about the relationship between politics and religion could be interpreted so differently.

Scene. The **scene** is the setting or situation in which the act occurred. In the preceding example, the scene is comprised of three elements: timing in the election, audience characteristics, and permitting questions (p. 498). Kennedy's speech came after he had firmly secured the nomination of his party; Romney's came before the first primary, before he had convinced his party that he should be the presidential nominee. Kennedy spoke to a predominantly Protestant audience traditionally opposed to Catholic candidates, whereas Romney addressed his friends and supporters George H. W. Bush Presidential Library. Kennedy permitted and answered critical questions from audience members; Romney spoke to an invited audience and did not allow questions.

Agent. The **agent** is the person or persons who commit the act. The agent must have the power or will to commit the act. In Kaylor's example, Kennedy and Romney were members of religions (Catholic and Mormon) that had never before held the office of president and, to some extent, regarded as marginal by the Protestant majority. They also both came from wealthy and politically-connected families, had resided in Massachusetts, and physically presented athletic and attractive personas.

Agency. The **agency** is the means by which the act is carried out. In this case, both speakers addressed an audience in a public context that was televised and repeated in broadcast for a much larger viewership.

Purpose. The **purpose** is the reason for the action that the agent can readily provide for the act. In this example, Kaylor argued that "while Kennedy's speech followed the rhetorical expectations of the civil-religious contract articulated by Hart (1977), Romney adopted a more confessional religious-political style characterized by a tone that was testimonial, partisan, sectarian, and liturgical" (p. 498). In this analysis, Kaylor claimed that Kennedy's refusal to discuss his personal religious beliefs and his avowal to keep his religion separate from public policy was reassuring to an audience acutely aware of his difference as a Catholic. By contrast, Kaylor demonstrated that Romney's open discussion of his religious beliefs linked to his political views was not as effectively persuasive for the larger audience.

When you select this form of criticism, your task as pentadic critic is to complete three main steps: (1) to identify and interpret the five elements of the pentad, (2) to apply the ratios or the relationships among the elements, and (3) to identify the motive based on examination of the ratios (S. K. Foss, 2009). The ratios are possible pairs of elements, like act—agent and act—scene, which are isolated to determine the effect each element has on every other element. By this process, the critic can discover which of the elements appear to be more important or significant than any other. Kaylor (2011) combined scene and agent, and then agency and purpose to reveal a sharp contrast between two speech acts about the relationship between a presidential candidate's religion and the political realm.

As you can see by the very few studies we have reviewed here, Burke (1969a, 1969b, 1970, 1973) addressed many issues and developed numerous conceptual theories that can be applied to the analysis of rhetorical texts. Undoubtedly, you will find other concepts from Burke not specifically mentioned in this section since he remains one of the richest sources of knowledge and interpretation applied in rhetorical criticism. To understand the worth of dramatistic criticism, we must consider the warrants most appropriate for this methodology.

Warrants

Because Burke's (1969a, 1969b, 1970) dramatism involves many interrelated complex conceptualizations, warrants for this type of research seem to rest in the *plausibility of various interpretations*. To establish the reasonableness of a claim, your role as critic would entail presenting Burke's concept as it is defined and explained by Burke with numerous references to original works Burke produced. You may also choose to cite accepted scholars, such as Rueckert (1982), who are recognized interpreters of Burke's books and essays, as a way of establishing the credibility of your interpretation. Additionally, the application of each Burkean concept or method requires a great deal of substantiation from the existing texts you wish to analyze. When Kenny (2000) advanced a claim about Kevorkian's character, he used most of the texts Kevorkian had produced up to that point as a way of building a case for the adequacy of his evidence.

Sometimes you would not be interested in making broad claims about rhetorical texts. As mentioned earlier, Kaylor (2011) demonstrated Romney's speech was unable to transcend political and religious opposition because his speech did not demonstrate the same level of coherence that Kennedy's earlier speech exemplified. Your explanation must fit the actual features of the text and add clarity and understanding.

In the next section, we examine another rhetorical critical method based on communication as a form of drama. With a focus on characters, plot, and setting, this third interpretive criticism methodology is narrative analysis.

Narrative Analysis

Contemporary studies of narratives represent widely varying theoretic bases and specific methodologies. Narratives are explored as myths, performed rhetorical texts, folklore, and social constructions of reality. Many disciplines have contributed to the study of narratives, such as literature and history, the social sciences of anthropology, psychology, and psychiatry. Narrative criticism had its origins in Greece and Rome with the writings of Aristotle and Quintilian. One of the first rhetorical critics to write about narratives in our field was Walter Fisher (1978, 1987, 1989). Fisher began his work on narratives by investigating the "American Dream." Rather than limiting the interpretation of narrative to a method of analysis, W. Fisher (1987, 1989) introduced the term **narrative paradigm** as a way of understanding human nature, including the central belief that humans are storytellers, that life is a continual process of recreating our own stories, that values change by context, and that ultimately our social realities construct and are constructed out of the narratives we tell. W. Fisher's initial contribution to narrative analysis has been complemented by the influences of Burke's dramatism and Bormann's (1972) fantasy theme analysis, the theory of symbolic convergence, and the cultural or ethnographic approach to narratives and narratives as performance. The interpretive framework for analyzing narratives that you use will depend in part on your understanding of the concept of narrative and your training as a methodologist. Generally, however, narrative criticism shares the basic assumptions about knowledge that we identify with the interpretive paradigm as we illustrate in the next section.

Claims and Data

As a narrative critic, you make your claim of interpretation when you formulate your purpose statement or research question. The data or evidence that you collect and analyze will be narrative rhetorical artifacts that may include spoken and/or written texts but also might include transcripts of conversations or songs, visual narratives represented in mediated forms (e.g., film), or even a representational space or place like a monument

Table 9.10 Steps in Narrative Analysis

Step 1	Select narrative as rhetorical text.
Step 2	Construct claims that link the narrative to objective and features of the narrative.
Step 3	Analyze the narrative by interpreting objective and features: a. Identification of narrative's objective b. Identification of narrative's features most relevant to accomplishing the objective c. redemption through purification (mortification, scapegoating, transcendence).
Step 4	Assess the significance of the narrative analysis in contributing to the understanding of the rhetorical texts.
Step 5 (optional)	Evaluate: a. the appropriateness of the narrative for the situation or context b. the alignment between the objective and the features of the narrative.

or a museum. Rybacki and Rybacki (1991) defined **narratives** as "rhetorical acts conceptualized in story form, that is, symbolic action in the words and deeds of characters that provide order and meaning for the audience, who then create, interpret, and live that action" (p. 108).

The steps for conducting narrative analysis are the same general steps for every method of rhetorical criticism, which include selecting rhetorical text (narratives), constructing claims, and supporting these with the application of the narrative framework. According to S. K. Foss (2009), this framework should include (1) identifying the objective of the narrative; and (2) identifying the features of the narrative to evaluate how they accomplish the objective (p. 310). In some cases, you may also include an evaluation of the appropriateness of the narrative for the context and the alignment between the objective and the features of the narrative as social critique (pp. 315–316). These steps are illustrated in Table 9.10.

Identifying the objective of the narrative means to interpret the intended effect or impact of a narrative. All stories are meant to accomplish some end, to perform some "rhetorical work." You can uncover this objective by the author's own identification, if it exists; you can assess it by evaluating the audience's reactions; and you can look at the context or situation. A standup comic will obviously tell a story differently than a surgeon at a medical conference. Foss identified a list of common narrative objectives, which included "to encourage action, to defend or justify an act, to comfort or bring relief, to challenge perceptions of a situation, to entertain, to manage or resolve conflict. . . . " (pp. 311–312). We haven't included the complete list here and the list is not exhaustive, but as you

can see from these few, narratives can accomplish many objectives.

Narrative analysis should also illustrate how the objective is accomplished by identifying the features or elements of a narrative. These can include the setting, characters, narrator, events, temporal relations (how events are connected in time), causal relations, audience, theme(s), and type of narrative, such as comedy, romance, tragedy (S. K. Foss, 2009, pp. 312–315). You need not include every feature in your analysis. Frequently, narrative themes are selected as central elements. For example, the themes of alienation and fragmentation appeared as central motifs in Stroud's (2001) narrative analysis of the film, *The Matrix*. Stroud identified themes of isolation and "solitary enlightenment" that separate the hero of the film from any community. In this analysis, the content of Stroud's rhetorical criticism deals with the significance of technology in our social narratives as applied to a film as text. In a more recent analysis of the same movie, Pierce and Kaufman (2012) claimed that the visuals elements depicting the setting, characters, and events were rhetorically compelling features. The use of color, camera angle and framing, and slow motion action added dimensions to the characters and plot that highly engaged film audiences. Daws (2007) used narrative analysis to explore the themes as features of Kanye West's music, including a "cynical attitude toward collegiate education, the positive role of Christ in the lives of both rappers and listeners, and commentary on the materialism that has manifested itself in our culture" (p. 90). It is clear that the narratives many contemporary studies can include both discursive and nondiscursive elements.

Increasingly, critics in narrative research may also construct evaluative claims from the critical paradigm to explore contemporary narratives as the "current socio-economic, political, cultural, aesthetic, and spiritual situation of the people central to the historical narrative and their relative position to the dominant society/ies that currently surround them" (Clair, 1997, pp. 323–324). Indeed, we will explore narrative analysis as a critical methodology in the next chapter on "How to Critique Texts." In this section, we will provide just a couple of examples to distinguish these approaches from the interpretive. Dickinson, Ott, and Aoki's (2005) analysis of the Buffalo Bill Museum showed that history is reconstructed through the myths or narratives suggested by the museum's exhibits. Dickinson et al. (2005) claimed that the themes reflected in these narratives privileged Whiteness and masculinity using "props, films, and posters of Buffalo Bill's Wild West to carnivalize the violent conflicts between Anglo Americans and Native Americans" (p. 87). From a critical paradigm perspective, narratives can appear to be authentic recreations of actual events but in fact serve as "collective memories" where memory is "selective, incomplete and partial," and where what is forgotten and omitted has "the potential to cleanse, absolve or relieve visitors of painful, conflictual histories," in this case, the violent colonization of the American Indians (Dickinson et al., 2005, p. 89). In another study, Burns (2009) claimed that NBC's use of Olympic athlete narratives in the 2006 Olympics were used to perpetuate the "rags-to-riches" American dream when in reality many athletes cannot gain access to the games because of their socioeconomic status. In this way, narrative analyses can explain themes of dominance and oppression or of voice and liberation. That emphasis places such studies clearly in the critical paradigm. We discuss those studies more fully in the next chapter, but before leaving narrative criticism, let's consider the warrants typically used to evaluate the effectiveness of this scholarship.

Warrants

The warrants or standards of evaluation have actually received more direct treatment by W. R. Fisher and his associates than even the theoretical components of narrative methodology. W. R. Fisher (1987) identified two standards to be applied to the evaluation of narratives: *coherence* and *fidelity*. From W. R. Fisher's (1987) perspective, coherence refers to a consistency or narrative rationality that can be applied to various aspects of the narrative. The narrative is judged for its ability to present a coherent "whole" as well as consistencies related to settings, characters, and temporal development of the plot. Fidelity refers to a narrative's ability to help the reader make sense of his or her experiences. If a narrative demonstrates both coherence and fidelity, it is judged to be an effective and satisfactory text. These are examined by judging whether the narrative's objective was reached successfully through its features. A narrative is also considered effective if it embodies values or ethical principles you judge to be worthwhile, whether it fulfills the goals of its creators, and whether it provides practical and useful suggestions for living everyday life (S. K. Foss, 2009, pp. 315–316).

In the narrative studies described in the previous section, the authors were concerned with establishing coherence and fidelity in answering their central claims. Stroud's (1995) study of *The Matrix* illustrated masterful use of plot and character to reinforce the themes of fragmentation and alienation. In Daws's narrative critique of Kanye West's music, the author demonstrated that the artist's lyrics revealed a consistency within and across songs for each theme. Moreover, Daws argued that the themes expressed fidelity for very different audiences, reinforcing realities and values of both mainstream and marginalized groups of young people, and therefore carried wide appeal. As with other methodologies in this chapter, narrative analyses have unique features that must be considered when the critic uses them in the examination of a rhetorical text to ensure the most effective application.

The narrative analyses that signal trends toward incorporating the assumptions of the critical paradigm also are less explicitly concerned with the warrants of coherence and fidelity (see Warnick, 1987, and Rowland, 1987, for criticisms of W.R. Fisher's concepts). Instead, they are frequently evaluated in terms of how well they can reveal the hidden agendas of the dominant social, economic, and political institutions that form the structure of any society (i.e., ideology, hegemony). For example, Dickinson et al.'s (2005) study of the Buffalo Bill museum showed how the inclusion and arrangement of the exhibits displaced violent with neutralized images in the narrative of "colonization and civilization," upholding the values of the dominant culture of "self-determination, rugged individualism, and heroism" (p. 103). And Burns's (2009) study of narratives in sports broadcasting revealed reinforcement of the hegemonic values that support the myth of the American Dream. Studies from the critical paradigm contain evaluative claims but they may also be reformist in directly arguing for the need for ideological and social change, claims investigated in much more detail in the next chapter. Remember that your ways of warranting a research argument will change as a function not only of the type of methodology you use but as a function of your underlying paradigmatic assumptions.

As a final consideration of this chapter, we return to the traditional components of rhetorical criticism to see how new theories of communication have reframed these foundational elements.

New Directions for Rhetorical Criticism

In the last section, we explored how the claims-data-warrants model shifted from a traditional conception of public speaking as the foundation of rhetorical criticism to interpretive paradigm perspectives that included mediated discourse (films, broadcast communications) along with oratory. In this section, we examine another shift as a bridge to the critical paradigm by transforming the traditional elements of context and audience. In redefining the rhetorical situation or context, we will consider McGee's (1980; 1982) cultural ideographic approach to criticism. As a second influence, we will examine Habermas's (1989) concept of the "public sphere" of communication as a transformation of traditional ideas of audiences.

Reconsidering Rhetorical Contexts

The traditional approaches to rhetorical criticism emphasized analysis of speeches as public address. As we have noted in earlier sections, our early use of data for rhetorical criticism primarily consisted of using speech outlines/transcripts/videotapes to recreate the rhetorical act within its context. Because of this approach, speeches were treated as fixed objects, atemporal and objective, with no consideration given to the ephemeral, transitory nature of speaking. One exception in the history of criticism is Ernest J. Wrage's "Public Address: A Study in Social and Intellectual History." Wrage (in Rostek, 1999) argued that rhetorical critics should engage "the whole ensemble of a culture, its 'mosaic of documents, including 'constitutions and laws, . . . scientific treatises, . . .

lectures, [and] sermons.' But . . . also its 'literature and song, . . . folklore, . . . speeches'—in short, all the artifacts of popular culture" (p. 230). Rostek continues by pointing to two important implications in Wrage's essay: (1) that analysts should select case studies that express culture, "privileging the *practice* of public culture above all else; and (2) that rhetorical criticism should focus on "the textualization of ideas within culture" (p. 231). As M. C. McGee (1999, as cited in Lucaites et al., 1999) pointed out, speaking is not thinking or writing. Its qualities are discursive (language based) and performative (a temporal act in a particular context targeted at a particular group or audience).

According to M. C. McGee (1999), the qualities of speaking that make it necessarily contextualized highlight the conditions of contemporary culture. We are not speaking to a large, homogenous group as an audience; from M. C. McGee's (1999) perspective, there is no "public sphere" but multiple, fragmented listeners, and public, political language is ideological; even the "American people" so frequently alluded to is a fiction. In another essay, M. C. McGee (1980) introduced the concept of an "ideograph." Because of the discursive and performative qualities of speech, M. C. McGee (1980) claimed that language cannot escape the contexts of ideology and power; symbolism is the necessary complement to political consciousness; and **ideographs** are words that operate as vectors of influence such as "liberty" and the "pursuit of happiness." We are immersed in our cultures where we learn political terms by association. Rather than be conditioned to belief or behavior, M. C. McGee (1980) asserted that we are shaped by "a vocabulary of concepts that function as guides, warrants, reasons, or excuses for behavior and belief" (p. 6). They are bound within the culture that they define through their usage. For example, Dubriwny (2005) used the ideographs of "women and children" and "rights" to illustrate Laura Bush's strategic use of discourse associated with feminism, "ideals of women's rights to education, health, and independence" and "maternal feminism" (p. 84).

McGee (1980, 1982) offered a critique to traditional rhetorical criticism, arguing that Bitzer's conception of a rhetorical situation did not extend far enough to consider cultural influence and the radicalization of rhetorical texts. As Keith and Lundberg (2008) note, "McGee expanded this approach by acknowledging persuasive processes that precede and move beyond a speech, mostly including cultural, ideological, and political predispositions that make up audiences and messages" (p. 30). From this cultural frame, you can see that rhetorical acts and how we are to understand them is much more complex, requiring understanding the standpoint perspectives of the message creator, its multiple audiences across multiple contexts from multiple cultural frames. The nature of those audiences has also been revolutionized by industrial and technological innovation, a transformation we shall now consider.

Audiences and the Nature of the Public Sphere

The concept of the "public sphere" came from Jüergen Habermas (1989), a philosopher writing in response to the modernism of the early twentieth century. Recall that modernism was described as a reliance on objectivism and the pursuit of universal truths earlier in this chapter. The contribution of Habermas's (1989) philosophy generally and his conception of the public sphere has had a profound effect on rhetorical criticism; in fact, DeLuca and Peeples (2002) recently claimed that the public sphere was "ubiquitous in contemporary social theory" (p. 127). Many of Habermas' ideas have resonated in a variety of ways and have met with many of the criticisms as you will see in our discussion.

Habermas (1989) believed that an idealized condition of society was possible through unrestricted debate of its individual members. Habermas termed this condition the **public sphere**, which happened in the past each time private individuals assembled publicly to discuss issues of general social importance. The idea of an audience has been radicalized by the advances of technology, moving it from the physical and temporal village sphere to the global and atemporal public sphere in which messages and texts are jointly shared by vastly greater numbers. Through freedom of assembly and expression of ideas, Habermas envisioned a "sovereign, reasonable public, nourished by the critical reporting of the press and engaged in the mutually enlightening clash of arguments" (as cited in S. K. Foss et al., 2002, p. 239). This level of engagement is now made possible with much larger and more accessible audiences through advances in wireless and mobile technologies, the Internet and social media; and these advances show remarkable ability for audience adaptation in ways that we have never before considered! A number of critics such as Eli Pariser, CEO of Upworthy (a website for political activism on the role of technology), are critical of Google and Facebook for creating filters that screen and personalizes information for each user.

There are four critical bases to the conception of the public sphere: (1) the autonomy of the public sphere, (2) the importance of rational debate, (3) the reliance on face-to-face dialogue, and (4) the belief that speech and reason would lead to universal truths (Sinekopova, 2006). The autonomy of the public sphere refers to Habermas's (1989) conception of one, uniform public. As we indicated in the previous section, rhetorical critics such as McGee now argue that Habermas's conceptions of the "public" do not address contemporary conditions of a pluralistic society in which there are many fractured, differentiated groups as audiences (see, e.g., McGee and Wander as cited in Lucaites et al., 1999).

Habermas (1989) believed that rational debate was at the core of an idealized public, that the emergence of ideas as universals was only possible through open access of all individuals to public forums: coffeehouses, salons, town hall meetings. But some critics have argued that by privileging rationality, Habermas promoted a Western view of "liberal democracy," one that is ethnocentric and exclusionary instead of global in its scope (Sinekopova, 2006). Moreover, Habermas believed that to have an open and accessible public sphere, communication had to happen face-to-face in dialogue. Habermas offered alternatives to the traditional conceptions of "speaker," "public address," and "audience" that were interactive and dialogic. However, recent critics have faulted Habermas for failure to consider multiple mediated and nondiscursive forms of communication made available through new technologies (DeLuca, 1999).

The final base of Habermas's public sphere was centered in his belief that speech and reason would lead to ultimate truths. Like Burke, Habermas believed that people were internally motivated by a desire for perfection and were therefore intent on "building a rational society where individuals can reason in universal terms and where everyone's needs are satisfied" (Sinekopova, 2006, p. 510). In his later writings, Habermas believed that the rise of capitalism has led to the decline of the public sphere: "Rational-critical debate had a tendency to be replaced by consumption, and the web of public communication unraveled into acts of individuated reception, however uniform the mode" (p. 163). Critics have offered alternatives to Habermas's predictions and have stated that the pluralism of society produces healthy differences in normative values, that there are other forms of thought and method distinct from rationality, and that multiple "public spheres" are emerging in the face of new technologies (DeLuca & Peeples, 2002;

Sinekopova, 2006). There are now many articles that address the positive contributions and dangers of various technologies and their effects on communication . . . the debate continues.

As you can see, the newest directions in ideological criticism have just begun to consider the implications of nontraditional and innovative texts, media, and technologies for expanding the applications of the methodologies discussed in this chapter. By considering new conceptions of discursive and nondiscursive texts and the public sphere, we can understand more fully how our traditional conceptions of rhetorical criticism must change. In this chapter, we traced the development of traditional and interpretive forms of rhetorical criticism through the claims-data-warrants model as applied to several methodologies in each paradigm. We ended the chapter by identifying several major developments in ideological research. In the next chapter, you will see how additional philosophical perspectives from the critical paradigm inform methodological analyses of communication as bases for social critiques and change.

Ethical Concerns in Rhetorical Criticism

From classical origins onward, the development of ethical theory has remained a central concern of rhetorical criticism. From the Sophists to the Romans and throughout the centuries of rule by the Christian churches, public ethos and concern for the moral good were conveyed through the process and substance of public speaking. In the eighteenth and nineteenth centuries, political and economic conditions that influenced the materialism of the industrial revolution gave rise to new philosophic speculations about what a public morality might mean. Religious authority was supplanted by scientific realism, and conceptions of a monolithic, unified "people" governed by a universal set of morals were challenged by an increasing awareness of multiple moralities emerging from distinctive cultures. The scientific rationalism of modernism and the burgeoning new technologies of the twentieth century resulted in a moral relativism of a fragmented global society. Christians, a rhetorical ethical scholar, asserted that "cultural relativity is unquestioned and celebrated—that is, the right and valid are only known in local space and native languages" and

consideration of universal principles has been "discredited as imperialistic" (2005, p. 5).

Cultural relativism has not provided means of coping with the social, political and economic crises on the global scene. Cultures with strong divergent beliefs are left to "duke it out" in deciding who will dominate through power and control. In an attempt to uncover a transcendent context for moral discourse, Christians (2005) claimed that rhetorical and media critics are in a special position to encourage the conversation about the development of not universal morals but an internationally inclusive set of ethical principles. Scholars in both of these areas contribute to discussion among world leaders about these issues.

For example, in 1998, the Global Ethics Foundation brought together an international group of ethicists who proposed four ethical guiding themes for a global society: (1) preservation of human rights; (2) emancipation of women; (3) realization of social justice; and (4) immorality of war (Christians, 2005, p. 6). Several other themes, such as the sacredness of life, have emerged in other discussions (pp. 7–9).

In recognition of the complexity of issues, Christians (2005) has identified three central problems in establishing internationally inclusive ethical principles: (1) the development of a knowledge base to support and defend this set of propositions; (2) the debate concerning the distinction between discovering essential values and constructing relative values, and 3) the question of whether the world is really one (underlying unity) or many (fragmented by distinct cultures); the enduring global vs. tribal issue. These problems lie at the very heart of the paradigmatic differences we have been discussing throughout the entirety of this book.

Rhetorical and media critics would seem especially positioned to highlight and address each of these problems in the discussions that ensue across global contexts. While there can be no one theory of universals, Christians (2005) has urged critics to consider multiple theories for emergent ethical guidelines, such as international human rights, that will serve as catalysts in coping with the issues and problems we all now share at global levels. "With its roots in language, culture, and the fundamentally human, communication ethics has the opportunity to set the standard for applied and professional ethics as a whole" (Christians, 2005, p. 13).

As summarized in Table 9.11, this chapter traced the development of traditional and interpretive forms of rhetorical criticism through the claims—data—warrants model as applied to several methodologies in each paradigm. We ended the chapter by identifying several major developments in rhetorical criticism and by suggesting the complexity of ethics in doing criticism. In the next chapter, you will see how additional philosophical perspectives from the critical paradigm inform methodological analyses of communication as bases for social critiques and change.

Table 9.11 Rhetorical Criticism Summary Table

Paradigm	Method	Claim	Data	Warrants
Discovery	Neoclassical	Explanatory	Public speeches	Validity and reliability
Discovery and Critical	Genre	Explanatory; Evaluative and reformist	Public speeches and discursive texts	Validity and reliability; coherence and change in awareness
Interpretive and Critical	Metaphoric	Interpretive; Evaluative	Discursive and nondiscursive texts	Adequacy of evidence; coherence; change in awareness and praxis
Interpretive and Critical	Dramatism	Interpretive; Evaluative	Discursive and nondiscursive texts	Adequacy of evidence; coherence; change in awareness and praxis
Interpretive and Critical	Narrative	Interpretive; Evaluative and reformist	Discursive and nondiscursive texts	Coherence and fidelity

Key Terms

Apologias
Archetypal or root metaphors
Artistic proofs
Canons of rhetoric
Cluster analysis
Deliberative rhetoric
Delivery
Enthymeme
Epideictic rhetoric
Ethos
Exigence
Figures
Forensic rhetoric
Generic application
Generic description
Generic participation

Genre
Identification
Ideograph
Inartistic proofs
Invention
Jeremiads
Logos
Metaphor
Mortification
Narrative
Narrative paradigm
Organization
Pathos
Pentadic criticism
Pentadic elements: Act, scene,
    agent, agency, purpose

Pollution
Public sphere
Purification
Redemptive cycle
Rhetoric
Rhetorical criticism
Rhetorical situation
Rhetorical theory
Style
Terministic screens
Transcendence
Trope
Victimage

Discussion Questions

1. According to neoclassical methodology, attention to the artistic forms of proof as support for the speaker's argument is vitally important. Why are moral or emotional appeals considered along with logical appeals? When would rational appeals grounded in evidence be superior to emotional appeals? When would emotional appeals be more effective than rational appeals?

2. Think of some common metaphors we use in language all of the time. Maybe you have heard sports metaphors applied to other contexts, such as saying "we want to be on the winning team" while working on a group assignment. What others can you think of? Are there any that specifically relate to being female or male? How do the metaphors we use help us construct meanings or interpretations of our experiences?

3. Think about your family get-togethers. What stories does your family tell about you? What do the stories say about your character, your aspirations, your humor? Explain how the stories your family tells are like the narratives W. R. Fisher (1989) discusses in his approach to narrative analysis. How do the stories of a family help constitute its culture?

4. What do you think about Habermas's concept of the public sphere? Is there one, uniform conception of the "American people"? Is technology promoting or negatively impacting democracy?

"Try It!" Activities

1. Find an article from a communication journal that uses neoclassical criticism. You may use any of the articles listed in the reference section for this chapter. Identify the concepts the critic makes use of from this methodology. Does the critic complete all three steps of the analytical process (reconstructing the context, analyzing the rhetorical artifact, and assessing its effects)? Does one of the canons (invention, organization, style, delivery) receive more emphasis than the others? Does the critic concentrate on one of the artistic proofs (logos, ethos, pathos) more heavily than the other two?

2. Choose any article listed in this chapter in the section on metaphoric criticism, or find an article from a communication journal that uses metaphoric criticism. Try to answer two or three of the following questions: What does the choice of metaphors tell you about the rhetor? What values or attitudes might be implicit in using specific metaphors? What do they tell you about the audience? Do the metaphors clarify or confuse the claim or thesis of the rhetor? Are there any visual or nonverbal metaphors?

3. Choose any article that shows how new technologies have contributed to social change. For example, awareness of sweatshop industries that support Nike, the Gap, and other multinational corporations has largely happened through groups of college students. One area of social concern you are likely to hear about frequently is global warming. What kinds of social events (e.g., documentary films) have raised social awareness?

10 How to Critique Texts

Introduction

In this chapter, you will learn more about how to closely read and evaluate texts, and how to suggest ways that communication might be reformed in order to achieve equal voice for all participants or to liberate some participants from an oppressive reality. As the idea of rhetoric changes, so does criticism. Here, theory and method intertwine, whether you evaluate language in use or aim to reform ideologies. We have organized this chapter around the distinction between structural and poststructural criticism because these two factions differ on a fundamental assumption (i.e., are social structures "real" or only temporarily constituted in language?). You will learn how to select and analyze mediated and nonmediated texts, including historical and present day actions and events, and your own experiences and beliefs, using deconstruction and narrative criticism. You also will learn to apply the critical paradigm warrants of coherence, researcher positionality, and impact.

Learning Outcomes

After completing this chapter, you should be able to:

» Compare and contrast at least one form of structural (e.g., Marxist, feminist) and one form of post-structural (postmodern, cultural, semiotic) criticism in terms of each method's assumptions about the nature of reality, role of the knower, and purpose of critiquing texts.

» Deconstruct and evaluate a set of actions or events, texts or your own experiences and beliefs in order to evaluate communication effectiveness, and/or to show how particular perspective(s) are being privileged and how other perspective(s) are being marginalized by either the social structure(s) or by language process(es) in that context.

» Given another person's narrative, evaluate the coherence, researcher positionality, and likely changes in awareness or praxis that would constitute successful intervention for either a social structure or a discourse process.

Outline

In Chapter 1, "Introduction to Communication Research," you learned that theories are sometimes quite distinct from the research methods used to develop, test, and revise them, but that sometimes theory and method are highly interconnected. Each critical method in this chapter relies on a different theory, and it's impossible to conduct each kind of criticism without knowing something about that theory. So when we interpret and critique texts, our theories and methods are inseparable. This connection between theory and method, and the analytic strategies of deconstruction and narrative analysis, are similar for interpreting and critiquing texts, so this chapter will build on what you gained from Chapter 9, "How to Interpret Texts."

Rhetorical criticism has long been used, not only to describe and interpret communication, but to evaluate its social and moral worth (Fisher, 1984). Many of the critical studies published today deal directly with ideology, and focus on issues of power, oppression, and privilege. They show how society's dominant power structures and discourses benefit some groups of people and oppress others, and how resistance to that oppression can be accomplished with communication. These studies tend to be one of two types: structural or poststructural. *Structural critics* believe that power imbalances are due to some aspect of an objectively real social structure, like the economy or gender arrangements. *Poststructural critics* reject the idea of social structures as objectively real, and instead, attribute power imbalances to the ways that language is used in a social setting or group.

Both structural and poststructural critics make *claims* of evaluation and reform. Structural critics intend for their evaluations to change people's awareness of, and perhaps the very structures of society, so as to equalize power relations among all members (e.g., debates over gender and wage equity seek to change the actual compensation afforded in jobs occupied by female and male employees). Poststructural critics, because they believe that all social structures are created and maintained through language, instead aim to evaluate and reform discourse processes, the way we talk about social structures and use language, in order to equalize power resources and opportunities for all participants. Here an example would be changing the way we speak about people who hold different jobs (e.g., replacing the terms waiter/waitress with waitstaff or waitperson).

Structural and poststructural critics both draw on the same sorts of *data* or *evidence,* including actions and events, texts, and their own experiences and beliefs. When you critique texts, you will need to embrace writing as your method of inquiry (Goodall, 2000; Groscurth, 2011). So your position in society, your language use, your national or regional affiliations, race, class, gender, sexuality, ability, and all of your lived experiences and beliefs will become the systematic, observable evidence against which you assess the need for social change. For this reason, in critical communication studies, we refer to the *evidence* upon which claims are based rather than to the *data*, per se.

Both structural and poststructural critics rely on the same *warrants* to connect their claims to evidence. Your coherent reasoning, your positionality as the critic, and your assessment of the likely impact that your critique will have on other people's awareness and praxis will help to determine the worth of your textual criticism. In the third section of this chapter, we will show you two basic analytic strategies you can use to critique texts: Deconstruction and narrative analysis. Both of these strategies are shared by interpretive rhetorical critics and discourse analysts. However, your use of deconstruction and narrative analysis to conduct communication criticism will be somewhat different. Interpretive analyses of texts will work to unpack and evaluate the *participants' meanings.* But your textual criticism will privilege *your* own interpretations and evaluations of the text(s) over the participants' meanings. You will work to evaluate people's communication effectiveness, reveal power-dominance relations, to describe participants' consciousness (or lack of it), and depict persuasive processes at work.

Sometimes, the persuasion you evaluate (or the communication you hope to change) operates in subtle ways that are below the conscious awareness of the participants. In that case, your critique will deal with hegemonic processes. **Hegemony** is the "process of domination, in which one set of ideas subverts or co-opts another" (Littlejohn & Foss, 2008, p. 331; see also Gramsci, 1971; Lears, 1985). The goal of critiquing texts is to enact the values of voice and liberation and to evaluate the effectiveness of communication or suggest the need for ideological change. Thus, the key purpose of communication criticism is to identify historical, economic, and political sources of power based in ideology,

whether that ideology is manifested in social structures or in discourse. An **ideology** is "a set of ideas that structure a group's reality, a system of representations or a code of meanings governing how individuals and groups see the world" (Littlejohn & Foss, 2008, p. 331).

As you know from reading the last chapter, "How to Interpret Texts," rhetorical critics who use historical, dramatistic, narrative, and metaphoric criticism to analyze artifacts do so to advance claims of interpretation and evaluation. The artifacts can include *linguistic texts* like public speeches, films or policy documents; but they also may include *nonlinguistic texts*, such as visual images and symbols, architectural features, even ways of enacting personal identities. Since interpretive rhetorical critics value subjectivity and rich descriptions of the artifact(s), they usually aim to show how their interpretation is the most plausible one or how more than one interpretation of an artifact is equally plausible. So it makes sense that the critic's training and experience, and his or her ability to write a coherent essay, serve as the main warrants for interpretive rhetorical criticism.

Today, critical studies in communication differ from interpretive rhetorical criticism, primarily in their urge to reform macro-level awareness and practice of communication. Both critical and interpretive textual analyses are used to advance claims of evaluation, but critical scholars take that evaluation one step further. They aim to change socially constructed realities, first by making people aware of how some people or groups are being oppressed by a situation or a set of practices, then by offering ways to change those situations and practices. If you compare the interpretive paradigm values of subjectivity and rich description with the critical paradigm values of voice and liberation, you can see why we make this distinction. Critical studies are thus warranted by their coherent arguments and by the researcher's standpoint, but also by their impact: Does the study raise awareness of effective persuasion, or of oppression? If so, what if anything is likely to change, as a result of that increased awareness?

New Directions: Bridges from Interpreting to Critiquing Texts

As we noted in the last section of Chapter 9, "How to Interpret Texts," traditional approaches to rhetorical criticism emphasized the analysis of speeches and other mostly linguistic texts as they are used in public address, political campaigns, and so on. Habermas's concept of the public sphere united much of that work by emphasizing how individuals in a capitalist democracy could participate, via discussion and debate, in evaluating the right courses of action, whether that meant talking about differences in political candidates' platforms, comparing the metaphors used to talk about social problems, or analyzing the stories people told one another about things of mutual interest. Notice that in traditional rhetorical criticism, analysis of a speech as artifact treated a speech as a fixed object, atemporal and objective, with no consideration given to the ephemeral, transitory nature of speaking. Many critics have analyzed Dr. Martin Luther King's "I Have a Dream" speech, for example. All of those analyses consider his words, and some focus on how he delivered the speech, but few critics explore how Dr. King embodied his identity as a minister, an African American man, or a civil rights activist.

However, speaking is not the same as thinking or writing (McGee in Lucaites, et al., 1999). Of course, speaking, thinking, and writing are all activities based in language. But speaking also includes nonlinguistic elements, like gestures, proximity, and vocal intonation. Speaking is a *discursive* activity, one that uses language but is also broader than just the words. Speaking is also *performative*; it happens in "real time," in a particular context or situation, and it is always targeted at a particular person or group. Treating communication as discursive and performative (rather than as a fixed artifact) forms the first part of our bridge from interpretive to critical paradigm studies of textual data.

Communication as Performative and Ideological

We have said that criticism is a way of making evaluative claims about belief systems, such as people's social, economic, political, and cultural interests. If you want to advance claims that evaluate who is benefitting from a particular ideology, and who is constrained by, or being oppressed by those beliefs, you will need to consider more than the words used to communicate those interests. In addition to the discursive aspects of ideology, you will need to evaluate how people embody those beliefs and attitudes. For example, you are a college student, probably between 18–25 years old, majoring in some aspect of communication study. Chances are good that you share certain social, economic, political, and cultural interests with other college students in the United States. How do you embody those interests? What aspects of your media and retail consumption habits, your ways of presenting yourself in public, or your political views mark you as a college student? A young person? A communication major?

Critical communication scholars analyze not only the ideological beliefs and attitudes shared by a group of people, but *how* those beliefs and attitudes are enacted and embodied in material terms. Performance studies deals with **aesthetic communication**, the kind of communication when texts, events, performers, or audiences, and maybe all of those, are considered artistic (Pelias & Vanoosting, 1987). Everyone participates. Performance studies "includes all members of a speech community as potential artists, all utterances as potentially theatrical, and all audiences as potentially active participants who can authorize artistic experience" (Pelias & Vanoosting, 1987, p. 221). For these reasons, Pelias and Vanoosting (1987) characterized performance studies as "radically democratic and counterelitist," even though performers "must also remain keenly aware that each performance amplfies some voices and stifles others" (p. 222). Performance scholarship isn't just for and about artists, though. Some performance studies works evaluate (and aim to reform) the ways that everyday communication is enacted and embodied.

Consider Lindemann's (2007) critical essay on the performance of homelessness by San Francisco men and women who sell *The Street Sheet*. Homeless individuals sell the weekly newspaper for spare change and they are allowed to keep most of the profits. The newspaper gives them a "voice to speak out against social injustices" (Lindemann, 2007, p. 42). Lindemann used ethnographic methods, participating with and observing homeless people selling *The Street Sheet,* interviewing some of the vendors, and analyzing the newspaper texts, along with memos about the newspaper circulated by the city's Coalition on Homelessness. But Lindemann's analysis went beyond interpreting the vendor's verbal messages and analyzing their artifacts, the newspapers. He also focused on the vendors' performance of authentic homelessness, that is, how they looked and acted the part of a homeless person: "In selling the Street Sheet, vendors likely must perform homelessness in a way that is nonthreatening yet sufficiently 'homeless-looking' to elicit sympathy and donations" (Lindemann, 2007, p. 42). In other words, vendors had to rely on stereotypes and act in ways that reinforced people's prejudices against homeless people. To sell the *Street Sheet*, they had to participate in their own oppression.

Take a look at the journal *Text & Performance Quarterly*. There you will find examples of other critical essays that analyze how ideologies and identities are embodied and enacted through people's communication practices (e.g., see Kilgard, 2011 on classroom pedagogy practices; Moreman & Non Grata, 2012, on the experiences of undocumented college students in California; or Vignes, 2008, on going through the aftermath of Hurricane Katrina in Mississippi). Those essays, and many others like them, claim to raise awareness of how some identities and ideologies are privileged or constrained in particular contexts. Some of their authors suggest ways to reform communication that will benefit members of the oppressed groups. A focus on changing social arrangements provides the second part of our bridge between interpretive rhetorical criticism and critical studies.

Communication as Social Change

Social change in the biggest sense is often provoked by the impact of various social movements. Rhetorical criticism of social movements has a long history in our field, beginning as early as the 1940s with the seminal work of Leland Griffin (Jensen, 2006). Griffin's first approach was from a traditional public address perspective, although he later adopted Burke's interpretive approach to study social movements as dramas. With the civil rights, antiwar and feminist protest movements of the 1960s, rhetorical scholars found less satisfying the kinds of rational analyses you learned about in the first part of Chapter 9. Plus, many of those and later movements relied increasingly on nondiscursive forms of protest, such as songs, visual icons, and events. Think about coverage you've seen of the Occupy movement, gay marriage, the Tea Party, or anti-abortion protests. The explosion of non-discursive protest forms, and new communications technologies during the last part of the twentieth century vastly increased the complexity and scope of studying social movements, so that interest in social change now includes issues of international scope (e.g., globalization, sustainability). Most recently, the evolving capacity of communication technologies being used to evaluate big data samples (e.g., *GoogleAnalytics*, or what's trending on *Twitter*?) is shifting how we can understand vast spatial and temporal social movements.

As you can see, the newest directions in rhetorical criticism, communication as performative and ideological, and social change movements have made critics consider the implications of new texts, new media, and new technologies on evaluating and reforming communication. Along with these considerations and developments come the obligation to grapple with a host of new ethical problems in rhetorical and media criticism, a point we will return to at the end of this chapter.

Claims in Critical and Cultural Studies

Keep in mind that in this section, you will be learning how to make claims for structuralist and poststructuralist textual criticism. Structuralist (aka modernist) criticism is based on Marxist theory, specifically the idea that socioeconomic and political structures are the root causes of unequal power distribution for individuals and groups. Some psychoanalytic, feminist, gender, and cultural criticism follows from this view (e.g., Abetz, 2012; Dow, 1990; Hatfield, 2010; L. McLaughlin, 1991). Poststructural criticism is based on the idea that "… there is no objectively real structure or central meaning and that oppressive 'structures' are ephemeral. There is a struggle, but it is not a struggle between monolithic ideologies. It is a struggle between fluid interests and ideas created in communication practices" (Littlejohn & Foss, 2008, p. 330). Researchers engaged in postmodern and postcolonial criticism follow this line of thinking as do critical discourse analysts and semioticians.

Unlike discovery paradigm adherents, critical and interpretive scholars embrace subjectivity (Peshkin, 1988). In doing criticism, you will find that your own subjective views are impossible to avoid. Quite the opposite, your subjectivity is a desirable asset in describing, evaluating, and reforming social systems. Whether you study social structures and institutions (e.g., politics, economics, education, healthcare, media) or the ideological beliefs associated with culture (race, class, gender, sexuality, ability, religion), your critical study will aim to evaluate communication effectiveness, and perhaps, to liberate oppressed people or groups by making them aware of their own oppression and/or reforming structures and symbols in a particular context.

As we pointed out in Chapter 4, "Making Claims," it is a little bizarre to classify some studies as exclusively interpretive or critical (Swanson, 1993), and the same thing is true for dividing critical studies into those that are clearly structuralist versus poststructuralist. Nonetheless, we are making this categorizing move, even though we feel it is illogical in some ways, because we want to make things as clear as possible for you while you are being introduced to this type of research. Rest assured that we expect to complexify or muddy these categories even as you read the rest of this chapter. As Thomas Merton wrote in a January 18, 1962, letter to Czeslew Milosz: "When I said I was fed up with answers, I mean square answers, ready-made answers, answers that ignore the question. All clear answers tend to be of this nature today, because we are so deep in confusion and grab desperately at five thousand seeming glimmers of clarity. It is better to start with a good acceptance of the dark (Merton, as cited in Bochen, 1993, p. 78).

Evaluating and Reforming Social Structures

The two structural forms of criticism we present here, Marxist and gender criticism, both work to show how privileged groups oppress marginalized groups based on socioeconomic, cultural, and political structures in a society (e.g., Balaji, 2011; Gilbert, 1997; Martino, 2008; Moreman & Non Grata, 2011). Some examples of social structure include legal status/citizenship, the structure of schools and other organizations, the nuclear family and so on, along with less obvious structures like, "wage structures, the design of housing, welfare/taxation policies and so forth" (Connell, 1987, p. 184, as cited by Hatfield, 2010, pp. 536–537). At present in the United States of America, some of the groups that are most constrained, or who may be marginalized by, social structures include people living in poverty, people of color, people with disabilities, females, anyone whose sexual orientation is not heterosexual, and members of the most recent groups to immigrate to this country.

When you conduct structural criticism, you will try to identify the social arrangements most responsible for unequal power distribution so that they can be changed or adapted, primarily by reforming economic, political, and cultural structures. Table 10.1 summarizes key theorists, claims, and research questions for these two types of structural criticism and suggests some sample readings that you should pursue if you want to conduct that type of criticism. Let's consider the key concepts of each form of structural criticism in turn.

Marxist Criticism

The writings of Karl Marx that were published in the late 1800s and early 1900s (i.e., *The Communist Manifesto, 1888; Capital, 1909*) have been used widely by scholars in many disciplines to critique dominant social structures. Marx's criticism focused explicitly on the economic basis of social structure. "Traditional Marxism separated 'society,' the material features of a socioeconomic system, and 'culture,' the sense-making processes members of a social collective employ to create meaning of their experiences and context" (Conrad, 1988, p. 180).

Table 10.1 Structural Critical Studies

Critical Studies Approach	Claims describe and evaluate social structures that most contribute to unequal power distribution in society. Evaluate who benefits and who is oppressed, and suggest how such structure(s) might be reformed.	Sample Readings
Marxist criticism (Karl Marx)	RQs: What are the means of production (e.g., capitalism)? What are the modes of production (i.e., sources and forms of labor)? Are workers aware of how the means and modes of production benefit some and oppress others? How is language used to make sense of those experiences?	McMillan & Cheney (1996) on the limits of the "student as consumer" metaphor
Gender/feminist criticism (Carol Gilligan, Sonja Foss). See also womanist and masculinist criticism	RQs: How do women and men differently participate in and benefit from the means and modes of production? How are gendered experiences reproduced in language (e.g., socialization)? What paradoxes exist for women in particular contexts?	Brasfield (2006) on paradoxes of feminism in *Sex & the City*; Hanke (1998) on *mock-macho* in *Tool Time*; Trujillo (1991) on Nolan Ryan's masculinity

Note: RQs = research questions.

Marx argued that a culture's key forms and artifacts reproduce the material or economic base of the social structure. Thus, the influence of social structure upon individuals was static, overt, deterministic, and unidirectional. For Marxists, working class groups are inherently oppressed in capitalist societies. In order for that power imbalance to be reformed, the people have to unite and revolt, changing the social structure from capitalism to socialism. However, individual people were viewed by Marx as "passive victims of social forces" (Conrad, 1988, p. 180) who did not realize that they were being dominated (or privileged) by the economic and political systems. Some critical scholars believe in liberation through awareness, the idea that once made aware, people in oppressed positions in society can unite to change those systems or can at least withdraw their participation from the oppressive social structures.

However, participating in or withdrawing from oppressive social structures is much more complicated than merely collaborating with others to achieve collective social power. Let's consider a local example. Imagine that you prefer to support a small, independently owned coffee shop instead of a large national chain. Perhaps you are trying to withdraw your participation from a structure of economic oppression. But we sometimes benefit from the structures that, at other times, limit or even harm us. Maybe the national coffee chain has several stores near where you live and work; perhaps their coffee is cheaper, they may offer a wider selection of flavors and products, or let you purchase their beans at the grocery store where you already shop. These access issues benefit you as you budget both time and money, and those benefits exist in tension with your belief that big national chain stores unfairly oppress small, independently owned local businesses. This simple, local example highlights economic structures and the complexity of trying to change them.

We hope you can see how the coffee store example illustrates the defining assumptions of the critical paradigm: There are multiple realities at work in any situation that are socially constructed. Realities are shaped by the knowers' standpoint, especially their economic and political locations in the social structure. The purpose of analysis is to reveal hidden constraints and structures, to raise awareness and perhaps, to instigate social change.

Let's look next at a model that highlights both social and biological structure, criticism aimed at the gender binary of male and female roles in society.

Gender and Feminist Criticism

As we mentioned earlier, many early feminist critics followed the Marxist idea that social structures control people's potential life experiences (e.g., M. Ferguson, 1990; Hanmer, 1990; Stoller, 1993). In this case, the lived experiences of women and men in patriarchal societies were seen as dictated by the hierarchy of the **gender binary**, the privileged position of males over females in education, medicine, religion, work, families, and all aspects of daily life. Structural gender criticism thus emphasizes the "gendered nature of institutional structures and practices" and the impact of "exclusionary norms" (Ashcraft & Pacanowsky, 1996, p. 217). Even **gender-benders**, people who purposefully violate and resist the gender binary by performing gender in ways that do not fit their biological sex, are thought to reinforce this social structure (Lorber, 1990, as cited by Hatfield, 2010). For example, if a woman intentionally dresses in a masculine style (because she works in a male-dominated industry, or because she wants to appear more authoritative), her fashion choices may do more to solidify the idea of masculine power than they do to change it.

In the past two decades or so, feminist criticism has been joined by masculinist, womanist, and queer communication criticism (including both structural and poststructural versions). So we use the term **gender and feminist criticism** in this section, as a more inclusive umbrella for these related forms of scholarship. In fact, some critical theorists use the term **hybridity** (aka intersectionality) to point to ways in which particular combinations of social category memberships work together to constrain people's options for communicating (Yep, Olzman & Conkle, 2012). No doubt, you have heard references to hybrid identities in your other classes or in the news (e.g., straight White men).

"Women and men experience a wide range of realities based on performance, class, and race" (Hatfield, 2010, p. 527). Thus, womanist criticism focuses on the domination of women on the basis of structural and cultural categories like gender roles, race, class, nationality, and sexuality and upon the ways in which those arrangements intersect within a patriarchal society (e.g., Anzaldua, 1987; O. I. Davis, 1999; hooks, 1990; W. S. Lee, 1998b; Moraga & Anzaldua, 1983; Sheared, 1994). Queer criticism also works to show how representations of gender and sexuality are power-laden, rather than neutral cultural artifacts (e.g., Booth, 2009; Vivienne & Burgess, 2012; Yep, Lovaas, & Ho, 2001; Yep,

Lovaas, & Pagonis, 2002). But queer criticism can also refer to criticism of "whatever is at odds with the normal, the legitimate, the dominant," in a social context (Halperin, 1995, as cited by Littlejohn & Foss, 2008, p. 94).

It's worth noting here that if you are treating gender, race, class or sexuality as comprised of discrete categories (e.g., gender as male/female, race as black/brown/white/yellow, sexuality as gay/straight), then your assumptions are more consistent with structural criticism than with poststructural criticism. If so, you probably will be more interested in revealing and changing social structures than in reinventing discourse processes pertaining to those structures.

Feminist, womanist and queer criticisms are further complemented by cultural studies of masculinity and hegemony (e.g., Collinson & Hearn, 1994; Hanke, 1998; Hatfield, 2010; Martino, 2008; Trujillo, 1991; J.T. Wood & Inman, 1993). It's important for you to notice that critical studies of intersectionality coexist within feminist, womanist, queer and masculinist criticism. Intersectional critics argue that gender and sexuality are fluid, performative constructs rather than binary categories dictated by cultural ideologies (e.g., Butler, 1990, 1993; Cooper, 2002; Sloop, 2000; Speer & Potter, 2000). Structural critics approach these categories as representations of material and cultural power. But poststructural critics believe that, although biological sex (M/F) remains more-or-less stable over time, verbal and nonverbal performances of gender are fluid; they shift over time and context as values and belief systems vary. In other words, gender and sexuality (and perhaps all cultural identity categories) are discursive performances. We learn to do them more or less effectively, and we adapt them, depending on time and place.

Criticism that emphasizes fluid performances, adapted over time, moves us toward poststructural assumptions about how values and belief systems, more so than material social structures, contribute to unequal power relations. If your criticism is based primarily on how people's language use exposes their values and belief systems, you probably will be most interested in poststructural criticism. Critiquing discourse processes will be the focus of our next section.

Evaluating and Reinventing Discourse Processes

Poststructural critics identify ideology, rather than material social structures, as the source of unequal power relations among people, as well as the means for resisting oppression. Poststructural critics evaluate and aim to reform the very ideas that structure a group's reality and the language or code of meanings through which all ideas, values, and beliefs are filtered. These scholars reject the idea that language has any definite meaning, and they resist assigning explanatory weight to material structures or any fixed category system. In fact, the tendency to reject fixed meanings and categories makes it really hard to introduce different forms of poststructural criticism, because any categorical distinctions that we create in this section can be easily torn apart. Nonetheless, we will sketch out some of the key concepts for three types of poststructural criticism in this section: postmodern criticism, cultural criticism, and semiotic criticism.

Table 10.2 presents the key theorists, claims, and research questions for each version of poststructural criticism and lists some sample readings that you should pursue if you want to conduct a study using one of those approaches.

Postmodern Criticism

Lyotard (1984) and Foucault (1980, 1983) are the theorists most closely associated with the movement known as postmodern criticism. Lyotard (1984) first coined the term **postmodern turn** to refer to a general movement away from social structure as the explanatory means of domination toward ideology, representation, and discourse as the sites of struggle for social power (e.g., Clair & Kunkel, 1998; Hallstein, 1999; Parker, 1992). For the postmodern critic, there is no one rational or correct view of the world, so ". . . power is not merely a top-down, repressive structural phenomenon, but an ever-present, relational, and productive social force negotiated between various orders of social discourse" (Groscurth, 2011, p. 301). The assumption that power is negotiated ongoingly makes postmodern critics interested in studying both how power is enacted and how it is resisted. Postmodernists view "all rationality as relative, or as a product of a given set of historically situated institutional practices" (Mumby & Putnam, 1992, p. 467). Foucault pointed out that, "the vision of each age is exclusive and incompatible with visions from other ages, making it impossible for people in one period to think like those of another" (Littlejohn & Foss, 2008, p. 342). It is also impossible to separate what we know from the language forms we use to think about and

Table 10.2 Poststructural Critical Studies

Critical Studies Approach	Claims describe the value and belief systems that most contribute to unequal power relations. Suggest how those values or beliefs might be reformed to distribute power more equally among all societal members.	Sample readings
Postmodern criticism (F. Lyotard, Michel Foucault)	RQs: How does discourse function in a given time and place? What do people "know," and what language forms are used to think about and express what they know (discursive formations)? How do speakers use language to resist oppression? What alternative vocabulary and ways of speaking would equalize power relations among speakers?	Herman & Sloop (1998) on postmodern authenticity; Kidder (2006) on bike messenger identities; Clair and Kunkel (1998) on child abuse; Mattson and Brann (2002) on managed healthcare and patient confidentiality
Cultural criticism (Stuart Hall)	RQs: How are cultural categories (e.g., class, race, sexual orientation) produced in the struggle among competing ideologies? How do some members participate in their own oppression by reifying categories? What internal contradictions exist? How do institutional changes in education, medicine, religion, government, or media perpetuate or change the dominant ideology? How can individuals disrupt the power held by members of more dominant groups?	Compare Sloop's (2000) and Cooper's (2002) analyses of the movie, *Boys Don't Cry;* see Watts & Orbe (2002) on the *Whassup?!?* Budweiser ads as spectacular consumption of African American cultural identity
Semiotic criticism (Roland Barthes, Umberto Eco, Christian Metz)	**RQs:** How do word choices, font, spacing, and layout work with visual images, sounds, and gestures to produce meaning in a given representation? How are those meanings *read*, or understood to mean something, differently in different cultures, times or places? Whose interests are served? What representations are present? Absent? What features of a multimodal text (images + words + sounds) give rise to different readings of that text? How does a coherent reading of the text rely on cues from different semiotic modes?	See Bianchi (2011) for a history of semiotics and its affinity to advertising studies, and look at film and art criticism, more generally. See Giradelli (2004) on the commodofication of Italian food in the United States for a sample study.

Note: The categories represented in Table 10.2 are provided to help you distinguish these critical methods, but the distinctions represented here collapse easily since poststructuralists resist all structures, including tables like this one.

express that knowledge. Foucault (1972) called such ways of knowing **discursive formations**, and he argued that power was an inherent part of all discourse. For example, a sense of formality (or social distance) is created discursively by using certain terms address ("sir" or "Professor"), formal grammar, politeness behaviors, and so on. The ways we use discourse to construct (or resist) formality are not the same today as they were 50 years ago. You can read about formality in Jane Austen novels, or ask your grandparents about how it was done in their day. But it is impossible for you to *think like* a person who lived in the Victorian era.

Cultural Criticism

Cultural criticism is used to investigate the ways cultures are produced through struggles among more-or-less dominant ideologies (S. Hall, 1986). Unlike interpretive ethnographers, who aim to describe cultures as systems of shared meanings, cultural critics explicitly aim to evaluate, and in some cases, reform cultural meanings and practices. Cultural critics acknowledge that meanings are contested rather than fully shared by all members. Thus, cultural critics try to change society by identifying internal contradictions and by providing descriptions that will help people see why change is needed (Littlejohn & Foss, 2008). Paradoxically, the struggles among competing ideologies are always happening, and so, the balance of power is always subject to change (fluidity).

Cultural critics often point to the discursive formations used in institutions like education, medicine, religion, the family, and government—and media, to the extent that media sources are often controlled by those institutions—as the social processes and practices that help to create, preserve, and change dominant ideologies. However, unlike Marxists, cultural critics see the relationships among social structures and individual actions as dynamic, bidirectional, and interdependent. The chief claims of cultural studies attempt to expose ways in which the ideologies of powerful groups are [un]wittingly perpetuated and to make people aware of ways to disrupt the power held by members of the dominant coalition.

High school and college courses in media literacy are an outgrowth of cultural criticism of the mass media. Those courses make learners aware of how the Internet, television, and other media sources frame what is good, bad, and who is central to a society versus who is a fringe element of society, questions that always lead to some evaluation of who benefits from the current frame. Those analyses can lead to reform efforts, as when public health practitioners work to reform alcohol advertising content guidelines (e.g., see Babor, Xuan, Damon & Noel's 2013 study of advertising code violations in beer ads televised college basketball games. The authors' research questions asked about "the prevalence of content code violations in beer ads" and "Which sections of the code were violated most often?" (p. e46).

Semiotic Criticism

Earlier in this chapter, we stressed that critical studies can incorporate an immense variety of texts, including, but not limited to, words. Semiotic criticism directly attacks our deeply entrenched "notion that language is *the* medium of representation and communication" (Kress, Leite-Garcia, & van Leeuwen, 1997, p. 257). Semiotics, like some of the other critical approaches you are learning about in this chapter, was first used in our field by interpretive rhetorical critics. In the 1970s, semiotic studies explored "a range of issues, including the semantics, rhetoric, style, ideological presuppositions, and the mythological nature of advertising" (Bianchi, 2011, p. 250). Bianchi (2011) provides a history of

semiotics and its affinity to advertising effectiveness studies, as well as cinema, cartoons, and other mass communication texts. These early semiotic studies fit the assumptions of poststructural criticism because they depended on Roland Barthes's (1957, 1964) theories of sign and code and they focused on how language was used.

But later, "[o]nce semiology had lost the prerogative of social criticism and its vocation for unmasking ideology, advertising seemed a less promising field for analysis than others" (Bianchi, 2011, p. 250). Today's semiotic theories are often used to conduct critical studies of *multimodality*, that is, all the different modes of representation within a given cultural context: This would include written and spoken language but would also address the material forms in which that language is realized (e.g., font, spacing, layout) as well as any visual, gestural, and sound images. In fact, "it has become impossible to read texts reliably by paying attention to written language alone" (Kress et al., 1997, p. 257). You may be able to see this with your own college textbooks, Blackboard websites or social media posts.

Some semiotic critics reject the rational notions of logic and linear order that are prominent in linguistic analyses. Because language depends on an alphabet, as well as sentence and paragraph structures, linguistic texts are constrained by the inherent order given by those structures. All semiotic criticism explores how power is instantiated in multimodal communication, so it includes the linear structures of language, but also the less linear and rational representations and significations in visual imagery. For example, when analyzing websites, your semiotic analysis will need to show how visual images are used differently than words or sounds, and how those three modes are most often used in combination. Which modes are more valued by advertisers, or news sites? In chatrooms or on film? How does all that change when we look at magazines or at the screens of our mobile phones, iPods, and PDAs? These questions are suitable for semiotic criticism because ideology is a factor in all modes of representation.

Now that you have some sense of how structural and poststructural critics stake out claims of evaluation and reform, let's consider what counts as data, or evidence, in critical studies. Table 10.3 shows you the overall steps to take in conducting textual criticism.

Table 10.3 Steps for Conducting Textual Criticism (Inductive Method)

1. Start by noticing a power difference in society;
2. Determine whether it is due to a social structure or is discursively maintained;
3. Deconstruct texts, actions, events and/or your own experiences and beliefs about this situation; or use narrative analysis to examine people's stories about the structure or discursive practices you want to critique;
4. Evaluate who is benefitting and who is being oppressed in the situation;
5. Offer alternative structures or discourse processes that would better serve everyone;
6. Acknowledge the particular ways that your standpoint shaped your interpretations of this situation.

Evidence in Critical Studies

The basic method for critical scholarship is to apply "an ideological perspective to some phenomenon in order to generate a value-based critique" (Fink & Gantz, 1996, p. 118). Some of the theorists we mentioned in the first section of this chapter have published 20 or more books, and you could spend a lifetime studying their ideas. Each type of criticism is itself an ideological perspective, so you will need to begin by reading some of the primary sources to apply those concepts to your own critical study. Ask your research methods and rhetorical theory instructors to help you select the right primary sources for the kind of analysis that you want to pursue.

As we mentioned in Part 1 of this book, two types of critical studies have emerged in communication studies: ideological critiques and empirical studies of communicative action based on ideological critique (Deetz, 2005). Both types of critical studies rely on the emancipatory values we identified in Chapter 6, "Warrants for Research Arguments" and both argue the ideological need for change in a given context. But these types of critical studies differ in their use of evidence and warrants. **Ideological critiques** use textual evidence to evaluate communicative phenomena and to argue the need for social change (Deetz, 2005). Ideological critiques are closely aligned with the more traditional forms of rhetorical criticism that you learned about in Chapter 9, "How to Interpret Rhetoric," so they primarily are warranted by coherence and researcher positionality.

Critical empirical studies of communicative action use some form of empirical data collected from participant observations, self-reports and other-reports, and textual evidence to describe and evaluate communication, and sometimes to suggest what reforms are needed in a particular context (Deetz, 2005). Thus, critical empirical studies employ a combination of warrants from the interpretive paradigm (i.e., researcher credibility, plausible interpretations, transferability) and the critical paradigm (i.e., coherence, researcher positionality, impact). Of course, readers of either type of critical study are free to disagree with the researcher's interpretations and evaluations.

In the next section, we elaborate on some of the evidence toward which you might turn your attention when conducting structural and poststructural critical studies, including actions and events, texts, and your own beliefs and experiences.

Actions and Events

One way to focus on the lived experience of real people, in context, is to conduct a case study of communicative action. As you know from Chapter 7, "Ethnography," case studies highlight the *actions* of individuals and groups and the *events* of which their actions are a part. Whether you consider actions and events that occurred in the past or in the present, their historical context will be an important feature of your critical analysis. For example, Ashcraft and Pacanowsky (1996) observed formal company meetings, informal work interactions, and a social function at a small business organization they called Office Inc. These actions and events formed the basis for their feminist critique of how present-day women participate in their own devaluation in the work setting. Some of the actions and events that Ashcraft and Pacanowsky observed during 6 months of participant observations at Office Inc. included the president's beginning a maternity leave and the termination of a lawsuit in an "agreeable settlement" (p. 224). Their case study applied the ideology of feminism to generate value-based critiques of present-day organizational actions and events.

Of course, you might select an action *or* event from the past for your analysis. W. S. Lee (1998b) advanced a feminist and postcolonial critique of discourse against footbinding, a longtime cultural practice in China. It was a "gendered practice that physically mutilated the feet of Chinese women in the Han ethnicity from middle- and upper-class families" for over 800 years (W. S. Lee, 1998b, p. 11). "It was a bone-crushing experience in a *literal* sense" (W. S. Lee, 1998b, p. 14). For centuries, opposition to the practice of footbinding was silenced, but in the late nineteenth century, a collective movement to speak up brought an end to footbinding for many Chinese girls and women. W. S. Lee's (1998b) analysis showed how the well-meaning antifootbinding discourse was at once emancipatory and oppressive, a site of identity struggle that implicated the race, class, and nationality of the dissenters as much as it did the women of the class and ethnicity whose feet were bound. W. S. Lee (1998b) used the case of footbinding to explore a paradoxical research question, "How is it possible to foster oppression in the midst of an emancipatory movement?" (p. 16). Your textual criticism might address a paradox from your own experiences, or you might locate paradoxical representations of reality in textual data.

Texts

Texts are discursive representations of the world. A text may refer to spoken language (e.g., in a telephone interaction, a film, a television commercial, a musical performance, organizational policy document). Texts can consist of life stories collected in oral history interviews, or narratives that emerge from your document analysis, but texts can also refer to symbolic representations (e.g., a gesture, a dance movement, architecture). Texts can be mediated or nonmediated, and the variety of texts available for analysis is theoretically endless.

The stories we tell to represent ourselves and our experiences of the world are texts that can be appropriated for critical analysis (e.g., Clair, 1993, 1994, 1997; Clair & Kunkel, 1998; Tretheway, 1997; Yep, Olzman, & Conkle, 2012). As such, stories are collected specifically for the purpose of critiquing the social structures and discourse processes that they represent. When we **appropriate** something, we make it our own or set it aside for a specific use. Rogers (2006) defined cultural appropriation as "the use of another culture's symbols, artifacts, genres, rituals, or technologies by members of another culture" (p. 474).

A number of critical studies have focused on how texts have been appropriated by specific people for their own uses (e.g., Delgado, 1998a; Herman & Sloop, 1998; Shugart, 1999). For example, Delgado (1998a) argued that a variety of Chicano artists have appropriated the rap music genre to articulate elements of Chicano ideology and help Mexican Americans see themselves as a unified, politically engaged group. In doing so, those rap artists promote Chicano political ideology and open a space in the mass media for that traditional, nationalist agenda to be heard and absorbed by contemporary Chicano audiences. Using stories as evidence for text criticism raises important ethical issues, such as whose stories can be used, and who can tell a story? (Leeman, 2011). In the last section of this chapter, we will give you some advice about how to approach those ethical dilemmas in your textual criticism.

Semioticians, on the other hand, are likely to analyze symbolic representations that are entirely nonlinguistic. For example, Drzewiecka and Nakayama (1998) argued that urban geographical spaces could be distinguished as modern or postmodern. The organization of neighborhood spaces in each city was the *text* to which Drzewiecka and Nakayama applied their ideological framework of postmodernism. San Francisco is a city with a "stronger modernist influence with their more traditional neighborhoods that are divided by social divisions" (p. 23). San Francisco has neighborhoods that are characterized by ethnicity and culture like Chinatown, Japantown, North Beach (Italian), the Castro (gay), Hunter's Point (African American), and the Mission (Latino/a). By contrast, the complexity and postmodernity of Los Angeles, and of Phoenix, was reflected in the blurring and fragmenting of traditional structural neighborhoods as well as the presence of multiplicitous, hybrid areas formed by highly mobile, multicultural groups of people (Drzewiecka & Nakayama, 1998). The *gentrification* of poor neighborhoods in many US cities tends to blur those more traditional, modernist neighborhood boundaries. Recently in San Francisco, the increasing presence of technology firms (now over 1900 strong) in downtown and the Mission neighborhood has been marked by competition for housing and transportation access. Political battles over changes like these underscore their relations to power and privilege (Knight, December 22, 2013).

Of course, more traditional means of collecting texts are also useful when conducting textual criticism. Participant observation and interviews are key routes by which you can access participants' lived experiences and stories. The field notes and interview transcripts that you create using those data collection strategies then constitute texts for analysis. As a case in point, Groscurth's (2011) critical discourse analysis triangulated participant-observations that he gained as an American Red Cross volunteer with "in-depth interviews with volunteers and paid staff who actively participated in the hurricane response" following Hurricane Katrina (p. 302). Those interview transcriptions served as the primary source of evidence for Groscurth's critique of how discourse and participation function in disaster relief contexts, and of "the communicative practices that produce racial paradox, tension and privilege" (p. 302). Groscurth's evaluation of communication in the aftermath of the hurricane does not suggest how disaster relief efforts should be changed. But his critique should raise readers' awareness of how relief efforts are likely to benefit some groups more than others.

Finally, you can collect texts in less intrusive ways, from archives, as is the case whenever newspapers, films, photos, television shows, song lyrics, and such are used (e.g., Carpenter, 1999; Conrad, 1988; Lewis, 1997; L. McLaughlin, 1991; Shugart, 1997; Tavener, 2000). Consistent with the critical paradigm assumption that truth is both personal and political, you will also use your own experiences and beliefs as evidence in making a critical argument.

Researchers' Experiences and Beliefs

The question of who has a right to assign meaning to actions, events, texts, and experiences is an important one for critical scholars, who refer to this issue as the **politics of representation**. All representations of actions, events, and texts are political because all of those representations broach the same questions: Whose voices should be heard? Whose interpretations are correct? Who says what reforms are needed in a society? At the crux of these debates are the issues of membership in and naming of a social category or group (e.g., Booth, 2009). Shane Moreman and Persona Non Grata (2011) described why they elected to name the second author *Persona Non Grata,* because she was an undocumented Latina attending college in California: "One difficulty, up front, is the need to disguise the student's name.... although Shane is a tenured professor, the student (Persona) has a tenuous presence in both the academy and in the United States" (p. 304). Moreman and Non Grata are both Latino/a, but they have different experiences because of their different social category memberships and positions, which they contrast in their essay.

Mumby (1993) asked, "How can researchers claim to speak for (i.e., construct representations of) social groups to which they do not belong?" (p. 18). Even if you are a member of the group you want to represent, how legitimate is it for you to represent the voices of research participants, the people whose stories you collect and in whose events you participate? We raise this question because your own experiences and beliefs are an important source of evidence in doing criticism (K. A. Foss & Foss, 1994). Your beliefs and experiences are not thought of as biases to be ignored or controlled, as might be the case in discovery research. Your experiences are not just acknowledged as they affect your interpretations, as would be the case in the interpretive paradigm (Peshkin, 1988). Rather, in critical studies, your experiences and beliefs are the basis for your analysis of communicative effectiveness, power, dominance, and any argued need for reforming ideology (Lannamann, 1991; K. A. Foss & Foss, 1994).

Analytic Moves in Critical Studies

Although there is no one exact method or procedure for conducting critical communication studies (Sprague, 1992), the steps we have outlined in Table 10.1 start with knowing something about a theory (e.g., Marxism, feminism, postmodernism, etc.), and then applying that theory to some evidence (i.e., texts, actions and events, your own experiences and beliefs). There are various ways to proceed in selecting textual evidence for critical analysis, just as there are different ways of analyzing those texts. You already know about several nonrandom data selection strategies (from Chapter 5, "What Counts as Communication Data"). So in this section, we will describe two data analytic strategies used in critical communication studies: (1) deconstruction, and (2) narrative analysis. Each of these analytic forms has a rich (and in some cases, lengthy) history of its own, to which we cannot do justice in this short space. So we will outline these two basic analytic strategies and provide you with two checklists to supplement the one you used in Chapter 8, "Conversation and Discourse Analysis: How to Interpret Talk." That checklist provided questions that you should ask yourself as you closely analyze linguistic and visual texts. The two new tables in this chapter will help you specifically deconstruct texts and closely read narratives as texts. Let's consider each of those analytic strategies in turn.

Deconstruction

Deconstruction is the critical studies term associated with unpacking, or taking apart, the meaning of a text (Derrida, 1972/1976, 1978, 1981). As the most basic analytic strategy for poststructural critical studies, deconstruction aims to show how texts have hidden dualisms and inner contradictions, or repressed meanings: "Meanings are not embedded within a text, but rather they are constructed through dichotomies or binary opposites that are constantly shifting. Derrida reasoned that textual meaning is only apparently stable because it "privileges" (makes present) one term over the other" (Mumby & Putnam, 1992, p. 468). Thus, deconstruction "always proceeds in an irreducible double gesture" (Gunkel, 2000, p. 52), because any attempt to merely break apart the two halves of a binary opposite constitutes *analysis*. But breaking apart the two halves of a binary distinction is not sufficient for deconstruction. Let's look at each half of this process.

The first part of deconstruction is inversion. Since two opposite terms are rarely equally valued, **inversion** is the attempt to "bring low what was high" (Derrida, 1981, p. 42, as cited in Gunkel, 2000). In an old Phil Donahue episode, the talk show host assumed the body posture and facial expression of a centerfold model, while fully clothed, onstage. It was a way of showing how that physical posture and facial expression functioned to present a nude female model as subservient. The image of an adult white male in that posture, showing that facial expression, fully clothed, made the function of the pose and the facial expression apparent to the audience and resulted in laughter. "This inversion, however, like all revolutionary operations, does little or nothing to challenge the system that is overturned" (Gunkel, 2000, p. 52).

In the second phase of deconstruction, known as **invention**, a new concept emerges that could never have been included in the previous dualism (i.e., the binary opposite terms that were unpacked during inversion). For example, Gunkel's (2000) essay showed how virtual reality is neither *real* nor *simulation* but something those two terms cannot fully encompass. Instead, virtual reality displaces the very metaphysical foundation it is based on, the hierarchical and causal relationship between real and represented.

Deconstruction is used as a general strategy for conducting cultural evaluation and critique. Deconstruction can help you evaluate dominant meanings and propose alternative interpretations that will better serve the interests of formerly marginalized groups (Yep, 1998). If your critique goes only so far as to invert the traditional relationship between two binary opposites (e.g., mind/body, male/female, self/other) then the point may simply be "to reject one ideology and embrace another" (Parks, 1997, p. 483). In the case of feminist deconstruction, "the point of such work is not simply to introduce women into the equation…but rather it is to rewrite the equation itself" (Mumby, 1993, p. 23). If the equation is not reinvented by feminist research, perhaps those studies function to "introduce radical doubt into segmented modes of thought" (Mumby, 1993, p. 24). Awareness of a need for change is, after all, the starting point for all reform (Mies, 1991; Ramazanoglu, 1992). Table 10.4, below, lists questions you can use to begin deconstructing linguistic and visual texts.

For example, Bajali (2011) deconstructed media representations of Haitians after the January 2010 earthquake in Port-au-Prince. Bajali unpacked the binary opposites of white/black in order to show how Haitians were depicted in US media representations as dysfunctional children,

Table 10.4 Questions to Ask as You Deconstruct Texts (Derrida, 1981)

Step One: Inversion	1. Closely examine the key terms used by this speaker/writer. Which terms does s/he use often, praise, or otherwise seem to value most? 2. What is the binary opposite of the speaker's most valued term(s)? What words or phrases would "bring low what was high" (Derrida, 1981, p. 42)? 3. Which groups are being elevated by the speaker's preferred terms? Which groups are being marginalized, suppressed or erased by the speaker's preferred terms?
Step Two: Invention	1. What words or phrases might the speaker use that would avoid the "high/low" trap of the binary opposite terms you identified in step one, inversion? In other words, what alternative words or meanings would serve the interest of the marginalized or oppressed group members? 2. Are there alternative language choices that would serve all groups more equitably?

"somehow hopelessly dependent upon the charity of whites" (p. 51). Having serving 10 years as a journalist, Bajali began by considering other historical cases where mediated representations of disaster, famine, land mines, and poverty have been racialized to differentiate "the pitied from those pitying" (p. 52). Arguing that pity and empathy cannot coexist, Bajali then argued that, "… we must examine whether such charity efforts do more harm than good when it comes to humanizing the victims. Pity becomes a powerful rhetorical device when organizations and individuals use it as a means of highlighting their good deeds (without giving the recipients of those deeds a voice)" (p. 55). In this study, however, Bajali did not offer any alternative ways of covering global disasters, alternatives that could better equalize representations of racial groups that "can help to construct narratives about shared humanity," rather than "those of victimhood and pathologies of Otherness" (Bajali, 2011, p. 64).

Narrative Analysis

We presented some interpretive uses of narrative analysis in Chapter 9. There, interpretive narrative analyses focused on the meanings people make through the stories they tell. Like other types of interpretive criticism, interpretive narrative analyses are warranted by their coherence and fidelity (Fisher, 1984). However, critical narrative analyses push the stories' meanings one step further, by examining the power struggles they contain. Thus, critical narrative studies are warranted by their authors' subjective standpoints, as well as by their values of voice and liberation. Narrative analysis is particularly appropriate for critical studies because "[t]he very nature of narrative is that it is the human way of dealing with disruption" (Leeman, 2011, p. 108). This makes narrative criticism especially relevant for mass media scholars (film, advertising, news).

Mumby's (1988, 1993) work on the political nature of storytelling in organizations was among the first to elaborate this strategy for doing critical studies outside mass media studies. His work has shown how the stories that get told over and over in organizations create and maintain power relations, and they perpetuate the interests of the dominant group members, management. Analyzing members' stories is one way that you can access people's lived experiences for critical studies of communication. Table 10.5, below, includes questions to ask yourself as you evaluate and seek to reform narrative texts, including questions about a story's structure, characters, setting, and bottom line (who benefits).

Table 10.5 Questions to Ask as You Analyze Narrative Texts (Stories)

Narrative Structure	1. Can you identify the story's beginning, middle and end? 2. What is the basic plot of the story? 3. What is the climax of the story? 4. What is the moral of the story?
Narrative Characters	1. Who are the main characters? Who are the supporting characters? 2. Which of the story's characters are being portrayed as "heroes"? 3. Which characters are "villains"? 4. How fully are the characters developed in the story (e.g., does the narrative text indicate a character's motives, or just her actions)?
Setting of the Story	1. Where does the action take place? 2. Does the character "belong" in this setting or not? 3. Is the character a member of one of the dominant groups in this setting?
Situated Story Telling Features	1. Who can tell this story? 2. When can this story be told? 3. Where might this story be told? 4. What is being accomplished in the telling of this story?
Bottom line	1. Who benefits from this story's structure, characters, or setting? 2. Who is being erased or marginalized by this story? 3. What is missing from this story?

A recent example from media criticism is Hatfield's (2010) narrative analysis of the television show, *Two and a Half Men*. Hatfield kept the story's *structure* intact (p. 530) by considering the show's portrayal of masculinities over five seasons, rather than during individual scenes, dialog passages, or even episodes. First, she reviewed 115 episodes of the show on DVD, looking for "narrative themes and exemplars" (p. 530). Then, Hatfield coded her notes for recurrring themes and storylines, and she organized her critical essay around three key themes, including gender performances, subordination, and social success. Her analysis ultimately showed how the two main *characters*, brothers Charlie and Alan, "each perform a different masculinity … Charlie's bachelor lifestyle rejects traditional values, whereas Alan contrasts this by mourning his divorce and continually hoping to remarry" (p. 530). As Hatfield unpacked the details of these portrayals with respect to each theme, she showed how the brothers' attire, aggressive banter, bonding activities, relationships with women and men, and their respective rewards and punishments, support her *bottom line* argument that, "only Charlie's version of masculinity is communicated as successful" (p. 530).

As you can see from Hatfield's study, the content of the stories we tell is just one feature of narrative analysis. Your critical narrative analysis might also address the situated features of storytelling such as, who can tell this story? When can this story be told? Where might the story best be told? What is being accomplished in the telling of this story? To illustrate this in a simple way, think of one joke that you find very funny. To whom, and in what times and places, would you tell this joke? In what situations would you avoid telling this joke or mask your true feelings if someone else shared the joke? The different answers you have for these questions may help you grasp the concept of *fluid, competing interests* and help you to see some situated features of narratives more critically.

Warrants for Critical Studies

The standards for evaluating critical textual analyses are still emerging, not only because poststructural critics resist any form of categorization or standardization, but because the standards for evaluating critical studies proceed from and build on interpretive paradigm warrants. In this section, we will show you how to demonstrate your coherence and researcher positionality, and

how you can use those standards to evaluate a critical study conducted by someone else. We will also show you how to estimate the likely change in awareness or praxis that could come from your critique of texts. Let's briefly consider each of these warrants.

Establishing Coherence

Deetz (1982) first pointed out that coherence, rather than accuracy, is the most appropriate warrant for critical studies. As we said in Chapter 6, "Warrants for Research Arguments," **coherence** means that our interpretations are logical, consistent, and intelligible. Of course, this raises the question, "*To whom* does this understanding of the text appear 'maximally reasonable and coherent'?" Fink and Gantz (1996) stated that "those who share the critical perspective of the researcher are free to accept or reject the argument" (p. 119). Those who disagree with the researcher's ideology, in all likelihood, will not see the researcher's interpretations as coherent. Bochner (1985) called this *free consensus,* which suggests that "verification can only be left to those who agree with that perspective" (as cited in Fink & Gantz, 1996, p. 129).

One way you can achieve coherence is to include some attention to the broader social systems of which your texts, actions, or experiences are a part. For example, how does your evidence relate to social structures like nationality, social class, education, skin color, and so on? Or if your assumptions better fit poststructural criticism, how is the act or event you analyze historically positioned? Even actions that appear unreasonable may be shown to be rational or necessary when their broader historical and social contexts are examined (Ramazanoglu, 1992). Some actions that appear irrational actually are reasonable responses to unreasonable situations (Clair, 1993, 1994; Yep, Lovaas, et al., 2002; Vivienne & Burgess, 2012). So "one should not pass judgment on an individual without understanding the inherent logic which makes his or her actions meaningful" (Deetz, 1982, p. 144). Conquergood's (1991) critical cultural ethnography of Latino gang members in Chicago showed how young men participated in gangs to fulfill their social needs for inclusion, affection, and control. His analysis was one early example of research that made coherent the seemingly incoherent, even life-threatening behavior of joining a street gang.

Another way you can achieve coherence is to become intimately familiar with the texts you analyze. In this case, membership in at least one of the social groups under study may be as important a warrant for your critical study as it is in interpretive research. For example, when Groscurth (2011) conducted participant-observations at a Midwest United States chapter of the American Red Cross (ARC), he served as a volunteer, "both a means for reciprocating the ARC for my intrusion and building rapport with staff members in the organization" (p. 302). Groscurth acknowledged that his experiences as a volunteer "both shaped and were shaped by my simultaneous collection and analysis of public discourse surrounding the ARC's involvement" in responding to Hurricanes Katrina, Rita, and Wilma during 2005 (p. 302).

Even as a member of one of the social groups under study, you will need to stay aware of multiple possible interpretations of the text. You must "search for the texts which best represent what is thinkable and doable" in that social situation (Deetz, 1982, p. 144). Only when you are intimately familiar with the situation, when you know "how to get things done . . . how to avoid unpleasant outcomes, how to recognize critical features," as well as "with whom to talk, what counts as adequate information" (Deetz, 1982, pp. 140–141) and so on, can you achieve a coherent interpretation. Without a coherent interpretation, you cannot possibly evaluate power imbalances or oppression or suggest what actions should be taken to reform those conditions.

Thus, coherence thus means several things. First, your criticism will need to be free of logical fallacies and contradictions. Second, you'll need to attend to the relationships between the texts you analyze and the broader social systems in which they exist. Third, you'll need to show your very close reading of the texts. Finally, coherence implies that your criticism is socially relevant, while remaining true to your experiences and values (i.e., you are a critic of good character).

Establishing Researcher Positionality

As you know from Chapter 6, "Warrants for Research Arguments," researcher positionality includes both your standpoint and your reflexivity about that standpoint. "The critical scholars make their social and political position explicit; they take sides, and actively participate, in order to uncover, demystify, or otherwise challenge dominance" (Van Dijk, 1997b, p. 22). In this section, we elaborate on some of the ways you can demonstrate both your standpoint and your reflexivity.

The idea of having some particular standpoint from which we view any evidence is familiar and common

sense to both interpretive and critical researchers. Because critical researchers believe it is neither possible nor desirable to eliminate subjectivity or to work around it when doing research, you will need to acknowledge your own subjective responses and include them in your analysis. You can start by becoming more aware of those occasions when your subjectivity has been engaged. You may notice, for instance, that you have positive or negative feelings toward some of the evidence you are analyzing, that there are some experiences you want more of, or some that you want to avoid (Peshkin, 1988). When you are interacting with members of marginalized groups, you may find yourself wanting to advocate for them or take on roles that go beyond your tasks as a researcher. Or when you interact with members of a dominant group, you may note your tendency to downplay their interpretations or their positions. You might catch yourself having a value conflict, such as debating whether to be completely honest about something you observed in data collection while wanting to portray your participants in a positive light (Gouldner, 1988). Peshkin (1988) advocated a disciplined, systematic self-monitoring of these cues to your subjectivity as a kind of workout, "so that I may avoid the trap of perceiving just that which my own untamed sentiments have sought out and served up as data" (p. 20). It's a good idea for you to keep track of your own subjective reactions as you do criticism. That way, your audit trail will help you to understand your own positionality, and to see how it is influencing your interpretations and evaluations of communication.

The second part of establishing your positionality as a researcher is to be reflexive about your standpoint. As we said in Chapter 6, "Warrants for Research Arguments," *reflexivity* refers to your own awareness of the specific ways that you are inseparable from the things you are trying to describe, evaluate, and ultimately, change. For example, Brenda Allen (1996) spoke "from her vantage point as an African-American faculty member at a predominantly White, research university" and "recounts her lived experiences to demonstrate the value of eliciting insight from an 'outsider within'" (p. 257). Allen (1996) was overtly subjective in her essay; she used the personal pronoun *I* repeatedly and used "self-interview data" (p. 258) to depict her experience of anticipating and being assimilated as a faculty member in a predominantly white research university. Allen (1996) wrote, "I speak from a perspective that 'I own and am rigorously reflective about'" (Marshall, 1993, p. 123, as cited in Allen, 1996, p. 261). Allen (1996) further acknowledged, "My experiences do not necessarily represent those of other women of color, of other women, or of other persons of color" (p. 261). Allen's comments demonstrated her recognition that her social location is distinct from another person's location and experience. As you read critical studies, you will notice that questioning the correctness of an interpretation receives far less attention than acknowledging multiple, plausible interpretations. This leads us to another way that you can be reflexive, which is to acknowledge your own and your readers' freedom of choice.

Critical essays often contain explicit admonishments to readers that they are free to choose another interpretation or to deconstruct the author's interpretation of the actions and events. As a critical scholar you are free to choose different actions, events, and texts as evidence for your analysis and to support the worth of your analysis with different warrants. But you must acknowledge the choices you have made and try to avoid presenting those choices as correct ones. If you make those choices thoughtfully, "rigor is possible in the maintenance of these principles rather than the following of a prescribed method or procedure" (Deetz, 1982, p. 143).

We hope these examples help to show how you might warrant your textual critique by establishing a coherent argument for why communication is effective or ineffective, and why ideological reform is needed. Both of those claims are relevant to your positionality as a researcher, in terms of your standpoint and your reflexivity. You also need to consider the interpretive paradigm warrants (i.e., researcher credibility, plausible interpretations, transferability), especially as those warrants are practiced in your particular critical method (e.g., critical ethnography, critical discourse analysis, semiotic criticism, etc.).

Establishing Impact: Changes in Awareness and Praxis

You probably realize that you, like most people, are somewhat resistant to change. After all, the familiar is often comfortable. But critical scholars who claim to evaluate and reform communication have to deal with people's aversion to change. Tompkins (1994) argued that changes in awareness and practice are "the least we can expect" from critical studies (p. 44). If your critique is approved by the people you studied or if you and they use the critique to change communication practices (what Tompkins called "pragmatic sanctions"), then your criticism is validated as worthwhile.

Changing awareness matters for the researcher, the oppressed group members, and members of more privileged groups. Oppressed group members may learn something about their own oppression that allows them to withdraw or adjust their participation in order to disrupt hegemonic practices. But increased awareness may lead members of the oppressive groups to become more entrenched in their attitudes, or to adjust their oppressive behaviors to more subtle forms that are harder to detect and resist. For instance, with increasing numbers of homosexual people in public life (e.g., in politics, sports, media or fictional representations) the word "gay" has become commonly used, but so has the phrase "that's so gay." Teenagers in schools often use "that's so gay" or "fag" and report no awareness of any potentially offensive meaning, or deny any intention of hurting another person with that phrase (Athanases & Comar, 2008). Athanases and Comar pointed out that,

> … injurious speech is enacted in an individual performance but its speaker is merely repeating what a community has developed. In this sense, (students) often mimicked homophobic language from discourses of local and larger institutions and communities without understanding roots, meanings, purposes, or impact of the language. This suggests that educators ultimately may need to target not individual "performances" of injurious speech but larger perspectives on language and power. (Butler, 1997, as cited in Athanases & Comar, 2008, p. 25)

Because the social construction of realities is gradual and usually incremental, oppression is evidenced in normative behavior. "Changing oppression, then, requires constantly working against the norm" (Kumashiro, 2002, p. 11).

Awareness is the first step to changing anything, but changes in communicative praxis also determine the worth of critical studies. For example, feminist communication research has led to changes in both awareness and praxis, over many years. The use of gender-neutral terms is accepted communication practice today in public life in the United States (e.g., flight attendant v. stewardess, congressperson, etc.). Likewise, the term "gay" and the acronym "GLBTQ" (gay-lesbian-bisexual-transgender-queer) have become much more commonly used during the last decade, in part due to national media coverage of school bullying cases and the political debates over gay marriage. Changing communication practices like job titles or social category names fits critical theorists' epistemology as social constructionists (i.e., new discursive choices create new realities), but those changes also have material consequences (see Dana Cloud's work on the materiality of discourse for more).

Finally, and as Rodriguez (2003) pointed out, any definition of social justice as helping marginalized groups relies on charity and fails to question the larger social, historical, and political forces that lead to such marginalization. "Communication should be more than merely the study of what is. It should ultimately be about what can be" (p. 32). You can start by assessing your own awareness and the impact that a study has on your communication practices: Did you learn something new? If so, how will your future interactions or messages be impacted by what you now know? For example, will you revise any of your language choices, or speak out when you hear someone else using language you feel is oppressive? (See DeTurk's 2011 study of how "allies work to promote social justice on behalf of others through … verbal and nonverbal tactics, and ranging from interpersonal support for individuals to actions intended to influence the culture as a whole," such as political or educational advocacy (pp. 580–581).

Ethical Issues in Critiquing Texts

Recall from Chapter 3 that ethical choices occur in every stage of research, planning your study, interacting with other people who participate and sharing the results of your research in written essays, speeches, or performances. Critical researchers acknowledge that they are inseparable from the settings, contexts, and cultures they want to understand and represent. For this reason, you must constantly interrogate yourself about why you have selected particular topics, how you go about gathering evidence to test or support your claims, and who is likely to benefit from your analysis. In the critical paradigm, there is less agreement about "the correct way" to select and analyze texts, or write essays, than in the interpretative or discovery paradigms. That means that your ethical choices also are less clear.

We said in Chapter 3 that communication research should maximize the good of society and minimize harm to individuals. But what is "good" for society is often contested in critical studies. So you must be reflexive about your standpoint. How did you come to your particular definition of "the good"? You must also consider the points of view of people who are likely to disagree with you about that social good (e.g., gun ownership).

Likewise, because you seek to understand and perhaps change arrangements of privilege and oppression, status differences will be inherently important to your critical studies project. Of course you will want to demonstrate respect for members of the oppressed group(s), but you must also show respect and inclusion for members of the privileged groups whose ideology and practices you want to critique.

Critical scholars understand their essays to be representations of the actions, events, and texts they study, representations that are inherently biased by their own experiences, values, and purposes. This does not mean that your critical essay will lack rigor or that you will intentionally abuse your power of representing actions and events through language. In fact, since critical scholarship is characterized by concerns about the *politics of representation,* every choice about what you say and what you leave out has ramifications that are linked to power and ideology. For example, Moreman and Non Grata (2011) acknowledged that they refused to put Spanish words in italic font, as directed by the Modern Language Association (MLA) format guidelines for their critical essay. "Our refusal nods toward the seamlessness of Spanish-English bilingualism in many people's lives in the Southwestern US. However, for the *Text and Performance Quarterly* audience, all Spanish words will be translated with a corresponding note" (p. 318).

One way that you can deal with the politics of representation in your writing is by being self-reflexive. The principle of rigorous self-reflection dictates that you examine your motives, word choices, and framing of an essay with immense care (Allen, 1996). Even then, you should not claim to have captured the true meaning of an act or event: "Objectivity is sustained in the inability of the [research] community to deny the results [of inquiry] through undistorted discussions of them" (Deetz, 1982, p. 147). Instead of assuming a false objectivity about the ideologies or communicative practices you study, approach your critical essay as an interesting fiction, to be evaluated for its ability to "read texts in their full variety, rather than to get beneath or behind them" (Deetz, 1982, p. 137). Specify in your essay the criteria by which your research may be evaluated. Make your descriptions of the texts, actions, events, or experiences "rich and compelling" (Deetz, 1982, p. 147).

Another strategy for ethical criticism is to interrogate yourself about your motives for doing a particular study: Is your purpose really to disrupt hegemonic relations? If so, will writing a critical essay be your best approach? Is there some other form of activism that would have a greater impact? If you are evaluating other people's communicative practices or critiquing their ideological choices, what are your ethical obligations to those persons? Rarely are there clear "either/or" answers to these questions. For example, Vivienne and Burgess (2012) examined "how queer storytellers balance privacy with the desire to have a voice and to be heard in public debates" (p. 362). Their dilemma is one of both wanting privacy, and wanting to have public voice. Similarly, let's say you are concerned with justice: If your work results in a power shift such that the oppressed group becomes the privileged group, and vice versa, is that *just*? To be an ethical critical scholar, you cannot simply be a crusader against oppression. You must be a reflective critic and advocate for social change (i.e., a moral person, yourself).

Finally, critical research studies are often exempt from IRB review, usually because the researcher is using publicly available texts as evidence or because the researcher does not aim to generalize knowledge to a whole population. Being exempt from IRB review does not excuse you from considering the ethics of your topic selection, your interactions with research participants, or your publication choices once you finish the analysis. For example, if you are observing and interviewing members of a minority group, how will you protect those participants' right to privacy and to be treated with respect? As Leeman (2011) pointed out: "I revel in the fact that I am able and available to give voice to the too-often unheard…. Yet I often have to stop and ask myself, what choice do my storytelling conversation partners really have?" (p. 108). You will need to think about how the stories you tell in your research might be viewed or used by others, whether those stories came from participant interviews or from publically available texts (e.g., chat room discourse, or blog entries). Even people in chat rooms and online forums, who usually do not get the chance to freely choose to participate in research, have some expectation of privacy and being treated honestly. So if you are participating in the chat room by pretending to be a regular member of the group, and if you do not disclose that you are conducting research (even though you aim to benefit members of that group through your study), then you have deceived other people, which is exactly the sort of oppression you seek to overturn.

Critical Studies Summary

This chapter, together with Chapter 9, "Rhetorical Criticism," shows you how rhetorical studies have bridged our three paradigms of discovery, interpretation, and criticism. Here, we focused only on critical paradigm analyses of textual data. These studies make claims of evaluation about social structures and discourse processes. Some of these studies also make reform claims (i.e., how social structures or discourse processes should be changed). Theories and methods overlap when doing criticism, so you will need to know something about both theory (e.g., Marxism, cultural studies, semiotics) and methods (e.g., deconstruction, narrative criticism) in order to conduct your own critical study. Finally, you'll need to combine what you know of interpretive and critical paradigm warrants to produce good criticism yourself, and to evaluate published critical scholarship. Table 10.6, below highlights the claims, data, warrants and manuscript form for structural and poststructural communication criticism.

Table 10.6 Summary Table. How to Critique Texts

Critical Paradigm	Claims	Data	Warrants*	Manuscript Format
Structural criticism	Describe, evaluate, and reform social structures	Primarily dialectical (paradox) analyses of actions, events, texts	Coherence, researcher positionality and impact	Critical essay
Poststructural criticism	Describe, evaluate, and reform symbol systems (i.e., discourse)	Deconstruction, paradox, speech act, and narrative analyses of actions, events, texts, and the critic's own experiences	Coherence, researcher positionality and impact	Critical essay

***Note:** Critical empirical studies of communicative action are warranted by coherence, researcher positionality (i.e., standpoint plus reflexivity) and impact (i.e., likely change in awareness and/or praxis), in combination with interpretive paradigm warrants.

Key Terms

Aesthetic communication	Gender and feminist criticism	Ideology
Appropriate (verb)	Gender binary	Invention
Coherence	Gender bender	Inversion
Critical studies of communicative action	Hegemony	Politics of representation
Deconstruction	Hybridity (aka intersectionality)	Postmodern turn
Discursive formation	Ideological critique	

Discussion Questions

1. Write a brief description of yourself that you would be willing to share with your classmates and instructor. Would you share the same description with your parents? Your employer? Your significant other? What are the politics of representing yourself? How different do you think those politics are when trying to represent another person or event outside yourself?

2. Consider Brenda Allen's (1996) assertion, "I speak from a perspective that 'I own and am rigorously reflective about'" (p. 261, citing Marshall, 1993, p. 123). What perspective do you own? What do you think it means to be rigorously reflective? How could we become more reflective about our own positions in our society?

3. An important question with respect to acknowledging subjectivity in critical studies concerns the practical problem of conflicting interpretations of the text (e.g., see Groscurth, 2011, p. 312, on racial subjectivity). Should critical scholars check their interpretations with others, such as the participants in their studies? If so, and participants disagree with the scholar, whose interpretation is correct? Whose ideas should be privileged in the written critical essay?

"Try It!" Activities

1. Think of one story you have told recently about some aspect of your real, lived experience. Analyze that story in terms of these six *W*s: To whom did you tell the story? When? Where? Why? What was the story about? What do you think you accomplished in telling this story? Does your story illustrate some hegemonic process? If so, what process and how does the story work to reinforce existing power relations?

2. In a small group of about five people, share the stories you analyzed in the previous activity. Rather than looking for commonalities (or generalizable features) in your group's stories, consider which stories provide the richest, most coherent and compelling interpretation of the social situation. How reflective are you and your group members about your own experiences and beliefs?

3. Look at several issues of one magazine or several magazines of the same genre (e.g., women fashions, beauty & health, sports, etc.). Use the RQs in Tables 10-1 and 10-2, and the textual deconstruction questions in Table 10.4 to analyze any assumptions you see in these magazines' representations of race, class, sex, gender, and ability. How are social categories being reproduced in the articles and advertisements published in those magazines? Note: You can also try this with different online chatrooms, blogs, or videogames.

4. Critique one movie of your choice (or your instructor's choice) as a narrative text. What social structures, events, or actions is that movie representing? What discursive formations doe the move rely upon? Use the questions in Table 10.5 to analyze the film's narrative structure, characters, setting, and bottom line message. Do the film writers or producers seem interested in evaluating and/or reforming social structures, events, or actions? Give reasons for your answer. What warrants can you identify for the worth or value of your analysis?

Part 3

How to Discover Communication

11 How to Design Discovery Research

Introduction

In this chapter, we will show you how to think like a discovery researcher, how to design empirical studies that use numbers to measure communication attitudes, beliefs, and behaviors. We explore how constructs are identified and defined through measurement. Next we discuss the importance of causal arguments and how this concern impacts choice of methods. In the last section of the chapter, we describe the elements of design control and discuss three design types for experiments: preexperimental, quasi-experimental, and true experimental research designs.

Learning Outcomes

After completing this chapter, you should be able to:

» Explain how variables are conceptually and operationally defined.

» Apply four levels of measurement scales in explaining how communication is operationalized in discovery research.

» Evaluate the strength of causal and associative arguments based on three required criteria: time order, covariation, and control of rival explanations.

» Critique the relative strengths of preexperimental, quasi-experimental, and true experimental designs based on the presence (or absence) of three control elements: pretests, random assignment, and comparison groups.

Outline

Whe you are in the very beginning stages of thinking about discovery research, it often begins by the desire to test a theory or experiment with an idea or interest. Keep in mind that testing your theory or idea may be a school project assigned by your instructor, or it can be testing a new product or campaign through surveys required by your team at work or your employer. Recall the assumptions that underlie the discovery paradigm we identified in Chapter 2 on paradigms in communication research. Your design choices will be influenced by these because, as a researcher, you value precision and accuracy by systematically observing communication.

Research Design as the Essential Framework

In this chapter, we will explore the essential features of designing research: measurement and the methodological framework that you choose. The relationships between these processes are often reflexive rather than linear and are depicted in Figure 11.1. You may begin with an interest in or theory that you can develop into a predictive claim about certain kinds of communication; the next step is to choose a research design to test your idea, such as an experiment or a survey. Your design choice influences how to measure the concepts and theories you are considering. Or your conceptualization might lead next to concerns for measurement and this set of decisions could influence your choice of design. This model then is a broad representation of the discovery research methods discussed in this section of the book: content analysis, surveys, and experiments; a

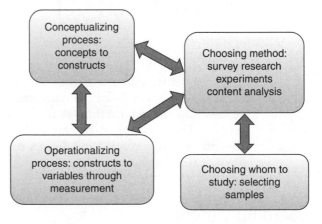

Figure 11.1 Designing Discovery Research

more elaborate version of this model is given to you in Chapter 14 when we discuss experimental research. It also provides the framework for the logic that underlies our discussion of hypothesis-testing in Chapter 15 on descriptive statistics.

We first turn to the term **measurement**, which grew out of the discovery-based assumptions that knowledge was gained by the precise and systematic study of the observed world; we began this discussion describing systematic data collection methods for discovery research in Chapter 5, "What Counts as Communication Data?" We now extend this conversation by considering the role of measurement. The most precise and accurate system developed in the science and social sciences is the quantification of data, yielding greater power through prediction and control. By adopting a systematic approach, we identify step-by-step procedures for making observations and assigning numbers to them.

Measurement

In the first step of beginning research, we develop a theory or an idea about observations of communication phenomena: Why do people interact the way that they do in a particular context? Our observations of communication translate to conceptualizations through discourse among social scientists interested in studying the same kinds of phenomena. Many communication phenomena are not directly observable because they entail complex internal processes like intention or emotion. Researchers in our field face the same problems with meanings of these indirectly observable, abstract concepts that we do in everyday life. How do I know what you mean by trusting or loving another person? When you say that news networks or advertising marketers have hidden agendas, what do you mean? In most of our day-to-day interactions, we settle for assuming that we understand one another unless, of course, we have a misunderstanding.

In empirical investigations, on the other hand, discovery researchers begin by assuming that the concepts and theories used to explain communication phenomena must be defined for precision linking definitions to systematic observation. By conducting and reporting on their studies, researchers work on clarifying their meanings often using other related concepts; you might us *reliance* for trust or *secret intentions* for hidden agendas in the examples above. This process is called conceptualization where we use theories and concepts to define other concepts and link these indirectly to our observations; when a group of scientists arrive at an agreed upon conceptual meaning, these concepts are called **constructs** (see Figure 11.1).

Certainly, you can directly observe some communication behavior, such as smiling at your best friend or counting the number of hours you watch television during a week. Kaplan (1964) long ago distinguished between phenomena that could be directly observed from those that required more complex, conceptual constructions. Because discovery researchers value precision, they cannot rely upon our everyday assumption of understanding what we mean. When a communication phenomenon cannot be observed directly, researchers look for key indicators of its presence or absence; for example, we might all agree that a trusting person is one who relies on others for information and assistance, or one who believes that the other will be respectful and caring, or one who confides in others about private experiences. All of these definitions are **key indicators** for trust because they identify other interactions that help us understand what we mean by trust.

You may think that trust includes some other dimensions of interaction (and it very well might), but a group of researchers may limit the definition to even one of those identified above for the purposes of a study. They may focus on the definition of trust as reliance on others for assistance and information and ignore the definition of trust and confiding in others because they are particularly interested in how trusting information sources can lead to important decisions. You can see then how this process of definition leads to greater precision in meaning; trust in this study is limited to X and not Z. Once researchers have an agreed upon meaning, they can develop procedures or methods that will capture their particular conceptualization of a construct. They might analyze various messages for content expressing key indicators of trust, or design a questionnaire to ask respondents about their experiences of these key indicators, or they might set up an experiment to test the effects of trusting another person on decision-making or relationship development. Further precision is added by measurement, by translating constructs into numbers. The process of specifying procedures used and instruments designed for measuring communication constructs is called **operationalization**. Once this process has been completed for a particular investigation, constructs are understood by their conceptual definitions and measured by their operational definitions.

Conceptual and Operational Definitions

As we stated above, **conceptual definitions** specify what a construct is and what it is not based on the agreed-upon meanings that have arisen in research discourse; to find out what "communication apprehension" means as a construct studied in our field, for example, you would conduct a literature review to determine how researchers are conceptually defining the construct. The next step in the operationalization process is to convert the construct to a variable. **Variables** are simply constructs that have been defined in measurable ways. As we pointed out earlier, some variables have essential characteristics that are directly observable, so there is no need to define them at a conceptual level. For example, observable and measurable characteristics already define biological sex, waving, font size, and the number of Tweets. But many of the things we study in communication cannot be directly observed or measured. For instance, we cannot cut open someone's head and see if the person is intelligent. We can only observe indirect *key indicators* of a person's intelligence. Almost every empirical research study in communication uses constructs; just a few examples include relational uncertainty, media presence, inoculation, and emotional labor.

One of these examples, uncertainty in interpersonal relationships, was first conceptualized as a theory (Berger & Calabrese, 1975) that many communication researchers used for explaining how relational partners communicated with each other based on a need to reduce the uncertainty they were experiencing. Recall that in Chapter 1, we began by explaining the process of building theory through research. In the original conceptualization of uncertainty theory, Berger and Calabrese defined three different types: self, partner, and relational uncertainty. Self-uncertainty occurred "when people are not able to describe, predict, or explain their own attitudes and behaviors" within a specific relationship; the conceptual definition for partner-uncertainty referred to "an inability to predict the other person's attitudes and behaviors within interaction," and finally, relational uncertainty was conceptually defined as "the doubt about the status of the relationship apart from either self or partner" (as defined in Knobloch & Solomon, 1999, p. 262). Several researchers worked to develop ways to measure uncertainty (Parks & Adelman, 1983; Clatterbuck, 1979), and through refinements, adaptations, and repeated empirical tests, researchers now often use instruments that measure one or more of the three types of interpersonal uncertainty by identifying key indicators for each of these (Knobloch & Solomon, 1999, 2003; Affifi & Schrodt, 2003; Bevan, 2004). We will show you one of these later on in our discussion of various measurement scales.

Operational definitions specify as precisely as possible every operation, procedure, and instrument needed to measure a construct. For example, Knobloch and Solomon (1999) developed self-, partner-, and relational-uncertainty scales as a type of survey instrument that consists of a series of statements related to each type of uncertainty: the self-uncertainty scale included questions like "How certain are you about how much you like your partner"; partner-uncertainty included statements like "How certain are you about how important is the relationship to your partner"; and relational uncertainty included statements like

"How certain are you about how you and your partner would describe this relationship." These three scales with 21 statements constitute an operational definition for the "respondent's uncertainty about his or her own relational involvement, the partner's relational involvement, and the relationship itself" (p. 268). Each of the responses ranged from 1 = "completely or almost completely uncertain" to 6 = "completely or almost completely certain"; each was statistically tested to ensure that they represented key indicators of the uncertainty variable.

Another familiar construct in interpersonal communication research is verbal aggressiveness. A recent study identified family patterns of communication that would predict the occurrence of this trait variable among the respondents (Schrodt & Carr, 2012). In this study, verbal aggressiveness was *conceptually defined* as "any communication behavior that attacks a person's self-concept to inflict psychological pain" that includes "character attacks, competence attacks, teasing, insults, and ridicule, to name a few" (pp. 54–55). Again, notice that all of the terms that we used to conceptually define verbal aggressiveness are abstract concepts as well. What counts as teasing, or profanity, must be further specified, so those concepts alone do not provide a definition that enables empirical measurement of verbal aggression. To measure a construct empirically (i.e., make it a variable), we need both a conceptual and an operational definition.

Operational definitions answer the question, "How will I recognize this concept or construct when I see it?" For example, Infante and Wigley's (1986) Verbal Aggressiveness Scale (VAS) is an *operational definition* for the construct verbal aggression. Similar to the uncertainty scale, the VAS is a written survey instrument that consists of 20 statements, each one a statement about how individuals try to get other people to comply with their wishes using aggressive tactics (e.g., "If individuals I am trying to influence really deserve it, I attack their character"; or, "I refuse to participate in arguments when they involve personal attacks"). Again, each statement was tested to make sure that it represented a key indicator of verbal aggressiveness. Five response choices for participants were provided for each item, from 1 = "almost never true" to 5 = "almost always true." You will learn more about this kind of measure, called a *Likert scale*, in the next section when we introduce you to the various scales used to measure communication variables as operationalizations.

Levels of Measurement

To operationalize a concept, construct, or variable, you will use one of four different levels of measurement: nominal, ordinal, interval, or ratio. These four levels of measurement are ordered from the least to the most precise empirical indicator, and Table 11.1 illustrates the characteristics of each of these levels of measurement.

Nominal and ordinal level measurement yield purely categorical variables and are used primarily to represent broad categorizations of data. Interval and ratio level scales yield continuously measured variables and provide the kind of precise measurements required for mathematical analysis, which is integral to discovery paradigm research. We will begin by defining some examples of each level of measurement, starting with the nominal level.

Nominal Level

Whenever we organize texts, direct observations of communicative behavior, or self-report or other-report data into separate categories, such as participant sex or marital status, we are dealing with **nominal level measurement**. Because the categories are separate, not overlapping, variables measured in this way are sometimes called discrete variables. Thus, nominal measures yield categorical variables, and the order of the categories is unimportant. When there are only two categories, it may be called a **dichotomous variable**, as is the case whenever we ask "yes" or "no" questions on a survey questionnaire

or during an interview. The only acceptable answer is either "yes" or "no." Respondents cannot choose "unsure," or "maybe" as an answer. Table 11.2 shows two examples of dichotomous variables.

Many nominal level measurements include more than two categories; asking people to identify their religious or political party affiliations, ethnicity, or club memberships (see Table 11.2 for examples). These **demographic variables** measure some preexisting characteristic of the research participant. Each characteristic category is assigned a unique number; so, for example, a "1" could be assigned to "Democrat," a "2" to "Republican," and so forth, until all possible political affiliations have been included. The numbers are assigned arbitrarily as the means by which the categories are identified. The "2's" in this case represent "Republicans" and carry no mathematical value.

We may also want to use **researcher-constructed categories** and ask people to classify themselves in ways that they may have never considered before they participated in our research study. For example, you might ask participants to answer questions about one of their interpersonal relationships and to indicate whether they are reporting about an acquaintance, a friendship, or a romantic relationship (see Table 11.2 for examples). Another kind of nominal variable with researcher-constructed categories are characterized by independent variables in traditional experimental research. As you will see later in this chapter in the experimental designs, the independent variable is defined and measured by treatment and control conditions. Each condition represents

Table 11.1 Characteristics of Four Levels of Measurement

Nominal level: Data are placed into discrete, unordered categories. Categories should be mutually exclusive, and the list of categories should be exhaustive.	Yields categorical data (see Table 5.2 for examples).	Least precise
Ordinal level: Has all of the characteristics of nominal level measurement plus the fact that the categories are ordered from least to most (for frequency, quantity, amount), from worst to best (for value), or from smallest to largest (for magnitude, size).	Yields categorical data (see Table 5.3 for examples).	▼
Interval level: Numbers represent precise measurements of interval points on a scale that are observable and equal.	Yields continuous data (see Tables 5.4, 5.5, and 5.6 for examples).	▼
Ratio level: Has all of the characteristics of interval level measurement plus the fact that an absolute zero point can be identified, indicating an absence of the variable being measured.	Yields continuous data (e.g., how many hours was your television on today?).	Most precise

Table 11.2 Examples of Nominal Level Measurement

1. **Dichotomous Variables:**
   (a). Did you consume alcohol today?
   _____ Yes _____ No
   (b). Indicate your employment status:
   _____ Full-time _____ Part-time
2. **Demographic Variables:**
   (a). Circle whether you are male or female: M or F
   (b). Indicate your religious affiliation:
   _____ Buddhism
   _____ Christianity
   _____ Hinduism
   _____ Judaism
   _____ Muslim
   _____ Other
   (c). Indicate your political party affiliation:
   _____ Not a registered voter
   _____ Registered Democrat
   _____ Registered Green Party
   _____ Registered Independent
   _____ Registered Republican
3. Researcher-Constructed Variables:
   (a). Indicate the type of relationship you are using as a basis for your responses:
   _____ Acquaintance
   _____ Friend
   _____ Romantic Partner
   (b). Indicate whether this e-mail message is mostly:
   _____ Task related
   _____ Socially related
   _____ Can't tell

a category of a nominally scaled variable. For example, an independent variable in a media effects experiment may control exposure to a media message. Viewers who see the clip represent one category and are assigned one number, whereas participants who do not view the clip represent a second category and are assigned a different number. Additionally, you should notice that both organismic and researcher-constructed categories can be dichotomous, but they may also be defined by more than two categories. Just imagine in our media experiment that participants are separated into three groups where two groups see different clips and the third sees no clip at all. We'll have more to say about this kind of variable a little later.

All nominal level measurements should satisfy two criteria: First, and ideally, the list of categories from which participants choose their responses, or into which

you are placing observations, should be an exhaustive list. It should include all possible categories of the variable. If your list leaves out an important category, then participants may not know how to respond, or the researcher will be unable to classify some behaviors or messages. This is why many nominal measures include an "other" category, as we did in the example of religious preference in Table 11.2.

The second standard for a good nominal level measure is that the variable categories be mutually exclusive, which means that each behavior, message, self-report, or other-report can be placed into one and only one category. In nominal level measurement, respondents must choose only one alternative from the list of categorical responses; if a person indicates membership in the Republican Party, then he or she cannot also be a Democrat. Likewise, if we are coding behaviors or texts, we cannot place a behavior or message into more than one category. For example, if we categorize a participant's conflict behavior as *avoiding*, we cannot also code that same act as *competing*.

Variables measured at the nominal level are simply treated as an organized set of categories and assigned numbers name or identify each distinct category (in fact, the term *nominal* comes from a Latin verb, "to give a name to"). For example, in content analysis you may want to study types of messages that occur in conflict scenarios. The messages that are collected as data are sorted into abstract categories of message types as the key indicators, and each category is assigned a number that names or identifies each message type. Then you would compare how frequently different categories of messages occur. In this case, you may count the frequency with which responses in each category appear, or the percentage of observations in each category. But the numbers assigned to each message type do not indicate anything about the size or value of the variable; the numbers simply represent the categories. To use numbers as indicators of quantity, we need at least an ordinal level measurement.

Ordinal Level

Ordinal level measurements rank order different categories of a variable; thus, ordinal measures provide some estimate of amount, such as frequency, magnitude, or value. With ordinal measures, the numbers you assign to variable categories are mathematically ordered. But the order is only approximate (e.g., least to most), so the mathematical relationship between categories is not very precise. For example, political communication and media researchers often ask respondents to rank from 1 to 5 the frequency with which they use a particular media source to get news information: The most frequent source of news information can be ranked "1," and the least frequent news source can be ranked "5." In much the same way, market and advertising researchers ask people to identify their favorite prime time sitcoms, websites, downloaded songs, and so forth.

Let's consider an example. Suppose we asked Maria, Alex, and Julian to indicate their use of different media channels as news sources. Suppose that they all indicate television as their most frequent news media choice, radio as their second choice, and newspapers as their third choice. Maria's ranking of 1, 2, and 3 may represent very different actual frequencies of TV, radio, and newspaper use than either Alex's or Julian's ratings indicate (see Table 11.3 for more). Even though the three participants indicated the same rankings, Maria's values of 1, 2, and 3 are not the same as Alex's 1, 2, and 3, or Julian's 1, 2, and 3. Ordinal level measurement gives us more precise information about amount or frequency of a variable than nominal level measurement, but ordinal measures are not as precise as the next two levels of measurement, interval and ratio level scales.

Table 11.3 Examples of Ordinal Level Measurement

Indicate the media sources you use as to get <u>news information</u> and rank each source starting with 1 as the most frequently used source:

Maria's response: __1__ television (Maria watches television news about 8 times a week)

   __2__ radio (Maria listens to the radio for news about 5 times/week)

   __3__ newspaper (Maria reads a newspaper about 3 times a week)

Alex's response: __1__ television (Alex watches television news about 5 times/week)

   __2__ radio (Alex listens to the radio for news about 4 times/week)

   __3__ newspaper (Alex reads a newspaper about 3 times a week)

Julian's response: __1__ television (Julian watches television news about 7 times a week)

   __2__ radio (Julian listens to the radio for news about 2 times/week)

   __3__ newspaper (Julian reads a newspaper about 1 time a week)

Interval Level

At the interval level of measurement, we can measure the amount or magnitude of a variable using attributes that have precise mathematical relationships to one another. Interval level measurement require a range or set of scaled responses that are ordered from least to most amount or from smallest to largest size. With **interval level measurement**, the distance between the points on the instruments is known and equal. You can think of interval measurement like temperature in which changes are measured accurately and equally by degrees. The units can vary depending on whether you are using a Fahrenheit or Celsius scale, but the meaning of "degree" stays the same for each scale regardless of where they are applied.

There are two types of interval scales that are frequently used in communication research today: the Likert scale and the semantic differential scale. Both Likert and semantic differential scales are used for self-report and other-report data collection in the discovery paradigm. Let's define and consider an example of each scale in turn.

Likert scales measure constructs by providing research participants with a set of statements designed to reflect the amount of the construct (see Tables 11.4 and 11.5 for two examples). Each statement is followed by a range of response choices that require participants to indicate the level at which they estimate they possess that construct (for self-report data) or the level at which they perceive that construct in another person (for other-report data). Recall that each response choice is assumed to be a *key indicator* of our variable. A shortened example of Infante and Wigley's (1986) Verbal Aggressiveness Scale (VAS) appears in Table 11.4.

Constructs that we measure with Likert scales can be either unidimensional or multidimensional. A **unidimensional variable** cannot be broken down into distinct factors or subconstructs because all of the items in the measure point to the same uniform conceptual definition. Infante and Wigley's VAS is a unidimensional measure, since all of the items in the VAS point to the same conceptual definition, a predisposition to attack other people with words. It is critical to note that effective scale construction means exploring the construct fully through the use of a number of statements, questions, or items that tap various aspects of its definition. Verbal aggressiveness, trust, and relational uncertainty could not be effectively measured by using just one

Table 11.4 Example of Interval Level Measurement: Unidimensional Likert Scale

Verbal Aggressiveness Scale (Infante & Wigley, 1986)
This survey is concerned with how we try to get people to comply with our wishes. Indicate how often each statement is true for you personally when you try to influence other persons. Use the following scale: 1 = almost never true, 2 = rarely true, 3 = occasionally true, 4 = often true, and 5 = almost always true.   _____ **1.** When individuals insult me, I get a lot of pleasure in really telling them off.   _____ **2.** When individuals are very stubborn, I use insults to soften their stubbornness.   _____ **3.** When I attack persons' ideas, I try not to damage their self-concepts.   _____ **4.** When others do things I regard as stupid, I try to be extremely gentle with them.   _____ **5.** If individuals I am trying to influence really deserve it, I attack their character.

Note: Items 3 and 4 are reverse worded, so scores for those items must be reversed before calculating a summary score on this measure.

statement or item. Imagine if you measured verbal aggressiveness with just one of the statements in Table 11.4. Rarely would a one-item scale for a complex construct withstand tests of validity.

However, some variables are **multidimensional**, which means that they have several distinct parts, or subconstructs. Each subconstruct represents a different dimension of the variable or construct you want to measure each with a distinct set of key indicators. For example, Knobloch and Solomon's (1999) relationship uncertainty measure that we described earlier is also a Likert scale; each type of uncertainty (self, partner, and relationship) contains a set of unique dimensions. The relationship uncertainty scale depicted in Table 11.5 has four dimensions: behavioral norms, mutuality, definition, and future. The behavioral norms subscale, for example, "emphasized the acceptable and unacceptable actions within the relationship" and the mutuality subscale "addressed the reciprocity of feelings within the relationship" (p. 270). Each dimension is measured with four statements. For example, items 8, 10, 18, and 20 correspond to the behavioral norms dimension; items 3, 12, 15, and 16 are used to measure the mutuality dimension, and so forth. This kind of measure allows the researcher to evaluate certain specific attributes or characteristics of relationship uncertainty that they believe will affect or be affected by other communication variables.

Another and perhaps easier example of a multidimensional construct is interpersonal attraction. McCroskey and McCain (1974) developed a multidimensional scale to measure this construct when they discovered three distinct types of attraction: physical, social, and task. Physical attraction is based on physical characteristics and dress or appearance; social attractiveness refers to personal liking of the other and likelihood of friendship; task attractiveness is related to "how easy or worthwhile working with someone would be" (p. 266). Each of these were measured by separate subscales; recently, the entire measure for the construct underwent further testing and refinement (2006), but importantly it still validated the original three types of interpersonal attraction.

The second type of interval scale that appears frequently in published communication research is the **semantic differential** scale, which consists of a series of bipolar adjectives placed at either end of a continuum. The adjectives act as anchors for feelings, attitudes or beliefs. Respondents are asked to indicate where along the continuum their responses lie or their perceptions of others' responses. Thus, semantic differential scales are also used for self-report and other-report data. As with Likert scales, semantic differential scales may be used to measure unidimensional or multidimensional constructs. An interesting use of a semantic differential was used by Smith, Nolan, & Dai (1996) who wanted to assess respondents' feelings toward job refusal or rejection letters received by applicants from an organization. Study participants were asked to evaluate the letters by ranking them on bipolar comparisons which included pairs like: wordy/concise, straightforward/devious, considerate/thoughtless, and blunt/tactful. A total of nineteen pairs were used on a 7-point scale with the positive pole scored as a "7" and the negative pole scored as a "1." By allowing participants a full range of responses, the researchers were able to capture a more nuanced, scaled ranking of

Table 11.5 Example of Interval Level Measurement: Multidimensional Likert Scale: Knobloch and Solomon's Relationship Uncertainty Scale

We would like you to rate how certain you are about the degree of involvement that you have in your relationship at this time. Please note, we are not asking you to rate how much involvement there is in your relationship, but rather how certain you are about whatever degree of involvement you perceive. It might help if you first consider how much of each form of involvement is present in your relationship, and then evaluate how certain you are about that perception.

The possible responses to the items were as follows: 1 = completely or almost completely uncertain, 2 = mostly uncertain, 3 = slightly more uncertain than certain, 4 = slightly more certain than uncertain, 5 = mostly certain, and 6 = completely or almost completely certain.

How certain are you about . . .

Behavioral Norms Subscale
  8. what you can or cannot say to each other in this relationship?
  10. the boundaries for appropriate and/or inappropriate behavior in this relationship?
  18. the norms for this relationship?
  20. how you can or cannot behave around your partner?

Mutuality Subscale
  3. whether or not you and your partner feel the same way about each other?
  12. how you and your partner view this relationship?
  15. whether or not your partner likes you as much as you like him or her?
  16. the current status of this relationship?

Definition Subscale
  1. the definition of this relationship?
  6. how you and your partner would describe this relationship?
  13. the state of the relationship at this time?
  17. whether or not this is a romantic or platonic relationship?

Future Subscale
  4. whether or not you and your partner will stay together?
  7. the future of the relationship?
  11. whether or not this relationship will end soon?
  19. where this relationship is going?

the refusal letters than if they had simply provided just the bipolar opposites by themselves (dichotomous). This semantic differential measure appears in Table 11.6. Interval level measures are widely accepted in discovery paradigm research, but there is one still more precise level of measurement, the ratio level scale.

Ratio Level

Ratio level measurement possesses all the characteristics of interval level measurement plus one additional element. Like interval scales, the response choices for a ratio scale have different values that represent points along a continuum from less to more (or small to large), separated by equal distances, known as intervals. But unlike interval level measurement, a **ratio scale** has a true or absolute zero point, which stands for a complete absence of the variable being measured. Ratio scales are used when we want to determine the frequency of some communication

behavior or when we want to measure duration in time. For example, how many texts do you send a day? Or how many times do you check Facebook per day? That variable can be appropriately measured with a ratio scale because it is possible that you *never* turned on the television today. You can see how much more precise this measure is compared to our example of ordinal level measurement in Table 11.3. Maria, Alex, and Julian provided only a general estimate of how frequently they used various forms of media rather than asking for an actual count.

Discovery researchers prefer to use interval and ratio level measures, whenever possible, because those scales provide the most precise measurement of constructs. Those scales also enable the data you collect to be analyzed in more complex statistical ways, which you will learn about in Chapters 15 and 16. Because interval and ratio scales do require great precision and accuracy, a lot of work goes into designing the scales themselves,

Table 11.6 Example of Interval Level Measurement: Semantic Differential Scale

Responses to Job Refusal Letters (Smith, Nolan, & Dai, 1996)
These semantic differential scales were used to access business communication students' affective responses to direct and indirect in the refusal letters.
Instructions: For each item below, please circle the number between each pair of adjectives that best represents your feelings about the content of the letter you have read. Numbers "1" and "7" indicate very strong feelings. Numbers "2" and "6" indicate strong feelings. Numbers "3" and "5" indicate fairly weak feelings. Number "4" indicates that you are undecided, or do not understand the adjectives themselves. Please work quickly. There are no right or wrong answers.

Efficient	1	2	3	4	5	6	7	Inefficient
Insincere	1	2	3	4	5	6	7	Sincere
Concise	1	2	3	4	5	6	7	Wordy
Valuable	1	2	3	4	5	6	7	Worthless
Straightforward	1	2	3	4	5	6	7	Devious
Selfish	1	2	3	4	5	6	7	Unselfish
Persuasive	1	2	3	4	5	6	7	Unconvincing
Timid	1	2	3	4	5	6	7	Bold
Good	1	2	3	4	5	6	7	Bad
Subtle	1	2	3	4	5	6	7	Obvious
Discourteous	1	2	3	4	5	6	7	Courteous
Organized	1	2	3	4	5	6	7	Disorganized
Pleasant	1	2	3	4	5	6	7	Unpleasant
Uninformative	1	2	3	4	5	6	7	Informative
Blunt	1	2	3	4	5	6	7	Tactful
Logical	1	2	3	4	5	6	7	Illogical
Considerate	1	2	3	4	5	6	7	Thoughtless
Unappealing	1	2	3	4	5	6	7	Appealing
Friendly	1	2	3	4	5	6	7	Unfriendly

selecting participants who will respond to the scales, and setting up the conditions in which the data will be collected. In fact, the phrase "research design" originally referred to those aspects of discovery scholarship; however, research design can be understood more generally, which we turn to in the next section.

Building Arguments Through Research Designs

As we noted in the beginning of this chapter, your **research design** is the methodological framework you will use to test your ideas or theories. In discovery paradigm research, there is a decided preference for causal arguments as we noted in Chapter 4 on claims and Chapter 6 on warrants. But let's take a step backwards here for a minute and think about what causal arguments enable you to do. Causal arguments make predictive control possible. If we can demonstrate what *causes* what, the claims shift from what is possible to what is likely or probable. Suppose a researcher constructs a causal model about the effects of media violence on aggressive behavior. A truly causal model allows us to develop understanding, and therefore planning and decision-making strategies. If we understand the link between high levels of exposure to media violence and the way that children act aggressively toward each other in play, then we can decide how to intervene most effectively by limiting media exposure. You can see in a very practical way through this simple example what the power of causal prediction might enable you to do.

A slightly different additional argument underlies the preference for causality in discovery research. It involves understanding the preference for directly observable phenomena. Recall our discussion of the key underlying assumptions from Chapter 2. One of these assumes that the real world consists of physical objects and observable interactions. A second assumption emphasizes that the world is *only* knowable through observation, and that the knowledge is gained through logical and empirical methods. As we discussed in the previous section, measurement is a method of building in precision for testing our claims. When communication phenomena cannot be observed directly, they *must* be defined as precisely as possible by key indicators of agreed upon meanings and based on more observable forms of interaction. Observing what constitutes variables is only part of the discovery claim process however; claims require stipulating the relationship that exists *between* the variables, and causal relationships permit the greatest degree of control possible, especially if the researcher controls the change in the cause or independent variable; ostensibly then the pattern of effects is also then controllable. In other words, discovery researchers prefer causal arguments to other kinds because valid causal arguments provide both prediction *and* control. Imagine that astrophysicists were not able to predict in causal ways how spacecraft must be constituted and how fuel must be formulated for space travel. Without causation, the likelihood of orbiting the earth or arriving on Mars successfully would be just remote possibilities rather than a set of probable outcomes.

Traditionally, causal arguments were tested using experiments because of the degree of control afforded to them in experimental designs; these are still considered optimal frameworks for testing causal relationships. As you will see in the last section, the components of experimental design were constructed precisely to provide greater identification of and control over presumed causes. However, with the advances of statistical analysis and control, not all causal claims are confined to experiments. You are likely to find these in survey research and some content analyses as you will see in the chapters that follow. Let us consider how claims and arguments influence research designs within these three methods.

Causal and Associative Arguments

From a discovery paradigm perspective, the most effective causal arguments are established by meeting three basic criteria (Lazarfield, 1959). You will see that when any of these are missing, the researcher is unable to make as strong a case for causality and therefore must relinquish some predictive control over changes that are expected to occur. The first of these criteria is the **time order** requirement, that change in the independent variable precedes the change in the dependent variable. The order of effects is invariant; the changes in the dependent variable cannot precede manipulation of the independent variable. To use an earlier example, if the researcher argues that certain family patterns cause verbal aggressiveness, they must make a strong case for the pattern preceding the development of verbal aggressiveness in children. We know from observing parents and children that many parental behaviors are reactions to children's behavior rather than the causes. And if verbal aggressiveness appeared before such family patterns were established, then the family patterns could not be the presumed cause.

Covariation is the second criterion; the changes in variables must happen together or be correlated. When the change in the independent variable occurs, it is must be followed fairly closely in time by the change in the dependent variable. In the preceding example, if there were periods where certain family communication patterns did not covary with verbal aggressiveness expression, it would be more difficult to tie the two together causally. You could argue that some developmental feature of personality traits, such as empathy, or peer friendship influence covaried or happened together more consistently with verbal aggressiveness than did family communication patterns. As we discussed in Chapter 4 on claims, researchers will often claim that two or more variables are correlated and test this relationship, without extending this claim to a causal argument. In those instances, researchers are making *associative* and not causal arguments.

The third criterion is **controlling competing explanations** or rival hypotheses. In the preceding example, if the researcher could not rule out personality trait development or peer friendship influence, these two variables would compete with the central claim about family communication patterns. When the researcher can control the change in the independent variable through manipulation and test its subsequent effects, then a stronger case can be made for a causal link. But when there is less control over competing explanations, the researcher must acknowledge that these competing possibilities may also just as effectively cause changes in verbal aggressiveness. The inability to control rival hypotheses considerably weakens the researcher's causal argument.

Content Analysis and Survey Research

The claims you will find in the methods that follow in this section of the book are primarily explanatory and predictive, but you will see that traditionally content analysis and survey research do not contain design elements that make for strong causal arguments. In content analysis, for example, you will see that researchers are interested in analyzing samples of messages by predicting types of messages or message characteristics that seem to be occurring under various conditions or from various sources. Often types of messages are collected and measured at nominal levels; the researcher collects messages as they occur naturally. Such a design does not permit manipulation of independent variables and therefore cannot be controlled experimentally. Similarly, survey research does not generally impose design control features that warrant strong causal arguments. Survey researchers often use passive data collection methods that do not involve intentional manipulation of the independent variables. They simply observe and collect information about key indicators of communication as it naturally occurs in the media or in organizations or in relationships. In some cases, the natural occurrence of a variable is the preferred choice for research because of ethical obligations. For example, researchers investigating the effects of stress may be more likely to find and study individuals who are already experiencing high levels of stress rather than trying to induce these experimentally. In order to avoid harming participants as the greater principle, we may accept less control in our study design.

By various methods and approaches, content analysis and survey research do attempt to provide stronger cases for their arguments by time order, covariance, and control of rival explanations. As you will see in the next chapter on content analysis, researchers frequently use an entire group or population of messages from an extended period of time to make a stronger argument for various patterns of messages occurring. For example, Gow (1996) used three sets of top 100 MTV videos over a 3-year period as his sample. An even longer period would help to establish the persistence in the pattern of effects he argued was occurring. As you learned in Chapter 5 on communication data, survey research may use a longitudinal design rather than a cross-sectional survey. For example, Groshek and Conway (2012) claimed that using a pervasive approach in teaching media ethics was more effective than offering a single course in media ethics; since the pervasive approach is to assess the cumulative effects of learning about ethics in a variety of curricular and extracurricular contexts, the researchers had to use a longitudinal survey to tap attitudinal changes over time, following the same group of students over time. It is not the strongest argument for causality; the researchers provided evidence of covariation and some basis for time order, but they had a difficult time ruling out rival explanations, like other changes in the curriculum or maturation over time, that might also explain how students' ethical reasoning and attitudes were changing. Longitudinal data collection is extremely difficult however, especially in survey research, and as a result, survey research may be unable to establish a true time order sequence as a criterion for causality.

As you can see with these approaches to survey research and content analysis, the arguments often satisfy the covariance requirement for causal arguments but may have more difficulty establishing time order and controlling for rival hypotheses. For example, a survey researcher may hypothesize the different conflict styles in romantic partners are associated with relational satisfaction, but have difficulty showing that changing one variable *causes* the change of the other variable. It may be that the preference for a conflict style precedes and changes satisfaction levels; however, it may equally plausible that relational satisfaction precedes and causes a preference for certain types of conflict styles. In another example, do website viewing preferences cause attitudinal shifts toward violence or do attitudes change first and cause viewers to select certain websites? In both of these cases, researchers may also have difficulty eliminating other potential causes of variable change. Are preferences for conflict styles the primary cause of relational satisfaction or is satisfaction influenced by other factors such as level of intimacy and degree of liking? Does website viewing cause attitudinal shifts in violence or are these more likely caused by parental interaction and peer influence?

Arguments for covariance or correlation are usually distinguished by *associative* claims as we explained in Chapter 4 on claims; tests of the hypotheses which include research designs from survey research or content analysis are generally not able to demonstrate the level of control evidenced in experiments. Traditionally, survey research was used on an exploratory basis to see what variables might be present and how they might be linked through association. The research design of an experimental study enables you to construct an effective experimental manipulation of the independent variable. Its primary purpose is to establish a strong base for causality through **experimental control**. As you will see in the next section, three procedural elements help to build a strong case for each of the required criteria for causality: time order, covariation, and control of rival explanations for the observed effects on the dependent variable. Additionally, many experiments check the manipulation of the independent variable for its effectiveness. If we show a clip of violent and nonviolent news stories, for example, we may want to have participants rate the violence in the clip in order to be sure they saw violence in the same way as we intended.

Experimental Research Design

Experimental control is acquired through three design elements: comparison groups, random assignment to independent variable conditions, and pretest-posttest administrations (Katzer, Cook, & Crouch, 1982, pp. 118–119). In the sections that follow, we will describe these elements and how they are employed with increasing levels of control across varying types of designs.

Design Elements

Comparison Groups. **Comparison groups** refer to groups of study participants who are exposed to the manipulated levels of the independent variable. Researchers vary the levels or conditions of the independent variable to observe the results for each variation on the group of participants. In a study by Limon and Kazoleas (2004), there were three experimental conditions to test exposure to public service announcements using different forms of evidence: one contained statistical evidence against the use of tanning beds, the second provided a case example as evidence against the use of tanning beds, and the third was considered a **control group**. When participants are not exposed to any variation of the independent variable, their group is called a control group. In this third condition, participants filled out the questionnaire about their attitudes but did not view any public service announcement. The group is held constant, with respect to the independent variable, as a baseline comparison for every other condition.

Groups that receive some exposure to the manipulation of the independent variable are sometimes called **treatment or experimental groups.** When you use comparison groups, you are trying to ensure that the groups are equivalent in every way except for exposure to the various levels or conditions of the independent variable. Isolating this single difference helps to build a strong case for a causal relationship between the independent variable and its effects on the dependent variable. Control groups are placed in the same setting and are responding to the same environmental cues except for the manipulation of the independent variable. For example, Banas and Miller (2013) used three different comparison groups, two of which received two distinctive versions of persuasive arguments against accepting media messages and one control group that received no persuasive argument before being exposed to the messages.

Sometimes, researchers go so far as to fool group members into thinking they have received a treatment when they have not. The false treatment is called a **placebo** and is used extensively in medical research in which many studies investigate the effectiveness of various medications. Placebos, in these cases, are treatments that appear to be medications but have no medical value ("sugar pills"). By administering a placebo, researchers hope to be able to distinguish between the psychological effects of believing medication has been ingested from the actual physiological effects of the drug. Occasionally, placebo groups are also used in communication research.

In a study in which the authors tested the effectiveness of various treatments of communication apprehension,

Heuett, Hsu, and Ayres (2003) had both a control condition and a placebo condition in addition to treatment levels of the independent variable. Study participants were exposed to one of four treatment conditions: (1) a treatment condition in which a videotaped visualization technique was viewed, (2) a treatment condition in which a videotaped systematic desensitization technique was viewed, (3) a treatment condition in which a videotaped procedure skills training was viewed, or (4) a multiple treatments condition in which all three of these videotapes were viewed.

A fifth group of participants was exposed to the placebo condition in which they viewed a videotape of great speeches. Heuett et al. (2003) pointed out that tapes of great speeches do not have any demonstrated effect on communication apprehension, but it could seem reasonable to students that viewing great speeches would produce the desired effect. In the sixth group tested as a *control* condition, participants were left alone with no interaction with the experimenter. You will hear about the use of placebos and control groups again later on in this chapter when you learn about the various ways of eliminating or reducing potential threats to validity. Researchers use comparison groups to strengthen their causal argument, but simply having groups to compare is an insufficient test. Experimental designs can also employ random assignment to treatment conditions.

Random assignment. A second design element, **random assignment**, refers to a procedure in which the researchers select participants on a purely random basis to participate in either treatment or control conditions. Random assignment is not the same thing as *selection* or *random sampling* that we discussed in Chapter 5, "What Counts as Communication Data?" Recall that the purpose of selection is to select people to participate in research study from the general population; when the selection process is random, participants will then more likely constitute a representative sample or group. Following the selection process, the researcher can randomly assign participants to experimental or control groups. Randomizing both the selection process and the assignment process helps to ensure that groups will not be biased in some way.

The main purpose of random assignment is to help establish equivalent groups at the beginning of the experiment. A sample that is not randomly assigned may have some type of selection bias, a characteristic present in one group but not the other. Students assigned from one school may represent real regional differences

compared to students from another school. In McDevitt and Chaffee's (2000) study, the researchers could not randomly assign students who would receive a new curriculum. As a result, they had to demonstrate that the student groups who were exposed to this special curriculum could not be distinguished in any other way from students who were not exposed. You will learn more about this problem later in the chapter on experimental research when we discuss threats to validity.

Pretesting. When researchers administer a **pretest**, they are assessing baseline or naturally occurring levels of the dependent variable before the independent variable is manipulated. They administer the very same test as a **posttest** following the manipulation. By using a pretest-posttest procedure, researchers want to establish a precise comparison between the first measurement of the dependent variable as a pretest and the second measurement as a posttest. If the participants are exposed to the manipulation of the independent variable while other environmental factors are held constant, then researchers can assume any change between pretest and posttest levels of the dependent variable is due to the influence of the independent variable.

Heuett and his colleagues (2003) used an elaborate experimental design that included pretests and treatment levels that included training participants in visualization, desensitization, and other skills. Participants were given the public speaking scale of McCroskey's *Personal Report of Communication Apprehension* (McCroskey, 1978) to first help the investigators screen those who had very high levels of communication apprehension, but the scores also served as a baseline comparison. Heuett et al. were able to precisely determine just how high subjects' levels of communication apprehension were prior to any exposure to treatment, and then they compared these scores with post-treatment levels of communication apprehension when the same participants filled out the same scale again following treatment.

Pretests can also help to assure that all comparison groups are equivalent before treatment exposure. If all treatment groups, the placebo group, and the control group in Heuett et al.'s (2003) study have approximately the same high levels of communication apprehension before any treatment is received, then the pretest is an additional way of demonstrating that no group was significantly different from any other at the onset of the study. In McDevitt and Chaffee's (2000) study, using a pretest was especially important because individual students could not be assigned to treatment conditions. The researchers were interested in testing the effects of the *Kids Voting* civics curriculum on a number of voting behaviors and attitudes, media use, and discussion with parents. By providing students with a pretest of these variables along with an analysis of other factors, the investigators could make a strong case that the school groups were equivalent before half of them were exposed to the *Kids Voting* curriculum.

As we mentioned earlier, *controlling* the manipulation of the independent variable is central to the causal argument made by experimental researchers. Implementing the elements of comparison groups, random assignment, and pretests-posttests along with the independent variable manipulation enables researchers to strengthen their claims that the independent variable is the source of the effects observed in the dependent variable. The absence or presence of these three elements changes the research design. Designs in which some or all of the elements are lacking result in weaker support for causal arguments; these are called preexperimental and quasi-experimental designs. Designs that make use of all three elements and employ random sampling methods provide the strongest evidence for causal arguments and are called "true experimental designs" (D. T. Campbell & Stanley, 1963, p. 8). We examine these more closely in the next section.

Types of Designs

Preexperimental Designs. Two preexperimental designs are for comparison: one-shot case study (or ex post facto design) and one group, pretest-posttest design. Both lack two elements described in the previous section (random assignment and comparison groups) and one design lacks all three. The designs are depicted in Table 11.7.

Table 11.7 Types of Preexperimental Designs

1. One-shot Case Study	O_1	X	O_1
2. One-group Pretest-Posttest Design		X	O_2

Based on D. T. Campbell & Stanley, 1963, p. 8.
Note: R = random assignment; O = observation or measurement of dependent variable; X = manipulation of independent variable.

One-shot case studies are those designs in which some change in the independent variable occurs and the researchers claim a particular set of effects on the dependent variable. The design does not include any of the control elements of pretesting, comparison groups, or random assignment. For example, suppose you wished to investigate the effects of a presidential candidate debate on voting behavior. The last debate is scheduled three weeks prior to the general election. After the debate, the majority of people vote for candidate B instead of candidate A. The researcher concludes that candidate B must have won the presidential election because of the debate. But can the researcher really support this claim based on the causal criteria we identified earlier? There does seem to be some support for time order: the debate preceded the vote. And since the two events happened fairly close together, we could also argue that the two covaried. However, many other events may have rivaled the debate as the cause. Perhaps the candidate who lost was given more negative media coverage or had less money and simply couldn't appear publicly as frequently as the other candidate in the final three weeks of the campaign. This type of design is also called the ex post facto design because they must argue the cause *after the fact* of observing the effects. The one-shot case study gives the weakest support for a causal argument.

The next design, the **one group pretest-posttest design**, adds an element that strengthens the investigator's causal argument. Using the voting example for the first design, the one group, pretest-posttest design would require that the researcher administer a pretest, such as a measurement of voter preference for the presidential candidates, prior to their viewing the debate. Then, after viewing the debate, the same survey could be given again to see whether voter preferences had changed; moreover, the actual vote 3 weeks later could be used as further corroboration. By administering the pretest, you have some baseline level of voter preference before exposure to the debate. The pretest makes it possible to determine whether there is a distinct change or no change between the pretest and the posttest measures. However, there are still many problems in assuming that the independent variable, *X*, is the source of those changes. You would still have the problem of not controlling rival explanations.

Quasi-experimental designs. This class of study design represents a step up in strengthening the causal argument. In this second group, we will consider two designs: the time series design and the nonequivalent control group design. There are actually many variations on these two themes, but the basic structures are depicted in Table 11.8. The **time series design** assesses levels of the dependent variable at several points in time prior to and following the manipulation of the independent variable. The rationale for this design is that if the dependent variable does not change over an extended period of time until the independent variable is manipulated and then it changes, you have more evidence that the change is from the independent variable and not some other competing factor. For example, a cluster of activities as the independent variable is given to students to help them become less apprehensive about public speaking. The treatment can be argued as the cause of reduced apprehension if, over time, the researchers can show that drops in apprehension were closely associated in time with the activity cluster (treatment). Such a design is particularly useful if the researcher suspects that some other factor, such as students' natural maturing over a semester, might compete with the treatment. That is, students' apprehension over time might naturally be reduced as they become accustomed to the idea of speaking publicly.

As another example, let's say you want to test the effects of media on children's remembering program material. A group of children are exposed to a visually rich online curricular program in the middle of the semester. If you have been measuring recall and retention abilities generally at several points in time before the children are exposed to the program and found that their ability levels are relatively stable, you are in a much stronger position to claim the effects of the program as the cause of any changes you see, especially if you find a significant change following exposure. The time series design permits you to demonstrate gains in retention

are not simply due to internal development in this age group of children. Even if the children's retention abilities are improving naturally over time, you will be able to estimate how much of the change in the dependent variable scores is due to the curricular program and how much is due to normal maturation, or age-related development. The time series design is still vulnerable to other problems, such as repeated testing, but using multiple pre- and posttests make it a design that is generally stronger than any of the preexperimental designs.

The second type of quasi-experimental design is called the **nonequivalent control group design.** In this case, you would use a control group not exposed to the independent variable manipulation or treatment. In the example we have already used several times, McDevitt and Chaffee (2000) were unable to randomly assign children to the treatment group (those who were exposed to *Kids Voting* curriculum) and the control group (those who were not). The researchers were very sensitive to the possibility that the two groups would not be equivalent and hence biased in some way. McDevitt and Chaffee had to conduct several analyses of both groups' characteristics before they could claim that these two groups did not differ in any way significant to their study. Fortunately, exposure to the curriculum was not dependent on any student's personal choice. Additionally, data was obtained on a variety of student and family characteristics such as their socioeconomic status, school grades, gender, ethnicity, or year in school. A statistical test showed that student participation in the curriculum was not related to any of these and that all of these characteristics were equally represented in each group. Without taking these additional measures, McDevitt and Chaffee would not have been able to establish that the treatment group could be compared to the control group. By using pretests and comparison groups, McDevitt and

Table 11.8 Quasi-Experimental Designs

1. Time Series:				O_1	O_2	O_3	X	O_4	O_5	O_6
2. Nonequivalent Control Group								O_1	X	O_2
								O_3		O_4

Based on D. T. Campbell & Stanley, 1963, p. 8
Note: R = random assignment; O = observation or measurement of dependent variable; X = manipulation of independent variable.

Chaffee used a design stronger than any preexperimental design.

True experimental designs. These designs are strongest in using all of the control elements providing the best evidence for causality. A true experimental design uses at least two and sometimes all three of the elements; these are the pretest-posttest control group design, the posttest-only control group design, and the Solomon four-group design (see Table 11.9).

The pretest-posttest control group design uses comparison groups, random assignment to place randomly selected participants into the treatment and control groups, and the pretest-posttest procedure (see Table 11.9). Random assignment and pretesting help to show that comparison groups are the same before the independent variable is manipulated; pretests also provide baseline levels of the dependent variable for precise comparisons; and comparison groups permit you to isolate the effects of the independent variable from other rival sources or causes. A variation of this type of design was employed by Heuett et al. (2003), who randomly assigned research subjects to six experimental conditions: three treatment conditions in which exposure to type of therapy for communication apprehension was varied, a placebo condition, and a control condition. This design has only one identifiable weakness: There is no way of assessing whether the pretest can interact with the effects of the independent variable through test sensitization when attempting to generalize the findings to any other group beside the study's sample. The problem occurs only when you try to assume the findings are representative of people outside of the current study.

To avoid this potential interaction, the second design, the **posttest-only control group,** removes the pretest (see Table 11.9). Random assignment helps to assure equivalence between groups; however, without a pretest, you have no baseline from which to calculate precise estimates of change in the dependent variable. In a study cited previously, Limon and Kazoleas (2004) used a posttest-only control group design in which participants were randomly assigned to one of three conditions: advertisements with statistical evidence, advertisements with a case example as evidence, and a control group. Without the pretest, it was not possible to assess precise changes in agreement with or counterarguments to tanning beds as a safe or dangerous practice.

To combine the strengths of both designs, the **Solomon four-group design** includes two groups that use the pretest-posttest control group design and two groups that use the posttest-only control group design. With this design, you can assess the specific effects of taking

Table 11.9 True Experimental Designs

1. Pretest-Posttest Control Group Design	R	O_1	X	O_2
	R	O_3		O_4
	R		X	O_1
2. Posttest-Only Control Group Design" should appear in Row 3, Column 1.	R			O_2
	R	O_1	X	O_2
3. Solomon Four-Group Design" should appear in Row 5, Column 1.	R	O_3		O_4
	R		X	O_5
	R			O_6

Note: R = random assignment; O = observation or measurement of dependent variable; X = manipulation of independent variable.

the pretest as a potential weakness of the design and eliminate it without sacrificing the information the pretest provides (see Table 11.9).

The greatest drawback to this design is the demands it makes in terms of time and effort. You must coordinate two test periods for two groups and one test period for two additional groups in a relatively comparable time frame. The number of subjects for each group must be fairly large so that the sample will reflect an adequate level of variation to establish confidence in your results. You will explore these design issues further when considering the warrants sections of the next three chapters on content analysis, survey research, and experimental research.

Summary

In this chapter, we introduced the concept of research design as the essential framework for discovery paradigm methods that use quantitative analysis. We explored how constructs are conceptually and operationally identified and defined through measurement. Next we discussed the importance of causal arguments and how this concern impacts choice of methods in content analysis, survey research, and experimental research. In the last section of the chapter, we described the elements of design control and discuss three design types for experiments: preexperimental, quasi-experimental, and true experimental research designs.

Key Terms

Comparison groups
Conceptual definition
Construct
Control group
Controlling competing explanations
Covariation
Demographic variables
Dichotomous variables
Experimental control
Experimental group
Interval Level Measurement
Key indicators
Likert Scales
Measurement
Multidimensional variable

Nominal Level Measurement
Nonequivalent control group design
One group pretest-posttest design
One shot case study
Operational definition
Operationalization
Ordinal Level Measurement
Organismic variables
Placebo
Posttest
Posttest-only control group design
Preexperimental designs
Pretest

Pretest-posttest control group design
Quasi-experimental designs
Random assignment
Ratio scales
Research design
Researcher-constructed categories
Semantic differential
Solomon four-group design
Time order
Time series design
Treatment group
True experimental designs
Unidimensional variable
Variables

Discussion Questions

1. Random assignment is an important consideration in making treatment groups equivalent and comparable. But random assignment is not always practical. Suppose, for instance, you wanted to test the effects of mediated messages in children's television programs on two separate day care groups using one of the groups as a control group. What kinds of problems might intervene in this type of situation?
2. Discuss how a true experimental design would provide better evidence for demonstrating cause-and-effect relations in some area of communication you care about. In your answer, be sure to apply the criteria and design elements.

"Try It!" Activities

1. Look up the following citation: Ayres and Heuett (2000), "An examination of the long term effect of performance visualization," *Communication Research Reports*, vol. 17, pages 229–236. On page 233 of this article, Ayres and Heuett identify their research design as "a pretest/post-test control group design." Explain this type of design and how it was applied to this study. Your explanation should include design elements (comparison groups, random assignment, and pretests) that were used. Identify the type of design it is (preexperimental, quasi-experimental, or true experimental), and explain the strengths and weaknesses of this particular design. How did they use placebo and control groups? Were these groups given access to treatment following the study's conclusion?

2. Select an area of communication that you find interesting. For this area, construct a hypothesis, identifying the variables with their conceptual and operational definitions, and a design that would permit you to test your prediction.

12 Content Analysis

Introduction

In this chapter, you will learn how to conduct content analysis. This discovery paradigm method focuses on message types or message characteristics, not on the communicators who send and receive messages. Following the research as argument model, you will learn to construct explanatory and predictive claims about the specific aspects of messages in particular contexts. We will consider the appropriate data sources for content analyses, and how you can select representative samples from message populations. You will learn to divide textual data into units of analysis and how to place those units into categories of a predetermined coding scheme. Depending on your claim, you may want to compare the frequency with which messages occur in different categories as a final step in your data analysis. You'll learn the statistical tests for those comparisons in Chapters 15 and 16. In the next section of this chapter, we will show you how to apply the warrants for content analysis: You will learn to assess the reliability of your coders' message unitizing and categorizing decisions, the content validity of your coding scheme, and the external validity of your data sample. We conclude this chapter by looking at some ethical issues for content analysis.

Learning Outcomes

After completing this chapter you should be able to:

» Develop your own explanatory and predictive claims that are well-suited for investigation with content analysis.

» Identify and locate representative samples of textual data that can be used to investigate a content analytic claim.

» Create a coding scheme that can be used to place units of textual data into discrete categories (and/ or identify a suitable coding scheme from previously published theory and research);

» Evaluate the face and content validity of a coding scheme.

» Unitize and categorize textual data (i.e., divide texts or messages into operational units and place each unit into a single category of a coding scheme).

» Work with another person to calculate intercoder reliability estimates for your unitizing and categorizing decisions.

» Use raw frequency data (or percentages) in each category of your coding scheme to make initial inferences about your claim.

Outline

Imagine that you want to understand a common type of message, like TV news, Facebook, or video games. You might be interested in how TV coverage of political campaigns affects voting (Benoit, 2003; Druckman, 2004). Or you might wonder how race is represented in television news (Dixon & Azocar, 2006). You might wonder how humor works in Facebook status updates (Carr, Shrock & Dauterman, 2013), or you could be curious about gender representations or profanity in video games (Ivory, 2006; Ivory, Williams, Martin & Consalvo, 2009). Content analysis will allow you to use textual data to make inferences about all of those messages, and more.

Content analysis is primarily a quantitative method of categorizing and comparing messages in specific contexts (Bereleson, 1952; Krippendorf, 2004; Neuendorf, 2002). It is especially prevalent among scholars of mass communication, where it has been "one of the most popular methods in top communication journals during the past quarter-century" (Conway, 2006, p. 186).

The textual data you will most likely select for content analysis is narrative discourse. **Narrative discourse** is "characterized by relatively fixed source-receiver roles" (Smith, 1988, p. 257). For example, public speeches are characterized by fixed roles because the speaker does all of the talking, and the audience typically just listens until the speech is over. The speaker is the source; the audience members are the receivers. Audiotaped or videotaped speeches are the physical records of narrative discourse. Speeches are often studied using content analysis. But far more common to content analytic studies are the texts produced or distributed by the mass media, including advertisements, newspaper stories and editorials, radio and television programs, films, websites, blogs and Tweets. By contrast, **interactive discourse**—in which the responsibility for speaking and listening is shared more equally among all participants—is more suitable for conversation analysis or experimental research methods, the focus of Chapter 8 and Chapter 14, respectively. Conversation and discourse analysts typically make interpretive or critical claims about how participants understand one another and coordinate their actions on a turn-by-turn basis (Schegloff, 2006; Sigman, Sullivan, & Wendell, 1988). Experimental researchers who study interactive discourse usually aim to explain and predict the causes of particular conversational behaviors and/or the effects of those behaviors (e.g., Burleson, Holmstrom & Gilstrap, 2005).

Content analytic research fits the epistemological assumptions of the discovery paradigm (see Table 2.2 for a review). Namely, content analysts believe that the nature of messages can be discovered by any careful knower through precise, systematic, repetitive observations. The goal of content analytic research is to sort messages into categories and compare the frequency with which different categories of messages occur. For example, Benoit (2003) collected presidential candidates' messages from television ads, campaign debates, and public speeches that spanned 62 candidates, from 1948 to 2000. He sorted the messages into two themes, talk about policy and talk about character. Benoit's (2003) analysis fits the discovery paradigm in several ways: First, his hypothesis was based on prior theory and research; second, he compared the relative proportions of policy and character discourse for campaign winners and losers; and third, his article is organized as a research report. Benoit's (2003) study also fits the assumption of discovery paradigm that researchers should aim to produce generalizable conclusions about communication, in this case, what sort of discourse makes voters elect the president. Content analysis is often used to study the content of political communications (e.g., Barnhurst, 2003; Benoit, 2003; Lasswell, 1927; Schenck-Hamlin, Procter, & Rumsey, 2000).

Before we look more closely at the claims content analysis can be used to support, let's briefly consider the history of this important method. Over 300 years ago, in Sweden, a group of scholars and clergy first used content analysis to examine a collection of 90 hymns called the *Songs of Zion*. The *Songs* were popular but controversial because they were not from the established hymnbook of the Swedish church. Critics charged that the *Songs* were blasphemous. To settle the controversy, the scholars and clergy members identified and counted the religious symbols in the *Songs* and compared them to the symbols used in the state-approved hymnal. When they found no significant differences between the symbols used in the *Songs* and the symbols used in the state-sanctioned hymnal, the researchers concluded that the *Songs of Zion* were acceptable alternatives to the established church music (Krippendorf, 2004).

From this beginning, content analysis was recognized as a legitimate way of analyzing the content of communication. In the early 1900s, as newspaper production and distribution in the United States expanded, so did the number of content analytic studies. Those early studies tracked the topics covered in the news and often described the amount of physical space devoted to a topic in terms of the number of column inches devoted to that topic. Later in the twentieth century, as radio, movies, and television grew more accessible and popular, so did the number of studies using content analysis. Today, you still will find content analytic studies of newspaper, television, film and radio discourse published in communication journals and presented at our professional association meetings. But you also will find more and more analyses of digital content (e.g., Ivory et al., 2009; Thackeray, Burton, Giraud-Carrier, Rollins & Draper, 2013).

The earliest content analytic studies in the United States were used mostly by journalists and other mass communications practitioners to evaluate and improve journalistic practice and to identify propaganda or unethical sources of influence. But the onset of World War II brought content analysis to bear on issues of national security. The Federal Communications Commission "relied primarily on domestic enemy broadcasts to understand and predict events within Nazi Germany" (Krippendorf, 2004, p. 16). For example, analyzing the speeches given by German leaders helped researchers accurately predict Germany's weapon production and use. Comparing the music played on different radio stations allowed US allies to gauge degrees of change in the troops amassed on the European continent. Charting the frequency of communication between Japan and various island bases helped to predict new operations planned between Germany and its allies. In the United States, content analyses of newspaper editorials and other print matter were accepted as evidence in court trials of suspected subversives (Krippendorf, 2004, pp. 5–10).

Indeed, there are modern parallels to those early content analyses conducted during World War II. You may be familiar with the controversy over journalists being embedded with US troops during our country's invasion and occupation of Iraq, beginning in 2003. Michel Haigh, then a doctoral student at the University of Oklahoma, along with her professor and students in a Joint Department of Defense class, examined the *Washington Post, New York Times, Los Angeles Times*, and *Chicago Tribune's* coverage of the war to see if coverage by embedded and nonembedded reporters was any different, and if so, how? In fact, their study did show significant differences in overall tone toward the military, trust in military personnel, framing, and authoritativeness between embedded and nonembedded reporters' articles (Haigh et al., 2006). The class also analyzed ABC, CBS, NBC, and CNN news coverage of the occupation and invasion and again found that embedded reporters generally depicted the US military more positively than the nonembedded reporters did (Haigh et al., 2005; 2006).

For over 70 years, then, content analysis has been the primary research method used to analyze newspaper articles and editorials, talk radio, television, film, and Internet content in order to explain and predict trends in coverage (e.g., Babor, Xuan, Damon & Noel, 2013;

Chang-Hoan & Hongsik, 2005; Druckman, 2004; Haigh et al., 2005, 2006; Ivory, 2006; Ivory et al., 2009; Kerbel & Bloom, 2005). All of these studies—from song lyrics, beer ads, and video games, to trends in how issues are covered in print and broadcast media or on the Internet—involve analyzing the content of narrative discourse.

Now that you know something about the history and scope of content analysis, let's look at specific claims you might want to investigate.

Content Analytic Claims: Explaining and Predicting Message Characteristics

Content analysts seek to explain and predict textual data by discovering how often certain kinds of messages occur in a specific context. Some content analytic studies aim to evaluate message characteristics in particular contexts, but those studies are based on explaining and predicting message frequencies, so they best fit the discovery paradigm assumption that there is one observable reality that can be known by any careful, systematic observer. Those studies usually employ some kind of statistical analysis and they are presented as research reports.

For example, Babor, et al. (2013) "evaluated advertising code violations using the US Beer Institute guidelines for responsible advertising" (p. e45). As in many industries, alcohol producers have developed voluntary standards about how they will market products, like the type of content they will portray in ads, or to whom those ads will be targeted. Babor et al. asked 15 public health professionals to rate the beer commercials that were broadcast in national markets during NCAA basketball games between 1999 and 2008. The purposes of the study were to "estimate the prevalence of content code violations in beer ads," and to "determine which sections of the code were violated most often, and whether one producer's ads were more likely to contain violations than others" (p. e46). All three elements of the claim are explanatory (i.e., whether the alcohol industry is following its own voluntary standards).

Some content analytic studies aim to go beyond explaining messages, and actually use messages to predict people's behaviors. For instance, Robinson, Turner, Levine and Tian (2011) tracked messages in a web-based interaction system between health-care providers (HCP)

and Native Americans who had recently been diagnosed with diabetes. The researchers wanted to assess the impact of person-centered communication (i.e., "messages uniquely developed and sent out to the individual" p. 128) on patients logging on to the web-based monitoring system. They also posed a research question, "What types of messages will best predict frequency of patient blood glucose monitoring?" (p. 128). Explaining and predicting HCP-patient interactions obviously has important implications for effective healthcare delivery.

But a vast number of message contexts have been studied with content analysis. We've already talked about content analyses that addressed newspaper stories, advertisements and political speeches. As we briefly mentioned, there also are a wealth of content analytic studies devoted to digital communication content (e.g., Chang-Hoan & Hongsik, 2005; Ivory, 2006; Ivory et al., 2009; Kerbel & Bloom, 2005; C. M. Stewart, Shields, & Sen, 1998; Thackeray et al., 2013; Wahl, McBride, & Schrodt, 2005; Weatherby & Scoggins, 2005–2006). The growth of health communication research over the past two decades has included content analyses of health care messages (e.g., Andsager & Smiley, 1998; Andsager & Powers, 2001; Anderson, 2001; Bannerjee, Greene, Hecht, Magsamen-Conrad, & Elek, 2013; Barker, 1998; Cegala, McGee, & McNeilis, 1996; Lesser, Zimmerman & Cohen, 2013; Thackeray et al., 2013). But you can find content analytic studies of just about any communication context, because narrative discourse exists in most every context. Table 12.1 contains some sample content analytic claims, most from published research studies; however, the last research question, and the last two hypotheses shown in that table, are claims that research methods students at San Francisco State University explored with content analysis during fall 2013.

Explaining message characteristics in different contexts is helpful for several reasons. A. J. Johnson, Smith, Mitchell, Orrego, and Yun (1999) pointed out some of these reasons in their content analytic study of television talk show experts: "These findings are designed to inform better those who create the shows, those who watch the shows, and those who critique the shows, the content and composition of the show. It also provides evidence for or against many claims made about experts and talk shows. . . ." (p. 94). Thus, the general claim of A. J. Johnson et al.'s (1999) study can be stated as "The content of televised talk shows is. . . ." However, A. J. Johnson et al. examined several specific

Table 12.1 Sample Content Analytic Claims

Research Questions (RQs)	Hypothesis (H)
RQ1: How prevalent are advertising code violations in beer ads shown during NCAA basketball games? (Babor et al., 2013) RQ2: "What kind of online messages from a health-care provider will predict frequency with which patients monitor their blood glucose levels?" (Robinson, et al., 2009, p. 128) RQ3: "Are individuals, organizations, or celebrities more likely to tweet about breast cancer during Breast Cancer Awareness Month?" (Thackeray et al., 2013, p. 1) RQ4: How do political campaigns affect voters by "priming" the criteria on which voters base their decisions? (Druckman, 2004) RQ5: "Are there more alcohol and tobacco advertisements in the Mission or Marina District of San Francisco?" (Foster, Hatcher & Lee, 2013, p. 1)	H1: "Presidential candidates who discuss policy more than their opponent(s) are more likely to win elections" (Benoit, 2003, p. 102). H2: Men swear more often than women do on prime-time television programs (Sapolsky & Kaye, 2005). H3: The horoscopes published in magazines that target working women depend more on the women's socioeconomic class than they do on the readers' zodiac signs (Evans, 1996). H4: "Expressive speech acts are the most frequently posted type of speech act in social network site status update messages" (Carr, Shrock, & Dauterman, 2012, p. 181). H5: "The number of person-centered messages received by their HCP positively predicts patients' login activities to a telemedicine system" (Robinson et al., 2011, p. 128). H6: "Community newspapers distributed in the Mission District feature stories which highlight a wider array of political and world issues than those in the Noe Valley neighborhood" (Alhammouri, Price, Siordia & Wexler, 2013, p. 2). H7: Takeout menus in the Marina District are more expensive to produce than takeout menus in the Mission District" (Abrahms, Barnes, Cruz & Nunez, 2013, p. 3).

research questions, so their claims can be further specified as:

1. The *issues* covered by television talk show experts are (e.g., family relationships, self-improvement, crime/safety).
2. The *qualifications* of television talk show experts are (e.g., PhD, health official, self-proclaimed).
3. The *nature of advice* given by television talk show experts is (e.g., specific or nonspecific).

Content analysts usually seek "to infer the effects of the messages that they have analyzed, although actual data about such communication effects are seldom available" (Rogers, 1994, p. 215). When we infer the effects of messages, we are offering an explanation after the fact. But content analyses can be used to support predictive claims. For instance, in political communication research, predictions about media usage, priming effects on voting behavior, and the like are often inferred from content analyses. In those cases, content analysts make explanatory and predictive claims simultaneously.

Anytime you study communication using textual data, you have to deal with the fact that there are layers of meaning in every message. In content analysis, those layers are divided into two types: manifest content and latent content. **Manifest content** meanings are, "those that are evident on the surface" (Clarke, 1999b, p. 63). Manifest meanings are apparent to just about anyone who encounters the message. But **latent content** meanings are those "below the threshold of superficial observation" (Merton, 1968, p. 105). To briefly illustrate the difference, consider the typical beer commercials you might see while watching college athletics on television. Quite often, you will see attractive people socializing, while a voiceover associates the beer with good times. The manifest content of most beer ads, then, is that beer is a refreshing beverage that complements almost any gathering. But there are innumerable latent meanings to those ads. For example, you might not notice that some of the people who appear to be drinking beer in the ads are underage, or that the ad content includes "symbols, language, or music considered to be appealing 'primarily to persons under the legal purchase age'" (Babor et al., 2013, p. e48). Babor et al. found that "ads with content violations were broadcast on average about twice as often as ads without violations" and that Anheuser-Busch had the most content violations.

If your claim about textual data goes beyond explaining and predicting message content to evaluating that content and suggesting how it should be reformed, you probably will want to know more about the interpretive rhetorical and critical methodologies outlined in Chapters 8–10 of this book.

Now that you have a sense of the claims you can explore with content analysis, let's move to the next element of the research-as-argument model, the data.

Data for Content Analysis

Because content analyses best fit the assumptions of the discovery paradigm, you will be trying to develop replicable explanations of communication with content analysis. In other words, another scholar could select a similar set of messages, unitize and categorize them in the same way that you did, thus replicating your analysis. To make replication possible, you should employ random selection methods and similar analytic strategies. (Refer back to Chapter 11 for details about random selection methods and their value in discovery paradigm studies.)

In this section, you will learn how to define a message population and select a representative sample of messages for content analysis. You also will learn to develop and use coding schemes. In Chapter 15, you will learn how to analyze your findings using descriptive frequencies and percentages, along with bar graphs and pie charts. In Chapter 16, you will learn to use chi-square and cross-tabs analyses to test your predictions. Both chi-square and cross-tabs are statistical tests that measure the goodness of fit between expected and observed distributions of message categories.

In the last section of this chapter, we will show you how to assess the consistency of your unitizing and categorizing decisions, since intercoder reliability is a primary warrant for content analysis. The sequence of operations for content analysis is outlined in Table 12.2.

Table 12.2 Steps for Conducting Content Analysis

1. State your explanatory and predictive claim(s) about message characteristics and their relative frequency of occurrence as either research questions or hypotheses.
2. Identify the unit of analysis into which you will divide textual data (i.e., physical, syntactical, categorical, or thematic).
3. Define the message population to which you hope your results will be generalized.
4. Find an existing coding scheme, or develop your own coding categories into which messages will be sorted. Ask your professor (or another expert) to help you assess the face and content validity of your coding scheme.
5. Select a representative sample of texts from the population, using one of the random selection methods or quota selection. If your message population is small, you may be able to study all the messages in the population.
6. Using only a small portion of your data, have at least one other coder (besides yourself) divide the textual data into units of analysis. Work independently at this step.
7. Assess the reliability of your *unitizing* decisions: Do you and the other coder consistently identify the same units in the data sample? If so, proceed to the next step. If you and your coders cannot reliably unitize the data at this step, retrain the coder, and/or revise your unit of analysis, so that you can reliably unitize the text with at least 70% agreement between you and the other coder.
8. Using the same small portion of your sample data from Step 6 (except that the texts have now been divided into units of analysis), have coders independently assign each data unit to one category of your coding scheme.
9. Assess the consistency of your *categorizing* decisions: Do you and the other coder(s) consistently categorize units the same way? If so, proceed to the next step. If you cannot reliably categorize the messages, either retrain your coder or revise your coding scheme so that you can reliably sort messages into categories with at least 70% agreement between you and the other coder.
10. Once you have established reliable unitizing and coding, you may unitize and categorize all of your sample data, either by yourself or sharing the work with other trained coders (aka research assistants).
11. Summarize the frequency with which units occur in each category of your coding scheme. Use a table, bar chart, or pie chart to visually represent the distribution of messages across your coding categories. Use these frequency data to make initial inferences about your research questions/hypotheses.
12. If you want to infer relationships among, or differences between, categories, compare the frequencies with which messages from different categories occur. You will compare the distribution of messages across categories observed in your data to the distribution you expected to observe (e.g., no difference in category frequencies).

Selecting a Representative Sample of Messages

Content analysis begins when you select a representative sample of textual data. If you are successful at representing a population of messages, then your results can be applied to the entire population of messages, not just the texts used in your study. To clarify how you might select appropriate texts for content analysis, let's begin by reviewing the concept of random selection. As you already know from Chapter 11, a population is a "comprehensive and well-defined group (a universal set) of the elements pertinent to a given research question or hypothesis" (Smith, 1988, p. 77). A **message population**, then, is a well-defined set of messages pertinent to a given research question or hypothesis. Just as the US population is defined by the Census Bureau, a population of particular kinds of messages must be defined by the researcher. For instance, Stern (2005) saw popular films as a potential influence on American teens' attitudes toward and initiation of substance abuse. Stern defined the message population as top-grossing films, because those films were likely to be seen by the greatest number of teens. Next, she identified 375 top-grossing films from the Nielsen ratings for 1999, 2000, and 2001. Then, "films that featured at least one teenager (ages 12–19) as a central character were isolated for inclusion in the sample" (Stern, 2005, p. 337). Forty-three films fit all of Stern's criteria and thus comprised the message population for her study.

A *representative* sample is a subset of population elements that has been "selected in such a way that it reflects well the characteristics of its parent population" (Smith, 1988, p. 78). The best way to ensure that a data sample represents the population from which it is selected is to give every element an equal chance to be included in the sample. If you use one of the random selection methods outlined in Chapter 11, you will be most likely to select elements that represent the population. You also will decrease the chance of selecting biased elements (i.e., elements that represent some, but not all, of the relevant population characteristics).

As you can imagine, an enormous array of message populations may be defined based on your research question or hypothesis. The two most important considerations when selecting a message population are the time frame for your study and the medium in which the messages appear. First, let's consider the time frame. If your claims address current issues, then you will want to work with texts that are produced now. For example, Babor et al.'s (2013) analysis of beer commercials in NCAA basketball games used ads that were broadcast between 1999 and 2008, and the authors used the 1997 and 2006 versions of the Beer Institute Code, voluntary standards set by the beer industry to regulate alcohol marketing. On the other hand, if your claim is about historical meanings of particular messages, then you will want to work with texts that were produced during the time frame relevant to your topic (e.g., Niquette & Buxton's 1997 analysis of print cartoons depicting nineteenth century world's fair visitors). Of course, you will also need to think about how frequently new content is produced or distributed. If your claim addresses an issue relevant to journalism, for example, you will want to consider the fact that newspapers are produced daily, or weekly, whereas broadcast news is produced hourly, or even continuously. If you ignore the production schedule for your message population, you're likely to select a sample of messages that does not represent the parent population.

The second dimension of defining a message population is the medium in which messages appear. Because mediated messages are so prevalent in society, they are a common source of data for content analysis. Those message populations tend to be defined by the type of media outlet, such as newspaper, television, radio, film, or the Internet. A population of messages within one media outlet may be further refined by considering genres or types of content. Just as the time frame for your message population depends on how time is relevant to your claim, defining a genre of messages depends on your research question or hypothesis. First, you may want to select one or more specific media outlets for your study. For example, if your claim addresses newspaper journalism, it won't be practical for you to examine every newspaper in the United States. But you may have reason to select specific titles, like the *New York Times*. Similarly, if your claim deals with Twitter messages, you won't be able to study them all! But you might isolate tweets on a particular topic (#BCAM, Thackeray et al., 2013) or tweets sent by celebrities with the largest number of followers (e.g., Katy Perry, Lady Gaga, or Justin Bieber).

A vast number of content analytic studies are contributing to our understanding of the nature of digitally mediated communication and its impact on society (e.g., Honeycutt, 2001; Kerbel & Bloom, 2005; Rossler, 2001; Wahl et al., 2005; Weatherby & Scoggins, 2005–2006). "Newspaper accounts, public opinion polls, corporate reports, files in government archives—all are now linked into networks that can be analyzed from numerous positions" (Krippendorf, 2004, p. xx). Like other media sources, the population of electronic texts can be further defined by type, such as email, listservs, discussion groups, chat rooms, blogs, Tweets and websites, as well as other distinctions of content or subject matter (e.g., support groups have their own blogs, listservs, etc.). Comparative content analyses of electronically mediated and face-to-face messages can help us assess the different uses and benefits of these different media (e.g., Honeycutt, 2001; C. R. Scott & Fontenot, 1999).

The second strategy to refine your selection of a particular medium, then, is to consider the genre or type of content. For example, within any newspaper, you can find articles, editorials, advertisements, and cartoons. On television, programs feature news, drama, comedy, and reality shows. Commercials appear on almost every channel, regardless of the program type. Even within one genre, such as comedy, there are situation comedies,

satires, stand-up monologues, animated series, and comedic variety shows. Again, you need to decide what is relevant for inclusion in your sample. Your topic may further delineate the message population if you are especially interested in mediated portrayals of gender, ethnicity, culture, etc. (e.g., Beasley & Standley, 2002; Billings, Halone, & Denham, 2002; Ivory, 2006; Nelson & Paek, 2005; Taylor & Bang, 1997). The best way to begin to define your message population is to ask yourself this question: "Once I have finished this study, where do I hope that my findings will be applied?" The population you need to represent is the one you hope your findings will address. Your selection decisions will all determine how your data sample is relevant to your claim.

Whether you are interested in analyzing digital or print media, there are many sources from which to sample message populations. Table 12.3 lists a number

Table 12.3 Examples of Message Populations Used for Content Analysis

Media sources:
- Newspaper stories (e.g., Druckman, 2005; Keshishian, 1997; McComas & Shanahan, 1999; Ramsey, 1999; Zoch & Turk, 1998)
- Magazine content (e.g., Clarke, 1999a; Deveau & Fouts, 2004; Evans, 1996; Nelson & Paek, 2005; Taylor & Bang, 1997)
- Films (e.g., Ramasubramanian, 2005; Stern, 2005; Weaver, 1991)
- Personal advertisements (e.g., Hatala, Baack, & Parmenter, 1998)
- Public health campaign messages (e.g., Apollonio & Malone, 2009; Bannerjee, et al., 2013)
- Song lyrics and music videos (e.g., Gow, 1996; Kubrin, 2005; McKee & Pardun, 1996)
- Television commercials (e.g., Babor et al., 2013; Cheng, 1997; Larson, 2001; Lin, 1997; Roy & Harwood, 1997)
- Television characters (e.g., Lichter, Lichter, & Amundson, 1997; Matabane & Merritt, 1996; Scharrer, 2001)

Surveys filled out by participants:
- Open-ended questionnaires (e.g., Chang-Hoan & Hongsik, 2005; Fiebig & Kramer, 1998; Hess, 2000)
- Health care patients' critical incident descriptions (e.g., C. M. Anderson, 2001; Ruben, 1993)
- Interaction diaries (e.g., Dainton, 1998)

Digital messages:
- Blogs (e.g., Kerbel & Bloom, 2005)
- CMC discussion groups (e.g., Honeycutt, 2001; C. M. Stewart, Shields, & Sen, 1998)
- Email messages (e.g., Robinson, Turner, Levine & Tian, 2009; Pragg, Wiseman, Cody, & Wendt, 1999)
- Facebook (e.g., Carr, et al., 2012)
- Twitter (Greer & Ferguson, 2011; Lewis, Zamith & Hermida, 2013; Thackeray, et al., 2013; Waters & Jamal. 2011)
- Video games & game reviews (e.g., Ivory, 2006; Ivory et al., 2009)
- Websites (e.g., Chan-Olmstead & Park, 2000; Wahl, McBride, & Schrodt, 2005; Weatherby & Scoggins, 2005–2006)
- Web-based interaction (Robinson, Turner, Levine & Tian, 2011)

Other sources:
- Coffee shop bulletin board postings (Kang, Maxwell, Reuther & Salazar, 2013)
- Jury deliberations (e.g., Sunwolf & Seibold, 1998)
- Audiotaped group discussions of HIV/AIDS (e.g., Pittman & Gallois, 1997)
- Semistructured, open-ended interviews (e.g., Graham, 1997)
- President speeches, campaign debates, and television ads (Benoit, 2003)

of message samples used in published content analyses. These examples are grouped according to their sources.

Collecting Texts

Once you have developed your selection method and defined a population of messages from which to draw your data sample, you can begin collecting texts. If your definition of the population is valid and if you select messages using some element of random chance then you should be able to select a representative sample of messages.

There are two ways to go about collecting texts. The traditional way of collecting texts for content analysis involved hand-on work with the original medium. For example, if you wanted to analyze what public health campaign messages appear in different neighborhoods of your city, you could walk or drive through the neighborhoods, taking photos of the messages you find. If you used a digital camera or mobile phone to snap the pictures, you would amass a sample of messages suitable for content analysis.

Today, most mass-media messages are readily available in digital formats. Furthermore, increasing amounts of content that was initially produced in print formats are being digitized. For example, Google recently won a lawsuit establishing their use of Google Books as fair use under US copyright law (Gershman & Trachtenberg, November 14, 2013). Thus, many books that were only available in print form are now searchable by keyword, and some of them are available in digital formats. Digitization greatly simplifies the task of collecting texts for content analysis. Entering keywords into a database search engine can eliminate a great deal of tedious hand searching, and may increase the reliability of selection decisions that human coders would otherwise make (Conway, 2006; Lewis et al., 2013).

Of course, you may want to analyze texts that are not yet digitized. If so, you will have to either capture those texts using digital photography (e.g., subway graffiti), or scan print documents into digital files. If you want to analyze the content of verbal interactions, you may need to transcribe the data into digital files. In that case, you will want to review the advice from Chapter 8, "Conversation and Discourse Analysis," about transcription practices. Once you have a collection of texts in digital format, you are ready to prepare your data for content analysis.

Data Treatment for Content Analysis

Content analysis proceeds in two phases: unitizing and categorizing bits of textual data. Both phases involve reducing complex, qualitative information into simplified themes or categories. When you plan to perform statistical analysis of those data, you will apply some kind of numerical code to those categories. Content analysts refer to both phases as coding the data.

In the first phase of coding, called **unitizing**, you divide texts into whatever **units of analysis** are relevant to your claim. For example, that could mean dividing newspaper articles into words, sentences, paragraphs, thematically coherent phrases, or passages. In the second coding phase, you **categorize** the data, assigning each unit to one category of a coding scheme. Typically, two coders work independently to unitize and categorize a small portion of the data, so that they can assess the percentage of agreement across their decisions, or intercoder reliability. You will learn about intercoder reliability in the warrants section of this chapter. Coding data is the most time consuming and tedious part of a content analysis, although using computers "can cut hours of human coding and analysis into seconds or minutes" (Conway, 2006, p. 186). Let's consider each step in detail.

Unitizing Messages

Content analysis actually begins when identify units of analysis. Unitizing textual data allows you to reduce complex messages to simpler categories, first isolating the features of text that are most relevant to your claim. Once you have identified these simpler units of analysis, you can place each unit into a single category of a coding scheme. Then, you will be able to compare the frequency with which particular message features occur in a data sample.

The first question to ask is, "What do I need to know about each message?" Krippendorf (2004) identified five potential units of analysis. Each of those units is defined and illustrated in Table 12.4.

The simplest units of analysis to isolate are based on physical or syntactic distinctions (Krippendorf, 2004). First, *physical distinctions* define content in terms of some physical medium, such as the amount of space or time given particular content. Counting how many lines of a transcript are devoted to a topic, or what number of column inches are allotted for a newspaper article, are examples of physical units for content

Table 12.4 Unitizing Textual Data for Content Analysis (Krippendorf, 2004)

Units of Analysis	Definition	Examples
Physical distinctions	The amount of space or time devoted to particular content	Column inches in a newspaper Amount of time devoted to a radio phone-in topic Position of television news story: Lead or not lead (Druckman, 2004)
Syntactical distinctions	Individual words, phrases, or sentences or individual images	Number of Tweets by unique users (Thackeray et al., 2013) Mentions of "wealth" in newspaper stories about any of three political candidates (Conway, 2006) Each sentence in a message sent by a healthcare provider to a patient (Robinson et al., 2011)
Categorical distinctions	Segments of text that share some important aspect (e.g., written by certain type of persons, written about certain places or things)	TV talk show "expert" qualifications: PhD, justice or health official, author, or self-proclaimed (Johnson et al., 1999) Presence/absence of profanity in video-game dialogue, background music & game text (Ivory et al., 2009)
Propositional distinctions	Sentence clauses	Mentions of gubernatorial candidate's Hispanic ethnicity (Conway, 2006) Expressive speech acts in Facebook status updates (Carr et al., 2013)
Thematic distinctions	Identifies topics within textual units based on their subjective meanings	Presidential candidates' *policy talk* and *character talk* (Benoit, 2003)

analysis. By themselves, physical distinctions do not reveal anything about the meaning of the text, but they may reveal something about the significance of the topic. For instance, Thackeray et al.'s (2013) analysis of tweets during breast cancer awareness month (BCAM) revealed more than 1.3 million tweets, most sent during the first few days of BCAM.

Syntactical distinctions also do not require us to judge the meaning of texts (Krippendorf, 2004). *Syntactical distinctions* define content units as discrete bits of text, such as individual words, phrases, or sentences for linguistic texts, or individual symbols for visual texts (Krippendorf, 2004). For example, Thackeray et al. (2013) used a series of key words (like "pink ribbon" and "mammogram") to obtain breast cancer tweets during BCAM. But human coders can also work with syntactic distinctions (e.g., while watching college athletics, notice how many fans are wearing the school colors of each team). If you are conducting your very first content analytic study, you probably will be able to achieve reliable unitizing decisions with either physical or syntactical

units of analysis. In other words, you and one other coder probably can divide your textual data into units of analysis with a high rate of agreement about how many units exist in your data sample. Of course, computers can divide textual data into syntactic units of analysis with perfect reliability (Conway, 2006). For example, computational methods have been used to examine Twitter feeds about certain topics (e.g., Thackeray et al., 2013, on breast cancer awareness month) or events (e.g., Papacharissi & de Fatima Oliveira, 2012, on the 2011 Arab Spring). Computers make it possible to analyze much larger data sets (aka big data). But analyzing a great deal of data is only helpful when your analysis is both consistent and accurate. For that reason, "blending computational and manual methods throughout the content analysis process may yield more fruitful results" (Lewis, Zamith & Hermida, 2013, p. 34).

However, you may want to analyze message content in ways that go beyond physical and syntactical distinctions. If so, then reliably dividing your data into units of analysis and putting those units into categories will be considerably more difficult and will require at least some decision-making by human coders. Krippendorf (2004) identified three other kinds of units for content analysis: categorical, propositional, and thematic distinctions.

Categorical distinctions divide texts into units that share some important aspect, such as the characteristics of their authors, the types of events described, or the types of issues discussed. The importance of any one type will depend on your claim. For example, if we analyzed your instructors' teaching evaluation comments, we could categorize all the references to your instructor by title, including "she," "Dr. X," "Professor X," or "the one who lectures." The resulting coding scheme would be a taxonomy (or classification scheme) of different ways of referring to a teacher. We could then compare the relative frequency of different forms of reference.

Propositional distinctions reduce complex sentences into smaller elements. At the simplest level, all sentences have a subject, verb, and object. But sentences also contain short phrases, called clauses, where the meaning depends on the linguistic construction of the clause. Roberts (1989, as cited in Krippendorf, 2004) identified four such clauses:

> A *perception* clause describes an activity (e.g., "Business-people vote predominantly Republican"). A *recognition* clause classifies a phenomenon as belonging (or not belonging) in a category (e.g., "He is a politician," or "This is not a scientific statement"). A *justification* clause classifies a phenomenon as reasonable or unreasonable, and an *evaluation* clause asserts how well a phenomenon fits a particular category. (p. 106)

First, let's consider an example using humor as a form of linguistic construction. When we find something humorous, it's often because we understand a certain form or pattern of delivery. Anecdotes, puns and one-liners are examples of propositional distinctions because the elements that make up these linguistic structures have certain, known semantic relationships to one another. For example, the first four turns of a "knock-knock" joke are recognizable to most speakers of the English language (i.e., "Knock-knock," "Who's there?" "Will this," Will this who?"). The last turn of the joke depends on some unexpected response to the third turn (e.g., "Will this be on the test?"). This example shows how important it is that you understand the syntax and semantics of the language you are analyzing when your unit of analysis is propositional. If you cannot recognize the parts of a complex assertion, then

you will not be able to reliably unitize or categorize your data. Here, computer-assisted content analysis is even less helpful: "Computers are best at counting words but cannot find an assertion" (Conway, 2006, p. 192).

Now think about another message you probably find familiar, the Facebook status update. What kind of speech acts do people use when updating their status? Carr et al. (2013) used propositional distinctions to code Facebook status updates posted by college students during a 2-week period.

> Status update messages were categorized into their component speech acts, because single status updates could contain more than one sentence and a sentence could contain more than one speech act. For example, a status update could read, "I've got a headache from last night, but I'm going to class anyway." In that status update there are two speech acts, the first referring to "a headache from last night," the second denoting the writer as "going to class." (Carr et al., 2010, p. 184)

The authors hypothesized that expression of feelings would be the most common speech act in those messages. Two people independently coded all the status updates, and they were able to consistently identify the same propositional units, the speech acts.

Of course, propositional distinctions also identify units of analysis in other research methodologies, such as conversation analysis, which you already learned something about in Chapter 8, "Conversation & Discourse Analysis." Briefly, if you wanted to analyze conversational data, your transcript of two people talking to one another might be divided into propositional units comprised of three sequential turns at talk, starting with Person A's utterance, but also including Person B's response, and A's acceptance or rejection of B's response.

Finally, *thematic distinctions* are used to divide texts into units based on the topics the text addresses. Themes are often identified within messages of a certain type, such as Benoit's (2003) two themes for presidential campaign discourse: policy talk and character talk. (Notice that this theme could be explored using newspaper, television, and advertising discourse; that is, across genres). Thematic distinctions afford rich descriptions of textual data: For example, you could analyze parents' emails to their college-aged students for the kinds of supportive messages the emails contain, such as instrumental, emotional, and material assistance. However, because thematic distinctions rely on subjective meanings, they are the hardest units to identify consistently and accurately.

In fact, Krippendorf (2004) noted that these five units of analysis can be organized from least to most complex: physical, syntactical, categorical, propositional, and thematic. Physical units are the easiest units to code reliably, but they may be of least interest if you want to explain the meaning of words as they are used in context. The opposite is true of thematic units; they may provide the most substantial data if you want to explore meanings, but at the same time, it is quite difficult to achieve consistent unitizing decisions.

Depending on your claim, you may need to divide your data into progressively smaller, more specific units of analysis. Let's consider an example from published research. In a study of how juvenile offenders from different racial groups were represented on Los Angeles, California, television news programs, Dixon and Azocar (2006) selected 205 television news programs from various channels, days, and times, all broadcast in the same two-year period. They recruited 10 undergraduate students, four White, four African American, one Latino, and one Asian to serve as coders. After an initial training session, the coders worked individually, each one viewing a randomly selected news program and dividing the text of that program into progressively more specific units of analysis. The three specific units were the crime stories themselves, then the race and juvenile status of the person accused of the crime.

First, the coders had to isolate the crime stories from all the rest of the content in the news program. They included only stories about crimes that are tracked by the US and California Justice Departments (e.g., murder, arson, robbery), and they eliminated all the news stories that were not about those kinds of crimes. The next unitizing decision that coders made was the race of the person accused of committing a crime, the perpetrator:

> Race included four categories: Black, White, Latino, and Other (e.g., Asian). All information contained in a news story was used to determine the race of perpetrators portrayed. These race indicators included (a) shown on videotape, (b) mug shot shown, (c) artist's sketch shown, (d) photo shown, and (e) race is stated. (Dixon & Azocar, 2006, p. 149)

Finally, coders had to determine the juvenile status of the accused perpetrators, as "over 18" or "under 18" years old.

> Coders were asked to determine the perpetrator's age by noting (a) whether the news story mentioned the suspect's precise age or (b) whether the news story mentioned the suspect's age range. In some cases visual inspection was used to determine the age of suspects. Coders relied strictly on visual inspection or age information stated by reporters in order to determine the age of suspects. (Dixon & Azocar, 2006, p. 149)

The coders could watch a program as many times as they wished to make their unitizing decisions.

As we mentioned in Table 12.2, "Steps for Conducting Content Analysis," after the coders have unitized a small portion of the sample data, you will need to assess whether coders are consistently identifying the same units of analysis (i.e., unitizing reliability). Once Dixon and Azocar's (2006) coders demonstrated their ability to reliably unitize the crime stories, race, and age of perpetrators, they then proceeded to divide all of the sample data into these units of analysis. We address the issue of reliable coding decisions in more detail later in this chapter. But you probably already appreciate, from this one example, how nicely content analysis fits into the discovery paradigm. Dividing textual data into units of analysis is a precise, systematic, and replicable process, one that can be completed by any careful, trained observers. Once you have reliably unitized your textual data, you are ready to begin categorizing those units.

Categorizing Messages

The next step in content analysis is to assign each text, or each unit of data, to its relevant category of your **coding scheme**. A coding scheme is a set of theoretic categories or types of messages. You will systematically examine every piece of text in your data sample in order to isolate its' unit of analysis (i.e., unitizing data) and identify its relevant categories (i.e., categorizing decisions). The process of coding is the same, whether you are working with original documents, print copies, or digitally stored data files.

Raw data is recorded onto standardized coding sheets. Your coding sheet (aka codebook) could come from another researcher's published work, or it could emerge inductively from the texts you collect. You might even combine categories suggested by past research with those you find in your data.

Just as we discussed in the previous section on unitizing data, you will first want to work with at least one other person to assign units of analysis to categories for a small portion of your sample data. This will allow you to check the consistency with which you and the other person assign textual units to the various categories of your coding scheme (i.e., categorizing reliability). In the

Dixon and Azocar (2006) study, for example, the authors had to be sure that their 10 undergraduate coders could agree on which stories were crime stories and which were not, as well as agreeing on the race (i.e., White, African American, Latino, or Asian) and age (i.e., under or over 18) of the accused perpetrators.

You may also need this pilot study of your sample data to test the workability of your prearranged coding scheme or to develop new content categories from your data. Whether your coding scheme is developed by you, or comes from prior research, you will want to make a standardized coding sheet for use by coders as they process the raw data. An example of a standardized coding sheet is provided in Table 12.5.

A Sample Coding Scheme

A. J. Johnson et al.'s (1999) study of television talk show experts provided a reasonably clear illustration of a coding scheme. The researchers measured three variables: First, the *issues* addressed on each talk show, a thematic unit of analysis, were coded into six categories (i.e., abuse, safety/crime, family relationships, romantic relationships,

drugs, and self-improvement or material improvement). Second, the *qualifications* of the talk show experts, a categorical distinction, were coded into four categories (PhD or formally trained, justice or health official, author/editor/teacher, and self-proclaimed/media/other). Finally, the *nature of advice* was categorized as either specific or nonspecific. A. J. Johnson et al. also counted the number of turns in each show and the number of expert turns. "A 'turn' was defined as the number of words spoken by an individual without being interrupted by someone else who then assumes the floor" (A. J. Johnson et al., 1999, p. 95). Thus, proportion of talk time, a physical unit of analysis, became another measure of being an expert. Table 12.5 shows what a standardized coding sheet for the A. J. Johnson et al. study might have looked like.

The process of entering raw data into a codebook is the actual categorizing of your data. By assigning each unit to one category of the coding scheme, you are reducing a complex message to a single idea—that we could code texts that refer to "Dr. So-and-so" as "1"; "Professor So-and-so" as "2"; "First name" as 3; etc. If the unit of analysis refers to some measure like column length or minutes of airtime, then you can code texts

Table 12.5 Standardized Coding Sheet

Program Title: _____
Host Name: _____
Date Program Aired: _____
Name of Expert: _____

Variable	Unit of Analysis	Categories
Issues addressed	Thematic	_____ Abuse _____ Safety/crime _____ Family relationships _____ Romantic relationships _____ Drugs _____ Self-improvement
Expert qualifications	Categorical	_____ PhD or formally trained _____ Justice or health official _____ Author/editor/teacher _____ Self-proclaimed/media/other
Nature of advice given	Thematic	_____ Specific _____ Nonspecific
Number of turns	Physical	_____ Turns in this show _____ Turns by this expert

Source: Constructed by Merrigan and Huston based on A. J. Johnson, Smith, Mitchell, Orrego, and Yun (1999).

with the actual ratio numbers taken during measurement (e.g., 4 column inches; 37 second phone-in call). Ultimately, the data you enter must be relevant to your unit of analysis, and should gather the information needed to test your claim.

There are computer software programs that perform the task of coding data. For example, VBPro is a popular open-source program for coding textual data, and Atlas.ti is a proprietary program. If your sample messages exist in digital format (or if you enter your messages in rich text format), then you may be able to use either of these programs to isolate physical and syntactical units of analysis. Obviously, programs like these can drastically reduce your workload! But software programs for analyzing content also have two important drawbacks. First, you need to understand how the computer software is making decisions when isolating units of text and coding them into categories. Second, you need to decide whether using a computer to unitize and categorize messages will threaten the validity of your content analysis, which is most likely if your analysis depends on the meaning of textual units (i.e., latent message content). Let's look at computer coding decisions first.

When you use computer software for content analysis, unitizing and categorizing phases of coding happen because you enter a list of key words that the computer will look for, either to find units, or to put them into categories. Let's consider two examples that will illustrate how these computer-software programs can be used for doing content analysis.

Andsager and Smiley (1998) used the free, open source software for content analysis called VBPro to first identify the most frequently occurring words in 106 news stories about silicone breast implants, published in six major US newspapers during 1991 through 1992. Andsager and Smiley then used VBPro's advanced statistical procedure, called *hierarchical cluster analysis*, to identify the clusters of terms that tended to occur most closely together in news stories published by three groups (i.e., medical groups, citizen groups, and Dow Corning, the leading global supplier of silicone products). Some of the term clusters they identified were named "Dow investigation," "side effects," and "risks." Andsager and Smiley's (1998) results showed that "Medical groups seemed to have exerted the most influence over news coverage, as shown by the frequency of mentions of terms in their frame." (p. 197). By contrast, citizen activist groups "seem to have had little influence over news coverage" (Andsager & Smiley, 1998, p. 198).

Szavo and Gerevich (2013) used *Atlas.ti 5.0* to examine how people with alcohol dependency used social words, "words referring to social connections" (p. 807). The authors hypothesized that "the frequency and pattern of social word usage typically differ in relapsed and recovered alcohol-dependent persons' autobiographies, thus predicting either a relapse or a recovery" (p. 807). They purposely selected two groups of participants who were similar in all respects except that the people in one group had maintained sobriety for at least two years, whereas participants in the other group had relapsed and received hospital treatment for alcohol dependency within the past year. You will learn more about this strategy of using comparison groups (aka quasi-equivalent groups) in Chapter 15, "Experimental Research." Szavo and Gerevich asked all their participants to write autobiographies, and they entered those messages into rich text format. They used the *Atlas.ti 5.0 word cruncher* function to find all the words referring to social connections in those autobiographies, and they created content categories for the words (e.g., "mother," "father," "family," "neighbor," "help," "love"). They compared the frequency and pattern with which the words were used in the two samples of autobiographies. Results showed that the relapsed patients wrote much shorter autobiographies and mentioned the word father more than recovered patients did. Recovered patients mentioned mother, children, and other relatives significantly more often than did relapsed patients, and words related to social groups, like team or community, were not found at all in the relapsed patients' autobiographies. Szavo and Gerevich argued that their findings contribute to the body of research that documents the importance of social relationships for individual well-being.

In some cases, you may use computer-assistance that does not involve a program like Atlas.ti or VBPro. As a case in point, Thackeray et al. (2013) used Twitter's application programming interface (API) to isolate tweets "five days before the start of BCAM in October 2012 (September 26) to 12 days after (November 12)" and to "filter the general Tweet-stream, to obtain only those tweets that contained keywords relevant to BCAM" (p. 579) They also had the computer identify unique users, using the senders' Twitter handles, and categorize tweets as "original" or "retweets." It was important for Thackeray et al. to understand how Twitter's API isolates tweets. If they disagreed with those methods, the data would be useless for their purposes.

In fact, Krippendorf (2004) distinguished four types of computer aids for content analysis. First, any word-processing program can provide counts of character strings that list, sort, count, and compare readings of linguistic texts. In this way, computers eliminate the most tedious work and increase the reliability of decisions that human coders would otherwise make. Character strings can answer research questions such as, "What terms are most (or least) frequently used?" or "What terms co-occur in a population of messages?"

Second, text searches scan large databases to find, count, and retrieve the messages you seek to analyze (e.g., when you use a search engine to locate primary source articles that might be relevant to your literature review). LexisNexis, for example, is a popular search engine for content analysts because it includes newspapers and magazines, popular press sources that comprise the population of messages for content analysis. Of course, your search engine must retrieve "*all* and *only* relevant textual documents" to provide valid data (Krippendorf, 2004, p. 276). You might use a text search to identify a relevant population of messages for content analysis, sample texts from that population that best represent whatever you are trying to study, and then analyze the attributes of particular messages within the population.

The third way that computers can aid you in doing content analysis is computational (Krippendorf, 2004; Leetaru, 2012). For example, computers can correct spelling and punctuation, add speaker names to turns at talk, mark the grammatical functions of words (e.g., verbs, nouns, adjectives), and drop all words that do not relate to your analysis, given your detailed instructions.

Last, computers can assist you in coding textual data using a dictionary approach (Krippendorf, 2004). In this case, a computer software program can replace all words that have common meanings with a single term, similar to a thesaurus, eliminating stylistic variations and simplify the way ideas are represented in a message sample. This might allow you, for example, to "rearticulate given texts in simpler terms and categorize them" according to your own needs (Krippendorf, 2004, p. 284). This example suggests how important it is for you to understand what choices the software is making and how you might tailor those choices, which Krippendorf refers to as *transparency* in computer-assisted content analysis. To better understand the dictionary approach, let's look at Conway's (2006) comparative study of content analysis, using human coders and software coding.

Conway (2006) ran a comparative study of newspaper agenda-setting in the TX Democratic gubernatorial primary race of 2002, "the first time in Texas history that two minority candidates ran against each other for a statewide office" (p. 188). His research question asked how each candidate was portrayed in the media. The data came from the *Austin-American Statesman* newspaper, January 1 through March 12, 2002.

> The coding unit was every paragraph mentioning a candidate. Because a single paragraph could have more than one reference to a candidate's image, the unit of analysis became the assertion. An assertion was any word, phrase, or sentence that conveyed an issue or attribute pertaining to the campaign or a candidate. (Conway, 2006, p. 188)

Four graduate students searched out the relevant articles: Two of them hand-searched issues of the paper, and two used Lexis-Nexis to find the articles using key words. The hand-search found six articles that the computer search didn't locate. The two teams of coders then categorized those articles using a list of 96 issues and attributes about the candidates. "The human coders and those using the computer program came up with dramatically different results on how the newspaper portrayed the candidates and issues during the campaign" (p. 189).

Conway outlined several reasons for those different findings. First, the computer found more instances of attributes and issues than the human coders found. But the human coders recognized differences that the computer didn't recognize. For instance, since humans can be trained to recognize assertions, but computers cannot, the computer team had to make lists of key words that would allow VBPro to recognize assertions. For example, in order to tell whether an article referred to the candidate's ethnicity, the computer team had to make a **word index**, a list of all the possible terms that might be used to refer to ethnicity, such as "Hispanic, minority, Latino," and so on. Conway pointed out that the tedious process of developing word indexes for all those attributes and issues would eliminate the speed benefit of using computer software to unitize and categorize the data.

More importantly, the results of the human and software analysis were different. For instance, the computer-assisted team in Conway's study created positive and negative word indexes (53 and 30 words, respectively) in order to code the affective tone of each news story.

The computer-coding showed more positive than negative coverage. But the human coder team found the overall coverage much more negative than positive, and the human coders used a category for "neutral" affect that the computer could not use. We hope this one example helps you to appreciate how computers can make content analysis much faster and easier, but may threaten the validity of your unitizing and categorizing decisions, if your analysis depends on the meaning of textual units. Whether you use a computer program like VBPro, or unitize and categorize your data by hand, the next step in content analysis is comparing the frequency with which different kinds of messages occur in your data sample.

Content Data Analysis

With unitized and categorized data in hand, you are ready to explore your research questions and/or hypotheses. As a content analytic researcher, you will be interested in both raw frequencies (i.e., the number of times a text unit falls into a particular category) and the percentage of units that fall into particular categories of your coding scheme. You also may want to compare the distribution of messages in categories that you observed in your sample data to a theoretic distribution, the one that you expected to observe in the data. For example, if you predicted that one type of message was more likely to occur than others, you will want to compare the proportion of units that occurred in each of your categories. You will be testing the null hypothesis that there is no difference in the frequency with which messages occur across categories, using the **chi-square** statistic. Chi-square is used to assess how well an observed distribution of messages fits an expected distribution of messages.

These days, nearly all statistical analyses in communication research are completed by executing computer programs like Statistical Package for Social Scientists (SPSS) or EXCEL. Software programs like these are used to test hypothesized relationships between message categories and/or differences in the relative frequencies with which message types occur. Such programs can produce visual data descriptions, too. SPSS is the most frequent choice for communication researchers, although EXCEL is sometimes used for small data sets and classroom projects, and it is often used in business environments

for statistical analyses of data. You will learn to use both (or either) of these programs in Chapters 15 and 16 of this book.

Some communication researchers use content analysis to sort textual units into categories using open-coding. They explore message data and try to develop a coding scheme that captures all of the different types of messages or texts in that population of discourse. Notice how this approach differs from applying an existing typology of message categories to a sample of textual data. One approach uses inductive reasoning, working from a set of messages to a category scheme. The other approach uses deductive reasoning, working from a set of categories to particular messages. When you want to develop a coding scheme inductively, you will apply some kind of thematic analysis to your collected data sample. If so, you'll want to refer to our discussions of analytic induction and grounded theory in Chapters 7, "Ethnography" and 8, "Conversation and Discourse Analysis," for more. Of course, if your content analytic claims are interpretive, you'll want to demonstrate the worth of your analysis using the interpretive paradigm values, form of argument, and standards for evaluating evidence, too.

For now, and with these broad ideas about how you can test your content analytic claims, let's consider how you can apply the discovery paradigm warrants to your content analytic study.

Warrants for Content Analysis

People who may want to use content analytic findings (e.g., judges in courts of law, advertising and public relations practitioners, reviewers of research funding applications) have to decide whether the findings are accurate and applicable. To that end, your ability to make generalizable explanations and predictions about textual data with content analysis depends heavily on three things: First, you must have consistency in the unitizing and categorizing decisions made by your coders (i.e., measurement reliability). Second, your coding categories must be internally valid. Third, your message sample must be representative if the results of your analysis are to be externally valid (aka generalizability). Since you already know about reliability and validity in a general sense, from Chapter 6, let's look at how you can apply each of these warrants to your content analytic study.

Intercoder Reliability

The results of content analyses depend heavily on measurement reliability, the consistency with which messages have been unitized and categorized. In its simplest form, intercoder reliability is calculated as the percentage of coding decisions on which all coders agree (e.g., A. J. Johnson et al., 1999). Sometimes, other, more complicated formulas are used, such as W. A. Scott's (1955) pi or Cohen's (1960) kappa, to assess intercoder reliability (e.g., Dixon & Azocar, 2006; Hess, 2000; McKee & Pardun, 1996; Pittman & Gallois, 1997). These are different ways of calculating the degree of agreement among coders, and estimating the degree to which coders' level of agreement about unitizing and categorizing decisions differs from the level of agreement likely to occur by chance alone (Krippendorf, 2004; Lombard, Snyder-Duch, & Bracken, 2002).

Let's consider an example from a student research project. Alhammouri, Price, Siordia and Wexler (2013) coded the stories in two community newspapers of San Francisco, the Mission and the Marina Districts, to test their prediction that the Mission's community newspaper, *El Tecolote*, featured a greater number of stories about political and world issues than did the Noe Valley community newspaper, *The Noe Valley Voice*. They used systematic sampling with a random start to select 10 issues of each newspaper from their respective online archives. They first unitized the data by separating "news stories" from other content, such as advertisements. Then they categorized each news story as "political news," "world news," or "other." The categories were mutually exclusive, so a story had to fit into one, and only one, of the three categories. Two of the student researchers are bilingual speakers (Spanish-English), so they coded the *El Tecolote* stories, since that newspaper serves a historically Latino/a neighborhood. The other two team members coded the *Noe Valley Voice* stories. Based on simple percentage of agreement, the team reported 98% reliability for categorizing decisions about the *Noe Valley Voice* stories and 94 percent agreement for decisions about the *El Tecolote* news stories. They achieved a high level of agreement, in part, due to their precise operational definitions of the three types of news stories.

To be categorized as a *political issue*, a story "had to meet at least three criteria of having a headline with words that indicated it was in this category, as well as significant evidence in the story to confirm it was 'political' and no words which blurred category lines" (p. 3). *World issues* were "defined as any news story from around the globe . . . all stories about crimes committed overseas, international protests, stories relating to race and equality, religion, sports and entertainment outside the U.S." (pp. 3–4). *Other issues* included "local human interest stories, local arts and entertainment, sports, home and garden, cooking, restaurant and store openings and nonpolitical community events, and local opinion pieces other than 'political' and 'world'" (p. 4).

Besides having precise operational definitions and coding your data very carefully, another way to assure a high degree of agreement among coders is to train the people who will code message content into units and categories. For example, in C. M. Anderson et al.'s (1998) content analysis of Chinese people's motivations for communicating with family and friends, the authors trained three graduate students to recognize the different motives, such as sharing ideas and interests, sharing feelings, and so on. As C. M. Anderson et al. read the participants' written reasons for why they talked to a best friend, the coders were able to agree which motive was represented in a response about 78 percent of the time. Anything over 70 percent constitutes an acceptable level of reliability for unitizing and categorizing message content.

Obviously, it will be easier to achieve a high level of agreement among coders if you have relatively few coding categories or if you are using physical or syntactical distinctions to unitize your data. Triangulating multiple investigator viewpoints in collaborative research teams also may help you achieve high reliability with more subjective units of analysis (i.e., propositional or thematic). Collaborative research and/or the use of computer software programs like VBPro and VBMap, two open-source software programs that can help you analyze larger data samples, which should contribute to greater generalizability of your findings. As we already noted, computer software programs can unitize and categorize physical and syntactic units of text with perfect reliability. But software cannot recognize assertions, so the consistency of computer-aided unitizing for propositional, categorical and thematic units will depend on the quality of the word indexes you build to locate those assertions (Conway, 2006). Depending on your claim, a combination of computer-assisted and human coding might provide the most reliable and valid data (Lewis et al., 2013). Computer algorithms can provide precision when sorting and categorizing texts from big data samples (like Twitter streams); human coders can evaluate whether those data are relevant for the context under study. Computers will be most useful for locating manifest content, whereas human coders are still needed to analyze latent content meanings.

Validity of the Coding Scheme

Two kinds of accuracy are important when conducting content analysis: The first issue is the *content validity* of your coding scheme. The second issue concerns the size of the coding scheme, including the size and contents of any "other" category. We use the term *parsimony* to refer to this issue. Since both of these ideas were introduced in Chapter 6, here we will elaborate on how you can apply them in your own content analytic study.

Content validity directly confronts the question, "Does my coding scheme accurately and completely specify the kinds of message content that I am trying to study?" For example, imagine that you want to categorize persuasive messages. You could just use three categories and restrict your coding scheme to threats, promises, and "other" messages. But that scheme would be much too simple to accurately and completely measure all persuasive strategies. So, your coding scheme would lack richness, and a panel of judges with even limited expertise in communication would likely see this problem.

Coding categories for content analysis typically should be mutually exclusive and exhaustive. If you have **mutually exclusive categories**, then a single textual unit can fit into one category and no other categories (e.g., if you are a college junior, you cannot also be a college senior). Overlapping categories make it more difficult to achieve intercoder reliability. For example, in A. J. Johnson et al.'s (1999) study of television talk shows, an expert could have been both a PhD and an author, in which case coders would have had to reliably recognize both membership categories. **Exhaustive categories** completely and comprehensively describe a message population (i.e., no legitimate types of messages from that population are left out of the coding scheme). Look back at Table 12.5: Can you think of other expert qualifications that should be represented in the A. J. Johnson et al. coding scheme? If not, then you can consider the categories listed there exhaustive.

Even as you attempt to represent the complexity of the message population that you are studying, you will have to balance that complexity against the value of parsimony, the discovery paradigm preference for a simple,

elegant explanation of social phenomena. One of the best ways to evaluate the parsimony of your coding scheme is to look at the presence or absence of the "other" category. If too much of your data fits into the "other" category, then your coding scheme may not be adequate to describe the message population. Indeed, your "other" category may be a sort of conceptual wastebasket, containing rich information that was not sorted out by your study.

Always watch out for the "other" category in a coding scheme. Analyze the messages that were placed there to see if there are commonalities that would point to a category you may have overlooked, one that should be added to the coding scheme. However, as we just said, too few categories will mean that your coding scheme lacks richness, but too many categories will threaten your scheme's parsimony. If you are designing your own coding scheme, you'll probably want to ask your professor to help you gauge whether your categories need to be mutually exclusive and exhaustive.

External Validity

Remember from Chapter 6 that external validity refers to the accuracy of applying the findings from one study to another setting, group of participants, or messages. The results of a study can be internally valid but still not be accurately applied in other settings or with other groups of people. In this section, we look at two factors you should consider to assess the external validity of your content analytic study: The degree of coder training required for your research project, and the representativeness of your sample data.

Coder Training

Many content analytic studies are premised on the notion that ordinary communicators interpret discourse categories in the same ways that trained coders interpret those categories (i.e., that anyone would be able to see these units of text and place them into these categories). If you make this assumption, but then require intensive training to achieve an acceptable level of intercoder reliability, your study can become suspect in terms of external validity. If your coders need extensive training to recognize a message as fitting into a particular category, then it is unlikely that communicators who are outside the study's context will recognize those messages in the same way. Therefore, the conclusions of a study in which coders are very extensively trained may be internally valid. But they may not be externally valid, or generalizable, because expert coders' interpretations will not match the judgments made by people in nonresearch contexts.

Sample Representativeness

To achieve a high degree of external validity, you will need to select a representative sample of messages that adequately represent the population about which you wish to make inferences. As you know from chapter 6, the surest way to garner a representative sample of a large population of elements is to introduce some element of chance, or randomization, into the sample selection process. But sample selection need not be purely random to be reasonably representative. For instance, Sunwolf and Seibold (1998) used a convenience sampling procedure to select citizens for participation in a content analytic study about jury deliberation rules: They recruited participants by requesting volunteers who had been summoned for jury duty, asking those who agreed to participate to complete an oral survey while they were waiting in the jury assembly room at the courthouse. It is highly likely that the volunteers in Sunwolf and Seibold's study represented the population of jurors in regular courtroom cases, the population the authors sought to represent. Sample size also has something to do with the likelihood of representation and thus with external validity. Usually, the larger the sample size, the better your chances of representing the parent message population.

To summarize, you will need to pay attention to three things to achieve externally valid conclusions in your content analytic study: First, you will need to ensure that your coders reasonably approximate the abilities of people interacting in natural contexts if you want to generalize those judgments from researchers to nonresearchers. Second, you will need select enough of the right kind of textual data to represent the population of messages to which you seek to generalize; and last, you will need to collect a large enough number of these messages to be reasonably sure you have given the possibility of random error an opportunity to work.

Ethical Issues in Content Analysis

Because content analytic research usually relies on existing message data that is publicly available, institutional review boards will likely either not want to review your research proposal or will consider your research study exempt. For example, "observations of online messages that cannot be linked to individuals, and that do not use identifiable examples, ... should not be considered human participant research" (Palomares & Flanagin, 2005, p. 174). But the fact that content analysis of publicly available messages is considered to pose minimal risk to research participants raises two important ethical issues related to your motives for research and your responsibility to protect participants' rights. First, you should *never* analyze message data simply because those data are conveniently available and you will not have to be reviewed by an institutional review board or because you will have an easier approval process. Instead, you should always aim to benefit the producers and/or consumers of the messages you analyze. If you look back at the student research claims in Table 12.1 (i.e., RQ5, H6–7), you will see that the researchers analyzed messages that are readily available to anyone in San Francisco, whether it was community newspapers, take-out menus, or advertisements visible from the street. But each of the research teams also tried to study communication that would matter to people who live in San Francisco, topics that were socially relevant. If you are to use content analysis ethically, you will need to notice when you are choosing expediency over beneficence, respect, or justice at any phase of your research project!

Similarly, with respect to expediency, unitizing and coding messages with a pen or pencil on a print copy is labor intensive compared to coding directly on your computer screen or using a computer software program to make coding decisions. But coding with pen and paper may result in more reliable coding decisions if you are making categorical, propositional, and thematic coding distinctions. Hand coding also *might* produce a better audit trail for your data analysis. "Sometimes, the old ways are best" (Neuendorf, 2002, p. 135).

Second, in terms of protecting human research participants' rights, you will need to think about how your content analytic study might threaten people's freedom of choice to participate in research or the privacy of the people whose messages you analyze: For example, if you are analyzing messages for which you know the authors' names, will you mask the names, or other identifying information, to preserve confidentiality for those communicators?

There are two additional ethical issues you should think about when reporting your content analytic study, whether you are presenting your findings to an audience or preparing a written research report for publication or other dissemination. First, consider whether and how your explanation and prediction of message frequency, structure, functions, or effects might impact the construction of messages in that context after your report is circulated. For example, if you successfully predict that deceptive messages will have greater persuasive impact, will those messages then likely increase in use? What efforts might you make to counter that possibility, given your expertise from the research (e.g., offer media literacy training to audiences who are the targets of those messages)?

Second, is it essential that you acknowledge clearly and fully the limitations of your study in your research report (i.e., any threats to measurement reliability or validity or external validity). If you do so, the people who consume your research will be cautioned and can make their own decisions about applying your research findings, especially without replication.

Table 12.6, below, summarizes this chapter.

Table 12.6 Content Analysis Summary Table

Paradigm	Claims	Data	Warrants	Manuscript Format
Discovery	Describe, explain, and predict	Representative samples of texts from message populations (i.e., archives)	Intercoder reliability, content validity of coding scheme, and sample representativeness	Research report

Key Terms

Categorize
Chi-square
Coding scheme
Content analysis
Exhaustive categories

Interactive discourse
Latent content
Manifest content
Message population
Mutually exclusive categories

Narrative discourse
Unitizing
Units of analysis
Word index

Discussion Questions

1. Why is it important that you know at the outset what type of claim you will be making in a content analytic study?
2. Why is it important to define a message population by its source as well as its time frame?
3. What are the advantages of using computer software to collect and code data for content analysis? What are some disadvantages of this work? How might using teams of human coders and computer software together help you to conduct effective content analyses?

"Try It!" Activities

1. *Data samples for content analysis.* Review the message samples listed in Table 12.3. For each sample, see if you can define that message population in one phrase or sentence. Check your population by answering this question: "Can you specify another subset of this message population from which you could sample messages to replicate the study's findings?"
2. *Designing a content analytic study.* Follow these steps to design a basic content analysis study of your own. Work with a partner for the best results:
   (a) First, use the following suggested *message populations* to brainstorm your own, more specific, list of 20 different message populations: interactions in contexts, such as interpersonal,

organizational, instructional; interactions via channels like face to face, CMC, telephone, and so on; mediated narratives in genres such as newspaper, radio, television, or Internet (and by type, such as news story, editorial, infotainment, commercial, etc.), possibly bracketed by time period (e.g., Facebook status updates posted within a student's first year at college).

(b) Join another pair of students, and review your combined lists of 40 message populations. Identify which, if any, of the suggestions on your combined list actually represent the *same population*. Which are *different populations*? Define the population characteristics that make this so.

(c) Work with your original partner to select one message population from all those you have identified so far. Develop three research questions (RQs) about that message population. Be creative! What would you like to know about messages of that sort? Clue: Make sure your RQs concern issues of frequency, degree, magnitude, and so on since these issues are appropriate for quantitative data analysis. If you cannot make a question suitable for quantitative analysis, you can save it for another chapter.

(d) Review Krippendorf's (2004) five units of analysis (i.e., physical, syntactical, categorical, propositional, and thematic), defined earlier in this chapter. For each RQ you wrote, identify the unit(s) of analysis needed to answer that question.

(e) Spend 1 to 2 hours with your partner and investigate your topic using a library database like Communication and Mass Media Complete (CMMC) or Academic Search Premier. Look for articles published in peer-reviewed, scholarly journals about the message population and unit(s) of analysis you want to study. Your goal is to determine whether any potential coding scheme for this message population already exists or can be identified from the existing literature.

(f) Create your own "standardized coding sheet" for your message population, using the categories you identified in your library search. If you didn't identify any existing coding scheme (or even categories), give a rough sketch of what categories you might look for in a small sample of pilot data.

(g) Last, write a paragraph that describes, in detail, your plan for acquiring a representative sample of the population of messages and, if needed, any additional steps you might have to take to prepare those messages for analysis (e.g., transcription).

3. *Coding data.* Read Carr et al.'s (2013) analysis of speech acts in Facebook status updates. Try replicating that analysis with your own Facebook friends.

(a) First, select a sample of Facebook status updates posted over one week's time (e.g., messages posted by your friends and family members);

(b) Identify the number of speech act(s) in each status update (i.e., propositional unit). Remember, ". . . status updates could contain more than one sentence, and a sentence could contain more than one speech act" (Carr et al., p. 184). For each status update, determine the number of speech acts (i.e., one or more), and then, assign each speech act to one of Carr et al.'s coding categories (i.e., assertive, directive, commissive, expressive, effective, or verdictive; see Carr et al.'s Table 1, p. 178, for definitions of the speech act types);

(c) Keep track of each one of your decisions using a coding sheet that shows a row for each status update and then indicates the number of speech acts in each update, and the type of each speech act.

(d) Work with one other student to code all (or a portion) of one another's data: What is your rate of agreement about the coding decisions you have made independently (i.e., the number of speech acts present in each update and the types of speech acts)?

(e) If at least 70 percent of your coding decisions are in agreement (reliable), compare your results with one another. Do your findings fit with Carr et al.'s findings? If "no," why not? What might explain the difference (e.g., coding reliability, sample validity)?

13 How to Construct Survey Research

Introduction

In this chapter, you will learn how to conduct survey research projects, building on what you already know about conceptual and operational definitions from Chapter 11, "How to Design Discovery Research." Survey research is the most common methodology used both in and outside academia. So it's an important method to know, whether you plan to become a researcher, run your own business, or work in government or not-for-profit organizations. You will learn more about how surveys are used to explore new topics and develop explanatory claims, usually claims of association, rather than full causal explanations. Then, you will learn about survey *data* collection sources and strategies, including cross-sectional and longitudinal research designs that we have discussed previously, sampling techniques, interviews and questionnaires, and instrumentation. We present three *warrants* for survey research, including assessment of response rate and measurement reliability and validity. The summary of this chapter will provide a Survey Study Worksheet that you can use to make all the decisions you need to design your own survey study, and will elaborate on what you learned in Chapter 1 about the elements of a research report.

Learning Outcomes

After completing this chapter, you should be able to:

» Distinguish between and provide examples of an associative claim and a causal claim using survey research as the methodology.

» Successfully apply the Survey Study Worksheet that will help you identify the sources, settings, design, sampling strategies, survey format, and instrument measures to your own survey project or to an example survey study.

» Identify at least two random and nonrandom sampling strategies and explain the preference for random data selection in survey research.

» Compare the relative advantages/disadvantages of face-to-face interviews, focus groups, mall intercept surveys, Internet questionnaires and questionnaires distributed by an in-person test administrator.

» Explain the effects of item- and total- response rates on the validity and reliability of a measure and the various steps that can be taken to help ensure these warrants are established for your survey.

» Articulate and defend at least two ethical issues in survey research.

Outline

We live in a world filled with survey invitations and survey results! Anyone on Facebook, LinkedIn, and Twitter knows that survey links abound. Businesses often invite visitors to take different types of surveys on customer service satisfaction, organizations survey their members about company climate, and educational institutions create alumni surveys on program home pages to invite their graduates to stay in touch. It is impossible to cruise through online news sources or periodicals without being asked for your feedback on some issue or problem. Even health providers are far more likely to routinely assess patient care partially through survey responses. You will learn in this chapter that there are sometimes great differences between the scientific surveys we conduct for the purposes of research and those you are likely to encounter elsewhere on the Internet, by phone or text, or even face-to-face.

Researchers use the term *survey* in a variety of ways. As you will see later in the chapter, surveys may take the form of interviews or questionnaires. Generally, **survey research** refers to the method of collecting information from certain groups of individuals or the general population about their knowledge, beliefs, attitudes, values, feelings, and perceptions. A recent analysis of survey research in communication (Macias, Springston, Lariscy, & Neustifter, 2008), showed that 565 survey studies appeared in 46 of the 54 journals studied during a 13-year period, with the bulk of these studies occurring in public relations, marketing, public opinion, advertising, and mass communication journals. Constructing surveys has never been easier, especially with the advent of software programs like Survey Monkey and Qualtrics. However, constructing a sound survey, one that will yield valid and reliable results means first thinking through the purposes of your survey (i.e., your claims), the questions that you want to ask, and the ways in which you wish to collect your data. Only then will you be able to assert strong conclusions based on the results that you have obtained. So let us first begin with the purposes and questions as embedded in the claims of survey research.

Survey Research Claims

In Chapter 11, we discussed general design considerations for discovery-paradigm research, including survey research. We explained that the design of research depends a great deal on the type of argument you wish to make. Often, we cannot meet all of the criteria for causality in a single study. So our purposes in conducting a survey may be exploratory: We might want to simply describe some communicators' attitudes, beliefs, or behaviors; or we might want to describe some message characteristics. Alternately, we might want to discover the associations that exist between various phenomena; for example, at your college or university, administrators may use student surveys to explore how different groups of students, such as athletes or first generation college students, experience their first year as a transition to college. You may have participated in surveys like these.

In communication research, we might want to know about how widespread communication apprehension is or how romantic couples experience relational uncertainty or the ways people assess speaker credibility or how they use various forms of media. In other cases, surveys are used with more explanatory purposes in mind, to explore whatever bases there may be for making a full cause-and-effect argument about some aspect of communication. We might ask how siblings differ from friends in responding to jealousy, for example, or if specific news agencies vary in race portrayals when reporting crime stories.

Survey research typically makes use of claims from the discovery paradigm about empirical or observable and quantifiable data, stated in the format of research questions and hypotheses. You may recall from Chapter 4 on "Making Claims" and Chapter 11 on "How to Design Discovery Research" that *research questions* frequently ask how a variable (or concept) can be classified (i.e., how does it fit into some typology or category scheme?) Research questions also may ask what relationships exist between various types of communication phenomena. *Hypotheses* make more precise and specific predictions about relationships among communication variables. We defined the term, *variable*, as any measurable construct, including examples such as age as measured in years, or college status as measured in number of units (e.g., sophomores are students who have earned about one-fourth to one-half of the total units required for graduation with a bachelor's degree). Scores on an aptitude test make up a variable of aptitude levels (e.g., the SAT or ACT college aptitude tests measure one's readiness for college-level academic work).

Generally, claims in survey research function in two ways: First, they are sometimes used for exploratory purposes, describing the characteristics of a certain group of individuals or messages. Second, they can be explanatory, including both associative and causal claims. Recall that in our discussion in Chapter 4, "Making Claims," we distinguished between *associative claims*, which predict phenomena that will occur together, and *causal claims*, which predict the influence of one phenomenon on another. Claims of association only assess covariation between a presumed cause and an effect. By contrast, full causal arguments explain and predict associations between cause and effect, but they also establish time-order (the cause happens or changes first). Causal arguments also attend to other possible explanations for the effects we study, something you will learn much more about in the next chapter on experimental research.

Claims in Exploratory Surveys

Researchers can construct surveys to simply explore and identify the unique characteristics of a particular group of individuals or messages. For example, Jones and Biddlecom (2011) conducted a survey to find out how teens used the Internet for sexual health information, specifically information about abstinence and contraception. The researchers wanted to know how teens evaluated the information they obtained in order to improve the accuracy of teen sexual health websites.

In another study, Ferris and Hollenbaugh (2011) distributed surveys to college students to discover motives for "drunk dialing" through application of uses and gratification theory. The researchers were interested in understanding this new and increasing phenomenon of calling while intoxicated. They believed that drunk dialing has become more prevalent because the nature of mobile phones make it easier for people to act impulsively. Among the motives for such calls were using these instances for entertainment, as a social lubricant, as a confession of emotion, and sexuality. The research was guided by two basic research questions about the motives for this behavior (refer to Table 13.1). Sex differences helped to explain differences for two of the motives, in which women were more likely to call to confess an emotion while men were more likely to phone for sexual reasons (e.g., hook up with someone).

Table 13.1 Claims in Exploratory Survey Studies

RQ1: What motives emerge for drunk dialing behavior?
RQ2: What motives predict frequency of drunk dialing behavior? (Ferris & Hollenbaugh, 2011, p. 108)

Note: RQ = research question.

In some cases, surveys can be used to map out specific conceptual territory. Just as Ferris and Hollenbaugh wanted to explore the new communication behavior of drunk dialing, you may want to discover what types of opinions, attitudes, or feelings people report having during certain interactions. For example, Kassing and Kava (2013) were interested in determining the ways in which employees expressed disagreements to their managers. This kind of communication is called *upward dissent* and is difficult to accomplish successfully because of the power differences between employees and the managers that supervise them. The researchers solicited 225 employees from over 20 different types of organizations, asking them questions related to upward dissent from several existing measures. Then they conducted an analysis of the factors or dimensions that are part of upward dissent. Recall that some variables are *multidimensional, a characteristic* that we described in Chapter 11. In this case, Kassing and Kava (2013) found that there were four factors that contribute to employees' upward dissent. Each factor was identified as one of four strategies that employees use when disagreeing with their supervisors: prosocial (using a direct and factual approach to solving the problem), threat (threatening resignation if changes do not occur), circumvention (going around or above supervisor), and repetition (voicing concern numerous times). By surveying employees from multiple organizations, the researchers hoped to establish their upward dissent scale as a valid and reliable measure, Once the measure is established, it can be used to explore the role of upward dissent in theorizing cause-and-effect relations (e.g., how does upward dissent make an organization more productive? How does it relate to employee satisfaction and turnover?).

Later in this chapter, you will learn how scales for other variables are embedded in questionnaires and how warrants provide criteria to evaluate the content and structure of the questionnaires. But first let's look at how explanatory claims are used in survey research.

Explanatory Claims

As you already know, there is strong a preference for causal arguments in discovery research. Some arguments fall short of the three criteria for establishing causality that we identified earlier in Chapter 11, "How to Design Discovery Research." Explanatory claims in survey research can be purely associative or they can test for causality, and they can be advanced as either research questions or hypotheses. In survey research, associative claims ask about, or predict that two or more variables are related to each other. This means that changes in one variable are accompanied by changes in the other variable. Often, these associative claims are preliminary tests of the covariance criteria for a causal argument; the researchers want to ensure that variables are correlated before more rigorous testing of time-order and control over competing explanations can begin.

Thus, associative claims express contingency relationships or correlations, a term you will learn about statistically in Chapter 16. Correlations refer to changes in variables that occur together in time. If the variables increase or decrease together, the type of association is said to be positive (see Table 13.2). For example, Clay, Fisher, Xie, Sawyer, and Behnke (2005) were interested in testing the relationships among various arousal levels in a speaker's sensitivity to punishment, the speaker's emotional intensity, and the act of giving public speeches. They hypothesized that there was a positive relationship between sensitivity to punishment and speaker sensitivity (arousal) during a public speech. Moreover, Clay et al. (2005) also hypothesized that speakers who were more likely to experience greater intensity of affect (emotions) also would be more likely to experience speaker arousal while delivering a public speech (p. 99). By testing first the association among arousal, emotions and sensitivity to punishment, the researchers are working toward a causal account of what makes some speaker better able to cope with anxiety about giving a speech. As the greatest fear of humans (more than death), that topic is important to college students, and everyone else!

If one variable decreases as the other increases, or vice versa, the relationship is identified as a negative correlation (see Table 13.2). For example, Rancer, Durbin, and Lin (2013) found a strong negative relationship between perceptions of difficulty and perceptions of understanding topics among students in research methods courses! They also found that math anxiety was negatively associated with students' understanding of research

Table 13.2 Explanatory Claims in Survey Research

Correlational Claims:

1. Positive correlation: Variables change together:

H1: A positive correlation exists between sensitivity to punishment and speaker sensitization during public performance (Clay, Fisher, Xie, Sawyer, & Behnke, 2005, p. 99).

2. Negative correlation: Variables change in opposite directions.

RQ1: What is the level of perceived difficulty among the 19 concepts or topics in an undergraduate communication research methods course?

RQ2: What is the relationship between self-reported math anxiety and perceived difficulty and understanding of topics covered in an undergraduate communication research methods course?

H1: There is a significant, negative relationship between students' perceived difficulty and their perceived understanding of those communication research methods topics (Rancer, Durbin, & Lin, 2013).

3. Causal claims:

H2: Fearful and dismissive individuals will be rated as less skilled in (a) expressiveness and (b) other-orientation than secure individuals (Guerrero & Jones, 2005, p. 310).

Independent variable: Type of attachment style.

Dependent variables: Expressiveness, other-orientation.

Note: RQ = research question; H = hypothesis.

methods topics. If you're following the definition, you can already see that students who find research methods more difficult are likely to understand less of the material; students with a high degree of math anxiety also are likely to report that they do not understand research methods!

Sometimes, the relationship is expected to be more complex, changing in several different directions. This type is called a curvilinear relationship. For example, Duggan and Le Poire (2006) found a curvilinear relationship between depression and partners' verbal strategies. Some helping and encouraging strategies were reported before the diagnosis of depression was given, the greatest amount of helping and encouraging strategies happened just following diagnosis, and then helping and encouraging strategies dropped off again during a period of frustration after initial attempts to help. Don't worry if this seems confusing for now. You will learn more about linear and curvilinear relationships in Chapter 16 when you learn about tests of correlation.

Surveys traditionally differ from experiments in that surveys do not involve any manipulation or controlled change in the variables or concepts studied.

"The important distinction between the survey and the experiment is that the survey takes the world as it comes, without trying to alter it, whereas the experiment systematically alters some aspect of the world in order to see what changes follow" (Simon as cited in A. A. Berger, 1998, p. 35). Because of the lack of experimental control, surveys have traditionally been thought of as a weaker form of study design by discovery scholars, because variable changes are not controlled and patterns of effects are not tested as they are in experiments. However, more complex ways of measuring variables with continuous scales, and more advanced data analysis techniques, such as regression and path analysis, can permit researchers to test more complex sets of causal relationships that exist naturally in the environment (but learning how to conduct these tests are beyond the level of an introductory course in research methods). Recall that causal claims must go several steps further than covariation: Causal claims have to establish evidence of time-order, by showing that a change in one variable (the independent variable, or predictor) precedes and influences change in the second variable (the dependent variable, or criterion). Causal claims also must show that the change in a dependent variable is not likely to be explained by the influence of any other factor (e.g., moderating variables, or selection bias).

In survey study designed to test causal relationships, Guerrero and Jones (2005) claimed that varying attachment styles, or approaches to forming intimate relationships (independent variable), would predict the use of conversational skills (dependent variables). They discovered that certain combinations of attachment styles were more likely to predict individuals with limited conversational skills. For example, fearful avoidants and dismissives (attachment styles) were less expressive and other-oriented during observed conversations than individuals with secure attachment styles. Because attachment style is thought to be a fairly stable trait of persons, developed over many years, attachment styles were the presumed cause, and conversational behavior in an intimate relationship was presumed to be the outcome, or effect of those attachment styles.

With the popularity of social networks and social media, one area of survey research that has undergone a major transformation is **network analysis**, a methodology that often tests complex patterns of association and causality. Social network analysis (SNA) involves the structural mapping and measuring the relationships and communication between "nodes" or individuals within a network

Table 13.3 Claims in Network Analysis (Holman & Sillars, 2012)

Exploratory research questions:

RQ1: How do college students define a hookup?

RQ2: What characteristics are reflected in hookup scripts?

RQ3: Do hookup scripts differ according to student attributes (gender, relationship status, sexual activity)?

RQ4: Is network range associated with participation in and attitudes toward sexual hookups?

RQ5: Does peer approval moderate the relationship of peer communication to hookup participation and attitudes?

Explanatory claims:

H1: More frequent peer communication about nonrelationship sex is associated with greater participation in sexual hookups.

H2: More frequent peer communication about nonrelationship sex is associated with more favorable attitudes toward sexual hookups.

H3: Perceived peer approval is associated with participation in sexual hookups.

H4: Perceived peer approval is associated with favorable attitudes toward sexual hookups.

H5: Peer closeness moderates the relationship between peer approval and participation in sexual hookups.

H6: Peer closeness moderates the relationship between peer approval and attitudes toward sexual hookups.

Note: RQ = research question; H = hypothesis.

(J. R. Lincoln, 1990; Wasserman & Faust, 1994; Doerfel & Barnett, 1999). Frequently, this methodology is combined with content analysis but may also use surveys to collect important but less apparent information. For example, Holman and Sillars (2012) used several different SNA network characteristics of college students' networks to predict likelihood of "hookup" behavior; frequency of communication, range of contacts, and closeness of network ties. The authors advanced five research questions and six hypotheses as explanatory claims about the ways in which these structural features of networks would be associated with and predict hooking up (nonrelationship sex). The authors' claims can be seen in Table 13.3. They asked participants to complete an online survey to examine the influence of network characteristics on their reported subsequent sexual behaviors.

In media research, surveys are often used to establish a more complete understanding of the factors that predict media usage. For example, Hmielowski, Holbert and Lee (2013) used phone surveys to assess the effects of 16 potential predictors of viewing TV political satire, specifically viewing *The Daily Show* and *The Colbert Report*. The predictors included variables such as demographics (sex, age, etc.), political orientations (e.g., Democratic, Republican, etc.), media exposure (broadcast television news, daily newspaper, internet), need for humor, affinity for political humor, and so on. By including several psychological attributes, such as need for humor, they hoped to strengthen the predictors of viewing certain media programming.

Claims in survey research will guide your project by helping you formulate what you want to ask your participants to report about themselves or other people. Whether they are associative or causal, your claims also will help you determine what variables you are interested in investigating and the types of relationships that may exist between them. These essential features will help you understand how to collect and measure the data and test your research questions/hypotheses using the appropriate statistical analysis. First, we will explore the steps in constructing surveys that will enable you to collect and analyze survey data.

Survey Research Data

Data treatment in survey research entails a lengthy process of preparation before the survey is ever administered. As part of this process, you must make some important decisions and take the following steps summarized in Table 13.4: (1) Identify data sources and settings, (2) select a general survey design, (3) decide on sampling strategies based on your ability (cost-wise) to randomize data, (4) identify data collection format as

Table 13.4 Steps in Survey Data Collection

1. Identify data sources and settings.
2. Select a general survey design.
3. Decide on sampling strategies.
4. Identify data collection format as interviews or questionnaires.
5. Develop data collection procedures and instruments.
6. Pilot any interview protocol or questionnaire.
7. Assess the validity and reliability of the data collection instruments.
8. Assess the generalizability of the sampled data (depends on sampling strategy selected).

interviews or questionnaires, (5) develop data collection instruments (interviews and/or questionnaires), (6) pilot test any interview protocol or questionnaire, (7) assess the validity and reliability of the data collection instruments using pilot data, and (8) assess the generalizability of the sampled data based on your sampling strategy selection. You must complete these steps before you can actually collect the data, and then analyze and interpret your findings. Each of these aspects of designing a survey study is examined in the sections that follow.

Sources for Data Collection

As we have indicated, the availability and ease of using survey software has resulted in making surveys a very common form of collecting data from the general public, both in and outside academia. Surveys usually take the form of questionnaires either self-administered by the research participant or administered by a member of the research team through an interviewing process. As you learned in Chapter 5, "What Counts as Data?" you can ask respondents to report on themselves, called *self-report data*, or on others they know, called *other-report data*. As we have shown in multiple examples, surveys typically assess characteristics or attributes of individual persons or groups in order to investigate how those characteristics are related to the communication process. These attributes or characteristics can refer to factual or observable features such as socioeconomic status or age or birthplace. Or they can be composed of ideas, attitudes, opinions, and emotions. Whether in questionnaire or interview format, surveys are useful ways to find out information from a sample of people when the population you aim to explain or make predictions about is too large to observe or test every member.

Settings for Data Collection

Laboratory and Field Settings

In survey research, choosing between laboratory and field settings is often mitigated by the data collection strategy itself, especially with the proliferation of email and internet surveys. When you put a survey link on Facebook, participants can answer it from any location, their work or home computer, or a mobile phone that they access from anywhere. So the data collection setting becomes far less relevant. In fact, accessibility to participants in their natural settings makes email and internet surveys more like field than laboratory studies; but the setting in these cases frequently has little to do with the study itself. For example, students can be evaluated for relationship uncertainty in their friendships via an email survey, but the fact that participants completed the survey by email or online is not directly relevant to the study design.

Sometimes the research setting does matter in survey research. As you learned previously, laboratories in communication research are seldom like the sterile environments portrayed in stereotypes of research facilities. They are very often offices or conference rooms or even classrooms in the academic department at the university where one of the researchers is a professor or graduate student. The role of the researcher varies depending on the paradigm assumptions that underlie the method of choice and depending on the type of survey used as well. Generally, the function of using a laboratory setting is to provide a more controlled environment and to facilitate the collection of data. As a direct test of survey methods, Chang and Krosnick (2010) brought participants to a lab setting to test the differences between self-administered computer-generated questionnaire and in-person interviews. We will outline the relative advantages and disadvantages of various survey methods later in this chapter, but if you want to see an overview of those, look ahead to Table 13.6.

You can also collect survey data directly in the field. Field research is any research that investigates communication in the setting where the interaction would most naturally occur. For example, Fix and Sias (2006) went directly to seven organizations in the field to recruit 120 employees for a survey about supervisor and subordinate communication variables, and Wright (2002) went online to recruit survey volunteers from an online cancer support group. It was important to approach participants in the field in these cases, and in the latter example, the online community was the field setting.

In the past, selecting the data collection setting was frequently dependent on the type of analysis: basic or applied research. Many academic programs still make a distinction between these two types of research, with applied contexts more likely in political polling, and the marketing and advertising industries.

Basic and Applied Research

Surveys traditionally have been used as a research tool for collecting and analyzing data from natural settings for the purposes of collecting applied research. **Applied research** focuses on satisfying practical outcomes or solving specific problems in field settings (Smith, 1988, p. 219). Experiments were conducted in the laboratory where a controlled environment was warranted, and were thought of as part of basic research. **Basic research** emphasizes investigating theoretic relationships among variables where practical outcomes in specific contexts may be implicit or unknown. So surveys were conducted in the field when researchers wanted to access groups in contexts not available through experimental research. By methodological tradition, field settings with survey instruments typified applied research, whereas laboratory settings in academic institutions were associated with basic research.

Two Types of Applied Survey Research

Applied research settings that use the survey method in communication research have been traditionally associated with political polling, consumer research, and action research. **Political polling research** refers to assessing political opinions and attitudes often to predict voter preferences. You are probably familiar with the Gallup poll, still one of the most prominent in predicting success for particular election candidates. In assessing journal scholarship since the year 2000, Price (2011), a former editor of *Public Opinion Quarterly*, noted three specific trends in public opinion research: expansive understanding of the survey response; challenges and opportunities for research in rapid changes in media communication; and quality of public opinion, particularly when subtly primed through political elites (pp. 846–847).

Advances in cognitive science and information processing helped researchers explore how survey respondents were likely to interpret (and misinterpret) the questions. Some studies focused on order effects, or the ways that early questions influence responses later in the survey, a pattern we will discuss in the next section. A second trend focused on the "seismic changes in communication and survey technology" (p. 849). There was certainly no disputing the increasing accessibility of collecting data via cell phones, email, and the Internet. However, the increase in channels brought new worries about the validity and reliability of these data collection strategies that challenged our conceptions of randomized, generalizable samples. A number of studies represented the third trend, exploring the quality of public opinion as our definitions of what constituted the "public" were fundamentally shaken. Price (2011) noted that many studies investigated a new political strategy aimed at influencing public opinion, called "*group-based priming*, and its role in shaping critical alignments and divisions among the population, especially within the electorate" (p. 850). This set of studies explored the ways in which political strategists used media to influence opinion in smaller, more homogenous groups of people with strongly held beliefs and attitudes by "priming" them with media environmental cues designed to evoke targeted responses. Price pointed to analyses of the candidacies of Barack Obama, Hilary Clinton, and Sarah Palin, and the rise of the Tea Party as illustrative examples.

Consumer research (also called marketing research) is designed to assess consumer attitudes and preferences for various products or services. Nielsen ratings, for example, help media and advertising organizations assess the characteristics and sizes of audiences who watch various television programming. Recently, Nielsen announced Nielsen Twitter TV Ratings, which "measure not only 'authors'—the number of people tweeting about TV programs—but also the much larger 'audience' of people who actually view those Tweets" (Nielsen, 2013). Initial results about episode viewing indicate that about 50 times the number of people tweeting about an episode make up the television audience; for example, 2,000 tweets predicts an audience of 100,000 episode viewers that are also viewing the tweets. Obviously, changes in media have heavily influenced communication consumer research.

In addition to the settings and applied or basic research emphases, survey research makes use of two designs discussed in earlier chapters, cross-sectional and longitudinal surveys.

Survey Research Design

In Chapter 5, *What Counts as Communication Data?*, you learned that a *research design* is the structural plan for conducting a test of the researcher's hypotheses or research questions. It specifies the procedures for collecting and analyzing the data. In Chapter 11 on designing discovery-based research, we talked about the preference for causal arguments in this paradigm and identified experiments as the primary design that optimizes control for making full good arguments about cause-and-effect sequences in communication. This does not mean that we ignore causality in survey research; we simply are unable to acquire the degree of control available to a researcher conducting an experiment within a laboratory setting. Additionally, most surveys are cross-sectional because of expediency, but as we will discuss in the next section, this type of design may not provide the same level of validity and reliability that longitudinal designs can afford.

Cross-Sectional Surveys

Cross-sectional surveys are the more prevalent of the two types of survey designs in all communication research. Collecting data one time only from one group of people is cheaper and less time consuming; and because of these factors, many surveys conducted in field settings are collected only once. Additionally, in cross-sectional designs, the researcher does not have to worry about loss of data over time as participants drop out or are lost from the original roster. But cross-sectional studies are limited in that they provide only a "snapshot" view of communication at a single point in time.

Longitudinal Surveys

Longitudinal surveys involve collecting data at more than one point in time, which can result in either a trend or panel design. **Trend studies** collect data at different points in time from different samples of individuals presumed to be from the same population (e.g., college students in the 1980s, 1990s, and the first decade of 2000s). **Panel studies** require collecting data from the same sample of individuals over several periods in time (e.g., survey cancer patients about their social support sources at diagnosis, and each month thereafter). As we stated earlier, longitudinal designs are presumed to be the stronger design choice for discovery research as opposed to cross-sectional, but this assumption is not always supported. Several researchers have argued that

a more complex set of factors should be compared when considering the two.

In a recent comparison of cross-sectional and longitudinal designs, Rindfleisch, Malter, Ganesan, and Moorman (2008) asserted that cross-sectional designs are usually critiqued as weak because the design does not permit the researchers to make causal influences by ruling out alternative explanations or hypotheses for observed effects. The authors decided to test a longitudinal design against a cross-sectional approach, assessing the validity threats to both sets of data focused on new product development. They offered eight guidelines which should inform researchers' decisions to use longitudinal research instead of cross-sectional. For example, cross-sectional data appear to have stronger validity and reliability when key constructs are more directly observable and concrete, when the survey format and measurement scales use certain features that reduce the chance of response bias, and when longitudinal studies cannot control for the likelihood of intervening events that can interfere with results collected over time. We focus on just a few factors here which should help you make choices about what type of longitudinal study is preferred.

Deciding which type of longitudinal survey study to conduct depends on sample size, characteristics of the sample, and the potential effect of participants' dropout rates. If the size of the population is very large, for example, the only feasible design is the trend study. The impracticability of surveying the same members of a large population, as you would do in a panel study, is fairly obvious. However, sometimes the claim you wish to test makes a panel study more advantageous. If you want to show, for instance, what types of networks individuals develop online over time, following the same group of individuals will allow you to map out gradual changes in network development.

A third consideration in deciding what type of longitudinal study to use concerns the effects of mortality or the dropout rate. You will learn more about this problem in the next chapter. If your research question or hypothesis poses a claim that is susceptible to this effect, selecting a panel format will be problematic. For example, if you want to see whether romantic couples' enrollment in a communication seminar influences relational satisfaction over the course of a semester, you will need to assure that your sample will not reflect only those who continue to be couples and participants in your study. Those who break up are least likely to be satisfied but would no longer qualify to be part of your study of couples. In this particular case, a trend study or even a cross-sectional design may be preferred.

Once you have decided which design best matches your claims and population characteristics, you must then select the sampling method you will use to construct a sample of people you will contact to take your survey.

Data Sampling Strategies

Design issues specify how data will be collected over time. You must also consider other data collection strategies such as sample selection and data collection formats.

Random Selection Methods

As we stated earlier, the primary purpose of surveys is to examine the characteristics or attributes of interest to our study from a sample that is representative of a larger population. Sample *representativeness* is, therefore, a key issue in survey research generally. In Chapter 5 on communication data, you learned about the general principle of representativeness. When a sample represents its population well, we say it provides a very good picture of what the whole group looks like even though we cannot test every member. The best way to ensure representativeness is to use random selection or another probability sampling method. When you select population members randomly to make up a sample, you are ensuring that every member of the population has an equal chance of being chosen for the sample.

Because representative samples provide such good pictures of the whole population, you can assume that the conclusions you reach about your observations have good external validity. External validity is the ability to generalize beyond what you see in your sample to the population at large. With strong external validity, you can say, for example, that your samples of voters, teenagers, women, television audiences, or whatever group you have selected will allow you to make accurate predictions about what all voters, teenagers, women, or television audiences generally will do even though you cannot test or observe every member of the whole group.

You may use any of the random sampling methods identified earlier: Simple random sampling and stratified sampling are among the most frequently chosen. Usually, researchers will select the method that is most cost effective and will satisfy the goals of obtaining a representative sample. For example, one set of researchers

(Atkin et al., 2002) used data collected from the National Family Opinion Research survey company to ensure a 70 percent response rate from samples tested for representativeness using US Census data. Atkin et al. were interested in surveying verbal aggressiveness in teens between the ages of 13 and 15 who were residents of Michigan, Ohio, and Illinois. Even though the number of states represented was small, Atkin et al. spent a considerable amount of time and money to ensure greater representativeness in their sample than you would ordinarily find in most survey research.

Many telephone survey studies make use of a procedure called random digit dialing (RDD). This procedure randomly identifies areas of a region to be sampled with their corresponding area codes and exchanges (first 3 numbers). Then, the last four digits of the telephone number are randomly generated. This procedure also enables you to access unlisted numbers. For example, Goidel, Freeman, and Procopio (2006) used RDD to obtain a representative sample of voting-age residents of Louisiana to assess the impact of television viewing on perceptions of juvenile crime.

With the advent of cell phone use, RDD has been modified as a procedure to account for these changes. In 2004, the National Health Interview Survey (NHIS), a large indexing firm for identifying common sample characteristics of American households, reported that about 50 percent of households owned one or more cell phones and about six percent had cell phones only (Brick, Brick, Dipko, Presser, Tucker, & Yang, 2007). By 2010, the National Center for Health Statistics (NCHS) reported that 24.5 percent of American households were cellular only, and "almost 15 percent of American households with a landline phone report receiving virtually all calls through cellular phone devices" (in Hmielowski, et al., 2011, p. 102). Many researchers argue that cell phone usage must be taken into account. In the study by Hmielowski and his colleagues (2011), a comparison of demographics between cell phone and landline users showed a mean age difference of 17 years between the two groups, critical to their study of younger viewer characteristics for *The Daily Show* and *The Colbert Report*. The researchers were careful to hire a private research firm that combined cellular and landline phone numbers in their RDD process, obtaining roughly equal subsamples of both groups.

RDD can also be adjusted to account for areas that have greater or lesser concentrations of various minority groups or other socioeconomic stratifications

(Mertens, 1998, p. 114). In some cases, survey researchers depend on samples previously drawn to recruit participants for new studies. For example, Dillard, McCaul, and Klein (2006) used data to assess perceived and actual smokers' risks from a large sample of data collected by the National Cancer Institute. The Health Information National Trends Survey dataset randomly sampled 6,369 respondents whose information was used in a number of health-related studies.

Random sampling methods enable you to estimate how far your sample characteristics (statistics) are likely to deviate from population characteristics (parameters). You will learn about this process in more detail in Chapters 15 and 16. For the time being, we want to identify the assumptions you will make in attempting to establish external validity: (1) Hypotheses are claims developed about relationships between population characteristics (parameters), (2) researchers specify the probability of error associated with sample characteristics (statistics), and (3) the probability of error permits researchers to reject or accept a hypothesis (Smith, 1988). These assumptions are grounded in random sampling, and they are inherent in most survey research. Why, then, would you choose a nonrandom sampling method in survey research?

Nonrandom or Purposive Selection Methods

One reason for choosing nonrandom sampling methods in survey research is because you cannot afford to use one of the random selection techniques, or constraints of the setting make random selection not practical (Fink & Gantz, 1996; Stake, 1998). This rationale will weaken your ability to generalize study results to the population due to self-selection bias, which means that people with certain characteristics (e.g., more altruistic or more invested in the topic or issue) will be more likely to respond and therefore will be overrepresented in the sample. We will discuss this error in more detail in the warrants section of this chapter. To compensate, you may take steps to help ensure representativeness in other ways. For example, Nathanson (1999) obtained a sample of elementary school-aged children from two communities outside of the university community to try to increase the variety of participants in her sample. She was interested in testing the effects of parental mediation on their children's television viewing. As Nathanson pointed out, samples within the university community were more likely to be "practiced" research

participants and be more educated, two factors the author believed might interfere with her investigation of parent mediation (control of and commentary about their children's television programs) and children's television viewing habits.

In some cases, survey research questions specifically call for a nonrandom sampling method. Network studies emphasize the uniqueness of each network as a whole system. In such studies, the selection method for network analysis is almost always purposive or snowball sampling, rather than random, because the network researcher aims to sample the entire social system. For example, Morton and Duck (2000) used a modified snowball sampling technique to recruit gay men for their sample. The researchers asked a group of gay men to refer other gay men that they knew personally; the researchers also solicited study participation from gay men through university campus groups. Morton and Duck used this procedure because they were interested in studying the effects of depending on the media on gay men's attitudes toward safer sex practices. As the researchers pointed out, if they had recruited their sample through mass-mediated sources, they may have obtained a sample already biased toward media dependency. In other network studies, however, representative sampling techniques can be used to select a subset of participants from a very large, loosely structured, social network (e.g., McLeod et al., 1999).

To summarize, the sample selection process for survey research can be accomplished by using either random or nonrandom sampling techniques. If you are interested in obtaining a sample that is a representative subset of its population, then random methods are preferred. If you are not interested in generalizing the study's findings beyond the particular communication context, or if there are special constraints on sampling imposed by the context, then you may select a nonrandom method.

Capturing Self-Reports and Other-Reports

As you know already, survey research is based on reports individuals give of their own or others' ideas, attitudes, beliefs, emotions, behaviors, or demographic characteristics. Gathering this information can be completed through *interviews* or by *questionnaires*. In the following section, you will learn about the types of interviews you may conduct and how these differ from administering print or digital questionnaires.

Types of Survey Interviews

When you collect survey data by interviews, you must make several decisions. The first decision concerns the setting for data collection. You can choose to meet participants face-to-face either in a laboratory setting or in the field. If a field setting is selected, you can intercept participants in a general public setting like a shopping center or mall, or you can solicit interviews over the telephone. You can meet with individuals, or in groups, or even conduct extensive interviews of whole networks. Second, you must decide what to ask during the interview. The format of questions can vary as well as your role as the interviewer. In preparing for the interview process, you must decide how structured the format will be, the degree of participation you will take as the interviewer, and how much training it will be necessary for you to receive. Each of these decisions comes with a set of distinctive advantages and disadvantages. You may find it advantageous to use a *Survey Study Worksheet*, such as the example in Table 13.5. It will help to organize your thinking as you work through the choices that you will have to make along the way.

Interviews can be arranged with individual participants, couples, or groups face-to-face in a field setting or in a laboratory setting. For example, Krcmar and Valkenburg (1999) interviewed children in their homes and in a day care setting to assess their perceptions of whether violence in television programs should be considered justified or unjustified. Duggan and Le Poire (2006) agreed to meet participants in their homes, at a coffee shop, or in a university setting to facilitate the interviewing process. Interviews that take place in natural settings are less likely to produce artificial effects due to the setting itself, but they are usually less controlled environments. So interviews in a field setting are subject to distractions and interruptions that interviews in more controlled setting do not face. Researchers frequently try to minimize the negative effects and maximize the positive effects of both settings by constructing laboratory settings that resemble the natural environment.

Face-to-face interviews with individual participants are also called *in-person* or *personal interviews;* they pose some unique advantages. It is much easier to establish a rapport and climate of trust between the interviewer and the participant if they meet personally than if they talk over the phone or by mailed questionnaire. Plus it is also more difficult not to answer all items, and so response rates are typically higher. You will also have access to more information from participants; you can probe for more in-depth responses, and you can easily monitor participants' nonverbal reactions for any expressions of confusion or concern. Participants can ask for clarification, too. This ability is especially important when participants cannot read fluently because, for example, English is not the participant's native language, or when the questions are especially complex or need further explanation (Mertens, 1998). Additionally, you can combine interview questions with some other form of media as part of the questioning, as when participants are asked to look at pictures or watch videotapes of interaction to then probe for a greater depth of information. Sometimes, face-to-face interviews can lead to more apprehension, especially when the questions are of a personal nature, or when researchers are asking to enter participants' homes (Watt & van den Berg, 1995). Depending on the nature of the study, it may be easier to interview participants collectively.

An interviewing strategy used with increasing frequency is the **focus group**, a small group of respondents (between 4 and 10 participants) who are selected by convenience, purposive, or snowball sampling methods. The format of the interview is generally loosely structured so that a wide range of information may be collected about a particular subject (Krueger, 1994; Morgan, 1988; Watt & van den Berg, 1995). For example, A. Hall (2006) used focus groups to explore what young adults value about reality television programming. Hall was interested in identifying attributes of various reality programs, how realism was evaluated, and which attributes were found most enjoyable.

Focus groups permit exploration of a conceptual area that has yielded inconsistent or contradictory evidence. In a study of media effects theory, Meirick (2006) used focus group interviews to clarify the beliefs of audience members about antisocial and prosocial media content. Meirick (2006) claimed that focus groups were used to "determine those beliefs and how they were expressed" (p. 633). Additionally, data from the focus groups "aided the development of reliable quantitative measures of schemas with perceived media effects as well as third-, first-, and second-person perceptions" (Meirick, 2006, p. 633).

Face-to-face interviews with individuals or focus groups can probe participants for information about themselves, about others, about groups to which they belong, or even about whole networks of which they are members. In their study of Latino expectations of

Table 13.5 Survey Study Worksheet

	**[Research Study Title]** **[Research Team Members]**
Research Questions/ Hypotheses		1. 2. 3....
Design	( ) Cross-sectional	( ) Longitudinal Panel	( ) Longitudinal Trend	( ) Other
Setting	( ) Laboratory	( ) Field	( ) Online	( ) Other
Sampling Strategy	( ) Random (list type):	( ) Nonrandom (list type):		
Questionnaire Type	( ) Distributed by test administrator	( ) Emailed administration	( ) Internet site	( ) Mailed administration
Questionnaire Format	( ) Open-ended	( ) Closed Format	( ) Question logic: Filter and Contingency Qs	
Interview Type	( ) Face-to-face dyads	( ) Focus Groups or ( ) Networks	( ) Phone (specify sample selection method):	( ) Mall intercept
Interview Format	( ) Structured	( ) Semistructured		
Variables	1. Independent:			
	2. Dependent:			
Variable Scales	1. Categorical Data	1. Nominal:		
		2. Ordinal:		
	2. Continuous Data	3. Interval:	Likert or Semantic differential items	
		4. Ratio:		
Descriptive Statistics Needed	Mean, median, mode, range, variance, standard deviation	Pie chart, Bar chart, Line graph, Frequency table		
Statistical Tests	RQ1/H1:			
	RQ2/H2:			
	RQ3/H3:			
Interpretation	For each RQ/H:	Significance of test statistic; Chance of Type I error; Rival hypotheses		

communicative competence, Bradford et al. (1999) listed three advantages of using focus groups. Bradford et al. noted that the "interactive effects of group settings" help to focus on participants' perceptions, attitudes, and behaviors to explore a specified concept from the perspective of the participants rather than the researcher. Focus groups may also increase the level of self-disclosure for participants from cultures that are more collective than individualistic. In this case, participants' responses are seen as parts of a whole group discussion rather than singular expressions. A final advantage Bradford et al. identified is that focus groups facilitate brainstorming around a specific concept or topic. As Bradford et al. (1999) noted, "people are more inclined to disclose information amid the security of others similar to themselves" (p. 105).

One of the disadvantages of face-to-face interviews for any study is that they are the most expensive form of data collection in terms of money and time. They also frequently require the most intensive form of interviewer training. Because using personal interviews nearly always means relying on nonrandom sampling methods, the sample obtained is often less representative and poses greater threats to external validity. The relative advantages and disadvantages of personal interviews and focus groups are listed in Table 13.6. In view

of these disadvantages, many researchers decide to use mall intercept surveys or telephone surveys instead.

As we discussed earlier, some survey researchers use **mall intercept surveys**, in which you find your participants at a shopping mall. They are less costly than personal interviews, and they provide relative anonymity to participants. The public setting reassures both participants and researchers about privacy and safety issues. However, some malls strictly prohibit administering surveys, shoppers are frequently pressed for time, and you must still be concerned about threats to external validity. You must take steps to ensure that the study's purpose will be addressed adequately by samples typically found in shopping malls, particularly at the locations you choose. And sampling should be scheduled across times and days the mall is open as a further hedge against selection bias. Many research teams using this method employ systematic sampling with a random start (from Chapter 5, this procedure means sampling every 7th person or every 14th person, and so on).

As an illustration, Kang, Cappella, and Fishbein (2006) were interested in collecting data about adolescents' judgments of anti-marijuana public service announcements. They used archived data created by the Annenberg School for Communication at the University of Pennsylvania through funding from the National

Table 13.6 Advantages and Disadvantages of Face-to-Face and Focus Group Interviews

Advantages:	Disadvantages:
Face-to-face personal interviews: 1. Easier to establish a rapport and climate of trust. 2. More difficult to avoid answering any item. 3. Can probe for more in-depth responses. 4. Can monitor participants' nonverbal reactions. 5. Can help to clarify any questions for participants. 6. Can combine interview questions with some other form of media as part of the questioning. *Focus groups:* 1. Loosely structured format for collecting wide range of information. 2. May help young children feel at ease with adult interviewers. 3. Group formats stimulate a greater variety of ideas. 4. Help to explore a specified concept from the perspective of the participants rather than the researcher. 5. May also increase the level of self-disclosure for participants from cultures that are more collective than individualistic.	*Personal interviews and focus groups:* 1. Can lead to more apprehension with sensitive questions. 2. Greater risk entering subjects' homes. 3. Most expensive form of data collection in terms of money and time. 4. Require the most intensive form of interviewer training. 5. Samples often less representative posing greater threats to external validity. 6. Some groups may exert conformity pressure over individual responses.

Institute on Drug Abuse. One sample was collected from shopping malls in four large urban locations while another sample was recruited from 15 different locations across the country. Together, data from more than 900 adolescents were used in the analysis, increasing sample representativeness and ensuring greater privacy through anonymity.

In many cases, **telephone surveys** may be more effective in soliciting needed information. Telephone surveys provide you with some distinct advantages. First of all, you can obtain more representative samples assuming that you take steps to systematically include cell phone numbers with landline numbers in your sampling frame. Recall the RDD procedure you learned about in the previous section. Telephone interviews also eliminate many privacy and safety concerns. Respondents may be more honest if the interviewer does not confront them personally, and the interviewer's appearance cannot influence the way in which questions are answered (though paraverbal characteristics may influence responses; see Pal & Buzzanell, 2013). Marketing firms that use phone interviewing often find the method provides more opportunities to enhance interviewer consistency. Interviewers are often located at a research center where supervisors may be available to answer any questions interviewers may have as they interact with participants. However, in a comparative study of RDD phone surveys versus face-to-face interviewing, there were some distinct disadvantages associated with phone surveys. Holbrook, Green, and Krosnick (2003) reported that phone respondents were more likely to provide no opinion or neutral responses, were less cooperative and engaged, were more likely to express dissatisfaction with the interview length (despite the shorter time spent on the phone), were more suspicious of the interview process, and tended to present themselves more favorably than in face-to-face interviews (p. 79). The relative advantages and disadvantages of mall intercept and telephone surveys are listed in Table 13.7.

Once you have decided on the type of survey interview you will conduct, you will then select a format that will determine how questions are asked and what their content will look like.

Formats for Survey Interviews

The format for asking questions can vary in three ways. Interviews can be structured, semistructured, or unstructured. **Structured interviews** have set formats called protocols or schedules that dictate what questions to ask when. They are defined by the following criteria: (1) The number of questions and their wording remains identical for all participants; (2) the questions are presented in the same order; and (3) researchers do not attempt to clarify or explain any question, even when asked, at any time during the interview process.

Table 13.7 Advantages and Disadvantages of Mall Intercept and Telephone Surveys

Advantages:	Disadvantages:
Mall intercept surveys: 1. Less costly than personal interviews. 2. Provide relative anonymity to participants. 3. Public setting reassures both participants and researchers about privacy and safety issues. *Telephone surveys:* 1. Provide more representative samples. 2. Eliminate many privacy and safety concerns. 3. Respondents may be more honest if they are not confronted personally by an interviewer. 4. Interviewer's appearance cannot influence the way in which questions are answered. 5. Interviewers are often located at the research center where supervisors may be available to answer any questions interviewers may have.	*Mall intercept surveys:* 1. Some malls strictly prohibit surveys. 2. Shoppers frequently pressed for time. 3. Samples still not representative. *Telephone surveys:* 1. Respondents may actually become less willing to disclose information because of less personal format. 2. Interview length cannot be as long as those conducted in person. 3. Greater distrust of telephone surveys as veiled marketing devices. 4. Respondents frequently use their answering machines to screen callers. 5. Can break it off at any point just by hanging up and blocking future attempts.

The rationale for such strict requirements is that you would be much less likely to interject any bias as the interviewer (Frankfort-Nachmias & Nachmias, 1996).

Semistructured interviews are also called the focused or "non-schedule-structured" interview (Frankfort-Nachmias & Nachmias, 1996, p. 234). This second type of interview format has four characteristics: (1) It asks respondents to reflect on an experience or a concept that they all have in common, (2) it refers to situations or constructs that have been analyzed and often defined prior to the interview, (3) it requires the interviewer to use a guide that specifies topics of interest rather than an interview schedule, and (4) it focuses on the participants' understanding or meaning of a particular concept or experience. For example, you might conduct semistructured interviews with students in your major to ascertain their strategies for "crashing" a course (i.e., getting into the course after it is already fully enrolled or after classes have begun).

In choosing a semistructured interview, you intentionally provide the respondents with more freedom because your research is generally more exploratory in nature. For example, Reich (2002) used a semistructured interview format to explore how women who have experienced violence are labeled and subsequently treated by the organizations that assist them. Participants were contacted through snowball sampling, and responded to 15 to 20 open-ended questions. The questions were based on previous research investigating the way organizations use language to label women as *victims* and the resulting effects on women's identities. The questions were meant to serve as a guide to stimulate discussion in each interview. After all participants had been interviewed, it was clear from the responses that thematic consistency could be established through recurrence, repetition, and forcefulness and that taping the interviews and contacting a subsample following the study to verify emerging themes helped to establish validity.

Unstructured interviews have the greatest amount of flexibility (also called the *nondirective interview*). In this type of interview, you will not have any prespecified set of questions; you will rely entirely on the participants to identify experiences and events that seem significant or meaningful. You may also use this format as a pilot survey to help construct questions as probes for subsequent interviews.

The purely nondirective approach to interviewing is more likely to be associated with more interpretive and critical methods such as ethnography and conversational and discourse analyses (see Chapters 7 and 8). From these paradigm perspectives, you are concerned with presenting the subjective points of view the participants express; it would not be important to you, therefore, to keep the structure of the interview uniform for every participant.

Uniformity and consistency is a general concern in discovery-based survey research. For this reason, it is important to examine the role of the interviewer and the amount of training required, which also varies depending on the type of interview and the format selected.

Training Survey Interviewers

Survey researchers who come from the discovery paradigm perspective have traditionally preferred structured interview formats. This type of interview requires extensive training to maintain consistency with generally one rule as the guiding principle: Intrude in the research process as little as possible. This means that "the interviewer should never direct the respondent toward an answer, should never be judgmental, [and] should not interpret the respondent's answers according to his or her own beliefs or values. The interviewer must be consistent in his or her communication style and language, so that each respondent is exposed to the same kind of measurement environment" (Watt & van den Berg, 1995, p. 359). With this approach, interviewers are given very specific sets of instructions on what to ask participants and how to state questions. Then, interviewers are usually required to complete practice interviews so that their performance can be thoroughly evaluated by the research team. Finally, the interviewer is required to repeat the practice trials until the researcher "is convinced that the interviewer is sufficiently low-key and consistent and will not bias the results" (Watt & van den Berg, 1995, p. 359).

Essentially, many discovery-based survey researchers believe that the interviewer should be a neutral medium and not affect responses in any way. This approach to survey research is based on the assumption that every question will mean the same thing to each participant and that the "interviewer's presence should not affect a respondent's perception of a question or the answer given" (Babbie, 1995, p. 264). The assumption of complete neutrality on the part of interviewers necessitates they play the role of detached observer. Even probes for more information or answers to respondents' requests for clarification must be carefully constructed so that they remain neutral and cannot "in any way affect the nature of the subsequent response" (Babbie, 1995, p. 267).

Because semistructured and unstructured formats are adopted from different paradigm perspectives, interviewers are generally concerned with using preconceived questions as guides only. Precision and consistency of wording are critically important in structured interviews and in the second main form of capturing self-reports and other-reports in survey data: the questionnaire.

Questionnaires

A second common way of capturing survey research data is the **questionnaire**, the self- or tester-administered form of self-report and other-report data collection. Questionnaires can be administered through email lists or Internet websites, taken in structured interview settings with or without in-person administrator or telephone mediation, or mailed out to participants. When using a questionnaire, you must also decide what the structure of the questionnaire should look like and how questions should be asked. You can use the Survey Study Worksheet in Table 13.5 to help organize your decisions. Every decision about using questionnaires has advantages and disadvantages just as interview decisions have.

The most prevalent increase in survey delivery formats during the last decade is the use of Internet surveys. This approach can occur in several different ways, either by posting a link to a survey within an email sent out to a panel of participants, embedding the link for a survey on a website and inviting individuals to participate, or by constructing a survey as part of a webpage and collecting the data directly into a spreadsheet. Survey software programs, such as *Survey Monkey* and *Qualtrics*, have made the construction and distribution of surveys relatively easy as data collection tools. You can see a screenshot of the many question formats available for selection using *Qualtrics* in Figure 13.1. This software allows you to choose between open- and closed-ended formats, items using multiple types of scales (nominal, ordinal, etc.), and a question logic that permits filtering portions of the

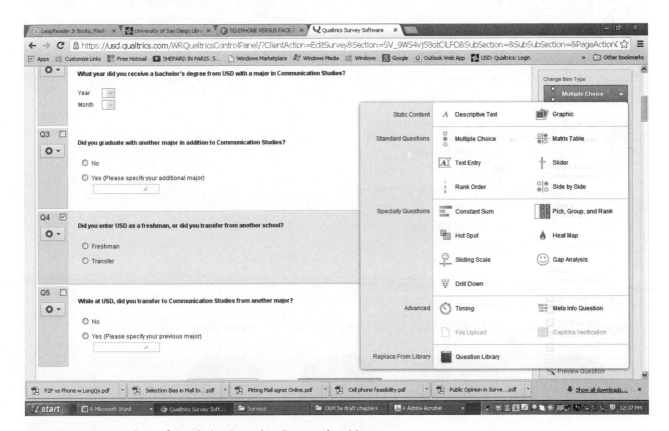

Figure 13.1 Screenshot of Qualtrics Question Formatting Menu

survey that will be screened by select participants. We will have more to say about these strategies in the sections that follow.

Additionally, survey software enables you to run some preliminary analyses, such as frequencies and averages for item responses. An example of this type of report appears in Figure 13.2. Survey programs also permit you to launch an open-invitation survey, so that anyone can respond, or panels of survey recipients. Panels can be emailed as part of the survey function, which will regulate the format and transmission of your email messages, including sending periodic reminders to participants who do not respond to initial invitations.

Unfortunately, most Internet surveys are taken voluntarily using nonprobability sampling techniques, which can seriously threaten the representativeness of the sample through selection bias. In a recent study of survey methods, a team of researchers (Yeager, Krosnick, Chang, Javitz, Levendusky, Simpser, & Wang, 2011) investigated the accuracy of survey findings collected from RDD and internet randomized samples and multiple internet non-probability samples. They used general population characteristics that were already known from several major national health surveys and then compared the demographics of the various samples they collected to these known characteristics. Probability sampling led to more accurate representations and predictions of certain variables than did nonprobability samples. However, they found that several procedures that we identified in Chapter 5, on communication data, helped to resolve the

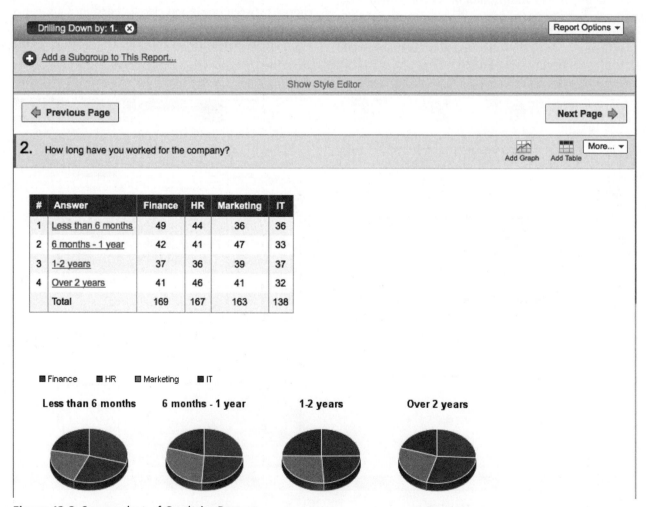

Figure 13.2 Screen shot of Qualtrics Report

differences in findings: quota sampling and post-collection stratified sampling. In the first instance, the researchers selected characteristics of the sample based on survey responses that repeated characteristics of the general population and discarded survey respondents who did not match those characteristics (e.g., if the population is one of low socioeconomic status, volunteer respondents from wealthier households would be eliminated from the study). In the second instance, the researchers identified a characteristic such as age, and then randomly sampled from all members based on that characteristic. In either case, sampling problems are one clear disadvantage of Internet surveys. Another is a lower response rate than face-to-face interviews when individuals are less-motivated to complete a survey or the survey is lengthy. It is simply easier to disengage from an online survey than refuse to answer an interviewer. Advantages of using online surveys include the relative ease of reaching large numbers of respondents in short periods of time by very economic strategies; it's also possible to reach respondents across geographic space using online surveys. Questionnaires keep the order and specific questions consistent, whereas consistency is sometimes a problem in face-to-face interviews. Some of the advantages and

disadvantages of Internet surveys appear in Table 13.8. As the frequency of using online surveys increases, we should remain vigilant about whether ethical principles are upheld in protecting participants and whether various groups will become inundated with survey requests.

Most academic institutions now have adopted survey calendars or schedules to help monitor when surveys are distributed and which populations have been targeted to help reduce survey overload. For instance, the use of telephone and online class registration systems provides easy access to a student population; but access to that population is tightly controlled, in part, so that fatigue will not reduce the students' willingness to respond to the most important survey items. We will also consider some of the ethical implications of survey research in the final section of this chapter.

General structure of questionnaires. The term **questionnaire architecture** has been used previously to capture the general structure of the questionnaire (Watt & van den Berg, 1995, p. 368). This term focuses very nicely on the attention you should pay to the structure of your questionnaire. You must consider three critical features: its general length, comprehensibility, and question order.

Table 13.8 Advantages and Disadvantages of Online Questionnaires vs. In-person Administration

Internet Questionnaires	In-person Test Administration
Advantages:	*Advantages:*
1. Provides easy access to a greater number of people.	1. Easier to control targeted groups for sampling.
2. May eliminate many privacy and safety concerns through greater anonymity or confidentiality.	2. Respondents may feel more motivated to take and finish the survey in the presence of a test administrator.
3. Respondents may be more honest if not in the presence of a test administrator.	3. Test administrator is on hand to answer any questions that may arise from respondents.
4. May be preferred in longitudinal studies in the place of personal diaries or journals, especially when the same information is repeatedly collected (software can automatically be set to prompt people to respond).	*Disadvantages:*
5. Respondents will not be influenced by test administrator characteristics.	1. May be more difficult to obtain larger samples of respondents.
	2. May be more costly to administer.
Disadvantages:	3. Respondents may feel less able to decline to participate.
1. May be difficult to obtain a representative sample with probability sampling.	4. May be influenced by test administrator characteristics.
2. Respondents may be less motivated to respond than with face-to-face context.	
3. Must maintain shorter length and therefore able to collect less information.	
4. Respondents can end survey easily at any time.	

First, you should regard *length* as a primary consideration. Questionnaires that are excessively long are fatiguing to individuals who may not complete certain items or who may decide not to complete the questionnaire at all because the task seems too demanding.

The second feature to consider is clarity. Because questionnaires often take the place of interviewers, both the questions themselves and the instructions to participants should be *easy to understand* and self-administer, or at least easy for your research team to administer with little advance training. The survey questionnaire should come with a cover letter and/or set of instructions that identify the basic purpose of the study and how to fill out the questionnaire. These should be *clearly worded* and use a vocabulary *appropriate* for the age, culture/language, and education level of the respondents. For the potential effects of length and clarity, all questionnaires should be pilot tested before they are administered to the study's selected sample. Because the structure of the questionnaire is important, you will need to be concerned with the *order* in which the questions are presented. Questionnaires in survey research are designed to measure concepts. When researchers construct a questionnaire, they have to be especially careful that questions asked early on will not adversely affect the way respondents answer later questions. These are called **order effects**. For example, asking respondents to indicate whether they believe disclosures about their sexual histories are part of practicing safe sex will likely influence later attempts to ask questions about how truthful they are in disclosing information about their sexual histories to new partners (Lucchetti, 1999).

However, the pattern of order effects isn't always clear. For example, asking in general how religious a person is can affect later specific questions regarding church attendance, but asking the more specific question first is just as likely to affect the later general response. People try to respond in ways that make them appear to be consistent. Sometimes, question sequences are randomized to eliminate order effects. However, randomizing the order can make the questions appear chaotic to respondents who have to jump from one topic to the next, and it does not guarantee that you have removed order effects. Researchers should pay more attention to constructing an order that participants find easy, interesting, and topically consistent or logically arranged (Babbie, 1995, p. 151; A. A. Berger, 1998, pp. 40–42).

Formats for survey questions. In this section, we examine the various types of questions based on their functions and the guidelines you should use in constructing these specific questions. There are several general types of question formats that can change how questions function depending on the purposes of the research. First, questions can be open-ended or closed format. **Open-ended questions** are defined as questions that ask respondents to provide unstructured or spontaneous answers to questions or to discuss an identified topic. For example, Harwood, Raman, and Hewstone (2006) distributed a questionnaire to college students with an open-ended question that asked them to "Please tell us any things that happen in communicating with your grandparents that make you aware of their age, or aware of the age difference between you" (p. 185). The responses to this question were analyzed and coded for content so that Harwood et al. (2006) could explore "communication phenomena associated with age salience" (p. 185). Open-ended questions ask respondents to report on an experience or concept in their own terms. Frequently, as you see in the preceding example, they are used in survey research as means of exploring new conceptual territory.

Closed-format questions (sometimes called *forced choice*) ask respondents to "choose from a fixed set of alternatives or to give a single numerical value" (Watt & van den Berg, 1995, p. 366). Questions that specify all possible response alternatives are scaled items. You will learn more about these types of responses in the next section of this chapter. Briefly, examples of closed-format questions include those that ask respondents to identify their biological sex or to indicate their level of agreement with various beliefs or attitudes. Generally speaking, open-ended questions are harder to code and can lead to greater problems with consistency as a result. Closed-format questions are much easier to handle but may be less rich, and possibly less accurate reflections of the respondents' perceptions and interpretations. This issue will surface again in your considering the warrants for survey research.

Network studies have their own versions of questions that are unique. The **roster method** is sometimes also known as the recognition technique. It is more like closed-format questions in that participants in the study are given a roster of all the members of their social system (e.g., all the employees in an organization or all the members of a sorority) and are asked to respond to questions about all the other members with whom they regularly interact. In this way, the participants are given an opportunity to recognize the members of their network. Alternately, the free-recall technique may be used. In this technique, the participants are asked to list all the members of their social network and then to answer a series of questions about each of those persons.

Questionnaires can also make use of filter and contingency questions, referred to as question logic in survey programs like *Qualtrics*. **Filter questions** direct people to respond to various portions of the questionnaire. For example, the question, "Do you own a DVD player? If yes, then skip to question #10" is a filter question (the "if . . . then" sequence is why this move is called question logic). The **contingency question** depends on responses to filter questions, and in most survey programs, is viewed only based on responses to filters. In the preceding example, Question 10 may ask respondents how long they have owned a DVD player as a contingency question. Open-ended and closed-format questions and filter and contingency questions are formats built into the survey software that make them easy to select for your own research purposes.

In general survey research, questions can also ask for different types of information. Three types of information are commonly sought: (1) Information that describes who participants are, called *demographics;* (2) information about behaviors participants engage in; and (3) information about participants' thoughts, feelings, beliefs, and attitudes. First, as a researcher, you may ask for descriptive information about the participants' *demographics.* As we mentioned earlier, demographics refer to personal characteristics of the respondents such as biological sex, ethnicity, education level, or socioeconomic status. When you construct surveys, it is important to become very sensitive about the ways in which individuals identify themselves along lines of race, class, religious affiliation, veteran status and disabilities. Mertens (1998) suggested broadening all of our classification codes and thinking generally about the way we use various categories like those that pertain to physical disabilities or learning disorders (pp. 121–122).

Second, you may want to know about participants' *behaviors.* When questions ask for information about specific behaviors or frequencies of behaviors, you should be aware of behaviors that respondents are likely to interpret as threatening as well as those behaviors that are not. Nonthreatening behaviors are those that are typical and easy to talk about like the number of times a week a person watches the evening news or how frequently a person emails friends. Threatening behavioral questions make participants feel defensive; obviously, what is threatening to one group of people might be less threatening to members of some other group When constructing questions, you should *avoid using provocative language* and make sure your questions are not leading. **Leading questions** direct respondents to answer in a specific way. Asking respondents, "How many times a week do you abuse drugs?" is obviously provocative *and* leading. It will very likely encourage participants to give you socially desirable responses regardless of the truth about their behaviors. Using leading questions typically occurs when those conducting a survey have an ulterior motive; for example, it is tempting in marketing surveys to lead consumers toward the benefits of a product you want them to begin to use. Likewise, training evaluations often lead participants to respond that the training was more-or-less effective, which is why those evaluations are referred to as "smile sheets" in the training industry. Leading questions are veiled (and not so veiled!) attempts at persuasion rather than direct and open-ended requests for information.

Sometimes you might be asking much subtler leading questions without realizing you are doing so. As an example, Oliver (1992) illustrated a contrast between questions worded in ways that implicitly locate blame for a physical disability within the person versus questions that locate the cause elsewhere. For example, notice the difference between asking, "What physical condition causes your difficulty in holding, gripping, or turning things?" and "What difficulties in the design of everyday things make it difficult for you to use them?" Oliver argued that questions that appear to be neutral in tone could still reflect researcher biases. One way to reduce the use of potentially threatening wording is to pilot your questionnaire with a sample of people representative of the population you wish to study.

When you construct a questionnaire, you can be extremely careful in your wording and still run into problems. Any questions that ask respondents to reveal the occurrence and frequency of undesirable behaviors—like questions about physical and sexual abuse, infidelity, drug use, sexual behavior, or criminal activity—are often underreported. There are a variety of ways to minimize the threat inherent in these questions. Asking open-ended questions instead of closed-format questions that ask how frequently a person engages in the undesirable behavior is one way to obtain more accurate information. Wording the question in such a way that provides a rationale for its importance or in a way that makes it all right to reveal the behavior asked for can circumvent tendencies to withhold information. For example, the question, "Many people complain that tax forms are just too complicated to figure out and compute accurately. What do you think about this problem?" may elicit more truthful tax practices than asking people directly if they fudge on their taxes. But it may also be leading and so you must test for this possibility with a pilot. Finally, preserving respondents' anonymity or at least assuring them of complete confidentiality makes it more likely they will disclose with greater accuracy when questions are threatening.

The third type of information you may want to find out about from respondents is about their *internal or mental states*, that is, their thoughts, beliefs, values, feelings, and attitudes or their perceptions of these in other people they know. Sometimes, the questions you will use are open-ended questions designed to explore a particular communication concept. Such questions can be used alone or in conjunction with closed-format questions. For example, Emmers-Sommer (1999) asked college students three open-ended questions regarding their perceptions of negative events in their relationships. This part of the questionnaire was used to confirm an existing classification scheme for negative relational events. Emmers-Sommer (1999) also asked them to complete the closed-format Miller Social Intimacy Scale that "examines individuals' feelings of psychological closeness" as an indicator of the feelings and attitudes the students had formed in their relationships (p. 290).

Ideally, all questionnaires are piloted to check for clarity of questions. In an unpublished study with Malcolm Parks, Huston had the experience of constructing a question designed to tap the concept of interpersonal commitment. Huston asked respondents to indicate how much they agreed with the statement, "I am afraid my relationship will end soon." In the pilot study, it became clear that this was an example of a **double-barreled question**, a question that asks two things simultaneously (Smith, 1988, p. 227). It asked respondents if they felt afraid about the relationship ending, and it also asked them if they expected the relationship to end soon. If she had not piloted the questions, this error would not have surfaced until the consistencies of the responses were checked. And then it would have been too late to correct.

To summarize, you should follow a few simple guidelines for questionnaire construction. These are

Table 13.9 Guidelines for Questionnaire Construction

1. Avoid making the questionnaire too lengthy.
2. Make the instructions and questions clear.
3. Make the instructions and questions easy to understand.
4. Consider the possibility of order effects, test for them, and make adjustments accordingly.
5. Avoid using provocative language.
6. Avoid leading questions.
7. Use open-ended questions and questions that provide support for answering truthfully when questions are potentially threatening.
8. Be sensitive to diversity issues when asking for information.
9. Avoid using double-barreled questions.
10. Pilot the questionnaire with a sample appropriate to the study.

listed in Table 13.9. In the next two sections of this chapter, you will learn how questionnaire items are constructed as instruments and how their use is validated. We will be using the measurement scales that we first introduced in Chapter 11, "How to Design Discovery Research."

Instrumentation and the Measurement of Survey Data

As a discovery-paradigm researcher, you will set up your survey study by using the survey to collect the data as a test of your claims as research questions and hypotheses. As you learned in Chapter 4, "Making Claims," your claims are assertions about the relationships between constructs or variables. We expanded on this explanation in Chapter 11 on designing discovery research by defining four measurement scales and providing multiple examples for each type from communication research. In survey research, each variable is *conceptually* and *operationally defined* and then embedded in interview questions or questionnaires through the process we earlier identified as operationalization.

Operationalization of Variables

When researchers specify the empirical characteristics of whatever communication phenomenon they have chosen to study, the process is called *operationalization*. Empirical indicators are observable and measurable.

Recall that conceptual definitions describe a communication construct by using other related concepts, just as a dictionary defines one word using other words Operational definitions specify the operations, procedures, and instruments needed to measure a communication construct. When you use empirical methods to test your evidence or data, the way that you measure the data will determine the kind of analysis that you can perform.

Levels of Measurement

Frequently in communication research, variables will be operationalized using several different measurement scales in one survey interview or questionnaire. From Chapter 11, you learned that measurement scales include nominal, ordinal, interval, and ratio levels of measurement. In an earlier example, Rancer and his colleagues (2013) were interested in examining students' perceptions of research methods courses. They first asked students about their *demographic* characteristics in a questionnaire administered in their classes. Students identified their age (interval), biological sex (nominal), and year in school (nominal). Likert scales (interval) were used to measure math anxiety, perceived topic difficulty, and perceived topic understanding.

In many media use studies, researchers will ask participants to indicate how frequently they view various forms of media. For example, Dupagne (2006) asked seven questions about media use, which included five questions based on ratio scales, such as "how many days a week, if any, do you read a daily newspaper?" and two interval scales, such as "On average, how often do you watch movies on television?" Responses could range over five points from "never" to "about every day" (Dupagne, 2006, p. 122).

Often, several items on a questionnaire will be combined to make up one variable measure. For example, Hmielowski and his colleagues (2013) measured "need for humor" (NFH) and "affinity for political humor" (AFPH) in their study of audiences for *The Daily Show* and *The Colbert Report*. The NFH measure consisted of 12 items or statements (e.g., "Sometimes I think up jokes or funny stories") measured with Likert scales (interval) whereas the AFPH measure included 11 items (e.g., "I appreciate political humor because it can aid me in reinforcing my political beliefs") on a Likert scale. After testing for consistency, the items are often summed and averaged to create one variable measure. In this same study, the researchers also used an ordinal scale to measure level of education which ranged from middle school to completing a doctorate (but without equal intervals). These various scales are illustrated in Table 13.10; however, this would also be a great time for you to review the measurement scale examples in Chapter 11, "How to Design Discovery Research."

Measurement scales provide you with a great deal of information, and they enable the data to be analyzed with more or less complex tests of the hypotheses. As you will see in Chapters 15 and 16 on descriptive statistics and statistical tests, nominal and ordinal scales create discrete categories of variables but they lack mathematical precision. Constructs measured with these two scales result in **categorical or discrete variables** (sometimes also called *nominal data*). Ratio and interval measurements give an array of information along a continuum instead of requiring the use of just one value to represent a whole group or sequence of numbers. Ratio and interval measures are more precise, which is why discovery paradigm scholars use those levels of measurement whenever possible. We can always reduce such rich, precise data to categories later. But we cannot capture that rich precision later if participants only give categorical responses. Because of this difference, it will be possible to make inferences not available when data is measured with nominal or ordinal scales. Constructs measured with interval and ratio scales are called **continuous** or **scaled** variables. This level of measurement has serious implications for the types of analyses that you can use to test your hypotheses.

As explained at the beginning of the section on survey data, a large amount of the work of survey research is done prior to the actual administration of the survey. From a discovery paradigm perspective, analyses of the data in survey research are direct tests of the claims. Depending on the scales used to measure each of the variables, certain statistical tests will be selected. For example, when your survey variables are all categorical, tests called *nonparametric statistics* are frequently used. When your measures are all continuous, you may use a correlation statistic or a regression test to find out whether the sampled data supports your claims. We reserve most of the discussion of statistical data analysis in survey research for Chapters 15 and 16.

Before statistical analyses can be performed, you must assess the validity and reliability of the sampling and data collection methods used in your survey to establish the worth of the data as evidence. Ideally, you will be using instruments that have been previously

Table 13.10 Survey Examples with Multiple Variables and Scales

---

Rancer et al., 2013: Study of Student Perceptions about Research Methods Courses

Demographic variables:

Age: number of years (interval scale)
Biological sex: Male or female (nominal scale)
Year in school: Freshman, sophomore, junior, senior (interval scale)

Dispositional variables:

Math anxiety
Perceived difficulty of topic
Perceived understanding of topic

Dupagne (2006): Study of Media Use and New Technology

Media use variable:

Respondents were asked seven questions about media use; each was accompanied by its own scale:

1. On average, how many days a week, if any do you read a daily newspaper? (Range: 0–7, ratio scale)
2. On average, how many hours a day, if any, do you watch television? (Range: 0–1,440 minutes {24 hours}, ratio scale)
3. On average, how often do you watch movies on television? (Range: 5-point scale from "never" to "about every day," interval)
4. On average, how often do you watch sport events on television? (Range: 5-point scale from "never" to "about every day," interval)
5. On average, how many days a week, if any, do you watch a news program on television? (Range: 0–7, ratio scale)
6. On average, how many hours a day, if any, do you listen to radio? (Range: 0–1,440 minutes {24 hours}, ratio scale)
7. On average, how many times a month, if any, do you go to see a movie in a theater? (Range: 0 to open ended, ratio)

Hmielowski et al., 2013

Respondents indicated level of agreement to the "need for humor" variable items and the "affinity for public humor" variable items with a Likert 5-point scale:

    1 = Strongly disagree
    2 = Disagree
    3 = Neutral
    4 = Agree
    5 = Strongly agree

Need for Humor (NFH): A sample of the 12 items:

1. Other people tell me that I say funny things.
2. Sometimes I think up jokes or funny stories.
3. I like to be around people who have a sense of humor.
4. I like situations where people can express their senses of humor.

Affinity for Political Humor: A sample of the 11 items:

1. I appreciate political humor because it can reveal the weaknesses of our political leaders and institutions.
2. I appreciate political humor because it can make me feel more knowledgeable about politics.
3. I appreciate political humor because it can aid me in reinforcing my political beliefs.
4. I appreciate political humor when it makes me aware that our political system is dysfunctional.

---

warranted before you collect your own data. These assessments often occur, in fact, in separate studies whose primary purpose is to validate the instrument. Validity and reliability assessments, as warrants in the research-as-argument model, are the last topic we consider in this chapter on survey research.

Survey Research Warrants

As you learned in Chapter 6 on "Warrants for Research Arguments," validity is a concern for accuracy or precision. It can refer to the *internal validity* of a survey study, which is the ability of the survey to accurately test claims in the form of hypotheses or research questions. In survey research, internal validity is almost synonymous with measurement validity because surveys are generally based on data collection strategies, not data manipulation.

In survey research, data collection strategies are aimed at maximizing response rates. In considering response rate, you will also become aware of the concern for *external validity* in survey research, which is the ability to generalize your results from representative samples to larger populations. *Measurement validity* specifically refers to the ability of a specific instrument or scale to accurately measure a variable. We will consider how survey research in particular is warranted through tests of measurement, internal, and external validity.

Response Rate as an Essential Contributor to Validity and Reliability

There are two types of response rates: total response rate and item response rate. The **total response rate** refers to the percentage of total survey interviews or questionnaires successfully completed and collected (or returned). The **item response rate** refers to the percentage of completed items or questions on each individual survey. Missing data in the form of whole surveys or specific items can affect the validity and reliability of any survey. You can influence the response rates, to some degree, by manipulating the format of the interview or the questionnaire. Considering the relative advantages of each type in Tables 13.6 to 13.8 and the guidelines in Table 13.9 will help you to maximize response rates.

For example, if your survey asks participants to respond to very complex and emotionally sensitive information, then arranging a smaller number of personal interviews will probably result in higher response rates than conducting a telephone interview or emailing out questionnaires. Interviews are more likely to increase response rates because as the interviewer, you are present to clarify any questions respondents may have about the survey, you can monitor respondents' nonverbal (or at least vocal) reactions, and you can probe respondents

for more information. Additionally, experienced interviewers that express confidence in their techniques are more likely to elicit fuller responses and more completed surveys than interviewers with less experience and confidence (Durrant, Groves, Staetsky, & Steele, 2010). Increasing the amount of information collected usually increases the internal validity and reliability of the responses. However, sometimes the interviewer possesses characteristics that can affect respondent choices in ways that directly interfere with results. Among Chinese respondents, Liu and Stainback (2013) found that women were more likely to respond positively about marital issues when interviewed by a female as opposed to a male, suggesting greater pressure to appear in a positive light when women are in interaction with other women. Of course, it's also possible that being interviewed by an in-group member could decrease respondents' willingness to disclose their attitudes or behaviors: You must carefully consider the questions in your survey, and think about how group memberships might impact responses from your participants.

You must also consider the assurance of anonymity that an emailed, mailed or web-based questionnaire provides. It may be easier to return a survey privately than to be singled out at a school or in a doctor's office, for example, for an interview. Other considerations in questionnaire construction already mentioned can affect response rates. Incomplete surveys or total nonresponses are more likely when the questionnaire is too long, or too complex, or too vague. Questions that are leading or provocative or are generally insensitive to respondents' diversity are also likely to diminish response rates.

Paying attention to these important factors will help to increase response rates as a function of the actual interview process. In the case of emailed questionnaires, you can also send out follow-up mailings to increase the total response rate. Adopting strategies like follow-up contacts to increase total response rates will also affect external validity. If you use a random sampling method, the higher the rate of return, the more likely the sample you obtain will be representative of the larger population.

How do you determine what return rate is acceptable? There are widely varying answers to that question. For example, Babbie (1995) recommended achieving a response rate of at least 50 percent. Babbie (1995) also added a warning that a high response rate is not the only goal; you should work for samples that are not biased by selection, and achieving a high response rate is only one means of achieving that end. Selection biases happen when a disproportionate number of respondents who share a certain characteristic are more likely to respond than those who do not have the characteristic. Individuals who have strong political attitudes or favorable/unfavorable experiences with various practices or policies are more likely to respond to a survey about these issues and choices than those who feel less strongly. That's why YELP reviews often come from consumers who really like or really dislike particular products or retail outlets. In a similar fashion, "RateMyProfessor.com" reviews can suffer the same type of bias. Selection biases can affect both internal and external validity. Recall that Internet surveys often make use of convenience or non-probability sampling. If you know certain population characteristics ahead of time, you can use quota sampling to try to obtain greater representativeness. So, for example, if you are at a college or university that has a 60/40 female/male ratio and you are interested in examining variables such as social climate, you could make sure that your Internet sample reflects the same proportion of the sexes as a potential influence on climate perceptions. While total response rates can affect external validity, item response rates affect measurement validity and reliability of a scale.

Establishing Valid Measurement

In Chapter 6, "Warrants for Research Arguments," you learned about several types of measurement validity that researchers from the discovery paradigm use as warrants for their arguments. Here, we only consider two points that address *how* measurement validity is established in survey research.

Our first point is that measurement validity requires that you construct a rationale for how you have arrived at your definition of a variable. This is most closely related to the idea of *richness*, as we presented it in Chapter 6, in considering *content validity*. You may also establish *criterion validity* by appealing to past and current conceptual and operational definitions of a variable. You may also want to assess *construct validity* by evaluating the structure of a variable, that is, by defining what a variable is and is not. For example, a research team (Levine et al., 2004) conducted two studies of the most commonly used measure of verbal aggressiveness: Infante and Wigley's (1986) 20-item Verbal Aggressiveness Scale, with a Likert-type format. Levine et al. compared aggressively worded

items on the scale with other antisocial measures (e.g., narcissism and obsessive relational intrusion) and the benevolently worded items on the scale with other prosocial measures (e.g., empathic concern and perspective taking). These comparisons permitted Levine et al. to assess the dimensionality or structure of the Verbal Aggressiveness Scale and to assess convergent and divergent validity by comparison with other related measures. In fact, Levine et al.'s findings indicated that the scale might be assessing two factors or variables instead of just one. There are a variety of techniques used to make these assessments, such as exploratory or confirmatory factor analysis, discriminant analysis, and multivariate correlation and regression analyses, but these are beyond the scope of your introduction to research methods.

The second point we make is that validity assessments are companions to reliability estimates. Validity tests establish warrants for *accuracy* of a study's measures, whereas reliability estimates establish warrants for the *consistency* of measurement. Ideally, you will strive for instruments that have high levels of both accuracy and consistency. Babbie (1995) illustrated the relationship between the two with the visual analogy of shooting at a bull's-eye. Measures that are high in reliability but are not valid show all of the shots clustered together but off center. The measures may be consistent, but they are consistently wrong. This type of error is called **constant error or bias**. Measures that are valid but not reliable are like shots that encircle the center but only diffusely. In this case, measures have small amounts of error that infiltrate from a variety of sources. This type of error is called **random error or noise**. And measures that are high on both dimensions show the shots dead on the center and clustered closely together (Babbie, 1995, p. 128). Measurements that are valid and reliable are not only accurate; they are consistently accurate. It is important, therefore, that we now consider the final element of this section, reliability estimates in survey research.

Establishing Reliable Measurement

Each of the types of measurement reliability you learned about in chapter 6 is relevant to survey research methodology. In this section, we briefly explore how researchers establish *stability*, *homogeneity*, and *equivalence* in measurement.

You may recall that *test-retest reliability*, a form of stability, occurs when a self-report survey instrument that has been administered to a group of people is given again, to those same people, on a later occasion. To the extent that the same people achieve consistent scores over time, test-retest reliability has been achieved. To demonstrate test-retest reliability, you need to consider what interval of time would be appropriate. If your measurement is repeated too soon, the participants may recall the items, and their scores may not have changed because of familiarity. But if too much time elapses before the second measurement, then real change on the variable being measured is likely to have occurred. Obviously, the appropriate time interval for demonstrating test-retest reliability will depend on the concept being measured. For example, children's reading ability is very likely to change over 6 months, but other variables, such as an adult person's willingness to communicate, or his or her credibility, are much more stable over time. So you will need to consider how much time to allow between your test and retest: Allow enough time that your respondents are not simply recalling the items on your survey; but do not wait so long that real change in the variable you are attempting to measure is likely to have occurred.

The second way to estimate reliability of a survey instrument is to assess the *homogeneity* (or internal consistency) of measurement. There are several methods used to check the patterns of response consistency in interval-level data scales such as the Likert-type and semantic differentials. Some of the survey items will correspond to a scale used to measure a variable associated with the study participants; for example, McCroskey's PRCA-24 scale consists of 24 Likert-type items used to measure communication apprehension. These 24 items are embedded in a survey that most likely asks for other information, such as participant demographics. To estimate the reliability of a scale, you could choose one of several techniques using *SPSS*, or other statistical software designed for this type of analysis; the SPSS reliability commands are found under the heading "Scale" under the Analyze tab (refer to the screen shot in Figure 13.3). One common technique is called the **split-half technique** in which one half of the items on a scale are randomly chosen and correlated with responses from the other half. Another more prevalent method is to calculate a **Cronbach's alpha**. This technique "randomly selects multiple pairs of subsets from an instrument, correlates each pair's scores, and then uses the composite correlation between all the paired subsets as an index" of consistency

(Smith, 1988, p. 47). As with any correlation, the closer the values are to 1.00, the higher the consistency estimate. Cronbach's alpha is so commonly used, it has many equivalent terms; whenever you see references to alpha reliabilities, reliability coefficients, alpha coefficients, *A*, or α, the authors are most likely referring to Cronbach's alpha.

The final way survey researchers assess the consistency or reliability of variable measurement is to establish *equivalence* of measurement. Recall that equivalence can estimate consistency in two ways, depending on the data source: Intercoder agreement verifies the agreement among judges about how qualitative data are interpreted or categorized; and alternate forms method verifies the consistency of measurement results yielded by more than one measure of the same construct. Whenever several coders are categorizing communication responses according to the operational definitions of the variables, we expect their responses to be equivalent or to agree. Intercoder agreement can be expressed as a correlation between the values of ±.00 and ±1.00. The closer the value approaches 1.00, the higher the level of agreement; but usually a value lower than .70 is considered too low to constitute reliable measurement. Other estimates can be used as well. Scott's pi, Krippendorf's alpha, and Cohen's kappa are all assessments of intercoder agreement. For example, Harwood et al. (2006) used Cohen's kappa to determine consistency across coder judgments for identifying and categorizing topics participants avoiding discussing. Just as Cronbach's alpha, a measure of relationship, is used to assess internal consistency of items in one Likert scale, correlation also can be used to assess the equivalence of two interval or ratio-level scales (i.e., two alternate forms). This is frequently used when researchers know of some existing measure, but want to use a shorter version of it (e.g., McCroskey's 24-item PRCA, or a 12-item version of that measure).

You should always provide some assessment of reliability and validity of your measures to establish warrants for connecting the data to your claims. As stated earlier, measurements that are valid and reliable are not only accurate; they are consistently accurate. Failure to estimate validity and reliability considerably weakens your argument that the instruments found in your survey will provide an adequate test of your study's claims. Additionally, survey researchers have an obligation to consider ethical issues affecting their participants.

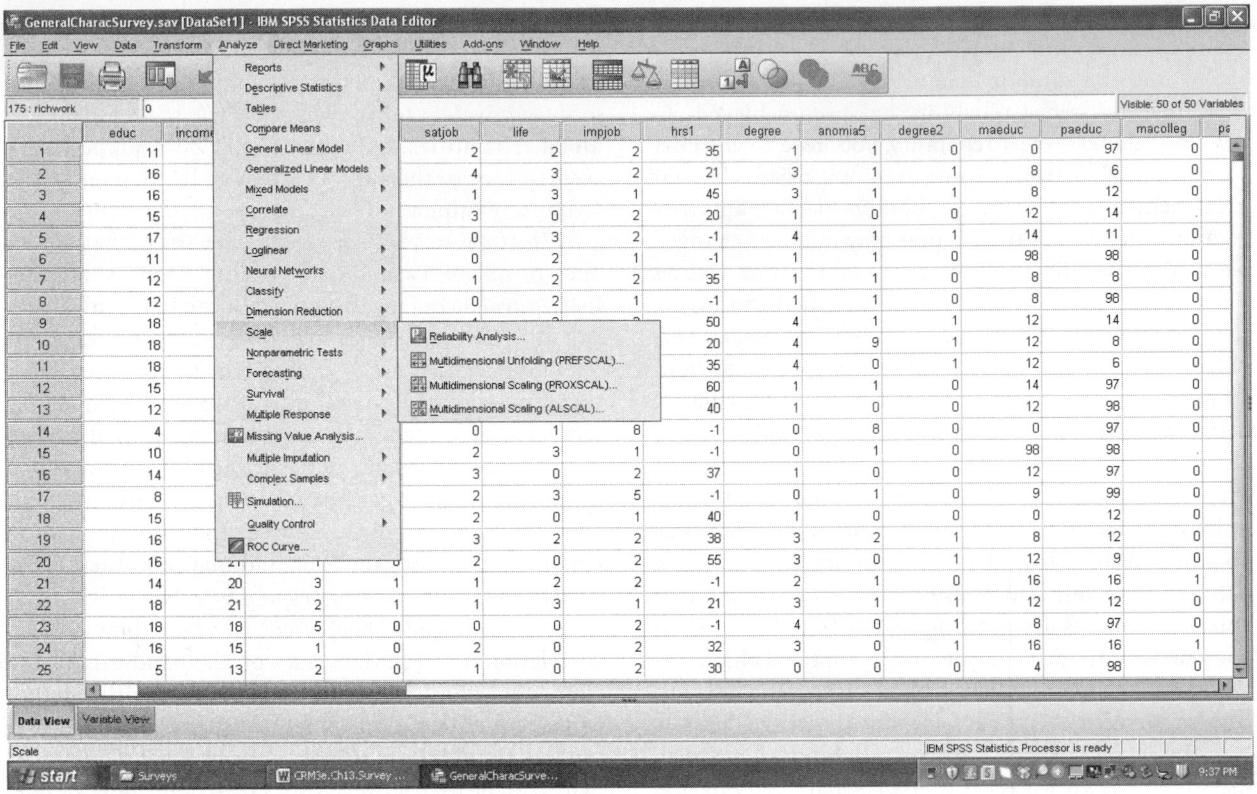

Figure 13.3 Screenshot of SPSS *Scale* Command for Reliability Tests

Ethical Issues in Survey Research

There are several ethical considerations you should make before conducting a survey study, primarily having to do with the way data are collected and reported. Recall from the second chapter on ethics and research the procedure of *informed consent*. Participation in research must be completely voluntary, which means that you have an obligation to inform individuals of any risks that their participation might entail. It also means that individuals can choose to stop participating at any point and that they will not be coerced in any way to participate or to continue to participate once the study has begun.

Most Internet, email/mail, telephone, and mall-intercept surveys can guarantee that participants' identity will be fully protected through *anonymity* in which identities are never revealed. However, when survey researchers are conducting face-to-face interviews or focus groups, the process of informed consent may be problematic if participants are not legally permitted to make their own informed decisions (e.g., if they prisoners, active duty military personnel, persons with mental illness, or if they are underaged children). Informed consent must be obtained from the guardians of persons who are not able legally to consent for themselves and from the parents of children participants. Sometimes, studies are about child or adolescent behavior that parents might want to know about, and so the researcher must be very careful not to violate the privacy rights of all parties involved. For example, suppose you were asking questions about teen "at risk" sexual behavior or drug usage. Even seemingly more benign questions, which ask about family coping mechanisms or other private family behaviors, may create a situation in which parents pressure their children to reveal what was told to the researchers.

In potentially face-threatening contexts, such as face-to-face interviews and focus groups, you must consider how you will protect your participants' *confidentiality*. One way to allay concerns is to guarantee that the study results only will be shared in such a way that participants' identities would not be revealed before they granted informed consent. For example, parents would still gain knowledge about adolescent or child behavior without assigning any set of answers to their own children. In many cases, researchers promise to provide access to mental health representatives if participants become uncomfortable with any aspect of the research process, and access often remains in place long after the conclusion of the data collection process. Protection of identities is a concern as long as the data exists, so researchers must guarantee safe, encrypted storage and, usually, destruction of the data when the analysis has concluded.

Researchers collecting survey data are expected to collect representative samples where possible, and that representation should not misrepresent minorities or socioeconomic groups by selective features. For example, health surveys conducted biannually by the National Cancer Institute using the RDD process described earlier in the chapter oversampled African Americans and Hispanics until percentages matching US Census figures were obtained. This procedure was critically important for studies assessing what health information about cancer had been received and understood (see, e.g., Viswanath et al., 2006).

A final consideration is accuracy in reporting. It is sometimes tempting to suppress or alter information that does not support our claims. But doing so violates a basic ethical tenet of research and would destroy your credibility as a researcher. Furthermore, unethical decisions like that reduce the confidence of people in all scientific research! In an analysis of 37 studies of the possible relationship between the lunar cycle and bizarre behavior, Rotton and Kelly (1985) refuted existing evidence by exposing errors in the data collection and analyses processes. For example, in one study, full moons in the lunar cycle coincided with weekends during data collection when that phase was correlated with a higher number of car accidents. But accident numbers tend to increase on weekends when the incidence of driving under the influence of alcohol and drugs also increases. Statistically, researchers should have analyzed the data using a time-series approach, but nearly none of them did. In one study that used the time-series analysis, a pattern emerged that did not fit the lunar phases of its cycle. One of the authors cited by Rotton and Kelly had conducted 48 tests of the "lunar lunacy" hypothesis and claimed significance. However, he failed to state that of the 48 tests, only 3 yielded significant results while 45 found no evidence to support the relationship between the moon's cycle and bizarre behavior. Even when a belief is robust and popular, researchers are obliged to be accurate and complete in reporting their results.

As you can see, from our summary in Table 13.11, when surveys are used in communication research, they require careful preparation and administration. In the preparation of surveys, you must decide what types of explanatory claims you will use: associative or causal. Once your claims and variables are identified, you must decide on the sources, settings, and design you will use in collecting the data. You must also carefully construct the instruments whether you are structuring questions for interviews or questionnaires. In operationalizing your constructs, you must decide on the levels of measurement you will use: nominal, ordinal, interval, and ratio. In administering the survey, you must establish warrants for the data collected in support of the study's claims by assessing the survey's validity and reliability. You will see in Chapters 15 and 16 that the specific tests of survey research questions and hypotheses are statistical analyses that require equal care in interpretation.

Table 13.11 Survey Research Summary Table

Paradigm	Claims	Data	Warrants	Manuscript Format
Discovery	Describe, explain, and predict	Representative samples from populations of people	Reliability established through stability, equivalence, and homogeneity. Content, criterion and construct validity of variable scales. Sample representativeness.	Research report

Key Terms

Applied research	Filter questions	Panel longitudinal designs
Basic research	Focus groups	Political polling research
Categorical or discrete	Internet surveys	Questionnaire architecture
variables	Interview formats: structured,	Questionnaires
Closed-format questions	semistructured,	Random digit dialing
Constant error or bias	unstructured	Random error or noise
Consumer research	Item response rate	Roster method
Contingency questions	Leading questions	Split-half technique
Continuous or scaled variables	Mall intercept surveys	Survey research
Cronbach's alpha	Network analysis	Telephone surveys
Double-barreled questions	Open-ended questions	Total response rate
Face-to-face interviews	Order effects	Trend longitudinal designs

Discussion Questions

1. Why are interviews taken "at random" on a street corner not really random?
2. Why do you think random sampling is essential from a discovery paradigm perspective and not essential from interpretive and critical paradigm perspectives?
3. If you wanted to conduct a survey study of children's reactions to frightening movies, what should you consider in deciding to use interviews or questionnaires?
4. Would researchers from a discovery paradigm prefer structured or unstructured interview formats? Explain your answer.
5. Because survey research is traditionally a discovery-paradigm situated form of research, how do the warrants of validity and reliability differ from those used in research from interpretive and critical paradigms?

"Try It!" Activities

1. Find a survey research report that identifies a claim in an exploratory study and one that identifies an explanatory or predictive claim. The two may be taken from the same article. Explain the difference between these two types of claims. Identify whether the explanatory claim is associative or causal.
2. Suppose you want to conduct a survey of attitudes toward rap music. Explain the various types of research designs you could use (cross-sectional or longitudinal). Explain the advantages and disadvantages of choosing each type.
3. Suppose you wanted to compare at-risk high school students with those not at risk for susceptibility to persuasive strategies. How would you go about defining and sampling both groups? What issues might require sensitivity to diversity?

14 How to Conduct Experimental Research

Introduction

In this chapter, we introduce you to experimental communication research, beginning with causal arguments, whose *claims* aim to explain and predict changes in communication attitudes and behaviors. Next, we explore how the processes of data collection and analysis are shaped by constructing research designs that support causal claims. Finally, we consider threats to internal and external validity, because those threats to accurate measurement compete with the research hypothesis as explanations for any observed change in a dependent variable.

Learning Outcomes

After completing this chapter, you should be able to:

» Explain how predictive claims in experimental research are grounded in deductive reasoning and causal arguments.

» Apply basic data elements (sources, settings, collection, and analysis) to experimental research examples contrasting their unique characteristics with other research methodologies.

» Use the warrants for internal and external validity to evaluate the strength of an experimental research design.

Outline

Experimental Research Claims
» Deductive Arguments
» Causal Arguments

Experimental Research Data
» Data Sources
» Data Settings
» Research Designs
» Data Collection and Analysis
    Data Collection Strategies
    Analysis of Variable Effects

Experimental Research Warrants
» Internal Validity Threats
    Time Progression Effects
        History
        Maturation
        Mortality
        Statistical regression
        Testing
        Instrumentation

When you conduct an experiment, control is a key element that will enable you to explain and predict what you see happening through your observations. Experimental research came about because of a desire to construct a sound causal argument. In other words, researchers were keenly interested in showing that variable X, and not W or Z, causes effects or changes in variable Y. The accuracy of your predictions is reflective of a strong causal argument based on the warrants of validity and reliability. From a discovery paradigm perspective, you will have succeeded in an accurate and precise representation of the "way things work" when you have warranted your causal argument by ruling out alternative or rival explanations.

Experimental Research Claims

Experiments are by their predictive nature designed to test the effect of one variable (or a set of variables) on another (or another set of variables). The claims explain the causal relationship between the variables under study, predicting the effect of the independent variable on the dependent variable. This form of argument relies on deductive reasoning, and establishing causality through the three criteria discussed in Chapter 11: time order, covariation, and control of rival explanations or hypotheses.

Deductive Arguments

Deductive reasoning begins with advancing a claim (generalization) supported through many observations for the purposes of reaching a conclusion. It is the cornerstone of all experimental research, in which predictive claims are constructed as hypotheses and tested through observations of the dependent variable so that a conclusion may be determined. Experiments are research designs that provide the level of precision and control necessary to assure that the hypotheses can be tested accurately. But every deductive process, every experiment, is made possible by theory-building and prior research. Virtually all experimental research relies on exploratory work that lays a foundation for constructing hypotheses. In one area of communication research, studying interpersonal communication led researchers to develop theories that would help to explain the changes they observed while people interacted with each other. Social exchange theories, for example, explain the tendency for people to "maximize their rewards" and "minimize their costs" in their relationships (Thibaut & Kelly, 1959; Blau, 1964). The theories were developed through **inductive reasoning**, in which many observed instances provided the basis for forming inferences or generalizations about communication behavior. Forming conjectural assumptions about what is being observed is considered exploratory work for discovery researchers. In this sense, interpretive paradigm research can contribute to the theory-building process. However, inductive observations do not permit the level of control needed to advance a causal argument. Hypotheses must be deduced from the theories, systematically tested through controlled experiments, and then statistically supported by the evidence to be accepted as valid and reliable.

To continue with the social exchange theory example, past experimental research has verified that relational partners perceive costs and rewards in relationships. Further experimentation has led to refining the theories across a variety of contexts and relationships and extended the theories to other constructs, such as equity, power and dominance. In one such experiment, Dunbar and Abra (2010), hypothesized that conversational partners express dominance by using a variety of strategies including "making suggestions, making demands, reasoning with their partner, disagreeing with their partner, ignoring, and expressing uncertainty" (p. 668). The researchers hypothesized that partners with perceived equal power (i.e., the ability to make decisions in solving a problem) would use more dominance strategies as attempts to gain control over the decision process. Partners in unequal power relationships wouldn't need to bargain for control as frequently because partners with high-power would make the decisions in the conversation and partners with low-power would permit this control. Dominance behaviors were coded by observers and included verbal and nonverbal behaviors like the number of illustrator gestures, body movement, number of reasons given, coded argumentativeness, vocal expressiveness, and speech fluency (p. 669).

The power balance was predicted as the cause that would affect the ways in which dominance was displayed. The researchers constructed an experimental design which would permit them to isolate and control the effects of varying the amount of power in a relationship (high and low) as they observed changes; they manipulated the independent variable to test its effect on the dependent variable. The researchers analyzed the results, producing a refinement of theory from which a new set of hypotheses can be derived and a new experiment conducted. Dunbar and Abra confirmed their central hypothesis that participants with less power were then also less dominant in conversational behaviors, but they also found that there was no difference in dominance between participants with more power and participants in equal power relationships. They suggested ways in which the experimental process could be improved to help strengthen their causal argument and that more research would be generally needed in order to understand the complex relationship between power and dominance. This deductive process in experimental research is the means for generating new knowledge in the discovery paradigm.

The experimental process is self-reflexive. It begins when you deduce a set of hypotheses from proposed theories and past research. The hypotheses predict the pattern of effects manipulating the independent variables will have on the dependent variables. You would then test the hypotheses by designing an experiment for

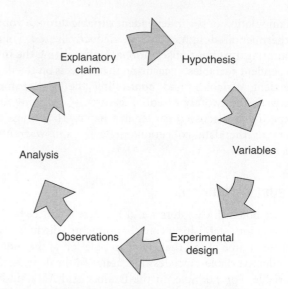

Figure 14.1 The Deductive Model of Experimental Research

observing those effects. The observations verify the explanatory predictions through precise and systematic analysis. This process is illustrated in Figure 14.1. Using our research-as-argument model, the deductive process begins with constructing claims that are verified through observations as data and warranted through tests of validity and reliability. Using an experimental model from Chapter 11, your instructor may guide you through these steps in constructing an experiment of your own. In this chapter, we will explore each of the components—claim, data, warrant—as they apply to experimental studies in our field.

In Chapter 13, "How to Construct Survey Research," you learned the difference between survey research and experimental research. Typically, surveys assess the world as it is; the variables are "givens" and are assumed to occur naturally. For example, survey researchers do not create relational power between partners; they would simply design an instrument scale to measure how this variable occurs in the general population. As an experimental researcher, on the other hand, you would be interested in exploring how relational power as a cause affects other variables, such as expressing dominance behaviors. Dunbar and Abra (2010) manipulated power in the relationship by exposing participants to a "high power" individual vs. a "low power" individual to test the effect of this manipulation on the participants' reactions. By controlling the manipulation of the independent variable through your experimental design, you can deductively test your claims against your observations. Manipulating the independent variables, measuring these effects on the dependent variables, and controlling the relationship between the two are essential features of designing an experiment discussed earlier in Chapter 11 and again here in the data collection strategies and warrants sections.

Causal Arguments

As we noted in Chapters 4 and 11, there are three basic criteria for establishing causal arguments. The first criterion is time order, that the manipulation of the independent variable precedes the change in the dependent variable. For example, in the Dunbar and Abra study (2010), the researchers had to expose participants to varying levels of relational power from their partners *first* to test the effect on the participants' conversational dominance behaviors, such as verbal argumentativeness, vocal expressiveness, and use of illustrators.

The second criterion for a causal argument is that variable changes must happen together; this correlation is the covariance requirement. Changes in the independent variable must be accompanied by changes in the dependent variable that occur close together. In our example, if too much time elapsed between the period that the participants experienced their partner's conversational "power" behavior and testing their perceptions of who was dominant, the causal link between these two would have been considerably weakened. A critic of your design would point out that perceptions of power were changed just by the passage of time or because the participants were affected by other partner behaviors unrelated to power. You will learn more about how causal arguments are strengthened or weakened in the section on warrants in this chapter.

The third criterion, controlling for competing explanations, refers to ensuring that the observed effect on the dependent variable can be accounted for only by the independent variable, not some third factor. In a study of teacher characteristics and their influence on students, Witt and Schrodt (2006) constructed a design to demonstrate the causal link between teacher immediacy behaviors and students' affective perceptions. Teacher immediacy behaviors include verbal support and expression of availability and nonverbal inviting behaviors, such as eye contact, smiling, and closeness in

proximity. The researchers had to take steps to effectively control for any rival explanations of cause and effect. They wanted to be sure that the pattern of effects observed were due to variations in the immediacy behaviors and not due to some other factor such as the gender of the teacher. **Intervening variables** are sometimes called rival factors or explanations; these are other potential causes or independent variables that could produce effects on the dependent variable. As a researcher, you would need to control for those potential effects by adopting one of the designs we discussed in Chapter 11, such as using random assignment, comparison groups and pretests-posttests. If you have not controlled these effects with your experimental design, your ability to make a causal argument will be considerably weakened.

Experimental researchers spend a great deal of time and attention to detail in constructing a design as a fair test of the data based on these three criteria: time order, covariation, and control over competing explanations. In experimental research, claims are most often found in the form of research questions or hypotheses, verified by some sort of observation. In traditional experimental designs, predictions are phrased as hypotheses in which at least one of the independent variables is manipulated while rival explanations are strictly controlled. This is the classic "wiggle" test. If we want to see what part of a machine causes changes in other parts, we can wiggle that part, systematically eliminating every other possibility until we can see what moves what.

In our earlier example, Witt and Schrodt (2006) constructed a research design to test the effects of teacher immediacy behaviors on student perceptions. They also tested the effects of a second independent variable, the use of instructional technology. By taking certain steps to hold other factors constant (steps you will learn about later on), Witt and Schrodt hoped to strengthen their claim that teacher behavior and the varying use of technology were the probable causes of change in the students' perceptions of the teacher and the course. Additional examples of hypotheses from experimental studies appear in Table 14.1. In each of these cases, the researchers presumed it was the manipulation of the independent variables that produced observed effects in the dependent variables.

In experimental research, the distinguishing factor from every other type of research, then, is that the researcher intentionally manipulates the independent variable for the purposes of testing its effect on the dependent

Table 14.1 Explanatory Claims in Experimental Research

H_1	: Young people have a stronger preference for negative content over neutral content [in news stories] than older people (Kleemans, Hendriks Vettehen, Beentjes, & Eisinga, 2012, p. 682).
	1. <u>Independent variable:</u> Age groups.
	2. <u>Dependent variable:</u> Negative content.
H_2	: Individuals will display more dominance (both verbal and nonverbal) in equal power relationships than in unequal relationships (Dunbar & Abra, 2010, p. 662).
	1. <u>Independent variables:</u> Equal/unequal power relationships
	2. <u>Dependent variable:</u> Dominance displays.
H_{3-4}	: Women playing with a same-sex avatar will exhibit greater presence and more aggressive thoughts than women playing with an opposite-sex avatar (Eastin, 2006, p. 355), and
RQ_{1-2}	: Does gender representation of opponent influence presence experienced and aggressive thoughts (Eastin, 2006, p. 356)?
	1. <u>Independent variables:</u> Sex of avatar, sex of opponent.
	2. <u>Dependent variables:</u> Presence and aggressive thoughts.
H_5	: The use of cute-flippant lines [in flirting] will be perceived as less (a) appropriate and (b) effective than the use of direct introductions and third-party introductions (Weber, Goodboy, & Cayanus, 2010, p. 185).
	1. <u>Independent variable:</u> Flirting strategies
	2. <u>Dependent variables:</u> Perceived appropriateness and perceived effectiveness.
RQ_3	: How, if at all, do differences in the use of instructional technology and teacher nonverbal immediacy behaviors interact to influence students' initial perceptions of affect for the teacher and course (Witt & Schrodt, 2006, p. 6)?
	1. <u>Independent variables:</u> Four treatment conditions of technology use (complete, moderate, minimal, no use) and two levels of teacher immediacy behaviors (high immediacy vs. low immediacy).
	2. <u>Dependent variable:</u> Students' perceptions of affect for the teacher and course.

Note: H = hypothesis; RQ = research question.

variable. The manipulation expresses control over the independent variable as the probable cause of change in the dependent variable. Additionally, the researcher uses experimental designs that we learned about in Chapter 11, "Designing Discovery Research." Elements such as pretests, random assignment, and comparison groups strengthen experimental control and hence the causal argument that the independent variable is the cause of any change in the dependent variable.

Besides these three control elements, researchers also frequently use **manipulation checks** to ensure that the manipulation of the independent variable has been successful. These include a variety of procedures that directly test whether the participants perceived the independent variable the way it was intended to be. In a complex experiment, Ramirez and Burgoon (2004) designed tests of an interactivity model of computer-mediated communication. They set up dyads (two people communicating) across one face-to-face and three mediated conditions for simultaneous interactions (these are also called synchronous interactions). Ramirez and Burgoon contacted one of the pair prior to the study to serve as a confederate. **Confederates** are

persons trained by the research team to behave in specific ways for research purposes while pretending to be study participants. The confederates were instructed to provide either positive or negative social information about themselves. Later in the study, the real participants (not confederates) were asked whether the information presented was positive or negative. By asking participants directly about the valence of the information provided by the confederates, Ramirez and Burgoon could make sure that the information was being perceived as they had intended it to be. The participants' evaluations of the information served as a manipulation check of the conditions of "positive information" and "negative information" varied by the confederates.

Not all causal arguments are tested with experiments. In the last chapter, you learned about a number of examples of survey studies that examined causal relationships. However, because of the central importance of establishing causal links in experimental studies, the strength of the causal argument that supports each hypothesis or claim rests in the design and analysis of experimental research data and the warrants for those claims. We first examine experimental research data.

Table 14.2 Experimental Conditions as Manipulation of the Independent Variable

Banas & Miller (2013) Study	Inoculation Message Type	Film Viewing of *Loose Change*
Condition #1	Fact-based Inoculation Message	Exposure to Film
Condition #2	Logic-based Inoculation Message	Exposure to Film
Condition #3: Control	No Inoculation Message	Exposure to Film

Experimental Research Data

The assumptions of causality and the requirements of experimental designs structure data in some very unique ways. We explore these by examining sources, settings, types of designs, data collection strategies, and data analysis in experimental research.

Data Sources

Sources of data for experimental studies vary by the type of variable you have selected to study. In our discussion of claims, you learned that the independent variable is constructed and manipulated by the researcher. Its manipulation is observed to see what effect it will have on the dependent variable. The changes in the state or conditions of the independent variable are based on its manipulation. The dependent variable is then assessed by the data sources of observation, self-report, or other-report to see what changes have occurred.

For example, Banas and Miller (2013) used inoculation theory to test the persuasiveness of the "9/11 Truth Conspiracy Theory" argument in the film, *Loose Change: Final Cut*. According to McGuire (Papageorgis & McGuire, 1961), inoculation theory explains how counterarguments can effectively contribute to resisting persuasive messages. Just as immunization shots provide protection against viruses, individuals can become inoculated against the argument in a persuasive message by hearing the counterargument first. Successful inoculations then act as warnings against the threat of a pending argument so that participants can initiate a defense. Banas and Miller manipulated the inoculation messages that participants received before they viewed the film. Each type of manipulation represented a different "condition" or "treatment" of the independent variable. For this experiment, there were a total of five

conditions, three of which will be described here and in Table 14.2. In the first condition, participants received a fact-based inoculation message before the film, consisting of a counterargument supported by "facts, evidence, concrete data, empirical reality, and specific examples" (p. 191). The second condition included a logic-based inoculation before being exposed to the film; the logic-based counterargument consisted of logical tests, deductive reasoning, sound argument, logical analysis, and critical thinking. The third condition was called the "control" condition, in which participants received no inoculation message prior to watching the film. When they had finished watching the film, participants' attitudes were measured to see to what degree they endorsed the central argument in *Loose Change*. Their attitudes toward accepting the central thesis of the film was the dependent variable. Participants who were "inoculated" were more able to resist the argument in the film than those who did not receive a counterargument (inoculation) before viewing the film. Moreover, those who had received a fact-based inoculation expressed greater resistance than those who had received a logic-based inoculation. The data sources for the dependent variables were the attitudinal self-report scales for participant perceptions of the argument in the film.

The Banas and Miller study reflects a classical approach to experimental research in which the independent variable is solely comprised of treatment conditions or manipulations of the independent variable. Manipulations are what make the variables *researcher-contrived*, as we discussed in Chapter 11 on how to conceptualize and operationalize variables. Frequently in communication experiments, researchers can construct messages that contain variable manipulations embedded within the message. For example, Weber, Goodboy, and Canayus (2010) varied videos of flirtatious "pick-up" lines in first encounter scenarios. In each case, the scene script was identical except for the flirting strategy used by males with females. An alternative to creating scenarios is to systematically vary the independent variable by training members of the research team to act as if they are a research participant to mask the real intent of the confederate's behavior. As we described earlier, confederate members were trained to provide positive information about themselves in one experimental treatment condition and negative information in another; in these conditions, the manipulation of the independent variable is achieved by the different behaviors displayed by the confederate members of the research team.

Sometimes variable groups occur naturally as internal characteristics of the research participants; they vary by types of characteristics that cannot be controlled by the researcher. If Banas and Miller had tested the effects of gender along with exposure to inoculation messages, participant gender would have been assessed as a participant characteristic. Some studies mix stimulus variables with participant characteristic variables; the resulting design is called a **mixed model paradigm** (G. R. Miller, 1970, as cited in Smith, 1988, p. 200). For example, Lehmann and Shemwell (2011) varied formats of print ads displayed in field settings with the gender and ages of participants viewing the ads. The formats (e.g., color vs. black-and-white) served as the stimulus variable and both gender and age were the organismic variables. The manipulation could only extend to the print format; gender and age were characteristics that were intrinsic to each participant.

Data Settings

In Chapter 5, "What Counts as Communication Data?" you learned that there are two basic settings: laboratory and field. The traditional setting for an experimental study is the laboratory. Laboratory settings permit researchers to exercise more control over environmental factors that might interfere with testing the causal relationship between the variables. Unfortunately, the control of extraneous factors achieved with the laboratory environment is sometimes offset by its artificiality. Participants often react in ways that they wouldn't ordinarily because there's just no place like home! Because of this problem, you might try to make the setting more natural. For example, in Dunbar and Abra's (2010) study of dyadic power described earlier in the chapter, participants were paired with confederates to engage in a conversation. The conversation took place in a "simulated living room environment with comfortable chairs that

face each other and is decorated with bookshelves, art on the walls, and an area rug. The room is designed to make the space appear home-like and encourage natural conversation" (p. 665). The cameras that they used for observation were unobtrusively placed so that participants would be more likely to remain unaware or forget that they were being watched. The conversational task that they were given, the Desert Survival Problem, is an engaging scenario which requires evaluating dilemmas and making decisions that are likely to lead to disagreements, ideal conditions for ordinary expressions of power and dominance. It was expected that these setting characteristics would help participants to respond as they would normally.

In some experiments, you might use a cover story that obscures the real testing situation so that the procedure will seem more natural to participants. **Cover stories** are deceptive strategies designed to reduce participants' reactions to the experimental situation while still maintaining control over manipulation of the independent variable. In the dyadic power study, Dunbar and Abra (2010) used confederates to create equal or unequal power conditions by explaining that one or both of them had emerged as the "leader" in solving the Desert Survival Problem individually. Those identified high in power "were told they had the ability to veto any decision made by the dyad" and how those decisions were reported to the research team. In the equal power condition, both the confederate and participants were told that they "were equals in the decision-making and that both people had the ability to say what was on the final list and had the ability to veto any decisions" (p. 666). If the researchers had not used trained confederates, they would not have been able to control the number and frequency of conversational disagreements that served as the basis for assertions of power and dominance displays. The confederates also underwent extensive training so that their performance was consistent and appeared as natural across all conversations with participants.

The cover story was given only to the **target** (or true) **participants**. The research assistant in the dyadic power study asked participants to wait while their partners finished their rankings; the short break was used secretly to determine a "dummy list" of confederate rankings so that these would match the participant's to "ensure consistent and identical differences between the two lists" across all of the conversations (p. 666). Though the confederate helped to ensure validity and consistency in responses, their identities were concealed from the target participants so that participant responses would not be affected by the design of the experiment.

You will learn more about laboratory setting effects in the discussion of validity and reliability in the warrants section of this chapter. Before leaving the topic of setting, however, we want to point out that a number of experimental studies are conducted in the field setting. For example, McDevitt and Chaffee (2000) went out to schools in the San Jose, California, unified school district and solicited students as participants who had been exposed to a particular curricular program on voting as well as student participants who had not been exposed. Adoption of the curriculum was not controlled by the researchers but by the teachers. McDevitt and Chaffee were fortunate to find equally large groups of students who had or had not been exposed to the program.

The weakness of field studies is a direct contrast with laboratory studies. In field studies, you do not have to recreate a natural environment for the sake of validity as you may have to in a laboratory study. But as a result, you will have much less control over extraneous factors in the field. McDevitt and Chaffee (2000) had to conduct special analyses to make sure that students exposed to the curricular program on voting did not differ substantially in characteristics from those other students not exposed to the curriculum; they also had to ascertain whether either group had been exposed to any events outside of the study that might influence the study's outcome (p. 269). We also elaborate on these potential setting effects when we discuss validity and reliability concerns in the warrants section.

Research Designs

The research design of an experimental study enables you to construct an effective experimental manipulation of the independent variable. Its primary purpose is to establish a strong base for causality through **experimental control**, which is achieved by checking the manipulation of the independent variable for its effectiveness, and through controlling alternative rival explanations for the observed set of effects on the dependent variables. In Chapter 11, we explained that experimental control is acquired through three procedural elements: comparison groups, random assignment to independent variable conditions, and pretest-posttest administrations (Katzer, Cook, & Crouch, 1982, pp. 118–119). In the

Banas and Miller study on inoculation effects described previously, participants were randomly assigned to the treatment conditions that varied exposure to inoculation messages. Random assignment assures that groups were equivalent at the onset of the study. Moreover, the researchers used a control group in which participants were not exposed to an inoculation message so that the effects of inoculation could be contrasted with this group. Using these two strategies helped the researchers isolate and control the effects of manipulating the independent variable. We will discuss this more thoroughly in discussing the warrants for experimental research.

To ensure that the manipulation of the independent variable has been successful, researchers will frequently use **manipulation checks.** These include a variety of procedures that directly test whether the participants perceived the independent variable the way it was intended to be. Again returning to the dyadic power study, Dunbar and Abra (2010) wanted to ensure that participants were accurately perceiving high-power, equal-power, and low-power conditions. They asked participants to evaluate their relative power positions and used these evaluations to substantiate the accuracy of perceptions about each of the conditions. In the inoculation study, Banas and Miller (2013) used manipulation checks to ensure that the inoculation messages were as they intended them to be. Both types (fact-based and logic-based) were validated by a team of experts. As noted earlier, successful inoculations should be perceived as warnings against the threat of a pending argument, in this case, warnings against the argument presented in the *Loose Change* film. The counterarguments act like flu shots that trigger defense strategies that keep us from getting sick. Statistical analyses helped to confirm that both inoculation messages resulted in perceptions of more perceived threat than the control condition. Manipulation checks help to ensure that the independent variable has been operationally defined accurately and consistently so that changes in the dependent variable can be attributed directly to changes in the independent variable.

Data Collection and Analysis

Data Collection Strategies

As we pointed out earlier, most experimental research involves the manipulation of the independent variable as a causal test of its effect on the dependent variable. Recall that the independent variable constructed by the researcher is called the *stimulus* variable. Or it can naturally occur as an assumed cause, such as the biological sex of the participants. In experimental research when there is more than one presumed cause, the independent variables are called **factors**, and the designs we discussed in the previous section are all types of **factorial designs** (Smith, 1988, p. 208).

In discussing experimental research, we often refer to one independent variable as if experiments are designed to test just the effect of one variable, *X*, on another. However, experiments frequently assess the effects of more than one factor. Look again at Table 14.1. In Eastin's (2006) study, the effects of two independent variables, the gender of a videogame avatar and the gender of the opponent character, on two dependent variables, presence and aggressive thoughts, were investigated. Witt and Schrodt (2006) tested the effects of two levels of teacher immediacy (immediate/nonimmediate conditions) and four levels of technology use (complete, moderate, minimal, no use) on student perceptions of affect for the teacher and the course.

Stimulus variables as independent factors in experimental research are traditionally categorical in nature. The experimenter constructs the treatment and control conditions. These are measured with a nominal scale, one of the measurement scales described in Chapter 11 on how to conceptually and operationally define variables. Each condition represents a separate category. To clearly display the number of independent variables tested by their specific number of categories per variable, researchers typically use a **research design statement.** It is usually expressed in numbers. For example, the Eastin (2006) study from Table 14.1 used a 2 × 2 design statement: one independent variable was the gender of the avatar game character (male, female) expressed as the first "2" and the second independent variable was the gender of the opponent game character (male, female) expressed as the second "2." The Witt and Schrodt (2006) study tested the effects of two independent factors: two levels of immediacy and four levels of technology use, resulting in a 2 × 4 research design statement.

Virtually every experiment has a research design statement that explains how many independent variables or factors will be tested and how many categories each independent variable will have. This statement is, in effect, a way of seeing how the dependent variable will be divided up or partitioned, in the analysis of the data, a topic to which we now turn our attention.

Analysis of Variance Effects

The traditional test of the effects of the independent variables on the dependent variable is called the *analysis of variance* (ANOVA), a test we explore at length in Chapter 16 on the statistical tests of group differences. In this section, you will learn how the results from this type of test are typically interpreted. When just one independent variable is manipulated and tested for effects, the analysis is called a *one-way* ANOVA. Defined in detail in Chapter 17, we say briefly here that the term, *one-way,* refers to one factor or independent variable. If there are two independent variables, then the test is called a two-way analysis. If there are three independent variables, then the test is called a three-way analysis, and so forth. Whenever there are more independent variables than just one, there are two types of effects researchers explore: main effects and interaction effects.

Main effects are the effects of each separate independent variable on the dependent variable. Suppose, for instance, you wanted to test the effects of instructor sex (female, male) and classroom size (small, large) on communication apprehension. This experiment has a 2 × 2 design statement. There are two factors, instructor sex and classroom size. You would therefore expect at the most two main effects, one for each factor. If you obtained a main effect for instructor sex, you would be saying that students' communication apprehension scores with female instructors would be significantly different than those students' communication apprehension scores with male instructors. The sex of the instructor would have a significant main effect on communication apprehension levels. On the other hand, if you obtained a main effect for classroom size, you would be saying that students in small classes would have significantly different communication apprehension scores than students in large classes. The size of the classroom would have a significant main effect on communication apprehension levels.

This 2 × 2 design results in four cells of data depicted in Figure 14.2. The mean, $\bar{X}$, in each cell of data is the average for all the scores represented by that cell. So $\bar{X}_1$ stands for the average communication apprehension score for the small class with the female instructor, and $\bar{X}_2$ stands for the average communication apprehension score for the small class with the male instructor. In the

2 x 2 Matrix of Data Cells

	Female Instructors	Male Instructors
Small Classes	$\bar{X}_1$	$\bar{X}_2$
Large Classes	$\bar{X}_3$	$\bar{X}_4$

Figure 14.2 A 2 × 2 Research Design

third and fourth cells, $\bar{X}_3$ and $\bar{X}_4$ stand for the average communication apprehension scores for the large classes with female and male instructors, respectively.

The second type of effect tested is an **interaction**, a combined effect of two or more independent variables on the dependent variable. There are a variety of different types of interactions. One possibility in the preceding example is that students in small classes with female instructors express the lowest levels of communication apprehension, whereas students with male instructors in small classes express just the opposite, the highest level of communication apprehension. This interaction effect is depicted in Figure 14.3.

Occasionally, factorial designs make use of **repeated measures**. In this type of design, the researcher exposes the same group of participants to several treatments, events, or time periods. The repeated measure becomes one of the independent factors. For example, a study by Knobloch-Westerwick and Crane (2012) tested the effects of prolonged exposure to thin-image ideals on body satisfaction and dieting. Women were exposed to sets of images from fashion magazines on seven different occasions. Effects of successive images were tested through repeated measures of the women's attitudes toward body satisfaction and dieting. This measure is called the **within-subjects factor**. The researchers were also interested in the effect of social comparison which they varied by two experimental groups: one which induced social comparison and one which did not. A third group which served as a control was exposed to images of women from news magazines that did not represent the thin-image ideal. These three conditions represented the **between-subjects factor**. When researchers use both types of factors as they did in this study, the design is called a **mixed independent groups/repeated measures design**.

There are three basic advantages in choosing a repeated measures design over other design types (Smith, 1988, pp. 209–210). In the first case, researchers do not have to worry about whether the groups are comparable. Since they are the same people across at least one set of differences, they are clearly comparable. Other potential problems may threaten the accuracy of the measures, as you will discover in the warrants section. A second advantage is that repeated measures may also require fewer subjects. If the researchers show three videotaped political advertisements to the same group of subjects, they will use fewer subjects than if they showed the advertisements to three separate groups.

Finally, the researcher may be interested in a variable that is, by its nature, best captured with a repeated measure. In the study of thin-image ideal effects identified earlier, the model of media effects proposed by the researchers hypothesized that it was precisely the repeated and prolonged exposure to media messages that led to perceptions of discrepancy in one's body with the idealized image resulting in greater levels of dissatisfaction. Using repeated exposures was the optimal design choice because of the very nature of the variables under examination.

In the last chapter on survey research, you learned about a variety of statistical software packages used for data analysis. Packages like *Statistical Analysis Software* (SAS) and *Statistical Package for Social Scientists* (SPSS) are the same software programs that are used for experimental data analysis. Just as survey research has relied

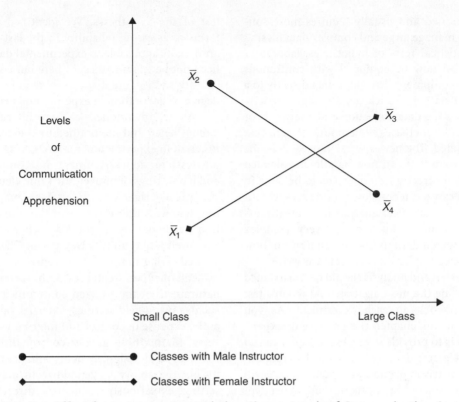

Figure 14.3 Interaction Effect for Instructor Sex and Class Size on Levels of Communication Apprehension

on correlational analysis and frequency counts in the past, experimental research has traditionally relied on various tests of group differences, most notably several different forms of analyses of variance. All but the simplest tests of differences will require software beyond *Excel*. In this chapter, we will briefly explore four different types of analysis that are available in two statistical packages: SAS and SPSS. Inexpensive packages are available to students which can be used in place of more expensive licensing agreements for the purposes of analysis at the level of this course and should be explored as viable alternatives. In some cases, cheaper software like *STATA* statistical software data analysis may be more readily available.

Researchers frequently use ANOVA to test differences among various groups or categories of the independent variable or variables for their effects on the dependent variable. As we explained earlier in this chapter, a one-way ANOVA is used when there is just one independent variable with more than two categories, groups, or levels. For example, we discussed three of the treatment conditions in the Banas and Miller

study on inoculation effects. Each of these represents a different level of one independent variable. If these had been the only independent variable in the study, the authors would have used a one-way ANOVA in the analysis of their results. This is one of the easier types of analyses to use in any of the statistical programs.

The assumption underlying the use of ANOVAs is that the independent variable is categorical, measured at the nominal or ordinal levels. When there are two or more categorical independent variables tested for their effects on the dependent variable, the ANOVA software programs are set up to statistically check for sets of main effects and complex interactions. Software programs can also be used to conduct an *analysis of covariance* (*ANCOVA*), a test that permits removing the effects of one or more independent variables to examine separately the effects of the remaining independent variables. When you want to test more complex relationships of multiple continuous and categorical independent variables on a dependent variable, you might use a *multivariate ANOVA* (*MANOVA*) in any of the software packages mentioned previously. This last test, however, is more sophisticated and usually requires more software support to manage large and complex data files.

Beyond statistical tests of hypotheses, laboratory environments can now be equipped with continuous video recording equipment that sends data directly to a preprogrammed statistical package. This new capacity really streamlines the data collection and analysis process and drastically increases the amount of data that can be incorporated. The newest version of SPSS is one example of software that can now handle downloaded video information directly into data sets to be used in analysis. As you can see, technological advances in software programs for statistical analysis have greatly expanded the possibilities for creating very complex experimental research designs not only in terms of how the data is analyzed but how it is collected as well.

Research design and analysis should be constructed carefully to provide the most accurate and reliable test of hypotheses possible in each experiment. As you learned earlier in this chapter, the purpose of experimental research is to provide strong evidence for causal arguments. By selecting design elements such as random assignment, comparison groups, and pretests, you will be attempting to isolate the effects of the independent variables while controlling for rival factors or causes. Establishing grounds for causality reflect the essential values of precision, power, and parsimony, which are assured using the standards of validity and reliability. It is to these warrants that our attention now must turn.

Experimental Research Warrants

Because controlling rival explanations is central to any causal argument, experimental researchers are especially concerned with a study's validity and reliability, as well as the discovery paradigm values of precision and parsimony introduced initially in Chapter 6, "Warrants for Research Arguments." *Validity* refers to the accuracy or truthfulness of the tests for claims, whereas *reliability* refers to the consistency of those tests. As you learned in Chapter 6, there are several different types of validity. *Internal validity* generally refers to the ability of a study to accurately assess the hypothesized relationship between the independent and dependent variables. *External validity* refers to how accurately the findings from one study can be generalized to a different setting or to the population at large. Generally, any study with strong internal and external validity is also considered a reliable

test of the hypotheses. We identified three different forms of assessing reliability in the last chapter, which are equally applicable to experimental data and so these need not be examined again here but considerations of validity and its potential threats require a much greater degree of elaboration in experimental research.

As we mentioned earlier, internal validity is strengthened and maintained by the degree of control inherent in experimental research design features (pre/posttests, random assignment, and comparison groups) and lab settings. However, the same elements that provide greater rigor over the variable manipulation also interfere with the relevance of the actual communication behaviors. Field studies such as Lehmann and Shemwell (2011) and McDevitt and Chaffee (2000) described earlier in the chapter, represent the paradoxical tradeoff of experimental research. As one increases the naturalness of the selected communication behaviors, such as using field settings, external validity increases at the expense of control and internal validity and vice versa. Maintaining greater control through lab environments and design elements enhances internal validity but the ability to generalize to other groups and settings is seriously challenged threatening external validity. We will consider specific threats to each in the next section.

Internal Validity Threats

In experimental research, your manipulation of the independent variable as a test of your causal claim is considered successful to the degree that you have established strong internal validity by controlling rival causes. In Chapter 6, you learned that measurement validity refers to the accuracy of measurement used in one study. When measurement validity is assessed, you are concerned with the presence or lack of bias, a threat to the internal validity of a study. You will learn a great deal about bias in Chapter 16, "Descriptive Statistics and Hypothesis Testing." For now, we will say that when a study's measures are biased, you are unable to rule out factors that potentially rival your independent variable as the cause of the observed pattern of effects. These factors are called **confounding variables** because they confound or interfere in the relationship between the independent and dependent variables.

In Chapter 11, we explained how using certain design elements used in experimental research help to establish valid and reliable tests of claims. In this section, you will begin to see how this process occurs. If the study is an experiment, the validity issues are directly related to design elements, and the potential threats are from biases that are reduced or eliminated by those design elements. There are essentially two types of bias that are related to the internal construction of experimental designs: effects related to time progression and threats called reactivity effects. They can affect both internal and external validity. A third set of effects specifically threatens the external validity of the study's claims.

Time Progression Effects

Time progression effects refer to those factors that rival independent variables as sources or causes of effects because the experiment takes place over a period of time. Preexperimental or quasi-experimental designs that make use of a pretest and posttest or a repeated measures design described in Chapter 11 are vulnerable to six of these time progression effects. Any experimental designs in which there is a time lapse between the manipulation of the independent variable and measuring the dependent variable can be vulnerable to these effects if specific precautions are not taken. Six of the most common time progression effects as threats to internal validity include history, maturation, mortality, statistical regression, testing, and instrumentation (Cook & Campbell, 1979). In each case, we will discuss the design elements that will help to reduce or eliminate each type of bias.

History. The effect of history refers to the occurrence of an event that happens during the course of the study that is external to the study but affects the outcome in such a way that the event rivals or threatens the independent variable as the source of influence on the dependent variable. To use an earlier example, supposed you wished to test the effects of a presidential debate on voter preference by identifying events after the fact in the field using a pre-experimental or quasi-experimental design. The threats to validity are immediately apparent in the weakness of these design selections. If any other event can rival the debate as a cause of voter behavior, such as a breaking news story that implicates one of the candidates in a scandal of some sort, or a dip in the economy, then the study's design is vulnerable to the history effect. One way to control for the effect of history is to use a control group that is exposed to all of the same events as the treatment group. You can then compare variable scores after those events have had their effect; presumably, dependent variable scores in a treatment

group (the group that viewed the debate) will change more than scores in a control group (the group that didn't), despite any history effect. Occasionally, studies will attempt to impose greater control in field settings. For example, Bailard's (2012) study of Internet use in voting behavior was an ambitious attempt to use random assignment to different field conditions. Participants in the treatment group were given first-time access to and trained in how to use the Internet in a region of Tanzania, whereas control group participants in the same area were not given access or training. Bailard was interested in seeing how Internet use might influence voting behavior in the Tanzanian elections. By using a control group and random assignment, she was better able to argue against extraneous history effects.

Maturation. This effect of maturation is obtained because of some naturally occurring developmental change that coincides with the administration of the independent variable and the test of its effects. The developmental change can be short-term and temporary or long-term and permanent. In the short term, participants who become fatigued because the experimental situation requires lengthy or complex testing are experiencing maturational changes. Sometimes, these rival the effects of the independent variable. For example, let's say you argued that teachers who were distant and unapproachable (nonimmediacy) adversely affect student performance, but then you gave students learning tasks that were too long or complex to comfortably complete. As a result, you could not tell whether the adverse effects were due to teacher style or task complexity. If the design included a control group who receives the same test of student performance without exposure to the teacher, then we would be able to discern the portion of the effects that were due only to teacher style.

You might run into a maturation threat over a longer period if you were assessing younger student performance over the course of a year, and improvement in scores could be explained simply by growing older and more competent generally. In illustrating the rationale for using a *time series design,* we explained that some studies are susceptible to developmental changes. If you wanted to test the effects of a certain type of curricular program over a long period (the school year), you would need to design your experiment in a way that would allow you to track changes due to the differences in curricular programs versus natural developmental changes in children's competence. If you did not collect repeated measures and had no control group for comparison, your study results would be confounded by a maturation effect.

Mortality. This is an effect in which subjects disproportionately drop out of an experiment. Suppose you wished to test the effects of teaching interpersonal negotiating strategies to romantic couples on the perceived satisfaction with their partners. First, you required participants to undergo three 1-hour training sessions, and over that period of time, a number of participants dropped out. As a rule in this type of study, those that drop out are also most likely to be those who are having relational problems or have broken up with their partners. The resulting scores of the remaining participants show increased levels of perceived satisfaction. Was this increase due to the effectiveness of the negotiating strategies or because those who were having the most relational difficulties dropped out? When the low scorers dropped out, it artificially inflated the average score for those who remained. The use of control groups and random assignment would help to separate time progression effects due to mortality from those due to manipulating the independent variable.

Statistical regression. The effect of statistical regression occurs when participants have been selected who represent the extremes on the dependent variable scale. These participants who receive extremely low scores on any measure are more likely to get higher scores the second time around just by chance. If you get a zero, the only direction you can go is up. Likewise, participants who score very high on some measure will most likely do worse on a subsequent measure. Statistical regression can sometimes rival the independent variable as an explanation for the observed effects.

For example, Heuett, Hsu, and Ayres (2003) tested the effectiveness of various treatment techniques for lowering communication apprehension. Heuett et al. also used multiple comparison groups and random assignment characteristic of a true experimental design so that they could rule out rival effects like statistical regression because they were interested in observing effects on participants who were extreme scorers on the communication apprehension scale. But suppose a researcher interested in the same relationship had not used random assignment and control groups and had selected a group of communicators who had scored extremely high on communication apprehension. Chances are without any therapy at all, the scores would naturally regress toward the middle or average score; that is, the scores would appear to show less communication apprehension simply because the initial scores were so high. Lower communication apprehension scores on the second collection could not be attributed to the manipulation of the independent variable.

Testing. *Testing* effects can happen any time the research design calls for a pretest. This effect occurs when participants become sensitized to the content of the test. In one type of testing effect, participants can improve their scores just from the *practice effect* of taking the test or measure more than one time. This is the rationale that underlies taking the Preliminary Scholastic Aptitude Test during the third year of high school. Practice usually helps to improve performance.

In another type of testing threat, the test actually acts as a cueing device to sensitize participants to the goals of the study so that they respond to the manipulation of the independent variable in some way they would not have if they had not taken a pretest. Suppose you wanted to find out about cheating behavior by placing participants in a situation in which they were given the opportunity to observe a confederate cheating. Before they witness any cheating, the participants take a pretest that measures their attitudes toward cheating. The test serves as a cue to be wary of cheating situations. When they are then confronted with a cheating confederate, they may be more likely to express harsher judgments toward the cheating they observed than they initially would have because of the pretest. You can minimize this testing effect by using random assignment and a control group and by using designs that do not rely just on the pretest/posttest design element.

Instrumentation. The instrumentation effect happens when the researcher changes the instruments used to measure the dependent variables between the pretest and the posttest. The instrument itself should remain constant across the duration of the study. If, for example, you evaluated communication competence with one scale in the pretest, the posttest should include the same measure of competence; otherwise, changes in the dependent variable could be attributed to scale content and construction characteristics rather than changes produced by manipulating the independent variable.

The instrumentation effect is of central importance when considering the stability or reliability of measurements as test-retest assessments. It is sometimes tempting to revise an instrument when you discover problems with its construction following a pretest. Rather than using the pretest to evaluate the scale's validity and reliability, you should use a pilot study or manipulation check with a separate group of participants as we have indicated earlier. In the last chapter, you learned in detail how the structure of an interview or questionnaire could adversely affect the validity and reliability of these measures.

If you think your experiment might be vulnerable to one or more time progression effects, we encourage you to use Table 14.3 to help you decide which design elements would help to reduce or eliminate these potential sources of bias.

Reactivity Effects

Reactivity effects are a set of effects or threats due to participants' responses or reactions to some design feature of the experimental situation. Participants may react very differently than they would in everyday life because they have been targeted for a study. In this section, we outline six of the most common reactivity effects, including the threats of selection, treatment diffusion, compensatory behavior, researcher attributes, demand characteristics, and evaluation apprehension (Cook & Campbell, 1979; Smith, 1988).

Selection. The effect of selection occurs when the researcher is unable to randomly assign subjects to treatment and control conditions. As you learned earlier,

random assignment helps to establish equivalent groups at the beginning of a study. Without this procedure, groups can differ in ways that systematically interfere with the effects of the independent variable. McDevitt and Chaffee's (2000) study of the effects of the *Kids Voting* curricular program with two different groups of high school students was vulnerable to a selection effect. That is why McDevitt and Chaffee went to such great lengths to assure that intact classrooms of students who could not be randomly assigned to groups did not possess any distinguishing characteristics. Potentially, any difference in the groups could have rivaled the independent variable in explaining the results they obtained.

Treatment diffusion. The treatment diffusion effect, sometimes called *contamination,* occurs when participants in the treatment group tell participants in the control group about the treatment, thereby "contaminating" the control group. Let's say you were interested in studying the effects of deception on suspicion. The participants in the treatment group were exposed to a confederate who fabricated a story to elicit suspicious responses. In the control condition, the confederate did not tell any lies. However, participants in the treatment condition told participants in the control condition about the lying confederate because both groups of participants shared a class together. After the treatment group contaminated the control group, participants in

Table 14.3 Time Progression Effect Solutions

Problem: Time Progression Effects	Design/Measure Solutions
History: was there a major uncontrollable event that could rival the independent variable as explanation for dependent variable effects?	Comparison groups and random assignment
Maturation: was there a developmental or fatigue effect on your participants?	Repeated measures design; control group
Mortality: did a drop-out rate affect your results?	Comparison groups; random assignment
Statistical regression: were initial samples that were pretested characterized by participants with extreme scores?	Comparison groups; random assignment
Testing: did taking a pretest result in test sensitization?	Comparison groups; random assignment; experimental designs that do not rely solely on pretest/posttest control measures
Instrumentation: did the experimenter change the independent variable measure between pre- and post-testing?	Pilot the instrument ahead of time and then do not vary the pretest/posttest measure

the control group showed greater suspicion of the confederate than they would have normally because they suspected deception based on what they had been told.

It is difficult to control this effect unless you can guarantee participants from both groups will remain separated during the duration of the study. Sometimes, this arrangement just isn't feasible; studies of married or cohabitating persons are especially vulnerable to this effect. In a study of fright reactions to films, Sparks, Pellechia, and Irvine (1999) attempted to control this effect by asking participants to refrain from discussing the experiment until they were informed in class that the experiment was over. These researchers were dependent on the good will of their study participants to follow their instructions.

Compensatory behavior. The compensatory behavior threat is actually a cluster of effects that can happen when the control group becomes aware that the experimental group is being treated differently. If the treatment seems to be a positive gain, then control groups can try to outperform the experimental group to receive the same treatment, or they can become frustrated and upset at the unequal treatment and withhold normal behaviors as a result. In either case, the unaffected behavior of the control group becomes decidedly influenced by the absence of the treatment. For example, let's say you wished to test the effects of using computer games to help students learn a series of math functions. Students in the control group are required to learn the same math functions without the benefit of the computer games. Suppose the control group discovered the treatment group was allowed to play computer games during the testing session; the control group participants might try harder at the learning tasks to be allowed to play the same games. Or they may become discouraged with no opportunity to play the games and try even less hard than they would have in the absence of the experiment. Again, the most effective way to eliminate this threat is to ensure that both groups have no contact while the study is ongoing.

Researcher attributes. Researchers can possess physical or psychological characteristics (aka researcher attributes) that may influence the way participants respond, thus affecting the outcome of the experiment. For example, Lucchetti (1999) asked personal questions about participants' sexual history as it related to knowledge about safe sex practices. Sometimes male participants are reluctant to discuss very detailed sexual behavior

with female researchers (and vice versa). In such cases, the study would benefit from a research team so that attribute effects could be distributed across the gender of the researchers, male and female. In this particular case, it would also be wise to assure participants of complete confidentiality as a means of gaining trust and establishing rapport.

Demand characteristics. In some cases, participants become aware of the goals of a particular study because the research team, the testing materials, the experimental design, or some combination of these factors inadvertently provides them with cues. If participants think that they know what the investigators are looking for, they can try to cooperate and give the researchers what they want, or they can resist complying to obstruct the research process, or the participants can simply try to forget what the goals are and act as they normally would. Obviously, researchers hope participants will choose the last option. Any time subjects vary their behavior because they are aware of the research goals, the effect is called demand characteristics. In a much-cited case, a study of workers at the Hawthorne Electrical Plant, demand characteristics were produced when employees became aware of the researchers' presence. Simple awareness of being targeted for research increased the employees' levels of productivity regardless of how environmental conditions were varied. The observed outcome of this study was called the **Hawthorne effect** (Frey, Botan, et al., 2000, p. 121).

Frequently, demand characteristics can be controlled by using research assistants who are blind to or unaware of the goals of a particular experiment so that they cannot cue subjects on how to respond. For example, in a study of fright reactions to film segments cited earlier (Sparks et al., 1999), the experimenter did not know the study's hypothesis and which participants had various coping styles. Participants were classified as having a repressor or nonrepressor coping style because of the tendency to repress or not repress emotion. Sparks et al. expected that repressors would experience greater levels of physiological arousal after exposure to frightening films than nonrepressors. By keeping the experimenter who collected the data unaware of the research goals, she could not cue participants to act in ways that would confirm researcher expectations. Sparks et al. confirmed no demand characteristics were present by using a *manipulation check* to see if participants had guessed what the study was about.

Another way to control this effect is to introduce a bogus treatment with a cover story or observe participants unobtrusively so that they will not learn the nature of the study. For example, in a study of compliance seeking and resisting behaviors in student drinking contexts, Wright and O'Hair (1999) disguised the purpose of the study by asking students unrelated questions about smoking and high calorie food consumption in addition to questions about their alcohol use. They felt that if student participants were aware the researchers were interested solely in drinking behavior, the participants might be more likely to alter their normal responses.

Evaluation apprehension. When researchers ask for information that is potentially embarrassing or negative in some way, then respondents often change their answers to give a more positive personal impression of themselves. This effect is called evaluation apprehension. In Chapter 14 on survey research, you learned about the importance of gaining participants' trust, especially when asking for sensitive information. Experimenters who examine socially negative behavior, like cheating and deception, may find participants' responses inhibited by apprehension about impressions they are giving. Likewise, measuring socially positive behavior, like comforting or altruistic behavior, may result in equally biased positive responses, as participants try to strategically influence impressions about their personal integrity. If, for example, you wanted to find out about communication problems in newlywed couples, you would need to be sensitive to the fact that most newlyweds in our society want to be seen as having few problems.

Considering potential reactivity effects will help guide you in deciding which design elements to target. To see which elements are recommended for each reactivity effect, consult Table 14.4.

In this section, we have explored six time progression effects and six reactivity effects as threats to the

Table 14.4 Reactivity Effect Solutions

Problem: Reactivity Effects	Design/Measure Solutions
Selection: was the experimenter unable to randomly select and then assign participants to comparison groups?	Repeat with random assignment; if not possible, then match participant characteristics (matched samples) for comparison groups.
Treatment diffusion: did treatment group members communicate with control group members in ways that could change the control group members' responses?	Separate comparison groups to ensure no contact until data is collected; ask members of both groups not to talk about study until data is collected; obscure independent variable manipulation in both groups (use a cover story).
Compensatory behavior: did the control group members become aware of treatment group conditions in ways that could change the control group members' responses?	Separate comparison groups to ensure no contact until data is collected; ask members of both groups not to talk about study until data is collected; obscure independent variable manipulation in both groups (use a cover story).
Researcher attributes: did physical or psychological characteristics of the researcher(s) change participant responses?	Use a team of researchers with varying characteristics to mitigate effects; if information collected is sensitive in nature, assure participants of complete confidentiality.
Demand characteristics: did participants' projections about the study's purpose change their responses?	Use manipulation checks to assess whether participants are responding as expected; use cover stories to obscure purposes; use random assignment and comparison groups.
Evaluation apprehension: did participants express a self-positive bias because of reporting on negative/positive social behavior?	Assure confidentiality/anonymity and establish trust with participants.

internal validity of an experimental design. Aside from the research progression and reactivity effects identified here, there are more complex effects due to the interaction of two or more of these. However, it is comforting to note that using the control elements of true experimental designs, comparison groups, random assignment, and pretests, greatly reduces the potential threat to the internal validity of the study as you can see in Tables 14.3 and 14.4.

External Validity Threats

Reactivity effects along with sampling deficiencies can also affect the external validity of the study's claims. As you learned in Chapter 6, "Warrants for Research Arguments," *external validity* refers to generalizing the results of a study to a larger population or across settings.

Sample Representativeness

Recall our discussion of representativeness from Chapter 5 on communication data. If a sample represents the parent population well, then the results obtained from a sample should also be representative of those you would find conducting the same test in the population. The best way to ensure representativeness is to use some form of random sampling. You learned about random sampling methods used by communication researchers in Chapter 5. When nonrandom methods are selected for experimental research, the samples are much more likely to be biased; that is, they are likely to vary in systematic ways that do not accurately represent the characteristics of the population from which they were drawn. This is called a **sampling effect**.

Many experiments in communication research are limited by the difficulties imposed on the researcher for obtaining random samples. It may be prohibitively costly in terms of time, effort, and money to obtain random samples. As a result, experimental researchers may depend on alternate means such as statistically assessing the amount of bias or noise present in a particular sample and using it to indicate whether results are generalizable.

Setting Appropriateness

Reactivity effects make it very clear that participants may be affected by the situational features of the experimental setting. Repeating a study's design in a different setting strengthens the claim that the study's results can be generalized across settings. When the same pattern of results is assured across settings, we say the study has strong *ecological validity,* a concept you learned about previously. Many researchers identify various strategies used to help participants experience the laboratory settings as more natural environments to avoid artificial setting effects. For example, Wright and O'Hair (1999) investigated student compliance gaining and resisting strategies in drinking situations. They constructed the laboratory to resemble a "small living room environment" with snacks and drinks on the coffee table and a bar containing a variety of alcoholic beverages. All laboratory sessions were conducted in the evening when drinking alcohol would seem more likely and appropriate under normal circumstances.

Replicating studies also helps to ensure ecological validity, and it is also a means of assuring reliability of research design and measurement as you may recall from Chapter 6 on research warrants. For example, Burleson, Holmstrom, and Gilstrap (2005) studied participant sex and message person-centeredness as a measure of support; in this investigation, they actually reported on four experiments: In the first study, participant sex and their scores on a gender scale were tested for their effects on how realistic various levels of comforting (person-centered) messages would seem to be. Studies 2, 3, and 4 refined this relationship by examining how interaction goals, plans, and actions might also mediate perceptions of comforting messages. Each study helped to confirm and enrich the understanding of previous results.

In experimental research, the necessity of building a strong case for causality requires careful consideration of the design and measurements used to test claims. By warranting these claims by demonstrating strong internal and external validity through experimental control, the researcher has developed a sound argument that the pattern of observed effects is best attributed to the experimenter's manipulation of the independent variable. Moreover, establishing validity internally and externally is a sound basis for assuring the reliability or consistency in the measurement of data.

Before we end this chapter, it is important to explore the major contributions of experimental research to the development of research ethics.

Ethics in Experimental Research

As outlined in Chapter 3, ethical principles in social science research were developed to address serious issues in research. Early social science research from the discovery paradigm stressed amoral and neutral objectivity in conducting experiments. Advancing knowledge became the justification for conducting experiments without adequate consideration of the potential harm to study participants. Early experiments to test the progression of syphilis, infectious hepatitis, and cancer were horrific examples of overlooking harm to participants for the "greater good" (National Institute of Health, 2002). As the experimental conditions and results were made public, the US government established policy as *The Belmont Report* to ensure that researchers would uphold three principles in the protection of human participants: beneficence, respect for persons, and justice.

The studies that led to the development of policy for the participants' protection violated the three principles by misleading individuals about the true nature of their participation, by withholding information about the potential risks that they could incur, and by actually harming them in the course of research. As you learned earlier in the chapter, experimental researchers may use a *cover story* to hide the exact purpose of a study. Cover stories are deceptive practices in which researchers mislead or mask intent; they do so when knowledge of the purpose or goals of the study are likely to influence the outcomes.

In a study of interpersonal relationships, Guerrero, Jones, and Burgoon (2000) invited romantic partners to the laboratory where they were told investigators were interested in how different types of romantic relationships discuss relational issues. After a brief discussion period, they were told that they would complete a personality inventory in separate rooms and then return for a discussion. One partner remained in the room to complete the inventory, while the other partner was taken to a separate room to be trained as a confederate. Recall that a confederate is someone who knows about and cooperates with the research team to manipulate one or more of the independent variables. Confederates were trained to either act more or less intimate with their partners when they returned for the second discussion to test the effects of varying levels of intimacy on the discussion.

Obviously, if participants had known about the true variable manipulation, they would have interpreted the increased or decreased intimacy as "fake" and responded accordingly. Prior knowledge would have compromised the validity of the variable tests. In this particular study, Guerrero et al. (2000) had to consider any potential harm that might arise, making a decision that any harm was very minimal and negated when participants were debriefed about the study's purpose following the study's conclusion. In this case, Guerrero et al. could argue that the benefits of the knowledge gained outweighed any potential risk, that respect for all had been upheld, and that both groups were given equal benefits at the end of their participation.

Using cover stories is a much-debated practice in social science research. Whenever deception is incorporated into the study design, you can seriously compromise the right of a participant to give "informed" consent and to participate voluntarily. In cases that are relatively benign like the one we just described, it can be argued that the benefits by far outweigh the costs. In other studies, some researchers try to equalize the risk/benefit ratio by providing follow-up treatment. As standard operating procedure, Hopf, Ayres, Ayres, and Baker (1995) offered to provide control and placebo groups with the same beneficial treatments to reduce communication apprehension that the experimental groups received once the study had been completed.

The process of balancing costs with benefits is subjective and therefore open to continual debate. As a researcher, you must carefully consider the consequences of an experiment for participants. The research community has come to general agreement about harm caused by specific experimental practice. For example, in the 1960s and 1970s, Milgram (1963, 1975) was heavily criticized for "duping" participants into situations in which they perceived they were harming others by their actions. Similarly, Reiss' (1971) study of police brutality raised serious ethical issues in the use of deception, lack of informed consent, and by decreasing public trust in scientific experimentation. In a famous experiment conducted at Stanford, Zimbardo (1973) simulated a prison environment to test its deleterious effects on ordinary college students, arguing that the environment and not personality characteristics would predict behavior. In the simulation, students were assigned to the roles of prison guards and prisoners. This induction produced such negative effects in both groups (sadistic brutality among the guards and severe depression among the prisoners) that the experiment was halted less than halfway through the simulation.

In some studies, however, the ethical line is less clear. For example, Heath and Davidson (1988) recruited college women to review one of three pamphlets that ostensibly would be published as part of a campus-wide, antirape campaign. Unknown to the participants, the pamphlet message varied by presenting rape as very controllable, somewhat controllable, and not at all controllable. The real purpose of the study was to test anxiety levels in women responding to rape as a controllable (or not) event. The researchers found that not only did anxiety increase when rape was perceived as uncontrollable but that such a perception might have actually influenced some women to see their own attempts to reduce rape (e.g., choices about time and location of being alone in public) as pointless.

A more recent study (Mulac, Jansma, & Linz, 2002) assessed the effects of men's exposure to nonsexual and sexually explicit, degrading, and nondegrading film content on their subsequent interactions with women. Following the film viewing, men were paired with women to complete problem-solving tasks in a business context. Unknown to the women, men who viewed sexually explicit films were more dominant, more focused on their partner's sexuality during problem-solving tasks, were more likely to ignore their partner's suggestions for solutions, and were more likely to touch their partners without looking at them. Although both men and women were thoroughly debriefed following the study, were the potential benefits of knowing how sexually explicit films influence male perception enough to outweigh the harmful effects the women experienced interacting with the men in this study? Mulac et al. argued that the study exposed a possible source of deleterious interactions many women already face in the workplace.

When considering the use of deception, you should ask three questions (Kelman, 1967): (1) How significant is the study? (2) Are there alternative research designs (such as role-playing) that would provide the same information? and (3) How great is the potential risk of harm to the participants? Additionally, you should also consider piloting the research design with individuals similar to your targeted participants. You can probe what the potential consequences of your design features, such as cover stories, might be before you actually deceive a larger number of people in your primary study. If you believe that deception is necessary for any reason, then you should debrief participants by providing complete disclosure as soon as possible (C. B. Fisher & Fryberg, 1994). Remember that in your role as a researcher, you have an ethical obligation to provide beneficence, respect for individuals, and justice for every person that participates in your study.

In this chapter, you learned about communication experimental research in terms of claims, data, and warrants from the research-as-argument model. As summarized in Table 14.5, our discussion of experimental research began with constructing causal explanatory claims that predict changes in communication attitudes and behaviors. We examined the sources and settings of experimental data, and we explored the data collection strategies by identifying and discussing the elements of research designs. We explored warrants for experimental research as controlling rival explanations for the observed effects on a dependent variable by establishing validity and reliability. We examined two sets of threats: time progression effects and reactivity effects. The preceding chapters on content analysis and survey research and this chapter on experimental research provide the conceptual framework and its application for understanding the forms of statistical analyses that appear in the next Chapters 15 and 16.

Table 14.5 Experimental Research Summary Table

Paradigm	Claims	Data	Warrants	Manuscript Format
Discovery	Explain, and predict	Representative samples from populations of people Design elements provide control over variable information.	Reliability established through stability, equivalence, and homogeneity and strong arguments for internal and external validity. Control of internal validity threats (time progression and reactivity). Control of external validity threats for sample representativeness and setting appropriateness.	Research report

Key Terms

Between-subjects factor
Compensatory behavior
Confederates
Confounding variables
Cover story
Deductive Reasoning
Demand characteristics
Evaluation apprehension
Experimental control
Factorial designs
Factors
Hawthorne effect

History
Inductive Reasoning
Instrumentation
Interaction
Intervening variable
Main effect
Manipulation checks
Maturation
Mixed independent groups/
    repeated measures design
Mixed model paradigm
Mortality

Reactivity effects
Repeated measures
Research design statement
Researcher attributes
Sampling effect
Selection
Statistical regression
Target participants
Testing
Time progression effects
Treatment diffusion
Within-subjects factor

Discussion Questions

1. Explain the three criteria for establishing causality described in this chapter. What makes an experiment a causal argument?
2. What do claims typically look like in experimental research? Why do experimental researchers construct claims in this way?
3. In constructing experimental data settings, identify some of the concerns a researcher might have. For example, why would you try to make a laboratory setting look more like a typical living room?
4. What is the difference between time progression effects and reactivity effects as threats to the validity of your research design? Is every design equally vulnerable to both types of effects?
5. Suppose a researcher wished to test the effects of watching violent cartoons on the subsequent behavior of children playing on a public playground. Discuss the ethical implications of this scenario.

"Try It!" Activities

1. A researcher wishes to assess the effects of biological sex and news stories with three types of endings on participants' level of recall. Identify the independent and dependent variables. Identify the factors, the design statement, the number of data cells, and possible main effects and interaction effects.
2. Suppose you want to study comforting strategy selection in interaction. You assess the baseline level of comforting strategies in your participants by using a pretest but you worried participants may not be truthful in their responses if they guess what behavior you are investigating. Many participants appear to be more comforting in the research context than they would actually be in a natural setting. Explain the type of research progression effect you are concerned about. Construct a plausible research design that would minimize this time progression effect.
3. Review the Mulac et al. (2002) study described in the chapter. Decide whether you think cover stories like the ones used by these researchers pose ethical problems in the practice of research. What problems are cover stories expected to solve? Could these problems be solved in any other way? Explain how.

15 Descriptive Statistics and Hypothesis Testing

Introduction

In this chapter, you will use what you have learned about measurement in Chapter 11 to examine your data and to prepare for statistical analyses. We start by exploring how data is visually represented in graphs. Next you will learn how to calculate descriptive statistics, or values that indicate important features about or characteristics of your data sample. These include measures of a distribution's central tendencies, dispersion, and shape. We will explain how you can find these with various software applications, many with simple operations in Excel. We conclude this chapter and transition to the next by introducing you to the reasoning underlying the steps in testing hypotheses.

Learning Outcomes

When you complete this chapter, you should be able to:

» Describe and explain the various visual representations of variables: pie charts, bar charts, and histograms.
» Calculate and interpret three types of descriptive statistics: measures of central tendency, shape, and dispersion.
» Apply steps to calculate descriptive statistics in Microsoft Excel and Statistical Package for Social Science (SPSS).
» Identify key ethical issues in representing data visually and statistically.
» Explain the basic logic of estimation and inference, and the steps required to test hypotheses.

Outline

ommunication research studies from the discovery paradigm that use some form of statistical analysis typically employ the methodologies examined in the last three chapters: content analysis, and survey and experimental research. **Statistical analysis** is defined as "the science of describing and reasoning from numerical data" (Smith, 1988, p. 93). Recall from Chapter 11 that studies in discovery-paradigm research share many assumptions about the types of claims you will make as a researcher, the nature of the data you will collect and measure, and the ways in which your arguments can be warranted. The definition of statistical analysis that we cite here identifies two functions or purposes: description and reasoning. In the first section, you will explore the descriptive function of statistics. In the last section, you will examine the reasoning process that underlies statistical analysis, which will allow you to draw inferences about what you are observing.

How to Describe Sample Data

In Chapter 5, "What Counts as Communication Data," we identified the process of sampling data in discovery paradigm research. We discussed the importance of *random sampling* to obtain representative samples from a larger group or population. The **samples** that we collect through this process provide us with a picture of what is happening in the larger group without having to look at every member. It is analogous to having jigsaw puzzle pieces. If you draw a random sample, the pieces will give you an idea of what the entire picture looks like instead of just a specific corner or its middle. Obviously, the more pieces that you have, the better your representation of the final picture, but a good random sample will be likely to capture more of the final picture than if you use a nonrandom method.

Instead of pieces of images like a puzzle, data samples are made up of numbers obtained when you convert the constructs you are studying to variables through operationalization. We described this process in detail in Chapter 11, in which any kind of communication you choose to study can be described by numbers using one of four measurement scales: nominal, ordinal, interval and ratio. In the methods chapters that ensued on content analysis, and survey or experimental research, we gave you many examples of the ways in which data is typically measured and the types of analyses that are likely to result. The samples of data collected for these analyses are first examined by evaluating their **descriptive characteristics**. The sample characteristics are called **statistics**; at the population level, the same characteristics are called **parameters**. Statistics of a sample should represent the parameters of the population from which the sample is drawn. For example, does the average age in this class (sample mean) represent the average age for Communication majors at this university (population mean)? You would be comparing the sample statistic to the population parameter.

Once you have completed the process of operationalizing your variables, the data will be distributed along one or more of the four measurement scales. Data measured with nominal or ordinal scales will result in groupings of the variables by discrete categories or ranked preferences. Recall that the data are not numerically related; numbers are assigned to categories in nominal scales purely to identify or *name* the distinct parts of the variable. Simple examples of variables measured this way include identifying "undergraduate" as "1" and "graduate" as "2" for levels of students, dichotomous responses ("yes" = 1/"no" = 2), experimental conditions (treatment = 1, control groups = 2), and messaging categories (texting = 1, e-mail = 2, phone call = 3). Ordinal scales include ranking of the sort that indicates preference. For example, you could indicate how often you use the messaging categories listed above, with 1 = the most frequently used message format (e.g., "texting") and 2 = the next most frequently used, and so forth.

When using descriptive statistics to explore nominal or ordinal level data, you must remember that your numbers are not mathematically related. The answer "no" is not numerically twice as much as the answer "yes." Data at this level are usually counted by their frequencies for each category; for example, you can count the number of text messages you have in your sample by identifying how many "1's" you have and how many emails by the number of "2's." Moreover, you can describe the frequencies of data in categories in several ways. Let's say we have a sample of 50 messages, where 35 of them are texts and 15 are emails. The frequency of 35 can also be expressed as a certain proportion or percent of the sample. In this case, 70 percent are text messages, and 30 percent are emails. The frequencies or proportions of various categories using nominal and ordinal data can be visually represented as well. Typically, these are depicted with pie charts and bar charts described in the next section.

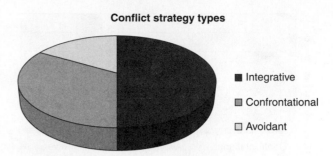

Figure 15.1 Pie Chart Display of Conflict Strategies

Visual Representations of Variables

The kinds of images you can use to represent sample data depend on how you measured the variables. In this section, you will learn about two images that you can use to represent data measured at the nominal or ordinal level: Pie charts and bar graphs. You will also learn about two images that you can use to represent data measured at the interval or ratio level: Histograms and frequency polygons.

Nominal and Ordinal Data

Pie charts. Suppose you wanted to visually represent the frequencies with which people in your sample chose three types of strategies to deal with a conflict: confrontational, avoidant, and integrative (Sillars, 1980). Pie charts make very good graphic representations of the frequencies or proportions of data.

Figure 15.1 is based on the following sample data: 8 of 24 people chose confrontational strategies, 4 out of 24 chose avoidant strategies, and 12 out of 24 chose integrative strategies; the frequencies and proportions are shown in Table 15.1 (also includes biological sex). The pie chart graph visually shows what proportion of the total circle is represented by each type of strategy. You can quickly see that integrative strategies make up the majority.

Bar charts. The bar chart in Figure 15.2 depicts the frequencies of strategy types. The *x*-**axis** (or *abscissa*) is the horizontal axis; the *y*-**axis** (or *ordinate*) is the vertical axis; and in the case of three-dimensional representations, the *z*-axis is the depth axis. Notice that the vertical bars are not connected along the *x*-axis. The separation between the bars denotes discrete groupings or categories of strategy types. As we explained earlier, the categories have no real mathematical relationship to each

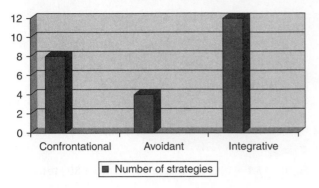

Figure 15.2 Bar Chart Display of Conflict Strategy Categories

Table 15.1 Frequency Table for Conflict Strategies

Type of Strategy	Frequency of Occurrence	Percentage of Sample
Confrontational	8	33.33
Males	6	25.00
Females	2	8.33
Avoidant	4	16.67
Males	1	4.17
Females	3	12.50
Integrative	12	50.00
Males	6	25.00
Females	6	25.00
Totals	24	100.00

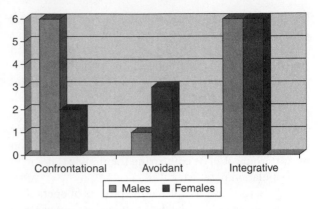

Figure 15.3 Comparison of Males and Females by Strategy Type

are represented along with the strategy types in Table 15.1. By using bar charts, you can visually compare how many males and females are using each type of conflict; this comparison is shown in Figure 15.3.

Pie charts and bar charts are easy to generate in both Microsoft Excel and SPSS (Statistical Package for Social Scientists), and bar charts are frequently used to report response results in survey programs such as Survey Monkey and Qualtrics (instructions for these can be found in the *Instructor's Manual*). They are often used to represent numerical data in textbooks, popular magazines, and online news reports. They are used less frequently in research journal articles. In their place, researchers may use a frequency summary table that indicates categories frequencies and percentages. For example, in a content analysis of messages individuals generated about family and work (Medved, Brogan, McClanahan, Morris, & Shepard, 2006), the research team used this type of table to show various family message categories (importance, permanency, prioritize family, etc.), work message categories (career enjoyment, work-career choice, etc.), and message categories about balancing work and life (work choice, life planning, stopping work, etc.). Just as graphics summarize data visually, the tables reveal at a glance which categories contain the majority of the participants' responses.

Interval and Ratio Data

When data are measured with interval and ratio scales, the descriptive and visual representations of these variables become more complex. Suppose you collected every final exam score in your communication class of 45 students. On a graph, the *x*-axis would stand for the

other on the *x*-axis. You could assign "6," "7," and "8" just as easily as "1," "2," and "3" to the three types of conflict strategies. The only real numbers (numbers with quantity values) on the graph are along the *y*-axis, which shows the frequency count for each type of strategy.

Unlike pie charts, bar charts can also be used to show how two or more groups compare across several categories. For example, suppose we found that 2 of the 8 people who used confrontational strategies were female, 3 out of 4 females used avoidant strategies, and 6 of the 12 used integrative strategies. Males and females

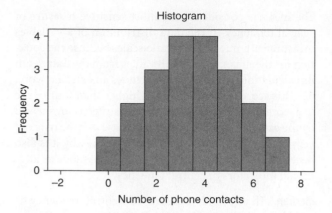

Figure 15.4 Histogram of Manager Contact

test score values ranging from 0 to 100 percent. The *y*-axis would stand for the number (or frequency) of students who obtained a certain score; for example, the *y*-axis would show you that the majority of students are scoring in the 70 percent range while very few are scoring at the very low or high ends of the sample.

The way the scores are distributed along the *x*-axis is called a **frequency distribution**. For example, let's say you wished to examine the pattern of phone conversations (as opposed to emails or texting) managers made with their employees throughout a workday. At the end of the day, each manager received a "contact score" that would represent the number of times the manager had spoken by phone with any employees. The graph in Figure 15.4 represents contact scores for 20 managers. You can see by reading the graphs that 1 manager made zero phone calls and one manager made seven phone calls with most managers making about 3 to 4 phone calls per day. The frequency distribution for this example is represented by a histogram in Figure 15.4.

Histograms. Any variables measured continuously can be represented by a histogram for the frequency distribution, which is like a bar chart for data measured with interval or ratio scales. Note the bars are connected along the *x*-axis. This is a visual illustration that there is a mathematical relationship between the intervals along the *x*-axis unlike the bars in a bar chart for data measured with nominal or ordinal scales. Because intervals are equidistant, the numbers stand for precise values. In the example illustrated in Figure 15.4, a manager who contacted employees four times during the day made twice as many calls as the manager who had only two phone contacts. The fact that the intervals along the *x*-axis are

mathematically precise makes many types of statistical tests possible, as you will see in the next chapter, "Inferential Statistics: Differences and Relationships."

It is not common that you will see data reported in communication research journals as histograms. Usually these graphs are tools that you can use in your preliminary data analysis to estimate the likelihood of error in your sample, a process we will explore in a later chapter section. However, you will see an occasional use of graphs in the research literature. For example, Crowell and Emmers-Sommer (2001) used histograms to visually represent heterosexual participants' scores on a number of variables including perceived risk of getting HIV, level of trust in partner prior to getting HIV, and perceived safety of their partners. The histograms helped to illustrate quickly that there was a relatively low level of perceived risk in getting HIV, a moderate level of perceived trust in their partners, and a relatively high level of perceived safety in their partners.

You are also more likely to see displays of histograms or even bar charts if you are taking a course that uses clickers in which students can be polled anonymously in large lecture formats. Communication instructors might show quiz score frequency, or attendance distributions for the class, or scores on interval-scaled measures like a test of communication apprehension (for a discussion of classroom clicker application, see Barrett, Bornsen, Erickson, Markey, & Spiering, 2005).

Data measured at interval and ratio levels can also be visually represented in another way. In the next chapter, you will learn about tests for the relationships between two or more continuous variables. The relationships between these variables can be described as linear or curvilinear, terms that refer to complex patterns of variable change. Instead of exploring their shapes and what these represent in this chapter, you will see how they are used to interpret tests of correlation and regression in the next chapter. In this chapter, you will be looking at distributions for just *one* variable.

Visual representations of all data from pie charts to histograms are easy to generate in Excel and SPSS. In subsequent sections, we will demonstrate how to obtain these using specific samples of data.

Numerical Representations of Variables

Sample distributions can be visually represented as we have seen in this section. They can also be characterized by using numbers (a.k.a. descriptive statistics). Using SPSS and Excel in a later section of this chapter, you will learn how to examine frequency distributions by tabled data and graphs and how to generate and interpret three types of descriptive measures: measures of central tendency, measures of shape, and measures of dispersion. But first we will describe how to calculate each of these measures and why you need to know them when beginning to analyze your data.

Measures of Central Tendency

When we use variables as data, we work with them as sets of numbers and we use several kinds of measures to help us understand how each variable is distributed. **Measures of central tendency** are descriptive statistics that reduce the data set to one number that best characterizes the entire sample. To return to our earlier example of final exam scores, if you knew that the average score was a 72 percent, you would probably infer that most people in the class earned a C on the exam. Measures of central tendency permit you to estimate what most of the sample looks like with just one score. There are three measures of central tendency: the mean, median, and mode.

Mean. The most sensitive measure of central tendency for data distributions is the **mean** or the arithmetic average. The mean can be written as M and $\overline{X}$. In this text, we use the latter symbol to denote the mean. You calculate the mean by summing all the scores in the data set, ΣX, and dividing by the total number of scores, n. Equation 15.1 is for calculating the mean:

$$\overline{X}_1 = \frac{\sum X_1}{n_1}$$

(15.1)

Suppose you wanted to calculate the mean for a set of scores you obtained from participants completing a relationship uncertainty scale; these included 12, 14, 18, 19, and 62. Using the equation for the mean, you would first sum the set of scores (ΣX):

$$12 + 14 + 18 + 19 + 62 = 125$$

The second step in calculating the mean requires dividing the sum (ΣX) by the total number of scores (n), which is equal to 5 scores. In this case, you would divide 125 by 5, or:

$$125/5 = 25.00$$

The mean is considered the most sensitive measure of central tendency in the data distribution of a variables measure with interval and ratio scales because the equation for the mean includes all values from the data set in its calculation. In this case, it includes an extreme score, 62. This score results in a mean higher than four of the five scores in this data set. The value is affected or skewed by the extreme score, and so in this case, the mean is not very representative of the data set. That is why it is also necessary to examine the median and the mode as additional indicators of central tendency.

Median. The second measure of central tendency is called the median, abbreviated as *Mdn*. The median is defined as the midpoint score where 50 percent of the scores in the sample distribution occur above the median and 50 percent appear below; in other words, it is the 50th percentile score, occurring exactly midway in the distribution. To return to the uncertainty data set we used earlier, you would first make sure all scores are listed from the smallest to the largest:

12   14   <u>18</u>   19   62

The first step is to determine whether you have an odd number or even number of scores (value of *n*). In this case, $n = 5$, and our median score is easy to find. The midpoint in a set of 5 scores is the third score (2 scores above and 2 below), and our $Mdn = 18$. For a set of 7 scores, it would be the score in the fourth position (3 above and 3 below). For a set of 9 scores, the median occurs at the fifth position (4 above and 4 below) and so forth. It is a little more complicated procedure when you are finding the median in an even number of scores. Suppose that we had an additional number in our data set:

12   14   16   18   19   62

In this data set, there are two middle positions: 16 and 18. In order to determine the median, you would calculate the average of the two middle positions:

$$\frac{16 + 8}{2} = 17$$

Even though the number 17 does not actually appear in the data set, it is a better estimate of the midpoint than either 16 or 18.

Median scores are reported in interval and ratio level measurements of data but not for categorically measured variables. Typically, median scores are reported along with means or averages to show that distributions do not contain extreme or outlying scores. For example, Hoffman and Heald (2000) used both mean and median score values for frequencies of tobacco advertisements, alcohol advertisements, and frequencies for both types per magazine issue targeted at African Americans. Hoffman and Heald showed that the data was distributed normally in each of the magazines examined because the mean and median values were close together.

Mode. The mode, abbreviated as *mo*, is usually the easiest to find in a distribution; it is the most frequently occurring score in one data sample. Suppose you consider our uncertainty data set with a slight modification:

| 12 | 14 | 16 | 16 | 18 | 19 | 62 |

In this set, the mode is 16 because it occurs twice. Samples often contain more than one mode characterized by scores that occur with a higher frequency than others. Consider an example of a study in which a researcher has collected data about communication satisfaction and other variables related to education and employment among married couples. The variable is continuous, measured at the ratio level, and is generated in SPSS for the wife's educational level in Table 15.2.

The score 12 appears 275 times, which is clearly the most frequently occurring score. It means that most women in this sample have completed high school, or 12 years of education. However, note that there are other higher frequencies of scores for 14 years and 16 years, which indicate that women complete associate's and bachelor's degrees at higher frequencies than other years-of-education scores. These three are considered peaks in the distribution and in this case, the researcher may report three modes. Distributions with two modes are called bimodal, and those with three like this distribution are called trimodal. Whereas having three modes is fairly common in large samples, distributions with numerous modes are not desirable, especially in small distributions, because it often indicates a flat or platykurtic curve, a shape discussed in the next section. It is also useful to know the mode for a distribution of nominal level data. Using our earlier pie chart example, consult Table 15.1 again. You can see that the most frequent strategy type is integrative strategies, occurring 12 out of 24 times. Modes in this kind of a distribution can quickly reveal scores with highest frequencies.

Table 15.2 Frequency Table for Wife's Years of Education

Number of Years	Frequency	Percent	Cumulative Percent
Valid 0	2	.1	.3
2	1	.1	.4
6	3	.2	.8
7	6	.4	1.5
8	22	1.5	4.3
9	24	1.6	7.4
10	35	2.3	11.9
11	20	1.3	14.4
12	275	18.3	49.5
13	69	4.6	58.3
14	103	6.9	71.4
15	29	1.9	75.1
16	118	7.9	90.2
17	27	1.8	93.6
18	34	2.3	98.0
19	10	.7	99.2
20	6	.4	100.0
Total	784	52.3	
Missing System	716	47.7	
Total	1500	100.0	

In our brief data set used for illustration for all three measures, you can see that the median and the mode are good estimates of the numbers in the set except for the extreme score of 62. Because of that score, the median is a much better estimate than the mean. Recall that the mean is considered the most sensitive measure of central tendency because it includes all scores in its calculation. But it can be misleading if your sample contains extreme scores or errors. The mean for this sample is 25.00 because the value is influenced by the extreme score of 62. You will often hear median scores reported for household income estimates or real estate prices because these samples frequently contain extreme scores.

To summarize, then, the measures of central tendency are used to characterize an entire sample with one best number or score value. Assessing these characteristics and applying them will help you to determine whether error is present, which we can further verify by examining their visual graphs. The presence of errors is considered in the next section of measures of shape.

Measures of Shape

As we mentioned in the last section, the measures of central tendency can be used to help you detect the presence of error in your sample distribution. Suppose that our sample of relational uncertainty scores included no extreme scores:

12   13   15   15   17   19

If you calculate the measures of central tendency for this set, the mean is 15, the median is 15 (midpoint scores are both 15) and the mode is 15. When the measures of central tendency are equal or nearly so in a data distribution, it is a general indication that our distribution is **normally distributed**, or contains little error; its curve

is **bell-shaped**. In Figure 15.5, the histogram from Figure 15.4 has been redrawn with a normal curve superimposed on it.

Recall from Chapter 6, "Warrants for Research Arguments," that there are basically two types of error that can enter the measurements of a variable: *bias, or constant error, and noise, or random error.* Bias occurs whenever the validity of the research design is threatened in some way; noise occurs whenever reliability is threatened. Distributions with constant or random error present will be shaped differently than the normal curve. **Measures of shape** that indicate the presence of error can be described in terms of two dimensions: skew and kurtosis.

Skew. When all three measures of central tendency are different values, it indicates that skew is present. Frequency distributions that are **skewed** display a horizontal shift in the majority of scores either to the right or left of the distribution's center, with a longer tail trailing away toward the opposite end of the distribution. **Positively skewed** data will have the majority of scores shifted to the left with the tail pointing in the direction of positive numbers as shown in Figure 15.6.

For example, in Chapter 14 on experimental research, you learned what would happen if research participants became afraid of being evaluated poorly by the researcher (evaluation apprehension). If the majority of participants experienced this apprehension in answering questions about personally undesirable behaviors, it would most probably result in an abnormal distribution of low scores, with very few middle or high scores represented (a positive skew). In other words, most people experiencing evaluation apprehension would report fewer of their undesirable behaviors (e.g., cheating, criminal history, child abuse, etc.).

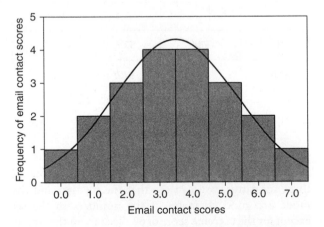

Figure 15.5 Histogram of Manager Contact with Normal Curve

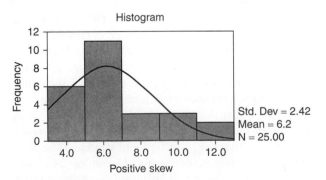

Figure 15.6 Positively Skewed Distribution

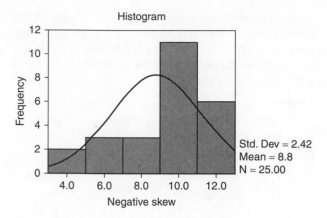

Figure 15.7 Negatively Skewed Distribution

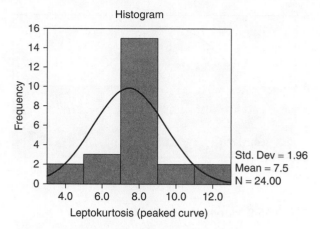

Figure 15.8 Leptokurtic or Peaked Distribution

Negatively skewed data will have the majority of scores shifted to the right with the tail pointing in the direction of negative (or smallest possible) numbers as shown in Figure 15.7.

A negatively skewed distribution would occur if scores were abnormally inflated because of a validity threat. For example, if you asked people to report their prosocial behaviors, such as helping or comforting behaviors or other "nice" behaviors, they could easily overestimate their frequency. In either case, whether it is positive or negative, a skew in the data distribution is an indication of bias in which some measurement resulted in a constant error. If you are interpreting a statistical analysis of skew on the computer, the numeric value of the skew measure is negative for a negative skew, positive for a positive skew, and equals zero when the shape of the distribution is normal or bell shaped. We will see these calculations generated in Excel and SPSS later in the chapter.

In skewed distributions, the mode and the median will be closer to the majority of scores (the highest part of the curve) while the mean will be pulled in the direction of the tail. In positive skews, the mean will fall to the right of the median and the mode; in negative skews, the mean will occur to the left of the median and the mode. In our previous example, the extreme score of 62 would pull the mean toward the right, and the skew would be positive. Thus, when you calculate all three measures of central tendency for your data, they will also corroborate your findings for skew either by looking at the graphs or by generating statistics for measures of shape. Values close to zero indicate no skew whereas positive or negative values will indicate what kind of skew you can expect to see in a histogram.

Kurtosis. If distribution skew represents abnormal shapes on the horizontal plane, kurtosis refers to abnormalities in the vertical dimension. Frequency distributions can be **leptokurtic**, or too peaked, and would look like the one depicted in Figure 15.8. Leptokurtic distributions tell you that there is not much score variation happening in your data distribution. The tendency for members of the same culture to interpret "beauty" or "intelligence" in very similar ways is like the tendency you are seeing in leptokurtic distributions. When distributions are too peaked, it means that majority of scores fall on one or two points or values, another indication of bias. Descriptive statistical analysis on the computer will report a positive value for kurtosis when the distribution is leptokurtic and zero when the curve is normal.

Frequency distributions can also be **platykurtic** (pronounced "plat" to rhyme with "flat"), or flat with "thick tails," like the one shown in Figure 15.9. When they are too flat, it can indicate noise or random error. A frequent source of random error is an instrument that is unreliable in its measurement because, for example, the questions asked are ambiguous, and several meanings can be given to the same question. The platykurtic shape indicates that each score is occurring with about equal frequency all along the x-axis. For example, if a scale designed to measure your level of communication competence had many ambiguous items included, you would not know how to answer the questions. You might be as likely to score low on this scale (on the right end of the x-axis), as you would be to score high on this scale (on the left end). In either case, your score would have little to do with your actual competence level. It would most likely be the result of too much random error present in

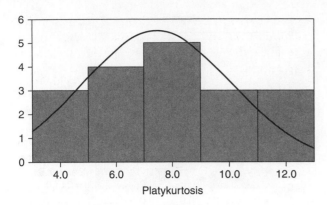

Figure 15.9 Platykurtic or Flat Curve

the data set. Computer descriptive statistical analyses will report kurtosis as a negative number when the shape is platykurtic.

The measures of central tendency and measures of shape will provide you with the important information about your sample, whether you are estimating what score value can best represent your entire sample or whether you are gauging how much error is present. You will need one last set of measures to complete the descriptive picture of your sample, the measures of dispersion. Just as the measures of central tendency describe the data by using just one score, the measures of dispersion explain how the scores are dispersed or scattered along the x-axis of the sample distribution.

Measures of Dispersion

The **measures of dispersion** are estimates of how much variation in scores is present in the sample distribution. These measures include: the range, the variance, and the standard deviation.

Range. The most general way of assessing the amount of variation in a sample is to calculate the range, which is obtained by subtracting the lowest score from the highest score. This is a "between two points" measure. Consider the following sample of the number of close friends reported by a group of five people:

$$2 \quad 4 \quad 4 \quad 4 \quad 6$$

The range is equal to $6 - 2 = 4$. The spread of close friends among the whole group is represented by the difference in the greatest and least numbers. The range is a weak estimate of the total amount of variation present in any data sample. It does not consider the frequency of scores

in its calculation. So even though some people in the group reported the same number of friends, the range does not capture that frequency; it is simply a calculation of the distance between the final data points in a distribution along the x-axis.

Variance. The sample variance is a measure of the distribution of scores around a single point in the distribution. It is denoted by s^2, and has a more complex calculation as denoted in Equation 15.2:

$$S^2 = \frac{\sum d^2}{n-1} \tag{15.2}$$

To obtain the variance of a set of scores, we must first calculate the deviation scores, d. The deviation scores are obtained by subtracting every x score from the mean as shown in Equation 15.3:

$$d = x - \bar{x} \tag{15.3}$$

Let's use the number of close friends sample to calculate these. First you would calculate the mean as $\sum X/n$, or $20/5 = 4$. Our mean for this sample is 4.0. Then subtract the mean from each score in the sample to obtain d: (2-4), (4-4), (4-4), (4-4), (6-4) results in {-2, 0, 0, 0, 2} as the set of deviation scores. These deviation scores are then squared and summed, $\sum d^2$ and this term is called the sum of the deviation scores squared:

$$\sum d^2 = (-2)^2 + (0)^2 + (0)^2 + (0)^2 + (2)^2$$
$$= 4 + 0 + 0 + 0 + 4 = 8.0$$

The next step requires dividing $\sum d^2$ by (n-1). Because there are 5 people in the sample, $n - 1 = 4$. The variance in this example is easy to calculate:

$$S^2 = \frac{\sum d^2}{n-1} = 8/4 = 2.0$$

The variance is equal to 2.0 in this distribution of close friends.

Variance scores are general indicators of how dispersed the scores are around the mean as the single central point of a distribution. However, we cannot simply subtract every score point from the mean. In calculating the variance, deviation scores are squared so that they will not cancel each other out when added together (you can see what would happened if we had not squared the values in our example; the -2 would have canceled out the +2). But squaring the values changes how the variable was originally measured. So to find an average distance measure in the original measuring units, we must take the square root of the variance. This measure is called the standard deviation.

Standard deviation. Once we have calculated the variance, the standard deviation is considerably easier to obtain. As we just explained, the standard deviation, s, is the square root of the variance. In our example:

$$s = \sqrt{s^2} = 1.41$$

The standard deviation is the best indicator of the total amount of variation within a given sample. It is used instead of the variance because it converts deviation units to standard distance measures from the mean and does so with the original units of measurement. So, for example, if you had a distribution of communication apprehension scores, the standard deviation would estimate distance intervals based on communication apprehension scores. In this case, we are estimating numbers of close friends. The standard deviation would estimate standard distances away from the mean in intervals based on the numbers of friends. We will have more to say about these standard distances in the next section on inferential statistics.

Means and standard deviations are the most commonly reported descriptive statistics in communication research. In a recent article, for example, Golish and Caughlin (2002) examined the topics stepfamilies avoided discussing with each other. The researchers reported means and standard deviations for every topic teens and young adults avoided talking about with their parents and stepparents. By looking at these, a comparison of means shows that participants reported avoiding discussing sexual issues, relationship issues, and negative experiences with their stepparents more frequently than any other topic, and they avoided these topics more frequently with their stepparents compared to their parents (see Golish & Caughlin's, 2002, table, p. 86). The standard deviations indicated the degree of variance in each variable's distribution. When these topics were tested for differences, both means and standard deviations are necessary as you will discover in Chapter 16. In the section on inferential statistics later in this chapter, we will explore the relationship between the means and standard deviations in more detail.

Now that you have some understanding of the measures of central tendency, shape, and dispersion, we can explore how easily these are calculated using SPSS and Microsoft Excel. These will also permit you to generate a series of graphs, like bar charts and histograms. Learning to use these programs will permit you to calculate descriptive statistics for large samples of numbers.

Using Excel and SPSS

You begin with a data set that your instructor will ask you to create or will be provided to you. We have provided you with two examples of frequency tables in Tables 15.1 and 15.2. We encourage you to try using the data in the activities at the end of the chapter and in the *Instructor's Manual* to build data sets so that you can experiment with the various statistical programs; we will examine generating frequency distributions and descriptive statistics in Excel and SPSS.

Excel

If your data set is in Excel, you should note that any missing data must be coded as a blank cell. If you are importing data from another source that fills "missing data" cells with any formatting, you should use the "Find" and "Replace" functions in Excel to remove it (see Figure 15.10).

Additionally, you will be using statistics from the Data Analysis tab in the Data menu. This subprogram is not automatically available in Excel, but you can install for free into almost any version of Excel software from the Microsoft Office website at http://www.office.microsoft.com. You should check to ensure you have the Data Analysis tab before you begin (see Figure 15.11).

The statistical tool kit is called the "Data Analysis ToolPak" for PCs and instructions for installation can be found on the website. For Mac users, you will be downloading a program called "StatPlus" available also for free from http://www.analystsoft.com. Finally, the instructions for various analyses will slightly vary depending on which version of Excel you are using. We will be using MS Excel 10 in our examples.

The data can first be compiled into a frequency distribution that will show you at a glance what values or scores you have for each of your variables and how often they are occurring. You will first need to open your data set. Each column represents a separate variable for which you can compute a frequency counts. To create both tables and charts, you will be using the Pivot Table and Pivot Chart functions illustrated in Figure 15.12.

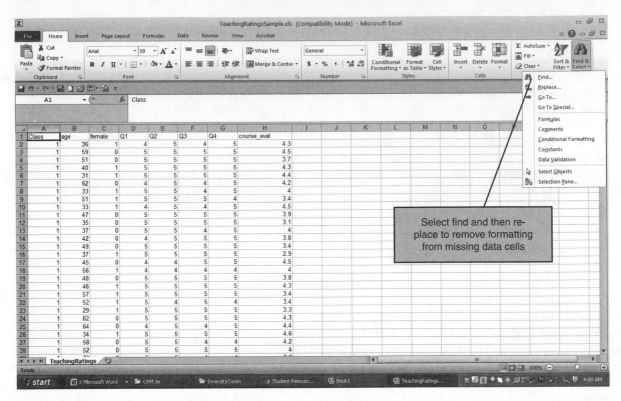

Figure 15.10 Screen Shot of Find and Replace Functions in Excel

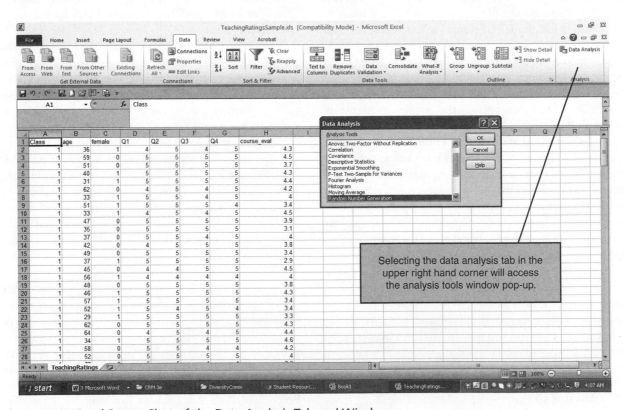

Figure 15.11 Excel Screen Shot of the Data Analysis Tab and Window

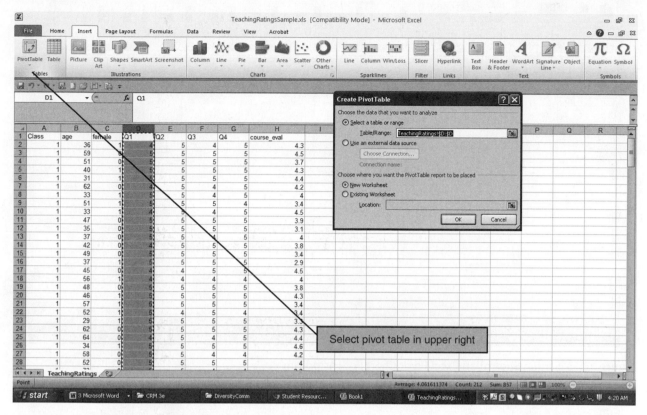

Figure 15.12 Excel Screen Shot of Pivot Table function

First you will select one column or variable from your data sheet. With the drop down menu that appears clicking on Pivot Table and Pivot Chart, make sure the box for "New Worksheet" is selected and then select OK. You will need to drag and drop the variable name into both the "row labels" and "values" boxes whether you are building a table or a histogram. The pivot chart result is illustrated in Figure 15.13.

Calculating descriptive statistics requires using the Data Analysis menu on the far right side. Highlight one of the variable columns and then select "Descriptive Statistics" from the Data Analysis menu. You will need to enter the column fields for your data. Once generated, the data appears tabled in a new worksheet (see Figure 15.14).

You can calculate descriptive statistics for large samples relatively easy with Excel. But the data is less manageable in Excel and it does require a few extra steps than statistical software packages, like SPSS.

SPSS

You will often see that communication researchers use SPSS to generate their statistical analyses and results.

SPSS provides you with many more options in calculating descriptive statistics, but the software may not be available through your department. Your instructor will indicate whether you are using this kind of software.

SPSS contains two types of files that we will be using throughout this section: data files and output files. Figures with screen shots of actions you will take are performed on the data files. The results of the calculations you generate appear in separate output files. These files will also keep a record of all actions that you take on the data files.

The frequency table in 15.2 is a good example of the output from SPSS. The process is relatively simple; from the menu at the top of the data set, you select "Analyze"; a drop-down menu will allow you to select "Descriptives" and from the third drop-down menu, you will select "Frequencies." You can see what this process looks like in the screen shot from Figure 15.15.

The frequencies tab will allow you to select from the range of variables you have in your data set. In Figure 15.16, you will see a window pop-up that contains the list of variables in your study in a box on the left and a box with four variables on the right.

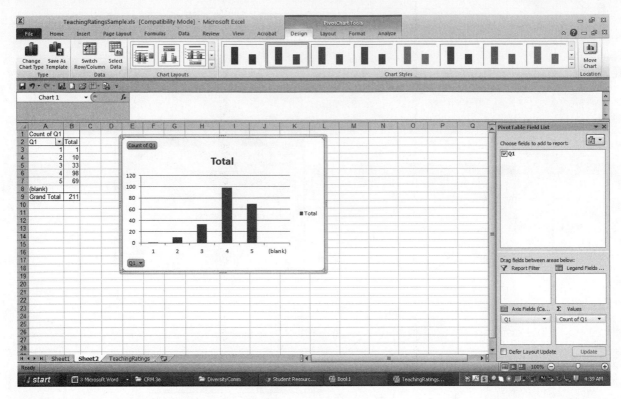

Figure 15.13 Screen Shot of an Excel Pivot Chart for Histogram

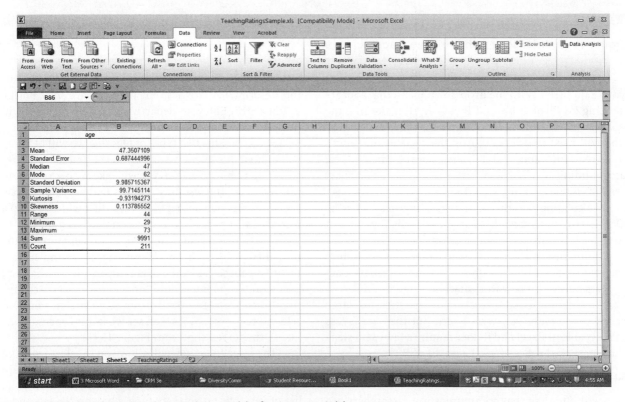

Figure 15.14 Excel Descriptive Statistics Table for Age Variable

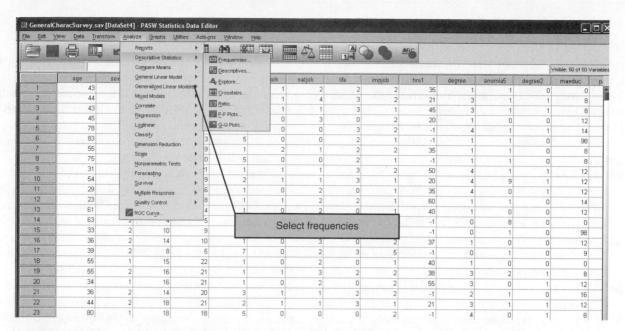

Figure 15.15 SPSS Screen Shot of Command to Generate Frequencies

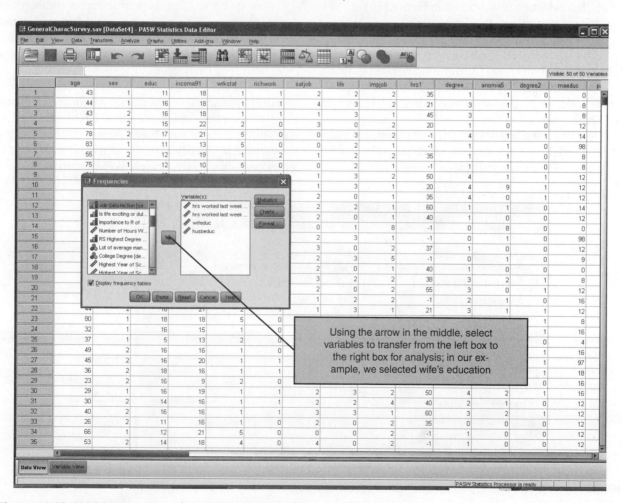

Figure 15.16 SPPS Screen Shot of Variable Selection for Frequencies

The four variables were transferred from the left box to the right box to indicate which variables were being selected for frequencies. You can see that in this case we have selected for variables at once to analyze. A close-up of this smaller window appears in Figure 15.17.

In the close up, you should note that the "Display frequency tables" box is checked in the lower left hand corner. This box must be selected in order to generate frequency tables for each variable. You can select as many as you wish and the program will generate frequency tables for each variable. The results of your frequency analysis will look like the table in Table 15.2.

SPSS provides you with greater selectivity in calculating the measures of central tendency, shape, and dispersion. Notice the alternatives available to you in the pop-up window illustrated in the Figures 15.16 and 15.17. In the upper right corner of this box, you will choose "statistics" to generate your selection of measures. This selection is illustrated in Figure 15.18.

When you select the "statistics" option, a new pop-up window will appear on your screen enabling you to choose all three sets of measures at once. You can also select percentiles values, ΣX, minimum and maximum values, and standard error of the mean in this window. These options are illustrated in Figure 15.19. Once you have made your selections, you will click "continue."

Just under the "statistics" option on the same pop-up window in Figure 15.18, you can select "charts" to generate graphs. This option is displayed in Figure 15.20.

A new pop-up window for charts will appear. This window will allow you to select bar charts, pie charts, and histograms. In the last instance, a normal curve will be superimposed on your histogram if you check the appropriate box under this option. These choices are illustrated in Figure 15.21. When you have made your selections, click "continue."

Now that your selections for statistics and charts have been made, you will return to the screen that appears in Figure 15.17 and select "OK." This final action on the pop-up screens will generate an output file with all three sets of descriptive measures and a graph. This summary table of statistics appears in Table 15.3. It contains information about four variables related to spouses' levels of education and number of hours worked during the week.

The output file will also contain a histogram with a normal curve like those that appear in Figures 15.5 through 15.9 depending on the type and degree of error present.

Now that you know how to interpret measures of central tendency and shape, what could you infer about the summary statistics that you see in Table 15.3? Without having to examine every piece of data in a sample of more than 1500 participants or visually graph the distributions, you can tell that there is some evidence of error because the means, medians and modes for the four variables summarized below are all different values. The types of error reveal a positively skewed distribution for the variable in the first column, nearly no skew for the second variable, and negatively skewed distributions in

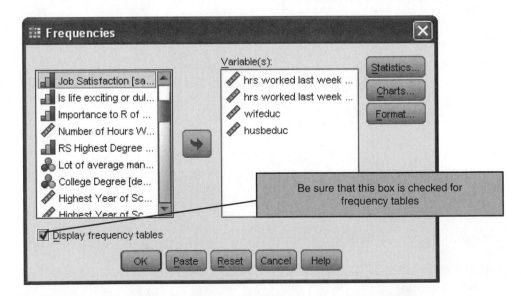

Figure 15.17 SPSS Close-up of Frequencies Pop-up Window for Variable Selection

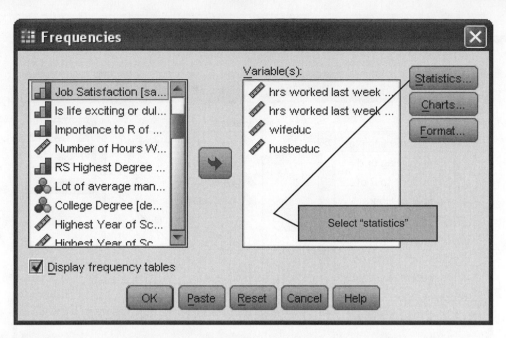

Figure 15.18 SPSS Screen Shot of Statistics Pop-up Window

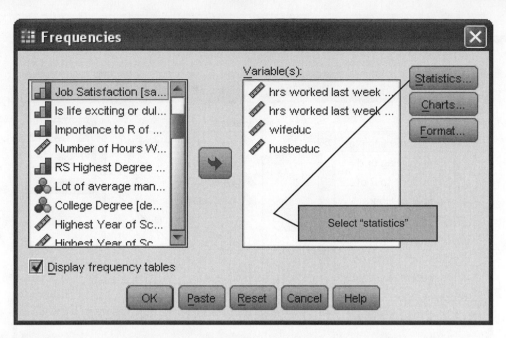

Figure 15.19 SPSS Pop-up window for "statistics" measures

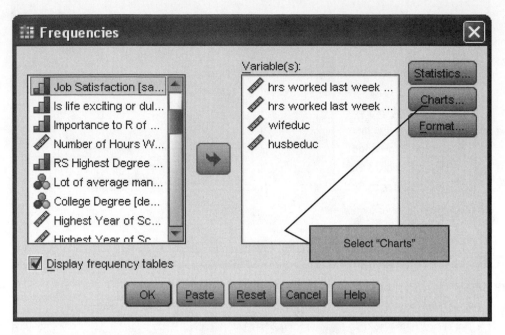

Figure 15.20 SPSS Screen Shot of Charts Pop-up Window

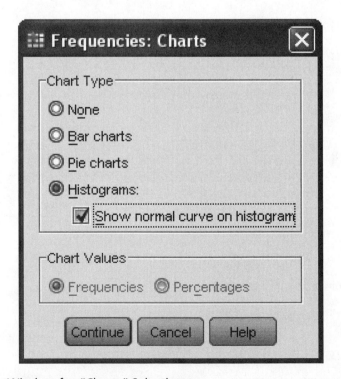

Figure 15.21 SPSS Pop-up Window for "Charts" Selections

Table 15.3 SPSS Descriptive Measures Summary Table

Statistics				
	Hrs Worked Last Week by Husband	**Hrs Worked Last Week by Wife**	**Wifeduc**	**Husbeduc**
Valid	381	381	784	784
N Missing	1119	1119	716	716
Mean	47.52	36.61	13.22	13.29
Median	45.00	40.00	13.00	13.00
Mode	40	40	12	12
Std. Deviation	12.648	13.703	2.675	3.286
Variance	159.961	187.770	7.157	10.801
Skewness	.245	−.009	−.251	−.365
Std. Error of Skewness	.125	.125	.087	.087
Kurtosis	1.127	.793	1.446	.632
Std. Error of Kurtosis	.249	.249	.174	.174
Range	83	76	20	20

third and fourth columns. The first and third variables are also more likely to more peaked distributions indicated by the positive kurtosis compared to the second and fourth distributions. When you examine the measures of dispersion, you can tell that there is more variation in scores between the hours worked per week by husbands and wives and the years of education both spouses have. The ranges and standard deviations for the first two variables are much greater than those in the second two variables. The distributions of hours worked per week are more spread out around the mean than the distribution of years of education. We will discuss score variation around the mean in the last section of this chapter but before we do, it is important that we consider the ethical issues researchers face when representing their data.

Some Ethical Issues

Now that you know how to visually and numerically describe data in a distribution, it's a good time to consider your ethical obligations as a quantitative researcher. You already know that precision is valued in discovery paradigm research. When you are dealing with quantitative data, precision and accuracy go hand in hand.

You should carefully proofread all of the data for your statistical analysis, and never falsify any data (i.e., "tweak the numbers" to support your predictions) even when it may be tempting to discard extreme scores as outliers. Honesty and accuracy are ethical obligations to your research participants and to those to whom you report your findings.

Furthermore, it's important that you disclose the nature and extent of missing (or unusable data) in your sample since knowledgeable readers will be able to tell whether those problems threaten the accuracy of your conclusions just as abnormal sample distributions do.

Finally, you may want to aggregate quantitative data and share only those aggregated results in your research report. For example, you might report only the group mean scores, and not the raw frequency data, as a way of protecting participants' privacy and anonymity, by not revealing any of the individual scores.

To summarize this first section on descriptive statistics, the general purpose of your calculations is to examine your data numerically and visually. At nominal and ordinal levels, frequency counts will quickly reveal how often various categories of your variables are occurring; for example, descriptive statistics on distributions for nominal variables will tell you how many females you have proportionally to males, how many prefer certain interaction strategy types to others, how many romantic partnerships you have relative to platonic friends, how many political ads are image-focused compared to issue-focused. Categorical variables have distributions that are easy to predict based on the laws of probability you are likely to know about if you play a game like poker. The likelihood that a person in your sample is a male is 1 in 2, or 50 percent; the probability that a certain strategy will be chosen from a set of 3 types is 1 in 3, or 33 percent. Calculating normal frequency distributions of these occurrences with discrete values is a simpler process than variables that fall along a continuous measure.

When your variables are measured at interval and ratio levels, in most cases your task in calculating descriptive statistics is to first verify that your data is distributed normally (there are a few exceptions to this rule not covered in this chapter). With normal curves, the probability that certain values will occur falls along a continuum of possibilities and the process of estimation becomes considerably more complex. The assumption that your data distributions have bell-shaped curves underlies the logic of hypothesis testing, the main process you will learn about in the second section of this chapter.

How to Estimate Population Differences and Relationships Using Sample Data: The Logic of Hypothesis Testing

At the beginning of this chapter, we introduced you to the terms *statistics* and *parameters*; statistics provide information about a *sample*, whereas parameters provide information about the *population* from which the sample is taken. Ideally, you want to be able to use your obtained sample of a normally distributed variable as a smaller representation of the total population; it is obviously much easier to examine a sample of participants who are experiencing communication apprehension, for example, than to try to measure every single participant who has ever experienced communication apprehension.

To use samples accurately, however, you must insure that they really do represent the population. You can reduce the possibility of error by random sampling, by your research design, and through careful measurement as we noted in earlier chapters. Graphing your variables and calculating measures of central tendency, shape, and dispersion allow you to further corroborate that your sample is normally distributed. When you are assured the level of error is minimal, you can then use your sample characteristics to estimate what is occurring generally in the population.

To understand this process more fully, it will be necessary for you to learn about three types of data distributions: sample, population, and sampling.

Three Types of Distributions

Sample Distributions

We have referred to the distributions of variables in our discussion of descriptive statistics; the distribution for one variable in your study is a **sample distribution**. Recall from Chapter 6 on "Warrants for Research Arguments" that samples are subsets or smaller grouping of members from a population. The measures of central tendency, dispersion, and shape are all characteristics of data samples based on data collected. For inferential statistics, there are two other kinds of distributions: population and sampling distributions.

Population Distributions

To measure a variable, we take a sample from the population to test. If we could test every member of the population, we would generate a **population distribution**. Our sample distributions should mirror the population distribution. In our example of communication apprehension, any sample of communication apprehension scores should be representative of what you would find at the population level. Incidentally, McCroskey and his colleagues (2009) spent a great deal of time and research effort verifying that communication apprehension was a normally distributed variable. Whenever you select a sample for studying some communication phenomenon, two different conceptions of a population come into play: target populations and survey populations.

A **target population** is "an idealized group representing the totality of target elements that interest a researcher," whereas a **survey population** is "an aggregation of all the elements from which a researcher's sample will actually be taken" (Smith, 1988, p. 77). Practically speaking, if you wanted to test gender differences in using persuasive strategies, it isn't possible to sample males and females from the target population of all women and men everywhere on earth! You are usually satisfied to obtain a random sample of available participants with as much variation as possible drawn from the survey population. For example, you might select women and men from the local telephone directory as a survey population, or use random digit dialing within your area code, if you wanted to include both land lines and mobile phone numbers. Because you can rarely sample all of the members of the target population or even the survey population, you will have to make inferences about their characteristics based on the data you have obtained in your sample.

In a sample distribution that is representative of the population distribution, the statistics will be accurate representations of the population parameters with some expected variation. The mean of the sample, $\bar{X}$, should reflect the mean of the population, μX, denoted by the Greek letter mu. The variance and standard deviation of the sample, $s2$ and s, should be good estimates of the population's variance and standard deviation, σ_X^2 and σ_X, denoted by the Greek letter sigma. In our communication apprehension example, the mean and standard deviation that we obtain from our sample should accurately reflect the population's mean and standard deviation. If our sample contains little error, then the mean and standard deviation values should be close estimates to other normally distributed samples of communication apprehension and to the population mean and standard deviation. This process of estimation is based on the third type of distribution, the sampling distribution.

Sampling Distributions

Sampling distributions actually can provide us with the ability to make more accurate inferences about population parameters from sample statistics. This is the core concept of inferential statistics and hypothesis testing. Based on probability theory and sampling techniques, you can estimate how far your sample statistics are likely to deviate from the population parameters; this general

estimation rule is called **sampling error**. The term is derived from a **sampling distribution**, which is a theoretic distribution of all possible values of any sample statistic from any given population; it specifies the probabilities associated with each of the sample's values.

Probability theory makes it possible to hypothetically construct a sampling distribution of sample means, sample variances, sample standard deviations, or any other sample statistic. By theoretically assuming that an infinite number of these statistics from samples is drawn from the same population, a sampling distribution can be constructed for any of these statistics. For example, in this way, we can construct a sampling distribution of means. Virtually any statistic that is obtainable at the sample level can provide the basis for a hypothetical sampling distribution of that statistic.

When we have obtained a sampling distribution of a statistic, we can "use the sampling distributions to calculate the probability that sample statistics could be due to chance and thus to decide whether something that is true of a sample statistic is also likely to be true of a population parameter" (McNeill, 2001. p. 8). This decision is an essential part of the statistical inference process that eventually leads to hypothesis testing.

Estimation and Inference

As we stated at the beginning of this chapter, statistics serve two functions. They can be used to describe data distributions as we have seen in the last section. They also permit us to make inferences about the population parameters to test a research hypothesis. Smith (1988) identified four assumptions governing sample distributions that will be used as a basis for inferential statistics:

> (1) All sample data are to be selected randomly, insofar as possible, from some well-defined population; (2) the characteristics of each random sample drawn from a population are related to the true population parameters; (3) multiple random samples drawn from the same population yield statistics that cluster around the population parameters in predictable ways; and (4) we can calculate the sampling error associated with a sample statistic, estimating how far a population parameter is likely to deviate from a given sample statistic. (p. 106)

Sampling errors are derived from sampling distributions based on the way multiple samples "cluster around the population parameters in predictable ways"; they are used to estimate the likelihood that certain statistics come from populations. As McNeill (2001) noted, "It is hard to overestimate the importance of sampling distributions of statistics. The entire process of inferential statistics (by which we move from known information about samples to inferences about populations) depends on sampling distributions" (p. 8). The predictability of statistical deviations from population parameters is the foundation for the logic of hypothesis testing.

The Logic of Hypothesis Testing

The reasoning process that underlies the steps researchers take to test their hypotheses includes two important concepts: the central limits theorem and the normal curve.

Central Limits Theorem

In addition to these assumptions, inferential statistics includes the **central limits theorem**, which states that larger samples have a greater chance of approximating the true population distribution (Kerlinger, 1973). Increasing sample sizes in random samples of the same variable results in distributions with normal curves. And the means and standard deviations of these more closely approximate the population's true mean and standard deviation. This theorem establishes normal curves as expected patterns of events increasing in probability with sample size randomly drawn.

The Normal Curve

Recall from the last section on descriptive statistics that normal distributions indicate little error in the data; this means that normally distributed data will yield statistics that are good estimates of the population parameters. Many continuous variables are assumed to have normal distributions. For example, communication apprehension, verbal aggressiveness, and relational satisfaction are variables that you can assume are distributed normally. Most people fall in the midsection of the bell-shaped curve for these communication variables, whereas just a few are assumed to represent the extremes. Two descriptive statistics, the mean and the standard deviation are used as critical indicators; the mean serves as the center of a normal distribution and the standard deviation provides an estimate of the ways in which scores vary around the mean.

Areas under the normal curve. Normal curves are so consistently regular that the areas under the curve can

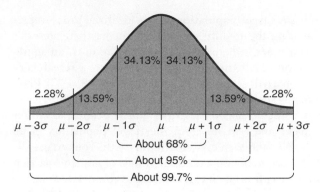

Figure 15.22 Areas under normal curve (image is from Google images)

be predicted at regular intervals. The distance measure used to evaluate these areas is the standard deviation of the sample. It allows you to estimate what proportion of scores will fall along various intervals of the distribution's measurement scale (x-axis). As you can see in Figure 15.22, approximately 68 percent of the sample's distribution of scores will fall between plus or minus (±) 1 standard deviation of the sample's mean, about 95 percent fall within ±2 standard deviations, and more than 99 percent fall between ±3 standard deviations. This is called the **empirical rule** of normal distributions (Holmes, 2001). These estimates enable you to determine those scores that are likely to be part of the sample distribution and those that are not, an important part of hypothesis testing.

How does this inference process work? Sampling distributions can be calculated to estimate the likelihood that sample statistics come from a particular population. Let's suppose you have hypothetically drawn 100 sample means from a population for your sampling distribution of means. Only one mean value will actually correspond to the population mean. The rest will cluster around this value in predictable ways (Smith, 1988). This sampling distribution of means is also normally distributed, so the sample means should conform to the empirical rule of normal distributions.

Standard error. The empirical rule of normal distributions enables us to predict how far a sample mean, $\bar{X}$, is likely to be from the population mean, μX (see Figure 15.22). With the sampling distribution of means, we can use the standard error to estimate the interval of distance between the sample mean and the population mean. The standard error is the standard deviation of the sampling distribution of means.

Confidence interval and level. To use a textbook case example, imagine that the standard error is calculated to be 0.5, and the sample mean is 3.0. By applying the empirical rule, we can estimate that 68.26 percent of the sample means will fall between $\pm 1\, S_{\bar{X}}$ (standard error), or between the values 2.5 and 3.5. This interval of means is called the **confidence interval**, and the percentage of means expected to fall within this interval (68%) is called the **confidence level** (Smith, 1988, pp. 106–109).

In analyzing the data, you will typically be interested in the intervals that have confidence levels of 95.44 percent and 99.72 percent, those levels that are associated with standard error estimates that are about ± 2 and ± 3 standard deviations away from the sample mean. For our preceding example, these correspond to regions between the intervals 2.0 and 4.0, or $\bar{X} \pm 2(s)$, and between the intervals 1.5 and 4.5, or $\bar{X} \pm 3(s)$, respectively. At these levels, we can say that we are 95.44 percent and 99.72 percent confident that the true population mean will fall within these intervals.

To summarize, the standard error is the standard deviation for sampling distributions. In a sampling distribution of sample means, the standard error estimates how far the sample mean is likely to deviate from the true population mean. As such, the standard error is an estimate of the sampling error associated with the distribution. The smaller the standard error, the closer the sample mean is to the population mean.

When you minimize sampling error, you are making the inferential process more accurate. You will be using what you know about sample statistics to estimate the characteristics or parameters of the population. You can also use inferential statistics to test your predictions, or hypotheses, about relationships between communication variables. It is the inverse process of estimation where you start with what is known (sample statistics) and predict what is unknown (population parameters). In hypothesis testing, you begin with a prediction and "then generate sample data to confirm or disconfirm our a priori assumptions" (Smith, 1988, p. 111).

Steps to Testing Hypotheses

To test hypotheses, you will complete four steps: (1) formulating hypotheses, (2) framing decisions by considering the likelihood of error, (3) calculating the test statistic, and (4) deciding whether hypotheses can be accepted or rejected.

Formulating Hypotheses

There are two basic types of hypotheses in formulating predictions about relationships between communication variables: the research hypothesis and the null hypothesis.

The research hypothesis. The **research hypothesis** is the prediction you are trying to test, often predicting "two or more populations are different in one or more respects" (Smith, 1988, p. 111). For example, Rosenfeld, Richman, and May (2004) hypothesized that office employees and employees in the field would need and receive different amounts and types of information. One of their research questions examined the relationship between the type of employee and the amount of information they received about organizational performance. What they found was that employees in the office $(\bar{X}_1)$ received more information than their counterparts in the field $(\bar{X}_2)$. This research hypothesis can be expressed as $H_1 : \bar{X}_1 > \bar{X}_2$. This hypothesis is **directional** in that one mean is projected to be greater (or less) than the other mean.

Nondirectional hypotheses are those that predict an inequality or difference but do not specify how that difference will occur: $H_1 : \bar{X}_1 \,^1 \bar{X}_2$. In our study example, a **nondirectional** hypothesis would be expressed by stating that the information received about organizational performance would be significantly different for office employees than for field employees, but the projected difference would not indicate which mean would be greater (or less) than the other. We have more to say about testing directional research hypotheses in the next chapter.

The null hypothesis. The **null hypothesis**, usually expressed as H_0, is "the antithesis of the research hypothesis," predicting no effects of one variable on another or no relationship between the variables (Smith, 1988, p.112). You should assume the null hypothesis is true until enough evidence is accumulated to reject it. As Smith noted, the analogy is like criminal court proceedings where the accused is presumed innocent and the burden of proof is to establish enough evidence to finally reject that conclusion. This concept is sometimes referred to as the *falsification principle* (Popper, 1962).

Framing Decisions Based on the Likelihood of Error

The second step of hypothesis testing is to estimate the probability of error associated with accepting or rejecting the null hypothesis. In the last section, you were shown how to calculate the sampling error associated with estimation. Using sampling distributions for testing the relationship between the variables, you can project a confidence level with its corresponding interval that will be associated with accepting or rejecting the null hypothesis. Depending on the actual statistics you obtain for your sample data, you can determine the probabilities that certain statistics like the mean are drawn from same or different populations.

By custom, researchers have agreed that the probability of error in supporting the research hypothesis should be less than 5 percent. Another way of stating this rule is that we can say we are 95.44 percent confident that we can reject the null hypothesis. When we make this decision, the probability level (called p or *alpha*) associated with this decision is less than .05 based on the areas under the normal curve (refer to Figure 15.22). This probability level is usually expressed with the test statistic as $p < .05$ (or some value smaller than .05).

Calculating the Test Statistic

The third step of hypothesis testing requires that you calculate the actual test statistic. There are two basic types of relationships between variables: tests of difference and tests of relationship. In Chapter 14, "Experimental Research," you learned about the first type of relationship as a causal prediction about the effects of an experimentally manipulated independent variable on a dependent variable. This type of explanatory or predictive claim requires a test of significant differences. You can also test the significance of the degree of association or relatedness between two or more variables. We explain these statistical tests in detail in the next chapter. Each test yields an obtained value that is associated with the correct p level of error (.05 or less) needed to reject the null hypothesis.

Deciding to Accept or Reject the Null Hypothesis

The fourth and final step in the hypothesis-testing process is to make a decision to accept or reject the null hypothesis. Statistical tests of hypotheses depend on sample data, but in most cases, these are used as evidence to support (or falsify) a generalizable claim about significant findings at the population level. You can accept the research hypothesis (and reject the null hypothesis); this decision is either correct or incorrect. Or you can fail to reject the null hypothesis (and not support the research hypothesis); similarly, this decision

Table 15.4 Decision Matrix for Type I and Type II Errors

Sample Statistics	Population Parameters	Outcome
No Significance	No Significance	Correct Decision
Significance	No Significance	Type I Error
Significance	Significance	Correct Decision
No Significance	Significance	Type II Error

will either be correct or incorrect. The matrix in Table 15.4 illustrates the decision possibilities.

Incorrect decisions result in two types of errors: Type I and Type II errors. A **Type I error** occurs when we decide to reject the null hypothesis but we shouldn't have; in truth, our research hypothesis cannot be supported. This type of error is sometimes called an *alpha* error because alpha corresponds to the p level, or probability level (Smith, 1988, p. 115). If you have established a probability level of significance at $p < .05$, the chance of making an error is less than 5 percent. However, when the error does occur, it is a Type I error. When tests of significance are conducted by using software like SPSS, then the reported p level is as low as it can be for the obtained calculation. Sometimes, the p level is $< .0001$, which means that you have less than one/ten-thousandth of a chance of committing a Type I error!

The second type of error, a **Type II error,** occurs when we fail to reject the null hypothesis but we shouldn't have; failure to reject the null hypothesis results in making an error in this case. Type II errors are also called *beta* errors (Smith, 1988, p. 116). When variable instruments have strong measurement validity and reliability, the chance of committing a Type II error decreases. The probability associated with not making a Type II error is called the **statistical power** of a variable. From the central limits theorem, we know that by increasing the sample size, the closer the sample statistics approximate the true population parameters. One good way to minimize the chance of a Type II error occurring is to use larger samples. By doing so, a researcher actually decreases the chances that either type of error will occur. Larger samples make statistics more stable generally and the decisions we make about them more accurate based on the Central Limits Theorem.

The four steps of hypothesis testing appear throughout the next chapter as the "steps to determine the significance" of the test statistics you will obtain. These steps complete the inferential process of estimation in helping you determine in very precise and systematic ways whether your data can statistically support your claims. You will learn how to complete each of these steps for two types of tests in the next chapter: tests of difference and tests of relationship.

In this chapter, we distinguished between the functions of description and inference as summarized in Table 15.5. The first part of the chapter returned you to the levels of measurement to understand the concept of frequency distributions for the variables you have selected for study. You examined frequency distributions visually in terms of graphs: pie charts, bar charts, and histograms. To statistically investigate the characteristics of your frequency distributions, you calculated three sets of measures: central tendency, shape and dispersion. You also considered the ethics of data representation. In the final section you learned about the reasoning or logic that is the foundation for testing hypotheses. These tests are the basis of the next and final chapter of the book.

Table 15.5 Descriptive Statistics Summary Table

Functions				
Description	Visual charts and graphs	Pie charts and bar charts for categorical variables	Histograms for continuous variables	
	Statistical measures	Central tendency (mean, mode median)	Dispersion (range, variance, standard deviation)	Shape (i.e., normal vs. skewed and/or leptokurtic)
Inference	Types of distributions (i.e., sample, population, sampling)	Estimating error when inferring population parameters		
	Logic of hypothesis testing	Four steps in hypothesis testing		

Key Terms

Bar chart	Measures of dispersion	Sampling distribution
Central limits theorem	Measures of shape	Sampling error
Confidence interval	Median	Skew
Confidence level	Mode	Standard deviation
Descriptive characteristics	Negative skew	Statistical analysis
Directional and nondirectional hypotheses	Normal or bell-shaped curve	Statistical power
	Null hypothesis	Statistics
Empirical rule	Parameters	Survey population
Falsification principle	Pie chart	Target population
Frequency distribution	Platykurtic distribution	Type I error
Histogram	Population distribution	Type II error
Kurtosis	Positive skew	Variance
Leptokurtic distribution	Range	x-axis or abscissa
Inferential statistics	Research hypothesis	y-axis or ordinate
Mean	Sample	z-axis
Measures of central tendency	Sample distribution	

Discussion Questions

1. In what ways are the visual descriptions (graphs) of nominal and ordinal level data different than the visual descriptions of interval and ratio level data?
2. Why is the mean considered the most sensitive measure of central tendency in a sample distribution?
3. Why is the range considered the weakest measure of dispersion? Why is the standard deviation used more frequently as a distance measure than the variance?
4. How is the sample distribution different from a population distribution and a sampling distribution? Try to come up with examples for each.
5. In the term *statistical inference*, what is the word *inference* referring to?
6. How is a Type I error different than a Type II error? What tells you what chance you have of committing a Type I error? What is one way you can minimize both types of error?

"Try It!" Activities

1. For the data distribution 13, 14, 15, 15, 16, 16, 17, 17, 17, 18, 18, 19, what is the median score?
2. A researcher studying phone conversations between students and teachers determines the average length of the conversations to be 7.3 minutes with a standard deviation of 1.20 minutes. What is the confidence interval for about 95% percent of the sample? What percent of the sample (confidence level) is characterized by the score range 6.1 minutes and 8.5 minutes (confidence interval)?
3. Try your Internet skills for obtaining a data set that you can use for calculating descriptive statistics. Go to http://www.math.yorku.ca/SCS/StatResource.html. At that URL, you will find a listing of many different types of statistical resources. Go to the subheading "Data." Click on the link to "The Data and Story Library." This is an online library of data files and stories that you may use for calculating any statistics. Under the "Datafile Subjects," click on "Consumer." Then select "Magazine Ads Readability." Calculate the measures of central tendency, dispersion, and shape on the number of sentences in advertisement copy for each of the three groups of educational levels (highest, medium, and lowest). You may calculate the three sets of measures by hand or by using a statistical software program like Excel, SPSS, or SAS. Explain which group has the greatest number of sentences based on the measures of central tendency. Explain which group has the most score variation based on measures of dispersion. Explain which group has the most error based on measures of shape.
4. Using the data distribution in Table 15.6 as your basis, find the descriptive statistics requested. Then draw and label histograms for each group's data on graph paper; each graph axis should also have a label. Finally, type a summary paragraph or two using the descriptive measures that you calculate to verbally describe the distributions. You should use the indexes of central tendency and dispersion as ways contrasting the differences between the two groups. Use them also in the discussion of the shape of the groups' distributions. Remember, the shape of the distribution will indicate presence or lack of

Table 15.6 Dating Couples' Distributions for Conflict Skills Training Study

Group #1: Control Group (No Training)				Group #2: Treatment Group (Training)			
0	3	5	7	3	7	6	7
2	3	4	6	8	6	7	7
1	3	4	6	3	6	7	7
1	2	2	4	4	6	5	8
3	4	5	5	6	7	7	3

error. Statistics that describe that shape will **NOT** let you make any claims about supporting or rejecting the research hypothesis.

Study Description: A researcher has selected two groups of dating couples to test the effects of training in interpersonal conflict skills. One of the groups of couples was exposed to a four-week conflict skills training workshop. During the workshop, the researcher stressed the importance of increasing communication with one's partner. The other group received no instruction on improving skills, nor were they exposed to any part of the four-week training session. Following the workshop, the researcher was interested in discovering how many contacts with one's partner were made by both groups over a five-day period. The researcher basically wanted to know whether the workshop had an effect on the number of contacts between dating partners. The independent variable is skills training workshop with two categories (exposure/no exposure). The dependent variable is the number of contacts in a five-day period. The data for the two groups is the following:

Answers to "Try-It!" Activities 1–2 and 4

1. The median for this data distribution is 16.5, calculated by $(16 + 17)/2$.
2. The confidence interval for 99 percent is between 3.7 and 10.9 ($\overline{X} \pm 3\ s$). The percentage of the sample for the interval between 6.1 and 8.5 minutes is 68 percent.
3. For the control group, the measures of central tendency are as follows: $\overline{X} = 3.5$, $mdn = 3.5$ and mos = 3 and 4. The measures of dispersion are as follows: range $= 7$, $s^2 = 3.421$, $s = 1.850$. For the treatment group, the measures of central tendency are as follows: $\overline{X} = 6.0$, $mdn = 6.5$ and mo $= 7.0$. The measures of dispersion are as follows: range $= 5$, $s^2 = 2.526$ and $s = 1.589$. The graphs show the control group has a fairly normal distribution, also indicated because the measures of central tendency all aligned. The treatment group graph shows the distribution is negatively skewed, which is an indication of bias or constant error. This is corroborated by the measures of central tendency, which are not aligned.

16 Inferential Statistics: Differences and Relationships

Introduction

In this chapter, you will review the four basic steps of testing hypotheses and apply these steps to analyzing group differences and linear relationships. You will learn how to calculate and interpret both nonparametric and parametric tests for analyzing group differences, including chi-square, *t*-test, and analysis of variance. You will also learn how to calculate and interpret the basic statistical test for associative relationships, the correlation. You will learn to recognize regression as a more complex causal test of linear relationships for multiple variables. Finally, we introduce the difference between bivariate and multivariate analyses; once you have completed this chapter, you will be able to appreciate the purposes of these tests when you read about them in original research reports.

Learning Outcomes

When you complete this chapter, you should be able to:

» Identify types and explain key distinctions between nonparametric and parametric tests of difference and tests of relationship.

» Calculate and interpret single- and multiple-samples of chi-square using appropriate software support from Microsoft Excel and SPSS and standard APA formatting.

» Calculate and interpret *t*-tests and analysis of variance using appropriate software support from Microsoft Excel and SPSS and standard APA formatting.

» Calculate and interpret correlation and regression using appropriate software support from Microsoft Excel and SPSS and standard APA formatting.

» Identify key ethical issues in using tests of difference and relationship.

Outline

Tests of Differences
» Nonparametric Tests
    Nature of Data and Assumptions
    Chi-Square
      Single-sample chi-square
      Multiple-sample chi-square

    SPSS and Excel chi-square steps
    Interpreting the results and APA formatting
» Parametric Tests
    Nature of Data and Assumptions
    t-test

I n the last chapter, you explored how statistics are used to describe samples and infer population characteristics through estimation. Estimation is generally a process that begins with what you know (sample statistics) to infer about what you don't know (population parameters). Hypothesis testing is the opposite procedure of making predictions about what you don't know to test these against what you do know (your data observations).

At the end of the chapter on descriptive statistics, you learned about the four steps necessary for testing research hypotheses: (1) formulating hypotheses, (2) framing decisions based on the likelihood of error, (3) calculating the test statistic, and (4) deciding whether the null hypothesis can be accepted or rejected.

In this sequence of steps, empirical research associated with the discovery paradigm begins with advancing one or more claims that can be statistically tested to see whether there is sufficient evidence to support them. There are generally two types of predictions that can be made: claims of difference and claims of relationship. In this chapter, you will explore both of these types of claims and the statistical analyses used to test them.

Tests of Differences

All statistical tests of difference are variations on basically the same proportion or ratio. The ratio is of observed differences between sample or group means to expected differences. Expected differences are calculated based on what you would estimate as the difference just from chance variation.

The ratio is expressed as:

$$\frac{\text{Observed group mean differences}}{\text{Chance mean differences}}$$

The observed group mean differences are usually referred to as the **between-groups variance**, and the chance mean differences, or sampling error, is called **within-groups variance**.

In certain types of tests, calculation of this ratio enables you to estimate whether the samples you are comparing are likely to be drawn from the same or different populations. In the last chapter, we explained that sampling distributions allow you to estimate the probabilities associated with any sample statistic that it is likely to have come from a given population. Sampling distributions also permit you to compare two statistics, like sample means, to decide whether they are likely to have been drawn from the same or different populations. Using sample distributions is the way in which statisticians establish "critical rejection regions," or areas under the normal curve that are associated with probability estimates that indicate the two statistics are not from the same population. The greater the ratio of observed sample mean differences to chance mean differences, the greater the likelihood that the means are significantly different. When means are significantly different, $\overline{X}_1 - \overline{X}_2$, we are saying that the sample means are not drawn from the same population. This all sounds pretty abstract, but we provide you with a number of examples for each test statistic to show you how the process works.

When deciding how to statistically analyze your data, the first step is to think about the way the data was originally conceptualized and measured. Ideally, this decision naturally develops out of the research design you construct to test your claims. Once you have reached the point of operationalizing your variables, you will assume certain statistical tests will follow. Nominal and ordinal scales will yield categorical variables; interval and ratio scales will yield continuous variables. When independent and dependent variables are categorical, they are analyzed using tests of differences between the frequencies of the various categories. Many of these are classified as nonparametric tests. When independent variables are categorical and the dependent variables are continuous, you will use distributions that test a more complex type of difference. These tests are referred to as parametric tests. In the next two sections of this chapter, you will learn some of the basic differences between nonparametric and parametric tests.

Nonparametric Tests

Nature of Data and Assumptions

From our discussion of measurement in Chapter 11 and in many of the examples of research from our previous chapters on content analysis, survey research, and experimental design, you have already been exposed to many examples of nominal scales. Dichotomous variables on surveys are measured by two response categories (e.g., "yes"/"no" or "true"/"false"). Some organismic or naturally occurring variables like biological sex, "male" and "female," are categorical variables. Remember that nominal categories don't indicate anything about amount or magnitude; they simply represent different categories. Ordinal measures, though, start to give some indication of amount or degree (e.g., always, sometimes, never).

Message categories used in content analysis employ nominal or ordinal scales. For example, Nastri, Pena, and Hancock (2006) conducted a content analysis of "away" messages used by students in instant messaging, and they identified four different types of speech acts in the messages: assertives ("at the library"), directives ("call my cell phone"), commissives ("going to the gym then class"), and expressives ("feeling hot today"). They were interested in finding out how frequently each of these message types occurred. To analyze the data, Nastri et al. selected a test of difference that matched the way the data was measured.

If the variables you are testing are all categorical (i.e., measured at the nominal or ordinal level), then there are several tests of difference you can select. A common and versatile one is the **chi-square**, χ^2, a nonparametric test. **Nonparametric** tests are used when you are able to make few assumptions about the way the parent populations are distributed. In the last chapter, you learned that normal distributions are assumed for most continuous variables measured at interval and ratio levels (G. A. Ferguson, 1981). But nonparametric tests are used when the data is not distributed in the same way as these continuous variables.

Chi-Square

The chi-square test can be used with a single sample or multiple samples. Because it is a nonparametric test, the chi-square is expressed as a ratio of the observed frequencies within variable categories over expected frequencies within variable categories. That means that we test the actual frequencies we have for each category and compare them to frequencies expected by chance alone to see if there are significant differences between the two. The formula for chi-square is expressed in Equation 16.1:

$$\chi^2 = \sum \left[\frac{(O - E)^2}{E} \right] \tag{16.1}$$

where O stands for the observed frequencies of the variable, and E stands for the expected frequencies by chance.

Single-sample chi-square. Single-sample chi-square analyses are relatively easy to calculate. For example, let's say that you have a sample or group of 30 people, and you want to know which of three conflict strategies these 30 people will choose in dealing with a fictitious conflict scenario you created for this study. If you used Sillars (1980) typology of conflict strategies (recall our pie chart example in the previous chapter), they would include a distributive (confrontational) type of strategy, an avoidant (withdrawing) type of strategy, and an integrative (negotiating) type of strategy.

The three types of strategies represent three mutually exclusive categories. The participants' responses can be placed in one, and only one, category. The data in Table 16.1 show that 4 people of 30 chose avoidant strategies, 19 of the 30 participants chose confrontational strategies, and 7 people chose negotiating strategies. Just by looking at these values, you can tell that these observed frequencies are different than the expected frequencies. But are they significantly different? To find the answer to that question, you will compare the actual strategies you obtained to their expected frequencies.

How can you calculate the expected frequencies due to chance variation among the three types of strategies? You must consider how likely it will be for each strategy to occur. The null hypothesis (H_0), "no difference," for this example is that all three strategy choices will occur equally as frequently. The expected frequencies for each choice, then, are the total number of participants (N) divided by

the number of strategy types or categories (k) as depicted in Equation 16.2:

$$E = \frac{N}{k} = \frac{30}{3} = 10 \tag{16.2}$$

In a group of 30 people, the laws of chance predict that each strategy will have 10 chances in 30 (or 1 in 3 chances) of being selected by the participants. Both the observed and expected frequencies appear in Table 16.1, and are used to complete the chi-square calculation.

The research hypothesis (H_1) states that the pattern of strategy selection will be significantly different than predicted by chance. The greater the value of the calculated or obtained chi-square, the less likely the differences are due to random or chance variation. In this single-sample of conflict strategy selection, the chi-square value calculated is 12.60. When you calculate this value on a computer using Excel or some other data analysis program such as SPSS as we do a little later on, the computer compares the calculated values for your observations to their expected values to test for significance. In this case, the value comparison is significantly different at $p < .005$ level, which means that we can be 99.5 percent confident that the difference shown in this sample probably exists in the parent population.

The expected values of the chi-square distribution are called *critical values* of the statistic. In order to find significance, the chi-square values you calculate based

Table 16.1 Calculation of a Single-Sample Chi-Square

	Types of Conflict Strategies		
	Avoidant	Confrontational	Negotiating
Observed frequencies (O)	4	19	7
Expected frequencies (E)	10	10	10
Single-Sample Chi-Square Calculation			

$$\chi^2 = \sum\left[\frac{(O-E)^2}{E}\right] = \frac{(4-10)^2}{10} + \frac{(19-10)^2}{10} + \frac{(7-10)^2}{10}$$

$$= \frac{(-6)^2}{10} + \frac{(9)^2}{10} + \frac{(-3)^2}{10}$$

$$= 3.6 + 8.1 + 0.9$$

$$\chi^2 = 12.60$$

on your observations must be greater than their expected critical values. To find the appropriate critical chi-square, computer analysis will determine the **degrees of freedom** (*df*), or the number of frequency categories that are free to vary. In a single-sample chi-square, the number of degrees of freedom is equal to the number of variable categories minus one: $df = (k - 1)$. In our example, the $df = 3 - 1 = 2.00$.

As one of the steps in determining the significance of the differences measured by a single sample chi-square, we are required to apply a decision rule that will estimate the probability of error in comparing the critical and obtained values. Remember that in the last chapter, you learned that researchers by agreement have standardized the acceptable level of error at no greater than .05, or 5 percent chance of a Type I error. When applied to a chi-square analysis, this rule means that the researcher may be wrong about 5 percent of the time in claiming that the observed frequencies are significantly different than those predicted by chance variation.

In our computer analysis, the lowest level of error is reported, which means the computer will find the lowest level of *p* associated with our calculated chi-square value. The *p* value associated with 12.60 is less than .05; in fact, it is less than .005, which significantly reduces the possibility of error in our conclusions. In this example, our test for significance was confirmed and the research hypothesis (H_1) was supported. We can conclude that in this sample of 30 people, there were significant differences in frequencies of the various conflict strategy types.

Another way of saying the same thing is that we can reject the null hypothesis. Again, the null hypothesis (H_0) for this example is that all three strategy choices will occur equally as frequently in our sample of people. The steps to determine the significance of our obtained chi-square are summarized in Table 16.2. The same general procedure is used to test multiple samples with chi-square.

Multiple-sample chi-square. When you wish to test the relationship between the frequencies of one categorical variable that is independent from another, you can choose the multiple-sample chi-square, or the chi-square test of independence. In SPSS, the test is called Crosstabs and in Excel, you will be using pivot tables, a function we demonstrated in the last chapter.

To demonstrate how the frequencies of multiple samples are compared using chi-square analysis, let's return to the example of conflict strategy selection. Suppose this time our research hypothesis states that women and men will make significantly different choices in the types of conflict strategies they select in resolving a conflict scenario, and let's add that the size of the two groups is different. The flexibility of the chi-square test permits it to handle different sizes of groups easily. Our new set of figures appears in Table 16.3.

There are several notable differences in a two-sample chi-square with unequal groups. We cannot determine the expected frequencies as easily as we could in the single-sample example. We must now use the expected frequency formula that appears below the rows and columns of data in Table 16.3. It is found by multiplying the row sum by the column sum and dividing that total by the grand sum. The grand sum is equal to adding across the column sums (10 + 25 + 15) *or* down the row sums (30 + 20); the grand sum is equal to 50 in this example.

Once the expected frequency values have been calculated for each of observed frequencies, we are ready to calculate the chi-square. The equation for a two-sample chi-square is identical to the one we used for the single-sample test. The steps for determining its significance are almost the same as well. The one distinction is in the formula for degrees of freedom, which is the number of rows minus one (number of rows − 1) multiplied by the number of columns minus one (number of columns − 1). The example of a two-sample chi-square calculation we have been using is presented in Table 16.4.

Table 16.2 Steps to Determine the Significance of χ^2

1. Calculate the value of the calculated or obtained (obt) chi-square: χ^2_{obt}
2. Determine the degrees of freedom (*df*): *df* = (No. of categories − 1) *df* = (3 − 1) = 2
3. Choose lowest possible probability level, *p* < .05 or smaller.
4. The computer will report whether the chi-square is significant when the *p* value associated with the obtained chi-square is less than .05. For example, $\chi^2_{obt} = 12.60 \, p < .01$.

Table 16.3 Data for Two-Sample Chi-Square with Expected Frequency Calculation

	Types of Conflict Strategies			
	Avoidant	**Confrontational**	**Negotiating**	**Row Sums**
Males: Observed frequency (O)	5	20	5	30
Expected frequency (E)	$E_1 = 6$	$E_2 = 15$	$E_3 = 9$	
Females: Observed frequency (O)	5	5	10	20
Expected frequency (E)	$E_4 = 4$	$E_5 = 10$	$E_6 = 6$	
				Grand sum
Column sums	10	25	15	50

Calculation for Expected Frequency

$$E = \frac{\text{row sum} \times \text{column sum}}{\text{grand sum}}$$

$E_1 = \dfrac{30(10)}{50} = \dfrac{300}{50} = 6$	$E_4 = \dfrac{20(10)}{50} = \dfrac{200}{50} = 4$
$E_2 = \dfrac{30(25)}{50} = \dfrac{750}{50} = 15$	$E_5 = \dfrac{20(25)}{50} = \dfrac{500}{50} = 10$
$E_3 = \dfrac{30(15)}{50} = \dfrac{450}{50} = 9$	$E_6 = \dfrac{20(15)}{50} = \dfrac{300}{50} = 6$

Table 16.4 Calculation of a Two-Sample Chi-Square with Steps to Determine Significance

$$\chi^2 = \sum \left[\frac{(O-E)^2}{E} \right]$$

$$\chi^2 = \frac{(5-6)^2}{6} + \frac{(20-15)^2}{15} + \frac{(5-9)^2}{9} + \frac{(5-4)^2}{4} + \frac{(5-10)^2}{10} + \frac{(10-6)^2}{6}$$

$$\chi^2 = \frac{1}{6} + \frac{25}{15} + \frac{16}{9} + \frac{1}{4} + \frac{25}{10} + \frac{16}{6}$$

$$\chi^2 = 0.1\overline{6} + 1.6\overline{6} + 1.7\overline{7} + 0.25 + 2.50 + 2.6\overline{6}$$

$$\chi^2_{obt} = 9.03$$

Steps to Determine the Significance of χ^2

1. Find the value of the obtained (obt) chi-square: $\chi^2_{obt} = 9.03$.
2. Determine the degrees of freedom (df): df = (No. of rows − 1)(No. of columns − 1) df = (2−1)(3−1) = 2.
3. Compare lowest possible probability level, $p < .05$ or smaller.
4. If computer calculated p is less than .05, the chi-square is significant.

It is important that we select the smallest probability level (*p*) for a Type I error in determining the significance of chi-square. Just as we explained for the single-sample test, any statistical software program, such as SPSS, will calculate and report the lowest *p* level associated with an obtained value. And if it is lower than .05, your obtained chi-square is significant. In that case, you will be able to reject the null hypothesis and accept your research hypothesis.

SPSS and Excel tests of chi-square. When you want to test differences among multiple samples of categorical variables, the calculations that we demonstrated in Table 16.4 easily become too complex to accomplish by hand. Let's imagine a similar example here. Suppose that a researcher wanted to test the difference between women and men on

the type of attachment relationship. Attachment styles refer to the kinds of connections people make based on their early relationships with their primary caregivers. In this study, three styles were studied: secure, avoidant, and anxious-ambivalent. Their names are largely self-explanatory where secures are characterized by healthy interdependence, avoidants withdraw from connecting with others, and anxious-ambivalents have contradictory patterns of approach and withdrawal based on overly dependent and protective relationships. As you can see by the nature of both variables, these are measured using nominal scales and are both categorical variables.

In SPSS, you will calculate a cross-tabs analysis for a two-sample chi-square. From the Analyze tab, select "Descriptives" and from that drop-down menu, select "Crosstabs" as illustrated in Figure 16.1.

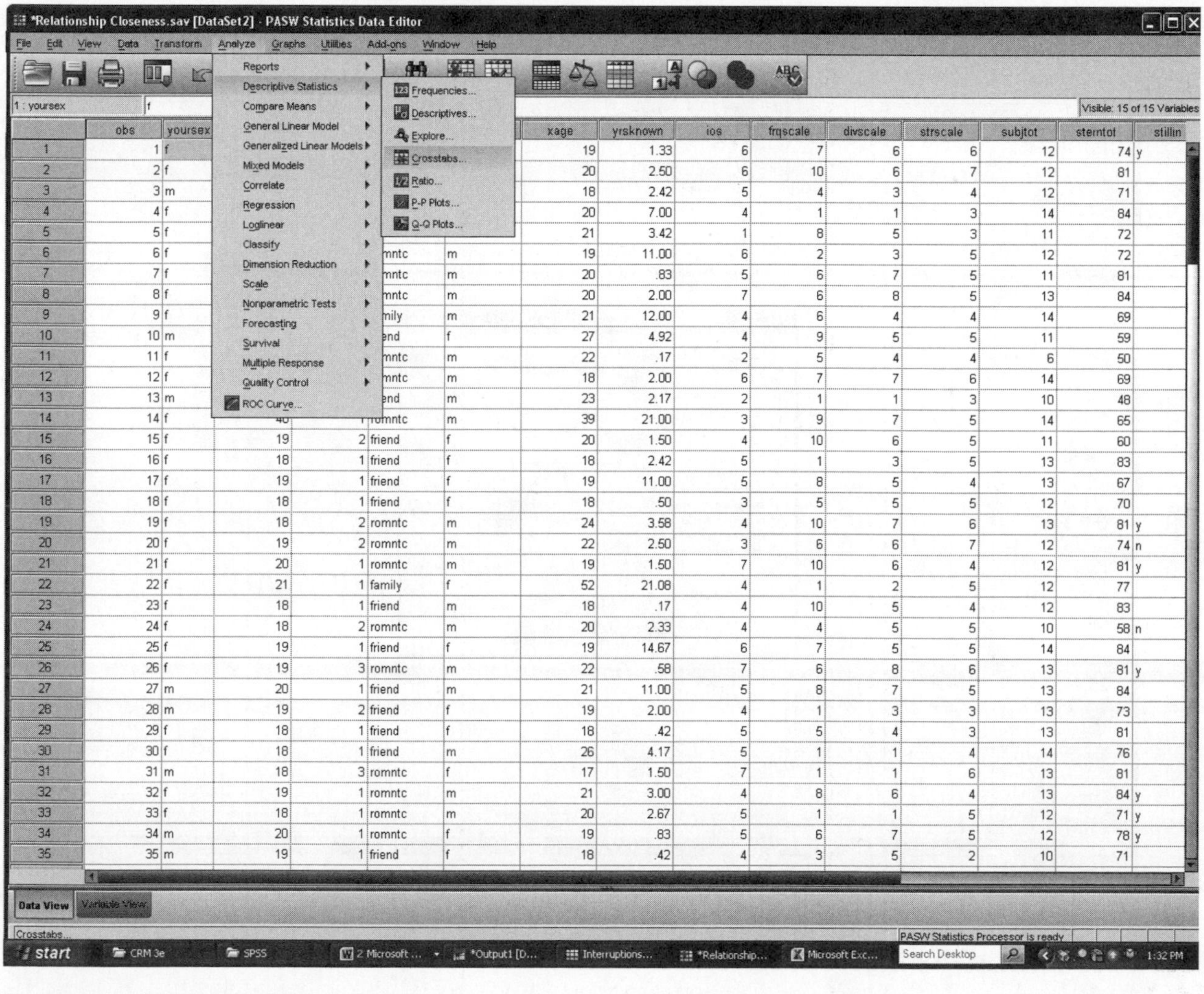

Figure 16.1 SPSS Crosstabs Command

As shown in Figure 16.2, a pop-up window will appear that will prompt you to select your variables by moving them from the left window to right window with the central arrow. It does not matter which you will select as the row variable and which you will select for the columns. In our example, we selected gender as the row variable and attachment style as the column variable (the term "shaver" was used as the variable name because Shaver's attachment style ratings were used to measure this variable).

After you have selected your variables, you will choose the "statistics" option and a new pop-up window with appear. You will check two boxes: chi-square and Cramer's V and phi (Φ) (see Figure 16.3). As we indicated earlier, the chi-square statistic will show you whether the observed frequency is significantly different than the expected frequency. Cramer's V and phi values will

actually help you determine how much of the difference (or variation) in one variable can be accounted for or explained by the variation in the other. In our example, it will show how much the change in attachment styles can be explained by whether you are male or female.

Once you have selected your test statistics, you will select the next tab under "statistics" on the main cross-tabs window. This tab is labeled "cells" and when you click on it will open a new pop-up window called the "Crosstabs: Cell Display" window (see Figure 16.4). The window should open with the "observed" box already checked. You will leave this checked and also check the box right underneath for "expected" frequencies, and then click "continue."

When you have completed the selections for "statistics" and "cells," you can now click on "ok" and the test statistics will be run. Your program will generate four

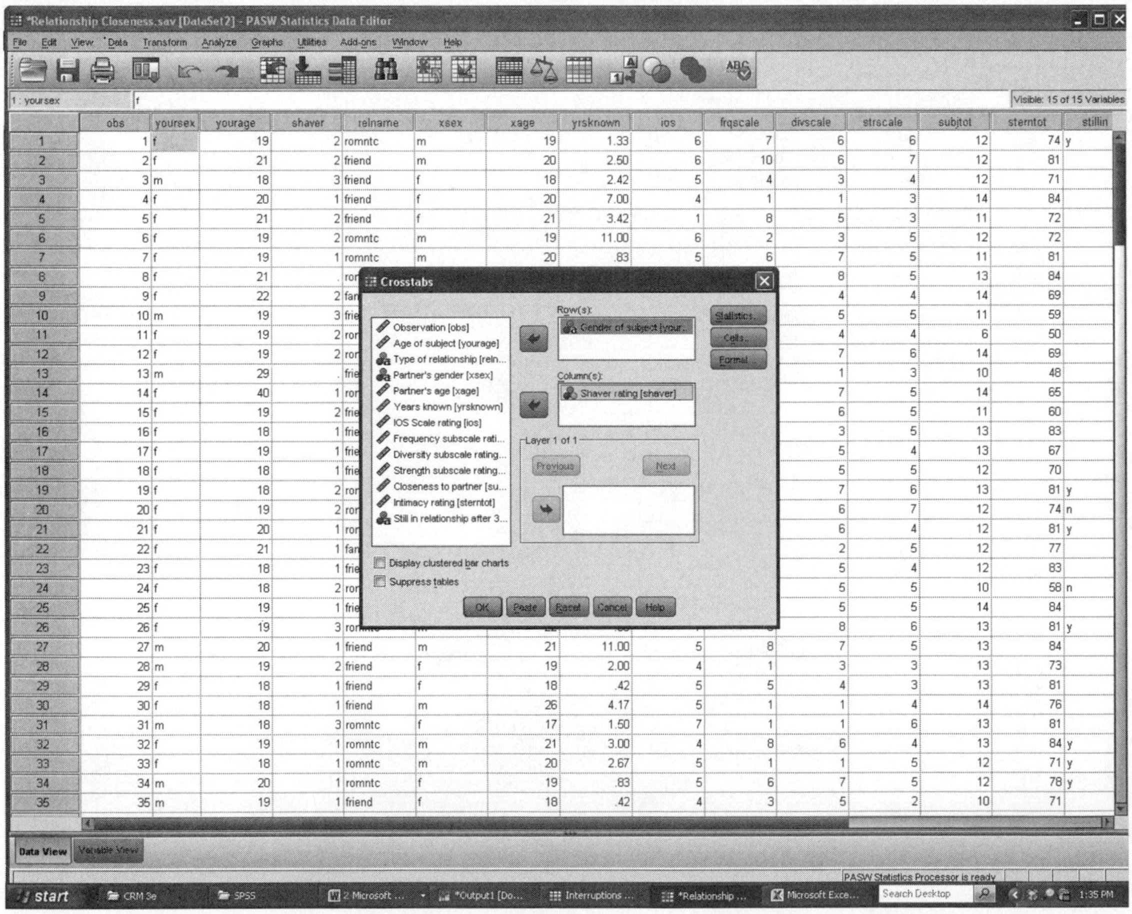

Figure 16.2 Crosstabs Pop-up for Matrix of Two Variables

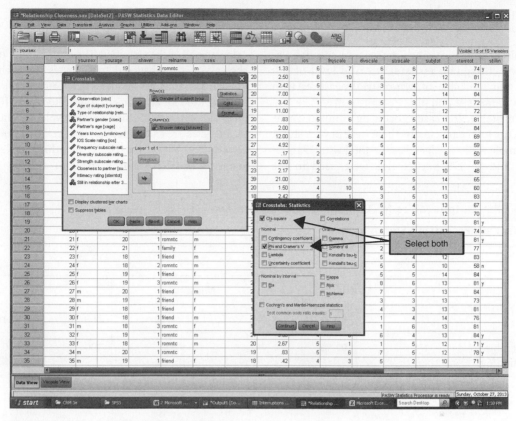

Figure 16.3 Selection of Chi-Square and Cramer's V

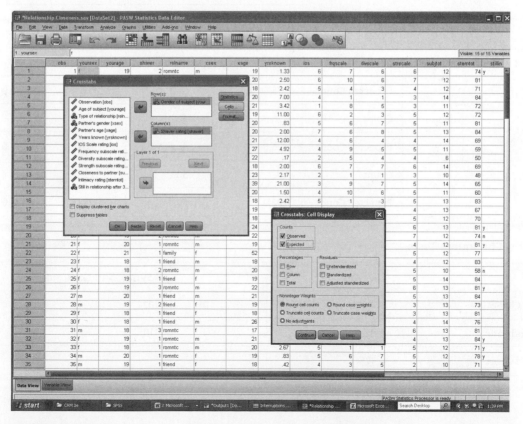

Figure 16.4 Crosstabs Cell Display Pop-up for Observed and Expected Frequencies

output tables: case processing summary, a crosstabulation matrix, chi-square test statistic and level of significance, and the table of symmetric measures with values for Cramer's V and phi.

The first table, the case processing summary, tells you how many total participants there were in your study. In our example, 190 were listed as the total with 15 missing cases, and so 175 participants were used in the

calculations of the statistics. The crosstabulations matrix shows you the observed frequencies for each category of each variable; for gender, there were 129 females and 46 males and for attachment styles, there were 102 secures, 50 avoidants, and 23 anxious-ambivalents. The expected frequencies are calculated for each cell in your gender by attachment styles matrix. In the third table, the chi-square statistic is reported as 4.561 and the p value is

Table 16.5 SPSS Output Tables for Two-Sample Chi-Square Analysis

Table 16.5a Case Processing Summary

	Cases					
	Valid		Missing		Total	
	N	Percent	N	Percent	N	Percent
Gender of subject * Shaver rating	175	92.1%	15	7.9%	190	100.0%

Table 16.5b Gender of Subject * Shaver Rating Crosstabulation

			Shaver Rating			
			Secure	Avoidant	Anxious-Ambivalent	Total
Gender of subject	Female	Count	76	40	13	129
		Expected Count	75.2	36.9	17.0	129.0
	Male	Count	26	10	10	46
		Expected Count	26.8	13.1	6.0	46.0
Total		Count	102	50	23	175
		Expected Count	102.0	50.0	23.0	175.0

Table 16.5c Chi-Square Tests

	Value	df	Asymp. Sig. (2-sided)
Pearson Chi-Square	4.561[a]	2	.102
Likelihood Ratio	4.274	2	.118
N of Valid Cases	175		

[a]0 cells (.0%) have expected count less than 5. The minimum expected count is 6.05.

Table 16.5d Symmetric Measures

		Value	Approx. Sig.
Nominal by Nominal	Phi	.161	.102
	Cramer's V	.161	.102
N of Valid Cases		175	

greater than .05. The test statistic in this case is not significant. You can see in the last table that the values for Cramer's V and phi are both very small (.161), a further indication that the results indicate that the observed frequencies equal the expected frequencies. Based on this sample of data, you must conclude that women and men do not differ significantly in their attachment styles (i.e., accept the null and reject your research hypothesis).

Chi-squares are also relatively easy to calculate in Excel, but they require a specific sequence of steps. First, we will select the same two variables used in the previous

illustration, the participant's sex and the attachment styles from Shaver's category scheme. You will begin by highlighting these two columns in your data spreadsheet and selecting "Pivot Table" from the Insert tab. This action will result in a pop-up table that will prompt you to enter the range values where your data begins and ends. In the example, we entered $B:$C as our range. It should be entered for you if you have highlighted the columns of data that you wish to use. You should also select "New Sheet" for the pivot table data output (see Figure 16.5).

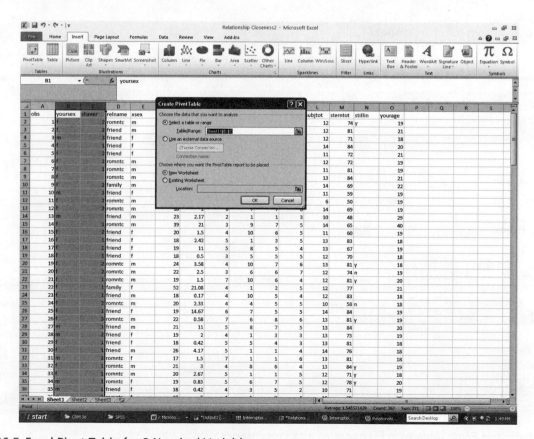

Figure 16.5 Excel Pivot Table for 2 Nominal Variables

On this new worksheet, you will have a dialogue box on the right side of the screen that will show "pivot table field list" for selecting sex and shaver as your row and column labels. You can do this by dragging and dropping your variables into these designated areas. Be sure to add your "sex" variable to the Σ values box by right clicking on sex and moving it to that designation. It should immediately display row and column counts plus their totals in the pivot table. You can convert these easily to percentages by copying the table below, placing your cursor on any value in the table, right-clicking on the value and selecting "percent of Grand Total" from the list. These pivot table areas are illustrated in Figure 16.6.

The next steps for calculating a chi-square in Excel are the most difficult. You must calculate an expected value for every cell of observed frequency data that you have in your rows and columns just as we did by hand. You will begin by copying your frequency count table into an empty space on your worksheet. Click on the first observed frequency; on our table, this first click is on the observed frequency of "26" as the value for males

x secures. You will remove the value of the 26 and replace it with a formula: = [row sum] * [column sum] / [grand sum]. This will require adding the coordinates for the row sum, in our case it is F5 * B9 / F9. You must repeat this action for every row sum and every column sum combination divided by the grand total. At the end of this action you will have completed a table of expected frequencies that will look like the set of calculations under the table in Figure 16.7.

In Excel, the last step is to calculate the probability level associated with the chi-square statistic. In this case, you will click on any empty cell below the tables of observed and expected frequencies. Type in = CHISQ .TEST ([Range of data cells from observed frequencies table, Range of data cells from expected frequencies table]). It might look something like this: = CHISQ.TEST (B5:E6, B23:E24) with whatever your actual score ranges are inserted between the parentheses. The statistic calculated is the probability level associated with the chi-square statistic. If it is less than .05, the test is significant; if it is greater than .05 (such as our example), the test is

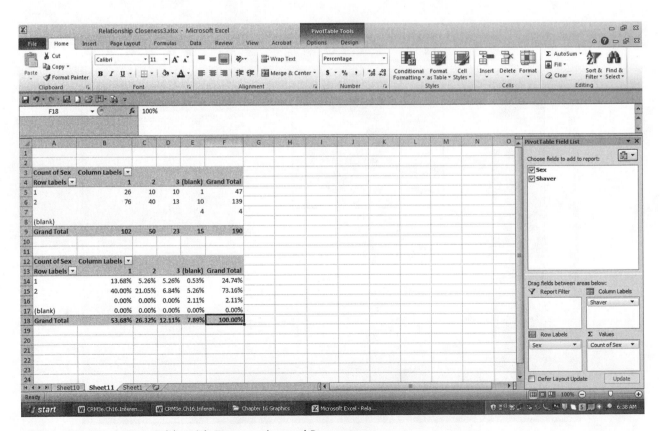

Figure 16.6 Excel Pivot Table with Frequencies and Percentages

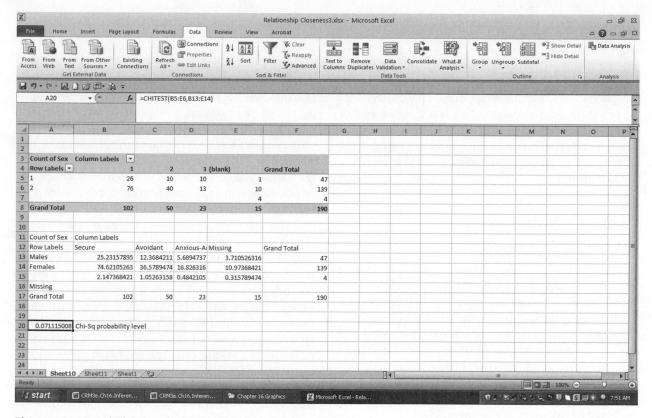

Figure 16.7 Excel Chi-Square Probability Level Calculation

not significant. We will discuss the meaning of significance in this next section.

Interpreting the results and APA formatting. As we have already pointed out in earlier chapters and examples, chi-square analysis is fairly frequent in content analyses in which variables are typically coded by categories using nominal scales. Our example of studying attachment styles in women and men showed that the groups did not significantly differ in their observed choices, ($\chi^2 = 4.56$. p $< .102$). You would also report Cramer's V as very small (.16), another indication that the observed and expected frequencies are equal. In the example cited earlier, Nastri et al. (2006) used chi-square analysis for a series of content categories depicting types of speech acts in "away" messages for instant messaging. Nastri et al. found that assertives were the most frequently occurring category, whereas expressives and commissives occurred far fewer times but more frequently than directives. The analysis showed that observed frequencies for all of these speech act types were significantly different than expected frequencies ($p < .05$).

Survey and experimental research also makes use of nominal variables. In an experimental design, K. Jones, Doughty, and Hicks (2006) asked male and female passers-by for a quarter to make a phone call. They either offered an exchange of 25 pennies or no exchange; these options were tested against whether the passers-by complied or didn't comply. In this multiple sample chi-square, K. Jones et al. found that compliance increased significantly when an exchange was offered regardless of gender as a test of the two independent variables: exchange/no exchange, male/female.

As we said at the beginning of this section, nonparametric tests do not make assumptions about the distributions of the parent populations from which samples are drawn; they simply test whether the distributions are equal (H_0), or they are not (H_1). Tests of nominal or ordinal level data are usually nonparametric because the researcher does not know much about the parent population or because it is known that the variable distributions under investigation deviate substantially from the shape of normal distributions we described in the last chapter (G. A. Ferguson, 1981). The data measured at these levels do not permit the researcher to use sample statistics to estimate population parameters (e.g., μ_X or σ_X) as we discussed in the last chapter, and so obtain the label "non-parametric." By contrast, tests of interval and ratio level data are more clearly articulated in relationship to population parameters, and so are called parametric tests.

Parametric Tests

Nature of Data and Assumptions

Parametric tests assume population distributions are shaped in a specific way; they have normal distributions. Moreover, because population distributions are assumed to be normal, their associated sampling distributions are also assumed to be normal. This means that you can estimate the population parameters from sample statistics and calculate the sampling error associated with each characteristic. This ability makes parametric tests more powerful, which is why they are preferred by discovery paradigm scholars.

We consider four parametric tests: two that test for the signficance of differences between group variances and two that test for significant degrees of association between variables. Parametric tests of difference include the t-test and the analysis of variance (ANOVA). The parametric tests of relationship that you will learn about include correlation and regression.

t-Test

Independent and paired samples. The *t*-test is used when the independent variable is categorical with two groups or categories, and the dependent variable is measured at the interval or ratio level (sometimes called scaled or continuous variables). The *t*-test can be used with samples that are not related, like students and teachers. This type of *t*-test is called an **independent-samples *t*-test**. Or the samples can be related or matched in some way, which occurs when the same sample is exposed to two different treatments. For example, A. Miller (2006) showed the same audience members a set of news stories that evoked fear and disgust responses to test how intently participants visually orientated to each type of story. Pairs of observations (one for disgust story

reactions and one for fear story reactions) permitted A. Miller (2006) to conclude that participants spent significantly more time looking at the screen when viewing the disgust news story. This type of *t*-test is called a **paired *t*-test**, because each participant provided a pair of scores, one for the fear story and another for the disgust story. The *t*-test can be expressed by the same ratio of observed mean differences as the numerator and chance differences or variation as the denominator that we used in calculating a chi-square. But in parametric tests, chance variation in the *t* distribution is assumed to be normally distributed and provides a much more powerful estimate of the sampling error.

You will find many more examples of independent-samples *t*-tests in the research literature. This type of analysis is used to see if the two groups of the independent variable exert independent and significantly different influences on the dependent variable. For example, Farley, Hughes, and LaFayette (2013) found that phone call raters could distinguish between phone calls directed toward romantic partners compared with phone calls directed toward close friends, based only on paraverbal cues. Once the content was masked, paraverbal qualities were rated for characteristics linked with "longing," such as approximating each other's vocal qualities (vocal convergence), and stress features. The researchers found that raters ranked calls to romantic partners as expressing both greater longing and stress cues. In another study, Scharrer, Kim, Lin, and Liu (2006) were interested in examining how women and men are depicted in doing household chores in television commercials. Using a *t*-test, they found that men were portrayed as less satisfactory in the performance of household chores, were met with greater disapproval, and were generally less successful than their female counterparts.

In conducting a *t*-test, we will be testing very specific assumptions about the null and research hypotheses. Let's consider an example. Suppose you wish to discover whether couples married for 10–15 years differ in the number of interruptions over several conversations than do couples married for 0–5 years. The *independent variable* contains two categories or groups: couples married for the longer time period or couples married for the shorter time period. The *dependent variable* is the number of interruptions measured with a ratio scale.

The null hypothesis in the *t*-test is expressed as random variation between the sample means. Another way of saying this is that the samples are both drawn from the same population, $H_0 : \mu_1 = \mu_2$. Applying this to the example, the null hypothesis predicts that couples married for longer amounts of time will interrupt each other equally as often during several conversations as will couples married for shorter periods. By calculating the t-test statistic, we are able to determine whether we can reject the null hypothesis and support the research hypothesis, $H_1 : \mu_1 \neq \mu_2$. The research hypothesis in this illustration predicts that the couples married for longer periods of time will significantly differ in the number of interruptions compared to couples married for shorter periods.

Remember that in the last chapter on descriptive statistics, you learned that research hypotheses can be directional or nondirectional for tests of difference. The directionality of the research hypothesis will determine what type of t-test you will conduct. In our example, we predict that shorter-term married couples will interrupt each other *more frequently* than longer-term married couples, or $H_1 : \overline{X}_1 > \overline{X}_2$. The research hypothesis (H_1) is directional in this case.

Directional tests of difference are called *one-tailed tests*; when the tests are nondirectional, they are called *two-tailed tests*. A **one-tailed test** is a "statistical test that takes the probability level required to reject the null hypothesis (p < .05) from the area under only one tail of the sampling distribution" (Smith, 1988, p. 115), whereas **two-tailed tests** use critical rejection regions under both tails of the normal curve distribution (Smith, 1988, p. 115). What this means is that it is actually more difficult to find support for your research hypothesis with a two-tailed test. In our example, you would conduct a one-tailed test.

The calculation of the independent-samples t statistic is an estimate of the probability that two means are from the same population. This is presented as the null hypothesis $H_0 : \mu_1 = \mu_2$. When the means are derived from random samples that are normally distributed with approximately equal variances, the formula for the t-test is expressed in Equation 16.3:

$$t = \frac{\left| \overline{X}_1 - \overline{X}_2 \right|}{\sqrt{\left(\dfrac{\sum d_1^2 + \sum d_2^2}{n_1 + n_2 - 2} \right) \left(\dfrac{n_1 - n_2}{n_1 n_2} \right)}} \qquad (16.3)$$

where $\left| \overline{X}_1 - \overline{X}_2 \right|$ is the absolute value (the positive value) of the difference between the means of the independent samples (or groups), $\sum d_1^2$ and $\sum d_2^2$ are the sums of the deviation scores from their means squared, and n_1 and

n_2 are the sizes of each sample (Smith, 1988, p. 127). This is an elaborate way of saying that the t-test is a calculation of the difference between the means for two samples proportionate to the amount of difference within each sample distribution (means by standard deviations), or the observed differences of sample means proportionate to the expected variation predicted by chance. It is the same ratio of difference that you will see expressed again in the F tests of the next section.

SPSS t-test. As you can see from the calculation, the test is not easy to construct by hand. It is a readily available test in many statistical software programs; in fact, the survey software, Qualtrics, discussed in the survey chapter now enables researchers to obtain simple t-test calculations. We will cover two approaches in this section: SPSS and Excel.

Let us consider a data sample for the example we introduced earlier in which we wish to test the frequency of interruptions between longer-term married couples ($\overline{X}_1$) and shorter-term married couples ($\overline{X}_2$) over several conversations. The SPSS data file is expressed in Figure 16-8. We expect that the mean for the shorter-term married couples will be higher than the mean for longer-term married couples, or $H_1 : \overline{X}_2 > \overline{X}_1$, and so we will conduct a one-tailed test.

To conduct a t-test in SPSS, you will first go to the "Analyze" tab on the top of the page. In the drop down menu, you will choose the "Compare Means" command which will enable you to scroll over and select "Independent Samples t-test" (see Figure 16.9). Once you select this test, a pop-up window will appear that will ask you to fill in several fields. Your first task is to select your variables from the left-hand box and place them into the appropriate boxes on the right-hand side. You will move your dependent variable(s) from the left to the right with the arrow for the "Test Variable" box. The independent variable move is a two-step process. First, move your variable with the arrow into the "Grouping Variable" box; a space and a "Define Groups" tab appear below the Grouping Variable box as shown in Figure 16.9.

Your second task is to define the two groups for your independent variable. Below the grouping variable window, you will see "Couple Types (?,?)" and below that, another button that says "Define Groups." Click on this second button, and another pop-up window entitled "Define Groups" will appear in the lower part of your screen. It will prompt you to enter the values you have assigned to your grouping variable. In our

Figure 16.8 SPSS Data File for *t*-Test

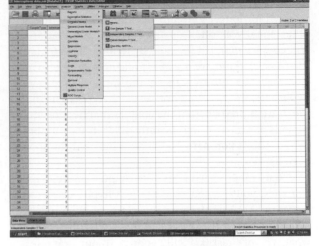

Figure 16.9 SPSS *t*-Test Command

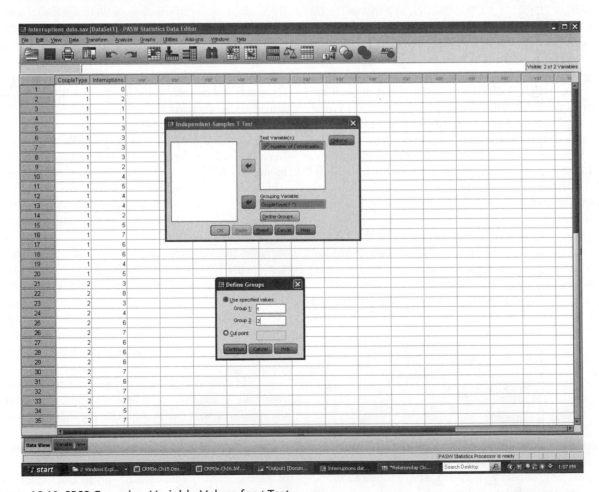

Figure 16.10 SPSS Grouping Variable Values for *t*-Test

example, a 1 = married couples (10–15 years) and a 2 = married couples (0–5 years). Couples married for different periods, such as 6–9 years and those married 16+ years, were not included in the study. You will enter these values into the pop-up window for the defining groups command and then click on "continue."

The next screen that appears will contain output files for the *t*-test statistic (see Table 16.6 a and b). The first table (.a) generated reports descriptive statistics for the two groups: total number in each group (N), and the means and standard deviations for each group. You can see from the reported values that the sizes of the groups are equal with 20 participants in each group. The mean of the first group (longer-term married couples) is 3.5 (average number of interruptions), and the mean of the second group (shorter-term married couples) is 6.0. The second output table (b) will contain the actual *t* statistic, which tests to see whether the groups are significantly different. On the output file, the *t* value = 4.585 (ignore negative values) and the significance level is reported at .000. In this case, we know that the probability level is less than .0005 because of the way that the computer reports numbers, so it is usually customary to round up and report at the nearest thousandth, in this case $p < .001$.

Please note in the second table that the program has automatically generated the Levene's Test for Equality of Variances. This statistic is checking to see if variances for the two groups can be assumed to be equal. If the *F* statistic (.872) reported in this table is not significant ($p > .05$ or $p = .356$) like our example, then we can report the t value for equal variances in the top row of the table. If the *F* statistic had been significant, then we would have had to use the *t* statistic reported in the second row for samples with unequal variances. In this latter case, p levels are calculated as a more conservative estimate making it harder to achieve significance because the assumption of equal variance in the two groups has been violated.

Excel t-Test. If you want to calculate the *t*-test in Excel, you will first start with a data set as depicted in Figure 16.11. Data sets for all tests that can be used for either SPSS or Excel are included in the Instructor's Manual and with the ancillary materials provided with the text. You can see in the figure that the first column of data represents the couple type with "1s" representing couples married for longer periods of time and "2s" representing couples married for shorter periods. The second column represents the interruptions count.

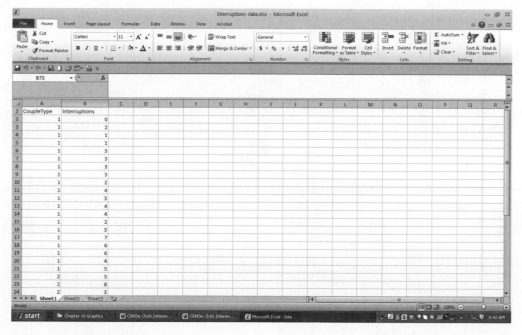

Figure 16.11 Excel Data File for *t*-Test

Table 16.6 SPSS Output Tables

Table 16.6a Descriptives for the Independent Variable Groups

Group Statistics

		Types of Married Couples	N	Mean	Std. Deviation	Std. Error Mean
Number of Conversational Interruptions	1	Couples 10–15 Yrs	20	3.50	1.850	.414
		Couples 0–5 Yrs	20	6.00	1.589	.355

Table 16.6b t-Test Statistic and Levene's Test

Independent Samples Test

		Levene's Test for Equality of Variances		t-Test for Equality of Means					95% Confidence Interval of the Difference	
		F	Sig.	t	df	Sig. (2-tailed)	Mean Difference	Std. Error Difference	Lower	Upper
Number of Conversational Interruptions	Equal variances assumed	.872	.356	−4.585	38	.000	−2.500	.545	−3.604	−1.396
	Equal variances not assumed			−4.585	37.159	.000	−2.500	.545	−3.605	−1.395

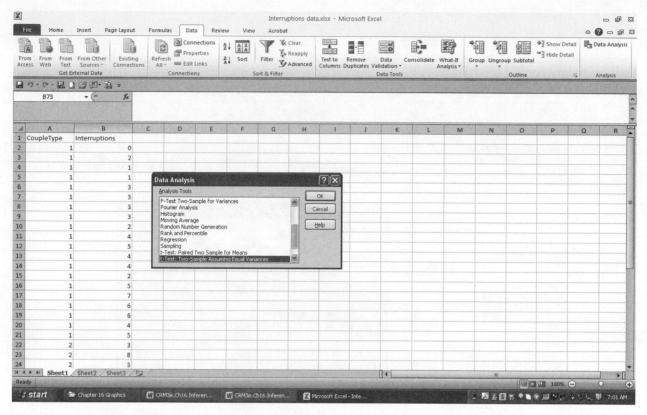

Figure 16.12 Excel *t*-Test Two-Sample Assuming Equal Variances

To conduct the *t*-test, click on the "Data" tab in Excel and choose the "Data Analysis" option from the toolbar for this window. A pop-up window should appear that will allow you to choose the "*t*-Test Two-Sample Assuming Equal Variances" option from the menu. This step is illustrated in Figure 16.12.

Note that you must decide initially whether to choose "assuming equal variances" or "assuming unequal variances" as separate options. Excel does not calculate the Levene's statistic as the SPSS *t*-test program does. You can use the more conservative test assuming unequal variances as the basic assumption but you won't know for sure whether this assumption is correct without a test like the Levene statistic.

Once you click on "OK" for the *t*-test option, a new pop-up window will appear that will prompt you to enter variable fields, identifying these as "Variable 1" and "Variable 2." Unfortunately in Excel, the categories of the one independent variable are named as separate variables. Do not be confused by this error (they are correctly called "groups" in SPSS). To complete this step,

you will click on the Variable 1 empty box, and then highlight all of the data in the "B" column that correspond to your 1s in the "A" column to identify the cell range for this first group. Then do the same for Variable 2. You can see in Figure 16.13 that cells B22 through B41 have been highlighted and then have appeared as a range in the Variable 2 box.

Check the "labels" box and note that the p level is automatically set at .05. Descriptive statistics and the *t*-test statistic will appear in a new spreadsheet as depicted in Figure 16.14. The *t* statistic is reported for both a one-tailed and a two-tailed test. You will see that the p level (or error term) is smaller for the one-tailed test than for the two-tailed test. In either case, the error term is so small that the choice between the two is inconsequential. If the p values were closer to the cut-off level (.05), we would choose the one-tailed test if the means were in the predicted direction, that the mean number of interruptions for the couples married 0–5 years is greater than the mean for the couples married 10–15 years, and it is in our example! Software programs such as SPSS

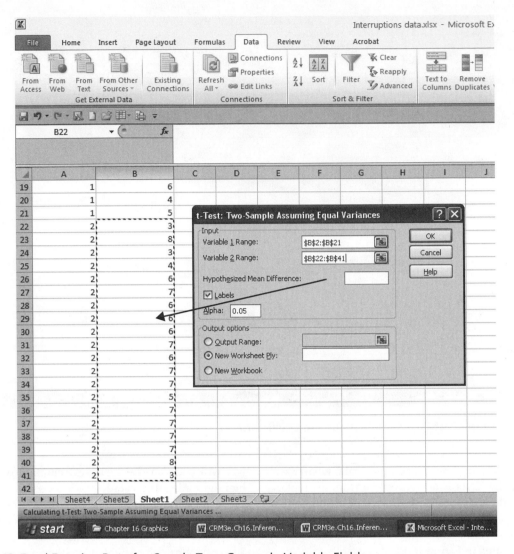

Figure 16.13 Excel Entering Data for Couple Type Groups in Variable Fields

and Excel greatly increase the accuracy in reporting both test statistics and the probability levels associated with each.

Interpreting the results and APA formatting. In our example, the *t* value we obtained, 4.585, is significant because p < .001. That means that we have reduced the chance of making a Type I error to less than one-tenth of 1 percent. According to our research hypothesis, we have supported our prediction that couples married for longer periods will interrupt each other significantly less ($\overline{X}_1 = 3.5$) than couples married for shorter periods ($\overline{X}_2 = 6.0$). We have therefore rejected the null

hypothesis that the two means are equal. Of course they are not equal, you might say, just look at them! But if you have very large samples in your comparison, means can look very different and still not vary significantly (i.e., not enough to conclude that their differences exist because they come from different populations of married couples, long- and short-term). Recall in our discussion of sampling frames that many samples can be drawn from the same population and their means will vary according to a normal distribution. A *t*-test statistic estimates how far sample means can differ and be from the same population vs. different populations.

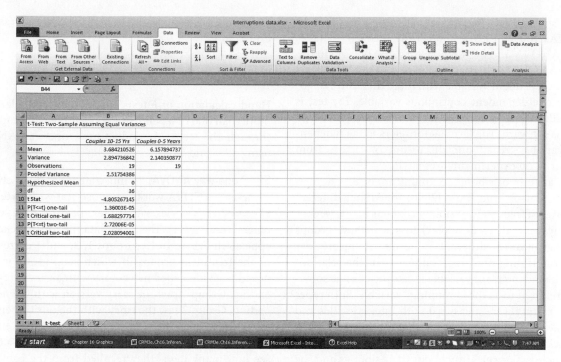

Figure 16.14 *t*-Test Output Table with Descriptives for Couple Type Groups

When researchers report *t*-test statistics, they usually identify the comparison of mean values to indicate the direction of the hypothesis, the *t* value, the degrees of freedom, and the size of the samples (n). For our example, the researchers would report that couples married 10–15 years ($M = 3.5$, $SD = 1.85$) were observed making significantly fewer interruptions than couples married 0-5 years ($M = 6.0$, $SD = 1.59$). The Levene's test was not significant and so the researchers could assume that variances were equal: $t = 4.59$, $p < .001$. Recall from the last chapter that the symbols for means can either be X-bar ($\overline{X}_1$) or M; you will be more likely to see the symbol *M* used in research articles.

In the last chapter, you were introduced to the term statistical power to refer to the probability of not making a Type II error. One way to increase the statistical power of the *t*-test is to increase the sample size. The *t* formula is dependent on sample size. The size of the sample will affect the degrees of freedom; the greater the sample size, the greater the degrees of freedom, which makes it easier to find significance at the .05 level. You will be less likely to make a Type II error as a result. If the sample size is very large ($n = 500$), the *t*-test becomes less accurate, and other tests of difference beyond the scope of this book, such as the *z* test, are preferred.

You can see now that *t*-tests are used when you have two groups or categories of data for your independent variable. But what happens when we wish to test an independent variable with more than two categories or samples, or if we want to determine the effects of more than one independent variable on the dependent variable? To address either of these possibilities, you will need to learn about the last test of group differences presented in this chapter, the ANOVA.

ANOVA

The analysis of variance (ANOVA) tests are also called *F* tests. These share some of the same assumptions of *t*-tests: (1) the distributions of the dependent variable scores are assumed to be normal, (2) the *F* statistic expresses the same ratio of group mean differences divided by chance differences, and (3) the greater the proportion of differences expressed by the *F* ratio the greater the likelihood that the groups were not drawn from the same population. The numerator of the ratio is called between-groups variance, and the denominator is called the within-groups variance. *F* tests can be calculated for independent samples or as repeated measures with the same sample.

One-way ANOVAs. There are basically two types of ANOVAs you will learn about in this chapter: single-factor ANOVA and multiple-factors ANOVA. A **single-factor ANOVA** is the statistic chosen to test the effects of one independent variable with more than two categories on one dependent continuous variable. The test is also called a **one-way ANOVA**, the term used in data analysis software. The term factor refers to the independent variable (recall our discussion of factors from Chapter 14 on experimental research).

In a study of sibling communication, Bevan, Stetzenback, Batson, and Bullo (2006) tested four different categories of frequency of sibling contacts (daily, weekly, monthly, several times a year) to see if these groups were significantly different in terms of uncertainty about the sibling and uncertainty about the relationship. The independent variable is categorical; it is sometimes referred to as the "grouping" variable. Both types of uncertainty were measured with interval scales and were therefore continuous or scaled variables. Bevan et al. found that siblings with daily and weekly contact had much less uncertainty about their siblings and the relationship than those with less contact (i.e., monthly and several times a year). Despite what might seem like the obvious, the amount of contact isn't always a good predictor of uncertainty; more contact can sometimes increase uncertainty depending on the circumstances and the relationship. Nonetheless, Bevan et al. could support the research hypothesis because the F values associated with the ANOVA they conducted were statistically significant.

To obtain the F statistic, the means and deviation scores squared are calculated for each group. These are used to find the SS_b, or **the sums of squares for between groups** (as the numerator portion of the test ratio), and the SS_w, or **the sums of squares for within groups** (as the denominator portion of the test ratio). Another way of expressing this ratio is to say that the SS_b is an estimate of the difference between group means, whereas the SS_w is an estimate of chance variation, or the sampling error.

The sums of squares for between and within groups are divided by the number of degrees of freedom associated with each estimate to find the mean squares. The df for between groups is called the **numerator df** and is calculated by $k - 1$, or the number of groups minus 1. The df for within groups is called the **denominator df** and is found by $N - k$, or the total number of scores across groups minus the number of groups. The mean squares

are used to determine the final F ratio as expressed in Equation 16.4:

$$F = \frac{MS_b}{MS_w} \qquad (16.4)$$

Hand calculation of F tests is onerous, particularly for more than one independent variable. We will guide you through the steps of conducting a one-way ANOVA using SPSS and Excel.

SPSS one-way ANOVA. To illustrate more precisely how a one-way ANOVA works, suppose you wish to test the effects of news stories with three types of endings on listeners' recall levels. The SPSS data file for this example appears in Figure 16.15. Groups 1, 2, and 3 correspond to the treatment groups in which each group was exposed to a videotaped news story with a varying type of ending: Group 1 saw the story version with the neutral ending, Group 2 saw the story with the positive ending, and Group 3 saw the version with the negative ending. Following the tape, all three groups were given a test to see how many items they recalled from the content of the news story. The independent variable is called "storyends," and the dependent variable is the number of recalled items is represented by the X scores for each of the groups (X_1, X_2, X_3). Your instructor may ask you to create your own data file. We have given several examples in the *Instructor's Manual*. This procedure will require creating independent and dependent variables with names of your choosing and your own data just as you see represented in the figure.

The null hypothesis is that the means of the three groups are equal, and the groups appear to be drawn from the same population, $H_0 : \mu_1 = \mu_2 = \mu_3$. If the obtained F statistic is associated with a p value less than .05, then at least two group means are significantly different and are assumed to represent different populations. Notice that the research hypothesis stipulates that just one contrast between two group means must be significantly different for H_1 to be supported regardless of how many categories or groups the independent variable has. In other words, the F statistic will tell us that at least one of the contrasts is significant, but it will not identify which or how many of the contrasts are different.

There are several ways to calculate an ANOVA in SPSS. One option appears under the "Compare Means" selection on the drop-down menu for "Analyze," just as you chose for the t-test earlier. However, the One-way

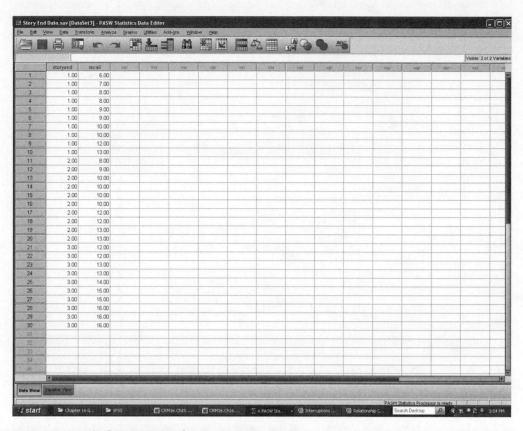

Figure 16.15 SPSS Data File for ANOVA of News Story Endings

ANOVA selection on that menu is limited and will not illustrate what test you would use for an analysis of variance with any number of independent variables. So for this reason we recommend this alternate procedure. First, select "Analyze" from the toolbar, and then select "General Linear Model" from the drop-down menu. This step will produce another sub-menu from which you will select "Univariate" as your test statistic. Clicking on this menu selection will open up a Univariate pop-up window in which you will move your variables in the left window into the appropriate boxes on the right (refer to Figure 16.16). Move your dependent variable to the "Dependent Variable" box with the arrow. In our example, this is the number of items recalled about the story. You will then move your independent variable to the "Fixed Factor" box. Note that you can enter more than one factor or independent variable into this box.

To the right of the "Fixed Factor box, you will see buttons for "Model," "Contrasts," "Plots," "Post Hoc" tests, "Save," and "Options." You will select the "Post Hoc" button which will prompt a pop-window entitled

"Univariate: Post Hoc Comparisons for Observed Means" to appear. After you have moved your factor(s) over to the right-hand window with the arrow for post-hoc analyses, you will see that several sets of tests are available: one for equal variances assumed and one for unequal variances (refer to Figure 16.16). Go ahead and selected "Tukey" for now and we will explain what this means in the interpretation of the results. Then click on "continue."

Scroll down the buttons listed on the Univariate window to the "Options" selection. You must again select your factor from the left window entitled "Factor(s) and Factor Interactions" and move it over to the right window termed "Display Means for" using the central arrow. Once our independent variable, "storyends," has been selected, then you will be able to choose from a number of options in the "Display" window below the two boxes (see Figure 16.17). Select "Descriptive statistics" and "Estimates of effect size," and then click on the "continue" button. This action will return you to the Univariate window and you are now ready to run the analysis by clicking on "ok."

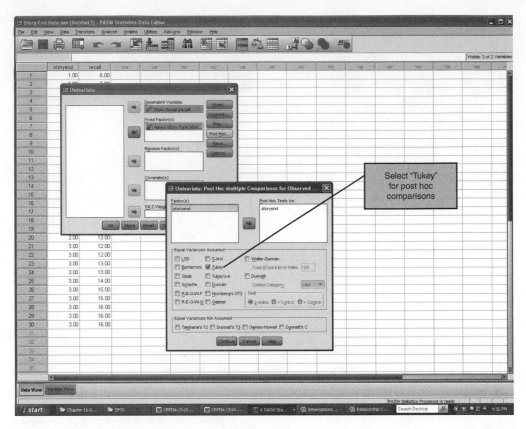

Figure 16.16 SPSS Univariate ANOVA Post Hoc Selections

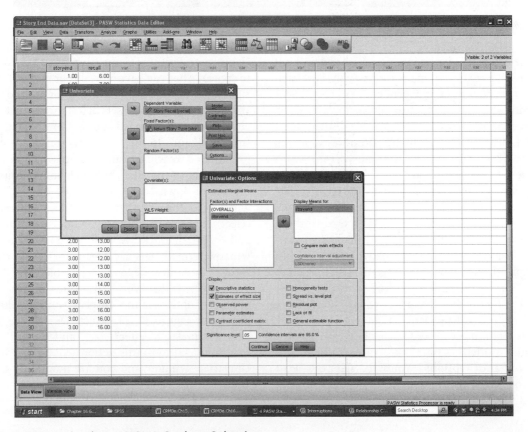

Figure 16.17 SPSS Univariate ANOVA Options Selections

Table 16.7 SPSS Univariate ANOVA Output Tables

Table 16.7a Between-Subjects Factors

		Value Label	N
News Story Type	1.00	NeutralEndStory	10
	2.00	PositiveEndStory	10
	3.00	NegativeEndStory	10

Table 16.7b Descriptive Statistics

Dependent Variable: Story Recall			
News Story Type	Mean	Std. Deviation	N
NeutralEndStory	9.2000	2.14994	10
PositiveEndStory	10.7000	1.70294	10
NegativeEndStory	14.2000	1.61933	10
Total	11.3667	2.77282	30

Table 16.7c Tests of Between-Subjects Effects

Dependent Variable: Story Recall						
Source	Type III Sum of Squares	df	Mean Square	F	Sig.	Partial Eta Squared
Corrected Model	131.667[a]	2	65.833	19.469	.000	.591
Intercept	3876.033	1	3876.033	1146.253	.000	.977
storyend	131.667	2	65.833	19.469	.000	.591
Error	91.300	27	3.381			
Total	4099.000	30				
Corrected Total	222.967	29				

[a]R Squared = .591 (Adjusted R Squared = .560)

Table 16.7d Estimated Marginal Means: News Story Type

Dependent Variable: Story Recall			95% Confidence Interval	
News Story Type	Mean	Std. Error	Lower Bound	Upper Bound
NeutralEndStory	9.200	.582	8.007	10.393
PositiveEndStory	10.700	.582	9.507	11.893
NegativeEndStory	14.200	.582	13.007	15.393

Once you have selected "ok," the program will generate a series of five output tables. The first two contain information about your variables; the third table is a summary table for the ANOVA or F test; the fourth table provides you with standard error estimates with score confidence intervals; the fifth and sixth will provide post hoc analyses. In the first table, the information shows that there were 10 participants in three groups or samples, and each group viewed a news story with a different type of ending (neutral, positive, or negative). The second table contains means and standard deviations for the number of recalled items in each group. The third table reports the F statistic and the probability level. You can see from the third table that the F statistic was 19.47 with a significance level of $p < .001$. The last column reports a value for a partial eta-squared (η) effect. In general, $\eta < .20$ is a small effect size, .50 is moderate, and .80 is a large effect size (Cohen, 1992). Our value was .59, a moderate effect size, which means that about 60 percent of the change in the dependent variable (recall) was explained by one or more of the story ending types. The fourth table shows confidence intervals at approximately the 5 percent error range predicted on the normal curve. This is the same type of calculation we estimated by hand in the previous chapter. We know at this point that the research hypothesis was supported. There are significant differences among the three news story types and their effects on listeners' recall.

The F statistic has provided evidence that a significant difference exists in comparing these three group means, but it does not tell you which comparisons of means was or was not significant. The possible comparisons include: the group who saw the neutral ending vs. the group that saw the positive endings ($\overline{X}_1 \neq \overline{X}_2$); the group that saw the neutral ending vs. the group that saw the negative ending ($\overline{X}_1 \neq \overline{X}_3$); or the group that saw the positive ending vs. the group that saw the negative ending ($\overline{X}_2 \neq \overline{X}_3$). To determine which pairs of group comparisons are significant, you will need the information from the post hoc multiple comparisons.

Multiple comparisons. The post hoc comparisons are reported in the fifth and sixth tables (Table 16.7e and f.). But before you can apply these results meaningfully, you will need to understand something about post hoc tests for the multiple comparisons necessary to determine which pairs of means are significantly different.

If you remember from the "Post Hoc Multiple Comparisons" pop-up box in the SPSS analysis above, you will recall that there were several tests available and you were directed to choose the Tukey test. The potential comparison tests all range from liberal to conservative estimates of difference in between-group comparisons. With liberal estimates, it is easier to obtain a significant test statistic; conservative tests make it harder to achieve significance. In other words, liberal tests increase your chance of making a Type I error whereas conservative tests decrease this chance. Four tests are common and are listed here in order from the least to most conservative: the Least Significant Difference (LSD) test, Student Newman-Keuls (SNK) test, the Tukey Honestly Significance Difference (HSD) test, and Scheffe's test. Without explaining the specifics of each test, Tukey's was chosen because it is more conservative, controlling more effectively for a Type I error. It will also indicate which group comparisons were significant.

Refer to the table in Table 16.7e. In the first column and first row, recall levels associated with the news story with the neutral ending are compared with recall levels for the news story with the positive ending and the news story with the negative ending in the second column. The comparisons are repeated for each possible combination. Across all comparisons, when recall levels from the stories with positive and neutral endings are compared, the p levels are not significant. However, comparisons between recall levels for the story with a negative ending are compared to either of the other two story types, the p levels are significant; for the negative/neutral comparison, $p < .001$, and for the negative/positive ending, $p = .001$. The last table, Table 16.7f, confirms this comparison outcome. Stories with positive and neutral endings do not differ in their effects on the number of recalled items; they are considered a homogeneous subset. But both groups are distinguished from the effects of the story with the negative ending, which was identified as a separate subset in the table.

Excel one-way ANOVA. Before we summarize our interpretations and show you APA formatting style, we will show you how to conduct a one-way ANOVA in Excel. You will begin by preparing your data file differently than it appears in SPSS (refer to Figure 16.18). Using the same news story example, the first column is your independent variable by news story type with three different endings. The second column is your dependent variable, the recall data for after being exposed to each story. You must also separate the dependent variable data by groups. In the figure, these correspond to columns D through F.

Table 16.7e Post Hoc Tests: News Story Type

					95% Confidence Interval	
(I) News Story Type	**(J) News Story Type**	**Mean Difference (I–J)**	**Std. Error**	**Sig.**	**Lower Bound**	**Upper Bound**
NeutralEndStory	PositiveEndStory	−1.50000	.82237	.181	−3.5390	.5390
	NegativeEndStory	−5.00000*	.82237	.000	−7.0390	−2.9610
PositiveEndStory	NeutralEndStory	1.50000	.82237	.181	−.5390	3.5390
	NegativeEndStory	−3.50000*	.82237	.001	−5.5390	−1.4610
NegativeEndStory	NeutralEndStory	5.00000*	.82237	.000	2.9610	7.0390
	PositiveEndStory	3.50000*	.82237	.001	1.4610	5.5390

*The mean difference is significant at the 0.05 level.

Table 16.7f Homogeneous Subsets

Story Recall			
Tukey HSD[a,b]			
		Subset	
News Story Type	**N**	**1**	**2**
NeutralEndStory	10	9.2000	
PositiveEndStory	10	10.7000	
NegativeEndStory	10		14.2000
Sig.		.181	1.000

Means for groups in homogeneous subsets are displayed.
Based on observed means.
The error term is Mean Square (Error) = 3.381.
[a]Uses Harmonic Mean Sample Size = 10.000.
[b]Alpha = .05.

To calculate the test statistic, click on the Data menu in the Toolbar, and select "Data Analysis" on the far right. From the drop-down menu, choose "ANOVA: Single Factor," and click "ok" (Figure 16.19). On the Anova: Single Factor pop-up window, you will highlight the columns of data that you have created for each group in columns D through F. These cells will automatically appear in the "Input Range" box as shown in Figure 16.20. Be sure that you have also checked the "Labels in First Row" box and "New Worksheet Ply" options, and then click on "ok."

Your output summary table will appear on a new worksheet. As you can see in Figure 16.21, the summary table provides group means and variance estimates, the *F* statistic, and the p value, which in this case was a very small value.

Interpreting the results and APA formatting. The one-way ANOVA is the preferred test when your independent

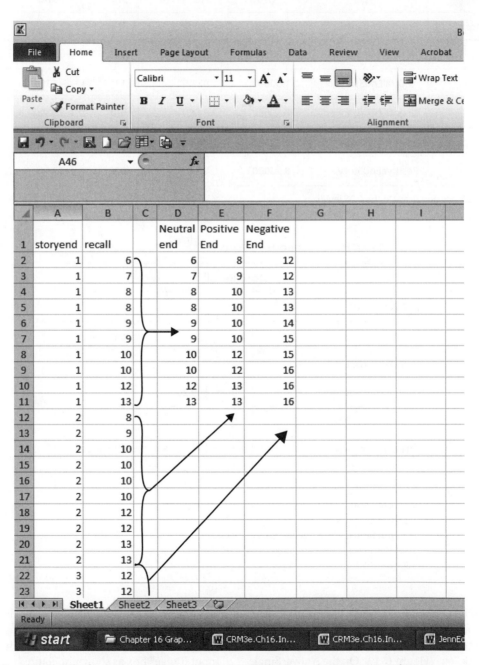

Figure 16.18 Excel Data File for Story Endings, Note: Group the Data in Separate Columns

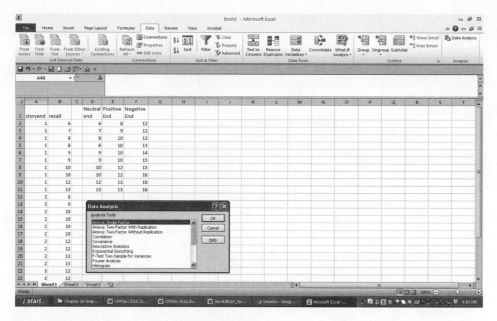

Figure 16.19 Excel ANOVA Single-Factor Data Analysis

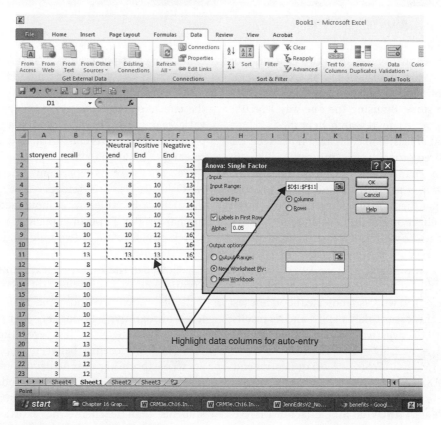

Figure 16.20 Excel ANOVA Enter Data Field

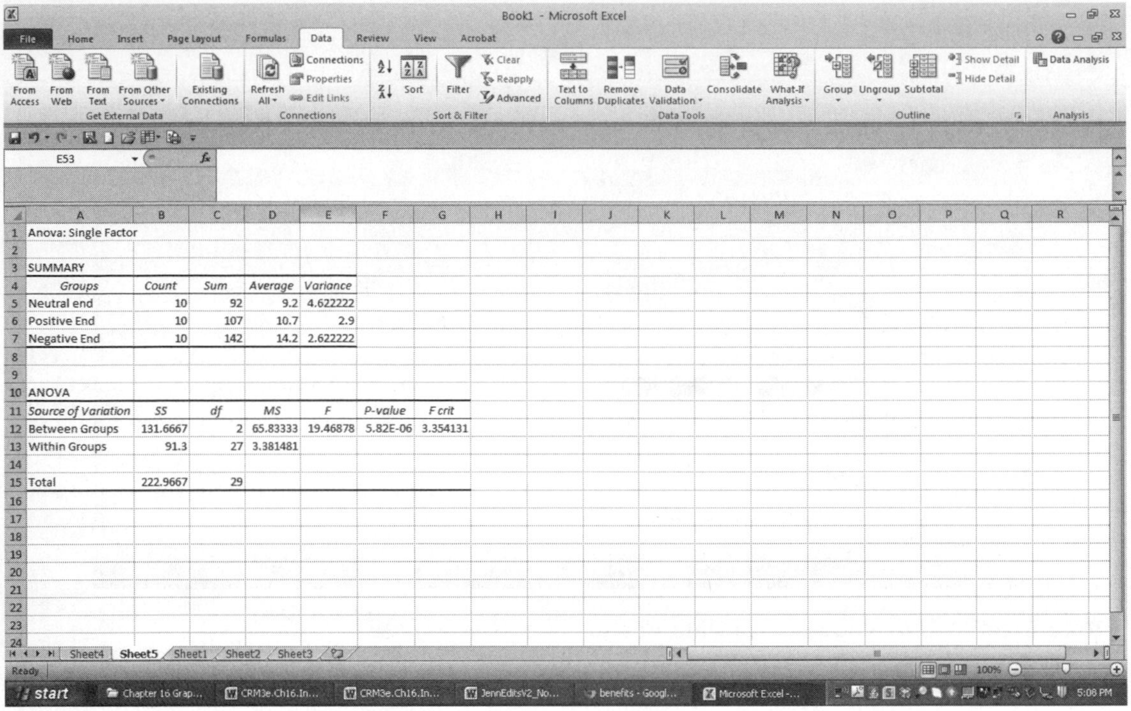

Anova: Single Factor

SUMMARY

Groups	Count	Sum	Average	Variance
Neutral end	10	92	9.2	4.622222
Positive End	10	107	10.7	2.9
Negative End	10	142	14.2	2.622222

ANOVA

Source of Variation	SS	df	MS	F	P-value	F crit
Between Groups	131.6667	2	65.83333	19.46878	5.82E-06	3.354131
Within Groups	91.3	27	3.381481			
Total	222.9667	29				

Figure 16.21 Excel ANOVA Summary Table

variable is categorical with more than two categories or groups. In our example, we tested the effects of news stories with different endings on the number of items recalled from each story. By using the one-way ANOVA analysis, we supported our research hypothesis ($H_1 = \mu_1 \neq \mu_2 \neq \mu_3$) that at least one comparison between the means for the three groups was significantly different than predicted by chance. We can reject the null hypothesis ($H_0 : \mu_1 = \mu_2 = \mu_3$). If this were a research report, you will report that the type of ending for news stories has a significant effect on the number of items recalled by stating the *F* statistic with its numerator and denominator degrees of freedom at the p level of significance indicated on your output table ($F_{2, 27} = 19.47$, $p < .001$). This is the *main effect* of the independent variable on the dependent variable. You will also indicate the ad hoc test that you used, in this case, Tukey's HSD, and its results; the new story with the negative ending resulted in more items recalled ($M_3 = 14.2$, $SD = 1.62$) than did the stories with the positive ($M_2 = 10.7$, $SD = 1.70$) or neutral endings ($M_3 = 9.2$, $SD = 2.15$).

Two-way (and greater) ANOVAs. Single-factor analyses are less common than the second type of ANOVA, called the **multiple-factors ANOVA**. It is considerably more complex than the single-factor, or one-way, ANOVA. Multiple-factors ANOVAs are computed for the effects of more than one independent categorical variable on a continuous dependent variable. The simplest of these designs can be illustrated by using a 2 × 2 research design matrix, a two-way ANOVA because there are two independent variables (three-way ANOVAs have three independent variables, and so forth). Recall your learning about factorial experiments in chapter 14, "Experimental Research." A 2 × 2 research design refers to two independent variables with two categories each.

Consider the following experiment conducted by Frymier and Houser (1998). They wished to test the effects of immediacy and topic relevance on students' levels of cognitive learning. Frymier and Houser (1998) defined immediacy as "the perception of physical and psychological closeness between people" (p. 122). Teachers who express high immediacy nonverbally smile and nod more in response to their students, have higher levels of eye contact, and move or stand closer to their students than teachers who express low immediacy nonverbally. Frymier and Houser chose a 2 × 2 design in which high and low levels of immediacy represented the two categories of the independent variable, and high and low levels of topic relevance represented the two categories of the second independent variable. The *dependent variable* is the level of learning measured on an interval scale as a continuous variable.

If you were calculating this two-way ANOVA in SPSS, you would select the General Linear Model and enter two factors, one for each independent variable in all of the appropriate selections for the descriptives, *F* test and post hoc comparisons. The main difference between a one-way and a two-way ANOVA is that those with two or more independent variables will report both main and interaction effects.

In our example, Frymier and Houser (1998) expected to find two *main effects*, one for immediacy and one for relevance, as predicted in the research hypotheses, H_1: Students who are exposed to teachers with higher levels of immediacy will experience significantly greater increases in their cognitive learning than students exposed to teachers with lower levels of immediacy; and H_2: Students who are exposed to teachers expressing higher levels of topical relevance will experience significantly greater increases in their cognitive learning than students exposed to teachers expressing lower levels of topical relevance. Recall that main effects are the predicted effects of each separate independent variable (immediacy or relevance) on the dependent variable (cognitive learning).

This two-way ANOVA also tests interaction effects. Recall from Chapter 14, "Experimental Research," that the *interaction effect* is the combined influence of two or more independent variables on the dependent variable. The interaction effect predicted in Frymier and Houser's (1998) study was stated in their third hypothesis, H_3: Students who are exposed to teachers expressing higher levels of both immediacy and topical relevance will experience significantly greater increases in their cognitive learning than students exposed to teachers expressing lower levels of immediacy and topical relevance.

SPSS and Excel generate summary tables that report F values for each main effect and the interaction effect (s) with their accompanying p values that you will read just as you interpreted them for the one-way test. *F* values for main and interaction effects with p < .05 are significant and the research hypotheses are supported. Those with significance levels higher than .05 are not significant and in those cases you have not rejected the null hypothesis.

From the Frymier and Houser example, you could draw the following conclusions: (1) Students who were exposed to teachers expressing higher levels of immediacy experienced significantly greater increases in their cognitive learning than students exposed to teachers expressing lower levels of immediacy (the F_{obt} value associated with the immediacy main effect is 7.81, significant at $p < .05$.; H_1 predicting a main effect for immediacy, was supported; (2) Students who were exposed to teachers expressing higher levels of topical relevance did not experience significantly greater increases in their cognitive learning than students exposed to teachers expressing lower levels of topical relevance; H_2, predicting a main effect for relevance, was *not* supported; (3) There were no significantly different combined effects for immediacy and topical relevance on cognitive learning. The probability associated with the interaction effect for relevance and immediacy was greater than .05; H_3, predicting an interaction effect for immediacy and relevance, was *not* supported.

More complex tests of difference are frequent in communication research and are applied with different research designs. Tests such as analysis of covariance allow researchers to clarify main effects by parsing out the variance that can be accounted for by a rival predictor variable (covariate). **Multivariate ANOVA** permits investigating the effects of independent variables on multiple dependent continuous variables. Calculation of these tests is beyond the scope of this textbook, but you will undoubtedly encounter them if you continue on in statistical methods, or you can read about them now in more advanced discussions (see, e.g., Pedhazur, 1982). At this point, we consider the second general type of claim made with inferential statistics, the claims of relatedness or association, and the tests of relationships used to assess their significance.

Tests of Relationships

The tests of relationships assess how changes in one scaled variable (interval or ratio-level data) are associated with or predict changes in a second (and more) scaled variables. Rather than use measures of central tendency, such as the *mean*, to examine differences between groups, tests of relationships make greater use of the entire amount of information about each variable that is available to you because the data is measured with interval or ratio scales. You will begin this section by learning about the general concept of **correlation**, also called covariance; you will explore ways of interpreting correlations and the types of possible relationships between variables; you will also examine tests of correlation or covariance; and you will conclude this chapter with a brief identification of more advanced methods.

Correlation

Nature of Data and Assumptions

When variables are correlated, it is assumed they covary, or have variance in common; that means that change in one of the variables is associated with change in the other variable. We can say the two variables systematically share variance. The statistics that estimate the degree of association are not direct tests of causality. In Chapter 11 on "How to Design Discovery Research" and in Chapter 14, "Experimental Research," you learned that causal claims require correlation as one condition of causality, but it is an insufficient condition by itself.

Many critics of social science underscore the importance of not assuming causality in correlations. For example, G. A. Ferguson (1981) noted that intelligence and motor abilities may be correlated because of the presence of some third and unacknowledged factor like age. Remove the factor of age, and the association disappears. Because of the complexity of human relationships, there are probably multiple causes for any event, and any event itself is probably composed of many variables. Assuming causality can lead to a spurious correlation, or two variables that appear to be associated when they are not causally related. G. A. Ferguson (1981) noted that both the birth rate and alcohol consumption rose after World War II, though establishing a causal link between the two leads to humorous if not dangerous conclusions (p. 138).

Associations of variance between just two continuous variables are called **bivariate relationships**; between more than two, the associations are called **multivariate relationships**. In this section, you will explore calculations and interpretations for statistics based on bivariate relationships.

Point-Biserial Correlation

For many bivariate relationships, the strength of this association is estimated with a statistic called a correlation coefficient. One of the most frequent tests of correlation begins with calculating a statistic, a coefficient that is

represented by an r for samples, and by ρ (Greek letter rho) at the population level. The formal name of the test statistic is the point biserial correlation, otherwise known as the Pearson's product-moment coefficient of correlation or simple, zero-order correlation.

SPSS and excel correlation tests. The test for correlation assumes the variables are normally distributed. The null hypothesis is written as $H_0 : \rho = 0.0$, and the research hypothesis is written as $H_1 : \rho \neq 0.0$ As an example, let's say that you wish to measure the strength or magnitude of the association between two continuous variables measured with interval scales, communication apprehension and level of procrastination in speech preparation, an example based on a study by Behnke and Sawyer (1999). They predicted that higher levels of communication apprehension would be associated with greater procrastination. We use Behnke and Sawyer's (1999) variables for SPSS example data file in Figure 16.22. The first column contains communication apprehension scores; procrastination scores constitute the second column of data.

In tests of difference, you observed how two or more samples were different on their dependent variable scores. For correlation, you will examine how the same sample of students varies on two separate measures: communication apprehension and procrastination. To calculate the r coefficient, the equation requires multiplying and summing deviation scores for both variables. The equation and values for our example appear in Table 16.8.

The procedure is very easy in SPSS. From the "Analyze" tab on the Toolbar, select "Correlate" from drop-down menu, and then "Bivariate" from the sub-menu (see Figure 16.23). This action will result in the appearance of a pop-up window entitled "Bivariate Correlations." You must move both of your continuous variables

Table 16.8 Calculation of the Correlation Coefficient r_{xy}

$$\text{Calculate } r_{xy}:$$

$$r_{xy} = \frac{\sum(d_x d_y)}{\sqrt{\left(\sum d_x^2\right)\left(\sum d_y^2\right)}}$$

$$r_{xy} = \frac{50.0}{\sqrt{300\,(10.5)}}$$

$$r_{xy} = \frac{50}{56.1249}$$

$$r_{xy} = +.89$$

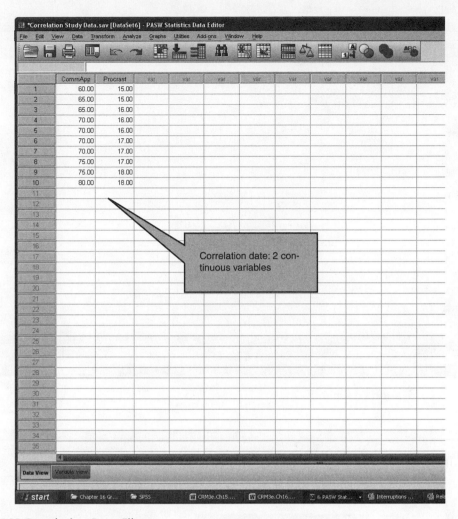

Figure 16.22 SPSS Correlation Data File

from the left window to the right window labeled "Variables" using the central arrow. Be sure to check "Pearson" if it is not checked; the default test of significance for correlation is two-tailed and check to have significant correlations flagged in the summary table (see Figure 16.24). To calculate the correlation between the 2 variables, click "ok."

The output file will contain a correlation matrix such as the one in Table 16.9. The correlation is the same as our tabled value, .891. We will have much to say about how to interpret this coefficient in the next section.

The operation for calculating a correlation in Excel is not much different. You will again create two columns of data, one for communication apprehension and the

second for procrastination. You will then select the Data tab from the Toolbar and then "Data Analysis" at the far right of the screen. Choose "Correlation" from the menu and then click "ok" (Figure 16.25).

A new pop-up window entitled "Correlate" will appear that will prompt you to enter the "Input Range" by highlighting both columns of variable data (see Figure 16.26). Be sure to check "Labels in First Row" and "New Worksheet Ply" for the output, and then click "ok."

The output table in Excel is minimal. It will identify the correlation but will not indicate its significance. To determine whether your correlation is significant, you would either have to use another program or you would

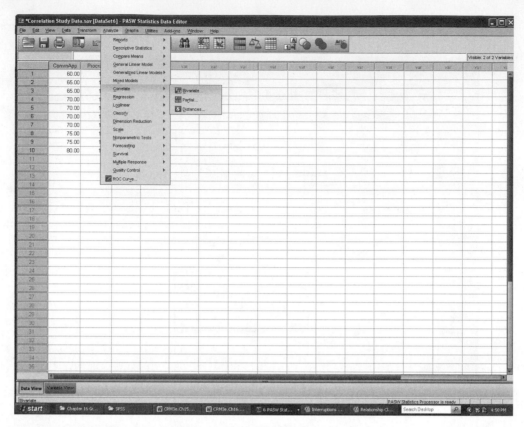

Figure 16.23 SPSS Correlation Command

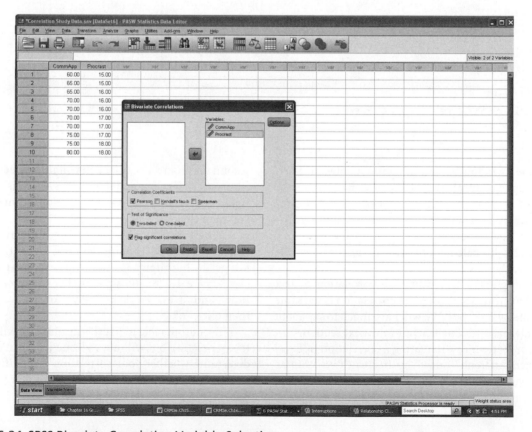

Figure 16.24 SPSS Bivariate Correlation Variable Selection

Table 16.9 SPSS Output Table for Correlation Coefficient

Correlations		CommApp	Procrast
CommApp	Pearson Correlation	1	.891**
	Sig. (2-tailed)		.001
	N	10	10
Procrast	Pearson Correlation	.891**	1
	Sig. (2-tailed)	.001	
	N	10	10

**Correlation is significant at the 0.01 level (2-tailed).

have to find a table of critical values for r_{xy}. These are readily available online. You will need to know the size of your sample and the degrees of freedom, *df*, calculated as n-2. In our example, n = 10, which means that there are 10 pairs of scores from ten participants, and the *df* = 8. The tabled critical value for correlation at p < .001 = .872. Since our value is .89, the correlation is significant at the p < .001 level.

Interpreting the results and APA formatting. When the researchers report a correlation such as the value we calculated in our example, they identify that the two variables were significantly correlated (r_{xy} = .89, p < .001). To interpret this correlation value further, you will need to examine three of its embedded characteristics: magnitude, sign, and coefficient of determination.

Magnitude. The correlation coefficient, *r*, is expressed as a value between +1.00 and −1.00; the value of *r* is its **magnitude** or strength. If it were possible and

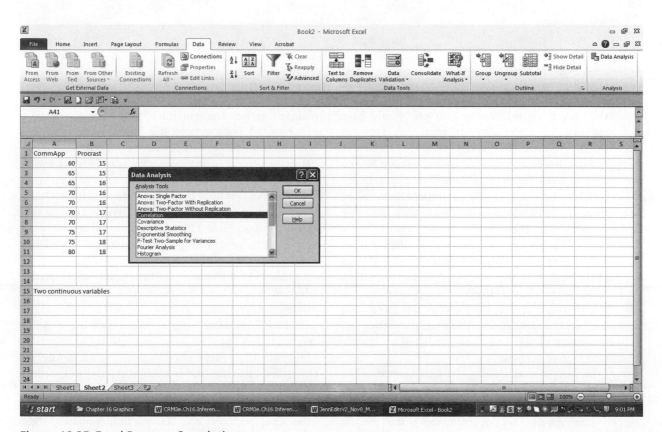

Figure 16.25 Excel Pearson Correlation

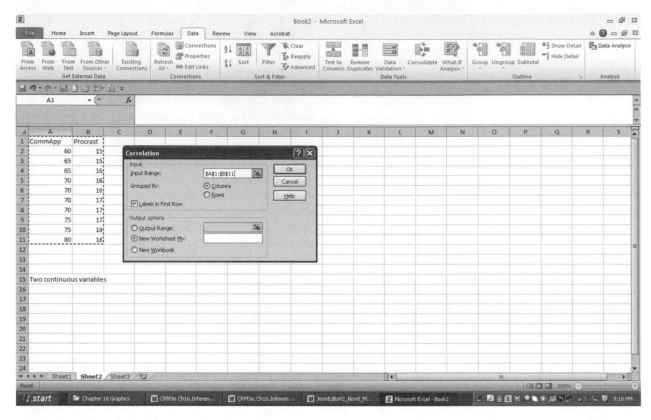

Figure 16.26 Excel Correlation Input Range

you calculated $r_{xy} = +1.00$ or -1.00, you would have obtained a perfect correlation, an ideal that does not occur in the practice of research. Perfect correlations happen when the changes in value that happen in one variable are *exactly the same as* those that happen in another variable, and that's why they represent ideal versus real values. If you obtained a correlation with the value of 0.0, it means that the variables are not related in any way. The change in one happens independently from the change in the other. We obtained an r_{xy} of +.89. The p level associated with this value of r_{xy} is less than .001, and so the research hypothesis is supported. In the example, this means that procrastination levels and communication apprehension levels vary together significantly more of the time than predicted by chance variation or error variance.

As we said in determining the significance of the correlation coefficient, the null hypothesis assumes the relationship is equal to zero at the population level, $H_0 : r_{xy} = 0.0$. Another way of saying this is that there is no association between the two variables; they do not

change together. The research hypothesis is expressed as $H_1 : r_{xy} \neq 0.0$. For example, it is fairly logical to assume that communication competence is not related to physical attractiveness in any systematic way. Persons may be considered attractive but not competent, or vice versa; they may possess both characteristics or neither. On the other hand, we might predict that general trait anxiety is strongly associated with communication apprehension and test this relationship by calculating a correlation coefficient.

Many variables in communication research are believed to be correlated. In one study, Kellas (2005) found moderate correlations among the variables associated with how families tell stories about each other. Kellas reported that families who use greater numbers of family identity statements ("We're a softball family") in their stories also had higher levels of engagement (defined as involvement and warmth), $r = .32$, and perspective-taking (defined as attentiveness to and confirmation of others' perspectives), $r = .33$. The family identity statements variable was measured with a ratio scale, and both engagement and perspective taking were measured with interval scales. Associations between these continuous variables were tested with correlations; and in this study, even though the correlations were of moderate magnitude, they were still significant associations.

Another study of correlational relationships (Rosenfeld, Richman, & May, 2004) reported moderate to weak relationships between sets of organizational variables. For example, organizational involvement (the "extent to which employees are concerned about and committed to their jobs"; Rosenfeld et al., 2004, p. 34) was only weakly correlated with organizational performance for workers in the field ($r = .15$) whereas supervisor support (the "extent to which management is supportive of employees and encourages employee supportiveness"; Rosenfeld et al., 2004, p. 34) was moderately correlated with office workers' personal performance ($r = .44$).

In our earlier illustration, Behnke and Sawyer (1999) found strong to moderate relationships among procrastination, communication apprehension, and perceived public speaking competence. Interpreting magnitude values is done using some established guidelines. Table 16.10 provides a typical set of ranges. The magnitude of the correlation we obtained in the example calculation was .89, a very strong relationship between communication apprehension and procrastination; in other words, students who express high levels of communication apprehension are also students who tend to procrastinate in preparing for presentations.

Sign. In addition to the magnitude or strength of the correlation, you also use the sign of the correlation to determine the type of relationship that exists between the variables. A **positive correlation** describes the relationship between variables that are changing in the same way; they are either increasing or decreasing together. In the example, you calculated a very strong positive correlation between public speaking procrastination and communication apprehension. This is similar to the value reported in the original study, $r = +.70$ (Behnke & Sawyer, 1999). The higher the students' levels of communication apprehension, the more likely they were to procrastinate in preparing their speeches. A positive correlation is graphically represented in Figure 16.27.

When the relationship between the variables is a **negative correlation**, it is called an inverse relationship in which variables are changing in opposite directions. As one increases, the other decreases, or vice versa. For example, Guerrero and Jones (2005) found a moderate negative correlation between attachment avoidance (discomfort with closeness) and expressiveness (appropriate use of verbal and nonverbal expressions); the correlation value was $r = -.44$. People who scored higher on the attachment avoidance scale were likely to score lower on the expressiveness measure. A negative correlation is graphically represented in Figure 16.28.

Positive and negative correlations express linear relationships. Occasionally associations between variables are more complex, expressing **curvilinear relationships**. The most common forms are the U-shape curve and the inverted U-shape curve. The inverted U-shaped correlation occurs when both variables initially increase together as a positive relationship, and then one variable declines over time, and the correlation becomes negative.

Table 16.10 Guidelines for Interpreting Correlation Magnitudes

0.0: No relationship
±.01 − .25: A weak relationship
±.26 − .55: A moderate relationship
±.56 − .75: A strong relationship
±.76 − .99: A very strong relationship
±1.00: A perfect relationship

Source: From *Contemporary Communication Research Methods*, p. 152, by M. J. Smith, 1988, Belmont, CA: Wadsworth, Inc. Copyright 1988 by Wadsworth, Inc.

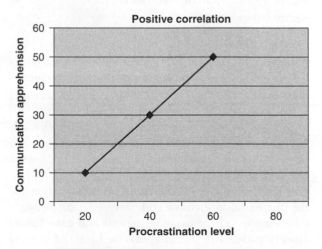

Figure 16.27 Graph of Positive Correlation

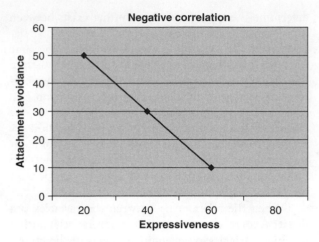

Figure 16.28 Graph of Negative Correlation

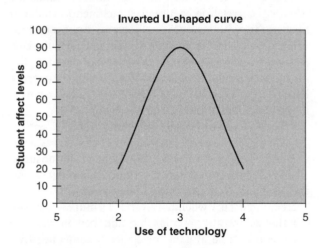

Figure 16.29 Graph of Inverted U-Shaped Relationship

A graph of this type of curvilinear relationship appears in Figure 16.29. For example, in a study of teacher immediacy and technology use, student affective learning began lower in the no-technology condition for both high- and low-immediacy teachers, increased with moderate use of technology, and then decreased again when the format was completely technologized, as in distance learning (Witt & Schrodt, 2006).

The U-shaped correlation reflects an association like the one found by Behnke and Sawyer (2000) between milestone speech preparation periods and anticipatory anxiety patterns in public speakers. Levels of anxiety were high after initially receiving the speech assignment.

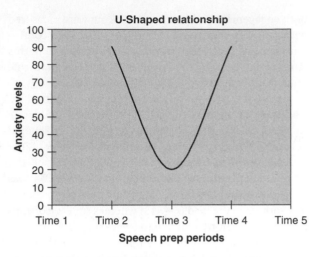

Figure 16.30 Graph of U-Shaped Relationship

These dropped off during speech preparation laboratory sessions, and then increased again significantly just before delivering the speech (see Figure 16.30). Curvilinear relationships express patterns between variables that shift in direction at several points across time.

Estimate of shared variance. The final way correlation coefficients are interpreted is by estimating the actual amount or proportion of variance two (or more) continuous variables have in common. The statistic used for this estimate is called the coefficient of determination, R. This coefficient is found by squaring r_{xy}. In Guerrero and Jones' (2005) study of the relationship between attachment avoidance and expressiveness, the coefficient of determination $(r_{xy})^2$ was equal to $(-.44)^2 = .1936$.

You can multiply the coefficient of determination by 100 and obtain a percentage: The estimate of shared variance between the two variables in the Guerrero and Jones' (2005) study was 19.36 percent. This percentage of shared variance can be graphically depicted by Venn diagrams (see Figure 16.31). In the example based on the Behnke and Sawyer (1999) study, the percentage of shared variance between procrastination and communication apprehension was $(.89)^2 \times 100 = 79.21$ percent, as depicted in Figure 16.32. Statistical researchers sometimes refer to shared variance as a way of highlighting the strength of a relationship between (or among) variables. In this example, if we knew a student's communication apprehension score, we would have a reasonably good chance (79%) of predicting his or her likelihood of procrastinating on a speech assignment.

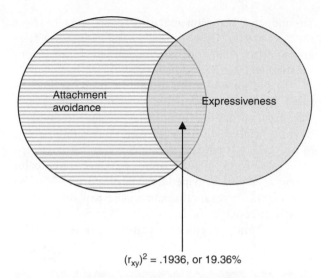

$(r_{xy})^2 = .1936$, or 19.36%

Figure 16.31 Venn Diagram of Shared Variance Estimate in the Guerrero and Jones (2005) Study

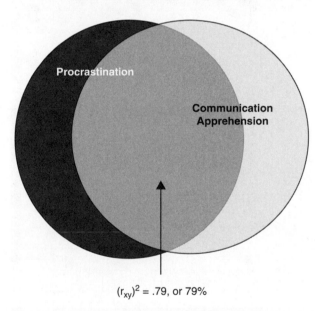

$(r_{xy})^2 = .79$, or 79%

Figure 16.32 Venn Diagram of Shared Variance Estimate in the Behnke and Sawyer (1999) Study

Magnitude, sign, and estimates of shared variance are attributes of a correlation coefficient that permit us to interpret more accurately the nature of the noncausal relationship between two or more continuous or scaled variables. More complex analyses are needed in considering tests of causality.

Causal Associations: Regression Analysis
Nature of Data and Assumptions

In bivariate and multiple correlation tests, the researcher is interested in assessing the degree of association between several continuous or scaled variables (measured at interval and ratio levels). Regression analysis permits tests of causality among sets of continuous or scaled variables.

Regression analysis is a common test statistic in communication research. With regression analysis, the researcher can actually predict unknown values of the dependent variables from the obtained values of one or more of its predictors. In causal tests of association, independent variables are sometimes termed the **predictor variables**, whereas dependent variables are called **criterion variables**. The variables are expected to covary, which means that they share some proportion of variance; common variance is the term we use when the sign and the magnitude of change happens in both variables at the same time. In regression analysis, the estimate of the variance they have in common is the amount of the criterion variable's variance that is *explained* by the variance in the predictor variable. Suppose, in our example for correlation, Behnke and Sawyer had decided to test the causal relationship between communication apprehension and procrastination, assuming that there were enough grounds to assume that communication apprehension was the cause or predictor variable and procrastination was the effect or criterion variable.

Like the correlation coefficient, regression analysis can be calculated for the relationship between one predictor and one criterion variable as in our example. This form is called linear or simple regression. It is expressed by Equation 16.5:

$$Y = a - bX \qquad (16.5)$$

where Y is the criterion variable along the vertical axis, X is the predictor variable along the horizontal axis, and a and b are **regression weights** or **beta coefficients**. This formula is actually an equation for a line in which a is the *intercept* (where the line intersects the vertical y-axis) and b is the *slope* of the line estimating how much change should occur in Y based on a unit of change in X. The line itself is the best estimate of the relationship between Y and X.

When conducting a regression analysis, the researcher is conducting a causal test of the relationship between two or more continuous variables. In a simple regression, the null hypothesis is that the predictor variable does not share any variance in common with the criterion variable, or $H_0 : R = 0$. The research hypothesis assumes that the predictor variable will be a better than chance predictor of the criterion variable. Regression will yield an estimate of the amount of variance that the predictor variable explains in the criterion variable. Let's try an example for testing in SPSS and Excel.

SPSS and Excel regression. For the purposes of illustration, we'll use the same data file that we used for correlation only this time we will identify communication apprehension as the predictor or independent variable, explaining greater than chance variation or change in the criterion or dependent variable of procrastination.

To conduct a regression analysis in SPSS, you will select the "Analyze" tab from the toolbar and then choose "Regression" from the drop-down menu, and "Linear" from the submenu (see Figure 16.33).

This action will result in a new pop-up window entitled "Linear Regression." Move your dependent variable, procrastination, from the left window to the right top box, labeled "dependent," using the middle arrow. Move your independent variable, communication apprehension from the left window to the second box on the right, labeled "independent" (see Figure 16.34). The click on "OK" to obtain the output tables explained below.

The first output table is labeled "Variables Entered/Removed" and identifies for you the variable that you

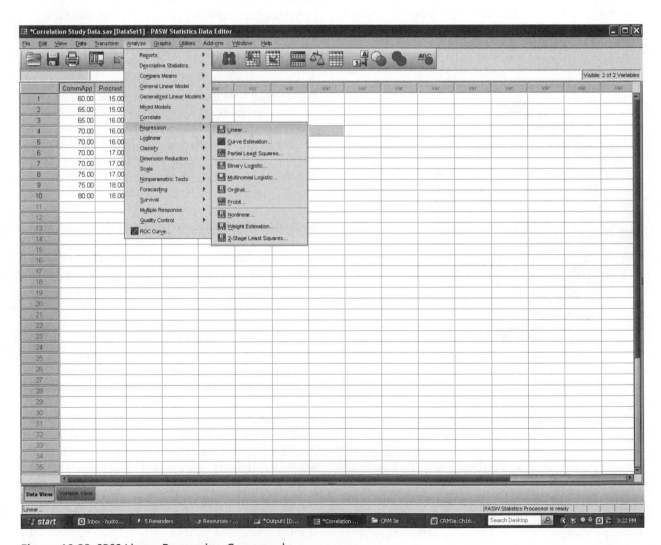

Figure 16.33 SPSS Linear Regression Command

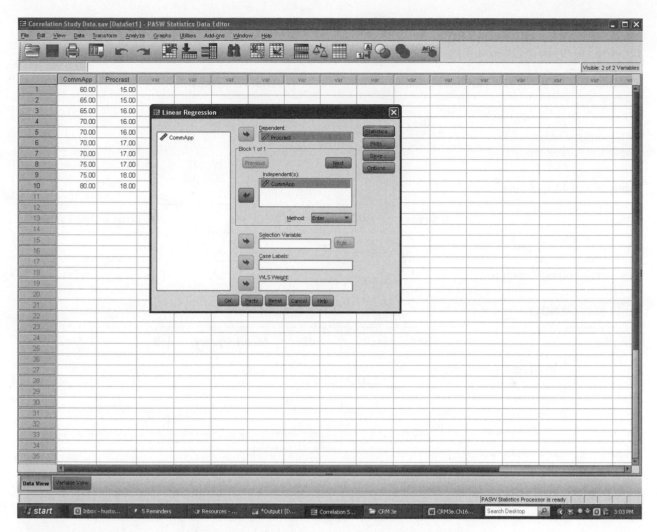

Figure 16.34 SPSS Regression Dependent and Independent Variable Selection

entered as the independent variable, in this case communication apprehension; below the table, procrastination is identified as the dependent variable (refer to Table 16.11a). The information in the second table is very important. Because you are testing the relationship between just two variables in this example, the R value in the first column, .891, is the same value as the correlation we calculated in the last section. Likewise, the R-squared value is the coefficient of determination for the regression, and its interpretation is similar to what we have said before (see Table 16.11b). In this case, the amount or proportion of change happening in your dependent variable (procrastination) can be explained by the causal relationship this variable has with the

independent variable (communication apprehension); because there are just two variables in this analysis, this is also called a bivariate regression. This relationship becomes much more complex when you test the effects of more than one independent variable in a regression analysis, a consideration for the next section.

The third table is used to determine the significance of the regression analysis. Like regressions, analyses of variance are also based on general linear models. Our F statistic is significant at $p < .001$ as reported in Table 16.11c. Finally, the last output table contains "coefficients," also a crucially important set of statistics for regression when you are testing more variables than two, or when you have a more complex regression than a bivariate analysis.

Table 16.11 SPSS Regression Output Tables

Table 16.11a Variables Entered/Removed[b]

Model	Variables Entered	Variables Removed	Method
1	CommApp[a]		Enter

[a]All requested variables entered.
[b]Dependent Variable: Procrast.

Table 16.11b Model Summary

Model	R	R Square	Adjusted R Square	Std. Error of the Estimate
1	.891	.794	.768	.52042

[a]Predictors: (Constant), CommApp.

Table 16.11c ANOVA[b]

Model		Sum of Squares	df	Mean Square	F	Sig.
1	Regression	8.333	1	8.333	30.769	.001[a]
	Residual	2.167	8	.271		
	Total	10.500	9			

[a]Predictors: (Constant), Communication Apprehension.
[b]Dependent Variable: Procrastination.

Table 16.11d Coefficients[a]

Model		Unstandardized Coefficients		Standardized Coefficients	t	Sig.
		B	Std. Error	Beta		
1	(Constant)	4.833	2.110		2.291	.051
	Communication Apprehension	.167	.030	.891	5.547	.001

[a]Dependent Variable: Procrast.

In multiple regression tests, the coefficients will help you interpret the individual effects of the multiple independent variables on the dependent variable. This more complex analysis is beyond the scope of this book but we will have a little more to say about these analyses a little later on.

It is also possible to calculate a simple linear regression in Excel. Using the same data set as we illustrated for the correlation example, you would select "Data" and then "Data Analysis" from the toolbar. From the menu in the pop-up window, select "regression" (refer to Figure 16.35).

In the Regression pop-up window that appears, you will need to enter the values for your "Input Y Range," by highlighting the values for procrastination as your dependent variable as $B1:$B11. You will do the same for

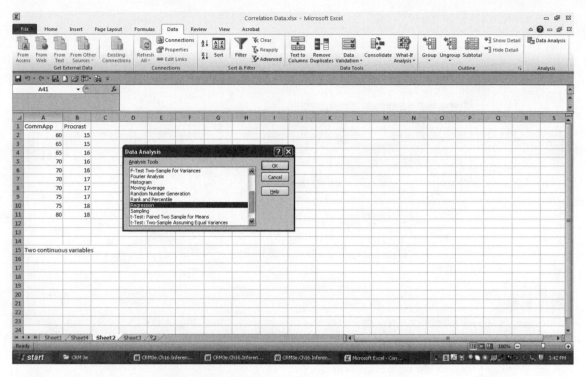

Figure 16.35 Excel Regression Command

the "Input X Range" box only this time highlighting the values for you independent variable, communication apprehension as $A1:$A11. Be sure to select the "Labels" check box and the New Worksheet Ply for the output option. Then hit "ok" (see Figure 16.36).

The output tables for your linear regression should appear in a new worksheet. You can see from the statistics in Figure 16.37 that we found the same values for the R (.89) and R-squared values (.79), the F statistic is significant, and there is one coefficient reported for the bivariate relationship just as in SPSS.

Interpreting the results and APA formatting. Using the same variables that we did in the correlation section, a causal relationship was assumed between communication apprehension and procrastination to calculate a regression. Our research hypothesis was significant, which means in this case that communication apprehension was a significant predictor of procrastination in speech preparation, or $H_1 : R \neq 0$. Recall our discussion of causality in Chapter 11. In order to allow the presumption of causality to stand, we must have evidence of covariation, time order, and the likelihood that we can rule out other rival independent variables for the effects on the dependent variable. We

know from our correlation analysis that the change in one variable is strongly associated with the change in the other; they do covary about 79 percent of the time.

Based on past research and by logical reasoning, we can also argue that communication apprehension (or the fear of speaking) is much more likely to cause procrastination in preparing a public speech than the other way around and we have found some preliminary support for this assumption in our regression analysis. However, we would also have to rule out other variables such as lack of experience or psychological factors such as introversion as important rival explanations for procrastination. In fact, we would have a much stronger study if we had measured these multiple predictors and allowed the regression analysis to help us estimate the contribution made by each independent variable. As we indicated earlier, this kind of analysis is called multivariate or **multiple regression analysis**.

Types of Regression Analysis

So now you see that there are bivariate and multivariate regression analyses. When we were discussing coefficients for the simple linear regression we computed, only one

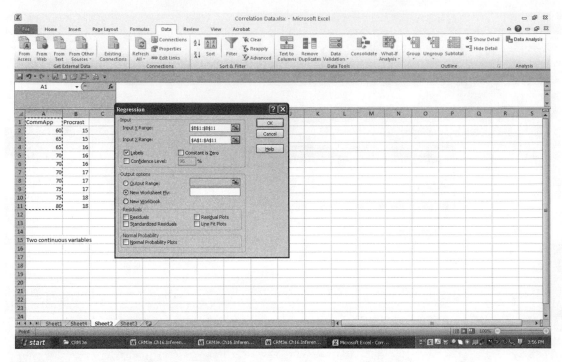

Figure 16.36 Excel Regression Variable Selection

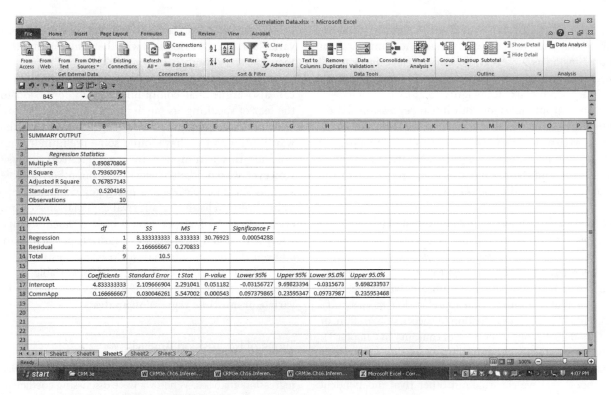

Figure 16.37 Regression Summary Output

coefficient emerged because we were testing just one independent variable effect on the dependent variable. However, multiple regression analysis derives regression weights (coefficients) from the linear equation so that we can assess how much of the total variance of the criterion variable can be explained by each individual predictor. Two of the more common forms of multiple regression analysis are stepwise regressions and hierarchical regressions.

Researchers using stepwise regression instruct the computer to try various combinations of predictors until it finds the "best fit" equation. Using a stepwise regression to test combinations of relationships, Weber (2004) tested the relationships among sets of teacher behaviors and student interest variables. Teacher behaviors were measured as "behavior alteration techniques" and were evaluated by students as either positive or negative attempts by the teacher to change student behavior. These were tested for their varying and complex effects on student interest as the dependent variable.

In a study of parental mediation and children's aggression, Nathanson (2001) used hierarchical regression, a form of multiple regression in which the researcher stipulates the order of variables entered into the linear equation based on theory and past research. The predictor variable that is assumed to be the primary or most important predictor is entered first to see if it does indeed explain a significant amount of the variance in the dependent variable. Nathanson was interested in testing the effects of parents who interpret television program content for their children and the presence of parents watching television with their children on children's aggressive behavior. The researcher first entered control or intervening variables (like violent TV watching, children's gender, age, and parental education) that she suspected would explain some of the variance in the children's aggressive tendencies. Past research has shown that each of these variables tends to influence children's expressed aggression.

Then, after removing the control variable effects, Nathanson (2001) found that two types of mediation still explained a significant amount of the remaining variance in children's aggressive tendencies, whereas coviewing did not make a significant contribution. Because she could construct an equation for each predictor, Nathanson (2001) found some evidence that the relationship between parental restrictive mediation (strict enforcement of viewing rules) and children's expressed aggressive behavior was curvilinear; that is, high and low levels of restrictive mediation in the parents were better predictors of aggression in their children than moderate levels of parental restrictive mediation. As you can see, Nathanson's research analysis represents a complex model of relationships between sets of independent variables and the dependent variable. Testing these assumptions is beyond the scope of this book but they are also commonly found in our research literature. If you decide to continue your training in research methods, you will undoubtedly come across these more advanced tests and applications.

Two Ethical Issues

Whenever you conduct statistical analyses and present your findings in a research report or at a professional association meeting, you have two specific ethical obligations, to *be honest* and to *do no harm*. In using inferential statistics, your obligations are to those who read (and use) your findings as well as to your participants. You can potentially harm the direction of social science research by misleading others or by misrepresenting your data.

For example, you should not use parametric statistics if your sample data is distributed abnormally. This determination will require exploring your data descriptively and testing various assumptions along the way. If your data do not meet the assumption of normal distribution, for example, then you may need to collect additional data, or eliminate outliers, scores that are above or below three standard deviations from the mean score for your sample. If your data sample is quite skewed, or abnormally peaked/flat, then you must acknowledge that limitation because it could mean that your statistical findings are less believable than they would be otherwise.

In any case, you must be forthright in acknowledging the limitations of your data as well as your chances of Type I (or Type II) error. Inferential statistics are based on probability, so any single conclusion is subject to error, even if the sample represents the population, and the measurement was highly reliable. If your measurement of variables was less than reliable, or your sample selection was biased, you must acknowledge those limitations and caution the people who read (or hear) your report about applying your findings before they are replicated since only replication will sort out which conclusions were Type I (or II) errors.

In this chapter, you have reviewed the essential steps of hypothesis-testing and learned how these steps apply to two types of statistical analyses: tests of

Table 16.12 Inferential Statistics Summary Table

Test	Variables	Hypotheses	Equation	Test Type	Causal
t-test	1 Independent: (2 Categories) 1 Dependent: (Interval/Ratio)	$H_1 : \overline{X}_1 \neq \overline{X}_2$ $H_1 : \overline{X}_1 > \overline{X}_2$ $H_1 : \overline{X}_1 < \overline{X}_2$ $H_0 : \overline{X}_1 = \overline{X}_2$	$\dfrac{\text{Between group differences}}{\text{Within group differences}}$	Parametric	Yes
F test **1-way ANOVA**	1 Independent: (3+ Categories) 1 Dependent: (Interval/Ratio)	$H_1 : \overline{X}_1 \neq \overline{X}_2 \neq \overline{X}_3$ $H_0 : \overline{X}_1 = \overline{X}_2 = \overline{X}_3$	$\dfrac{\text{Between group differences}}{\text{Within group differences}}$	Parametric	Yes
F test **2+ way ANOVA**	2+ Independent: (2+ Categories) 1 Dependent: (Interval/Ratio)	$H_1 : \overline{X}_1 \neq \overline{X}_2, \overline{X}_3, \overline{X}_4$ $H_0 : \overline{X}_1 = \overline{X}_2, \overline{X}_3, \overline{X}_4$	$\dfrac{\text{Between group differences}}{\text{Within group differences}}$	Parametric	Yes
Chi-square χ^2 **One sample**	1 Variable	$H_1 : O \neq E$ $H_0 : O = E$	$\dfrac{\text{Observed frequencies}}{\text{Expected frequencies}}$	Nonparametric	No
Chi-square χ^2 **Two samples**	1 Independent: (2+ Categories) 1 Dependent: (2+ Categories)	$H_1 : O \neq E$ $H_0 : O = E$	$\dfrac{\text{Observed frequencies}}{\text{Expected frequencies}}$	Nonparametric	Yes
Correlation r_{xy}	2+ Continuous (Interval/Ratio)	$H_1 : r_{xy} \neq 0$ $H_0 : r_{xy} = 0$	$\dfrac{\text{Cross products}}{\text{Sums of squares}}$	Parametric	No
Regression R	1+ Independent: Continuous 1 Dependent: Continuous	$H_1 : R \neq 0$ $H_0 : R = 0$	$y = a + bx$	Parametric	Yes

Note: ANOVA = analysis of variance.

difference and tests of relationships. Using a statistical software program such as SPSS or Excel, you also learned step-by-step procedures for conducting nonparametric and parametric tests of group differences: chi-square, *t*-test, one-way ANOVA, correlation, and simple regression. Table 16-12 effectively summarizes the essential information for each of these test statistics. We concluded the chapter by considering ethical issues in statistical analysis. Once you have achieved the chapter's outcomes, you will be able to understand the purposes of and apply many of these statistical tests in engaging in research.

Key Terms

Analysis of variance (ANOVA)	Factors	Negative correlation
Beta coefficients	Follow-up tests	Nonparametric tests
Between-groups variance	Hierarchical regression	Numerator degrees of freedom
Bivariate relationships	Independent samples *t*-test	One-tailed test
Chi-square statistic	Inverted U-shaped correlation	One-way ANOVA
Coefficient of determination	Linear relationships	Outliers
Contingency table analysis	Magnitude	Paired samples *t*-test
Correlation coefficient	Mean squares between groups	Parametric tests
Covariance	Mean squares within groups	Point-biserial correlation
Criterion variable	Multiple regression analysis	Positive correlation
Curvilinear relationship	Multiple factors ANOVA	Post hoc comparisons
Degrees of freedom	Multiple-sample chi-square	Predictor variable
Denominator degrees of freedom	Multivariate relationships	Regression analysis

Regression coefficients or weights (see beta coefficients)	Standard error of difference between means	Sums of squares within groups
Significant difference	Statistical significance	*t*-test
Single-factor ANOVA	Stepwise regression	Two-tailed test
Single-sample chi-square	Sums of squares between groups	U-shaped correlation
Spurious correlation		Within-groups variance

Discussion Questions

1. Explain the main difference between parametric and nonparametric tests.
2. For tests of difference, explain the main distinctions among the following: *t*-tests, and *F* tests. In what ways are these tests similar? How do they differ?
3. What is the essential difference between tests of difference and tests of relationship? How do the data requirements change for each?
4. Review the underlying assumptions of the discovery paradigm from chapter 1, "Introduction to the Field of Communication." See if you can explain why statistical analysis is used in many methodologies associated with this paradigm.

"Try It!" Activities

1. This first problem is a relatively easy chi-square analysis you should be able to compute by hand (with the aid of a calculator) or easily with either *Excel* or *SPSS*. A researcher recently asked 500 Republicans and 500 Democrats if they were "for" or "against" (two categories) the president's domestic policy: 100 Republicans were "against," whereas 400 Republicans were "for." Alternately, 300 Democrats were "against," and 200 Democrats were "for." [Hint: these are the observed frequencies.] Solve for the expected frequencies for Republicans and Democrats for and against the president's domestic policy (see Table 16.3). Once you have calculated the expected frequencies for each cell, calculate the chi-square statistic. If you enter the same data using a statistical software program, the analysis will provide you with a *p* value associated with your statistic. What value would it have to have for your test statistic to be significant?
2. This next problem set can also be calculated by *Excel*. This problem asks you to calculate a *t*-test. A researcher is interested in finding out whether there are significant differences between romantic partners and close friends in terms of communication frequency. The research hypothesis is $H_1 : \overline{X}_2 > \overline{X}_1$. Use the data from Table 16.13. Calculate the *t*-test statistic. If you enter your data using Excel, you can determine the *p* value associated with your *t* statistic. Have you supported (failed to support) the research hypothesis, and what does this mean?

Table 16.13 Communication Frequency by Relationship Type

Romantic Partners	Close Friends
5	2
6	2
7	3
8	3
9	5

3. In this sample problem, you will calculate a simple correlation (can be completed in *Excel*) for the data set in Table 16.14. Once you have obtained the correlation coefficient, interpret it in terms of magnitude, sign, and coefficient of determination. A researcher wishes to measure the degree of association between two variables. One is measured by a scale to assess relational uncertainty; the other is a scale that measures degree of liking. Both of these are Likert-type scales, which is an interval-level measurement scale. It is predicted that as relational uncertainty decreases, the level of liking will increase. The following set of scores was obtained from a sample of 10 people.

Table 16.14 Correlation Data for Two Relational Variables

Uncertainty	Liking
5	1
4	1
5	1
4	2
3	3
3	4
2	4
1	5
1	4
2	5

Answers to "Try It!" Activities

1. Chi-square = 400
2. t obt = 4.49
3. Correlation = −0.91

Glossary

Abscissa: Horizontal axis of a graph.

Abstract: A brief paragraph, usually 100 to 120 words, that provides readers with an overview of the study in much the same way that a speech introduction gives listeners an overview of the speaker's purpose, argument, and conclusions.

Action research: Research that is conducted for the purpose of its more practical and applied outcomes rather than for the sole purposes of developing theory or increasing knowledge, sometimes known as evaluation research. An example of action research would include assessing the performance of individuals within various program, organizational, or institutional units.

Adequacy (aka, adequacy of evidence): Demonstrated when a researcher has collected enough evidence to account for and understand multiple plausible interpretations.

Adjacency pairs: Two-part conversational structures in which the first pair part calls for or invites the second pair part.

Aesthetic communication: Artistic texts, events, performers, or audiences,

Alternate forms method (aka, equivalence): Different measures of the same variable produce similar results, a measure of reliability.

Analysis of variance (ANOVA): A statistical test that tests the effects of one or more categorical independent variables on a continuous dependent variable; also called an F test, expressed as the ratio of the differences in group means divided by chance differences.

Analytic induction: *See* Inductive reasoning.

Anonymity: Protecting human subjects' privacy by purposely not collecting any identifying information about individuals or by collecting such information in a way that is it does not become known to the researcher.

Apologias: In genre criticism, speeches made in self-defense.

Applied research: Research that focuses on satisfying practical outcomes by solving specific problems in field settings.

Appropriate (verb): To make something your own or set it aside for a specific use.

Archetypal or root metaphors: Metaphors assumed to be so primal any individual in any context could understand its meaning.

Archival documents: Written or symbolic records of communication such as letters, newspapers, websites, billboards, or memos.

Archive: A preexisting collection of textual data or evidence.

Artifact: Any object made by human work, and used by group or cultural members, such as clothing, jewelry, buildings, photographs, tools, or toys, which can be read as texts for the purpose of cultural analysis or criticism.

Artistic proofs: *Logos, ethos,* and *pathos* as internal constructions of the speaker in neo-Aristotelian criticism.

Associative claim: A claim that two communication phenomena are in some way related; a change in one phenomenon is accompanied by a change in the other phenomenon, although one change does not necessarily "cause" the other.

Audit trail: Documents the development and progress of an interpretive research project including the field notes from participant observation and/or interviews, classification schemes, drafts of data analysis at various stages, permissions/agreements with participants, and so on.

Autoethnography: An ethnographic study of a social setting or situation for which the key informant is the researcher himself or herself.

Bar chart: Visually depicts the frequencies of categories with bars along the horizontal axis for nominally and ordinally scaled variables.

Basic research: Research that emphasizes investigating theoretic relationships among variables in which practical outcomes in specific contexts may be implicit or unknown.

Bell-shaped curve: The shape of a data distribution that is normally distributed along the horizontal axis.

Benchmarking: The process of measuring and validating strategic performance indicators in a given business or industry.

Beta coefficients: In the formula $Y = a + bX$ for linear regression, the beta coefficients are a and b, where a is the *intercept* (the point at which the line intersects the vertical y-axis) and b is the *slope* of the line (estimation of how much change should occur in Y based on a unit of change in X); also called *regression weights*.

Between-groups variance: Observed differences between group means.

Between-subjects factor: An independent variable comprised of different treatment conditions in which groups of participants are separately assigned to each condition.

Bias: Systematic or constant error in the measurement of a variable; a threat to measurement validity.

Bivariate relationships: Associations of variance between just two continuous variables.

Bracket: The act of setting aside one's own understandings and preferences in order to privilege research participants' views or their meaning of the situation.

Breaching: Deviating from the principles on which ethnomethodology is based.

Canons of rhetoric: Invention, organization, style, delivery, and memory.

Case study: A narrative account of the communication practices in a particular setting and among specific participants.

Categorical variables: Variables measured at the nominal and ordinal levels.

Categorizing: Grouping units into different categories.

Causal claim: A claim that predicts that a change in one communication phenomenon is preceded and influenced by a change in another.

Central Limits Theorem: Large and randomly selected samples have greater chances of approximating the true population distribution.

Chi-square statistic: A comparison of the actual distribution of the sample data (i.e., observed units per category) to the predicted distribution (i.e., expected units per category).

Claim: The central assertion or premise of an argument; in the research-as-argument model presented in this book, claim is a central assertion or premise that is argued in a research report or critical essay.

Closed-format questions: Questions that provide specific response options to research participants; multiple-choice questions are examples of closed-format questions.

Cluster analysis: In Burkean dramatism, a form of analysis in which the rhetor examines key terms, groupings of those terms, and whole language patterns in one or several rhetorical texts, which are presumed to reflect the rhetor's meanings, motives, and attitudes.

Code of conduct: A policy that translates an organization's values into social actions.

Codeswitching: Mixing the rules of one speech community with the rules of another.

Coding scheme: A set of categories into which message units are placed.

Coding: Reducing many specific observations into themes or categories.

Coefficient of determination: In tests of correlation, an estimate of the actual proportion of variance that two continuous variables have in common.

Coherence: The degree to which a researcher's interpretations of actions, events, or texts are logical, consistent, and intelligible.

Collaborative ethnography: A form of team research in which multiple researchers provide viewpoints on a setting or similar settings.

Comment sheets: Records for the researcher to jot down notes after interviews, perhaps concerning the emotional tone of the interview, insights and reflections about any difficulties encountered during the interview, and so on.

Communal function of communication: The ways that communication is used to create and affirm shared identities.

Communication code: The set of rules for speaking and interpreting others' speech within a particular speech community.

Comparison groups: Groups of study participants who are exposed to the manipulated levels of the independent variable.

Compensatory behavior: A cluster of confounding effects that can happen when the control group becomes aware that the experimental group is being treated differently. If the treatment seems to be a positive gain, then control groups can try to outperform the experimental group to receive the same treatment, or they can become frustrated and upset at the unequal treatment and withhold normal behaviors as a result.

Conceptual definition: A description of a construct that relates it to other abstract concepts.

Concurrent validity: Accuracy warranted by presenting an existing measuring instrument as validation of a newly created instrument because the two instruments produce similar results.

Conditions of causality: Time order, association, ruling out competing claims.

Confederates: People who pose as naïve study participants when, in fact, they have received special instructions to help the researchers manipulate the independent variable without the real or targeted study participants' knowledge; often used to create a plausible cover story.

Confidence interval: The interval of distance between various proportions of sample means and the population mean.

Confidence level: The percentage of sample means associated with each of the confidence intervals.

Confidentiality: Protecting research participants' privacy by withholding their identifying information from the transcripts, field notes, or written research reports.

Confirmability: The degree to which findings that a researcher posits, based on analysis of data, can be confirmed, or echoed by another person who had similar access to those same data sources.

Confounding variables: Factors that interfere in the relationship between the independent and dependent variables as rival causes or sources of influence.

Constant error: Bias or systematic error in the measurement of a variable; a threat to measurement validity.

Construct: Phenomenon that can only be observed indirectly.

Construct validity: Accuracy warranted by establishing that the results from an instrument's administration converge with, or diverge from, the results achieved by other instruments that measure different, but theoretically related, concepts.

Consumer research: Research designed to assess consumer attitudes and preferences for various products or services.

Content analysis: A primarily quantitative method of categorizing and describing communication messages in specific contexts.

Content validity: A form of measurement validity; it is achieved when the items that make up a measuring instrument represent the full range of the behavioral domain that the researcher is trying to measure.

Contingency questions: Questions that depend on responses to filter questions.

Contingency table analysis: Multiple-sample chi-square.

Continuous variables: Constructs measured with interval and ratio scales.

Control group: A comparison group that is not exposed to the manipulation of the independent variable but is in every other way the equivalent of the treatment group(s).

Controlling competing explanations (aka, rival hypotheses): Attempts to account for possible reasons that a dependent variable score might change; control is usually accomplished by measuring other variables that could also help to explain a change in dependent variable scores following manipulation of the IV.

Convenience samples: Selection of whatever data is easily accessible to the researcher.

Conversation: Interactive discourse, usually telephone or face-to-face interactions between two or more participants (Woofit, 2005).

Conversation Analysis (CA): Scientific, or discovery paradigm, method that aims to describe and explain how people accomplish social actions and events by collaboratively organizing sequences of talk-in-interaction (Schegloff, 2006).

Conversational trouble: Usually, interrupted sequences of interaction caused by problems of understanding or offense (Schegloff, Jefferson, & Sacks, 1977).

Corrective justice principle: Sometimes called restorative justice; the idea that those who have benefited least in the past, or who have been most harmed by past practices, should be benefited most in present decisions.

Correlation coefficient: An estimate of the strength of the association between two continuous variables, expressed as r_{xy}, showing the degree to which two variables are systematically related to one another or covary.

Counterclaims: Other interpretations that could be potentially supported by a data set.

Counterexamples: Instances of data that do not fit the researcher's claim and which might support a competing explanation or interpretation of the talk.

Covariance: *See* Correlation coefficient.

Covariation: A relationship that exists when two or more concepts or variables are related to one another such that changes in one variable are accompanied by changes in the other variable.

Cover story: A deceptive story designed to reduce participants' reactions to the experimental situation by obscuring the real testing situation so that the procedure will seem more natural to participants.

Criterion variable: In tests of association, the term for dependent variable.

Criterion-related validity: Accuracy warranted by the measuring instrument's relationship to other instruments that have already been shown to be valid.

Critical Discourse Analysis (CDA): A method of analyzing texts in order to evaluate the social construction of reality and to suggest how texts and practices should be reformed (Fairclough, 1995; Habermas, 1979).

Critical empirical studies of communicative action: Data collected from participant observations, self-reports and other-reports, and texts are used to evaluate communication, and sometimes, suggest reforms (Deetz, 2005).

Critical essay: A manuscript based primarily (or only) on textual data sources, whether the text being analyzed is a speech, an artifact, or the researcher's experience as evidence given in support of a claim.

Cronbach's alpha: A coefficient that measures the internal consistency or homogeneity of an interval scale.

Cross-sectional studies (aka, cross-sectional research design): A research design where a sample of data collected at one point in time is used to draw inferences about the research question.

Culture: A system of shared meanings (webs of significance) that are held in common by group members.

Curator's exhibitionism: An ethical problem in field research that happens when a researcher or performer "sensationalizes the cultural experiences that supposedly define the cultural world of the other" (Denzin, 2003, p. 55).

Curvilinear relationships: A complex relationship between two variables that changes directions at several points during their association.

Custodian's rip-off: An ethical problem in field research that happens when researchers look for *good* texts to study and perform, often "denigrating family members or cultural groups" in the process (Denzin, 2003, p. 55).

Data collection settings: The places where observation, self-, and other-report data are gathered or found.

Data collection sources: The points from which the data originate.

Data collection strategies: How data for a study are gathered.

Data logging: Carefully recording various forms of data including field notes from participant observations, write-ups from interviews, maps, photography, sound recordings, document collections, and so on.

Data memo: Refers to interpretive and critical researchers' notes about their initial impressions when analyzing a text or observing participants' communication.

Data: The evidence or grounds for a claim.

Debriefing: Telling participants the full truth after their responses have been collected, and giving them a chance to withdraw from the study once they know about the researcher's omission or deception.

Deconstruction: Unpacking, or taking apart, the meaning of a text.

Deductive reasoning: Begins with a conclusion and then tests to see if the evidence for the conclusion is valid.

Degree of membership: The extent to which one belongs to a social group.

Degrees of freedom: The number of frequency categories that are free to vary.

Deliberative rhetoric: Political discourse, a genre of speeches given on the floor of the legislative assembly for the purpose of establishing or changing a law.

Delivery: The rhetor's presentation, including presentation format and nonverbal cues, as one of the five canons of rhetoric.

Demand characteristics: Confounding effects in which research participants vary their normal behavior because they think they have discovered the research goals.

Demographic variables: Measuring general characteristics common to any group of people such as age, biological sex, socioeconomic class, level of education, and ethnicity.

Denominator degrees of freedom: The total number of scores across all groups (N) minus the number of groups (N-k); part of a formula that tests for significance of difference(s).

Dependent variable: A communication phenomenon that has been influenced by a change in another communication phenomenon; the "effect."

Descriptive claim: Assertions about how to define some particular communication phenomenon.

Descriptive statistics: A description of how the collected sample data appears, both visually and in numerical terms; the characteristics of sample data.

Deviant case sampling: Selecting people or messages (i.e., cases) that are extremely different from those already included in an existing data sample.

Dichotomous variables: Responses to survey questions based on two choices.

Directional hypothesis: A prediction that specifies the exact nature of a relationship between variables or a difference between groups. In tests of relationship, directional hypotheses specify either positive or negative relationships between variables. In tests of group differences, directional hypotheses predict that one mean will be greater/lesser than the other(s).

Discourse analysis (DA):   An umbrella term for the analysis of textual evidence, usually based on a social constructivist epistemology (Berger & Luckmann, 1967). The term is used in anthropology, applied linguistics, communication, discursive psychology, and sociology.

Discourse: ". . . an interrelated set of texts, and the practices of their production, dissemination, and reception, that brings an object into being" (Phillips & Hardy, 2002, p. 3, citing Parker, 1992).

Discrimination: Sorting objects by their differences.

Discursive formation: The language forms (specific to a historical time period) that allow people to think about and express their knowledge.

Distributive justice principle: The idea that the costs and benefits of a decision should be distributed fairly.

Double-barreled questions: Questions that ask two things simultaneously.

Ecological validity: The accuracy of applying results gained in one setting to people or messages in another setting.

Emic view of culture: Ingroup members' understandings of a social situation are privileged over an outside observer's understandings of the same situation (*see also* Etic view of culture).

Empirical rule: The rule of distributions that approximately 68 percent of the sample's distribution of scores will fall within ±1 standard deviation of the sample's mean, about 95 percent will fall within ±2 standard deviations, and more than 99 percent will fall within ±3 standard deviations.

Enthusiast's infatuation: An ethical problem in field research that happens when an ethnographer trivializes other people's experiences by presenting surface interpretations or stereotyped representations of things she or he does not understand well.

Enthymeme: A form of deductive reasoning that is based on a syllogism in which at least one of three parts—observation, generalization, and inference—is omitted so that the audience must participate by filling in the blanks.

Epideictic rhetoric: Ceremonial speech genre given on special occasions to praise or blame another's actions, to uphold an individual as virtuous, or condemn an individual as corrupt.

Equivalence: Consistency of measurement across measuring scales or across researchers.

Ethnographic interviews: Informal conversations and storytelling between participants and researchers.

Ethnography of communication: A specific theoretic approach to ethnography that focuses on speech communities.

Ethnography of speaking: A specific theoretic approach to ethnography that uses Dell Hymes's (1962) S-P-E-A-K-I-N-G framework in data collection and analysis.

Ethnography: A way of studying social settings or situations that privileges the participants' meanings by using participant observations, perhaps along with interviews and/or textual analysis.

Ethnomethodology: A way of studying people's ordinary daily practices.

Ethos: One of the artistic proofs that refers to the character or credibility of the rhetor.

Etic view of culture: Outsiders' understandings of a social situation are privileged over an insider or member's understandings of the same situation.

Evaluation apprehension: As a confounding effect, the tendency for respondents, when asked for information that is potentially embarrassing or negative in some way, to change their answers to give a more positive personal impression of themselves.

Evaluative claims: Claims establishing a set of criteria or standards and rendering judgments about how well or how poorly a communication phenomenon meets those standards.

Ex post facto design: A type of preexperimental study, also called a one-shot case study, in which there is virtually no control over the manipulation of the independent variable or over the observation of the change in the dependent variable; one of the weakest causal arguments.

Executive summaries: Brief overviews of research used to publicize communication research to audiences who do not regularly read scholarly journals.

Exempt vs. nonexempt research: A designation given by the Institutional Review Board (IRB) that refers to the amount of risks for human and animal research participants; exempt research involves minimal risks to participants, and includes educational settings, educational testing, the use of existing data that is publicly available, or consumer taste testing studies.

Exhaustive categories: All possible categories of the variable are listed from which the research participant (or researcher/coder) will choose a response.

Exigence: A problem requiring change; it is the basis for any persuasive communication.

Expedited v. full IRB review: Refers to approval process for a research study by an IRB Committee; studies deemed exempt or low-risk to participants are given expedited review by the IRB chair or a subgroup of the IRB. Studies deemed nonexempt are reviewed by the full IRB committee.

Experimental control: A research objective achieved by checking the manipulation of the independent variable for its effectiveness and through controlling alternative rival explanations for the observed set of effects on the dependent variable.

Experimental group: Group that receives some exposure to the manipulation of the independent variable.

Explanatory and predictive claims: Claims explaining the relationships between various communication phenomena, often by identifying reasons or causes for communication phenomena.

External validity: Accuracy of applying conclusions from one study to another setting (as in *ecological validity*), or to other people (sometimes called *generalizability*).

Face sheets: Records containing details about the interviews such as a code or name for the participants; the date, place, and time of the interviews; and any relevant demographic information about the interviewees.

Face validity: The degree to which a measuring instrument appears to be accurate in the view of those asked to use it, or to permit is use.

Face-to-face interviews: Personal interviews between the interviewer and the participant.

Facework: The use of politeness behaviors to show respect for and avoid offending other people.

Factorial designs: Experimental research designs that frequently contain multiple independent variables manipulated for their effects on one or more dependent variables.

Factors: The term used to refer to independent variables when there are two or more within the experimental design.

Faithfulness: The degree to which researchers remain steadfast in their commitment to conduct an important, believable study during ethnographic data collection, analysis, and reporting.

Falsification principle: The assumption that the null hypothesis is true until enough evidence is accumulated to reject it.

Fidelity: Accomplished when interpretations of the evidence are coherent and help readers make sense of their own experiences (Fisher, 1987).

Field settings: Sites for data collection in the places where communication occurs just as it would when research was not being conducted.

Figures: In metaphorice criticism, the creative arrangements of words in phrases or sentences that catch the audience's attention and focus it on key ideas. Examples of figures include repetition of sounds, words, or phrases for dramatic effect to engage listeners more effectively.

Filter questions: Questions that direct people to respond to various portions of a questionnaire.

Focus group: A small group of respondents (4 to 10 participants) who are selected by convenience, purposive, or snowball sampling methods and interviewed, generally with a loose structure, so that a wide range of information may be collected about a particular topic.

Follow-up tests: *See* Post hoc comparisons.

Forensic rhetoric: The genre of legal discourse in courtroom proceedings.

Formulas: Mathematical principles used in physical and applied sciences.

Frequency distribution: The way that scores are distributed along the x-axis.

Frequency table: Useful quick references summarizing the frequencies and percentages of data that are visually displayed in pie chart or bar chart graphs.

Fronting: Participants' attempts to avoid telling the whole truth when being interviewed.

Gaining access (or entry): The process of getting permission and approvals for doing research in a particular setting.

Gatekeepers: The participants who have power to grant or deny access to a setting.

Gender and feminist criticism: A broad term that refers to feminist, masculinist, womanist, and queer communication criticism (both structural and post-structural types).

Gender benders: People who purposefully violate and resist the gender binary by performing gender in ways that do not fit their biological sex.

Gender binary: Classifying sex and/or gender into two separate and disconnected categories, male and female, or masculine and feminine; may also refer to the privileged position of males over females in education, medicine, religion, work, families, and all aspects of daily life.

Generalizability: Findings from one study may be applied to other similar messages or persons because the sample selected adequately represents the population of interest.

Generalization: Grouping or categorizing objects together by their similarities.

Generic application: Deductively explaining how the characteristics of genre should be applied to a specific rhetorical text to assess whether it is a good or poor fit.

Generic description: Analyzing several rhetorical texts to determine inductively whether a genre exists.

Generic participation: A deductive process of comparing the characteristics of several genres with the characteristics of several rhetorical artifacts or texts for the purpose of classifying the artifacts by genres.

Genre: A common pattern in rhetorical texts across similar types of contexts.

Grounded-theory approach: A research method in which the investigator builds theory by systematically and repeatedly gathering and analyzing field data during the data collection process; thus, the theory is grounded inductively in the data.

Group: A set of "3–12 people who interact regularly over a period of time and conceive of themselves as a social entity" (Lofland & Lofland, 1995, p. 107).

Hawthorne effect: A specific example of a demand characteristic effect in which simple awareness of being targeted for research increased the employees' levels of productivity regardless of how environmental conditions were varied.

Hegemony: A (usually hidden) form of power that comes from privileging one ideology over another.

Hermeneutic circle: Movement back and forth between the general and specific meanings of messages or texts, usually done in order to examine in detail the embedded historical and sociocultural contexts in which they were created.

Hierarchical regression: A form of multiple regression in which the researcher stipulates the order of variables entered into the linear equation based on theory and past research.

Histogram: Visual representation of variables measured with interval or ratio level scales where numbers along the x-axis are true values mathematically related to each other at equidistant intervals.

History: A time progression effect, when the occurrence of an event external to the study affects the outcome in such a way that the event rivals or threatens the independent variable as the source of influence on the dependent variable.

Homogeneity (aka, internal consistency): The degree to which each item in a measuring instrument consistently refers to the same underlying concept.

Hybridity (aka, intersectionality): The ways that particular combinations of social category memberships work together to constrain people's options for communicating.

Hypotheses: Statements that make specific predictions about relationships between communication variables.

Identification: In Burkean dramatism, the process of finding common ground and acting in concert with other individuals by following an established set of rules or principles.

Ideograph: "A vocabulary of concepts that function as guides, warrants, reasons, or excuses for behavior and belief" (McGee, 1980, p. 6); used in rhetorical criticism of social movements; a word that operates as a vector of social influence, such as "liberty" or "the pursuit of happiness."

Ideological criticism: The analysis of discourse that emerges from social groups united by ideologies (i.e., shared beliefs and values).

Ideological critique: The use of textual evidence to evaluate communicative phenomena and to argue the need for social change (Deetz, 2005).

Ideology: A group's system of beliefs and values, the ideas on which a social system is based.

Inartistic proofs: External forms such as testimony from witnesses or key documents.

Independent samples *t*-test: A test of difference between an independent variable with two samples, or groups of an independent variable that are unrelated, for their effects on a continuous dependent variable.

Independent variable: A communication phenomenon presumed to be the source or cause of change in another communication phenomenon.

Inductive reasoning: Starts with a set of specific observations and derives general interpretations or claims from those observations.

Inferential statistics: Numerical estimates of population characteristics, based on the characteristics of sampled data.

Informed consent: The process of communicating potential risks and benefits, answering prospective participants' questions, and securing their written permission to be observed, interviewed, and so forth as part of a research study.

Institutional frame: A macro-level context for discourse analysis that refers to some form of professional talk. For instance, a discourse may be framed in legal, journalistic, medical, or educational terms.

Institutional Review Board (IRB): Committee charged with the protection of human subjects (aka research participants) in research.

Instrumentation: A confounding effect that happens when the researcher changes the instruments used to measure the dependent variables between the pretest and the posttest.

Interaction effect: Two or more independent variables acting together to impact the dependent variable.

Interactive discourse: Discourse in which all interactants share responsibility for speaking and listening.

Intercoder reliability: The agreement among two or more researchers who are categorizing messages.

Internal consistency (aka, Homogeneity): The degree to which each item in a measuring instrument consistently refers to the same underlying concept.

Internal validity: The ability of a study to accurately test its claim(s) including the validity of the research design, procedures, and measurement.

Internet surveys: Surveys distributed online.

Interpretive claims: Claims about how communicators create and interpret meanings.

Interpretive community: A group of people who share rules for how to encode meanings or interpret meanings when decoding others' messages. *See also* Speech community.

Interrater reliability: The agreement among either research participants or researchers who rate communication characteristics of a single target (see intercoder reliability).

Intertranscriber reliability: Consistent transcription of videotaped or audiotaped conversation into a written record by two or more people.

Interval level measurement: Placing texts, observations of communicative behavior, self- or other-report data into categories that have precise mathematical relationships to one another (e.g., least to most, or smallest to largest).

Interval scales: Scales used to measure communication variables that express values of magnitude and have equal distances between each value.

Intervening variable(s): Other independent variable(s) that produce effects in the dependent variable that are not controlled and so weaken the cause-and-effect relationship observed in the study.

Interview formats: Question formats that range from structured sets of questions (with fixed types and order) to unstructured sets of questions (varying types and order).

Invention: One of the canons of rhetoric that refers to the speaker's ideas or main points of an argument; in deconstruction, invention refers to the second move, articulating new concept(s) that emerge from analysis of binary opposites, and which could not have been included in the previous dualism.

Inversion: The first move in performing deconstruction, in which researchers attempt to show how one half of a binary opposite has been privileged over the other half.

Inverted U-shaped correlation: Two variables initially increase together as a positive relationship, and then one variable declines over time and the correlation becomes negative.

Item response rate: The percentage of completed items on each individual survey.

Jeremiads: A speech genre consisting of castigating a group of people by announcing their violation of social norms, reviewing their punishment, detailing the violation, and urging them to repent.

Key indicators: Variables which are statistically related to a variable that cannot be directly observed; instead, the other variables are used as proxies, or indicators of the variable of interest.

Key informants: Informed, articulate members of the culture or group a researcher wants to understand.

Knowing by authority: Believing something is true because someone regarded as an expert thinks it is true.

Knowing by criticism: The method of knowing by increasing our awareness of the ways in which society or the dominant group constructs our realities, primarily through the processes of privilege and oppression.

Knowing by discovery: The method of knowing by discovering objective reality through precise, systematic, and repetitive observations of communication phenomena.

Knowing by interpretation: The method of knowing by understanding multiple interpretations people attach to their subjective experiences of the world.

Knowing by tenacity: Customary knowledge; knowing something is true because it is commonly held to be true.

Knowing on a priori grounds: Testing claims against standards of reasonableness derived from logic, aesthetics, or moral codes.

Kurtosis: The vertical dimension of a sample distribution's shape that refers to how peaked or flat it is when error is present.

Laboratory settings: Sites for communication data collection that are selected and controlled by the researcher(s).

Language and Social Interaction (LSI) research: "... studies of speech, language, and gesture in human communication; studies of discourse processes, face-to-face interaction, communication competence, and cognitive processing; conversation analytic, ethnographic, microethnographic, ethnomethodological, and sociolinguistic work; dialect and attitude studies, speech act theory, and pragmatics" (LeBaron, Mandelbaum, & Glenn, 2003, p. 2).

Latent content: The meaning of messages or texts that become apparent only upon careful analysis and synthesis of messages.

Laws: The immutable, physical laws of nature (gravity, for example).

Leading questions: Questions that direct respondents to answer in a specific way.

Leptokurtic distribution: A sample distribution that is too peaked because the distribution is biased.

Liberation: Overcoming oppression, gaining equal rights.

Likert scales: A type of interval scale that asks the study participant to indicate varying levels of responses to questions. Typically, the scale asks for varying levels of agreement (i.e., Strongly Agree, Agree, Neutral, Disagree, Strongly Disagree) or frequency (e.g., Always, Sometimes, Never).

Linear relationships: A simple association between two continuous variables where they change together proportionately in the same or opposite directions.

Literature review: A review of the existing published works that are most closely related to a research topic.

Logos: One of the artistic proofs referring to the logical or rational appeals a speaker makes by identifying the central claims made and the evidence used to support them.

Longitudinal research designs: Research designed so that data are collected at several points in time.

Macroethnography: A form of ethnographic research that involves years of field research, sometimes by numerous ethnographers; *contrast with* Microethnography.

Magnitude: The size or strength of the correlation coefficient.

Main effect: The change in the dependent variable that is directly attributable to each separate factor or independent variable.

Mall intercept surveys: Surveys in which participants are found in shopping malls.

Manifest content: The overt, surface-level meanings of messages or texts.

Manipulation check: Procedure that directly tests whether the manipulation of the independent variable by the researcher was perceived by participants as intended.

Maturation: A confounding effect due to time progression; it happens when a naturally occurring developmental change accounts for some, or all, of the observed effect on the independent variable.

Mean squares between groups: The sum of squares, divided by the degrees of freedom (i.e., k-1), for the numerator portion of a formula that tests for significant difference(s).

Mean squares within groups: The sum of squares, divided by the degrees of freedom (i.e., N-k), for the denominator portion of a formula that tests for significant difference(s).

Mean: Arithmetic average of variable values used as a measure of central tendency for a sample distribution.

Measurement: Assigning numbers to objects or events.

Measurement reliability: Consistency in research observations over time, across settings, subjects, and instruments.

Measures of central tendency: Descriptive statistics that reduce the data set to one number that best characterizes the entire sample (i.e., mean, median, or mode).

Measures of dispersion: Assessments of how much variation in scores is present in a sample distribution, including range, variance, and standard deviation.

Measures of shape: Assessments of skew and kurtosis to indicate the presence or absence of error in a sample distribution.

Median: The midpoint score used as a measure of central tendency for a sample distribution.

Member checks: Allowing your research participants to review, and perhaps verify, some or all of the materials that you have prepared such as field notes, interview transcripts, and narrative research reports.

Message population: A well-defined set of messages pertinent to a given research question or hypothesis.

Metaphor: An analogy created by linking two or more symbols through language to add meaning.

Method of science: Testing claims for reasonableness through logical consistency, observation, systematic analysis, and experience.

Microethnography: A form of ethnographic research that is short in duration, conducted by one researcher, and focuses on a single social situation; *contrast with* Macroethnography.

Misconduct: Acts that violate a code of conduct; in academic research, misconduct refers to fabrication, falsification or plagiarism.

Mixed independent groups/repeated measures design: A research design using both within-subjects and between-subjects factors.

Mixed method research: Using more than one data source, setting, or investigator (*see also* triangulation).

Mixed model paradigm: A design mixing stimulus variables with organismic variables.

Mode: The most frequently occurring score used as a measure of central tendency for a sample distribution.

Mortality: A confounding effect due to time progression, such that subjects disproportionately drop out of an experiment affecting the sum total of change measured in the dependent variable.

Mortification: In Burkean dramatism, a person's act of self-sacrifice to expiate guilt and find redemption.

Multidimensional variable: Variables with different subconstructs to represent each of the different dimensions of the variable.

Multiple regression analysis: A test of the relationship between a set of predictor (independent) continuous variables and the criterion (dependent) continuous variable.

Multiple-factors ANOVA (aka, MANOVA): A test of group differences for the effects of more than one independent categorical variable on a dependent continuous variable.

Multiple-sample chi-square: A test of the relationship between the frequencies of two or more categorical variables that are independent from one another.

Multivariate relationships: Associations of variance between more than two continuous variables.

Mutually exclusive categories: Categorizing characteristics that require each data entry be placed in one and only one category.

Narrative discourse: Discourse in which one participant has greater responsibility for speaking than do other participants.

Narrative Paradigm: A way of understanding human nature that includes as a central belief that humans are storytellers and that our social realities construct and are constructed out of the narratives we tell.

Narrative: Symbolic acts told in story form that have significant meanings for the societies in which they appear.

Naturalistic inquiry: Inductive method for studying human behavior in specific contexts.

Negative case analysis: A conscientious search for counterexamples.

Negative correlation: An association between two continuous variables where the change in one variable is accompanied by an inverse change in the other; for example, as one variable increases in frequency, the other variable decreases in frequency.

Negative skew: A shift in the majority of scores to the right with a tail pointing in the direction of negative numbers.

Network analysis: An approach that aims to describe and explain communication processes and structures by collecting data about the relationships among people, symbols, or groups.

Network sampling: Selecting people to participate in a study and asking each person to solicit additional participants (perhaps with similar characteristics); also called snowball sampling.

Noise: Measurement error derived from random sources; a threat to reliability.

Nominal level measurement: Created by placing texts, observations of communicative behaviors, or self- or other-report data into unordered categories.

Nondirectional hypothesis: A hypothesis that predicts an inequality or difference between two or more group means without specifying the exact nature of the difference (which group will be more or less).

Nonequivalent control group design: A type of quasi-experimental research design using a control group and a treatment group but whose participants were not randomly assigned to either group. The equivalence of groups is thus not assured.

Nonparametric tests: Statistical tests where all of the variables are categorical (measured with nominal or ordinal scales) from which no assumptions about populations can be made.

Nonrandom selection methods: Ways of selecting people and texts that do not ensure that the resulting data sample represents some theoretically generalizable population.

Normal or bell-shaped curve: Presumed shape of many continuously measured variables when there is little error present and that therefore yield statistics that are accurate and reliable estimates of the population parameters.

Null hypothesis: A prediction that there is no relationship between two or more variables, or the logical opposite of the research hypothesis.

Numerator degrees of freedom: The number of groups minus one (i.e., k-1); part of a formula that tests for significance of difference(s).

Objectivity: A philosophical concept or assumption that things or objects exist in reality separate from our perceptions and interpretations of them.

Observed communication behaviors: Researcher's representations of the verbal and nonverbal messages, channels of communication, or communicators that they have seen or heard (compare with self-report and other-report data sources).

One-group pretest-posttest design: A type of pre-experimental design in which administration of the pretest enables the researcher to discover a distinct change or no change between the pretest and the posttest measures. However, there are still many problems in assuming that the independent variable, X, is the source of those changes.

One-shot case study: A type of preexperimental study, also called an ex post facto design, in which there is virtually no control over the manipulation of the independent variable or over the observation of the change in the dependent variable; one of the weakest causal arguments.

One-tailed test: A test that uses critical rejection regions under only one tail of the normal curve distribution.

One-way analysis of variance (aka, one-way ANOVA): A test of group differences between one independent categorical variable, having three or more levels, and one continuous dependent variable.

Open-ended questions: Questions that ask respondents to provide unstructured or spontaneous answers or to discuss an identified topic.

Operational definition: A precise specification of every operation, procedure, and instrument needed to measure a construct.

Operationalization: The process of specifying the operations, procedures, or instruments used to measure communication phenomena as variables.

Order effects: The adverse effects of earlier questions on the way respondents answer later questions in a questionnaire.

Ordinal level measurement: Created by placing texts, observations, self- or other-report data into approximate, rank-ordered categories, thus, giving some estimate of a variable's amount, magnitude, or value.

Ordinate: Vertical axis.

Organismic variables: Variables that represent organic or natural differences in the participants' internal characteristics or characteristics that the participants have chosen for themselves (such as marital status).

Organization: One of the five canons of rhetoric referring to the structure or general pattern of the various components in a rhetorical text.

Other-report: Perceptions about other people's behavior, beliefs, and/or characteristics.

Outliers: Scores that are above or below three standard deviations from the mean score in a sample distribution.

Paired samples t-test: A test of group differences between an independent variable with two groups that are related or matched in some way and a continuous dependent variable; for example, between pretest and posttest scores for the same group of participants.

Panel longitudinal designs: Studies that examine the same sample of individuals over time.

Panel of judges: A group of people selected to evaluate the content validity of a measuring instrument because they have particular knowledge or expertise on the topic being measured.

Paradigms: Different ways of knowing based on different sets of interrelated assumptions about theory and research.

Paradox: Something possessing inherently contradictory qualities.

Parameters: Characteristics of a population expressed in numbers.

Parametric tests: Statistical tests where at least one variable is continuous, allowing assumptions to be made about the way populations are distributed.

Parsimony: The combination of precision and power valued in discovery research.

Participant observation: The process of watching and learning about the setting and participants while the researcher is participating in the daily realities he or she is studying.

Pathos: One of the artistic proofs referring to the emotional appeal of a speaker.

Pentadic criticism: Applying the pentadic elements of drama to any symbolic act or text to understand the underlying motivation.

Pentadic elements: Act, scene, agent, agency, and purpose.

Performance ethnography: A critical paradigm method that uses performative writing and public performances of participants' cultural meanings, to evaluate those meanings and to "make sites of oppression visible" (Denzin, 2003, p. 14).

Performance tests: A form of member checking in which the researcher enacts specific behaviors to confirm his or her interpretations of how those behaviors will be received by members of the social situation.

Periodicity: A recurring pattern or arrangement that exists naturally in the sampling frame, and which can cause a bias in selecting sample messages or persons.

Pie chart: Visually depicts the frequencies of categories with proportions of a circle for nominally and ordinally scaled variables.

Placebo: A false treatment given to one of the comparison groups for the purpose of fooling group members into thinking they have received a treatment when they have not.

Plagiarism: The act of representing another person's words, ideas, or work as one's own, or failure to properly credit the source of one's ideas and/or words.

Platykurtic distribution: A distribution that is too flat, indicating the presence of noise or random error.

Point-biserial correlation: Otherwise known as the *Pearson's product-moment coefficient of correlation or simple, zero-order correlation*; the simplest test of a linear relationship between two continuously measured variables.

Political polling research: Research designed to assess political opinions and attitudes, often to predict voter preferences.

Politics of representation: The issue of who has a right to name, or to assign meaning to actions, events, texts, or experiences.

Pollution: In Burkean dramatism, the consequence of rejecting social hierarchical order, regarded as a social "fall from grace."

Popular press publications: Secondary sources that are aimed at the general public, largely without regard to their readers' fields of academic study or particular occupations.

Population: The entire set of cases or instances that the researcher is attempting to represent with a data sample. *See also* Survey population and Target population.

Positive correlation: An association between continuous variables that are changing proportionately in the same direction (increasing or decreasing together).

Positive skew: A shift in the majority of scores to the left with a tail pointing in the direction of positive numbers.

Post hoc comparisons: Tests of individual contrasts between pairs of groups following the calculation of the *F* statistic.

Postmodern turn: A general movement away from social structure as the explanatory means of domination, toward ideology, representation, and discourse as the sites of struggle for social power.

Poststructural criticism: A critical paradigm perspective that directly critiques rationalism, especially attempts to identify any foundational structure of language, discourse, and society; instead, poststructural critics attribute power imbalances to the ways that language is used in social settings or groups.

Posttest: An assessment of scores on the dependent variable after the independent variable has been manipulated.

Posttest-only control group design: A type of true experimental design in which participants are randomly assigned to comparison groups. The pretest is eliminated as an attempt to control for the test sensitization effect.

Power: The broad scope of a definition or measurement, which is most valued in discovery research.

Praxis: The use of theoretical knowledge in social action.

Precise, systematic, and repetitive observations: Specific or detailed observations made carefully, on more than one occasion, for the sake of accuracy.

Precision: The detailed and accurate definitions and measurements of communication variables valued in discovery research.

Predictive validity: Accuracy warranted by showing that a measuring instrument predicts scores on some other variable in the way that a theory predicts it should work; sometimes called the *known-groups method* because the predictor variable scale is validated by testing groups of people already known to possess the construct's characteristics.

Predictor variable: In tests of association, the term for the independent variable.

Preexperimental designs: Designs in which two or three of the elements of experimental control (comparison groups, pretest/posttest, random assignment) are missing, resulting in very weak support for causal arguments.

Preference organization: A way of making sense of conversational behavior, based on some existing contextual standard for behavior (e.g., the preferred or dispreferred second-pair parts that are expected whenever a first-pair part is observed). *See also* Breaching and Conversational trouble.

Pretest: An assessment of the baseline or naturally occurring levels of the dependent variable before the independent variable is manipulated.

Pretest-posttest control group design: A type of true experimental design that uses comparison groups, random assignment to place participants into the treatment and control groups, and the pretest-posttest procedure.

Primary sources: Original research reports or critical essays written by the researcher, which describe the claims, data, warrants, and backing for a research study.

Principle of covariation: A prediction of relationship between two or more concepts or variables; the assertion that changes in one variable are accompanied by changes in the other variable.

Principles: Legal rules and statutes.

Procedural justice principle: The idea that a process should be fair, even if some people will benefit more from the outcome of that process than others.

Professional associations: A dues-paying group of academic, business, or industry practitioners in a particular field of study.

Proprietary research: Research conducted in business or industry where procedures and findings are owned by the organization; proprietary research may not be not disseminated so as to protect the organization's competitive advantage.

Public sphere: An idealized condition of society formed from the unrestricted debate of its individual members.

Purification: In Burkean dramatism, the absolution of guilt through mortification or victimage and transcendence.

Purpose statements: Declarative sentences that succinctly outline the researcher's goal(s) for a study.

Purposive samples: Select the particular people or messages needed to test a claim about communication within one specific context.

Quasi-experimental designs: Designs in which one or two of the elements of experimental control (comparison groups, pretest/posttest, random assignment) are missing, resulting in weaker support for causal arguments.

Questionnaire architecture: The general structure of a questionnaire: its length, comprehensibility, and question order.

Questionnaires: Written paper-and-pencil measures for data collection.

Quota sampling: A nonrandom sampling method for small, well-defined populations in which key population characteristics are proportionally represented in the data sample.

Random assignment: A procedure in which the researchers select subjects on a purely random basis to participate in either treatment or control conditions.

Random digit dialing: A procedure that first randomly identifies areas of a region to be sampled with their corresponding area codes and exchanges (first three numbers) and then randomly generates the last four digits of the telephone number.

Random error (aka, noise): Measurement error that constitutes noise or interference with the variable's true values; a threat to reliability.

Random selection: Use of procedures that use some element of chance to select sample data that will represent a population.

Range: A measure of dispersion in a sample distribution, obtained by subtracting the lowest score from the highest score.

Rapport: A sense of comfort and trust between researcher(s) and participant(s), valuable in ethnographic data collection.

Ratio scales: Created by placing texts, observations of communicative behaviors, self-, or other-report data into precise, ordered categories that have a mathematical relationship to one another and that have a true zero point, indicating the absence of the thing being measured.

Reactivity effects: Effects or threats due to participants' responses to some design feature of the experimental situation.

Redemptive cycle: In Burkean dramatism, a repeating social drama characterized by the stages of order, pollution, guilt, purification, and redemption.

Reference list: A section appearing at the end of written research reports and critical essays and containing the full citations for all the works cited in the manuscript.

Reflexivity: A process by which researchers recognize that they are inseparable from the settings, contexts, and cultures they are attempting to understand and represent; sometimes called *self-reflexivity.*

Reformist claims: Evaluative claims that identify negative consequences of the existing social system as a way of instigating change.

Regression analysis: A statistical test of association between continuous variables where one or more predictor variables (independent variables) are used to assess the values of the criterion variable (dependent variable).

Regression coefficients or weights: *See* Beta coefficients.

Relevance: The degree to which ethnographic interpretations are germane, or salient, to the people in the group or culture being studied.

Reliability: Consistency of measurement; a standard for evaluating discovery research.

Repair: Work, or actions that interlocutors take, to fix disruptions in interaction, either because a speaker feels he or she has violated a norm or is being accused of such a violation by someone else in the conversation.

Repeated measures: An experimental design in which the researcher exposes the same group of participants to several manipulations of the independent variable(s).

Representative sample: A sample whose characteristics are good estimates (valid and reliable) of the population characteristics.

Request for proposals: Documents funding agencies distribute in order to announce funded research programs.

Research design statement: A numerical statement of the number of independent variables by the specific number of categories per variable found in an experimental study; for example, a 2 × 3 research design statement refers to two independent variables, the first having 2 categories or levels and the second having 3 categories or levels.

Research design: The logical sequence used to connect a researcher's claim, data or evidence, warrants, and background reasoning.

Research hypothesis: The predictive claim about the relationship between two or more variables to be tested with a statistical analysis.

Research protocol: Documents submitted to an IRB which who will be invited participate in a study, how participants will be recruited or selected, the methods for collecting and analyzing data, and all potential risks and benefits to participants, as well as means of protecting participants' rights.

Research questions: Questions that ask how a concept chosen for study can be classified or ask what relationship exists between various types of communication variables.

Research report: Written summary of a research project that includes some form of data collection from self-reports, other-reports, or observations, or from a combination of those sources, perhaps with textual data as well.

Research sources: Research reports and critical essays (primary sources), as well as encyclopedias, magazine and newspaper articles, websites, and so on (secondary sources), which can be examined in the process of conducting a literature review.

Research strategies: Techniques for searching the communication literature at the library, on the Internet, and via electronic databases.

Researcher attributes: A reactivity effect which can happen when researchers possess physical or psychological characteristics that influence the way participants respond, thus affecting the outcome of the experiment.

Researcher credibility: An umbrella term used in field research to cover a number of concerns, including authenticity, training and experience, and the like.

Researcher positionality: Both the researcher's standpoint and his or her reflexivity.

Researcher-constructed categories: Categories that have been created by the researcher for the purpose of conducting research (e.g., relationship types of friend, romantic partner, relative).

Rhetoric: The "human use of symbols to communicate" (Foss, 2009, p. 3).

Rhetorical criticism: The systematic application of theory to persuasive communication.

Rhetorical situation: Theory describing how the situation contributes to the persuasiveness of the message;

the concept includes three components: exigence, audience, and constraints.

Rhetorical theory: Explanations and interpretations of the ways in which messages or texts are persuasive.

Rich description: Descriptions of data or evidence that address every aspect of a social situation or text, such as the setting, the participants, their actions, relationships, and roles (Geertz, 1973); most valued by interpretive researchers.

Root metaphor: *See* Archetypal metaphor.

Roster method: A technique in which participants in the study are given a roster of all the members of their social system and are asked to respond to questions about all the other members with whom they regularly interact.

Rules: General prescriptions for behavior that must be elaborated in context if they are to be applied (Garfinkel, 1967); more generally, rules are reasons that people are likely to accept as a basis for action.

Sample distribution: The actual data set the researcher obtains when conducting the study, a small portion, or subset, of the population distribution.

Sample: A subset or smaller grouping of members from a population.

Sampling: Selecting a relatively smaller number of cases to represent some larger group of cases or instances of phenomena.

Sampling distribution: A theoretic distribution of all possible values of any sample statistic from any given population, specifying the probabilities associated with each of the values.

Sampling effect: A confounding effect that occurs when nonrandom methods are used to collect samples; these samples are much more likely to be biased, or they are likely to vary in systematic ways that do not accurately represent the characteristics of the population from which they were drawn.

Sampling error: Estimation of deviation between sample statistics and population parameters.

Sampling frame: A list of all members of the population.

Scene: One of five key elements in the pentad of Burkean dramatism referring to the setting or situation in which an act occurred.

Scholarly journals: Journals published under the sponsorship of professional associations in a given discipline, with the purpose of conveying the very best theoretic and research scholarship in that field to a community of scholarly peers.

Secondary sources: Another writer's summary and interpretations of an original research project.

Selection: How researchers decide which people or messages to include in a research study.

Selection bias: A confounding effect that can happen when researchers are unable to randomly assign subjects to treatment and control conditions. Without this procedure, the experimental groups can differ systematically in ways that interfere with the effects of the independent variable.

Self-reflexivity: *See* Reflexivity.

Self-report: Data gained from asking people to report their own perceptions, behaviors, beliefs, and/or characteristics.

Semantic differential: Scales consisting of a series of bipolar adjectives placed at either end of a continuum. The adjectives act as anchors for extremes; the respondents indicate where along the continuum between the extremes their perceptions lie.

Sequence organization: "the ways in which turns-at-talk are ordered and combined to make actions take place in conversation, such as requests, offers, complaints, and announcements" (Schegloff, 2006, p. 1).

Significant difference: Refers to a statistical finding indicating that the difference in mean scores for two or more sample groups is large enough to conclude that it is not due to chance alone, but to the influence of the independent variable.

Simple random selection: A random sampling method in which each person (or text) in the population has an equal chance of being selected for inclusion in a study.

Single-factor analysis of variance (aka, single factor ANOVA): Test of the effects of one independent variable with more than two categories on one dependent continuous variable; also called a one-way analysis of variance.

Single-sample chi-square: A test of the difference between expected frequencies and obtained frequencies for one categorical variable.

Skeptic's copout: An ethical problem in field research that happens when researchers are too detached or cynical in interactions with participants or when reporting their study's findings.

Skew: A horizontal shift in the majority of scores either to the right or left of the distribution's center with a longer tail trailing away toward the opposite end of the distribution.

Snowball sampling: A nonrandom sampling method in which each subject selected to participate in a study also solicits additional subjects (perhaps with similar characteristics) to participate in the same study; also called network sampling.

Solomon four-group design: A type of true experimental design that includes two groups that use the pretest-posttest control group design and two groups that use the posttest-only control group design.

Spectrogram: Visual description of data that shows speakers' vocal volumes and/or pitch ranges.

Speech community: A group of people who share rules for using and interpreting speech.

Split half technique: A procedure to assess the internal homogeneity of a measurement scale where one half of the items are randomly chosen and correlated with responses from the other half.

Sponsors: Participants who actively help the ethnographic researcher establish credibility with other participants, identify key informants, arrange interviews, and so on.

Spurious correlation: Two variables that appear to be associated when they are not actually related in any way.

Stability (aka test-retest method):   Consistency of results obtained by one measuring instrument over time, a measure of reliability.

Standard deviation: A measure of dispersion; it is the most accurate indicator of the total amount of variation within a given sample distribution, obtained by taking the square root of the variance.

Standard error (aka standard error of difference between means):   An estimate of distance between the sample mean and the population mean. The standard error is the standard deviation of the sampling distribution of means.

Standpoint: The material and social/symbolic circumstances that shape how members of a group think, act and feel (Wood, 1997).

Statistical analysis: Describing and inferring about data based on characterizing the data sample numerically.

Statistical power: The probability associated with not making a Type II error.

Statistical regression: A time progression effect that occurs when participants have been selected who represent the extremes (extreme high or extreme low) on the dependent variable scale during pretesting. Subsequent posttests are likely to show change in the direction of the mean; very high scores are likely to change to somewhat lower scores and very low scores are likely to change to somewhat higher scores simply because the pretest levels were so extreme.

Statistical significance: Refers to the high probability that observed variation is greater than what would be expected by chance alone.

Statistics: Characteristics of a sample expressed in numbers.

Status differentials: A situation where one party to an agreement has more power resources than the other(s).

Stepwise regression: A common form of multiple regression analysis in which researchers instruct the computer to try various combinations of predictors until it finds the "best fit" equation.

Stimulus variable: A variable manipulated to provoke a targeted response.

Stratified sampling: A random selection method in which the population is first divided into relevant subgroups so that each person or message within each subgroup has an equal chance of being selected for the data sample.

Strict empirical requirement: Conversation analysts' agreement that interpretations of talk be grounded in the data on the page and/or the audio- or videotape. Compare with discourse analysts' use of their own cultural knowledge to make sense of talk.

Strutural criticism: Textual analysis based on the idea that power imbalances in society are rooted in some aspect of an objectively real social structure, like the economy or gender arrangements (*see* Poststructural criticism).

Style: One of the canons of rhetoric referring to the language the rhetor uses.

Subjectivity: Our human ability to know using our minds, based on our thoughts and feelings.

Sums of squares between groups: In tests of difference, an estimate of the difference between group means.

Sums of squares within groups: In tests of difference, an estimate of chance variation, or the sampling error.

Survey population: A large collection of population members from which the sample is actually drawn; it is usually a subset of the target population.

Survey research: Method for collecting information from certain groups of individuals or the general population about their knowledge, beliefs, attitudes, values, feelings, and perceptions.

Systematic sampling with a random start: A random selection method in which the researcher selects the first element from a sampling frame by chance and thereafter selects each next element systematically (i.e., each "kth element").

Target participants: Naive or true participants from whom researchers collect a sample of data to assess as the basis of the experiment.

Target population: The complete set of population members forming an "ideal" population.

Taxonomy: In the data collection process, a categorizing scheme for identifying communication phenomena (behaviors, roles, events, texts, dispositions, or messages) that are related theoretically or conceptually; also see "coding scheme."

Telephone surveys: Interviews conducted by telephone using random or nonrandom selection methods.

Terministic screen: Language choices made to describe any event.

Testing: Two types of time progression effects, both resulting from a pretest. In one type of testing effect, participants can improve their scores just from practicing taking the test or measure more than one time. The second type of testing effect occurs when the test actually acts as a cueing device to sensitize participants to the goals of the study so that they respond to the manipulation of the independent variable in some way they would not have if they had not taken a pretest, sometimes called sensitization.

Test-retest method (aka stability):   Equivalence across multiple administrations of the same measure in the same group of subjects.

Text: Written or spoken words, performances, and visual/pictorial symbols used as evidence to support communication research claims.

Textual analysis: Any of several methodologies, such as discourse analysis or rhetorical criticism, that systematically explore written or spoken words, performances, and visual/pictorial symbols to be used as evidence in support of research claims.

Theoretical sampling: Process of collecting the additional data specifically needed to fill out one part of an emerging theory (Glaser & Strauss, 1967).

Theoretical saturation: The point in data collection when any new data adds little that is new or useful to the explanation or categories that have already been generated.

Theories: Descriptions and explanations for how things work, what things mean, or how things ought to work differently.

Time order: One of the three criteria for making a causal argument, the requirement that change in the independent variable precedes the change in the dependent variable.

Time progression effects: A set of confounding effects that rival the independent variable as sources or causes of effects because the experiment takes place over a period of time.

Time series design: A research design that assesses levels of the dependent variable at several points in time prior to and following the manipulation of the independent variable.

Title page: A page including the title of the paper, the writer's name and institutional affiliation, as well as contact information such as address, telephone number, and email address.

Total response rate: The percentage of total surveys successfully completed and collected.

Trade journals: Written publications aimed at practitioners in a particular business or industry.

Transcendence: In Burkean dramatism, the state of transforming the social hierarchy into a higher moral order through the redemptive cycle.

Transcription veracity: The degree of correspondence between the words typed on a page (or in a computer file) and those recorded on a segment of audiotape or videotape.

Transcription: The process of converting audiotaped or videotaped interactions into verbatim digital or print form.

Transcripts: The translated spoken words and sounds in written form.

Transferability: The ability to apply confirmable, relevant insights from one study to other settings, participants, or texts.

Treatment diffusion: A reactivity effect that can occur when participants in the treatment group tell participants in the control group about the treatment, thereby "contaminating" the control group; also called contamination.

Treatment groups: Groups that receive some exposure to the manipulation of the independent variable.

Trend longitudinal designs: Studies conducted by examining several different representative samples from the same population at different points in time.

Triangulation: The use of several different kinds of evidence to support a research claim.

Trope: A metaphor used as an ornamental literary device.

True experimental designs: Research designs that make use of comparison groups, random assignment, and pretests-posttests and that employ random sampling methods.

_t_-test: A statistical test of the effects of one categorical independent variable with two groups or samples on a continuous dependent variable.

Two-tailed test: A test that uses critical rejection regions under both tails of the normal curve distribution.

Type I error: An incorrect decision to reject the null hypothesis; that is, identifying a significant difference or relationship in the sample data when no difference or relationship exists in the population.

Type II error: A failure to reject the null hypothesis when it should have been rejected; that is, overlooking a significant difference or relationship that probably does exist in the population.

Unidimensional variable: Variables that cannot be broken down into subconstructs or factors.

Unit of analysis: The basic element, or part of a thing, to be analyzed.

Unitizing: Dividing texts into units of analysis.

U-shaped correlation: A curvilinear relationship expressing patterns between continuous variables that change in direction at several points across time, first by decreasing together, then flattening out, and finally by increasing together.

Utilitarian ethics: An approach to ethical behavior based on creating the greatest good for the greatest number of people, and for the right of researchers to exercise individual freedoms, so long as no harm is done to another person.

Validity: Accuracy of measurement, and/or accuracy of applying conclusions from one study to other settings, persons, or situations; a standard for evaluating discovery research.

Variables: A communication phenomena with a set of characteristics or groupings or scores; a construct that can take on an array of numerical values.

Variance: A measure of dispersion, obtained by summing the squared deviations of all scores in a distribution, and dividing by one less than the total number of scores (for a sample) or by the total number of scores (for a populations).

Victimage: In Burkean dramatism, the suffering of a scapegoat so that society can be redeemed.

Voice: The right to express one's own view, choice, wish, or opinion.

Warrant: Standards for evaluating the worth of the data as evidence of the claim.

Within-groups variance: In tests of difference, random variation or chance mean differences in sample distributions, also known as sampling error.

Within-subjects factor: An independent variable comprised of different treatment conditions in which one group of participants is exposed to all conditions sequentially.

Word index: List of all the terms that might be used to refer to a variable.

x-axis (aka abscissa): Horizontal axis of a graph.

y-axis (aka ordinate): Vertical axis of a graph.

z-axis: Depth axis of a graph.

References

Abelson, R. P. (1995). *Statistics as principled argument*. Hillsdale, NJ: Lawrence Erlbaum.

Abetz, J. (2012). Everyday activism as dialogic practice: Narratives of feminist daughters. *Women's Studies in Communication, 35*, 96–117.

Abrahms, S., Barnes, B., Cruz, I., & Nunez, M. (2013). *A Content Analysis of the Production Cost of Menus in the Marina and Mission District*. Unpublished student research project; San Francisco State University.

Adler, P. A., Adler, P., & Fontana, A. (1987). Everyday life sociology. *Annual Review of Sociology, 13*, 217–235.

Afifi, T. D., & Schrodt, P. (2003). Uncertainty and the avoidance of the state of one's family in step-families, postdivorce single-parent families, and first-marriage families. *Human Communication Research, 29*, 516–532.

Agar, M. H. (1983). Ethnographic evidence. *Urban Life, 12*, 32–48.

Alexander, B. K. (2003). Fading, twisting, and weaving: An interpretive ethnography of the Black barbershop as a cultural space. *Qualitative Inquiry, 9*, 105–129.

Alhammouri, A., Price, N., Siordia, L., & Wexler, I. (2013). *Community Newspapers' Political & World News Coverage in San Francisco: El Tecolote vs. The Noe Valley Voice*. Unpublished student research project; San Francisco State University.

Allen, B. J. (1996). Feminist standpoint theory: A black woman's (re)-view of organizational socialization. *Communication Studies, 47*, 257–271.

Almeida, E. P. (2004). A discourse analysis of student perceptions of their communication competence. *Communication Education, 53*, 357–364.

Amason, P., Allen, M. W., & Holmes, S. A. (1999). Social support and acculturative stress in the multicultural workplace. *Journal of Applied Communication Research, 27*, 310–334.

American Psychological Association. (2010). *Publication manual of the American Psychological Association* (6th ed.). Washington, DC: Author.

Amidon, P. (1971). Nonverbal interaction analysis coding system. In *Nonverbal interaction analysis* (chapter 4). Minneapolis, MN: Paul S. Amidon & Associates, Inc.

Anastasi, A. (1976). *Psychological Testing* (4th ed.). New York: MacMillan.

Andersen, K. E. (2000). Developments in communication ethics: The ethics commission, code of professional responsibilities, credo for ethical communication. *Journal of the Association for Communication Administration, 29*, 131–144.

Anderson, C. M. (2001). Communication in the medical interview team: An analysis of patients' stories in the United States and Hong Kong. *The Howard Journal of Communication, 12*, 61–72.

Anderson, C. M., Martin, M. M., & Zhong, M. (1998). Motives for communicating with family and friends: A Chinese study. *Howard Journal of Communications, 9*, 109–122.

Anderson, J. A. (1987). *Communication research: Issues and methods*. New York: McGraw-Hill.

Andrews, J. R., Leff, M., & Terrill, R. (1998). *Reading rhetorical texts: An introduction to criticism*. Boston: Houghton Mifflin.

Andsager, J. L., & Powers, A., (2001). Framing women's health with a sense-making approach: Magazine coverage of breast cancer and implants. *Health Communication, 13*, 163–185.

Andsager, J., & Smiley, L. (1998). Evaluating the public information: Shaping news coverage of the silicone implant controversy. *Public Relations Review, 24*, 183–201.

Ang, I. (1990). Culture and communication: Towards an ethnographic critique of media consumption in the transnational media system. *European Journal of Communication, 5*, 239–260.

Anzaldua, G. (1987). *Borderlands/La frontera: The new mestiza*. San Francisco: Spinsters/Aunt Lute.

Aoki, E. (2000). Mexican-American ethnicity in Biola, CA: An ethnographic account of hard work, family, and religion. *Howard Journal of Communications, 11*, 207–227.

Apollonio, D. E., & Malone, R. E. (2009). Turning negative into positive: Public health mass media campaigns and negative advertising. *Health Education Research, 24*, 483–495.

Aristotle. (1991). *On rhetoric: A theory of civil discourse*. Trans. by G. Kennedy, New York: Oxford University Press.

Arnold, L. B., & Doran, E. (2007). Stop before you hurt the kids: Communicating self-control and self-negation in femininity, mothering, and eating disorders. *Women's Studies in Communication, 30*, 310–339.

Asante, M. K. (1999). An Afrocentric theory of communication. In J. L. Lucaites, C. M. Condit, & S. Caudill (Eds.), *Contemporary rhetorical theory: A reader* (pp. 552–562). New York: Guildford.

Ashcraft, K. L., & Mumby, D. K. (2004). Organizing a critical communicology of gender and work. *International Journal of the Sociology of Language, 166*, 19–43.

Ashcraft, K. L., & Pacanowsky, M. E. (1996). A woman's worst enemy: Reflections on a narrative of organizational life and female identity. *Journal of Applied Communication Research, 24*, 217–239.

Athanases, S. Z., & Comar, T. A. (2008). The performance of homophobia in early adolescents' everyday speech. *Journal of LGBTQ Youth, 5*(2), 9–32.

Atkin, C. K., Smith, S. W., Roberto, A. J., Fediuk, T., & Wagner, T. (2002). Correlates of verbally aggressive communication in adolescents. *Journal of Applied Communication Research, 30*, 251–268.

Atkinson, J. M., & Drew, P. (1979). *Order in the court: The organization of verbal interaction in judicial settings.* London: Macmillan.

Atkinson, J. M., & Heritage, J. (Eds.). (1984). *Structures of social action: Studies in conversation analysis.* Cambridge, England: Cambridge University Press.

Babbie, E. (2001). *The practice of social research* (9th ed.). Belmont, CA: Wadsworth.

Babbie, E. (2013). *The basics of social research* (6th ed.). Belmont, CA: Cengage.

Babor, T. F., Xuan, Z., Damon, D., & Noel, J. (2013). An Empirical Evaluation of the U.S. Beer Institute's Self-Regulation Code Governing the Content of Beer Advertising, *American Journal of Public Health, 13*(10), e45–e51.

Bailard, C. S. (2012). A field experiment on the Internet's effect in an African election: Savvier citizens, disaffected voters, or both? *Journal of Communication, 62*, 330–344.

Bakardjieva, M., & Smith, R. (2001). The Internet in everyday life: Computer networking from the standpoint of the domestic user. *New Media & Society, 3*, 67–83.

Bakhtin, M. (1981). Forms of time and chronotope in the novel (C. Emerson, Trans.). In M. Holquist (Ed.), *The dialogic imagination* (pp. 84–258). Austin: University of Texas Press.

Bakhtin, M. (1984a). *Problems of Dostoevsky's poetics* (C. Emerson, Trans. and Ed.). Minneapolis: University of Minnesota Press.

Bakhtin, M. (1984b). *Rabelais and his world* (H. Iswolsky, Trans.). Bloomington, IN: Indiana University Press.

Bakhtin, M. (1987). *Speech genres and other late essays* (V. W. McGee, Trans., & C. Emerson & M. Holquist, Eds.). Austin: University of Texas Press.

Bakhtin, M. M. (1981). *The dialogic imagination: Four essays.* (C. Emerson & M. Holquist, Trans., & M. Holquist, Ed.). Austin: University of Texas Press.

Balaji, M. (2011). Racializing pity: The Haiti earthquake and the plight of "others." *Critical Studies in Media Communication, 28*(1), 50–67.

Bales, R. F. (1950*). Interaction process analysis: A method for the study of small groups.* Reading, MA: Addison-Wesley.

Bannerjee, S. C., Greene, K., Hecht, M. L., Magsamen-Conrad, K., & Elek, E. (2013). "Drinking won't get you thinking": A content analysis of adolescent-created print alcohol counter-advertisements, *Health Communication, 28*(7), 671–682.

Banus, J. A., & Miller, G. (2013). Inducing resistance to conspiracy theory propaganda: Testing inoculation and meta-inoculation strategies. *Human Communication Research, 39*, 184–207.

Barge, J. K. (2004). Reflexivity and managerial practice. *Communication Monographs, 71*, 70–96.

Barker, D. C. (1998). Political talk radio and health care (un)reform. *Political Communication, 15*, 83–97.

Barker, J. R. (1993). Tightening the iron cage: Concertive control in self-managing teams, *Administrative Science Quarterly, 38*(3), 408–437.

Barnhurst, K. G. (2003). The makers of meaning: National Public Radio and the new long journalism, 1980–2000. *Political Communication, 20*, 1–22.

Barrett, M. S., Bornsen, S. E., Erickson, S. L., Markey, V., & Spiering, K. (2005). The personal response system as a teaching aid. *Communication Teacher, 19*, 89–92.

Barthes, R., (1964). *Elements of semiology.* London: Cape.

Bastien, D. T., & Hostager, T. J. (1992). Cooperation as a communicative accomplishment: A symbolic interaction analysis of an improvised jazz concert. *Communication Studies, 43*, 92–104.

Bavelas, J. B., Black, A., Chovil, N., Lemery, C. R., & Mullett, J. (1988). Form and function in motor mimicry: Topographic evidence that the primary function is communicative. *Human Communication Research, 14*, 275–300.

Baxter, J. (2002). Competing discourses in the classroom: A post-structuralist discourse analysis of girls' and boys' speech in public contexts. *Discourse & Society, 13*, 827–842.

Baxter, L. A., & Goldsmith, D. (1990). Cultural terms for communication events among some American high school adolescents. *Western Journal of Speech Communication, 54*, 377–394.

Baxter, L. A., & Montgomery, B. M. (1998). A guide to dialectical approaches to studying personal relationships. In B. M. Montgomery & L. A. Baxter (Eds.), *Dialectical approaches to studying personal relationships* (pp. 1–15). Mahwah, NJ: Lawrence Erlbaum.

Beach, W. A. (1989a). Orienting to the phenomenon. In J. A. Anderson (Ed.), *Communication Yearbook* (v. 13, pp. 216–234). Newbury Park, CA: Sage.

Beach, W. A. (1989b). Sequential organization of conversational activities. *Western Journal of Speech Communication, 53*, 85–246.

Beach, W. A. (2003a). Making the case for airline compassion fares: The serial organization of problem narratives during a family crisis. *Research on Language & Social Interaction, 36*(4), 351–393.

Beach, W. A. (2003b). Communication and cancer? Part II: Conversation analysis. *Journal of Pychosocial Oncology, 21*(4), 1–22.

Beach, W. A., & Good, J. S. (2004). Uncertain family trajectories: Interactional consequences of cancer diagnosis, treatment, and prognosis. *Journal of Social & Personal Relationships, 21*, 8–32.

Beasley, B., & Standley, T. C. (2002). Shirts vs. skins: Clothing as an indicator of gender role stereotyping in video games. *Mass Communication & Society, 5*, 279–293.

Beck, C. (1996). "I've got some points I'd like to make here": The achievement of social face through turn management during the 1992 vice presidential debate. *Political Communication, 13*, 165–180.

Behnke, R. R., & Sawyer, C. R. (1999). Public speaking procrastination as a correlate of public speaking communication apprehension and self-perceived public speaking competence. *Communication Research Reports, 16*, 40–47.

Behnke, R. R., & Sawyer, C. R. (2000). Anticipatory anxiety patterns for male and female public speakers. *Communication Education, 49*, 187–195.

Bennett, J. A. (2006). In defense of gaydar: Reality television and the politics of the glance. *Critical Studies in Media Communication, 23*(5), 408–425.

Benoit, W. L. (1995). *Accounts, excuses, and apologies: A theory of image restoration strategies.* Albany: State University of New York Press.

Benoit, W. L. (2003). Presidential campaign discourse as a causal factor in election outcome. *Western Journal of Communication, 67*, 97–112.

Benoit, W. L., & Currie, H. (2001). Inaccuracies in media coverage of presidential debates. *Argumentation & Advocacy, 38*, 28–39.

Bereleson, B. (1952). *Content analysis in communication research.* New York: Hafner.

Berger, A. A. (1998). *Media research techniques* (2nd ed.). Thousand Oaks, CA: Sage.

Berger, C. R., & Calabrese, R. J. (1975). Some explorations in initial interaction and beyond: Toward a developmental theory of interpersonal communication. *Human Communication Research, 1*, 99–112.

Berger, P., & Luckmann, T. (1967). *The Social Construction of Reality.* London: Allen Lane.

Berry, J. (1990). Psychology of acculturation: Understanding individuals moving between cultures. In R. Brislin (Ed.), *Applied cross-cultural psychology* (pp. 232–253). Newbury Park, CA: Sage.

Best, J. (2013). Constructionist social problems theory. *Communication Yearbook, 36*, 237–269.

Bevan, J. L. (2004). General partner and relational uncertainty as consequences of another person's jealousy expression. *Western Journal of Communication, 68*, 195–218.

Bevan, J. L., Stetzenback, K. A., Batson, E., & Bullo, K. (2006). Factors associated with general partner and relational uncertainty within early adulthood sibling relationships. *Communication Quarterly, 54*, 367–381.

Bianci, C. (2011). Semiotic approaches to advertising texts and strategies: Narrative, passion, marketing, *Semiotica, 183*(1/4), 243–271.

Billig, M. (1999). 'Whose terms? Whose ordinariness? Rhetoric and ideology in conversation analysis', *Discourse and Society, 10*, 543–558.

Billig, M., & Schegloff, E. A. (1999). Critical discourse analysis and conversation analysis: An exchange between Michael Billig and Emanuel A. Schegloff. *Discourse & Society, 10*, 543–582.

Billings, A. C., Halone, K. K., & Denham, B. E. (2002). "Man, that was a pretty shot": An analysis of gendered broadcast commentary surrounding the 2000 men's and women's NCAA Final Four Basketball Championships. *Mass Communication & Society, 5*, 295–315.

Bilmes, J. (1976). Rules and rhetoric: Negotiating the social order in a Thai village. *Journal of Anthropological Research, 32*, 44–57.

Bitzer, L. F. (1959). Aristotle's enthymeme revisited. *Quarterly Journal of Speech, 45*, 399–408.

Bitzer, L. F. (1968). The rhetorical situation. *Philosophy and Rhetoric, 1*, 1–14.

Black, E. (1978). *Rhetorical criticism: A study in method.* Madison: University of Wisconsin Press.

Blackwell, R. D., Hensel, J. S., & Sternthal, B. (1970). Pupil dilation: What does it measure? *Journal of Advertising Research, 10*(4), 15–18.

Blau, P. M. (1964). *Exchange and power in social life.* New York: Wiley.

Blommaert, J. (2005). *Discourse: A critical introduction.* Cambridge: Cambridge University Press.

Bochner, A. P. (1985). Perspectives on inquiry: Representation, conversation, and reflection. In M. L. Knapp & G. R. Miller (Eds.), *Handbook of interpersonal communication* (pp. 27–58). Beverly Hills, CA: Sage.

Bode, D. (1990). The world as it happens: Ethnomethodology and conversation analysis. In G. Ritzer (Ed.), *Frontiers of social theory: The new synthesis* (pp. 185–213). New York: Columbia University Press.

Boicu, R. (2011). Discursive norms in blogging. *Romanian Journal of Journalism & Communication, 6*, 54–62.

Bok, S. (1979). *Lying: Moral choice in public and private life.* New York: Vintage Books.

Bolden G. B., & Robinson, J. D. (2011). Soliciting accounts with *why*-interrogatives in conversation. *Journal of Communication, 61*, 94–119.

Bolkan, S., & Goodboy, A. K. (2013). No complain, no gain: students' organizational, relational, and personal reasons for withholding rhetorical dissent from their college instructors, *Communication Education, 62*(3), 278–300.

Booth, E. T. (2009). On stability, fluidity, and public stumbling. *Spectra, 45*(8), 1 & 6.

Booth, W. C., Colomb, G. G., & Williams, J. M. (1995). *The craft of research.* Chicago: University of Chicago Press.

Bormann, E. G. (1972). Fantasy and rhetorical vision: The rhetorical criticism of social reality. *Quarterly Journal of Speech, 58*, 396–407.

Bostrom, R. N. (2004). Empiricism, paradigms, and data. *Communication Monographs, 71*, 343–351.

Bowman, M. S. (1996). Performing literature in the age of textuality. *Communication Education, 45*, 96–101.

Bowman, M. S., & Kistenberg, C. J. (1992). "Textual power" and the subject of oral interpretation: An alternate approach to performing literature. *Communication Education, 41*, 287–299.

Boyd, E., & Heritage, J. (2004). Talking the Patient's Medical History: Questioning During Comprehensive History Taking. In J. Heritage & D. Maynard (Eds.), *Communication in Medical Care: Talk and Action in Primary Care Encounters.* Cambridge: Cambrige University Press.

Bradford, L., Meyers, R. A., & Kane, K. A. (1999). Latino expectations of communicative competence: A focus group interview study. *Communication Quarterly, 47*, 98–117.

Braithwaite, C. (1997a). Blood money: The routine violation of conversational rules. *Communication Reports, 10*, 63–73.

Braithwaite, C. (1997b). Sa'ah Naaghai Bik'eh Hozhoon: An ethnography of Navajo educational communication practices. *Communication Education, 46*, 1–15.

Braithwaite, C. (1997c). Were *you* there?: A ritual of legitimacy among Vietnam veterans. *Western Journal of Communication, 61*, 423–447.

Braithwaite, D. O., Dollar, N. J., Fitch, K. L., & Geist, P. (1996, February). *Case studies for "ethics in qualitative research."* Panel presented at the annual meeting of the Western States Communication Association, Pasadena, CA.

Brasfield, R. (2006). Rereading: *Sex and the City:* Exposing the hegemonic feminist narrative. *Journal of Popular Film & Television, 34*(3), 130–139.

Brick, J. M, Brick, P. D., Dipko, S., Presser, S., Tucker, C., & Yuan, Y. (2007). Cell phone survey feasibility in the U.S.: Sampling and calling cell numbers versus landline numbers. *Public Opinion Quarterly, 71,* 23–39.

Brock, B. L. (1990). Rhetorical criticism: A Burkeian approach revisited. In B. L. Brock, R. L. Scott, & J. W. Chesebro (Eds.), *Methods of rhetorical criticism: A twentieth-century perspective* (3rd ed., pp. 183–195). Detroit, MI: Wayne State University Press.

Brock, B. L., Scott, R. L., & Chesebro, J. W. (1990). *Methods of rhetorical criticism: A twentieth-century perspective* (3rd ed.). Detroit, MI: Wayne State University Press.

Brodkey, L. (1987). Writing ethnographic narratives. *Written Communication, 4,* 25–50.

Brown, P., & Levinson, S. C. (1987). *Politeness: Some universals in language usage.* Cambridge: Cambridge University Press.

Browning, L. D., & Beyer, J. M. (1998). The structuring of shared voluntary standards in the U. S. semiconductor industry: Communicating to reach agreement. *Communication Monographs, 65,* 220–243.

Bruess, C. J. S., & Pearson, J. C. (1997). Interpersonal rituals in marriage and adult friendship. *Communication Monographs, 64,* 25–46.

Brummett, B. (2010). *Techniques of close reading.* Los Angeles: Sage.

Brummett, B. (2011). *Rhetoric in popular culture.* (3rd ed.). Thousand Oaks: Sage.

Bryant, D. C. (1953). Rhetoric: Its function and scope. *Quarterly Journal of Speech, 39,* 401–424.

Bryman, A. (2007). Barriers to integrating quantitative and qualitative research. *Journal of Mixed Methods Research, 1,* 8–22.

Bucholtz, M. (2000). The politics of transcription. *Journal of Pragmatics, 32,* 1439–1465.

Bulmer, M. (1979). Concepts in the analysis of qualitative data. *Sociological Review, 27,* 651–677.

Burgoon, J. K., & Le Poire, B. A. (1999). Nonverbal cues and interpersonal judgments: Participant and observer perceptions of intimacy, dominance, composure, and formality. *Communication Monographs, 66,* 105–124.

Burgoon, J. K., Buller, D. B., Guerrero, L. K., & Feldman, C. M. (1994). Interpersonal deception VI: Effects of pre-interactional and interactional factors on deceiver and observer perceptions of deception success. *Communication Studies, 45,* 263–280.

Burgoon, J. K., Johnson, M. L., & Koch, P. T. (1998). The nature and measurement of interpersonal dominance. *Communication Monographs, 65,* 308–335.

Burgoon, J. K., Parrott, R., Le Poire, B. A., Kelley, D. L., Walther, J. B., & Perry, D. (1989). Maintaining and restoring privacy through communication in different types of relationships. *Journal of Social and Personal Relationships, 6,* 131–158.

Burgoon, M., & Bailey, W. (1992). PC at last! PC at last! Thank God almighty, we are PC at last! *Journal of Communication, 42,* 95–104.

Burke, K. (1969a). *A grammar of motives.* Berkeley: University of California Press.

Burke, K. (1969b). *A rhetoric of motives.* Berkeley: University of California Press.

Burke, K. (1970). *The rhetoric of religion: Studies in logology.* Berkeley, University of California Press, 1970.

Burke, K. (1973). *The philosophy of literary form: Studies in symbolic action.* Berkeley: University of California Press.

Burke, K. (1989). Language as action: Terministic screens. In J. R. Gusfield (Ed.), *Kenneth Burke: On symbols and society* (pp. 114–125). Chicago: University of Chicago Press.

Burleson, B. R., Holmstrom, A. J., & Gilstrap, C. M. (2005). "Guys can't say *that* to guys": Four experiments assessing the normative motivation account for deficiencies in the emotional support provided by men. *Communication Monographs, 72,* 468–501.

Burns, M. K. (2009). Gold medal storytelling: NBC's hegemonic use of Olympic athlete narratives. *Journal of the Communication, Speech & Theatre Association of North Dakota, 22,* 19–29.

Bute, J. J. (2013). The discursive dynamics of disclosure and avoidance: Evidence from a study of infidelity. *Western Journal of Communication, 77* (2), 164–185.

Butler, J. (1990). *Gender trouble: Feminism and the subversion of identity.* New York: Routledge.

Butler, J. (1993). *Bodies that matter: On the discursive limits of "sex."* New York: Routledge.

Butler, J. (1997). *Excitable speech: A politics of the performative.* New York: Routledge.

Butler, J. (2005). *Giving an account of oneself.* New York, NY: Fordham University Press.

Buttny, R. (1987). Sequence and practical reasoning in account episodes. *Communication Quarterly, 35,* 67–83.

Buttny, R. (1993). *Social accountability in communication.* London: Sage.

Buzzanell, P. M., Burrell, N. A., Stafford, S., & Berkowitz, S. (1996). When I call you up and you're not there: Application of communication accommodation theory to telephone answering machine messages. *Western Journal of Communication, 60,* 310–336.

Buzzanell, P. M., Waymer, D., Paz Tagle, M., & Liu, M. (2007). Different transitions into working motherhood: Discourses of Asian, Hispanic, and African American women. *Journal of Family Communication, 7,* 195–220.

Buzzanell, P., & Liu, M. (2005). Struggling with maternity leave policies and practices: A poststructuralist feminist analysis of gendered organizing. *Journal of Applied Communication Research, 33,* 1–25.

Calas, M. B., & Smircich, L. (1996). From "the woman's" point of view: Feminist approaches to organization studies. In S. Clegg, C. Hardy, & W. R. Nord (Eds.), *Handbook of organization studies* (pp. 218–257). London: Sage.

Calhoun, L. R. (2005). Will the real Slim Shady please stand up? Masking whiteness, encoding hegemonic masculinity in Eminem's Marshall Mathers LP. *Howard Journal of Communication, 16,* 267–294.

Campbell, D. T., & Fiske, D. W. (1959). Convergent and discrimnant validation by the multitrait-multimethod matrix. *Psychological Bulletin, 56,* 81–105.

Campbell, D. T., & Stanley, J. C. (1963). *Experimental and quasi-experimental designs for research*. Chicago: Rand McNally.

Campbell, K. K. (1973). The rhetoric of women's liberation. *Quarterly Journal of Speech, 59*, 74–86.

Campbell, K. K. (1974). Criticism: Ephemeral and enduring. *Speech Teacher, 23*, 9–14.

Campbell, K. K., & Jamieson, K. H. (1978). Form and genre in rhetorical criticism: An introduction. In K. K. Campbell & K. H. Jamieson (Eds.), *Form and genre: Shaping rhetorical action* (pp. 18–25). Falls Church, VA: Speech Communication Association.

Canary, D. J. (2003). Introductory comments. *Western Journal of Communication, 67*, xi.

Canovar, N. (2012). *Business writing in the digital age*. Sage: Thousand Oaks, CA.

Cappella, J. N. (1990). The method of proof by example in interaction analysis. *Communication Monographs, 57*, 236–242.

Carbaugh, D. (1987). Communication rules in Donahue discourse. *Research on Language and Social Interaction, 21*, 31–62.

Carbaugh, D. (1988). Cultural terms and tensions in the speech at a television station. *Western Journal of Speech Communication, 52*, 216–237.

Carbaugh, D. (1993). "Soul" and "self": Soviet and American cultures in conversation. *Quarterly Journal of Speech, 79*, 182–200.

Carbaugh, D. (2005). *Cultures in conversation*. Mahwah, NJ & London: Lawrence Erlbaum Publishers.

Carbaugh, D. (2007). Six basic principles in the communication of social identities: The special case of clinical discourses. *Communication and Medicine, 4*, 111–115.

Carbaugh, D., Berry, M., & Nurmikari-Berry, M. (2006). Coding personhood through cultural terms and practices. *Journal of Language & Social Psychology, 25*, 203–220.

Carbaugh, D., Gibson, T. A., & Milburn, T. (1997). A view of communication and culture: Scenes in an ethnic cultural center and a private college (pp. 1–24). In *Emerging theories of human communication*, Ed. B. Kovacic. Albany: SUNY Press.

Carpenter, N. (1999). Pictures of prostitutes: The discursive battle of subject position. *Communicate, 28*(2), 21–44.

Carr, C. T., Shrock, D. B., & Dauterman, P. (2012). Speech acts within Facebook status messages. *Journal of Language & Social Psychology, 31*, 176–196.

Carter, D. (2005). Living in virtual communities: An ethnography of human relationships in cyberspace. *Information, Communication, & Society, 8*, 148–167.

Cegala, D. J., McGee, S., & McNeilis, K. S. (1996). Components of patient's and doctor's perceptions of communication competence during a primary medical care interview. *Health Communication, 8*, 1–27.

Cezec-Kecmanovic, D., Treleaven, L., & Moodie, D. (2000). Computer-mediated communication: Challenges of knowledge-sharing. *Australian Journal of Communication, 27*, 51–66.

Chandler, D. (1995). *The act of writing: A media theory approach*. Aberystwyth: University of Wales.

Chang, H. J., & Johnson, J. D. (2001). Communication networks as predictors of organizational members' media choices. *Western Journal of Communication, 65*, 349–369.

Chang, L., & Krosnick, J. A. (2010). Comparing oral interviewing with self-administered computerized questionnaires: An experiment. *Public Opinion Quarterly, 74*, 154–167.

Chang-Hoan, C., & Hongsik J. C. (2005). Children's exposure to negative Internet content: Effects of family context. *Journal of Broadcasting & Electronic Media, 49*, 488–509.

Chan-Olmstead, S. M., & Park, J. S. (2000). From on-air to online world: Examining the content and structures of broadcast TV stations' web sites. *Journalism & Mass Communication Quarterly, 77*, 321–339.

Cheney, G. (2004). *Australian Journal of Communication, 31*(3), 35–40.

Cheng, H. (1997). Toward an understanding of cultural values manifest in advertising: A content analysis of Chinese television commercials in 1990 and 1995. *Journalism and Mass Communication Quarterly, 74*, 773–796.

Cheng, K., & Powers, J. H. (2012). Persuasion in Hong Kong medical encounters, *Journal of Communication in Healthcare, 5*(3), 147–162.

Chien, S. C. (1996). Code-switching as a verbal strategy among Chinese in a campus setting in Taiwan. *World Englishes, 15*, 267–280.

Childress, H. (1998). Kinder ethnographic writing. *Qualitative Inquiry, 4*, 249–264.

Christians, C. G. (2005). Ethics and politics in qualitative research. In N. K. Denzin & Y. S. Lincoln (Eds.), *The landscape of qualitative research: Theories and issues* (2nd ed., pp. 208–243). Thousand Oaks, CA: Sage.

Chua, C. E. H. (2009). Why do virtual communities regulate speech? *Communication Monographs, 76*, 234–261.

Chung, G., & Grimes, S. M. (2005). Data mining the kids: Surveillance and market research strategies in children's online games. *Canadian Journal of Communication, 30*, 527–548.

Clair, R. P. (1993). The use of framing devices to sequester organizational narratives: Hegemony and harassment. *Communication Monographs, 60*, 113–136.

Clair, R. P. (1994). Resistance and oppression as a self-contained opposite: An organizational communication analysis of one man's story of sexual harassment. *Western Journal of Communication, 58*, 235–262.

Clair, R. P. (1997). Organizing silence: Silence as voice and voice as silence in the narrative exploration of the Treaty of New Echota. *Western Journal of Communication, 61*, 315–337.

Clarke, J. N. (1999a). Breast cancer in circulating magazines in the U.S.A. and Canada: 1974–1997. *Women and Health, 28*, 113–130.

Clarke, J. N. (1999b). Prostate cancer's hegemonic masculinity in select print mass media depictions (1974–1995). *Health Communication, 11*, 59–74.

Clatterbuck, G. W. (1979). Attributional confidence and uncertainty in initial interaction. *Human Communication Research, 5*, 147–157.

Clay, E., Fisher, R. L., Xie, S., Sawyer, C. R., & Behnke, R. R. (2005). Affect intensity and sensitivity to punishment as predictors of sensitization (arousal) during public speaking. *Communication Reports, 18*, 95–103.

Clayman, S. (1993). Reformulating the question: a device for answering/not answering questions in news interviews and press conferences. *Text, 13*(2), 159–188.

Clayman, S., & Heritage, J. (2002). Questioning presidents: Journalistic deference and adversarialness in the press conferences of Eisenhower and Reagan. *Journal of Communication, 52*(4), 749–775.

Clifton, J. (2012). Conversation analysis in dialogue with stocks of interactional knowledge: Facework and appraisal interviews, *Journal of Business Communication, 49*, 283–311.

Cloud, D. L. (2004). "To veil the threat of terror": Afghan women and the clash of civilizations in the imagery of the U.S. war on terrorism. *Quarterly Journal of Speech, 90*, 285–306.

Cohen, J. (1960). A coefficient of agreement for nominal scales. *Educational & Psychological Measurement, 20*, 37–46.

Cohen, J. (1992). A power primer. *Psychological Bulletin, 112*(1), 155–159.

Collinson, D., & Hearn, J. (1994). Naming men as men: Implications for work, organization, and management. *Gender, Work, and Organization, 1*, 2–22.

Communication Studies 298. (1999). Shopping for family. *Qualitative Inquiry, 5*, 147–180.

Condit, C. (2006). Contemporary rhetorical criticism: Diverse bodies learning new languages. *Rhetoric Review, 25*, 357–387.

Connell, R. W. (1987). *Gender and power.* Palo Alto, CA: Stanford University Press.

Conquergood, D. (1988). Health theater in a Hmong refugee camp. *The Drama Review, 32*, 174–208.

Conquergood, D. (1991). Rethinking ethnography: Towards a critical cultural politics. *Communication Monographs, 58*, 179–194.

Conquergood, D. (1992). Life in Big Red: Struggles and accommodations in a Chicago polyethnic tenement. In L. Lamphere (Ed.), *Structuring diversity: Ethnographic perspectives on the new immigration* (pp. 94–144). Chicago: University of Chicago Press.

Conquergood, D. (1994). Homeboys and hoods: Gang communication and cultural space. In L. R. Frey (Ed.), *Group communication in cultural context: Studies of natural groups* (pp. 23–55). Hillsdale, NJ: Lawrence Erlbaum.

Conquergood, D. (1995). Between rigor and relevance: Rethinking applied communication. In K. N. Cissna (Ed.), *Applied communication in the 21st century* (pp. 79–96). Mahwah, NJ: Lawrence Erlbaum.

Conquergood, D. (Producer), & Siegel, T. (Producer & Director). (1990). *The heart broken in half* [Videotape]. Chicago: Siegel Productions; New York: Filmmakers Library.

Conrad, C. (1988). Work songs, hegemony, and illusions of self. *Critical Studies in Mass Communication, 5*, 179–201.

Conway, M. (2006). The subjective precision of computers: A methodological comparison with human coding in content analysis. *Journalism & Mass Communication Quarterly, 83*(1), 186–200.

Cook, T. D., & Campbell, D. T. (1979). *Quasi-experimentation: Design and analysis issues for field settings.* Chicago: Rand McNalley.

Cooper, B. (2002). *Boys Don't Cry* and female masculinity: Reclaiming a life & dismantling the politics of normative heterosexuality. *Critical Studies in Mass Communication, 19*, 44–63.

Cooper, B., & Descutner, D. (1997). "Strategic silences and transgressive metaphors in *Out of Africa*: Isak Dinesen's double-voiced rhetoric of complicity and subversion. *Southern Communication Journal. 62*, 333–343.

Corman, S. (2005). Postpositivism. In S. May & D. K. Mumby (Eds.), *Engaging organizational communication theory and research* (pp. 15–34). Thousand Oaks, CA: Sage.

Couldry, N. (2010). *Why voice matters—Culture and politics after neoliberalism.* Sage Publications: Thousand Oaks, California.

Covarrubias, P. (2007). (Un) biased in Western theory: Generative silence in American Indian Communication. *Communication Monographs, 74*, 265–271.

Covarrubias, P. (2008). Masked silence sequences: Hearing discrimination in the college classroom, *Communication culture & critique, 1*, 227–252.

Cox, J. L. (2012). Politics in motion: Barack Obama's use of movement metaphors. *American Communication Journal, 14*, 1–14.

Craig, R. T. (1999). Communication theory as a field. *Communication Theory, 9*, 119–161.

Crawford, L. (1996). Personal ethnography. *Communication Monographs, 63*, 158–170.

Creswell, J. W. (2009). *Research design: Qualitative, quantitative, and mixed methods approaches.* (3rd ed.). Thousand Oaks, CA: Sage.

Crick, N. (2010). The Sophistical attitude and the invention of rhetoric. *Quarterly Journal of Speech, 96*, 25–45.

Crowell, T. L., & Emmers-Sommer, T. M. (2001). "If I knew then what I know now": Seropositive individuals' perceptions of partner trust, safety and risk prior to HIV infection. *Communication Studies, 52*, 302–323.

Dainton, M. (1998). Everyday interaction in marital relationships: Variations in relative importance and event duration. *Communication Reports, 11*, 101–109.

Dangle, L. F., & Haussman, A. M., (1963). *Preparing the research paper* (3rd ed.). Fairfield, NJ: Cebco Standard Publishing.

Davis, F. (1973). The Martian and the Convert: Ontological polarities in social research. *Urban Life, 2*, 333–343.

Davis, O. I. (1999). In the kitchen: Transforming the academy through safe spaces of resistance. *Western Journal of Communication, 63*, 364–381.

Daws, L. B. (2007). The college dropout: a narrative critique of the music of Kanye West. *Florida Communication Journal, 36*, 90–99.

De Jong, P. J. (1999). Communicative and remedial effects of social blushing. *Journal of Nonverbal Behavior, 23*(3), 197–217.

Deetz, S. (2005). Critical theory (pp. 85–111). In S. May & D. Mumby (Eds.), *Organizational communication theory and research: Multiple perspectives.* Thousand Oaks, CA: Sage.

Deetz, S. A. (1982). Critical interpretive research in organizational communication. *Western Journal of Speech Communication, 46*, 131–149.

Delgado, F. P. (1998). When the silenced speak: The textualization and complications of Latina/o identity. *Western Journal of Communication, 62*, 420–438.

DeLuca, K. (1999). *Image politics: The new rhetoric of environmental activism.* New York: Guilford.

DeLuca, K., & Peeples, J. (2002). From the public sphere to the public screen: Democracy, activism, and the "violence" of Seattle. *Critical Studies in Media Communication, 19*, 125–151.

Denman, A., & Wilkinson, R. (2011). Applying conversation analysis to traumatic brain injury: investigating touching another person in everyday social interaction, *Disability & Rehabilitation 33*(3), 243–252.

Denzin, N. K. (1978). *The research act* (2nd ed.). New York: McGraw Hill.

Denzin, N. K. (1997). *Interpretive ethnography: Ethnographic practices for the 21st century.* Thousand Oaks, CA: Sage.

Denzin, N. K. (1999). Two-stepping in the '90s. *Qualitative Inquiry, 5,* 568–572.

Denzin, N. K. (2003). *Performance ethnography: Critical pedagogy and the politics of culture.* Thousand Oaks, CA: Sage.

Denzin, N. K., & Lincoln, Y. S. (1998a). "Introduction: Entering the field of qualitative research," (pp. 1–34) in N. K. Denzin & Y. S. Lincoln (Eds.*), Strategies of qualitative inquiry.* Thousand Oaks, CA: Sage.

Denzin, N. K., & Lincoln, Y. S. (2003). Introduction: The discipline and practice of qualitative research (2nd ed., pp. 1–46) in *Collecting and interpreting qualitative methods.* Thousand Oaks, CA: Sage.

Denzin, N. K., & Lincoln, Y. S. (Eds.). (1998b). *Strategies of qualitative inquiry.* Thousand Oaks, CA: Sage.

Derrida, J. (1976). *Of grammatology* (G. Spivak, Trans.). Baltimore: Johns Hopkins University Press. (Original work published 1972).

Derrida, J. (1978). *Writing and difference* (A. Bass, Trans.). Chicago: University of Chicago Press.

Derrida, J. (1981). *Positions* (A. Bass, Trans.). Chicago: University of Chicago.

Derrida, J. (1982). *Margins of philosophy* (A. Bass, Trans.). Chicago: University of Chicago Press.

DeTurk, S. (2012). Allies in action: The communicative experiences of people who challenge social injustice on behalf of others. *Communication Quarterly, 59,* 569–590.

DeTurk, S. (2012). Allies in action: The communicative experiences of people who challenge social injustice on behalf of others. *Communication Quarterly, 59*(5), 569–590.

Dixon, T., & Azocar, C. L. (2006). The representation of juvenile offenders by race on Los Angeles area television news. *Howard Journal of Communications, 17,* 143–161.

Dodemaide, P., & Crisp, B. R. (2008). Living with suicidal thoughts. *Health Sociology Review, 22*(3), 308–317.

Doerfel, M. A., & Barnett, G. A. (1999). A semantic network analysis of the International Communication Association. *Human Communication Research, 25,* 589–603.

Dollar, N. J. (1995, February). *"What a long strange trip it's been": Understanding the expression of cultural identity.* Paper presented at the annual meeting of the Western States Communication Association, Portland, OR.

Dollar, N. J. (1999). "Show talk" and communal identity: An analysis of Deadheads' ways of speaking. *Journal of the Northwestern Communication Association, 26,* 101–120.

Dollar, N. J., & Beck, C. (1997, February). *Advancing and supporting claims in ethnography of communication.* Workshop presented at the annual meeting of the Western States Communication Association in Monterey, CA.

Dollar, N. J., & Merrigan, G. (2002). Ethnographic practices in group communication research. In L. Frey (Ed.), *New directions in small group communication research* (pp. 59–78). Mahwah, NJ: Lawrence Erlbaum.

Dollar, N. J., & Zimmers, B. (1998). Social identity and communicative boundaries: An analysis of youth and young adult street speakers in a U.S. American community. *Communication Research, 25,* 596–617.

Dorazio, P., & Stovall, J. (1997). Research in context: Ethnographic usability. *Journal of Technical Writing and Communication, 27,* 57–67.

Douglas, J. (1967). *The social meanings of suicide.* Princeton, NJ: Princeton University Press.

Douglas, J. D. (1976). *Investigative social research: Individual and team field research.* Beverly Hills, CA: Sage.

Dow, B. J. (1990). Hegemony, feminist criticism, and "The Mary Tyler Moor Show." *Critical Studies in Mass Communication, 7,* 261–274.

Drew, P., & Heritage, J. (Eds.) (1992). *Talk at work: Interaction in institutional settings.* Cambridge, England: Cambridge University Press.

Drew, P. (1992). Contested evidence in courtroom cross-examination: The case of a trial for rape. In P. Drew & J. Heritage (Eds.), *Talk at work: Interaction in institutional settings* (pp. 470–520). Cambridge, England: Cambridge University Press.

Drew, P. (1997). 'An "Open" class of repair initiation in conversation: Sequential sources of troubles in understanding.' *Journal of Pragmatics, 28,* 69–102.

Drew, P. (1998). 'Out-of-hours' calls to the doctor: misalignments between callers and doctor during diagnostic questioning. In S. Cmejrková, J. Hoffmannová, O. Müllerová & J. Svetlá (Eds.), *Dialoganalyse VI (Volume 2) Proceedings of the 6th International Congresss of IADA (International Association for Dialog Analysis)* (pp. 65–77). Tübingen: Niemeyer.

Druckman, J. N. (2004). Priming the vote: Campaign effects in a U.S. Senate election. *Political Psychology, 25*(4), 577–594.

Druckman, J. N. (2005). Media matter: How newspapers and television news cover campaigns and influence voters. *Political Communication, 22,* 264–481.

Drzewiecka, J. A., & Nakayama, T. K. (1998). City sites: Politics of urban space and communication of identity. *Southern Journal of Communication, 64,* 20–31.

Dubriwny, T. (2005). First ladies and feminism: Laura Bush as advocate for women's and children's rights. *Women's Studies in Communication, 28,* 84–114.

Duggan, A. P., & Le Poire, B. A. (2006). One down, two involved: An application and extension of inconsistent nurturing as control theory to couples including one depressed individual. *Communication Monographs, 73,* 379–405.

Duits, L. (2009, May). Much ado about media? The importance of media in everyday girl culture. Paper presented at the annual meeting of the International Communication Association: Chicago, IL.

Dunbar, N. E., & Abra, G. (2010). Observations of dyadic power in interpersonal interaction. *Communication Monographs, 77,* 657–684.

Dupagne, M. (2006). Predictors of consumer digital television awareness in the United States. *Communication Research Reports, 23,* 119–128.

Duranti, A. (1997). *Linguistic anthropology.* Cambridge, England: Cambridge University Press.

Durrant, G. B., Groves, R. M., Staetsky, L., & Steele, F. (2010). Effects of interviewer attitudes and behaviors on refusal in household surveys. *Public Opinion Quarterly, 74,* 1–36.

Dutta, M. J., & Harter, L. M. (2009). *Communicating for social impact: Engaging communication theory, research and pedagogy.* Cressgill, NJ: Hampton Press.

Eastin, M. S. (2006). Video game violence and the female game player: Self- and opponent gender effects on presence and aggressive thoughts. *Human Communication Research, 32,* 351–372.

Eckstein, N. J. (2004). Emergent issues in families experiencing adolescent-to-parent abuse. *Western Journal of Communication, 68,* 365–388.

Eco, Umberto. 1990. *The limits of interpretation.* Bloomington: Indiana University Press.

Edwards, D., & Fasulo, A. (2006). "To be honest": Sequential uses of honesty phrases in talk-in-interaction. *Research on Language & Social Interaction, 39,* 343–376.

Eisenberg, E. (1990). Transcendence through organizing. *Communication Research, 17,* 139–164.

Eisenberg, E., Murphy, A., & Andrews, L. (1998). Openness and decision making in the search for a university provost. *Communication Monographs, 65,* 1–23.

Ellingson, L. L. (1998). "Then you know how I feel": Empathy, identification, and reflexivity in fieldwork. *Qualitative Inquiry, 4,* 492–514.

Ellis, C. (2004). *The Ethnographic: I. A methodological novel about autoethnography.* Walnut Creek, CA: Alta Mira Press.

Ellis, C., & Bochner, A. P. (2003). Autoethnography, personal narrative, and reflexivity: Researcher as subject. In *Collecting and interpreting qualitative methods* (2nd ed., pp. 199–258). Thousand Oaks, CA: Sage.

Ellis, D. G. (1976). *An analysis of relational communication in ongoing group systems.* Unpublished doctoral dissertation, Department of Communication, University of Utah, Salt Lake City.

Ely, R. J. (1995). The power in demography: Women's social constructions of gender identity at work. *Academy of Management Journal, 38,* 589–634.

Emmers-Sommer, T. M. (1999). Negative relational events and event responses across relationship-type: Examining and comparing the impact of conflict strategy-use on intimacy in same-sex friendships, opposite-sex friendships and romantic relationships. *Communication Research Reports, 16,* 286–295.

Evans, W. (1996). Divining the social order: Class, gender, and magazine astrology columns. *Journalism and Mass Communication Quarterly, 73,* 389–400.

Fairclough, N. (1995). *Critical discourse analysis: The critical study of language.* London, England: Longman.

Farley, S. D., Hughes, S. M., & LaFayette, J. N. (2013). People will know we are in love: Evidence of differences between vocal samples directed toward lovers and friends, *Journal of Nonverbal Behavior, 37,* 123–138.

Favero, L. W., & Heath, R. (2012). Generational perspectives in the workplace: Interpreting the discourses that constitute women's struggles to balance work and life. *Journal of Business Communication, 49,* 332–356.

Feldman, H. K. (2012). Customers' Participation in Organizational Structure: A Conversation Analytic Approach for Understanding the Action of Service Inquiries. *Communication Reports, 25*(1), 14–26.

Feldman, M. S. (1995). *Strategies for interpreting qualitative data* [Qualitative Research Methods Series No. 33]. Thousand Oaks, CA: Sage University Paper.

Ferguson, G. A. (1981). *Statistical analysis in psychology and education* (5th ed.). New York: McGraw-Hill.

Ferguson, M. (1990). Images of power and the feminist fallacy. *Critical Studies in Mass Communication, 7,* 215–230.

Ferris, A. L., & Hollenbaugh, E. E. (2011). Drinking and dialing: an exploratory study of why college students make cell phone calls while intoxicated. *Ohio Communication Journal, 49,* 103–126.

Fiebig, G. V., & Kramer, M. W. (1998). A framework for the study of emotions in organizational contexts. *Management Communication Quarterly, 11,* 536–572.

Fine, G. A. (1993). Ten lies of ethnography: Moral dilemmas of field research. *Journal of Contemporary Ethnography, 22,* 267–293.

Fink, E. J., & Gantz, W. (1996). A content analysis of three mass communication research traditions: Social science, interpretive studies, and critical analysis. *Journalism & Mass Communication Quarterly, 73,* 114–134.

Fisher, B. A. (1970). The process of decision modification in small groups. *Journal of Communication, 20,* 51–64.

Fisher, C. B., & Fryberg, D. (1994). Participant partners: College students weigh the costs and benefits of deceptive research. *American Psychologist, 49,* 417–427.

Fisher, W. R. (1978). Toward a logic of good reasons. *Quarterly Journal of Speech, 64,* 376–384.

Fisher, W. R. (1984). Narrative as a human communication paradigm: The case of public moral argument. *Communication Monographs, 51,* 1–22.

Fisher, W. R. (1987). *Human communication as narration: Toward a philosophy of reason, value, and action.* Columbia: University of South Carolina Press.

Fisher, W. R. (1989). Clarifying the narrative paradigm. *Communication Monographs, 56,* 55–58.

Fisher, W. R. (1989). The narrative paradigm: An elaboration, *Communication Monographs, 52,* 347–367.

Fitch, K. L. (1994). Criteria for evidence in qualitative research. *Western Journal of Communication, 58,* 32–38.

Fix, B., & Sias, P. M. (2006). Person-centered communication, leader-member exchange, and employee job satisfaction. *Communication Research Reports, 23,* 35–44.

Floyd, K. (2006). Human affection exchange XII: Affectionate communication is associated with diurnal variation in salivary free cortisol. *Western Journal of Communication, 70,* 47–63.

Ford, C. E. (2004). Contingency and units in interaction. *Discourse Studies, 6*(1), 27–52.

Forman, M. (2007). 'Hood work: Hip-Hop, youth advocacy, and model citizenry. *Communication, Culture & Critique, 6,* 244–257.

Foss, K. A., & Foss, S. K. (1988). Incorporating the feminist perspective in communication scholarship: A research commentary. In C. Spitzack & K. Carter (Eds.), *Doing research on women's communication: Alternative perspectives in theory and method* (pp. 65–92). Norwood, NJ: Ablex.

Foss, K. A., & Foss, S. K. (1994). Personal experience as evidence in feminist scholarship. *Western Journal of Communication, 58,* 39–43.

Foss, K. A., Foss, S. K., & Griffin, C. L. (1999). *Feminist rhetorical theories.* Thousand Oaks, CA: Sage.

Foss, S. K. (2009). *Rhetorical criticism: Exploration and practice* (4th ed.) Long Grove, IL: Waveland.

Foster, K., Hatcher, K., & Lee, A. (2013). *Alcohol & Tobacco Billboards in Two S.F. Neighborhoods: The Marina & the*

Mission Districts. Unpublished student research project; San Francisco State University.

Foucault, M. (1972). *The Archaeology of Knowledge*, (A.M. Sheridan Smith, Trans.) New York: Pantheon Books.

Foucault, M. (1979). *Discipline and punish: The birth of the prison* (A. Sheridan, Trans.). New York: Random House.

Foucault, M. (1980). *Power/knowledge: Selected interviews and other writings, 1927–1977* (C. Gordon et al., Trans., & C. Gordon, Ed.). New York: Pantheon.

Foucault, M. (1983). The subject and power. In H. Dreyfus & P. Rabinow (Eds.), *Michel Foucault: Beyond structuralism and hermeneutics* (2nd ed., pp. 208–226). Chicago: University of Chicago Press.

Frankfort-Nachmias, C., & Nachmias, D. (1996). *Research methods in the social sciences* (5th ed.). New York: St. Martin's Press.

French, S. L., & Brown, S. C. (2011). It's all your fault: Kenneth Burke, symbolic action, and the assigning of guilt and blame to women. *Southern Communication Journal, 76*, 1–16.

Frey, L. R. (1994a). The call of the field: Studying communication in natural groups. In L. R. Frey (Ed.), *Group communication in context: Studies of bona fide groups* (2nd ed., pp. ix–xiv). Mahwah, NJ: Lawrence Erlbaum.

Frey, L. R. (1994b). The naturalistic paradigm: Studying small groups in the postmodern era. *Small Group Research, 25*, 551–577.

Frey, L. R., & Carragee, K. M. (2007). *Communication activism, Volume I: Communication for social change.* Cresskill, NJ: Hampton.

Frey, L. R., Adelman, M. B., Flint, L. J., & Query, J. L., Jr. (2000). Weaving meanings together in an AIDS residence: Communicative practices, perceived health outcomes, and the symbolic construction of community. *Journal of Health Communication, 5*, 53–73.

Frey, L. R., Botan, C. H., & Kreps, G. L. (2000). *Investigating communication: An introduction to research methods* (2nd ed.). Boston: Allyn & Bacon.

Frymier, A. B., & Houser, M. L. (1998). Does making content relevant make a difference in learning? *Communication Research Reports, 15*, 121–129.

Fuchs, S. (2001). What makes sciences "scientific"? In J. H. Turner (Ed.), *Handbook of sociological theory* (pp. 21–35). New York: Kluwer Academic/Plenum.

Gale, K., & Bunton, K. (2005). Assessing the impact of ethics instruction on advertising and public relations graduates. *Journalism & Mass Communication Educator, 60*, 272–285.

Galvin, J. (1999). *Writing literature reviews: A guide for students of the social and behavioral sciences.* Los Angeles: Pyrczak Publishing.

Garcia, A. C. (2012). Advice-giving and disputant empowerment in divorce mediation sessions, *Language & Dialogue, 2*(3), 398–426.

Garcia, C. (2010). Pope Benedict XVI on religion in the public sphere. *Journal of Communication & Religion, 33*, 87–107.

Garfinkel, H. (1967). *Studies in ethnomethodology.* Englewood Cliffs, NJ: Prentice-Hall.

Gee, J. P. (2011). *How to do discourse analysis: A toolkit.* New York: Routledge.

Geertz, C. (1973). *The interpretation of cultures: Selected essays.* New York: Basic Books.

Geraghty, S., & Velez, M. (2011). Bringing transparency and accountability to criminal justice institutions in the south. *Stanford Law & Policy Review, 22*(2), 455–488.

Gershman, J., & Trachtenberg, J. (Nov. 14, 2013). Google Books: Court dismisses authors' lawsuit: Judge says database of scanned works helps writers and "provides significant public benefits." *Wall Street Journal*

Getis, A. (1995). *The tyranny of data.* San Diego, CA: San Diego State University Press.

Ghareeb, P. A., Bourlai, T., Dutton, W., & McClellan, W. T. (2013). Reducing pathogen transmission in a hospital setting. Handshake verses fist bump: a pilot study. *Journal of Hospital Infection, 85*(4), 321–323.

Gibaldi, J. (2009). *MLA handbook for writers of research papers* (7th ed.). New York: Modern Language Association of America.

Gilbert, J. R. (1997). Performing marginality: Comedy, identity, and cultural critique. *Text and Performance Quarterly, 17*, 317–330.

Gill, A. (1994). *Rhetoric and human understanding.* Prospect Heights, IL: Waveland Press.

Gillen, J., & Merchant, G. (2013). Contact calls: Twitter as a dialogic social and linguistic practice. *Language Sciences, 35*, 47–58.

Gilligan, C. (1982). *In a different voice: Psychological theory and women's development.* Cambridge, MA: Harvard University Press.

Gilligan, C. (1983). Do the social sciences have an adequate theory of moral development? In N. Haarn, R. N. Bellah, P. Rainbow, & M. Sullivan (Eds.), *Social science as moral inquiry* (pp. 33–51). New York: Columbia University Press.

Girardelli, D. (2004). Commodified identities: The myth of Italian food in the United States. *Journal of Communication Inquiry, 28*, 307–324.

Glaser, B. G., & Strauss, A. L. (1967). *The discovery of grounded theory: Strategies for qualitative research.* Chicago: Aldine.

Glionna, J. M. (November 13, 2000). Dot-com spurs angry protests: S.F. locals upset over rising land prices in city. *L A Times*, p. 02D.

Godard, D. (1977). Same setting, different norms: Phone call beginnings in France and the United States. *Language in Society, 6*, 209–219.

Godley, A. J., Carpenter, B. D., & Werner, C.A. (2007). "I'll speak in proper slang": Language ideologies in a daily editing activity. *Reading Research Quarterly, 42*, 100–131.

Goetz, J. P., & LeCompte, M. D. (1984). *Ethnography and qualitative design in educational research.* Orlando, FL: Academic.

Goffman (1967). *Interaction ritual.* Chicago: Aldine.

Goffman, E. (1961). *Asylums: Essays on the social situation of mental patients and other inmates.* New York: Doubleday.

Goffman, E. (1971). *Relations in public.* New York: Harper and Row.

Goidel, R. K., Freeman, C. M., & Procopio, S. T. (2006). The impact of television viewing on perceptions of juvenile crime. *Journal of Broadcasting & Electronic Media, 50*, 119–139.

Golish, T. D., & Caughlin, J. P. (2002). "I'd rather not talk about it": Adolescents' and young adults' use of topic avoidance in step-families. *Journal of Applied Communication Research, 30*, 78–106.

Goodall, H. L. (2000). *Writing the new ethnography.* Walnut Creek, CA: AltaMira Press.

Goodwin, C. (1979). The interactive construction of a sentence in natural conversation. In G. Psathas (Ed.), *Everyday language: Studies in ethnomethodology* (pp. 97–121). New York: Irvington Publishers.

Goodwin, C. (1980). Restarts, pauses, and the achievement of a state of mutual eye gaze at turn-beginning. *Sociological Inquiry, 50,* 277–302.

Goodwin, C. (1981). *Conversational organization: Interactions between speakers and hearers.* New York: Academic.

Goodwin, C. (1993). Recording interaction in natural settings. *Pragmatics, 3*(2), 181–209.

Goodwin, C., & Heritage, J. (1990). Conversation Analysis. *Annual Review of Anthropology, 19,* 283–307.

Goodwin, M. H., & Goodwin, C. (2012). Car talk: Integrating texts, bodies, and changing landscapes. *Semiotica, 191* (1–4), 257–286.

Goodwin, M. H., & Goodwin, C. (1986). Gesture and co-participation in the activity of searching for a word. *Semiotica, 62*(1–2), 51–75.

Gordon, J. (2002). From gangs to the academy: Scholars emerge by reaching back through critical ethnography. *Social Justice, 29,* 71–82.

Gould, S. J. (1999). *Rocks of ages: Science and religion in the fullness of life.* New York: Ballantine.

Gould, S. J. (2003). *The hedgehog, the fox, and the magister's pox: Mending the gap between science and the humanities.* New York, NY: Harmony Books.

Gouldner, A. W. (1988). The sociologist as partisan: Sociology and the welfare state. *American Sociologist, 3,* 103–116.

Gow, J. (1996). Reconsidering gender roles on MTV: Depictions in the most popular music videos of the early 1990s. *Communication Reports, 9,* 151–162.

Graham, E. E. (1997). Turning points and commitment in post-divorce relationships. *Communication Monographs, 64,* 350–368.

Gramsci, A. (1971). *Selections from the prison notebooks* (Q. Hoare & G. Nowell Smith, Trans.). New York: International.

Grano, D. A., & Zagacki, K. S. (2011). Cleansing the Superdome: The paradox of purity and post-Katrina guilt. *Quarterly Journal of Speech, 97,* 201–223.

Greer, C. F., & Ferguson, D. A. (2011). Using Twitter for promotion and branding: A content analysis of local television station's Twitter sites, *Journal of Broadcasting & Electronic Media 55*(2), 198–214.

Grice, H. (1975). Logic and conversation (pp. 41–58). In P. Cole & J. L. Morgan (Eds.), *Syntax and semantics: Speech acts. Volume 3.* New York: Academic.

Griffin, E. (2000). *A first look at communication theory* (4th ed.). Boston: McGraw-Hill.

Griffin, R. A. (2012). I AM an angry black woman: Black feminist autoethnography, voice and resistance. *Women's Studies in Communication, 35,* 138–157.

Griffiths, S., Barnes, R., Britten, N., & Wilkinson, R. (2011). Investigating interactional competencies in Parkinson's disease: The potential benefits of a conversation analytic approach, *International Journal of Language & Communication Disorders, 46*(5), 497–509.

Groscurth, C. R. (2011). Paradoxes of privilege and participation: The case of the American Red Cross. *Communication Quarterly, 59,* 296–314.

Groshek, J., & Conway, M. (2013). The effectiveness of the pervasive method in ethics pedagogy: A longitudinal study of journalism and mass communication students, *Journalism, 14,* 330–347.

Guerrero, L. K., Jones, S. M., & Burgoon, J. K. (2000). Responses to nonverbal intimacy change in romantic dyads: Effects of behavioral valence and degree of behavioral change on nonverbal and verbal reactions. *Communication Monographs, 67,* 325–346.

Gumperz, J. J., & Field, M. (1995). Children's discourse and inferential practices in cooperative learning. *Discourse Processes, 19,* 133–147.

Gunkel, D. J., & Gunkel, A. H. (1997). Virtual geographies: The new worlds of cyberspace. *Critical Studies in Mass Communication, 14,* 123–137.

Guralnik, D. (Ed.). (1986). *Webster's new world dictionary* (2nd ed.). New York: Simon and Schuster.

Habermas, J. (1989). *The structural transformation of the public sphere.* Cambridge, MA: MIT Press.

Haigh, M. M., Pfau, M., Danesi, J., Tallmon, R., Bunko, T. Nyberg, S., et al. (2006). A comparison of embedded and nonembedded print coverage of the U.S. invasion and occupation of Iraq. *Harvard International Journal of Press/Politics, 11,* 139–153.

Hall, A. (2006). Viewers' perceptions of reality programs. *Communication Quarterly, 54,* 191–211.

Hall, B. J., & Noguchi, M. (1993). Intercultural conflict: A case study. *International Journal of Intercultural Relations, 17,* 399–413.

Hall, S. (1986). *Cultural studies: Two paradigms.* London: Sage.

Hallmark, J. R., & Armstrong, R. N. (1999). Gender equity in televised sports: A comparative analysis of men's and women's NCAA Division I Basketball Championship broadcasts, 1991–1995. *Journal of Broadcasting and Electronic Media, 43,* 222–235.

Hallstein, L. (1999). A postmodern caring: Feminist standpoint theories, revisioned caring, and communication ethics. *Western Journal of Communication, 63,* 32–56.

Halpern, D. J. (1995). *St. Foucault: Towards a Gay Hagiography.* New York: Oxford University Press.

Hanke, R. (1998). The "mock-macho" situation comedy: Hegemonic masculinity and its reiteration. *Western Journal of Communication, 62,* 74–94.

Hanmer, J. (1990). Men, power, and the exploitation of women. *Women's Studies International Forum, 13,* 443–456.

Hart, P. S., & Leiserowitz, A. A. (2009). Finding the teachable moment: An analysis of information-seeking behavior on global warming related websites during the release of *The Day After Tomorrow, Environmental Communication, 3,* 355–366.

Hart, R. P. (1971). The rhetoric of the true believer. *Speech Monographs, 38,* 249.

Harter, L. M., Berquist, C., Titsworth, B. S., Novak, D., & Brokaw, T. (2005). The structuring of invisibility among the hidden homeless: The politics of space, stigma, and identity construction. *Journal of Applied Communication Research, 33,* 305–327.

Harwood, J., Raman, P., & Hewstone, M. (2006). The family and communication dynamics of group salience. *Journal of Family Communication, 6,* 181–200.

Haskins, E. (2006). Choosing between Isocrates and Aristotle: Disciplinary assumptions and pedagogical implications. *Rhetoric Society Quarterly, 36,* 191–201.

Hatala, M., Baack, D., & Parmenter, R. (1998). Dating with HIV: A content analysis of gay male HIV-positive and HIV-negative personal advertisements. *Journal of Social & Personal Relationships, 15,* 268–276.

Hatfield, E. F. (2010). "What it means to be a man:" Examining hegemonic masculinity in *Two and a Half Men*. *Communication, Culture, and Critique, 3*, 526–548.

Hauser, G. A. (1991). *Introduction to rhetorical theory*. Prospect Heights, IL: Waveland Press.

Heath, L., & Davidson, L. (1988). Dealing with the threat of rape: Reactance or learned helplessness? *Journal of Applied Social Psychology, 18*, 1334–1351.

Hefner, V., & Wilson, B.J. (2013). From love at first sight to soul mate: The influence of romantic ideals in popular films on young people's beliefs about relationships. *Communication Monographs, 80*, 150–175.

Heritage, J. (1984). *Garfinkel and ethnomethodology*. Oxford, England: Basil Blackwell.

Heritage, J. (1985). Recent developments in conversation analysis. *Sociolinguistics, 15*, 1–18.

Heritage, J. (2002). Ad hoc inquiries: Two preferences in the design of 'routine' questions in an open context. In D. Maynard, H. Houtkoop-Steenstra, N. K. Schaeffer & H. van der Zouwen (Eds.), *Standardization and Tacit Knowledge: Interaction and Practice in the Survey Interview* (pp. 313–333). New York: Wiley Interscience.

Heritage, J. C. (1998). Oh-prefaced responses to inquiry. *Language in Society, 27*, 291–334.

Heritage, J. D., & Robinson, J. D. (2006). The structure of patients' presenting concerns: Physicians' opening questions. *Health Communication, 19*, 89–102.

Heritage, J., & Maynard, D. (2006). *Communication in medical care: Interaction between physicians and patients*. Cambridge, England: Cambridge University Press.

Heritage, J., & Roth, A. (1995). Grammar and institution: Questions and questioning in the broadcast news interview. *Research on Language and Social Interaction, 28*(1), 1–60.

Heritage, J., & Sorjonen, M. L. (1994). Constituting and maintaining activities across sequences: And-prefacing as a feature of question design. *Language in Society, 23*, 1–29.

Herman, A., & Sloop, J. M. (1998). The politics of authenticity in postmodern rock culture: The case of Negativland and the Letter "U" and the Numeral "2." *Critical Studies in Mass Communication, 15*, 1–20.

Hess, J. A. (2000). Maintaining nonvoluntary relationships with disliked partners: An investigation into the use of distancing behaviors. *Human Communication Research, 26*, 458–488.

Heuett, B. L., Hsu, C.-F., & Ayres, J. (2003). Testing a screening procedure in the treatments for communication apprehension. *Communication Research Reports, 20*, 219–229.

Hewitt, J. P., & Stokes, R. (1975). Disclaimers. *American Sociological Review, 40*, 1–11.

Hinkle, L. (1999). Nonverbal immediacy communication behaviors and liking in marital relationships. *Communication Research Reports, 16*, 81–90.

Hmielowski, J. D., Holbert. R. L., & Lee, J. (2011). Predicting the consumption of political TV satire: Affinity for political humor, *The Daily Show*, and *The Colbert Report*. *Communication Monographs, 78*, 96–114.

Hochmuth Nichols, M. (1955). *A history and criticism of American public address* (Vol. 3). London: Longmans-Green.

Holbrook, A. L., Green, M. C., & Krosnick, J. A. (2003). Telephone versus face-to-face interviewing of national probability samples with long questionnaires comparisons of respondent satisficing and social desirability response bias. *Public Opinion Quarterly, 67*, 79–125.

Holling, M. (2006). *El Simpatico* boxer: Underpinning Chicano masculinity with a rhetoric of *Familia* in *Resurrection Blvd*. *Western Journal of Communication, 70*, 91–114.

Holman, A., & Sillars, A. (2012), Talk about "hooking up": The influence of college student social networks on nonrelationship sex. *Health Communication, 27*, 205–216.

Holmes, S. (2001). *Empirical rule*. [Online]. Available from www.stat.stanford.edu/~susan/courses.html.

Honeycutt, L. (2001). Comparing e-mail and synchronous conferencing in online peer response. *Written Communication, 18*, 26–60.

hooks, b. (1989). *Talking back: Thinking feminist, thinking black*. Boston: South End Press.

hooks, b. (1990). *Yearning: Race, gender, and cultural politics*. Boston: South End Press.

hooks, b. (1994). *Outlaw culture: Resisting representations*. New York: Routledge.

hooks, b. (2000). *Where we stand: Class matters*. New York: Routledge.

Hopf, T., Ayres, J., Ayres, F., & Baker, B. (1995). Does self-help material work? Testing a manual designed to help trainers construct public speaking apprehension reduction workshops. *Communication Research Reports, 12*, 34–38.

Hopper, R. (1992). *Telephone conversation*. Bloomington: Indiana University Press.

Hopper, R. (1993). Conversational dramatism and everyday life performance. *Text & Performance Quarterly, 13*, 181–183.

Hopper, R. (1999). Going public about social interaction. *Research on Language & Social Interaction, 32*, 77–84.

Hopper, R., Doany, N., Johnson, M., & Drummond, K. (1990/91). Universals and Particulars in Telephone Openings. *Research on Language and Social Interaction, 24*, 369–87.

Hopper, R., Koch, S., & Mandelbaum, J. (1986). Conversation analytic methods. In D. Ellis & W. Donohue (Eds.), *Contemporary issues in language and discourse processes* (pp. 169–200). Hillsdale, NJ: Lawrence Erlbaum.

Houtkoop-Steenstra, H., & Antaki, C. (1997). Creating happy people by asking yes-no questions. *Research on Language and Social Interaction, 30*(4), 285–313.

Hsieh, Y.-C., Hsieh, C.-C., & Lehman, J. A. (2003). Chinese ethics in communication, collaboration, and digitalization in the digital age. *Journal of Mass Media Ethics, 18*(3–4), 268–285.

Huspek, M. R. (1986). Linguistic variation, context, and meaning: A case of *ing/in'* variation in North American workers' speech. *Language in Society, 15*, 149–164.

Hutchby, I., & Wooffitt, R. (1998). *Conversation analysis: Principles, practices, and applications*. Cambridge, England: Polity Press.

Hymes, D. (1962). Models of the interaction of language and social life. In J. J. Gumperz & D. Hymes (Eds.), *Directions in sociolinguistics* (pp. 35–71). New York: Holt, Rinehart & Winston.

Hymes, D. (1974a). *Foundations in sociolinguistics: An ethnographic approach*. Philadelphia: University of Pennsylvania Press.

Hymes, D. (1974b). Ways of speaking. In *Foundations in sociolinguistics: An ethnographic approach*. Philadelphia: University of Pennsylvania Press.

Infante, D., & Wigley, C. J., III. (1986). Verbal aggressiveness: An interpersonal model and measure. *Communication Monographs, 53*, 61–69.

Ivory, J. D. (2006). Still a man's game: Gender representation in online reviews of video games. *Mass Communication & Society, 9*, 103–114.

Ivory, J. D., Williams, D., Martins, N., & Consalvo, M. (2009). Good clean fun? A content analysis of profanity in video games and its prevalence across game systems and ratings. *Cyberpsychology and Behavior, 12*(4), 457–460.

Jackson, S. (1986). Building a case for claims about discourse structure. In C. H. Tardy (Ed.), *Contemporary issues in language and discourse processes* (pp. 129–147). Hillsdale, NJ: Lawrence Erlbaum.

Jaffe, A. (2007). Codeswitching and stance: Issues in interpretation. *Journal of Language, Identity, & Education, 6*, 53–77.

Jaksa, J. A., & Pritchard, M. S. (1994). *Communication ethics: Methods of analysis.* (2nd ed.). Belmont, CA: Wadsworth.

Jamieson, K. H. (1973). Generic constraints and the rhetorical situation. *Philosophy and Rhetoric, 6*, 162–170.

Jamieson, K. H., & Campbell, K. K. (1982). Rhetorical hybrids: Fusion of generic elements. *Quarterly Journal of Speech, 68*, 146–157.

Janesick, V. J. (1998). The dance of qualitative research design: Metaphor, methodalatry, and meaning. In N. K. Denzin & Y. S. Lincoln (Eds.), *Strategies of qualitative inquiry* (pp. 35–55). Thousand Oaks, CA: Sage.

Jarmon, L. (1996). Performance as a resource in the practice of conversation analysis. *Text and Performance Quarterly, 16*, 336–355.

Jefferson, G. (1983). *Issues in the transcription of naturally occurring talk: Caricature versus capturing pronunciational particulars.* Tilburg Papers in Language and Literature 34: Tilburg University, Tilburg, Netherlands.

Jefferson, G. (1985). An exercise in the transcription and analysis of laughter. In T. A. Dijk (Ed.), *Handbook of Discourse Analysis, Volume 3* (pp. 25–34). New York: Academic Press.

Jefferson, G. (1996). On the poetics of ordinary talk. *Text & Performance Quarterly, 16*, 1–61.

Jefferson, G. (2004). Glossary of transcript symbols with an introduction. In G. H. Lerner (Ed.), *Conversation Analysis: Studies from the first generation* (pp. 13–31). Amsterdam/Philadelphia: John Benjamins Publishing Company.

Jenkins, M. (1999). What to do if you find out you have breast cancer. *Magazine, 17*, 197–201.

Jenkins, M. (2005). Menopause and desire or 452 positions on love. *Text & Performance Quarterly, 25, 254–281.*

Jenkins, M. (Producer). (2000). *A credit to her country.* A staged play based on oral history interviews.

Jensen, R. J. (2006). Analyzing social movement rhetoric. *Rhetoric Review, 25*, 357–387.

Johannesen, R. L. (2001). Communication ethics: Centrality, trends, and controversies. *Communication Yearbook, 25*, 201–235.

Johnson, A. J., Smith, S. W., Mitchell, M. M., Orrego, V. O., & Yun, K. A. (1999). Expert advice on daytime talk television: A beneficial source of information for the general public? *Communication Research Reports, 16*, 91–101.

Johnson, D., & Sellnow, T. (1995). Deliberative rhetoric as a step in organizational crisis management: Exxon as a case study. *Communication Reports, 8*, 54–61.

Johnson, E. P. (2003). *Appropriating Blackness: Performance and the Politics of Authenticity.* Durham, NC: Duke University Press.

Jones, K., Doughty, A., & Hickson, III, M. (2006). The effects of age, gender, and economic status on generosity in the presence of exchange: A pilot study. *Communication Quarterly, 54*, 257–264.

Jones, R. K., & Biddlecom, A. E. (2011). Is the internet filling the sexual health information gap for teens? An exploratory study. *Journal of Health Communication, 16*, 112–123.

Jorgensen, D. L. (1989). *Participant observation: A methodology for human studies.* Newbury Park, CA: Sage.

Kang, J., Maxwell, S., Reuther, W., & Salazar, K. (2013). *Coffee Shop Advertisements and Community Involvement.* Unpublished student research project; San Francisco State University.

Kang, Y., Cappella, J., & Fishbein, M. (2006). The attentional mechanism of message sensation value: Interaction between message sensation value and argument quality on message effectiveness. *Communication Monographs, 73*, 351–378.

Kant, I. (1993). *Grounding for the metaphysics of morals: On a supposed right to lie because of philanthropic concerns* (J. W. Ellington, Trans.). Indianapolis, IN: Hackett. (Original work published 1785)

Kaplan, A. (1964). *The conduct of inquiry.* San Francisco: Chandler.

Kassing, J. W., & Infante, D. A. (1999). Aggressive communication in the coach-athlete relationship. *Communication Research Reports, 16*, 110–120.

Kassing, J. W., & Kava, W. (2013). Assessing disagreement expressed to management: Development of the Upward Dissent scale. *Communication Research Reports, 30*, 46–56.

Katriel, T. (1995). From "context" to "contexts" in intercultural communication research. In R. Wiseman (Ed.), *Intercultural communication theory* (pp. 271–284). Thousand Oaks, CA: Sage.

Katriel, T., & Philipsen, G. (1981). "What we need is communication": "Communication" as a cultural category in some American speech. *Communication Monographs, 48*, 301–317.

Katzer, J., Cook, K. H., & Crouch, W. W. (1998). *Evaluating information: A guide for users of social science research* (4th ed.). Boston: McGraw-Hill.

Kaylor, B. T. (2011). No Jack Kennedy: Mitt Romney's "Faith in America" speech and the changing religious- political environment. *Communication Studies, 62*, 491–507.

Kearney, M. S., & Levine, P. B. (2014). Media influences on social outcomes: The impact of MTV's *16 and Pregnant* on teen childbearing, *Working paper 19795 in NBER Working Paper Series* (http://www.nber.org/papers/w19795), National Bureau of Economic Research.

Keith, W. M., & Lundberg, C. O. (2008). *The essential guide to rhetoric.* Boston: Bedford/St. Martin's.

Kellas, J. K. (2005). Family ties: Communicating identity through jointly told family stories. *Communication Monographs, 72*, 365–389.

Kelman, H. (1967). Human use of human subjects: The problem of deception in social psychological experiments. *Psychological Bulletin, 67*, 1–11.

Kennamer, D. (2005). What journalists and researchers have in common about ethics. *Journal of Mass Media Ethics, 20*, 77–89.

Kennedy, G. (1963). *The art of persuasion in Greece.* Princeton, NJ: Princeton University Press.

Kenny, R. W. (2000). The rhetoric of Kevorkian's battle. *Quarterly Journal of Speech, 86*, 386–401.

Kerbel, M. R., & Bloom, J. D. (2005). Blog for America and civic involvement. *Harvard International Journal of Press/Politics, 10*(4), 3–27.

Kerlinger, F. N. (1986). *Foundations of behavioral research* (3rd ed.). New York: Holt Rinehart, & Winston.

Keshishian, F. (1997). Political bias and nonpolitical news: A content analysis of an Armenian and Iranian earthquake in the *New York Times* and the *Washington Post. Critical Studies in Mass Communication, 14*, 323–343.

Kidder, J. L. (2006). Bike messengers and the really real: Effervescence, reflexivity, and postmodern identity. *Symbolic Interaction, 29*, 349–372.

Kienzler, D. S. (2004). Teaching ethics isn't enough. *Journal of Business* Communication, *41*, 292–301.

Kilgard, A. (2011). Chaos as Praxis: Or, Troubling Performance Pedagogy: Or, You Are Now, *Text & Performance Quarterly, 31(3)*, 217–228.

Kim, L. S. (2003). Multiple identities in a multicultural world: A Malaysian perspective *Journal of Language Identity & Education, 2*, 137–158.

Kim, M. S. (1999). Cross-cultural perspectives on motivations of verbal communication: Review, critique, and a theoretical framework. *Communication Yearbook, 22*, 51–89.

Kim, Y. Y. (1995a). Cross-cultural adaptation: An integrative theory. In R. Wiseman (Ed.), *Intercultural communication theory* (pp. 170–193). Thousand Oaks, CA: Sage.

Kim, Y. Y. (1995b). Identity development: From cultural to intercultural. In H. Mokros (Ed.), *Information and behavior: Vol. 5. Interaction & identity* (pp. 347–369). New Brunswick, NJ: Transaction.

Kim, Y. Y., Lujan, P., & Dixon, L. D. (1998). "I can walk both ways": Identity integration of American Indians in Oklahoma. *Human Communication Research, 25*, 252–274.

Kirkman, B. L., & Shapiro, D. L. (2000). Understanding why team members won't share. *Small Group Research, 31*, 175–210.

Kirzner, L. G., & Mandell, S. H. (2010). *The Brief Wadsworth Handbook* (6th ed.). Belmont, CA: Wadsworth-Cengage Learning.

Kitzinger, C. (2005). "Speaking as a heterosexual": (How) does sexuality matter for talk-in-interaction? *Research on Language and Social Interaction, 38*, 221–265.

Kleemans, M., Hendriks Vettehen, P. G. J, Beentjes, J. W. J., & Eisinga, R. (2012). The influence of age and gender on preferences for negative content and tabloid packaging in television news stories. *Communication Research, 39*, 679–697.

Knight, H. (December 22, 2013). Listening to the many sides in the great tech debate. www.sfgate.com (downloaded 01/16/14).

Knobloch, L. K., & Solomon, D. H. (2003). Responses to changes in relational uncertainty within dating relationships: Emotions and communication strategies. *Communication Studies, 54*, 282–305.

Knobloch, L. K., & Solomon, D. H. (1999). Measuring the sources and content of relational uncertainty. *Communication Studies, 50*, 261–278.

Knobloch-Westerwick, S., & Crane, J. (2012). A losing battle: Effects of prolonged exposure to thin-ideal images on dieting and body satisfaction. *Communication Research, 39*, 79–102.

Krcmar, M., & Valkenburg, P. M. (1999). A scale to assess children's interpretations of justified and unjustified violence and its relationship to television viewing. *Communication Research, 26*, 608–634.

Kress, G., Leite-Garcia, R., & van Leeuwen, T. (1997). Discourse semiotics (pp. 257–291). In T. A. van Dijk (Ed.), *Discourse as structure and process. Discourse Studies: A multidisciplinary introduction, Volume 1*. London: Sage.

Krippendorf, K. (2004). *Content analysis: An introduction to its methodology* (2nd ed.). Thousand Oaks, CA: Sage.

Krueger, R. A. (1994). *Focus groups: A practical guide for applied research*. Newbury Park, CA: Sage.

Kruml, S. M., & Geddes, D. (2000). Exploring the dimensions of emotional labor. *Management Communication Quarterly, 14*, 8–50.

Kubrin, C. (2005). Ganstas, thugs and hustlas: Identity and the code of the streets in Rap music. *Social Problems, 52*, 360–378.

Kuhn, T. S. (1970). *The structure of scientific revolutions* (2nd ed.). Chicago: University of Chicago Press.

Kumashiro, K. (2002). *Troubling Education: "Queer" activism and anti-oppressive pedagogy*. New York: Routledge.

Lannamann, J. W. (1991). Interpersonal communication research as ideological practice. *Communication Theory, 3*, 179–203.

LaRose, R., & Whitten, P. (2000). Re-thinking instructional immediacy for Web courses: A social cognitive exploration. *Communication Education, 49*, 320–338.

Larson, M. S. (2001). Interactions, activities, and gender in children's television commercials: A content analysis. *Journal of Broadcasting and Electronic Media, 45*, 41–56.

Lasswell, H. D. (1927). *Propaganda techniques in the World War*. New York: Knopf.

Lattin, B. D., & Underhill, S. (2006). The soul of politics: The Reverend Jim Wallis's attempt to transcend the religious/secular left and the religious right. *Journal of Communication and Religion, 29*, 205–223.

Lawes, R. (1999). Marriage: An analysis of discourse. *British Journal of Social Psychology, 38*, 1–20.

Lawrence, T. B., Phillips, N., & Hardy, C. (1999) Watching whale-watching: A relational theory of organizational collaboration. *Journal of Applied Behavioral Science, 35*(4): 479–502.

Lazarsfield, P. F. (1959). Problems in methodology. In R. K. Merton (Ed.), *Sociology today*. New York: Basic.

Lears, T. J. (1985). The concept of cultural hegemony: Problems and possibilities. *American Historical Review, 90*, 567–593.

LeBaron, C. D., Mandelbaum, J., & Glenn, P. J. (2003). An overview of language and social interaction research. In P. Glenn, C. D. LeBaron, & J. Mandelbaum (Eds.), *Studies in language & social interaction: In honor of Robert Hopper* (pp. 1–39). Mahwah, NJ: Lawrence Erlbaum.

Lechte, J. (1994*). Fifty key contemporary thinkers: From structuralism to post-modernity*. London: Routledge.

LeCompte, M. D., & Goetz, J. P. (1982). Problems of reliability and validity in ethnographic research. *Review of Educational Research, 52*, 31–60.

Lee, W. S. (1998b). Patriotic breeders or colonized converts: A post-colonial feminist approach to antifootbinding discourse in China. *International and intercultural annual, 21*, 11–33.

Leeman, M. A. (2011). Balancing the benefits and burdens of storytelling among vulnerable people. *Health Communication, 26*, 107–109.

Leetaru, K. H. (2012). *Data mining methods for the content analyst: An introduction to the computational analysis of content*. New York: Routledge.

Lehman, D., & Shemwell, D. J. (2011). A field test of the effectiveness of different print layouts: A mixed model field experiment in alternative advertising, *Journal of Promotion Management, 17,* 61–75.

Leidner, R. (1991). Serving hamburgers and selling insurance: Gender, work, and identity in interactive service jobs. *Gender & Society, 5,* 155–177.

Lesser, L. I., Zimmerman, F. J., & Cohen, D. A. (2013). Outdoor advertising, obesity, and soda consumption: a cross-sectional study, *BMC Public Health, 13,* 20–26.

Levin, L. A., & Behrens, S. J. (2003). From swoosh to swoon: Linguistic analysis of Nike's changing image. *Business Communication Quarterly, 66,* 52–65.

Levine, T. R., Beatty, M. J., Limon, S., Hamilton, M. A., Buck, R., & Chory-Assad, R. M. (2004). The dimensionality of the verbal aggressiveness scale. *Communication Monographs, 71,* 245–268.

Lewis, C. (1997). Hegemony in the ideal: Wedding photography, consumerism, and patriarchy. *Women's Studies in Communication, 20,* 167–187.

Lewis, S. C., Zamith, R., & Hermida, A. (2013). Content analysis in an era of big data: A hybrid approach to computational and manual methods. *Journal of Broadcasting & Electronic Media, 57*(1), 34–52.

Lichter, S. R., Lichter, L. S., & Amundson, D. (1997). Does Hollywood hate business or money? *Journal of Communication, 47,* 68–84.

Licoppe, C., & Morel, J. (2012). Video-in-Interaction: "Talking Heads" and the Multimodal Organization of Mobile and Skype Video Calls. *Research on Language & Social Interaction, 44* (4), 399–421.

Limon, M. S., & Kazoleas, D. C. (2004). A comparison of exemplar and statistical evidence in reducing counter-arguments and responses to a message. *Communication Research Reports, 21,* 291–298.

Lin, C. A. (1997). Beefcake versus cheesecake in the 1990s: Sexist portrayals of both genders in television commercials. *Howard Journal of Communication, 8,* 237–249.

Lin, Y. P., & Tsai, Y. F. (2011). Maintaining patients' dignity during clinical care: A qualitative interview study. *Journal of Advanced Nursing, 67*(2), 340–348.

Lincoln, Y. S., & Guba, E. G. (1985). *Naturalistic inquiry.* Beverly Hills, CA: Sage.

Lindemann, K. (2007). A tough sell: Stigma as souvenir in the contested performances of San Francisco's "Street Sheets," *Text & Performance Quarterly, 27* (1), 41–57.

Lindlof, T. R. (1995). *Qualitative communication research methods.* Thousand Oaks, CA: Sage.

Lindlof, T. R., & Schatzer, M. J. (1998). Media ethnography in virtual space: Strategies, limits, and possibilities. *Journal of Broadcasting & Electronic Media, 42,* 170–193.

Lindsley, S. L. (1999). A layered model of problematic intercultural communication in U.S. owned *maquiladoras* in Mexico. *Communication Monographs, 66,* 145–167.

Lindstrom, A. (1994) Identification and Recognition in Swedish Telephone Conversation Openings, *Language in Society, 23,* 231–52.

Littlefield, R. S., & Quenette, A. M. (2007). Crisis leadership and Hurricane Katrina: The portrayal of authority by the media in natural disasters. *Journal of Applied Communication Research, 35,* 26–47.

Littlejohn, S. (2002). *Theories of human communication* (8th ed.). Belmont, CA: Wadsworth Thompson.

Littlejohn, S. W., & Foss, K. A. (2008). *Theories of human communication* (9th ed.). Belmont, CA: Thomson Learning.

Liu, M., & Stainback, K. (2013). Interviewer gender effects on survey responses to marriage-related questions. *Public Opinion Quarterly, 77,* 606–618.

Lofland, J., & Lofland, L. H. (1995). *Analyzing social settings: A guide to qualitative observation and analysis* (3rd ed.). Belmont, CA: Wadsworth.

Lofland, J., Snow, D., Anderson, L., & Lofland, L. H. (2006). *Analyzing social settings: A guide to qualitative observation and analysis* (4th ed.). Belmont, CA: Thomson.

Lombard, M., Snyder-Duch, J., & Bracken, C. C. (2002). Content analysis in mass communication: Assessment and reporting of intercoder reliability. *Human Communication Research, 28,* 587–604.

Lorber, J. (1990). "Night to his day": The social construction of gender. In S. E. Case (Ed.), *Performing feminisms: Feminist critical theory and theatre* (pp. 53–68). Baltimore: The Johns Hopkins University Press.

Lucaites, J. L., Condit, C. M., & Caudill, S. (Eds.). (1999). *Contemporary rhetorical theory: A reader.* New York: Guilford.

Lucchetti, A. E. (1999). Deception in disclosing one's sexual history: Safe-sex avoidance or ignorance? *Communication Quarterly, 47,* 300–314.

Lyotard, F. (1984). *The Postmodern condition: A report on knowledge* (G. Bennington & B. Massumi, Trans.). Minneapolis: University of Minnesota Press.

Lyu, J. C. (2012). Mainland China and Taiwan: The melamine-tainted milk-powder crisis in China. *Public Relations Review, 38,* 778–791.

Macias, W., Springston, J. K., Lariscy, R. W., & Neustrifter, B. (2008). A 13-year content analysis of survey methodology in communication related journals. *Journal of Current Issues and Research in Advertising, 30,* 79–94.

Madison, S. (2005). *Critical ethnography: Method, ethics, & performance.* Thousand Oaks, CA: Sage.

Malinowski, B. (1922). *Argonauts of the western Pacific.* London: Routledge.

Mandelbaum, J. (1987). Couples sharing stories. *Communication Quarterly, 35,* 144–170.

Manusov, V., & Trees, A. R. (2002). "Are you kidding me?": The role of nonverbal cues in the verbal accounting process. *Journal of Communication, 52,* 640–656.

Markham, A. (1996). Designing discourse: A critical analysis of strategic ambiguity and workplace control. *Management Communication Quarterly, 9,* 389–421.

Marshall, J. (1993). Viewing organizational communication from a feminist perspective: A critique and some offerings (pp. 122–143) in S. Deetz (Ed.), *Communication Yearbook, 16,* Newbury Park, CA: Sage.

Martino, W. J. (2008). Male teachers as role models: Addressing issues of masculinity, pedagogy, and the re-masculinization of schooling. *Curriculum Inquiry, 38*(2), 189–223.

Marx, K. (1888). *The Communist Manifesto.* London: Reeves.

Marx, K. (1909). *Capital.* Chicago: Kerr.

Matabane, P., & Merritt, B. (1996). African-Americans on television: 25 years after Kerner. *Howard Journal of Communication, 7,* 329–337.

Mathison, S. (1988). Why triangulate? *Educational Researcher, 17*(2), 13–17.

Mattson, M., & Brann, M. (2002). Managed care and the paradox of patient confidentiality: A case study analysis from a communication boundary management perspective. *Communication Studies, 53,* 337–358.

May, R. A., & Pattillo-McCoy, M. (2000). Do you see what I see? Examining a collaborative ethnography. *Qualitative Inquiry, 6,* 65–87.

Mayer, V. (2005). Research beyond the pale: Whiteness in audience studies and media ethnography. *Communication Theory, 15,* 148–167.

Maynard, D. W. (1997). The news delivery sequence: bad news and good news in conversational interaction. *Research on Language and Social Interaction, 30*(2), 93–130.

Maynard, D. W. (2003). *Bad news, good news: Conversational order in everyday talk and clinical settings.* Chicago: University of Chicago Press.

Maynard, D. W., & Clayman, S. E. (1991). The diversity of ethnomethodology. *Annual Review of Sociology, 17,* 385–418.

Maynard, D. W., & Heritage, J. (2005). Conversation analysis, doctor-patient interaction and medical communication. *Medical Education, 39,* 428–435.

Mazer, J. P. (2013). From apologia to farewell: Dan Rather, CBS News, and image restoration following the 60 Minutes "memogate" scandal. *Ohio Communication Journal, 51,* 168–185.

McComas, K., & Shanahan, J. (1999). Telling stories about global climate change: Measuring the impact of narratives on issue cycles. *Communication Research, 26,* 30–57.

McCormick, A. C. (2010, Nov./Dec.). Here's looking at you: Transparency, institutional self-presentation, and the public interest. *Change,* 36–43. (www.changemag.org).

McCroskey, J. C., & McCain, T. A. (1974). The measurement of interpersonal attraction. *Speech Monographs, 41,* 261–266.

McCroskey, J. C., & Young, T. J. (1981). Ethos and credibility: The construct and its measurement after three decades. *Central States Speech Journal, 32,* 24–34.

McCroskey, J. C. (1978) Validity of the PRCA as an index of oral communication apprehension. *Communication Monographs 45,* 192–204.

McCroskey, J. C. (1982). *An introduction to rhetorical communication* (4th ed.). Englewood Cliffs, NJ: Prentice Hall.

McCroskey, L., McCroskey, J., & Richmond, V. (2006). Analysis and improvement of the measurement of interpersonal attraction and homophily. *Communication Reports, 54,* 1–31.

McDermott, R. P., Gospodinoff, K., & Aron, J. (1978). Criteria for an ethnographically adequate description of concerted activities and their contexts. *Semiotica, 24,* 245–275.

McDevitt, M., & Chaffee, S. (2000). Closing gaps in political communication and knowledge. *Communication Research, 27,* 259–293.

McGee, M. C. (1980). The "ideograph": A link between rhetoric and ideology. *Quarterly Journal of Speech, 66,* 1–16.

McGee, M. C. (1999). Text, context and the fragmentation of contemporary culture. In J. L. Lucaites, C. M. Condit, & S. Caudill (Eds.), *Contemporary rhetorical theory: A reader* (pp. 65–78). New York: Guilford.

McGee, M. C. (1982). A materialist's conception of rhetoric. In R. E. McKerrow, Ed. *Explorations in rhetoric: Studies in honor of Douglas Ehninger* (pp. 23–48). Glenview, IL: Scott, Foresman.

McIntosh, P. (1992). White privilege and male privilege: A personal account of coming to see correspondences through work in women's studies. In M. Anderson & P. Hill-Collins (Eds.), *Race, class and gender: An anthology* (pp. 70–81). Belmont, CA: Wadsworth.

McKee, K. B., & Pardun, C. J. (1996). Mixed messages: The relationship between sexual and religious imagery in rock, country, and Christian videos. *Communication Reports, 9,* 163–172.

McLaren, P., & Kincheloe, J. L. (2007). *Critical pedagogy: Where are we now?* New York: Peter Lang.

McLaughlin, L. (1991). Discourses of prostitution/discourses of sexuality. *Critical Studies in Mass Communication, 8,* 249–272.

McLaughlin, M. L. (1984). *Conversation: How talk is organized.* Beverly Hills, CA: Sage.

McLeod, J. M., Scheufele, D. A., Moy, P., Horowitz, E. M., Holbert, E. M., Zhang, W., et al. (1999). Understanding deliberation: The effects of discussion networks on participation in a public forum. *Communication Research, 26,* 743–774.

McMillan, J. J., & Cheney, G. (1996). The student as consumer: The implications and limitations of a metaphor. *Communication Education, 45,* 1–15.

McNeill, K. (2001). *Statistical concepts.* Available from www.wizard.ucr.edu/~kmcneill/stats.html.

Mead, G. H. (1934). *Mind, self, and society from the standpoint of a social behaviorist.* Chicago: The University of Chicago Press.

Medved, C. E., Brogan, S. M., McClanahan, A. M., Morris, J. F., & Shepard, G. J. (2006). Family and work socializing communication: Messages, gender, and ideological implications. *Journal of Family Communication, 6,* 161–180.

Meirick, P. A. (2006). Media schemas, perceived effects, and person perceptions. *Journalism and Mass Communication Quarterly, 83,* 632–649.

Mertens, D. M. (1998). *Research methods in education and psychology: Integrating diversity with quantitative & qualitative approaches.* Thousand Oaks, CA: Sage.

Merton, R. K. (1968). *Social theory and social structure.* New York: Free Press.

Merton, T. (1993). *The courage for truth: Letters to writers* (Selected and edited by Christine M. Bochen). New York: Farrar, Straus & Giroux.

Messner, B. A. (1996). "Sizing up" codependency recovery. *Western Journal of Communication, 60,* 101–123.

Messner, N., & DiStasio, M. (2013). Wikipedia versus Encyclopedia Britannica: A longitudinal analysis to identify the impact of social media on the standards of knowledge. *Mass Communication & Society, 16*(4), 465–486.

Metz, C. (2009). "The Imaginary Signifier" in *Film Theory and Criticism* (L. Braudy & M. Cohen, Eds.). New York/Oxford: Oxford University Press.

Mies, M. (1991). Women's research or feminist research? The debate surrounding feminist science and methodology. In M. M. Fonow & J. A. Cook (Eds.), *Beyond methodology: Feminist scholarship as lived research* (pp. 60–84). Bloomington: Indiana University Press.

Miles, M. B., & Huberman, A. M. (1994). *Qualitative data analysis: An expanded sourcebook* (2nd Ed.). Thousand Oaks, CA: Sage.

Milford, M. (2009). Sarah Palin as mascot: Burkean symbolic boasting and community identity. *Florida Communication Journal, 37,* 43–53.

Milford, M. (2012). The Olympics, Jesse Owens, Burke, and the implications of media framing in symbolic boasting. *Mass Communication and Society, 15,* 485–505.

Milgram, S. (1963). Behavioral study of obedience. *Journal of Abnormal and Social Psychology, 67,* 371–378.

Milgram, S. (1975). *Obedience to authority.* New York: Harper & Row.

Miller, A. (2006). Watching viewers watch TV: Processing live, breaking, and emotional news in a naturalistic setting. *Journalism & Mass Communication Quarterly, 83,* 511–529.

Miller, C. R. (1998). Genre as social action. In T. B. Farrell (Ed.), *Landmark essays on contemporary rhetoric* (pp. 123–141). Mahwah, NJ: Lawrence Erlbaum.

Miller, C. W., & Roloff, M. (2007). The effect of face loss on willingness to confront hurtful messages from romantic partners. *Southern Communication Journal, 72,* 247–263.

Miller, D. L., Creswell, J. W., & Olander, L. S. (1998). Writing and retelling multiple ethnographic tales of a soup kitchen for the homeless. *Qualitative Inquiry, 4,* 469–491.

Miller, G. R. (1970). Research setting: Laboratory studies. In P. Emmert & W. Brooks (Eds.), *Methods of research in communication* (pp. 77–104). Boston: Houghton Mifflin.

Miller, G. R. (1975). Humanistic and scientific approaches to speech communication inquiry: Rivalry, redundancy, or rapprochement. *Western Speech Communication, 39,* 230–239.

Miller, J. M. (2000). Language use, identity, and social interaction: Migrant students in Australia. *Research on Language and Social Interaction, 33,* 69–100.

Miller, K. (2002). The experience of emotion in the workplace: Professing in the midst of tragedy. *Management Communication Quarterly, 15,* 571–600.

Miller, M. (1995). An intergenerational case study of suicidal tradition and mother-daughter communication. *Journal of Applied Communication Research, 23,* 247–270.

Mitchell, C. J. (1983). Case and situation analysis. *Sociological Review, 31,* 187–211.

Mongeau, P. A., Hale, J. L., & Alles, M. (1994). An experimental investigation of accounts and attributions following sexual infidelity. *Communication Monographs, 61,* 326–344.

Mongeau, P. A., Serewicz, M. C. M., & Therrien, L. F. (2004). Goals for cross-sex first dates: Identification, measurement, and the influence of contextual factors. *Communication Monographs, 71,* 121–147.

Monto, M. A., Malachek, J., & Anderson, T. L. (2013). Boys doing art: The construction of outlaw masculinity in a Portland, Oregon graffiti crew. *Journal of Contemporary Ethnography, 42,* 259–290.

Moore, M. P. (2006). To execute capital punishment: The mortification and scapegoating of Illinois governor George Ryan. *Western Journal of Communication, 70,* 311–330.

Moraga, C., & Anzaldua, G. (Eds.). (1983). *This bridge called my back: Writings by radical women of color.* New York: Kitchen Table.

Moreman, S., & Persona Non Grata (2011). Learning from and mentoring the undocumented AB540 student: Hearing an unheard voice. *Text & Performance Quarterly, 31*(3), 303–320.

Morgan, D. L. (1988). *Focus groups as qualitative research.* Newbury Park, CA: Sage.

Morgan, M. (2010). The presentation of indirectness and power in everyday life. *Journal of Pragmatics, 42,* 283–91.

Morse, J. M. (1998). Designing funded qualitative research. In N. Denzin & Y. Lincoln (Eds.), *Strategies of qualitative inquiry* (pp. 56–85). Thousand Oaks, CA: Sage.

Morton, T. A., & Duck, J. M. (2000). Social identity and media dependency in the gay community: The prediction of safe sex attitudes. *Communication Research, 27,* 438–460.

Mumby, D. K. (1988). *Communication and power in organizations: Discourse, ideology, and domination.* Norwood, NJ: Ablex.

Mumby, D. K. (1993). Critical organizational communication studies: The next 10 years. *Communication Monographs, 60,* 18–25.

Mumby, D. K. (1997a). Modernism, postmodernism, and communication studies: A rereading of an ongoing debate. *Communication Theory, 7,* 1–28.

Mumby, D. K. (1997b). The problem of hegemony: Rereading Gramsci for organizational communication studies. *Western Journal of Communication, 61,* 343–375.

Mumby, D. K., & Putnam, L. L. (1992). The politics of emotion: A feminist reading of bounded rationality. *Academy of Management Review, 17,* 465–486.

Mumby, D., & Stohl, C. (1991). Power and discourse in organizational studies: Absence and the dialectic of control. *Discourse & Society, 2,* 313–332.

Munshi, D., & Kurian, P. (2005). Imperializing spin cycles: A postcolonial look at public relations, greenwashing, and the separation of publics. *Public Relations Review, 31,* 513–520.

Murillo, E. G., Jr. (November, 1996). *Pedagogy of a Latin-American festival: A Mojado ethnography.* Paper presented at the Annual Meeting of the American Educational Studies Association in Montreal, Quebec, Canada.

Nakayama, T. K. (1997). Les voix de l'autre [The voices of the other]. *Western Journal of Communication, 61,* 235–242.

Nakayama, T. K., & Krizek, R. L. (1995). Whiteness: A strategic rhetoric. *Quarterly Journal of Speech, 81,* 291–309.

Nakayama, T. K., & Martin, J. N. (1999). *Whiteness: The communication of social identity.* Thousand Oaks, CA: Sage.

Nastri, J., Pena, J., & Hancock, J. T. (2006). The construction of away messages: A speech act analysis. *Journal of Computer-Mediated Communication, 11,* 1025–1045.

Nathanson, A. I. (1999). Identifying and explaining the relationship between parental mediation and children's aggression. *Communication Research, 26,* 124–144.

Nathanson, A. I. (2001). Parents versus peers: Exploring the significance of peer mediation of antisocial television. *Communication Research, 28,* 251–274.

National Institute of Health. (2002). *Human participant protections education for research teams.* Washington, DC: US Department of Health & Human Services.

Nelson, M. R., & Paek, H. J. (2005). Cross-cultural differences in sexual advertising content in a transnational women's magazine. *Sex Roles, 53,* 371–383.

Neruda, P. (1972). *New poems: 1968–1970* (B. Belitt, Ed.). New York: Grove Press.

Neuendorf, K. A. (2002). *The content analysis guidebook.* London: Sage.

Neuman, W. L. (1994). *Social research methods*. Boston: Allyn & Bacon.

Newman, I., & Benz, C. R. (1998). *Qualitative-quantitative research methodology: Exploring the interactive continuum*. Carbondale: Southern Illinois University Press.

Nielsen. (October 7, 2013). Nielsen Launches 'Nielsen Twitter TV Ratings.' Retrieved from http://www.nielsen.com/us/en/press-room/2013/nielsen-launches-nielsen-twitter-tv-ratings.html.

Nielson, M. F. (2013). "Stepping stones" in opening and closing department meetings. *Journal of Business Communication, 50* (1), 34–67.

Niquette, M., & Buxton, W. J. (1997). Meet me at the fair: Sociability and reflexivity in nineteenth-century world expositions. *Canadian Journal of Communication, 22,* 81–113.

Norwood, K. M., & Baxter, L. A. (2011). "Dear Birth Mother": Addressivity and meaning-making in online adoption seeking letters. *Journal of Family Communication, 11,* 198–217.

Nunnally, J. C. (1972). *Educational measurement and evaluation* (2nd ed.). New York: McGraw Hill.

O'Keefe, D. (1980). Ethnomethodology. *Journal for the Theory of Social Behavior, 9,* 187–219.

Ochs, E. (1979). Transcription as Theory (pp. 43–72). In *Developmental Pragmatics*, edited by E. Ochs and B. B. Schieffelin. New York: Academic Press.

Oliver, M. (1992). Changing the social relations of research production? *Disability, Handicap, & Society, 7,* 101–114.

Osborn, M. (1967). Archetypal metaphor in rhetoric: The light-dark family. *Quarterly Journal of Speech, 53,* 115–126.

Owen, A. S., (2002). Memory, war, and American identity: Saving Private Ryan as cinematic jeremiad. *Critical Studies in Media Communication, 19,* 249–282.

Pal, M., & Buzzanell, P. M. (2013). Breaking the myth of Indian call centers: A postcolonial analysis of resistance. *Communication Monographs 80,* 199–219.

Palmgreen, P. (1984). Uses and gratifications: A theoretical perspective (pp. 20–55) in R. N. Bostrom (Ed.), *Communication Yearbook, 8,* Beverly Hills, CA: Sage.

Palomares, N. A., & Flanagin, A. J. (2005). The potential of electronic communications and information technologies as research tools: Promise and perils for the future of communication research (pp. 147–185) in *Communication Yearbook, 29,* Beverly Hills: Sage.

Papacharissi, Z., & de Fatima Oliveira, M. (2012). Affective news and networked publics: The rhythms of news storytelling on Egypt. *Journal of Communication, 62*(2), 266–282.

Papageorgis, D., & McGuire, W. J. (1961). The generality of immunity to persuasion produced by pre-exposure to weakened counterarguments. *Journal of Abnormal and Social Psychology, 62,* 475–481.

Park, H. W. (1998). A Gramscian approach to interpreting international communication. *Journal of Communication, 48,* 79–99.

Park, Y. Y. (2002) Recognition and identification in Japanese and Korean telephone conversation openings (pp. 25–47) in K. Kwong Luke and T. S. Pavlidou (Eds.) *Telephone Calls: Unity and Diversity in Conversational Structure across Languages and Cultures.* Amsterdam: John Benjamins.

Parker, M. (1992). Post-modern organizations or postmodern organizational theory? *Organization Studies, 13,* 1–17.

Parks, M. R. (1997). Ideology in interpersonal communication: Beyond the couches, talk shows, and bunkers. *Communication Yearbook, 18,* 480–497.

Parks, M. R., & Adelman, M. B. (1983). Communication networks and the development of romantic relationships: An expansion of uncertainty reduction theory. *Human Communication Research, 10,* 55–79.

Parks, M. R., Faw, M., & Goldsmith, D. (2011). Undergraduate instruction in empirical research methods in communication: Assessment and recommendations. *Communication Education, 60*(4), 406–421.

Patterson, B. R., Neupauer, N. C., Burant, P. A., Koehn, S. C., & Reed, A. T. (1996). A preliminary examination of conversation analytic techniques: Rates of inter-transcriber reliability. *Western Journal of Communication, 60,* 76–91.

Patton, M. Q. (1990). *Qualitative evaluation and research methods* (2nd ed.). Newbury Park, CA: Sage.

Patton, O. (2004). In the guise of civility: The complications of maintenance of inferential forms of sexism and racism in higher education. *Women's Studies in Communication, 27,* 60–87.

Pavitt, C. (2004). Theory-data interaction from the standpoint of scientific realism: A reaction to Bostrom. *Communication Monographs, 71,* 333–342.

Pearce, W. B. (1998). On putting social justice in the discipline of communication and putting enriched concepts of communication in social justice research and practice. *Journal of Applied Communication Research, 26,* 272–278.

Pearson, J. C., Child, J. T., & Kahl, D. H., Jr. (2006). Preparation meeting opportunity: How do college students prepare for public speeches? *Communication Quarterly, 54,* 351–366.

Pearson, J. C., Child, J. T., Mattern, J. L., & Kahl, D. H., Jr. (2006). What are students being taught about ethics in public speaking textbooks? *Communication Quarterly, 54,* 507–522.

Pedhazur, E. J. (1982). *Multiple regression in behavioral research: Explanation and prediction* (2nd ed.). New York: Holt, Rinehart, & Winston.

Peirce, C. S. (1992). *Reasoning and the logic of things: The Cambridge Conference lectures of 1898* (K. L. Ketner, Ed.). Cambridge, MA: Harvard University Press.

Pelias, R. (2003). The academic tourist: An autoethnography. *Qualitative Inquiry, 9,* 369–373.

Pelias, R. J., & Vanoosting, J. (1987). A paradigm for performance studies. *Quarterly Journal of Speech, 73,* 219–231.

Pepper, G. L., & Larson, G. S. (2006). Cultural identity tensions in a post-acquisition organization. *Journal of Applied Communication Research, 34,* 49–71.

Perez, G. J. (1997). Communication ethics in a Latin American context. In C. G. Christians & M. Traber (Eds.), *Communication ethics and universal values* (pp. 159–169). Thousand Oaks, CA: Sage.

Peshkin, A. (1988). In search of subjectivity—one's own. *Educational Researcher, 17,* 17–22.

Petersen, J. L. (2009). "You have to be positive": Social support processes of an online support group for men living with HIV. *Communication Studies, 60*(5), 526–541.

Philipsen, G. (1975). Speaking "like a man" in Teamsterville: Cultural patterns of role enactment in an urban neighborhood. *Quarterly Journal of Speech, 61,* 13–22.

Philipsen, G. (1976). Places for speaking in Teamsterville. *Quarterly Journal of Speech, 62,* 15–25.

Philipsen, G. (1977). Linearity of research design in ethnographic studies of speaking. *Communication Quarterly, 25,* 42–50.

Philipsen, G. (1982). The qualitative case study as a strategy in communication inquiry. *The Communicator, 12,* 4–17.

Philipsen, G. (1989). An ethnographic approach to communication studies. In B. Dervin, L. Grossberg, B. J. O'Keefe, & E. Wartella (Eds.), *Rethinking communication 2: Paradigm exemplars* (pp. 258–267). Newbury Park, CA: Sage.

Philipsen, G. (1992). *Speaking culturally: Explorations in social communication.* Albany: State University of New York Press.

Philipsen, G. (1997). A theory of speech codes. In G. Philipsen & T. Albrecht (Eds.), *Developing communication theories* (pp. 119–156). Albany: State University of New York Press.

Phillips, A. (2012). Visual protest material as empirical data. *Visual Communication, 11*(3), 2–21.

Phillips, N., & Hardy, C. (2002). *Discourse analysis: Investigating processes of social construction.* Thousand Oaks, CA: Sage.

Pierce, D. L., & Kaufman, K. (2012) Visual persuasion tactics in narrative development: An analysis of *The Matrix. Visual Communication Quarterly, 19,* 33–47.

Pitcher, K. C. (2006). The staging of agency in *Girls Gone Wild. Critical Studies in Mass Communication, 23,* 200–218.

Pittman, J., & Gallois, C. (1997). Language strategies in the attribution of blame for HIV and AIDS. *Communication Monographs, 64,* 201–218.

Pollach, I. (2005). A typology of communicative strategies in online privacy policies: Ethics, power and informed consent. *Journal of Business Ethics, 62,* 221–235.

Pomerantz, A. (1978). Compliment responses: Notes on the co-operation of multiple constraints. In J. Schenkein (Ed.), *Studies in the organization of conversational interaction* (pp. 79–112). New York: Academic.

Pomerantz, A. (1990). Chautauqua: On the validity and generalizability of conversational analysis methods. Conversation analytic claims. *Communication Monographs, 57,* 231–235.

Popper, K. (1962). On the sources of knowledge and ignorance. *Encounter, 19,* 42–57.

Potter, J., & Wetherall, M. (1987). *Discourse and social psychology.* Newbury Park, CA: Sage.

Pragg, L., Wiseman, R. L., Cody, M. J., & Wendt, P. F. (1999). Interrogative strategies and information exchange in computer-mediated communication. *Communication Quarterly, 47,* 46–66.

Preston, D. (1982). Mowr and mowr bayud spellin': Confessions of a sociolinguist. *Journal of Sociolinguistics, 4*(4), 615–621.

Preston, D. R. (2000). Three kinds of sociolinguisitics and SLA: A psycholinguistic perspective. In B. Swierzbin & F. Morris & M. Anderson & C. Klee & E. Tarone (Eds.), *Social and Cognitive Factors in Second Language Acquisition: Selected Proceedings of the 1999 Second Language Research Form* (pp. 3–30). Somerville, MA: Cascadilla Press.

Price, V. (2011). Public opinion research in the new century: Reflections of a former POQ editor. *Public Opinion Quarterly, 75,* 846–853.

Prividera, L. C., & Howard, J. W., III. (2007). Masculinity, whiteness, and the warrior hero: Perpetuating the strategic rhetoric of U.S. nationalism and the marginalization of women. *Women and Language, 29,* 29–37.

Psathas, G., & Anderson, W. T. (1987). The "Practices" of Transcription in Conversation Analysis. *Semiotica, 78,* 75–99.

Puhl, R. M., Luedicke, J., & Heuer, C. A. (2013). The Stigmatizing Effect of Visual Media Portrayals of Obese Persons on Public Attitudes: Does Race or Gender Matter? *Journal of Health Communication, 18*(7), 805–826.

Pyrczak, F., & Bruce, R. R. (1992). *Writing empirical research reports: A basic guide for students of behavioral and social sciences.* Los Angeles: Pyrczak Publishing.

Ralston, S. M. (2000). The "Veil of Ignorance": Exploring ethical issues in the employment interview. *Business Communication Quarterly, 63,* 50–52.

Ramasubramanian, S. (2005). A content analysis of the portrayal of India in films produced in the West. *Howard Journal of Communications, 16*(4), 243–265.

Ramazanoglu, C. (1992). On feminist methodology: Male reason versus female empowerment. *Sociology, 26,* 207–212.

Ramirez, A., Jr., & Burgoon, J. K. (2004). The effect of interactivity on initial interactions: The influence of information valence and modality and information richness on computer-mediated communication. *Communication Monographs, 71,* 422–447.

Ramsey, S. (1999). A benchmark study of elaboration and sourcing in science stories for eight American newspapers. *Journalism & Mass Communication Quarterly, 76,* 87–98.

Rancer, A. S., Durbin, J. M., & Lin. Y. (2013). Teaching communication research methods: student perceptions of topic difficulty, topic understanding, and their relationship with math anxiety. *Communication Research Reports, 30,* 242–251.

Rasmussen, D. M. (1996). Critical theory and philosophy. In D. M. Rasmussen (Ed.), *The handbook of critical theory* (pp. 11–38). Oxford, England: Blackwell.

Raymond, G. (2000). *The Structure of Responding: Type-Conforming and Non-Conforming Responses to Yes/No Interrogatives.* PhD dissertation, Department of Sociology, University of California, Los Angeles.

Reich, N. M. (2002). Toward a re-articulation of women as victims: A thematic analysis of the construction of women's identities surrounding gendered violence. *Communication Quarterly, 50,* 292–311.

Reiss, A. J. (1971). *The police and the public.* New Haven, CT: Yale University Press.

Retrieved from http://online.wsj.com/news/articles/SB100014240527 02303289904579197942487038488).

Rettinger, S. (2011). Construction and display of competence and (professional) identity in coaching interactions: *Journal of Business Communication, 48*(4) 426–445.

[Rhetoric] Glossary of terms. Retrieved from http://wac.colostate.edu/books/ramage_argument/glossary.pdf .

Rindfleisch, A., Malter, A. J., Ganesan, S., & Moorman, C. (2008). Cross-sectional versus longitudinal survey research: Concepts, findings, and guidelines. *Journal of Marketing Research, 45,* 261–279.

Ritter, K. W. (1980). American political rhetoric and the jeremiad tradition: Presidential nomination acceptance speeches, 1960–1976. *Central States Speech Journal, 31,* 153–171.

Roberts, C. W. (1989). Other than counting words: A linguistic approach to content analysis. *Social Forces, 68,* 147–177.

Roberts, F., & Robinson, J. D. (2004). Interobserver agreement on first-stage conversation analytic transcription. *Human Communication Research, 30*(3), 376–410.

Robinson, J. (2004). The sequential organization of "explicit" apologies in naturally occurring English. *Research on Language and Social Interaction, 37*, 291–330.

Robinson, J. D. (1998). Getting down to business: Talk, gaze, and body orientation during openings of doctor-patient consultations. *Human Communication Research, 25*, 97–123.

Robinson, J. D. (2003). An interactional structure of medical activities during acute visits and its implications for patients' participation. *Health Communication, 15*(1), 27–57.

Robinson, J. D. (2006). Managing trouble responsibility and relationships during conversational repair. *Communication Monographs, 73*, 137–161.

Robinson, J. D., & Stivers, T. (2001). Achieving activity transition in physician-patient encounters: From history-taking to physical examination. *Human Communication Research, 27*, 253–298.

Robinson, J. D., Turner, J. W., Levine, B., & Tian, Y. (2011). Expanding the walls of the healthcare encounter: Support and outcomes for patients online. *Health Communication, 26*, 125–134.

Rodriguez, A. (2003). Social justice and the challenge for communication studies. In O. Swartz (Ed.), *Social Justice & Communication Scholarship* (Chapter 2, pp. 21–34). New York: Lawrence Erlbaum Associates.

Rogers, E. M. (1994). *A history of communication study: A biographical approach*. New York: Free Press.

Rogers, R. A. (2006). From cultural exchange to transculturation: A review and reconceptualization of cultural appropriation. *Communication Theory, 16*, 474–503.

Romaine, S. (1982). What is a speech community? In *Sociolinguistic variation in speech communities* (pp. 13–24). London: Edward Arnold.

Rosenfeld, L. B., Richman, J. M., & May, S. K. (2004). Information adequacy, job satisfaction, and organizational culture in a dispersed-network organization. *Journal of Applied Communication Research, 32*, 28–54.

Rossler, P. (2001). Between online heaven and cyberhell: The framing of "the Internet" by traditional media coverage in Germany. *New Media & Society, 3*, 49–66.

Rostek, T., Ed. (1999). *At the intersection: Cultural studies and rhetorical studies*. New York. Guilford.

Rothman, B. K. (1986). Reflections: On hard work. *Qualitative Sociology, 9*, 48–53.

Rotton, J., & Kelly, I. W. (1985). Much ado about the full moon: A meta-analysis of lunar lunacy research. *Psychological Bulletin, 97*, 286–306.

Rowland, R. C. (1987). Narrative: Mode of discourse or paradigm? *Communication Monographs, 54*, 264–275.

Roy, A., & Harwood, J. (1997). Underrepresented, positively portrayed: Older adults in television commercials. *Journal of Applied Communication Research, 25*, 39–56.

Ruben, B. D. (1993). What patients remember: A content analysis of critical incidents in health care. *Health Communication, 5*, 99–112.

Rubin, R. B., Palmgreen, P., & Sypher, H. E. (2004). Source credibility scale: 15-item semantic differential (pp. 338–339). In *Communication Research Measures: A Sourcebook*. Mahwah, NJ: Lawrence Erlbaum Associates.

Rubin, R. B., Rubin, A. M., & Jordan, F. F. (1997). Effects of instruction on communication apprehension and communication competence. *Communication Education, 46*, 104–114.

Rubin, R. B., Rubin, A. M., & Haridakis, P. (2010) *Communication Research: Strategies and Sources* (7th ed.). Belmont, CA: Cengage Learning.

Rueckert, W. H. (1982). *Kenneth Burke and the drama of human relations* (2nd ed.). Berkeley: University of California Press.

Rusted, B. (2006). Performing visual discourse: Cowboy art and institutional practice. *Text & Performance Quarterly, 26*, 115–137.

Ruud, G. (1995). The symbolic construction of organizational identities and community in a regional symphony. *Communication Studies, 46*, 201–222.

Rybacki, K., & Rybacki, D. (1991). *Communication criticism: Approaches and genres*. Belmont, CA: Wadsworth.

Sacks, H., Schegloff, E., & Jefferson, G. (1974). A simplest systematic for the organization of turn taking for conversation. *Language, 50*, 696–735.

Sapolsky, B. S., & Kaye, B. K. (2005). The use of offensive language by men and women in prime time television entertainment. *Atlantic Journal of Communication, 13*, 292–303.

Saunders, C. M. (2008). Forty Seven Million Strong, Weak, Wrong, or Right: Living Without Health Insurance. *Qualitative Inquiry, 14*, 528–545.

Scanlon, J. (1993). Challenging the imbalances of power in feminist oral history: Developing a give-and-take methodology. *Women's Studies International Forum, 16*, 639–645.

Scharrer, E. (2001). From wise to foolish: The portrayal of the sitcom father, 1950s–1990s. *Journal of Broadcasting and Electronic Media, 45*, 23–40.

Schegloff, E. A. (1979). Identification and Recognition in Telephone Openings (pp. 23–78). In G. Psathas (Ed.), *Everyday Language: Studies in Ethnomethodology*. New York: Erlbaum.

Schegloff, E. A. (1982). Discourse as an interactional achievement: Some uses of 'uh huh' and other things that come between sentences. In D. Tannen (Ed.), *Analyzing Discourse (Georgetown University Roundtable on Languages and Linguistics 1981)* (pp. 71–93). Washington DC: Georgetown University Press.

Schegloff, E. A. (1997). Whose text? Whose context? *Discourse & Society, 8*, 165–187.

Schegloff, E. A. (1999a). "Schegloff's texts as Billig's data": A critical reply. *Discourse & Society, 10*, 558–572.

Schegloff, E. A. (1999b). Naivete vs. sophistication or discipline vs. self-indulgence: A rejoinder to Billig. *Discourse & Society, 10*, 577–582.

Schegloff, E. A. (2006) *Sequence organization in interaction: A primer in Conversation Analysis I*. Cambridge, England: Cambridge University Press.

Schegloff, E. A. (2006). *Sequence organization in interaction: A primer in conversation analysis I*. Cambridge, England: Cambridge University Press.

Schegloff, E. A., & Sacks, H. (1973). Opening up closings. *Semiotica, 8*, 289–327.

Schegloff, E. A. (1997). Whose Text? Whose Context? *Discourse & Society 8*, 165–187.

Scheibel, D. (1994). Graffiti and "film school" culture: Displaying alienation. *Communication Monographs, 61*, 1–18.

Scheibel, D. (1996). Appropriating bodies: Organ(izing) ideology and cultural practice in medical school. *Journal of Applied Communication Research, 24*, 310–331.

Scheibel, D. (1999). "If your roommate dies, you get a 4.0": Reclaiming rumor with Burke and organizational culture. *Western Journal of Communication, 63*, 169–192.

Schely-Newman, E. (1997). Finding one's place: Locale narratives in an Israeli Moshav. *Quarterly Journal of Speech, 83*, 401–415.

Schenck-Hamlin, W. J., Procter, D. E., & Rumsey, D. J. (2000). The influence of negative advertising frames on political cynicism and politician accountability. *Human Communication Research, 26*, 53–74.

Schenkein, J. (1978). Sketch of an analytic mentality for the study of conversational interaction. In *Studies in the organization of conversational interaction* (pp. 1–6). New York: Academic.

Schiffrin, D. (1997). Theory and method in discourse analysis: What context for what unit? *Language & Communication, 17*, 75–92.

Schlegloff, E. A., Jefferson, G., & Sacks, H. (1977). The preference for self-repair in the organization of conversation. *Language, 53*, 351–362.

Schmidt, M. (2005). Individuation: Finding oneself in analysis—Taking risks and making sacrifices. *Journal of Analytical Psychology, 50*, 595–616.

Schrodt, P. (2006). A typological examination of communication competence and mental health in stepchildren. *Communication Monographs, 73*, 309–333.

Schrodt, P., & Carr, K. (2012). Trait verbal aggressiveness as a function of family communication patterns. *Communication Research Reports, 29*, 54–63.

Schrodt, P., Braithwaite, D. O., Soliz, J., Tye-Williams, S., Miller, A., Normand, E. L., et al. (2007). An examination of everyday talk in stepfamily systems. *Western Journal of Communication, 71*, 216–234.

Schutz, A. (1967). *The phenomenology of the social world* (G. Walsh & F. Lehnert, Trans.). Evanston, IL: Northwestern University Press.

Schwartz, H. S. (1987). [Review of the book *The reflective practitioner: How professionals think in action*]. *Administrative Science Quarterly, 32*, 614–617.

Schwartzman, H. B. (1993). *Ethnography in organizations* [Qualitative Research Methods Series No. 27]. Thousand Oaks, CA: Sage.

Scolo, M. (2011). Cultural approaches to discourse analysis: A theoretical and methodological conversation with special focus on Donal Carbaugh's Cultural Discourse Theory. *Journal of Multicultural Discourse, 6*(1), 1–32.

Scott, C. R., & Fontenot, J. C. (1999). Multiple identifications during team meetings: A comparison of conventional and computer-supported interactions. *Communication Reports, 12*, 91–100.

Scott, W. A. (1955). Reliability of content analysis: The case of nominal scale coding. *Public Opinion Quarterly, 19*, 321–325.

Scotton, C. M. (1985). What the heck, sir: Style shifting and lexical colouring as features of powerful language. In R. L. Street & J. N. Capella (Eds.), *Sequence and pattern in conversational behavior* (pp. 103–119). Baltimore, MD: E. Arnold.

Seale, C. (1999). Quality in qualitative research. *Qualitative Inquiry, 5*, 465–478.

Sequeira, D. L. (1993). Personal address as negotiated meaning in an American church community. *Research on Language and Social Interaction, 26*, 259–285.

Sheared, V. (1994). Giving voice: An inclusive model of instruction—A womanist perspective. *New Directions for Continuing and Adult Education, 61*, 27–37.

Shimanoff, S. B. (1980). *Communication rules*. Beverly Hills, CA: Sage.

Shimanoff, S. B. (1985). Rules governing the verbal expression of emotions between married couples. *Western Journal of Speech Communication, 49*, 147–165.

Shugart, H. A. (1997). Counterhegemonic acts: Appropriation as a feminist rhetorical strategy. *Quarterly Journal of Speech, 83*, 210–229.

Shugart, H. A. (1999). Postmodern irony as a subversive rhetorical strategy. *Western Journal of Communication, 63*, 433–455.

Sigman, S. J. (1985). Some common mistakes students make when learning discourse analysis. *Communication Education, 34*, 119–127.

Sigman, S. J. (1987). *A perspective on social communication*. Lexington: Lexington, MA.

Sigman, S. J., Sullivan, S. J., & Wendell, M. (1988). Conversation: Data acquisition and analysis. In C. H. Tardy (Ed.), *A handbook for the study of human communication: Methods and instruments for observing, measuring, and assessing communication processes* (pp. 163–192). Norwood, NJ: Ablex.

Sillince, J. A. (2007). Organizational context and the discursive construction of organizing. *Management Communication Quarterly, 20*, 363–394.

Simmerling, M., Schwegler, B., Sieber, J. E., & Lindgren, J. (2007). Introducing a new paradigm for ethical research in the social, behavioral, and biomedical sciences: Part I. *Northwestern University Law Review, 101*, 837–859.

Sinekopova, G. V. (2006). Building the public spheres: Bases and biases. *Journal of Communication, 56*, 505–522.

Skovholt, K., & Svennevig, J. (2006). Email copies in workplace interaction. *Journal of Computer-Mediated Communication, 12*, 42–65.

Sloop, J. M. (2000). Disciplining the transgendered: Brandon Teena, public representation, and normativity. *Western Journal of Communication, 64*, 165–189.

Smith, G, N., Nolan, R. F., & Dai, Y. (1996) Job-refusal letters: Readers' affective responses to direct and indirect organizational plans. *Business Communication Quarterly. 59*, 67–73.

Smith, M. J. (1988). *Contemporary communication research methods*. Belmont, CA: Wadsworth.

Smith, V. (2007). Aristotle's classical enthymeme and the visual argumentation of the twenty-first century. *Argumentation and Advocacy, 43*, 114–123.

Snow, D. A. (1980). The disengagement process: A neglected problem in participant-observation research. *Qualitative Sociology, 3*, 100–122.

Soukup, C. (2006). Hitching a ride on a star: Celebrity, fandom, and identification on the World Wide Web. *Southern Communication Journal, 71*, 319–337.

Sparks, G. G., Pellechia, M., & Irvine, C. (1999). The repressive coping style and fright reactions to mass media. *Communication Research, 26*, 176–193.

Speer, S. A., & Potter, J. (2000). The management of heterosexist talk: Conversational repairs and prejudiced claims. *Discourse & Society, 11*, 543–572.

Spitzberg, B. H. (2000). What is good communication? *Journal of the Association for Communication Administration, 29*, 103–119.

Spitzberg, B., & Cupach, W. (1984). *Interpersonal communication competence*. Beverly Hills, CA: Sage.

Spitzberg, B., & Hecht, M. (1984). A component model of relational competence. *Human Communication Research, 10*, 575–599.

Spradley, J. P. (1980). *Participant observation*. New York: Holt, Rinehart & Winston.

Sprague, J. (1992). Critical perspectives on teacher empowerment. *Communication Education, 41*, 181–203.

Stablein, R. (1996). Data in organization studies. In S. R. Clegg, C. Hardy, & W. R. Nord (Eds.), *Handbook of organization studies* (pp. 347–369). London: Sage.

Stage, F. K., & Russell, R. V. (1992). Using method triangulation in college student research. *Journal of College Student Development, 33*, 485–491.

Stake, R. E. (1998). Case studies. In N. Denzin & Y. Lincoln (Eds.), *Strategies of qualitative inquiry* (pp. 86–109). Thousand Oaks, CA: Sage.

Stamp, G. H. (1999). A qualitatively constructed interpersonal communication model: A grounded theory analysis. *Human Communication Research, 25*, 531–547.

Stern, S. R. (2005). Messages from teens on the big screen: Smoking, drinking, and drug use in teen-centered films. *Journal of Health Communication, 10*, 331–346.

Stewart, A. (1998). *The ethnographer's method* [Qualitative Research Methods Series No. 46]. Thousand Oaks, CA: Sage.

Stewart, C. M, Shields, S. F., & Sen, N. (1998). Diversity in on-line discussions: A study of cultural and gender differences in listservs. *Electronic Journal of Communication, 8*(3/4), File Stewart V8N398, 1–15.

Stiles, W. B. (1980). Comparison of dimensions derived from rating versus coding of dialogue. *Journal of Personality and Social Psychology, 38*, 359–374.

Stivers, T., & Heritage, J. (2001). Breaking the sequential mold: answering "more than the question" during medical history taking. *Text, 21*(1/2), 151–185.

Stoker, K. (2005). Loyalty in public relations: When does it cross the line between virtue and vice? *Journal of Mass Media Ethics, 20*, 269–287.

Stokoe, E. H., & Smithson, J. (2001). Making gender relevant: Conversational analysis and gender categories in interaction. *Discourse & Society, 12*, 217–244.

Stoller, E. P. (1993). Gender and the organization of lay health care: A socialist-feminist perspective. *Journal of Aging Studies, 7*, 151–170.

Stormer, N. (2013) Recursivity: a working paper on rhetoric and mnesis. *Quarterly Journal of Speech, 99*, 27–50.

Strauss, A., & Corbin, J. (1998). Grounded theory methodology: An overview. In N. K. Denzin & Y. Lincoln (Eds.), *Strategies of qualitative inquiry* (pp. 158–183). Newbury Park, CA: Sage.

Stroud, S. R. (2001). Technology and mythic narrative: *The Matrix* as technological hero-quest. *Western Journal of Communication, 65*, 416–441.

Stuckey, N. P., & Daughton, S. M. (2003). The body present: Reporting everyday life performance. In P. LeBaron, C. D. LeBaron, & J. Mandelbaum (Eds.), *Studies in language & social interaction* (pp. 479–492). Mahwah, NJ: Lawrence Erlbaum.

Sunwolf, & Seibold, D. R. (1998). Jurors' intuitive rules for deliberation: A structurational approach to communication in jury decision making. *Communication Monographs, 65*, 282–307.

Swanson, D. L. (1993). Fragmentation, the field, and the future. *Journal of Communication, 43*, 163–192.

Szabo, J., & Gerevich, J. (2013). Alcohol dependency, recovery, and social words. *Journal of Applied Social Psychology, 43*, 806–810.

Tardy, R. W., & Hale, C. L. (1998). Getting "plugged in": A network analysis of health-information seeking among "stay-at-home Moms." *Communication Monographs, 65*, 336–357.

Tavener, J. (2000). Media, morality, and madness: The case against sleaze TV. *Critical Studies in Mass Communication, 17*, 63–85.

Taylor, C. R., & Bang, H. (1997). Portrayals of Latinos in magazine advertising. *Journalism and Mass Communication Quarterly, 74*, 285–303.

Taylor, S. J., & Bogdan, R. C. (1998). *Introduction to qualitative research methods: A guidebook and resource* (3rd ed.). New York: Wiley.

ten Have, P. (1999). *Doing conversation analysis: A practical guide*. London: Sage.

Thackeray, R., Burton, S. H., Giraud-Carrier, C., Rollins, S., & Draper, C. R. (2013). Using *Twitter* for breast cancer prevention: an analysis of breast cancer awareness month. *BMC Cancer, 13*(1), 1–18.

Thibaut, J. W., & Kelley, H. H. (1959). *The social psychology of groups*. New York: Wiley.

Thomas, J. (1993). *Doing critical ethnography*. Newbury Park, CA: Sage.

Thomas, S. (1994). Artifactual study in the analysis of culture: A defense of content analysis in a postmodern age. *Communication Research, 21*, 683–697.

Thonssen, L., & Baird, A. C. (1948). *Speech criticism*. New York: Ronald.

Tinney, J. (2008). Negotiating boundaries and roles. *Journal of Contemporary Ethnography, 37*(2), 202–225.

Tompkins, P. (1994) Principles of rigor for assessing evidence in "qualitative" communication research. *Western Journal of Communication, 58*, 44–50.

Toulmin, S. E. (1972). *Human understanding*. Oxford: Clarendon Press.

Toulmin, S. E., Rieke, R., & Janik, A. (1984). *An introduction to reasoning* (2nd ed.). New York: Macmillan.

Tracy, K., & Haspel, K. (2004). Language and Social Interaction: Its institutional identity, intellectual landscape, and discipline-shifting agenda. *Journal of Communication, 54*, 788–816.

Tracy, K. (1995). Action-implicative discourse analysis. *Journal of Language & Social Psychology, 14*, 195–216.

Tracy, K., & Tracy, S. J. (1998). Rudeness at 911: Reconceptualizing face and face attack. *Human Communication Research, 25*, 225–251.

Tracy, S., Myers, K. K., & Scott, C. W. (2006). Cracking jokes and crafting selves: Sensemaking and identity management among human service workers. *Communication Monographs, 73*, 283–308.

Tretheway, A. (1997). Resistance, identity, and empowerment: A postmodern feminist analysis of clients in a human service organization. *Communication Monographs, 64*, 281–301.

Trethewey, A. (2001). Reproducing and resisting the master narrative of decline: Midlife professional women's experiences of aging. *Management Communication Quarterly, 15*, 183–207.

Trujillo, N. (1991). Hegemonic masculinity on the mound: Media representations of Nolan Ryan and American sports culture. *Critical Studies in Mass Communication, 8*, 290–308.

Trujillo, N. (1992). Interpreting (the work and the talk of) baseball: Perspectives on ballpark culture. *Western Journal of Communication, 56*, 350–371.

Trujillo, N. (1993). Interpreting November 22: A critical ethnography of an assassination site. *Quarterly Journal of Speech, 79,* 447–466.

Trujillo, N. (1999). Teaching ethnography in the twenty-first century using collaborative learning. *Journal of Contemporary Ethnography, 28,* 705–719.

Trumbo, C. W. (2004). Research methods in mass communication research: A census of eight journals, 1990–2000. *Journalism & Mass Communication Quarterly, 81,* 417–436.

Turner, V. W., & Bruner, E. M., Eds. (1986). *The anthropology of experience.* Urbana: University of Illinois Press.

Turowetz, J., & Hollander, M. (2012). Assessing the experience of speed dating. *Discourse Studies, 14*(5), 635–658.

Valdes, G., & Pino, C. (1981). *Muy a tus ordenes:* Compliment responses among Mexican-American bilinguals. *Language and Society, 10,* 53–72.

Van Dijk, T. A. (1997b). The study of discourse. In *Discourse as structure and process* (pp. 1–34). London: Sage.

Van Dijk, T. A. (Ed.). (1997a). *Discourse as social interaction.* Thousand Oaks, CA: Sage.

Van Lear, C. A., Sheehan, M., Withers, L. A., & Walker, R. A. (2005). AA Online: The enactment of supportive computer mediated communication. *Western Journal of Communication, 69,* 5–26.

Van Maanen, J. (1988). *Tales of the field: On writing ethnography.* Chicago: University of Chicago Press.

Van Oosting, J. (1996). Acoustic writers and electronic readers: Literature through the back door. *Communication Education, 45,* 108–111.

Veatch, R. M. (1996). From Nuremberg through the 1990s: The priority of autonomy. In H. Y. Vanderpool (Ed.), *The Ethics of research involving human subjects: Facing the 21st century* (pp. 45–58). Frederick, MD: University Publishing Group.

Verbeke, W., & Bagozzi, R. P. (2000). Sales Call Anxiety: Exploring What It Means When Fear Rules a Sales Encounter. *Journal of Marketing, 64*(3), 88–101.

Vevea, N. N., Pearson, J. C., Child, J. T., & Semlak, J. L. (2009). The only thing to fear is public speaking? Exploring predictors of communication in the public speaking classroom. *Journal of the Communication, Speech & Theatre Association of North Dakota, 22,* 1–8.

Vignes, D. S. (2008). "Hang it out to dry": Performing ethnography, cultural memory, and Hurricane Katrina in Chalmette, Louisiana. *Text and Performance Quarterly, 28* (344–450).

Viswanath, K., Breen, N., Meissner, H., Moser, R. P., Hesse, B., Steele, W. R., et al. (2006). Cancer knowledge and disparities in the information age. *Journal of Health Communication, 11,* 1–17.

Vivienne, S., & Burgess, J. (2012). The digital storyteller's age: Queer everyday activists negotiating privacy and publicness. *Journal of Broadcasting and Electronic Media, 56*(3), 362–377.

Voosen, P. (September 20, 2013). Researchers struggle to stanch data leaks. *Chronicle of Higher Education*, pp. A2 and A4.

Wahl, S. T., McBride, M. C., & Schrodt, P. (2005). Becoming "point and click" parents: A case study of communication and online adoption. *Journal of Family Communication, 5,* 279–294.

Ware, B. L., & Linkugel, W. A. (1973). They spoke in defense of themselves: On the generic criticism of apologia. *Quarterly Journal of Speech, 59,* 273–283.

Warnick, B. (1987). The narrative paradigm: Another story. *Quarterly Journal of Speech, 73,* 172–182.

Warren, J. T. (2006). Introduction. Performance ethnography: A *TPQ* Symposium. *Text & Performance Quarterly, 26*(4), 317–319.

Wasserman, S., & Faust, K. (1994). *Social network analysis: Methods and applications.* Cambridge: Cambridge University Press.

Waters, R. D., & Jamal, J. Y. (2011). Tweet, tweet, tweet: A content analysis of nonprofit organizations' Twitter updates. *Public Relations Review, 37*(3), 321–324.

Watt, J. H., & van den Berg, S. A. (1995). *Research methods for communication science.* Boston: Allyn & Bacon.

Watts, E. K., & Orbe, M. P. (2002). The spectacular consumption of the "True" African American culture: "Whassup" with the Budweiser Guys? *Critical Studies in Mass Communication, 19,* 1–20.

Weatherby, G. A., & Scoggins, B. (2005–2006). A content analysis of persuasion techniques used on white supremacist Web sites. *Journal of Hate Studies, 4*(1), 9–31.

Weaver, J. B., III. (1991). Are "slasher" horror films sexually violent? A content analysis. *Journal of Broadcasting and Electronic Media, 35,* 385–392.

Weber, K., Goodboy, A. K., & Cayanus, J. L. (2010). Flirting competence: An experimental study on appropriate and effective opening lines. *Communication Research Reports, 27,* 184–191.

Wei, L. (2002). "What do you want me to say?" On the conversational approach to bilingual interaction. *Language in Society, 31,* 151–180.

West, C. (1982). Why can't a woman be more like a man? *Work and Occupations, 9,* 5–29.

West, C., & Zimmerman, D. (1983). Small insults: A study of interruptions in cross-sex conversations between unacquainted persons. In B. Thorne, C. Kramarae, & N. Henley (Eds.), *Language, gender, and society* (pp. 102–117). Rowley, MA: Newbury House.

West, M., & Carey, C. (2006). (Re)enacting frontier justice: The Bush administration's tactical narration of the Old West fantasy after September 11. *Quarterly Journal of Speech, 92,* 379–412.

Whalen, M., & Zimmerman, D. (1987). Sequential and institutional contexts in calls for help. *Social Psychology Quarterly, 50,* 172–185.

White, S. J. (2012). Closing Surgeon-Patient Consultations, *International Review of Pragmatics, 4* (1), 58–79.

Whiteman, N. (2009). The De/Stabilization of identity in online fan communities. *Convergence: The Journal Of Research Into New Media Technologies, 15*(4), 391–410.

Wichelns, H. A. (1925). The literary criticism of oratory. In A. M. Drummond (Ed.), *Rhetoric and public speaking in honor of James A. Winans* (pp. 181–216). New York: Century.

Wiemann, J. M. (1981). Effects of laboratory videotaping procedures on selected conversational behaviors. *Human Communication Research, 7,* 302–311.

Williams, D. J. (2006). Autoethnography in offender rehabilitation research and practice: Addressing the "us vs. them" problem. *Contemporary Justice Review, 9,* 23–38.

Witmer, D. F. (1997). Communication and recovery: Structuration as an ontological approach to organizational culture. *Communication Monographs, 64,* 324–349.

Witt, P. L., & Schrodt, P. (2006). The influence of instructional technology use and teacher immediacy on student affect for teacher and course. *Communication Reports, 19*, 1–15.

Witteborn, S., Milburn, T., & Ho, W. (2013). The ethnography of communication as applied methodology: Insights from three case studies. *Journal of Applied Communication Research, 41*(2), 188–194.

Wittgenstein, L. (1953). *Philosophical Investigations*. Translated by G. E. M. Anscombe. New York: Macmillian.

Wittig, M. (1990). The straight mind. In R. Ferguson, M. Gever, T. T. Minh-Ha, & C. West (Eds.), *Out there: Marginalization and contemporary culture* (pp. 51–58). Cambridge, MA: MIT Press.

Wolfe, D. (2008). The ecological *jeremiad*, the American myth, and the vivid force of color in Dr. Seuss's *The Lorax. Environmental Communication, 2*, 3–24.

Wong, J. (2000). The token "yeah" in nonnative speaker English conversation. *Research on Language & Social Interaction, 33*, 39–67.

Wood, A. F., & Fassett, D. L. (2003). Remote control: Identity, power, and technology in the communication classroom. *Communication Education, 52*, 286–296.

Wood, J. K. (2005). Balancing innocence and guilt: A metaphysical analysis of the U.S. Supreme Court's "ruling on victims" impact statements. *Western Journal of Communication, 69*, 124–126.

Wood, J. T. (1997). *Communication theories in action: An introduction.* Belmont, CA: Wadsworth.

Wood, J. T., & Inman, C. C. (1993). In a different mode: Masculine styles of communicating closeness. *Journal of Applied Communication Research, 21*, 279–295.

Wooffitt, R. (2005). *Conversation analysis and discourse analysis: A comparative and critical introduction.* Thousand Oaks, CA: Sage.

Wright, K. (2002). Social support within an on-line cancer community: An assessment of emotional support, perceptions of advantages and disadvantages, and motives for using the community from a communication perspective. *Journal of Applied Communication Research, 30*, 195–209.

Wright, K. B., & O'Hair, D. (1999). Seeking and resisting compliance: Selection and evaluation of tactics in a simulated college student drinking context. *Communication Research Reports, 16*, 266–275.

Yang, C., & Brown, B. B. (2013). Motives for using Facebook, patterns of Facebook activities, and late adolescents' social adjustment to college. *Journal of Youth and Adolescence, 42*, 403–416.

Yeager, D. S., Krosnick, J. A., Chang, L., Javitz, H. S., Levendusky, M. S., Simpser, A., & Wang, R. (2011). Comparing the accuracy of RDD telephone surveys and internet surveys conducted with probability and non-probability samples. *Public Opinion Quarterly, 75*, 709–747.

Yep, G. (1997). My three cultures: Navigating the multicultural identity landscape. *Magazine, 15*(2), 43–55.

Yep, G. (1998). Freire's Conscientization, Dialogue, And Liberation: Personal Reflections on Classroom Discussions of Marginality. *International Journal of Sexuality and Gender Studies, 3*, 159–166.

Yep, G. A. (2003). The violence of heteronormativity in communication studies: Notes on injury, healing, and queer world-making (pp. 11–60) in G. A. Yep, K. E. Lovaas, & J. P. Elia (Eds.), *Queer Theory and communication: From disciplining queers to queering the discipline(s).* Binghamton, NY: Haworth Press.

Yep, G. A., Lovaas, K. E., & Ho, P. C. (2001). Communication in "Asian American" families with queer members: A relational dialectics perspective. In M. Bernstein & R. Reimann (Eds.), *Queer families, queer politics: Challenging culture and the state* (pp. 152–172). New York: Columbia University Press.

Yep, G. A., Lovaas, K. E., & Pagonis, A. V. (2002). The case of "riding bareback": Sexual practices and the paradoxes of identity in the era of AIDS. *Journal of Homosexuality, 42*(4), 1–14.

Yep, G. A., Olzman, M., & Conkle, A. (2012). Seven stories from the "It Gets Better" project: Progress narratives, politics of affect, and the politics of queer world-making. In R. A. Lind (Ed.), *Producing theory in a digital world: The intersection of audiences and production in contemporary theory* (pp. 123–141). New York: Peter Lang.

Zand-Vakili, E., Kashani, A. F., & Tabandeh, F. (2012). The Analysis of Speech Events and Hymes' SPEAKING Factors in the Comedy Television Series: *Friends. New Media & Mass Communication, 2*, 27–43.

Zimbardo, P. (1973). On the ethics of intervention in human psychological research: with special reference to the Stanford prison experiment. *Cognition, 2*, 243–256.

Zoch, L. M., & Turk, J. V. (1998). Women making news: Gender as a variable in source selection and use. *Journalism & Mass Communication Quarterly, 75*, 762–775.

Index